CALIFORNIA STUDIES IN URBANIZATION
AND ENVIRONMENTAL DESIGN

American City Planning since 1890

MEL SCOTT

AMERICAN
CITY PLANNING
SINCE 1890

A history commemorating the
Fiftieth Anniversary
of the American Institute of Planners

UNIVERSITY OF CALIFORNIA PRESS   BERKELEY, LOS ANGELES, LONDON   1971

University of California Press
Berkeley and Los Angeles, California

University of California Press, Ltd.
London, England

Copyright © 1969, by
The Regents of the University of California

First Paperback Printing, 1971

Designed by Ikuko Workman
ISBN: 0–520–01382–4 (cloth)
        0–520–02051–0 (paper)
Library of Congress Catalog Card Number: 70–84533
Printed in the United States of America

This publication was made possible
by the cooperation of the University of California
with the Fiftieth Anniversary Commemoration Committee
of the American Institute of Planners.
Of the branches of the University which
contributed to the preparation of the work,
the Institute of Governmental Studies provided
the chief support for a period of four years.
The Department of City and Regional Planning,
the Institute of Urban and Regional Development,
and the Center for Planning and Development Research
also aided in the undertaking.

CONTENTS

LIST OF ILLUSTRATIONS

PREFACE

This volume presents a personal view of the growth of a significant profession and the development of the planning function in modern government. The American Institute of Planners commissioned the work as part of a program celebrating a half century of professional activity (the volume appears, unfortunately, two years after the fiftieth anniversary of the founding of the organization). A committee of Institute members offered criticisms while the writing was in progress, but the finished product is in no sense an "official" history expressing the ideas of a governing board, a special committee, or a group of academicians. I have been free at all times to exercise my own judgment regarding the choice and treatment of subject matter. For two main reasons the choice has been unavoidably individual. No one can liberate himself entirely from his biases, attachments, and limitations, no matter how earnestly he attempts to be thorough, dispassionate, and intellectually honest. The very abundance of material—far more, I am sure, than most city planners ever imagined—has multiplied the opportunities for personal preferences and prejudices to assert themselves. Inevitably, each reader will say to himself at times, Why was this included? or Why was that omitted? Let him be assured that there was no intention to be capricious or arbitrary in the selection of material, but integrity compels the acknowledgment that one's peculiar cast of thought may unwittingly compromise intention.

The work is perhaps twice as long as the subcommittee on publications desired. Certainly, it is a great deal longer than I had originally contemplated, yet it is, as I have often said to the chairman of the subcommittee and my colleagues in the University, no more than a sketch. A truly comprehensive history of American city planning since 1890 would encompass at least five or six volumes, perhaps as many as ten. Planners themselves have written a vast number of reports and books, newspaper and magazine articles, letters, journals, bulletins, and speeches. Journalists, historians, professors, members of allied professions, and countless other people have poured forth torrents of comment and criticism for the past seventy or eighty years. The record of the planning field is, in fact, so voluminous that I recall with wry amusement the solicitous query of a past president of the American Institute of Planners a few months after I had begun my research: "Are you finding enough material?" My reply was that I was being buried alive in it.

The problem, I soon discovered, was not only to visit numerous cities and to examine all the obviously important sources but also to ferret out old newspaper editorials, articles in ephemeral magazines, minutes of the meetings of civic committees, the proceedings of local and regional conferences, and long-forgotten municipal, state, and federal reports that would illuminate the historical context in which city planners put forth their proposals and succeeded or failed in influencing the course of growth and development in American urban areas. The search for such usually neglected material was less difficult than I had expected, since I had access to one of the largest libraries in the United States, that of the University of California, Berkeley. Moreover, I pursued my investigations of some matters in sufficient detail to convince myself that I was merely working the exposed surface of a rich historical lode. Untold treasure yet awaits urban historians. Until they give more attention to the story of city planning in our metropolitan communities, the social history of the United States will remain decidedly unbalanced. Even the least successful attempts at planning reveal the play of highly complex social, economic, and political forces and invariably foreshadow movements and struggles of national significance.

There is, of course, material for many other histories of American city planning or for an encyclopedic work bringing together much more information than I could compress within the covers of this volume—a pioneer effort to survey the rise of a relatively new profession. The future will disclose new vantages from which the record of city planning should be examined. I hope that others will accept the challenge of making their own assessments, because adequate understanding of a field comes only from viewing it through many intellects.

I could not have appropriately commemorated a milestone in the history of the American Institute of Planners if I had not noted particularly the contributions of its members to the development of city planning as an art and science. Yet one of the most striking facts which emerges is that persons outside the profession—financiers, industrialists, merchants, members of other professions, writers, professors of political science, economics, sociology, and law, legislators, mayors, governors, and presidents—have influenced the development of planning perhaps as much as the recognized practitioners and their cohorts, the professors of city and regional planning in our universities. The variety of participants in the long-term effort to make planning more effective is in itself evidence that the planning function in our society touches almost all interests, affects almost all aspects of our lives, and holds enormous potential for improving our institutions and our environment. If today planning appears to be a field of indeterminate breadth and depth, it is because hosts of allies have helped planners to move it more and more into the forefront of American life and to arm it with some of the most far-reaching legislation on the statute books. The field may sometimes dismay practitioners with its increasing comprehensiveness, but they cannot complain about lack of opportunity. Their chief concern should be to continue to attract highly creative minds to their ranks, so that development can be as dynamic from within the fold as from without.

Acknowledgments

At various times in the past four years I have been anything but grateful to my colleague Corwin Mocine for suggesting that the subcommittee on publications of the Fiftieth Anniversary Committee of the American Institute of Planners commission me to prepare this history. As an undertaking which I had originally believed could be completed in two years began to stretch into a third year and then a fourth, I had dark thoughts about Mocine and rued the day that I had been tempted by a letter from Russell Van Nest Black, chairman of the subcommittee. But now that the pleasure and pain of writing have come to an end, I realize how much I am indebted to Mocine, to Black and his fellow committeemen, Tracy B. Augur and Charles W. Eliot II, and to the Anniversary Committee, which approved the contractual arrangements recommended by the subcommittee. Thanks to all these members of the Institute, I have enjoyed an unparalleled opportunity to expand my own knowledge of city planning and American cities. I trust that others will also benefit from my acceptance of the invitation to write this volume.

The preparation of a manuscript would not have been possible, however, without the cooperation of several of my associates at the University of California, Berkeley. A group of six helped me to work out a memorandum of understanding with the Fiftieth Anniversary Committee, of which Harland Bartholomew was chairman. The agreement provided that the committee would pay for research assistance and travel and would make a grant to the university to finance my appointment as a part-time research associate in the Center for Planning and Development Research for two years. The Institute of Governmental Studies agreed to contribute half my time for two years—and later took over full support of the project for almost as long a period. The Department of City and Regional Planning released me from most of my teaching duties and contributed part of my time to the project. When these arrangements were made in 1964 those who aided me were Dr. Martin Meyerson, Dean of the College of Environmental Design; Dr. William L. C. Wheaton, Director of the Institute of Urban and Regional Development; Dr. Dwight Waldo, Director of the Institute of Governmental Studies, and Stanley Scott, Assistant Director; Dr. John Dyckman, Director of the Center for Planning and Development Research; and Professor T. J. Kent, Chairman of the Department of City and Regional Planning. Dr. Waldo and his successor, Dr. Eugene C. Lee, were especially generous in extending the original commitment of the Institute of Governmental Studies.

Robert L. Williams, Executive Director of the American Institute of Planners, assisted in working out the memorandum of understanding, helped me in negotiations with the University of California Press for the publication of this book, and publicized it in newsletters of the Institute, other planning publications, and exhibitions at conferences. I am grateful to him for his friendly interest in the project, his wise counsel, and his forbearance over the long delay in the completion of the work.

From time to time throughout the protracted period of writing, Harland Bartholomew, Russell Black, and Professor John T. Howard, head of the City and Regional Planning Department of the Massachusetts Institute of Technology, carefully read each chapter and gave me detailed criticisms. Since all three have long been leaders in the city planning profession, their comments were exceedingly helpful. They also provided me with useful personal reminiscences, suggested sources of material, and saved me the embarrassment of some errors of fact, though I daresay that in a large work such as this some readers will find a few slips of which none of us was aware.

I asked several authorities on particular periods or movements to read and criticize certain chapters. Professor John W. Reps, of the Department of City and Regional Planning of Cornell University, reviewed the first two chapters, giving me the benefit of all the knowledge represented by his recent book about the national capital and his earlier work, *The Making of Urban America.* Professor Howard K. Menhinick, of the School of Architecture of the Georgia Institute of Technology, appraised chapter 4 from the unique vantage of having done the field work for that landmark volume of the 1920s, *Our Cities To-day and To-morrow,* by Theodora Kimball Hubbard and Henry Vincent Hubbard. Professor Coleman Woodbury, of the Department of City and Regional Planning of the University of Wisconsin, read chapter 5 with the authoritative eye of a deeply committed leader in the struggle for public housing in the early days of the New Deal. Professor Victor Jones, of the Department of Political Science of the University of California, Berkeley, scrutinized the last chapter and made welcome suggestions for some revisions. Dean William Wheaton filled the margins of the first three chapters and the seventh with pertinent criticisms which led to some substantial alterations of the text. My colleagues in the Institute of Governmental Studies, Dr. Lee and Stanley Scott, and my friend Dr. Albert Lepawsky, of the Political Science Department on the Berkeley campus, gave me their expert advice whenever I needed it. To all these valued allies in the pursuit of truth it is difficult to say thank you adequately because each one has many demands upon his time and must make a personal sacrifice whenever he consents to review anything.

Early in my research, when I traveled from city to city in search of material, many planners who remember some of the early developments in city planning granted me interviews and lent me rare reports, letters, and memoranda. Among them were Frederick Adams, Tracy Augur, Harland Bartholomew, Russell Black, Walter Blucher, Charles Eliot, Professor Howard, Harold A. Merrill, C. McKim Norton, Paul Oppermann, Lawrence Orton, and Flavel Shurtleff. Others whom I consulted during my travels were Norman Beckman, Stuart H. Brehm, H. Alden Deyo, Cushing N. Dolbeare, Edward Foster, William R. B. Froehlich, Fritz Gutheim, Eric A. Grubb, Professor Malcolm G. Little, Jr., Rodney O'Hiser, Thomas H. Roberts, Matthew Rockwell, John D. Spaeth, and Marvin R. Springer. The names of several other planners who wrote letters containing information I especially wanted appear in a section of the bibliography listing manuscripts. I herewith express my gratitude to all these contributors to this work.

As in any undertaking, there were times when my spirit drooped. Grant Barnes, Social Science Editor of the University of California Press, provided encouragement when I especially needed it; I am grateful to him for his patience, thoughtful criticisms, and moral support.

My good friend Nick Crump laid the groundwork for my labors by carrying on research under my direction for several months before I was able to free myself from other commitments. His further assistance for more than two years enabled me to tap resources of the University of California Library that I little dreamed of. Later Sam C. Anugwelem was assiduous at finding material required for the concluding chapter. To both I am indebted for much more than services well performed: a very deep interest in the progress of my endeavors.

Barbara Hudson and the staff of the Library of the Institute of Governmental Studies and Charles Shain of the Library of the College of Environmental Design were at all times helpful to Crump, Anugwelem, and myself. I appreciate their resourcefulness and efficiency.

Mrs. Hazel Karns, head of the Institute's secretarial staff, facilitated my efforts by her unfailing willingness to arrange for the typing of manuscript. Among those to whom I am especially grateful for neatly typed pages are Jewel Boyd and Mrs. Jacqueline Berner.

Mrs. Henry Castor, who edited the manuscript, has earned my thanks for respecting my general style while saving me from certain idiosyncratic constructions and various inconsistencies in small but important matters of usage. I hope that she remembers what the Bible says about the last being first.

CHAPTER 1

THE SPIRIT OF REFORM

Steps Toward City Planning

In that painful decade now ironically called the Gay Nineties there were few urban Americans who would have subscribed to the belief, or hope, that entire cities and metropolitan regions can be developed and renewed by a continuous process of decision-making based on long-range planning, and there were no men who professed to be city planners. Yet there were some architects, landscape architects, and engineers then practicing who would soon be widely known as the pioneers of a new profession of city planning. In a kind of apprenticeship for their later endeavors, they were designing parks and boulevards, or areawide park systems, or the streets of outlying, undeveloped sections of cities. Their fellow citizens, troubled

1

by problems as disturbing as those which beset urban residents today, for the most part applauded their efforts and yearned for mitigating beauty amid the utilitarian drabness of their surroundings.

It was a time of arrogant and callous trusts, corrupt but sometimes benevolent political bosses, bewildered and exploited immigrants, and embittered famers. It was also a period in which, at long last, groups were forming in city after city to combat fraudulent elections, institute civil service in municipal government, improve sanitation and water supplies, promote education for citizenship, and force predatory utilities to reduce their rates. Indeed, the spirit of reform had been gathering force ever since the 1870s, and as the cities increased in complexity, their industries multiplying, their slums spreading, and their central areas becoming intolerably congested, this spirit suddenly invested every aspect of urban life, even the least political. Mainly it directed its energies against the more obvious evils, however, and left to later generations various problems of less compelling immediacy.

In the preceding decade many cities had grown phenomenally, for those times. Enterprising farm boys and girls left the rural areas to seek jobs in factories and offices. Immigrants poured into the ports of the Atlantic seaboard or joined relatives in the big industrial cities of the Middle West. In sheer numbers, Chicago's gain of almost 600,000 topped all others, including increases of more than 300,000 in New York City, 240,000 in Brooklyn, and 200,000 in Philadelphia. Six other cities — Baltimore, Buffalo, Cleveland, Minneapolis, Omaha, and St. Louis — each added more than 100,000 to their populations. In older cities such as Cleveland and Buffalo even the addition of 100,000 or more represented only a 63 or 65 per cent increase, whereas a similar augmentation of the population in Minneapolis represented a gain of 251 per cent and in Omaha a startling rise of 360 per cent. Such proportionately great strides made even Chicago's 118 per cent increase seem rather modest. Moreover, detractors could point out that the Illinois metropolis had swelled its numbers by annexing many small communities.

Almost everywhere the upsurge in population had touched off orgies of land platting and selling, in many places well beyond the city limits, though usually near railroads. The subdivision of land long before more home sites were really needed was such a common practice that few voices were raised against speculators. Ever since the days of the canals and early railroads urban growth had stimulated feverish trading in land. In the mushrooming midwestern cities, curbs on the indiscriminate creation of lots and streets would be some time in coming, but in the slower growing, more experienced eastern seaboard cities, such as Boston, Baltimore, New York, Washington, and municipalities in Pennsylvania, the local authorities began in the early nineties to pay some attention to the quality of platting. Generally, their attempts to exercise stronger control represent some of the first steps toward modern city planning.

Early street commissions, acting under laws applying only to public streets, usually found themselves powerless to prevent private owners from subdividing land and designating the streets as private streets or from laying out streets which caused drainage and traffic problems or made difficult the installation of utilities. The new boards of survey that were established as the decade opened were authorized not only to check such abuses but also to assure orderly expansion in the future.

But the cities undertaking to provide for better development soon discovered that although some of their citizens approved of regulations designed to improve tenements and would even support the condemnation and demolition of insanitary structures to make space for parks and playgrounds in immigrant neighborhoods, another category of citizens bitterly resented any limitation on private initiative and displayed militant impatience with governmental restraint. The whole course of national development—a restless quest for new frontiers, greater opportunity, and sudden riches—reinforced this tendency to license when rules and regulations threatened to interfere with personal ambitions. Yet, paradoxically, Americans had an almost childlike reverence for Law in the abstract—for principle rather than the whim of a tyrant or a latter-day political boss, for truth and justice as the ultimate refuge of the wronged and oppressed.

The experience of the board of survey that was created in Boston in 1891 foreshadowed the difficulties the first recognized city planners were to encounter as they sought to carry out their plans and assert the primacy of the public interest over the rights of private-property holders in an era of extreme judicial conservatism. Established under special authorization of the state legislature, the board was charged with making "plans showing the location of highways which the present and future interests of the public require" in outlying areas then comparatively unoccupied.[1] A section of the act under which the board operated provided that after public hearings had been held on the plans, and the mayor and the board had signed them, no damages would be awarded for a building erected at a different grade from that established in the plan "or for a building erected within the boundary of a way shown on a plan after the filing of said plan."[2] But the Massachusetts Supreme Court invalidated this no-damages provision as an unconstitutional and ineffectual attempt to avoid the taking the taking of property under the right of eminent domain.[3] (Nowadays, of course, state laws permit municipalities to prevent the erection of buildings within the rights-of-way of mapped streets by regulations under the police power rather than by the costlier method of eminent domain. In other words, the establishment of a

[margin note: how Boston got around court ruling]

[margin note: New York]

[margin note: Baltimore]

mapped-street line does not in itself constitute a taking of land. One of the purposes of such laws is to assure that land needed for street widening and for future streets will be available at the price of vacant land.)

Faced with this judicial deterrent to farsighted planning, the city of Boston then did what many other cities in the same predicament were forced to do, with varying success: it refused to cooperate with nonconforming property owners in constructing and maintaining water, sewer, and lighting systems. Among respectable property owners, however, the official plans had standing; and cautious banks in Boston declined to lend on property subject to a board-of-survey line unless the building plans showed observance of the line. Gradually, violations of the street lines became infrequent because most property owners recognized the economy of a planned street system.

In 1891 New York City took the less impressive step of appointing a commissioner of street improvements for upper Manhattan and the Bronx, but it was not until toward the end of the decade, after the state legislature approved a charter for Greater New York, that a bureau was established to complete a plan of streets and parks for the entire city.

In 1893 Baltimore emulated Boston by creating a topographical survey commission to make a complete street plan of the city, including approximately seventeen square miles of undeveloped territory annexed in 1888. In that city, too, some property owners behaved as individualistically as some of those in Boston; and unfortunately for Baltimore, the Maryland Court of Appeals was as zealous in safeguarding private property as the Massachusetts Supreme Court. The justices struck down a no-damages provision in an act of the General Assembly of Maryland prohibiting the city from accepting a deed of dedication or the opening in any manner of a street which did not conform to the general plan prepared by the survey commission and duly approved by the city council. Recalcitrant property owners laid out private streets in open defiance of the survey commissioners and even built houses in the beds of platted streets. When the commissioners decided to block the inharmonious plan of one property owner by opening one of the established streets of the general plan by condemnation, he got wind of their intentions and thwarted them by hastily erecting several houses in the bed of the city's proposed street. As the city council thought that condemning the structures would be too costly for the benefit derived, his triumph over orderly processes was complete.

Only in certain sections of the annexed territory did the survey commission rarely encounter "the old bugbear of personal liberty." Previous to the annexation, the county authorities had laid down an officially adopted plan of many streets that were extensions of those in the old

[margin note: all fought mapping of official street maps]

city, all conforming to "the unsightly gridiron method," as the chief engineer of the survey commission observed.[4] The northeast corner of these streets had been marked on the ground by stone monuments which, though they in no way dedicated the streets for public use, impressed most property owners with the idea that the streets would actually be opened on the ground at some future time. The topographical survey commission therefore had few problems in areas where the stone markers were conspicuous, but elsewhere it was plagued by the opposition of property owners for two decades or more.

Matters were altogether different in Washington once Congress decided to have a plan prepared for the forty-five square miles of the District of Columbia lying beyond the boundaries of the area initially planned in 1791 by General Washington's aide, Major Pierre Charles L'Enfant — who, incidentally, had lacked authority to enforce his plan and had had difficulties with officials and property owners which led to his dismissal and the continuation of his work by his assistant, Andrew Ellicott. From the time of the Civil War until 1888 subdivisions "grew in fantastic shapes" in many parts of the city.[5] In that year Congress declared that no more street plans should be recorded unless they conformed to the general plan of the city, but the legislators failed to authorize the preparation of such a plan. Five years later they did so, creating a commission to devise a system of highways "as nearly in conformity with the [original] street plan of the city of Washington" as they deemed advisable and practicable.[6] The members were the Secretary of War, the Secretary of the Interior, and the Chief of Engineers of the Army. Their plan of 1898, while extending the main avenues and thoroughfares delineated by L'Enfant, included many dull checkerboard arrangements and provided in only a few sections of rough topography for curvilinear streets and varying sizes of blocks. Although there was no statutory prohibition of buildings in the bed of mapped streets, the commission and the District Government avoided the problems encountered in other cities by resolutely refusing to install sewers, water mains, paving, and other improvements unless property owners conformed with the plan.

Of the large cities in the East, Philadelphia was perhaps unique in having unquestioned authority to enforce street planning. It had a tradition of orderly urban expansion going back to an act of the colonial assembly of February 24, 1721, providing for "surveyors and regulators" to establish streets and building lines in the city. The number of these officials was increased not only in Philadelphia but also in adjacent municipalities, and their duties were gradually broadened until the consolidation act of 1854 created a department of surveys for the enlarged city of 129 square miles. Each of the twelve districts into which the city was divided had a surveyor and regulator, and the twelve officials together formed a board of surveyors under the presidency of the chief engineer and surveyor of the city.

The Pennsylvania legislature on May 16, 1891, hastened the formation of similar boards in other cities by enacting a statute requiring that "every municipality shall have a general plan of its streets and alleys."[7] The law included the usual no-damages provision applying to buildings constructed within the lines of any located street or alley after councilmanic approval of a plan. The state supreme court, respecting the pre-revolutionary origins of the Philadelphia precedent, repeatedly upheld this act, as did the United States District Court.

Commenting on the statute in 1917, when municipalities in many other states were still struggling to regulate subdivisions and curb indiscriminate street openings by private owners, Andrew Wright Crawford, a city solicitor of Philadelphia, said that he had often been puzzled to know why admirers of the Pennsylvania legislation had not adopted "the perfectly simple process of securing state constitutional amendments" granting cities of their own states the same legal sanction to plat and protect undeveloped streets.[8] But broad public support for adequate power to plan and carry out plans was slow to evolve in some states owing to the general fear that planning would unduly curtail individual freedom.

Crusaders in the Slums

The ancient notions of property rights which at times impeded better development of the peripheral areas of cities proved less troublesome in the more popular struggle to regulate tenement houses and improve the living conditions of the urban poor. In the interest of public health and safety, cities had enacted laws in the early days of the republic providing for the inspection of boarding and lodging houses and had occasionally instructed officials to remove dangerously dilapidated buildings. Through the years the legal precedents for requiring improvements in ventilation, sanitation, and cleanliness had accumulated. By 1867, there was a strong movement for the enactment of a first tenement-house law for the cities of New York and Brooklyn. Not that this measure was any great obstacle to the renting of damp cellars and the erection of more railroad flats with a succession of dark, windowless interior rooms, but at least its very deficiencies suggested additional goals for the philanthropists, church folk, and physicians who had agitated for its adoption, after conducting house-to-house investigations which indicated an alarming correlation between cheap, crowded living quarters and a high incidence of communicable disease and mortality.

In the seventies a magazine entitled the *Plumber and Sanitary Engineer* joined the crusade for better housing for working people by sponsoring a competition among architects to develop an ideal plan for tenement houses. From this effort at reform came the "dumbbell" tenement, so named because its side walls were idented to provide a narrow light-well between buildings and afford interior rooms a modicum of natural illumination and ventilation. Made mandatory by a new tenement-house law in 1879, the dumbbell type at first seemed a true symbol of progress. But structures five or six stories high on lots twenty-five by a hundred feet were only slightly better than the old railroad flats. Little sunshine penetrated the deep air shafts between the dumbbell tenements at any time of the year. In summer when the mercury soared, the occupants all but suffocated in the ovenlike interiors. Still more space would be required around all buildings, and certainly more toilets and bathtubs and washbasins in the apartments.

In the late eighties and early nineties, after the first settlement houses had been established to aid the immigrant in his adjustment to a strange land, social workers took up positions in the vanguard of the housing reform movement, bringing to it a heightened awareness of the shortcomings of the tenement-house environment, especially the lack of play space for children, the inadequacy of school grounds, and the absence of social centers for adults. The contribution of these humanitarians to the incipient city planning movement was to be a strong expression of the necessity of preventing further congestion of population.

Not only in New York but also in other cities civic leaders and voluntary associations cried out for action to improve the housing and surroundings of the "new Americans" from Europe, and of the native poor, victims of the industrialization begun before the Civil War and enormously accelerated by that conflict and the subsequent period of reconstruction and headlong economic expansion. In Boston the Massachusetts Bureau of Statistics of Labor conducted an investigation of tenement houses in 1891. The findings were promptly translated into legislation prohibiting nonfireproof tenements. In 1892 a similar investigation in Buffalo, inspired by an imminent cholera epidemic, resulted in the adoption of a housing ordinance by the city council the following year. Many other cities passed regulatory measures after police reporter Jacob Riis spurred on the reformers with his *How the Other Half Lives.* This sensational bestseller, a vivid, anecdotal account of the squalor and degradation of life in the East Side wards of Manhattan, caused citizens throughout the country to look about in their own localities and discover slums every bit as bad as those he described.

In 1892 the Congress responded to the national sense of shame, though with a firm grip on the purse strings. The lawmakers granted the Bureau of Labor the paltry sum of $20,000 for a study of slum areas in all cities with a population of 200,000 or more. As the amount was altogether insufficient for an investigation of the sixteen cities in that category, the federal agency was obliged to select only four: New York, Philadelphia, Chicago, and Baltimore.

The investigators approached their task with a certain bureaucratic detachment, ruling out "inquiries looking to causes why people are found in the slum districts of cities, what brought them there, the experience which leads to such a residence," and similar troublesome questions as being "too vague for the application of the statistical method."[9] The findings, accordingly, were almost guaranteed to eliminate serious repercussions when they were published in 1894.

The bureau's report presented thirty-three tables, twenty-three of which concerned the foreign-born of slum areas chosen in consultation with city authorities. The figures confirmed the popular understanding that immigrants were mainly concentrated in such areas, that overcrowding was a serious problem, that the proportion of arrests was far higher in slum areas than elsewhere, and that New York tenements had a large number of sleeping rooms with no outside windows—6,576 out of 28,050 surveyed, to be exact. But the tone of the report was not urgent. It stated that "the earnings of the people living in the slum districts canvassed are quite up to the average earnings of the people generally. . . ."[10] It presented the reassuring finding of a physician that "the almost complete absence of pathogenic germs in the air of the slums is astonishing."[11] By way of explaining why some families "of the highest respectability" still lived amid depressing surroundings, it mentioned only once that many formerly prosperous areas in all four cities had steadily decayed and become hopelessly blighted.

A companion study, authorized at the same time that the investigation of American slums was ordered, appeared in 1895. Entitled *The Housing of the Working People,* it described model housing developed by private industry, cooperative associations, and citizens' groups in Great Britain, France, Germany, Holland, Sweden, and Denmark. The author was Elgin Ralston Lovell Gould, a political scientist and expert in municipal government, who admired the earlier efforts of Alfred T. White of Brooklyn and various philanthropic companies and associations to provide commercially profitable model tenements for "thrifty and socially ambitious" artisans. Like most well-intentioned intellectuals of his era, Gould believed that if the workingman was to have decent housing, private enterprise rather than government must provide it, at dividends limited to 4 or 5 per cent, even though venture capital in America had shown little enthusiasm for the modest returns offered by model tenements. Certainly, very few had been built. Yet Gould, in asking the rhetorical question will improved housing pay? stoutly maintained that "only in case an affirmative response is forthcoming can we augur a successful issue to the housing problem."[12] His faith in profitable philanthropy was, indeed, so strong that he contended that renovated housing could be provided for the casual worker, who might be somewhat lazy, careless, or inclined to run into debt, if companies or associations attempting to meet his needs would employ "lady rent collectors with wise heads and sympathetic hearts," like those Octavia Hill, Ruskin's friend, found to manage the dilapidated houses she rehabilitated for the London poor.[13]

Gould's building moderate income housing

But Gould expected improvement in the housing situation not alone from benevolent landlordism. He hoped that the development of rapid transit in American cities would afford opportunities for well-paid workers to move to the suburbs, thereby making older dwellings in central areas available to the lowest paid. He was fearful, though, that American builders were being allowed to create "insanitary property" for later generations by laying out poorly planned developments on unsewered land, whereas some German and English cities provided improvement plans and prohibited building in areas without sewers.

Gould himself demonstrated his confidence in limited-dividend philanthropy by forming the City and Suburban Homes Company in 1896 and building the first of several model apartments in Manhattan. Later his company sought to set an example for other groups interested in relieving the congestion of the older areas of New York City. The firm purchased a 530-acre tract in Brooklyn on which it erected 250 cottages for sale on liberal payment terms. Advanced as some of his apartment developments were (they had all necessary sanitary conveniences and were two rooms deep to assure ample light and good cross-ventilation), they were priced beyond the means of the average tenement-dweller and were redolent of capitalist efforts to sanctify plutocracy. Among Gould's associates was Cornelius Vanderbilt, for whom Richard Morris Hunt had designed the lavish Breakers at Newport, a pile costing millions at a time when laborers were lucky if they earned $500 a year.

The results of Gould's experiment

Neither Gould's report for the Bureau of Labor nor that agency's own study of slums caused the federal government to intervene in the struggle for better housing for working people. The impetus for improvement continued to come from the press, settlement-house workers, public health officials, sanitarians, professional men, and assorted lay reformers, to all of whom the badly planned, pathogenic tenement house represented the prime social evil. A few, such as Robert W. de Forest, president of the New York Charity Organization Society, increasingly realized the need for planning the larger urban environment and reconstructing slum neighborhoods, but the majority steadfastly pursued the goal of higher

where support for reform came from

standards for tenement houses, scarcely understanding that requirements for better construction, more sanitary facilities, and more space
would result in rents above the reach of low-income families.

Congestion, Playgrounds, and Parks

Prodded by the reformers, the New York state legislature in 1894 authorized the governor to appoint another tenement-house committee (there
had been two earlier commissions, in 1884 and 1887) to investigate conditions and recommend remedial legislation. Its findings, far more detailed
than those of the Bureau of Labor, filled no fewer than six hundred pages
and focused public indignation on the growing congestion of the tenement districts and the shocking fact that Trinity Church, wealthiest in
America, obtained a large proportion of its income from "old and rickety"
tenements. The agitation over congestion was especially significant because it was to provide much of the stimulus for the organization of the
first national conference on city planning fifteen years later. The outrage
against Trinity Church was to energize the housing reform movement
until the end of the decade, when still another tenement-house commission, not content with recommending superficial changes in regulations,
would propose outlawing the dumbbell tenement altogether.

The Tenement House Committee of 1894 disclosed that the population
density of Manhattan Island — 143.2 persons per acre — exceeded that of
the most crowded cities of France, Germany, and England. The residential tenth ward, with a density of 626 per acre, was 30 per cent more congested than a similar section of Prague, generally considered the worst
in Europe. One section of the eleventh ward had a density of 986.4 per
acre and was even more crowded than the Koombarwara district of
Bombay, which in 1881 had a density of 759.66 persons per acre and was
one of the most overpopulated spots on earth. Still more disquieting was
the revelation of a police census, made in April, 1895, that half of the
population of the entire city lived in certain wards whose total area was
less than a tenth of the territory within the city boundaries.

Small wonder, then, that the state legislature that year authorized the
expenditure of $5,000,000 for the expropriation of unfit tenements and
the establishment of small parks in the most crowded sections of the
slums. But New York was not the first big city to awaken to the need
for play space for children in congested areas. The Boston Park Department in 1889 converted a ten-acre tract on the Charles River into an
open-air gymnasium for residents of a nearby densely populated section.
In Chicago the civic-minded William Kent (who later presented the
famous Muir Woods near San Francisco to the American people for a
national park) four years later gave land to Jane Addams, the founder
of Hull House, for the first playground in that city. And school properties

THE SPIRIT OF REFORM   11

in cities throughout the country were soon being used after hours for children's play, Boston leading the way in 1894, Chicago following suit in 1897, San Francisco in 1898, and New York in 1899. Many states in those years also passed laws permitting school buildings to be used in the evenings as social centers for adults living in crowded areas.

All these progressive actions, as well as others aimed at abolishing sweatshops, strengthening the labor movement, providing more manual and trade instruction, and improving education, together constituted a *fin de siècle* approximation of present-day antipoverty programs. Viewing the "broad-minded administration" of Boston in 1898, Robert A. Wood, the head of a settlement house in the South End, was thankful that local officials espoused "the principle that the modern city must be more and more socialized, must more and more minister directly to the comfort and pleasure of its inhabitants."[14] Yet there was nothing truly novel about the trend of the times; the growing sense of responsibility for the public welfare had been nurtured for three or four decades by interrelated movements for developing pure water supplies, controlling contagious diseases, creating effective sewerage systems, and providing parks, particularly large, romantic pleasure grounds, such as Central Park and Franklin Park, which Frederick Law Olmsted, America's first great landscape architect, thought of as offering city dwellers the equivalent of a day in the country. The park movement, especially, prepared middle- and upper-class Americans for the reform efforts to establish small parks and playgrounds in immigrant neighborhoods and other congested areas.

In Chicago, for example, the campaign that gathered momentum after the turn of the century to develop active recreation centers in the "river wards" and similarly crowded sections of the city might have met with an indifferent response if the more established citizens, having long ago learned to value the chain of parks brought into being by an older generation, had not finally realized that most of these parks were too distant from the congested districts to serve them adequately. Even as a young city Chicago had acquired many small parks and "beauty spots" at street intersections. In the late sixties, after the city had developed Lincoln Park, the first of its larger pleasure grounds, the public imagination had been captivated by a proposal for a system of parks and connecting boulevards. In response to popular demands, the state legislature in 1869 created three special metropolitan park authorities, so that desirable sites outside the municipal boundaries could be obtained without waiting for the city to expand. By 1880 Chicago boasted some two thousand acres in parks and ranked second only to Philadelphia in park area. But this proud showing lulled Chicagoans to comparative inactivity until torrential immigration and overcrowding awakened them to the needs of the deprived districts.

Chicago was advanced, however, in creating the first links of a metropolitan park chain while it was still in its lusty adolescence. In the 1870s and 1880s most cities struggled arduously merely to acquire a few small parks or to develop a single great park, though a few municipalities were fortunate in obtaining the services of landscape architects who proposed complete park systems. Horace W. S. Cleveland, who had been among the thirty or more designers competing in the 1850s with Frederick Law Olmsted and Calvert Vaux for the commission to plan Central Park in New York City, outlined a system of parks and parkways for Minneapolis in 1883 and a regional park system for both that city and St. Paul in 1887, but the twin cities were not then ready for regional planning. Minneapolis alone immediately availed itself of Cleveland's plan, by 1893 acquiring and developing twenty-nine parks embracing a total of twelve hundred acres. Omaha, Nebraska, also gave this designer the opportunity to plan a comprehensive park system. And in 1890 Kansas City, Missouri, turned to George Edward Kessler, a landscape architect with a European education, to prepare a city-wide plan of parks and boulevards.

These were unusual men, far ahead of their contemporaries in realizing the need for city planning as well as park planning. In 1873 Cleveland wrote, in a series of essays brought together under the title *Landscape Architecture,* "Certainly no people ever before possessed such facilities as are placed in our hands for carrying through to a successful result a prearranged plan of town construction, and no people ever before had such control of all the requisite material for the purpose. We have our choices of sites in a virgin region [the Middle West], comprising every variety of soil, climate, and topographical character."[15] But his fellow citizens in the rapidly growing mid-continental areas were too busy subduing a new environment to accept his ideal of comprehensive planning. Cleveland observed with dismay how railroad surveyors laid out towns with "no regard . . . to the topography of the ground; no reference . . . to future interests or necessities of business or pleasure; no effort . . . to secure the preservation of natural features which in time might be invaluable as a means of giving to the place a distinct and unique character."[16] Only after thoughtless planning and building had destroyed much of the pristine beauty of the urban setting did officials and townsmen awaken to the need for restoring some of the natural charm lost in the initial period of settlement. Cleveland was able to fulfill their desire for parks and tree-lined boulevards, but he understood that these should be "integral portions of the city, instead of being merely ornamental appendages."[17] Had he lived at a later time (he died in 1900), he would unquestionably have been a leading city planner. Denied the opportunity to enjoy a broader career, he surely contributed to the development of that milieu of progressive thought from which the city planning movement sprang.

George E. Kessler, only eleven years old when Cleveland penned his ideas about "the art of town arrangement," spanned parts of two centuries and succeeded in making the transition from landscape architect to city planner, being much in demand by city planning commissions from 1910 until his death in 1923. His mother, ambitious for his success in life, took him in his middle teens from the frontier town of Dallas, Texas, to Germany, where she gave him an education in forestry, botany, civil engineering, and landscape design, not to mention travel throughout Europe with a private tutor, studying civic design in all the great cities. Upon his return to the United States at the age of twenty, he spent a few months working in Central Park under Olmsted's direction, and while there he may have absorbed the older landscape architect's conception of a city-wide system of parks and parkways, the germ of which appeared in a plan prepared for the City and County of San Francisco in 1865–1866. Though Olmsted invited the young man to stay on in New York, Kessler yearned for the trans-Mississippi regions he had known as a boy. He went to work in the raw, unlovely Kansas of the early 1880s for the Kansas City, Fort Scott, and Gulf Railroad, transforming "some nondescript acreage" near the town of Merriam, Kansas, into a delightful railroad excursion park "supplied with . . . every attraction and convenience for outdoor meetings."[18]

A few years later Kessler was landscaping a rugged hollow in a new, high-priced residential section of Kansas City, Missouri, and designing the grounds of the home of the chairman of the newly established park board, a dynamic, European-educated, multimillionaire businessman

1. George E. Kessler, landscape architect

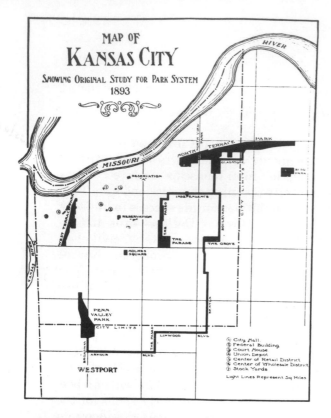

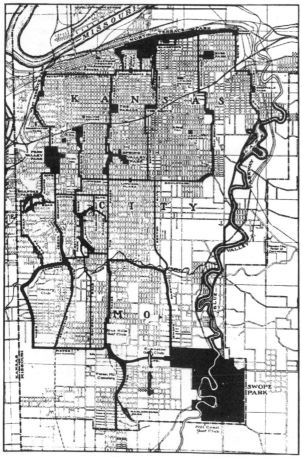

2. (upper) Kessler's study for the Kansas City park system, 1893; (lower) Kansas City park system, 1917

named August Robert Meyer. The young man's big opportunity came when the board engaged him as "secretary" and "engineer," at a salary of $200 a month, to design the park system of Kansas City. In a little more than three years he produced a report that was "vastly more than a plea for a few parks." It was, according to one authority, "a detailed and comprehensive look at Kansas City's topography and traffic patterns, population density and growth, its industrial and residential sections, and its prospects for future development . . . in a word, planning."[19]

Kessler's achievements in the next twenty years made Kansas City famous and inspired cities from Salt Lake City to Toledo and from Indianapolis to Mexico City to seek his services, but neither he nor the various park boards he served in Kansas City can be credited exclusively with arousing the desire for parks, boulevards, and playgrounds. For more than twenty years before his original report was issued in October, 1893, the press and numerous civic leaders of Kansas City had agitated for parks. And when at last the city had a sweeping plan showing "selections for public purposes, their most satisfactory distribution, and the dependence of one improvement upon another,"[20] progressive citizens discovered that political boss James Pendergast was allied with them in supporting the plan, for one reason because the creation of a park system would provide jobs for deserving followers. Not even the backing of Pendergast was sufficient, however, to insure smooth sailing for the Kessler plan. For several years mossbacks and taxpayers employed obstructionist tactics and legal actions to hinder execution of the plan, but by the end of 1900 effective resistance ceased.

Meanwhile, the city had received, in June, 1896, a princely gift of land from "a shy, wispy bachelor" named Thomas H. Swope — more than two square miles of beautiful, wooded land, bisected by the Blue River. Developed as a large suburban park, Swope's lands handsomely supplemented the five interior parks, many small squares, and boulevards of Kessler's original plan. And in time, of course, the city limits expanded to envelop this outlying preserve.

In the city itself the most ornamental feature of the park system was The Paseo, a dual boulevard that replaced an area of slums and shanties. Extending for nine blocks through the north-central section, this broad drive was really a chain of small parks, as Kessler himself said. At one intersection was a formal sunken garden, at another an enormous fountain reminiscent of those at Versailles, and at still others small fountains or distinctive green rectangles. The Pergola, a double colonnade with a trellis roof, graced one side of the route, between Tenth and Eleventh streets, providing welcome shade on hot summer days. The whole scheme, flavored with European touches, bestowed on Kansas City an urbanity that was the envy of lesser cities in the unsophisticated midlands of America.

3. West Bluff, Kansas City, in the early 1890s *(Parks and Recreation Department, Kansas City, Missouri)*

4. Tenth Street outlook, West Terrace Park, Kansas City, 1921 *(Parks and Recreation Department, Kansas City, Missouri)*

Metropolitanism in the Boston Area

Though the park systems designed by Cleveland and Kessler exemplified for Middle Western and Southwestern cities all that was worthwhile in civic improvement, for other parts of the United States the Boston metropolitan park system developed in accordance with plans proposed by Charles Eliot, landscape architect, and Sylvester Baxter, journalist and editor, was the ideal in urban regional amenity. To Eliot, an apprentice of Frederick Law Olmsted's before he opened his own office in 1886 at the age of twenty-seven, belongs the chief credit for realizing that the rapid expansion of Boston and surrounding towns would soon deprive an ever increasing population of "riches of scenery such as Chicago or Denver or many another American city would give millions to create, if it were possible."[21] Eliot took the initiative in organizing, first, a group known as the Trustees of Public Reservations to acquire and hold, for the benefit of the public, beautiful and historical places in Massachusetts, and then, when the limitations of wholly private financial support became obvious, the movement that resulted in the establishment of a

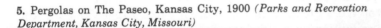

5. Pergolas on The Paseo, Kansas City, 1900 *(Parks and Recreation Department, Kansas City, Missouri)*

temporary state commission to investigate and report on the need for a publicly financed metropolitan park system.

Eliot and Baxter and their supporters followed local precedent in proposing a regional authority to provide Boston and thirty-eight surrounding cities and towns with public open spaces. As early as the 1840s Boston and some of its suburbs had encountered another regional problem that demanded a regional solution—pollution of the Charles River and its tributaries. Year by year the problem grew worse, until the Boston Board of Health noted in one of its annual reports that "large territories have been at once, and frequently, enveloped in an atmosphere of stench so strong as to arouse the sleeping, terrify the weak, and nauseate and exasperate everybody."[22] Various outlying areas became parts of the city by annexation between 1868 and 1874, in order to contribute through their municipal taxes to the building of an interceptor sewer designed to reduce the pollution of the river. But independent communities to the north and in the southern sector of the region would neither cease their pollution of the river nor assent to consolidation with Boston, as suggested by a study commission in 1874. The alternative was a special metropolitan authority similar in administrative organization to the London Metropolitan Police District established in 1829 and the Metropolitan Board of Works formed in the British capital in 1855. Still, the opponents of annexation were lukewarm toward this new form of metro-

6. Charles Eliot, landscape architect

politan organization. Neither they nor the state legislature accepted it until two additional investigatory commissions and the state board of health had reported that a much-needed great northern interceptor sewer and the enlargement of the southern interceptor built by Boston should be undertaken by a state agency operating regionally and financed by a series of annual payments from the towns benefited. Thus, in 1889, the Boston region finally overcame local jealousies and achieved, with state assistance, a form of areawide government capable of being adapted to the solution of other regional problems as well.

Taking the Metropolitan Sewerage Commission as his model, Eliot on December 16, 1891, called together members of the park commissions of various suburban communities to consider petitioning the legislature to create a metropolitan park authority. Their plea to the lawmakers stated:

> The undersigned petitioners respectfully represent that the seashores, the river-banks, the mountain-tops, and almost all the finest parts of the natural scenery of Massachusetts are possessed by private persons, whose private interests often dictate the destruction of said scenery or the exclusion of the public from the enjoyment thereof. In the opinion of the undersigned, the scenes of natural beauty to which the people of the Commonwealth are to-day of right entitled to resort for pleasure and refreshment are both too few in number and too small in area. . . .[23]

7. Sylvester Baxter

Appearing before the legislature, Eliot pointed out that the whole metropolitan region was likely to be deprived of the open spaces it needed because existing legislation limited local park commissioners to action within the bounds of their own towns and cities, whereas it was self-evident that those boundaries bore no relation to the scenery of the district they divided.[24] The best lands for park purposes were along the banks of rivers and brooks, but where town boundaries followed the channels of streams, it was almost certain that a town on one side would not acquire waterside properties unless the town on the opposite side agreed to do so, and one or the other was almost sure to feel that its burden of expense would be out of proportion to the benefit accruing to it. The only answer therefore was an areawide park authority with power to acquire desirable areas anywhere in the metropolitan region.

Unmoved by the young landscape architect's plea for swift action, the legislators chose to appoint a study commission to present a detailed case for such an authority. The three members of course selected Eliot to project a system of scenic and recreational areas. To Baxter fell the task of marshaling all the pertinent facts of metropolitan growth and adducing the arguments for "laying out ample open spaces for the use of the public"[25] in an area then containing almost 900,000 residents, with prospects of "a million and a half within a measurable time."[26]

Eliot's scheme of proposed reservations reflected the general desire of the park commissioners of the cities and towns in the region to integrate city and country. Along the streams would be "a whole series of public promenades and playgrounds for the use of the population which tends to crowd into the valleys." Since the main watercourses flowed toward the heart of Boston, waterside roads would constitute "a series of sorely needed pleasant routes leading from the country, through the suburbs, to the city, and even to the bay or oceanside beyond."[27]

Baxter emphasized the importance of a metropolitan tax base for acquiring and developing an areawide park system by describing the restricted financial resources of the outlying cities and towns. Their treasuries were "strained to the utmost extent to meet the demands imposed by their rapid increase in population."[28] Painting a picture of the Bostonian suburbia of the early 1890s which might be mistaken for a description of some present-day suburbia, he wrote: "The overflow of Boston into the surrounding country, the attractions of cheap lands and the consequent facilities for the building of low-priced houses in the suburban districts, has caused these various communities to fill up rapidly with a population composed of persons, for the most part, in very moderate circumstances. Therefore, in many of these suburban cities and towns the increase in valuation has not been at all commensurate with the increase of population."[29] On nearly every side one heard complaints

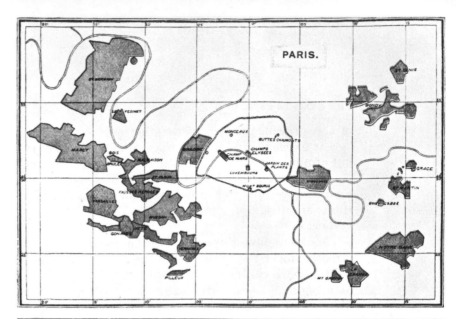

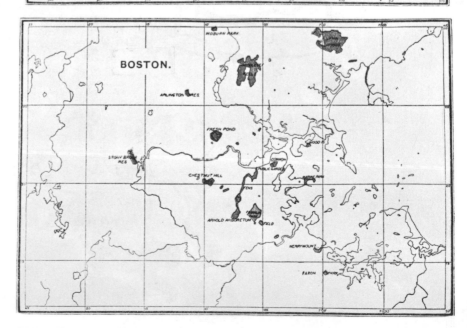

8. Park systems of Paris (upper), London (middle), and Boston (lower), 1890

of the growing burden of taxation as suburban communities incurred "great expenditures for the erection of new school-houses, for the laying out of new streets and building of sidewalks, for the extension of water-supply service, for the construction of sewers, etc." Without a metropolitan governmental unit to provide parks for their residents, many of these small jurisdictions would probably forgo recreation areas altogether.

Thanks to Baxter's persuasive pen, the Boston region in 1893 achieved, directly under the authority of the commonwealth, a permanent metropolitan park commission capable of financing the acquisition of parks on a regional basis, but his part in this great endeavor has usually been overlooked. In many ways his was a broader vision than Eliot's, encompassing social needs to which Eliot merely alluded, foreseeing opportunities for regional planning not even mentioned by the landscape

9. Boston metropolitan park system, 1902, as developed in accordance with Eliot's plan

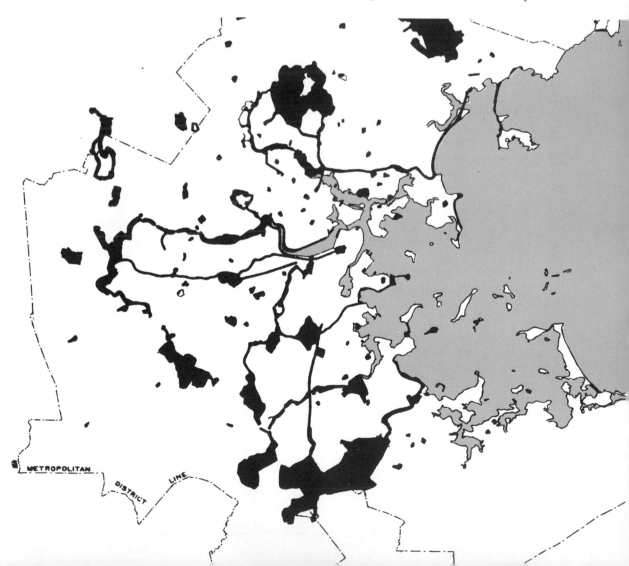

architect. Baxter rather than Eliot worried because "the suburban movement has already converted the outlying sections very extensively into
tenement-house regions,"[30] and it was Baxter who pleaded for the construction of blocks of dwellings like those of the Co-operative Building
Company of Boston and the Victoria Square dwellings of Liverpool—
projects distinguished by central garden courts "where children may be
safely left to play together, while adult residents may frequent the place
for out-door rest and relaxation."[31] Baxter particularly appreciated the
work of the Boston Board of Survey in planning the street systems of
outlying sections of the city and suggested the desirability of establishing a metropolitan board of survey to plan the highway system of undeveloped areas of the metropolitan region. Such a regional board, he
wrote, could "co-ordinate its work with that of the Metropolitan Parks
Commission, so that at the same time the latter could designate the most
suitable sites for . . . local pleasure grounds, and make the reservations
accordingly."[32]

A man with such wide-ranging interests in housing, parks, playgrounds, regional circulation systems, sanitation, government, and finance was well ahead of the vast majority of his contemporaries, though
the very selection of his type as secretary of an important investigatory
commission was prophetic of regional planning programs on which many
metropolitan communities would embark in the future.

The regional park system he and Eliot envisaged took shape swiftly.
Within a year the permanent Metropolitan Park Commission acquired
five reservations ranging in size from fifty-nine acres to forty-three hundred acres and aggregating more than seven thousand acres. The commission also took immediate action to obtain Revere Beach, five miles
from the State House in Boston, and the lower banks of the Charles River,
and to provide direct parkways, with central space reserved for electric
cars, from Blue Hills and Middlesex Fells to the edge of the densely
populated area of Boston. By 1902 the system embraced approximately
fifteen thousand acres, including a total river frontage of thirty miles,
ten miles of ocean shoreline, and twenty-two miles of right-of-way for
parkways.

The urban regionalism manifested in this outer-park movement reflected, in some measure, the typical late nineteenth century American
uneasiness about "the poisonous excitement of city life" and the search
for antidotes to "the noisy ugliness of towns," as Eliot expressed it.[33]
The metropolitanism associated with a third regional undertaking, the
formation of an areawide water supply district, was, on the other hand,
a hardheaded recognition of political, fiscal, and environmental realities.
Since 1886 the state board of health had been allocating a dwindling
number of uncontaminated local sources of water supply among the

10. Beaver Brook, Boston metropolitan park system, 1895 *(Metropolitan District Commission of Massachusetts)*

11. Echo Bridge in Hemlock Gorge, Boston metropolitan park system, 1896 *(Metropolitan District Commission of Massachusetts)*

contentious suburban communities around Boston. Early in 1893 the state legislature directed the board to investigate the advisability of a metropolitan system administered by a district corresponding to the sewer district previously established and the park district then under discussion. Boston agreed to turn over to the proposed water supply district the great waterworks it had already constructed, and smaller localities badly in need of water expressed eagerness to join. But others in fair or relatively good positions bargained for concessions or opposed the scheme until a severe drought and water famine later in the year clearly demonstrated the need to develop a new water supply for the entire metropolitan district. In 1895 the legislature created the desired special agency, controlled by the state but serving cities and towns throughout the Boston region.

While this third metropolitan district was under consideration, the state legislature approved an act which was potentially one of the most significant ever passed by a group of lawmakers. It authorized the governor to appoint a commission of three members to investigate forms of metropolitan organization; and it specifically charged the members to consider two possibilities: "that of establishing for the metropolitan district . . . a general government with limited powers . . . allowing each municipality [in it] independence in local affairs, but conferring upon the general government authority in matters which could be administered to better advantage by a general government;" and that of "uniting such cities and towns into one municipality by annexing them to the city of Boston."[34]

Thus, in 1895, one of the oldest metropolitan regions in the United States began to debate alternative forms of metropolitan government, one of which, a multipurpose jurisdiction with limited powers, remains to this day an ideal sought by many regional planners, since comprehensive planning without responsible areawide government to carry out a general scheme of development is a venture characterized more by extravagant hopes than by assurance of success.

The investigatory commission appointed in the Boston area in 1894 submitted a report in 1896 opposing both a supercity created by annexation and further state administration through so-called metropolitan commissions. Instead, the group recommended a government modeled after that of Greater London, centralizing functions of areawide importance and guaranteeing local autonomy in matters deemed to be wholly of local concern. Each city or town in the Boston metropolitan district, the commission pointed out, "has its own peculiar local needs and aspirations, which are known to its own people much better than they are or can be known to those who live outside its borders."[35] The commission believed that by thus suggesting the continuance of long-established local governments and the preservation of community identity, it would win acceptance of its proposal to rearrange county boundaries and transform all of Suffolk County and parts of Essex, Middlesex, and Norfolk counties into a new metropolitan county to be known as the County of Boston.

To assure every section of this extensive jurisdiction direct representation, the commission recommended a large county council somewhat similar to the ancient New England county courts and to the new English county councils. The functions of the metropolitan sewer, park, and water supply commissions would be transferred to this governing group, and "when an evident need arose," it would, upon authorization of the legislature, assume "other duties that were undeniably of a metropolitan character," such as maintenance of main highways and "possibly questions of metropolitan transportation."[36]

Rather than have the legislature impose the proposed new form of government on the region, the commission suggested a referendum by the people of the metropolitan district on the question, "Shall a new county be formed of the cities and towns which make up the metropolitan district?" But the commission's remedy for the trend toward state control of metropolitan functions was too novel for most Bostonians and, as might have been expected, aroused strong opposition among county officials and officeholders in many of the smaller communities, who feared that the representatives of Boston would dominate the proposed county council. A bill calling for a referendum on the formation of the metropolitan county failed in the legislative session of 1896. The defeat of the measure ended, until the latter half of the twentieth century, any prospect of creating an all-embracing jurisdiction capable of undertaking integrated planning and development of all truly metropolitan facilities, though later merger of the three special metropolitan districts was a partial victory for the idea of coordinated planning.

Borough Government and Hopes for a City Plan

More favorably disposed toward proposals for metropolitan unification, the New York state legislature only a year later authorized a borough form of government for the densely settled territory comprising Greater New York, thereby arousing some hopes that large-scale public works serving a vast territory would be carried out in accordance with a "city plan." Now thought of as a form of municipal government, the "borough plan" of New York City was at the time it was instituted essentially a type of metropolitan government. The greater part of the territory socially and economically related to the central city was included in the consolidation—approximately 315 square miles in all. The census of 1900 showed 3,437,200 of the 4,607,804 persons in the metropolitan district living in the five boroughs of Manhattan, the Bronx, Brooklyn, Queens, and Richmond. Further growth later extended the populated area into a widespread region embracing parts of three states, but in the late nineties New York City enjoyed the distinction of being one of the few metropolitan communities in which an overall government served the greater proportion of the regional population.

The smaller New York and environs of earlier days had, however, had a foretaste of metropolitanism. The state legislature in 1857 had established a metropolitan police district embracing New York City, Brooklyn, and the counties of Kings, Westchester, and Richmond. In 1865 New York and Brooklyn were included in a metropolitan fire district; and from 1866 to 1870 a metropolitan health district served the same area as the metropolitan police district created in 1857. But none of these districts had endured, because New York politicians complained bitterly about them and finally succeeded in having them abolished.

As examples of areawide jurisdictions, these special districts appealed to a Consolidation Inquiry Commission selected in 1890 to consider the expediency of combining New York City with its suburbs. The commission suggested no local autonomy whatsoever. The borough form of government established in Greater New York on January 1, 1898, under a charter approved by the state legislature in 1897 was a compromise forced by Brooklyn and other communities fearful of losing control of all local matters. The charter provided for powerful central agencies of government, such as a municipal assembly of two houses, a board of estimate and apportionment, and a board of public improvements, but granted each borough a measure of home rule, though not enough to satisfy local interests.

In a charter revision three years later the mighty Board of Public Improvements, on which served the heads of the departments of water supply, highways, street cleaning, sewers, public buildings, and bridges, was eliminated as inconsistent with the plan of autonomy for the boroughs in matters of public improvements, but for a brief period this auspicious agency seemed to bring into "intelligent and comprehensive relationship nearly all the most important constructive departments of the city government."[37] Contemplating the scope of the board's authority, architect Julius F. Harder was moved to believe that no obstacles existed to a beginning of city planning. "Civic pride and interest in municipal affairs will in time evolve a logical city plan," he predicted in the Reform Club's publication, *Municipal Affairs*.

A prophet now all but forgotten, Harder had studied L'Enfant's plan of Washington, Haussmann's plan of Paris, and the plans of many other cities. From them he had drawn inspiration for his own plan for transforming Manhattan from an island constricted by a gridiron street pattern into an urban area served by several convenient diagonal routes and graced by a civic center in the general area of Union Square.

"The system of diagonal avenues results, aside from its practical and economic superiority, in conditions known as 'Vistas,'" he explained. At the intersections of main diagonals the central spaces would be so large that important structures could be erected in them. The views down these broad avenues thus would focus on monumental buildings instead of "terminating in a perspective nothing." Even the intersections of the diagonals with the streets of the rectangular system would afford greater length of vision and bring "larger objects or an increased aggregate within the extended angle of sight."[38]

Though Harder was intrigued by the aesthetic possibilities of his plan, he was by no means interested only in the appearance of the city. He fully appreciated the economic functions on which the prosperity of New York depended and was well aware that these were determined in large measure by a location enabling the metropolis readily to tap the resources of a vast continent and to carry on maritime trade with the whole world. "These are conditions, eminently practical, which in wise conjunction with interior and local requirements preclude haphazard methods in the new plan and are entitled to the profound study of the best qualified brains of the time," he urged. "These conditions will impose imperatively the location and extent of docks, of railroads, of bridges, of ferries, of warehouses and markets, of the manufacturing districts, and finally of the system of streets and intra-mural communications, the seat of City Government, private buildings and residence, of the parks and other systems."[39]

As if countering skepticism about the wisdom of attempting to prepare a long-range plan, he asserted, "While it is fair to admit that such a plan must contain a certain elasticity, both in original intention and in the mode of application, to permit of the incorporation of future development which it must ever remain impossible to foresee; still, in the main, it may proceed upon theories of tolerable certainty. Such for instance, that the southerly end of Manhattan Island will remain the nucleus of anticipated accumulation and that the area directly contributory to the city's activity will extend in a radius of at least 50 miles from it."[40]

Had Harder been writing more than twenty years later, when Thomas Adams and other city planners were preparing the first great regional plan of New York and its environs, he could hardly have been more cognizant of the regional influence of the nation's largest center of population. He was amazingly perceptive, too, in pointing out that almost the entire city "will be rebuilt from two to eight times within a century, and the most radical changes can thus be accomplished with the slightest hardship to individuals or the public."[41] Then, perhaps expecting objections to that statement, he observed,

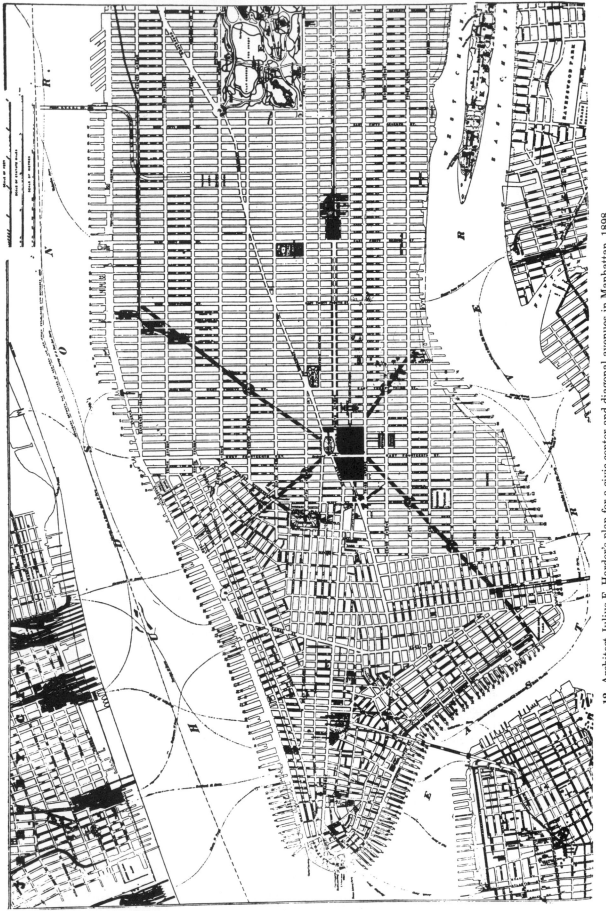

12. Architect Julius F. Harder's plan for a civic center and diagonal avenues in Manhattan, 1898

While it is true that the execution of radical measures must result inevitably in greater restrictions upon individuals and corporations, and thus interferes with that liberty which is the essence of American institutions, still, against this is to be urged the usual argument, that the resulting increased value of the whole returns again to the greater number. We will be told that the proposition is an idle dream. But the function of all law is the greatest good for the greatest number, and the fact that the citizen has awakened at all is by reason of an appreciation that in this matter the interests of the citizens collectively are identical with and supersede those of the individual.[42]

This farsighted architect concluded that "the mere establishment of a comprehensive general proposition for improvements will result in voluntary conformity to it in many cases where such conformation will be simpler and more economical than to do otherwise."[43]

Apparently no one in the reorganized city government shared Harder's vision of a metropolis "planned . . . with due consideration of the comparative and just importance of its related elements,"[44] though the various agencies of government moved quickly to meet certain obvious area-wide needs. The inadequate water supplies of Brooklyn, Queens, and Richmond were augmented, and plans were prepared for a new water supply system to serve the entire enlarged area of the city. City engineers set to work on plans for bridges to link Manhattan Island with the Bronx, Brooklyn, Queens, and Richmond, while agitation for public construction of a subway system serving Manhattan, Brooklyn, and the Bronx spurred official efforts to prepare the blueprints for such a system. Adna F. Weber, author of *The Growth of Cities in the Nineteenth Century,* hailed plans for rapid transit from the business center to the residential outskirts as the only effective solution of the problem of congestion of population. "Adequate space for the housing of the people lies at the basis of all reform," he noted, adding that other remedies were mere palliatives.[45]

The thrust of the metropolis was outward into the sparsely settled areas, but in a haphazard manner, with almost no official consideration of the amenities. One newspaper pointed out that

The site of a future city north of the Harlem offers a field for improvement more magnificent than that for which Nero destroyed imperial Rome. With a Haussmann or L'Enfant in our three millions of population, the ideal city, the city beautiful and perfect, would at least be suggested, but what are we doing with it? We are plodding along on village lines, with village methods, marring with patchwork improvements that disfigure, ignoring all the teachings of the past, unconscious of all the possibilities of the future. We are laying out the new districts of the Greater New York, not as the ideal city or the city beautiful, or even as the city of common sense. We are merely permitting it to grow up under the stimulus of private greed and of real estate speculation.[46]

In characteristic fashion, private enterprise duplicated in some of the newly developing districts the very crowding decried in the older neighborhoods.

In lower Manhattan tall, steel-frame office buildings, like those originating in Chicago, signified the intensification of commercial activity in a restricted area and presaged still further concentration and congestion at other locations farther uptown in years to come. Called "skyscrapers" by an article in *Harper's Weekly* in 1894, these bold structures gave the metropolis a new and awesome "skyline"—another term added to the vocabulary in the nineties.[47] But with all its zest for experimentation, invention, and innovation, New York had already been superseded by Chicago in foreshadowing the potentialities of the "City Beautiful" and large-scale planning.

A Momentous Civic Venture in Chicago

Even earlier than Boston and New York, the midwestern metropolis had sought political union with the villages and unincorporated areas lying in the path of its eventual development, and with what success! "Between the rising and the setting of yesterday's sun Chicago added 130 square miles of land to its area and a quarter of a million souls to its population,"[48] the *Chicago Tribune* announced triumphantly on June 30, 1889, celebrating a consummation that was to prove but the beginning of a dramatic new civic venture—an exposition destined to influence cities throughout the nation and to contribute enormously to the emergence of city planning as a new activity of municipal government.

Until Chicago annexed Hyde Park, Lake View, Lake, Jefferson, and a part of Cicero and overnight expanded to "a city . . . twenty-four miles one way and from four to eight and a half the other,"[49] its public officials and leading citizens had not bestirred themselves greatly to win the honor of commemorating, in 1892, the four hundredth anniversary of Columbus' discovery of America. But when Chicago surpassed Philadelphia as the second city of the nation and became the undisputed mistress of the West, their civic pride at once catapulted them into a contest with New York, Philadelphia, and Washington for the privilege of being designated by Congress as the city to hold the proposed exposition. By midsummer a citizens' committee of three hundred, authorized by the city council and appointed by Mayor De Witt C. Cregier, was enthusiastically at work "to get that fair in spite of Washington bluff and New York bluster and braggadocio," as the *Tribune* put it.[50] Among the committee members were some leading residents of Milwaukee and citizens of Iowa, for even though St. Louis suddenly appeared as a new competitor for the Congressional subsidies expected to finance the exposition in part, most Midwesterners believed Chicago to be the logical place. The *Toledo Blade,* for instance, had endorsed Chicago as "the only city in the West that could accommodate the crowd such an enterprise would attract. . . . She has the ability to plan and the enterprise to carry out mammoth undertakings."[51]

In the exuberance of its new glory as a supercity of 170 square miles and a million residents, Chicago relished mammoth undertakings. Four months after the extensive annexations were approved, the electorate voted overwhelmingly to create a sanitary district even larger than the expanded city. To this new jurisdiction the metropolitan community entrusted the construction of a multimillion-dollar sanitary and ship canal to reverse the flow of the Chicago River and prevent it from further polluting Lake Michigan, source of the city's water supply. The municipality utilized its own taxing and borrowing capacity to fulfill other expectations of its new residents, who had been promised nothing less than "all the benefits of a great city—purer water, cheaper gas, more police and firemen, lower insurance rates, 5-cent car fare, less taxes, more improvements, better drainage, no more typhoid-fever epidemics."[52] In the next few years the city laid hundreds of miles of water mains and sewers, surfaced almost six hundred miles of streets, constructed more than twenty-two hundred miles of sidewalks (almost all of wood), replaced kerosene streetlamps in some of the annexed areas with gas lights, installed a fire-alarm system and fire-alarm boxes throughout the annexed territory, and exercised its corporate powers to force gas companies to reduce their rates to households in outlying districts.

The businessmen of the city, realistically appraised as "hustlers" by the *New York Times*,[53] matched this outburst of municipal activity by the vigor with which they organized to vanquish all other competitors for the world's fair, particularly New York. The *Chicago Tribune* saw "not so much a fight between Chicago and New York as between the West and the East."[54] Overlooking no opportunity to mobilize support, the Chicago promoters appointed various subcommittees to lobby in Congress, to propagandize editors, and to flood railroads, hotels, and chambers of commerce throughout the nation with "information showing the advantage of a Chicago site to the nation."[55]

The booster spirit of the city triumphed. On February 24, 1890, the House of Representatives voted to designate Chicago as the site of the exposition, and two months later the Senate confirmed the selection. But lest anyone think that Chicago merchants and industrialists had in mind creating merely "a shop window on a grand scale," the *Tribune* proclaimed that the fair would be "a vast museum, showing the products of the soil, the mines, and the seas, and the inventive skill of America. It is to cover square rods where the Paris Exposition [of 1889] covered square yards. It is to reveal the material wonders of the continent, while that displayed the artistic skill of a city."[56]

Three years later and, because of unavoidable delays, one year after the quadricentennial of Columbus' landing in the New World, twenty-one and a half million Americans flocked to the "White City" on the shores of Lake Michigan. In this temporary wonderland of grand perspectives and cross axes, this incredible transformation of swamps and sandbars into shimmering lagoons and monumental palaces, they were less impressed by the products of the soil, the mines, and the seas than by the magnificent ensemble. Here was an enthralling amalgam of classic Greece, imperial Rome, Renaissance Italy, and Bourbon Paris, as improbable in the Midwest as a gleaming iceberg would be in the Gulf of Mexico, yet somehow expressive of the boastfulness, the pretentions, the cultural dependence, the explosive energy, and the ingenuous optimism of industrial America. Unacquainted with the Rome of the Caesars and the Popes, the gardens of Versailles, and the legendary marvels of Venice, the millions gaped and admired and almost disbelieved that so much beauty and splendor had sprung up in Chicago, city of grain and lumber and meat, city of railroads and smoke and grime. The entire enchanting spectacle was a thrilling revelation of the power of architects, landscape architects, sculptors, and painters to evoke rapture and delight. True, the Midway offered carnival vulgarity, and Little Egypt, the ecdysiast, shocked native prudery, but the brilliant image of symmetrical edifices, colossal statues, and stupendous domes burned in memory long after the summer pilgrims had returned to their lackluster commercial cities, dreary mill towns, and homely prairie villages.

Plaster fantasy that it was, the World's Columbian Exposition touched the deep longing of a nation suffering from a loss of continuity with history for visual assurance of maturity and success. Not the creative and original office blocks in downtown Chicago but the specious classicism of the fair satisfied the hunger for cultural security and self-approbation. It was a classicism transmuted by the Ecole des Beaux-Arts of Paris, imported by successful New York and Boston architects, and eagerly accepted by the self-made millionaires of Chicago because it represented, above all, organization—the kind of large-scale, masterly ordering of complex elements that men who had developed great industries, built transit systems, and made fortunes in real estate could appreciate. Yet some talents distinctly indigenous helped fashion this anachronistic symbol of accomplishment: Frederick Law Olmsted, who recommended the site in an undeveloped section of Jackson Park and saw the possibilities of dredging the marshes to form lagoons and canals; John Root, of the architectural firm of Burnham and Root, who sketched the rough plan showing the principal buildings arranged around a formal canal and a great basin; Daniel Hudson Burnham, his partner, who chose the architectural firms commissioned to design the major

[handwritten note: planners of "White City"]

13. Court of Honor, World's Columbian Exposition, Chicago, 1893 (*Scientific American*)

14. Grand Basin, World's Columbian Exposition, Chicago, 1893 (*Scientific American*)

structures and coordinated their efforts, first as chief of construction and later as director of works; and Louis Henri Sullivan, who with Dankmar Adler created the one important building not in the neoclassic tradition, the Transportation Building, with rich polychrome decoration on its walls and a great arched doorway intricately ornamented with arabesques and bas-reliefs. Rebellious from the beginning against the decision of the Eastern architects to adopt historic forms, Sullivan doubtless had the sympathy of Olmsted, who wrote to his partners from Paris in 1892 expressing his fears that the snowy palaces were "going to look too assuming of architectural stateliness and to be overloaded with sculptural and other efforts for grandeur and grandiloquent pomp."[57] Sullivan later charged that the exposition set off "a violent outbreak of the Classic and the Renaissance in the East, which slowly spread westward, contaminating all that it touched" and wreaking damage that would "last for half a century."[58] But his indictment was only half true, since Chicago architects and many others continued to design office buildings in the functional vernacular they had evolved in the 1870s and 1880s; and even after some classical trappings crept into later designs, it was difficult not to accede to the demands of the steel cage.

The convocation of many "congresses" in Chicago in 1893 reinforced the popular feeling that henceforth public buildings should resemble the Parthenon, the Baths of Caracalla, or St. Peter's. Susan B. Anthony and other militant feminists, Frances Willard and her following of temperance reformers, social workers troubled about juvenile delinquency and crime, labor unions, bankers, and religious leaders of all faiths assembled to exhort, to view with alarm—and to extol the majestic harmonies of the fair. Its imperial richness was especially comforting to the bankers, harried by the panic that was filling the streets with beggars and the pawnshops with the watches and keepsakes of the unemployed. If America could produce this capsule of abundance, surely the country could not be so plundered and demoralized as the Farmers' Alliance and the fanatical Populists maintained. The financial mind had always had a penchant for structures of classical stability, and in the colonnades and pediments of the White City it perceived the enduring soundness of the nation. The whole regal scene was, indeed, a prophecy, a forecast of monumental city halls, public libraries, museums, union stations, banks, and academic halls to be built in the next twenty or thirty years. As clearly as a royal edict, the fair proclaimed the aesthetic principles that would govern the design of civic centers, malls, boulevards, university and college campuses, waterfronts, and other expositions for two decades or more. It powerfully persuaded visitors from Omaha, Buffalo, St. Louis, Portland, Seattle, San Francisco, San Diego, and other cities that they, too, must commemorate great events in similar fashion, as in time they did. And each of these successive expositions disclosed new miracles of American technology, helped to expand the national economy, introduced millions to unfamiliar areas of the country, strengthened local pride, and left its legacy of civic improvements and plans for the future.

Burnham's New Interest in the Urban Environment

Daniel H. Burnham, whose organizing genius had achieved a comprehensive unity in the White City by fusing the talents of architects from Boston, New York, Chicago, and Kansas City, emerged from the fair as a man with a new professional competence. His fellow members of the American Institute of Architects, holding their annual meeting in Chicago in July, 1893, elected him their president, and the next year some of them joined with him and Charles F. McKim in founding the American School of Architecture in Rome, later the American Academy, whose coveted fellowships still attract men of high capabilities in painting, sculpture, architecture, and landscape architecture. But Burnham was now more than the designer of individual buildings or groups of buildings; he was deeply interested in the larger urban environment and was to become, step by step, an architect-city planner, as he indicated by accepting his friend James E. Ellsworth's suggestion that he make a plan for the eight miles of lakefront from the Chicago River to Jackson Park, site of the exposition.

At a dinner given by Ellsworth in 1896, Burnham presented a scheme destined to burgeon into a plan for the whole Chicago region, but he himself then probably little realized how far his interest in enhancing the lakefront would carry him. To George Pullman, Marshall Field, Philip D. Armour, and other millionaire merchants and manufacturers he unfolded a proposal for creating a great boulevard east of the Illinois Central Railroad tracks and developing a long, narrow park on filled land in the lake, so as to form a lagoon for boating between the park and the boulevard. Various members of the group expressed willingness to aid in carrying out the plan, thereby encouraging Burnham to work further on it.

The architect, however, did more than refine his plan; he immediately initiated a public project related to it, as an entry in his diary discloses:

> On the election of Mayor George B. Swift, an old school boy companion of mine, I urged that ordinances looking toward the improvement [of the lakefront] be adopted at once. The Mayor, the Commissioner of Works Kent, and Campbell, Chairman of Council Committee, came, looked over the plans, were enthusiastic, and the Mayor then made an arrangement with the Illinois Central Road which resulted in commencing work on the breakwater [for the boulevard]. This night, July 27, an ordinance prepared here in this office passed the Council, giving the Lake Front to the South Park [District], with a reservation for

the [Field Columbian] Museum and the Illinois Militia, all of which is in accordance with the design . . . and in the line of carrying it out; a great public work which will be memorable if finished according to our designs as now seems probable.[59]

In December, 1896, Burnham presented his proposal to the Literary Club, the Art Institute, and the Back Lot Club of Evanston in a paper entitled "The South Shore Drive." Still later, in April, 1897, he spoke to the Merchants' Club and to a large public meeting at the Auditorium of his hopes to make Chicago "the most attractive town in the world."[60] The talks revealed how greatly he was indebted to ancient Greece and Rome — and to the Paris of Napoleon III — for inspiration:

> At the southern end of the Lake Front will begin the Shore Drive, which, going above the Illinois Central Railway to the Lake, will extend over a stone bridge of the old Roman pattern to the first great outer concourse, and thence south seven and a half miles, to the lower end of Jackson Park. . . .

> The driveway itself should be protected by a sea-wall, designed to express dignity as well as to afford security. Behind it should be a broad terrace, supporting seats made in the old Grecian pattern, so placed that the sitter might look out to sea. Next this wall should be a space, planted with tall shrubs, disposed partly to conceal and partly to reveal the Lake. Next this, a bicycle course and a greensward, covered with flowering plants. Next to this plantation should be an equestrian way, and west of it should be the great Avenue itself, with its broad green lawns and its rows of stately trees. Besides the Drive, on the west of it, should be another terrace, with here and there old Greek resting-places, some curved into the banks, out of which should flow fountains of water. The floor of this walk and of the recesses should be paved with small colored pebbles, in geometrical patterns. The wall itself, which is to be next west of the walk, should be built of long slivers of sparkling stone, like those encircling the Roosevelt farms that skirt along the Hudson, north of Poughkeepsie.[61]

Though Burnham could fire the imaginations of some of his hearers, he failed to move the correspondent of the *American Architect and Building News*, who reported that Chicago was filled with rumors and talk about lakefront improvement "which sound like plans from fairy-land, rather than the sober schemes of the inhabitants of a city whose chief occupation is supposed to be pig-sticking."[62] Of all these plans, Burnham's was the most dreamlike, the journal commented.[63] Snidely it suggested that the sometime director of works at the World's Columbian Exposition was hardly the man to divert Chicago from its preoccupation with hog-butchering: "Mr. Burnham is leaving no stone unturned to arouse enthusiasm in this scheme, and enthusiasm in the idea that he is the man to do it, irrespective of the fact that the two men who, as his partners, made the name of the firm noted for its artistic work are now beyond giving any help in making Chicago a beautiful city. Mr. Burnham may have discovered some other genius whose work will some day delight us as that of Mr. Root's and Mr. Atwood's has done, but it would seem a little risky to trust such a tremendous undertaking as this would be to less tried hands."[64]

The implication that Burnham without his now dead partners was a designer not to be taken seriously overlooked the considerable drive, leadership, and civic devotion he combined with his passion for Beaux-Arts aesthetics and Haussmannesque urban planning. Chicago in 1897 was not yet ready to attempt full development of its lakefront, but the plan on which Burnham had begun working with Charles Atwood in 1894 was not to die. Rather, it was to lie dormant for almost a decade, then to be resurrected as the point of departure for a great city planning effort. In the meantime, Burnham became engrossed in the practice of architecture and was for several years so busy supervising the work of his office and conferring with clients in all the large cities of the Middle West and East that he was obliged to curtail his civic activities and slight his predilection for urban design.

15. Daniel Hudson Burnham
(Art Institute of Chicago)

The Gathering Forces of Municipal Reform

Chicago, like many other American cities in the late nineties, had its political stables to clean — a task requiring the time, energy, and concerted attention of its better citizens. Even if, as Burnham contended, the metamorphosis of the lakefront would bring wealth to Chicago's hotelkeepers and railway systems, there would be little point in further enriching the city as long as police graft and administrative abuses sapped the public treasury and directly or indirectly victimized legitimate businesses. In 1895 the Municipal Voters' League, a nonpartisan organization with a platform of municipal reform, had been founded to strike at one of the chief sources of corruption, the city council, which abounded in aldermen willing to grant outrageous contracts to certain construction and utilities companies. Branding as thieves fifty-seven of the sixty-eight aldermen, the League succeeded in defeating all but six of the undesirable politicians. By 1899 it could command a clear majority in the council, and in 1900 it controlled two-thirds of the aldermen. But it did not win its victories unaided; it had the support of other reform groups, such as the Civic Federation and the Municipal Order League, an organization that had fought for an appropriation for the construction of the first free public bath and for the installation of drinking fountains throughout the city.

Generally, reform groups concentrated on overhauling local government first, relegating to second place the needed physical improvements, though municipal park movements, housing reform efforts, and other civic causes all made advances throughout the decade. In 1888 Lord Bryce had called municipal government in the United States the "one conspicuous failure," and in 1890 Andrew D. White had indicted it as being not only the most inefficient in Christendom but also, with few exceptions, the most expensive and the most corrupt. To such stinging criticisms, other observers added wholesale condemnation of the maldistribution of wealth in America and the domination of state and local governments, and at times even the national government, by giant corporations and syndicates. James Muirhead, an English visitor in 1893, scored "manifestations of economic slavery, of grinding the faces of the poor, of exploitation of the weak, . . . of unjust monopoly, of unequal laws, of industrial and commercial chicanery. . . ."[65] Henry Demarest Lloyd, predecessor of the muckrakers of the first decade of our century, assailed laissez-faire capitalism in his carefully documented, morally indignant *Wealth Against Commonwealth* and declared that "when capitalists combine irresistibly against the people, the government, which is the people's combination, must take them in hand."[66] In more than five hundred pages exposing the Standard Oil Trust, Lloyd raised the question, "Can we forestall ruin by reform? If we wait to be forced by events we shall be astounded to find how much more radical they are than our utopias. Louis XVI waited until 1793, and gave his head and all his investitures to the people who in 1789 asked only to sit at his feet and speak their mind. Unless we reform of our own free will, nature will reform us by force, as nature does."[67] These and other warnings that American democracy was threatened, particularly in the cities, goaded the municipal leagues and civic federations to greater and greater effort, increasingly directed toward the reorganization of the structure of local government and the enactment of remedial legislation rather than merely toward the removal of unfit politicians and the exposure of corruption.

As early as 1892 political scientist Frank P. Prichard concluded, "The ordinary administrative machinery of the government, constructed for a less complex condition of society, is proving inadequate. A more scientific construction and a more systematic operation is imperative." He went on to say,

> The probable growth of the city, the social conditions which may affect its future needs, the probability of constant changes in its administrative force, the necessity for a scientific organization of the work which will enable it to be carried on with some uniformity in spite of such changes, the equitable distribution of expenses among the citizens themselves and between the present and future generations; all these are considerations which enter into the problem of muncipal government and render its operation a science, involving, indeed, many branches of scientific knowledge, but possessing an individuality distinct from all of them. To understand and to apply this science requires a thorough knowledge, obtained by a careful study of past and existing facts; an investigation of previous experiments, with their results; a comparison of observations, and the working out of rules of general application. This would seem almost self-evident, yet there has been in the past a general tendency to ignore this truth and to assume that all our difficulties of administration come from dishonesty in our officials. Year after year we spend a large part of our energy, and some of our substance in the vain attempt to elect first-class men by means of second-class political machinery, and when occasionally we succeed we flatter ourselves that we have solved the problem of municipal government, as if all its principles were so simple and so well understood that any man of ordinary business sagacity could administer them if only he were honest.[68]

By 1899 the National Municipal League, which had been formed in 1894 with sixteen local leagues and had grown in its first year alone to include 180 branches, promulgated a model city charter designed to correct some of the more glaring weaknesses of municipal government. It provided for expanded home rule, a stronger mayor and council, trained administrators, and more advisory divisions of government under the authority of the mayor and council. The emphasis on qualified personnel and their selection by civil service was especially significant because it heralded the entry of many classes of "experts" into municipal government in later years, including city managers, city planners, budget and efficiency analysts, public health statisticians, and men capable of operating publicly owned street-railway systems, water and power departments, and other highly technical enterprises. But there were as yet few specialists in city halls and few professors in American universities who shared Prichard's hope of seeing "the states and municipalities establishing schools and offering scholarships for the purpose of filling their administrative offices with trained and competent men."[69]

The increasing interest in the "science" of administration disclosed a need for many kinds of information about cities then difficult to obtain. Few cities kept orderly records or made any attempt at systematic compilation of data that would be useful to mayors and department heads. Dr. Edward M. Hartwell, a Boston educator, traveled throughout Europe in 1897 studying the municipal statistical offices of capital cities and upon his return published a lengthy article describing them as serving "much the same purposes as does the 'headquarters staff' in the administration of modern military affairs. That is to say, being organized as 'intelligence departments,' they furnish the executive department of the city government with such information as it requires for devising and conducting its plan of campaign against ignorance, disease, crime, pauperism, and extravagance." Hartwell found these agencies "also capable of rendering important aid to the electorate in arriving at intelligent conclusions as to the degree of fidelity and efficiency shown by its public servants in the discharge of their duties." He concluded that the "establishment by Boston and other great cities of the United States of similar offices could hardly fail to conduce to better government and a more enlightened public spirit, provided the teachings of the best European experience in this field were clearly apprehended and consistently applied in their organization and management."[70]

In the same year that Hartwell wrote his article the League of American Cities adopted a constitution stating that one of its objects would be the "maintenance of a central bureau of information for the collection and compilation and dissemination of statistics, reports and all kinds of information relative to municipal government."[71] The publications of the Bureau of the Census, the association explained, "neither convey a complete picture of the city, nor are they intended to give a general view of it."[72] In this dissatisfaction with federal research on the city might be noted the origin of future demands for the establishment of a federal department concerned solely with the problems and needs of urban areas, though even the most radical reformers of 1897–1899 probably would have been unwilling to grant the federal government an important role in urban affairs. Indeed, most reformers were struggling to divorce municipal politics altogether from national politics, since the bosses of the corrupt machines were invariably allied with national political organizations; and even "good government" men who suggested state supervisory or statistical agencies serving cities met resistance to the idea. Home rule, with as few ties as possible to the state capital or Washington, D.C., was the paramount goal in a nation in which the cities of only four states—Missouri, California, Washington, and Minnesota—enjoyed freedom from interference by the state legislature. The plans of a private association to meet a national need for useful factual information about municipal governments and cities of all classes represented an acceptable solution for the times and laid the foundation for the widespread collection and analysis of urban data essential to later city and regional planning programs.

The Municipal Art Movement

In the closing years of the nineteenth century, when reform groups had begun to celebrate some of the initial victories in their drives to modernize and uplift municipal government, the civic endeavors marking the beginnings of city planning were, however, mainly aesthetic rather than analytical or "scientific," though they were not devoid of broad social motivation and, frequently, a concern for municipal efficiency and economy. Burnham, for instance, believed that his proposed lakefront development would be "a new and beneficent element to individual lives in the city" and would "restore to the people" a shoreline from which they had long been barred by railroad tracks.[73] The young architects who held a competition in Cleveland in 1895 for a proposed arrangement of public buildings sought to emulate the imposing groupings at the Chicago fair, but they did not fail to suggest that relating governmental structures one to another would facilitate the transaction of public affairs. After the Cleveland chapter of the American Institute of Architects endorsed the general idea and the Cleveland Chamber of Commerce showed its interest in the construction of a new city hall, courthouse, public library, and post office around a beautiful park extending from the heart of the downtown area to the lake, all that was needed to impel the city toward its famous "Group Plan," one of the first civic centers inspired by the Chicago exposition, was for President McKinley to sign the bill authorizing a new post office for Cleveland. Though this and other structures did not materialize until after the turn of the century, many civic leaders had already accepted the proposition that grandeur, convenience, and efficiency could be combined in a stately arrangement of public buildings. Nor were the societies promoting the planting of street trees and the es-

tablishment of municipal forestry departments composed wholly of "beau-
tifiers"; many of their members also supported park movements, in the
conviction that open spaces and trees have therapeutic as well as aesthetic value for city dwellers.

The upsurge of interest in improving the appearance of cities in the
late nineties is so often erroneously attributed solely to the influence of
the World's Columbian Exposition that it is well to note what Charles
Mulford Robinson, once a reporter and editorial writer for Rochester
and Philadelphia newspapers, said in 1899 in the last of a series of articles on the improvement of cities: "It is common to hear it [the fair]
spoken of as 'the white city' and even 'the dream city.' In these terms was
revealed a yearning toward a condition which we had not reached. To
say that the world's fair created the subsequent aesthetic effort in municipal life were therefore false; to say that it immensely strengthened,
quickened, and encouraged it would be true. The fair gave tangible shape
to a desire that was arising out of the larger wealth, the commoner travel,
and the provision of the essentials of life; but the movement has had a
special impetus since 1893."[74]

Municipal art societies spearheaded the effort to make streets and other
public areas more rewarding to the eye. The first of these organizations
was formed in New York the year of the Chicago exposition and was enlarged in 1898. A second appeared in Cincinnati in 1894, and others in
Cleveland, Chicago, and Baltimore in 1899. In December of that year the
Baltimore society invited all the others, as well as the municipal art
commissions of Boston and New York, to "a conference on various subjects relating to the artistic development of cities."[75] Delegates discussed
public squares and buildings, color in architecture, municipal bridges,
artistic street signs, art as an educator—"It has helped men to think"—
and the ways in which civic art "pays" by attracting tourists and a desirable class of residents and by increasing real estate values. Various
speakers recommended construction of memorial arches and the enrich-
ment of public buildings with sculpture and mural paintings. But Sylvester Baxter of Boston spoke of fundamentals. Citing Olmsted's plan as
the basis for "the wonderful artistic success" of the Chicago fair, he told
those who were thinking mostly of adorning the city, "Therefore, it is
easy to see that the plan is the first thing to be considered in the beautification of a city; the other things, the architecture of the buildings and
their interior decorations, should spring from the ground plan; we should
not think of landscape architecture as something that is a mere embellishment, something to be added as a sauce to the pudding."[76]

Probably few of Baxter's hearers appreciated the wisdom of his words.
Edwin Howland Blashfield, writing in the issue of *Municipal Affairs*
containing a summary of the Baltimore conference, expressed the popular

feeling: "Beauty in high places is what we want; beauty in our municipal buildings, our parks, squares, and courts; and we shall have a national school when, and not until when, art, like a new Petrarch, goes up to be crowned at the capitol."[77]

George Kriehn, another writer in the same periodical, knew precisely the city for Americans to copy: "Of all modern cities, Paris, more than any other, deserves the title of 'The City Beautiful.' With its clean paved streets, with its public places surrounded by buildings in harmonious style and decorated with statuary which represents the highest development of modern art, with its river so beautifully bridged, with its old cathedral of immense proportions, it comes nearer than any other to reaching the ideal which is the object of this municipal art movement, 'The City Beautiful.' "[78]

A nation grown rich by the development of its natural resources and its industries, a nation at last critical of its municipal institutions and determined to remold them to serve broader public purposes stood optimistically at the threshold of a new century, elated by its recent victory in the Spanish-American War and dazzled by its heightened status in the world community. Patrick Geddes, the Scottish biologist and organizer of the first great international exhibitions on town planning, wrote to his wife after a Boston lecture in 1899 of the "great ferment of changes" taking place in this vast land, as yet "the martyr of her own progress" and the producer of the "pandemonium city."[79] But the people were "moving fast in thought," and the chaotic, congested city spawned by the nineteenth century was soon to become the object of intense concern and the subject of innumerable muckraking articles, social surveys, civic improvement schemes, reform campaigns, and innovative laws, all aimed at making the urban environment worthy of a great and powerful country. If the initial drive was for a city outwardly more pleasing, perhaps it was because Americans needed something more soul-satisfying than trunk sewers, elevated railways, and metropolitan water supply systems to stimulate their local pride and induce them to continue the work of providing the utilitarian essentials of urban growth. They also needed, for their spirits, more parks and playgrounds, and if they could afford them, handsome boulevards, civic centers, and decorative monuments, but, of course, they had already started developing most of these evidences of sophisticated urban life well before the end of the century. The "City Beautiful" movement now capturing their imaginations was but a continuation or broadening of the park and boulevard movements, augmented by a fresh interest in malls, lordly public buildings, and all the street furnishings—fountains, ornamental benches, statues, and memorials—common in European cities. The emphasis on aesthetics tended to negate an earlier, more humanitarian tone and was almost certain to alienate some social workers, tenement-house reformers, and budding sociologists, yet without this reorientation America might not have entered the twentieth century with the prospect of evolving a new municipal function of city planning and a new professional corps dedicated to improving the city.

CHAPTER 2

THE HEYDAY OF
THE CITY BEAUTIFUL

A Plan in the Grand Manner

If the leaders of the municipal art movement had been given millions and told to try their hands at creating an American equivalent of Paris, "the City Beautiful," unquestionably they would have selected Washington, D.C., as the city most suitable for their demonstration project. Its baroque plan, prepared by Major Pierre Charles L'Enfant, a native of the French capital and the son of a painter, sprang from the same traditions of design as those employed by Napoleon III and Baron Haussmann in transforming Paris into "the Queen City of the World." The

47

shade of Andre Le Nôtre, Louis XIV's celebrated landscape architect, subtly influenced L'Enfant when he planned the capital of the United States in 1791, and it must surely have offered guidance in 1853 when the emperor and his prefect of the Seine discussed proposals to slash broad boulevards through the congested French capital. But it was by coincidence rather than by careful decision that Washington, D.C., became the scene of the first great effort to achieve the "City Beautiful" in this country, and it was not the enthusiasts of the municipal art societies and civic art commissions who took charge of the work but some of the experienced designers who had given neoclassic form to the Chicago world's fair. They could not, certainly, have had a more appropriate urban setting in which to pursue their passion for magnificent effects and axial arrangements, because the national capital, though growing rapidly, was still a comparatively small city—population 218,000 in 1900—with none of the formidable industrial and commercial complexes which elsewhere might have presented obstacles to the formulation of a plan in the grand manner.

The year after the Chicago exposition the secretary of the American Institute of Architects, Glenn Brown, was preparing a history of the United States Capitol when he rediscovered, as it were, L'Enfant's original plan of Washington and was impressed by the skillful way in which the young veteran of the Revolutionary War had adapted his scheme to the topography, placing the "Congress House" and the "President's Palace" on sites commanding extensive prospects, devising avenues of direct communication to connect the most distant objects with the principal, and everywhere preserving "a reciprocity of sight" or unobstructed views.[1] Brown's fancy kindled as he thought of certain features of the plan only vaguely indicated by L'Enfant, such as the mall stretching westward from the Capitol toward the Potomac. He wrote in his history:

> It is easy to imagine the magnificence of a boulevard 400 feet wide beginning at the Capitol and ending with the [Washington] Monument, a distance of nearly a mile and a half, bounded on both sides by parks 600 feet wide. . . . Looking from the boulevard across the park a continuous line of beautiful buildings was to have formed the background. They were not to have been deep enough to curtail either the natural or artistic beauties of the parks, or to encroach upon the people's right to an air space. By this time such an avenue would have acquired a world-wide reputation, if it had been carried out by competent architects, landscape architects, and sculptors consulting and working in harmony with each other.[2]

L'Enfant's plan could be "commended for other reasons than those of beauty," however, because it had "every advantage in point of economy in maintenance, repairs, supervision, inter-communication, transportation, and accessibility of the Departments to each other and to the public."[3] Brown concluded that it would be feasible to carry out the original scheme, or one closely allied to it, in the erection of future government buildings.

In 1898, as all Washington began to look forward to the commemoration, two years later, of the one hundredth anniversary of the removal of the seat of government from Philadelphia to the District of Columbia, Brown suggested that the American Institute of Architects hold its annual meeting in the national capital in the centennial year. A man possessed by an idea, he wished to use the occasion to propose a revival of the L'Enfant plan, particularly that part indicating an arrangement of government buildings around the mall. Since his recommendation met with the approval of the directors of the Institute, he set about developing a program to further his objective, while official Washington planned commemorative exercises and debated various suggestions for constructing some large building or memorial but came to no agreement on a specific project.

When members of the architectural profession convened in the capital in December, 1900, Brown had made certain that their deliberations would come forcibly to the attention of Congress and the American people. At an evening session well attended by journalists, several distinguished architects presented papers, illustrated with lantern slides, on the grouping of buildings in great cities and on "monumental grouping of buildings" in Washington in particular. Frederick Law Olmsted, Jr., discussed landscape in Washington, and H. K. Bush Brown discoursed on sculpture in Washington. At the Cosmos Club on Lafayette Square, Brown staged an exhibition of plans entered in the Phoebe Apperson Hearst Competition in 1898 for a plan of the campus of the University of California at Berkeley. The winning scheme, by French architect Emile Bénard, showed the sort of imposing placement of buildings along a strong main axis and various minor axes that might be achieved in Washington. The report of the board of directors of the Institute, disclosing the fine hand of Brown, pointed out that the drawings gave "a clear idea of the effectiveness which may be produced by an intelligent grouping of buildings."[4] The next paragraph expressed the conviction that "the Institute should put itself on record as advocating the formation of a commission, composed of experts who shall be architects, landscape architects, and sculptors who are recognized by the professions, as well as by the community, as men of skill, intelligence, and experience in such work, to either formulate or approve a plan for the future arrangement of such art features in the National Capital."[5] Not surprisingly, the membership assented to the appointment of a committee to draft a bill providing for such a commission, and the committee met immediately with "several gentlemen of influence" but discovered that Congress had too much business at the current session to consider the measure.

Brown nevertheless had succeeded in arousing great interest in the future of Washington. A resolution adopted by the American Institute of Architects indicated that not only the location and grouping of public buildings but also "the ordering of landscape and statuary, and the extension of the park system in the District of Columbia" were matters of national concern and should therefore be made in accordance with "a comprehensive artistic scheme."[6] All the more responsive to the Institute's demand for the best obtainable general design because of the prevailing emphasis on improving the federal city, various members of Congress expressed willingness to further the preparation of a general plan, but none was more enthusiastic than Senator James McMillan of Michigan, chairman of the Senate Committee on the District of Columbia. He had been a member of the park commission in Detroit in the 1870s when Frederick Law Olmsted the elder prepared the plan for Belle Isle Park. In recent years he himself had worked out a scheme for a "centennial boulevard" running through the mall west of the Capitol.

The senator was especially concerned about the park system of the city. From time to time the government had acquired various park lands, including the still undeveloped Rock Creek Park of 1,600 acres and the National Zoological Park of 175 acres, but no provision had been made for connecting the scattered park areas into a genuine city-wide system or for relating such a system to the street plan prepared by the Highway Commission for the unbuilt sections of the District of Columbia. Nor had anyone yet decided what to do about the reclaimed Potomac flats and the malarial swamps along the Anacostia River, with their "deposits of mud, slime, and putrifying organic matter."[7] In conferences with the group appointed by the American Institute of Architects to seek creation of a commission to prepare a general design for the capital, Senator McMillan worked out a resolution to submit to his fellow lawmakers, directing his committee to "report to the Senate plans for the development and improvement of the entire park system of the District of Columbia."[8] The resolution, adopted by the Senate on March 8, 1901, also authorized the committee to secure the services of such experts as might be necessary.[9]

The practitioners who were selected upon the advice of the American Institute of Architects, Daniel H. Burnham and Frederick Law Olmsted, Jr., soon made it clear that in a ceremonial city such as Washington, D.C., they were concerned with parks in their relation to public buildings, as well as with large recreation areas. Empowered to add to their number, these two invited Charles F. McKim, of the New York architectural firm of McKim, Mead, and White, to join them, and later asked

Augustus St. Gaudens, the sculptor, to become a fourth member of what became known as the Senate Park Commission. All except the younger Olmsted had been associated at the Chicago exposition, and he, of course, had followed closely the work of his father in that precedent-setting venture. From the beginning there was a harmony of thought in the group, in no way disturbed by the addition of Senator McMillan as a kind of ex officio member and keen participant in important decisions.

Although they were planning for the future of a capital serving an extraordinarily dynamic nation, with enormous industrial and technical resources, the members of the group were fettered from the beginning by an overwhelming sense of the historic past, as they revealed later in their report: "The very fact that Washington and Jefferson, L'Enfant and Ellicott, and their immediate successors, drew inspiration from the world's greatest works of landscape architecture and of civic adornment made it imperative to go back to the sources of their knowledge and taste in order to restore unity and harmony to their creations and to guide future development along appropriate lines."[10]

First, Burnham and his associates sought clues to the taste of the founding fathers by visiting places familiar to them, such as estates on the Potomac and James rivers and the old colonial towns of Annapolis and Williamsburg. But the modest scale of these early American towns suggested little to designers struggling to evolve grand concepts and already besieged by government officials desiring advice about the location of new buildings and memorials. Burnham therefore determined that the group should go to Europe and there study every great example of civic design and park planning that might aid them in solving the problems of the capital.

As St. Gaudens was in poor health, Charles Moore, clerk of Senator McMillan's Committee on the District of Columbia (who was later to be Burnham's biographer), accompanied Burnham, McKim, and Olmsted on their five-week trip abroad. The four visited Paris, Rome, Venice, Vienna, Budapest, Frankfurt, Berlin, and London, but since they were pressed for time, they omitted St. Petersburg, in whose baroque plan they might have noted certain resemblances to the original plan of Washington.

The illustrations in their report indicate what impressed them: the gardens of Versailles, Fontainebleau, Compiègne, Vaux-le-Vicomte, the quays of Venice, Budapest, and Paris, the Memorial Walk in the Thiergarten in Berlin, and the great mall at Cirencester, England. From all these legacies of autocrats and nobles, from all these seemingly timeless survivals of departed or decayed societies they hoped to fashion on the banks of the Potomac an expression of the republican ideal, a city honoring men who had revolted against a tyrant, others who had fought to preserve a Union, and still others who had more recently humbled a

Spanish monarch. No wonder Washington, D.C., is the supreme paradox among cities! And one of the least American.

Above all else, the problems of central Washington challenged the designers, as they had L'Enfant, whose plan featured two great axes, one drawn through the center of the Capitol and the other drawn through the center of the White House, intersecting at the site originally selected for an equestrian statue of George Washington. Near this site but not at the precise intersection of the axes stood the tremendous obelisk begun in 1848, somewhat off center because the engineers had despaired of securing on the proper site a foundation capable of supporting the immense weight of the monument and had had to select a firmer base. From the towering shaft to the Potomac stretched a mile of land reclaimed since 1881 and not shown at all on L'Enfant's plan, which had provided for a view from the White House of broad reaches of the Potomac. Between the monument and the Capitol the mall that Glenn Brown had imagined as an avenue as splendid as the Champs Elysées was filled with unrelated informal parks and groves planned in 1851 by Andrew Jackson Downing, a landscape gardener who had probably never seen L'Enfant's plan. But the most incongruous and offensive element was the rail line of the Baltimore and Potomac, crossing the area on grade at Sixth Street. Moreover, the railroad had recently received permission to erect a great viaduct and a train shed, 160 feet high, in a strip of land 600 feet wide extending all the way across the mall.

Fortunately, while the designers were in London, they had found a way to eliminate this most discordant feature, or rather President Cassatt of the Pennsylvania Railroad had proposed a bold solution of their difficulty. His line operated the Baltimore and Potomac Railroad and had recently acquired controlling interest in the Baltimore and Ohio, which had already been granted permission to construct its new station north of the Capitol. Cassatt suggested to Burnham — who had designed the new Pennsylvania Railroad station at Pittsburgh and had already been engaged to prepare plans for a new Baltimore and Potomac station in Washington — that all the lines be combined in a new union station north of the Capitol. The railroad president's only condition was that Congress pay part of the cost of the necessary tunnel to the station site from the south — a condition willingly accepted by legislators who appreciated Cassatt's decision, as a patriotic American, not to obstruct the efforts of the designers to "restore, develop, and supplement" L'Enfant's historic plan.

The proposal for a union station introduced new elements into the emerging scheme, which was fast becoming not a revival of the original plan but a wholly new one. Burnham, who was to design the terminal, saw an opportunity to make it a dramatic gateway fronting upon a plaza six hundred feet wide and twelve hundred feet long, from which the arriving visitor would catch his first glimpse of the Capitol dome. This conception necessitated, first, finding a site different from that already designated by Congress for the Baltimore and Ohio Railroad and then clearing many buildings between the new site on Massachusetts Avenue and the Capitol to make way for the great plaza, in which inaugural parades would assemble and distinguished diplomats would be welcomed. But the commission did not hesitate to suggest this important change in the city, and the station which began to rise only seven or eight months after the planners completed their work was essentially as Burnham had portrayed it in the report submitted to Congress—a monumental structure a few inches longer than the Capitol itself, with a central portico reminiscent of a Roman triumphal arch, sheathed in Vermont white marble, decorated with allegorical draped figures, and edified by inscriptions selected by the former president of Harvard University, Charles W. Eliot. This was not the first of the big terminals—St. Louis had opened one in 1896 housing all connecting railroads, and Boston had inaugurated its imposing South Station in 1898; but Burnham's edifice was the prototype of all the imperial wonders to come later, such as McKim, Mead, and White's Pennsylvania Station in New York, Warren and Wetmore's and Reed and Stern's Grand Central Terminal, Jarvis Hunt's union station in Kansas City, and many others.

The mall that the designers had struggled to retain as the principal feature of their plan became, in the hands of Charles McKim, an element the Sun King himself would have admired. By shifting the axis slightly, McKim brought the Capitol in line with the Washington Monument and a proposed memorial to Abraham Lincoln near the banks of the Potomac. Had this classicist been less intent on rigid alignment, the huge stone needle would not now slice the dome of the Capitol as seen from the shrine of the Great Emancipator, but though McKim could justify tilting an axis, he could not defend, even to himself, allowing one of the great triumvirate of structures to stand to one side of the imaginary line. At the eastern end of the mall, at the foot of the Capitol, appeared a plaza that was to be the American equivalent of the Place de la Concorde, a "Union Square" with equestrian statues of generals Grant, Sherman, and Sheridan. From there to the Washington Monument extended a tapis vert three hundred feet wide, framed by double rows of elms and enlivened by fountains, but not inviolate to cross streets. At the base of the monument was a sunken garden enriched by more fountains and temple-like structures, and beyond, to the west, a long, shallow, reflecting basin similar to that in which the Lincoln Memorial is mirrored. From the memorial a new bridge arched the Potomac to Arlington National Cemetery, directly in line with Robert E. Lee's mansion.

The cross axis of this formal composition, marked by the White House at the northern end, terminated south of the Washington Monument in an edifice that was to be either a memorial to a single great national hero or a pantheon to the authors of the Constitution. In the triangle between Pennsylvania Avenue and the mall the commission grouped important federal buildings and structures serving the District of Columbia.

Presented in superb drawings and models, these central elements of "the great consistent scheme" attracted more attention than any others when the planners exhibited their work at the Concoran Gallery of Art after their report had been handed to Congress. The proposals were everything that the Chicago world's fair had led the public to expect, but whereas the exposition had been a spectacle designed to entertain the summer crowds, these monuments, malls, and plazas were intended to glorify forever the national history and to intimate heroic events of the future. That they did so in foreign accents and in conceits more compatible with the ideologies of Pope Sixtus V, Louis XIV, or the Duke of Marlborough than with the democratic traditions of twentieth century Americans was almost beside the point. The designers proffered grandeur such as the national spirit craved — authentic, somewhat overpowering, and obviously expensive grandeur, confirming in white marble and verdure and sparkling water the American preeminence in government by popular consent, no matter how tarnished that exalted reputation might be at the moment by dollar diplomacy in Latin America and Rooseveltian imperialism generally. The scale of the proposed developments both reduced the citizen to insignificance and inflated his self-esteem as a member of a society ennobled by great men. Fundamentally, however, these drawings informed him that if he would re-create the city as a work of art, he must achieve, to use Olmsted's words, "a sophisticated self-restraint with regard to each part of . . . the design as a whole,"[11] permanently abjuring temptations to introduce new elements, make drastic modifications, or even to indulge in minor adjustments required by new technology.

The Washington of the Senate Park Commission — a kind of national civic center in a vernacular city in which that harbinger of dispersion, the automobile, had already made its prophetic appearance — was to be an historical artifact, an elaborate set piece immune to the whims of time and chance, a sacrosanct expression of the national past and the national destiny, though there was nothing about it that so much as suggested the influence of the rough frontier, the diversity of regions and peoples encompassed between the Atlantic and the Pacific, or the inevitability of economic and social upheavals. In a nation undergoing enormous changes, "the large design" promised, indeed demanded, immutability, at least outwardly, in the heart of the capital. And that, apparently, was a de-

mand to which Congress and the American people seemed eager to accede. Throughout the country there was acclaim for the commission's
plan and a desire to develop local schemes resembling it.

Somewhat overlooked in all the discussion of the plan was its most
commendable feature — Olmsted's scheme for a park system extending
beyond the boundaries of the District of Columbia to include scenic areas
along the Potomac River from Great Falls to Mount Vernon. The landscape architect's part in shaping the plan for the mall and Washington's
formal parks has been called "mysterious" because the design of these
areas is "uncharacteristic" of his work and indicates, as one authority
suggests, that he may have been unsympathetic to the ideas of McKim
and Burnham or ineffective in opposing them.[12] But his plan for the overall park system is the unambiguous embodiment of the vision of a broad-
scale planner and humanitarian.

As consulting landscape architect to the Metropolitan Park District
of Boston and to park departments in many other large cities, Olmsted
was especially qualified to envisage a park system meeting the long-

16. Senate Park Commission's general plan of Washington, 1902

term needs of the national capital. He identified the main problems of developing the system as selecting and acquiring areas best fitted for connections between existing parks, preserving and improving the chain of Civil War forts encircling the District, bringing into use for pleasure purposes "the wild and picturesque banks of the Potomac," and obtaining many small parks and squares throughout the city. Noting that development was taking place rapidly, he warned in language that would be familiar to conservationists today, "Whatever of natural beauty is to be preserved and whatever park spaces are still to be acquired must be provided for during the next few years or it will be forever too late."[13]

His solicitude for the comfort of Washingtonians obliged to suffer "the physical strain caused by summer heat" is shown in the various palliatives he suggested: "the maintenance of shade, the preservation of many hilltops where breezes may be caught, preservation of many of the deep, shady valleys in which the cooler air appears to settle on summer afternoons, and the liberal use of fresh running water all about the city and in its parks, whether in the form of springs and brooks or of fountains and basins."[14]

It is a tribute to the foresight of this distinguished son of a great father that in the next half-century almost all the areas he recommended for acquisition and development were added to the recreation resources of the city, besides many others. In fact, the District of Columbia today bears unmistakably the stamp of the McMillan Park Commission, to both its advantage and its disadvantage. The union station and plaza, the triangle of massive, neoclassical federal buildings, the mall (wider and bleaker than proposed, and lacking fountains), the Lincoln Memorial and the memorial bridge to Arlington, the Jefferson Memorial as a substitute for the pantheon to the authors of the Constitution, but in a somewhat different location—all these testify to the strength of the commission's ideas, sometimes enthusiastically and sometimes grudgingly accepted by Congress and carried out piecemeal in the next four decades.

But in an air age the station has lost its importance as a gateway; the mall divides rather than unites the city; the neoclassical edifices, mostly erected long after Americans had ceased to think of themselves as latter-day noble Romans, appear pompous and sterile; and the automobile is out of place in the whole central composition—a mechanism voraciously demanding parking space where the need for it was not foreseen. How strange that Burnham and his colleagues and Senator McMillan, witnessing momentous changes all about them, should have believed that their plan would be a boon almost indefinitely! Yet such was the faith of those days in that new thing, the city plan. Burnham thought of it as "a noble, logical diagram" to be used year after year, even decade

THE HEYDAY OF THE CITY BEAUTIFUL 57

after decade, as an oracular instrument for improving and embellishing a city.

Inspiration to Other Cities

As newspapers and magazines throughout the country published pictures of the handsome plan of Washington and poured forth columns of laudatory comment, appeals went up in cities large and small for the preparation of a city plan. In some of the larger cities, particularly, the planning movement resulted in new plans and new projects or in the revival of old schemes such as Burnham himself might have conceived.

In the nation's largest city the *New York Times* proposed the appointment of a commission similar to the McMillan group and suggested that since Charles McKim and Augustus St. Gaudens were residents of New York City, they should of course be asked to serve on it. The newspaper commented, resignedly, that it was by no means to be expected that the results would be comparable to those possible in Washington, because New York was cursed with a rectangular street plan that had acted as a blight upon the city ever since its adoption. Furthermore, the city was primarily a commercial town and would probably continue to be afflicted with considerable squalor and confusion. The *Times* believed, nevertheless, that it would be quite possible to do a good deal to relieve the inconveniences as well as the ugliness of the existing city.[15]

With the approval of the mayor, the board of aldermen created the New York City Improvement Commission in December, 1903, and gave it, as Olmsted said, the staggering duty of preparing in one year a comprehensive plan for the entire city. Twelve months later the commission presented a preliminary report in which Olmsted found "the aesthetic element . . . as clearly over-emphasized as it had been under-emphasized in the current routine planning."[16]

Granted a more extended tenure, the commission submitted a final report in 1907 in which it recommended main thoroughfares in each borough and a system of arteries connecting the various boroughs, parkways linking park systems in each of the boroughs, and a civic center formed around City Hall Park in Manhattan. But aside from the widening of Fifth Avenue, the improvement of one area of the waterfront, and the construction of a few outlying streets, the proposals of the commission were ignored.

In Philadelphia the City Parks Association issued a report severely condemning the rigidity of the street system and suggesting the need for new diagonal thoroughfares like those in the national capital. Although the association was especially critical of the abandonment of a number of old diagonal roads when the city was extended northward and southward of William Penn's original gridiron, it was chiefly interested

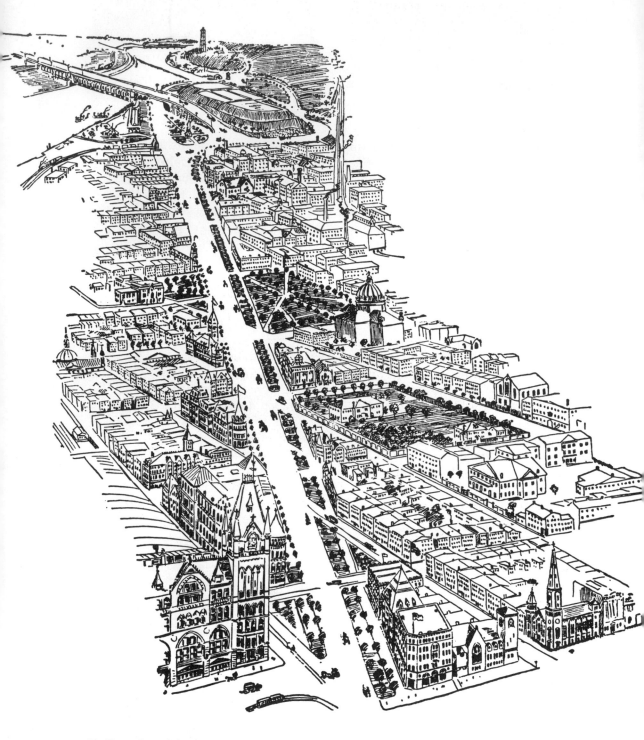

17. First plan of the Fairmount Parkway, Philadelphia (now Benjamin Franklin Parkway), by James H. Windrim, 1892 *(Free Library of Philadelphia)*

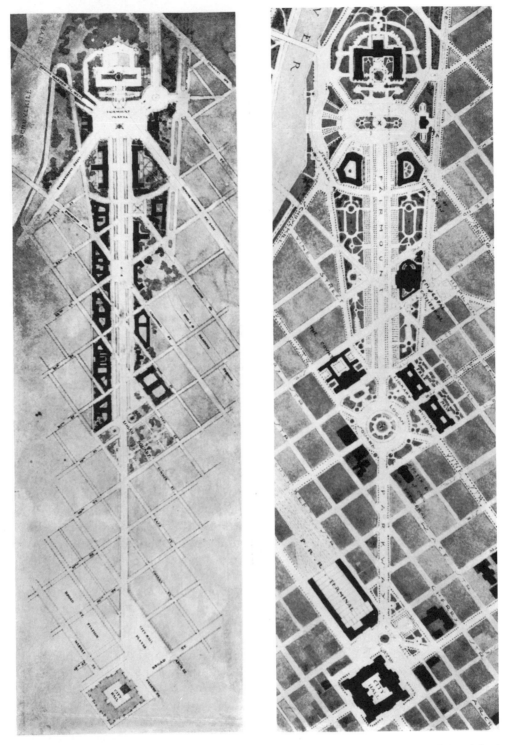

18. (left) Plan of Fairmount Parkway by Paul P. Cret and other architects, 1908; (right) architect Jacques Gréber's plan, 1917 *(Fairmount Park Art Association)*

in the provision of additional radial routes in rapidly growing suburban districts and in the creation of some important diagonal boulevards in the heart of the city.

A proposal dear to the hearts of the members was one that had been much discussed in the early 1890s — a plan for a parkway 160 feet wide extending from the City Hall to Fairmount Park. From 1892 until 1894 a design of James H. Windrim, director of public works, for this grand boulevard, "with well-shaded walks and roads, and park places . . . embellished by landscape gardening,"[17] had actually been placed on the official city map, but disagreement between the mayor and councils over financing had caused the parkway to be stricken from the map. In the renewed interest in civic development aroused by the McMillan Commission's report, Philadelphians again placed the parkway on the street map in 1904. Two years later the lines of the proposed thoroughfare were revised. In 1907 Paul P. Cret and other architects produced a rather elaborate design for the project, which went through various modifications in subsequent years until, finally, in 1917 French architect Jacques Gréber devised a scheme that was approved. Now known as the Benjamin Franklin Parkway, the great avenue was opened for its entire length in 1919, though it was not completed until several years later.

The extensive park proposals in the report of the McMillan Commission inspired the Municipal Art Society of Baltimore to revive a scheme it had considered two years earlier. Its executive committee had thought of recommending that the city purchase a belt of suburban property, reserve certain areas for parks, and lease other parts, thereby "getting park lands practically free of cost."[18] In May, 1902, the society decided to employ the firm of Olmsted Brothers itself to make a careful general examination of the outlying areas of Baltimore and adjacent county territory having a "close organic connection" with the city and prepare a report suggesting reservations for park purposes and main lines of communication, together with "location plans upon a small scale but sufficiently definite to serve as a basis for approximate estimates of area and cost of land."[19] After studying the report, the society proposed to determine whether to advocate municipal acquisition and control of the development of suburban lands.

The Olmsteds reported mainly on Green Spring Valley, one of the sources of the city's water supply. This area was then in large estates but was in danger of being subdivided into small plots as the city expanded, thus becoming useless as a watershed and losing forever its rural charm. The landscape architects tentatively suggested that "a commission under proper legislative authority by right of eminent domain might impose certain restrictions limiting the percentage of land to be occupied by buildings, excluding from the operation of such restrictions a reasonable amount of land in and around each of the villages."[20] By exercise of the police power the commission might also require proper treatment of sewage and prevent pollution of streams, and might itself construct intercepting sewers for the larger villages. Finally, the commission might lay out and maintain public roads and reservations along streams and in other scenic areas. Thus the whole valley could be kept in low-density development, could be saved as a source of water supply, and could be made useful as a recreation area.

The proposal for a public commission to plan and control the development of an entire suburban territory was indeed farsighted in 1903 — so farsighted, in fact, that no American city has yet established anything of the kind. But the Olmsteds reflected the cautiousness of their time in suggesting that landowners should be paid damages under eminent domain for restricting the speculative value of their holdings. Early tenement-house regulations under the police power had limited the percentage of the lot to be occupied by the building, but the application of such controls to rural property no doubt seemed out of the question in the early years of the century. Therefore, only payment of damages — in effect, purchase of certain development rights — appeared to be a reasonable means of achieving long-term control. Indeed, it may be the best way nowadays, considering the ease with which speculators induce politicans to change zoning ordinances supposedly enacted to maintain some fringe areas as agricultural land or as semirural acreage.

The Olmsteads were unable to include in their report precise indications of park sites and a road system to replace the gridiron pattern already extended, at least on paper, to the outlying areas. Detailed topographical surveys of many parts of the outlying areas had not yet been made, and the landscape architects themselves could not afford surveys. Their report nevertheless enabled the Municipal Art Society to persuade the city fathers to authorize $1,000,000 for the acquisition of park lands. No attempt was made, however, to create a development commission, especially after a disastrous fire swept central Baltimore in 1904 and placed the city under great financial strain.

The civic leaders of Cleveland pursued all the more intently their goal of a splendid group of public buildings after the plan of Washington appeared. Under authorization of the state legislature, Governor Nash of Ohio in June, 1902, appointed a commission of architects to complete plans for the project. The members included Burnham, who had already been commissioned to design a union station on the lakefront whenever the city and the railroads reached an agreement on property rights; John M. Carrere, who had been chief architect for the Pan-American Exposition at Buffalo in 1901; and Arnold W. Brunner, architect for the new Cleveland post office.

Burnham, by the force of his personality, cast the entire scheme in the familiar configuration of the World's Columbian Exposition. The grand basin of the fair became a mall leading from the proposed station to the post office and public library, near the center of the city; the columns of the terminal resembled the colonnade at the opposite end of the basin from the domed administration building of the exposition. A city hall east of the mall complemented a courthouse on the west; and between these structures and the station extended a formal esplanade. An even more elaborate esplanade graced the lakefront on the opposite side of the terminal. Parisian in its order, the plan revealed its origins especially in the mall, whose lawns and rows of trees were modeled after the gardens of the Palais Royal. As for the architecture, probably everyone expected it to be "derived from classic Rome" and to have a uniform scale and a prescribed cornice height for all the buildings.

This civic center project, the prototype of dozens of others in the first two decades of our century, was also a slum clearance effort. On the forty-four-acre site between Superior Street and the lakeside railroad tracks stood many old buildings, including a five-story light manufacturing structure not razed until 1936, several years after a revised Mall Plan was completed. Progress was slow, and the post office was not dedicated until 1911. The courthouse was opened on New Year's Day, 1912, the city hall on the Fourth of July, 1916; and not until 1925 was the public library completed. In the meantime, a Federal Reserve Building and a public auditorium not contemplated in the original plan were added to the group of structures. But all hope of realizing the scheme as Burnham and his colleagues had envisaged it was shattered when the Van Sweringen brothers, having daringly acquired the Nickel Plate Railroad, decided in the twenties to build the central railroad station of Cleveland on the Public Square, five blocks from the location shown on the Mall Plan. Somewhat to one side of the spot on which Burnham's monumental terminal would have risen, a municipal stadium was constructed in 1931. Today the mall, refurbished in modern style, has only an expansive view of Lake Erie at its northern terminus—charming, but not the climactic element the grandiose composition demands. Yet this civic center has fared better than many others conceived in the fulsome days of the "City Beautiful" movement. Only a lone city hall or courthouse bears witness to the enthusiasm with which some were begun; and an incalculable number remained nothing but architectural drawings.

The present view of these early schemes as civic extravaganzas obscures an aspect highly important to progressive citizens of Theodore Roosevelt's day. Grouping public buildings was one way to outwit "local rings of real estate interests" who wanted to scatter public structures in order to "divide the benefit of their presence" among various sections of the city.[21] The civic center was not only a symbol of local pride; it was also a tangible municipal reform.

Burnham, Carrère, and Brunner soon discovered that they were needed to make decisions about many things besides the Group Plan. Acting very much like a city planning commission, they gave advice about a proposed lakeshore boulevard and lakefront parks, the terminus of the High-level Bridge, and the design and location of branch libraries, schools, markets, and minor public buildings. However, these architects actually thought of themselves as performing the functions of a municipal art commission, for aesthetic judgments outweighed more practical considerations.

San Francisco was the next city to become interested in Burnham's services as a planner. This time his assignment was to propose not merely a park system or the arrangement of public buildings but a plan for the entire territory within the combined city and county. His invitation to

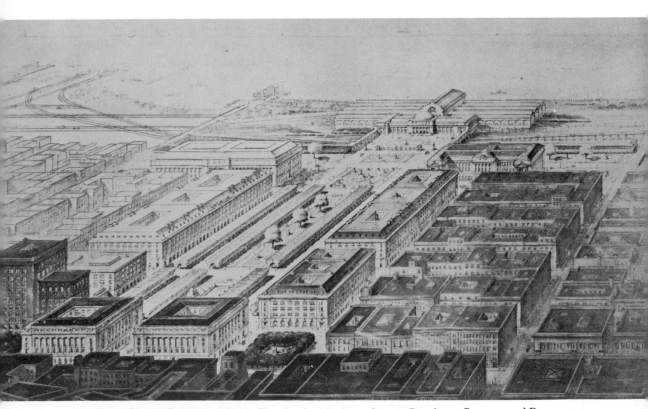

19. Group Plan of Public Buildings, Cleveland, 1903, by architects Burnham, Carrere, and Brunner *(Cleveland City Planning Commission)*

set forth graphically and in writing what the metropolis might become in another half-century came from a private group, the Association for the Improvement and Adornment of San Francisco, rather than from the city administration, then fast becoming one of the most corrupt in the nation.

This circumstance — the unofficial sponsorship and the lack of direct participation in the planning effort by any members of the city government — tended to invest the plan with a certain visionary quality. San Francisco had its problems, but none of them posed the urgency of the mall situation in Washington, D.C., for example; nor were public officials clamoring for advice about the location of proposed civic structures. Burnham and his young architectural associates, Edward H. Bennett, Willis Polk, Henry Gutterson, and others, encountered few restraints on their imaginations as they gazed at the city from their specially built studio or "shanty" on Twin Peaks in 1904 and 1905 and dreamed of slicing great diagonal boulevards through the gridiron street pattern laid over the hills and valleys of the city. James Duval Phelan, the wealthy former mayor who headed the improvement and adornment group, occasionally objected to some of these augustan proposals, but Burnham

20. Bird's-eye view of the Burnham plan of San Francisco, 1905

always convinced him that anything was possible in a city destined to double or triple in population and to extend its economic influence in all directions. The completed plan, suggesting a Parisian complex of radial boulevards and round points, civic buildings distributed around a small inner circuit, another great park three times the size of Golden Gate Park, and parkways connecting hilltop parks, had, as Professor John Reps has observed, more merit as an abstract design than as a serious proposal for public improvement.[22]

What the fate of this ambitious scheme might have been if San Francisco had not experienced a catastrophic earthquake and fire eight months after the members of the Association for the Improvement and Adornment of San Francisco and their political enemy, Mayor Eugene Schmitz, extolled it at a gala dinner on September 27, 1905, no one can say. Schmitz and other officials of the stricken city made only a brief effort to avail themselves of the plan as they set about rebuilding, and most businessmen impatiently demanded that it be disregarded altogether, at least in the downtown area. Yet initially there was widespread interest in Burnham himself and in his labors in behalf of the city.

When Burnham addressed a public meeting in May, 1904, and asked members of the audience to inform him about the needs of San Francisco, delegates from a score or more of civic organizations enthusiastically contributed advice and described worthwhile projects on which there was already considerable agreement. Many of these spokesmen represented improvement clubs in the humbler neighborhoods of the city, whereas the City Beautiful movement is sometimes protrayed as a patrician cause which achieved indifferent success because it attracted support chiefly among the well-to-do. The diversity of the San Francisco audience revealed, in fact, that newspapers, magazines, and the bulletins of reform associations had widely disseminated the gospel of municipal improvement and beautification.

The Literary Road to City Planning

Foremost among those who did missionary work in the field of civic betterment was Charles Mulford Robinson. A prolific writer, he soon found himself functioning in the dual capacity of public educator and planner, although he was a man with no specific professional education, either as a landscape architect or as an architect or an engineer. The success of Robinson's series of articles about municipal improvements in the United States in the *Atlantic Monthly* in 1899 brought him an invitation from *Harper's Magazine* to go abroad and prepare a similar series about municipal developments in Europe. Having collected much more material than he could use in the magazine, he decided to write his first book, which he entitled *The Improvement of Cities and Towns*. It was, as its subtitle indicated, a treatise on the practical basis of civic aesthetics and had chapters on the influence of the site on the beauty of a city, types of street plans, the importance of fine architecture, street trees, parks, gardens, playgrounds, and sculpture, the control of advertisements and utilities, and various means of educating the public to appreciate and demand civic art. But since the subject matter was then so new that no publisher would take the financial risk of publication, Robinson himself issued the book — and to his great surprise discovered that he had written a best-seller. Within a year the book was in its third printing and in subsequent years was revised and reprinted again and again. Not only did it create a wide readership for Robinson's second book, *Modern Civic Art,* published in 1903, but it also stimulated the formation of improvement groups and civic art societies throughout the United States, some of which later engaged him to prepare city plans.

According to the preface of this second work, there were at the time of its publication upwards of twelve hundred local "improvement" societies in the United States.[23] By 1906 Robinson was able to report in a new edition of *The Improvement of Cities and Towns* that there were no fewer than two thousand. The increase of these organizations can be attributed in part to the activities of the American League for Civic Improvement, formed in 1900 as the National League of Improvement Associations and combined in 1904 with the American Park and Outdoor Art Association under the new name of the American Civic Association, which Robinson himself served for a few months as temporary secretary. But his suc-

21. Charles Mulford Robinson
(Public Library, Rochester, New York)

cessor, J. Horace McFarland, was as amazed and mystified by the rapid multiplication of improvement groups as anyone in the land and could explain the popularity of the movement only by voicing his belief that "in the fulness of time God has put it into the hearts of our American citizens . . . to make the habitations of men more cleanly, more sightly, and more comfortable; to act for all the people in unselfishness; to endeavor in some sense to give us here on earth in our urban habitations conditions at least approximating those of the beautiful wild into which our forefathers came a few generations ago."[24] Some religious motivation there may have been for the great civic awakening of which McFarland spoke, but it is more realistic to assume that public-spirited citizens gradually became aware of the gross deficiencies in their environment and determined to remedy matters.

Writing of his own city of Harrisburg, Pennsylvania, McFarland said that in 1901 "we had no parks worthy of the name; we were drinking typhoid-polluted water, commingled with coal dust; we had no system of street cleaning and but few paved streets; our drainage system was weak in places and conspicuously bad in one important part of the city."[25] Similar conditions in hundreds of other cities and towns became increasingly intolerable to citizens as the reform agitations begun in the 1880s and 1890s gathered momentum and swept the country. Contributing to the rising dissatisfaction with municipal inadequacies were the articles of the muckrakers, Ida M. Tarbell, Lincoln Steffens, Ray Stannard Baker, Upton Sinclair, and others, whose writings collectively protrayed alliances between corrupt political machines and equally corrupt big businesses. Another potent influence of the times was the enthusiasm for the commission form of government first instituted in Galveston, Texas, after the disastrous flood of 1900. Widely adopted in cities of the Middle West and West, especially, this more "efficient" type of local government, with responsibility centered in five decision-makers, gave many communities the clean water, cheaper transportation, more numerous parks, and decent law enforcement they wanted.

Caught up in the Progressivism pervading America, the improvement associations sometimes joined the general drive to revamp governmental institutions, curb the profiteering of trusts, and safeguard natural resources. In a nation still greatly affected by its Puritan heritage, citizens could muster tremendous moral indignation not only against individual sinners who gambled or imbibed too freely but also against corporate malefactors. Some of the latter, besides bribing inspectors and selling inferior products at high prices, blackened the atmosphere with smoke from their factories, defiled rivers, and dumped refuse in conspicuous places. Outraged as well as aesthetically offended, a few improvement groups went all the way to the statehouse to stop pollution or prohibit dumping, but most preferred to work locally; and altruism rather than righteous anger provided the motive power for their programs.

By temperament Robinson was equipped to inspire the nonmilitant rather than the shrill crusaders. His message struck the proper idealistic note: "Civic art is not a fad. It is not merely a bit of aestheticism. There is nothing effeminate and sentimental about it. . . . It is vigorous, virile, sane. Altruism is its impluse, but it is older than any altruism of the hour—as old as the dreams and aspirations of men."[26]

Robinson made civic art especially appealing to his countrymen by telling them that it joins utility to beauty. He thereby satisfied their practical bent. "If the end be to clothe utility with beauty," he wrote, "and in providing the beautiful to provide also that which will add to the convenience and comfort of the citizens, we shall best find its opportunities for usefulness by studying what has been happily called the anatomy of cities. In this there appear three groups of requirements: Those that have to do with circulation, those that have to do with hygiene, and those that have to do distinctly with beauty. No hard lines separate these classes. . . ."[27]

The means of uniting good circulation and "urban hygiene" with beauty was "a well thought out, artistically conceived general plan." "It has been necessary," Robinson explained, "to divide the city into parts, according to the purposes it serves; and each of these parts has presented a question of development by itself, while the great, all-embracing urban problem has proved to be the co-ordination of these into a single scheme comprehensive and harmonious."[28] Such a scheme would "weld together in a harmonious system the street plotting of the different districts," show the future development of all the public and semipublic institutions, and indicate "a degree of recognizable uniformity" in the design of public buildings.[29]

In thus restricting the city plan to two principal elements, circulation and community facilities, plus some standards of design for public buildings, Robinson seemed to be no broader in his thought than the members of the McMillan Comission. But a chapter in *Modern Civic Art* entitled "Among the Tenements" reveals that he approved of efforts to relieve the congestion of tenement districts by removing factories and workers to suburban areas, that he followed closely the progress of regulatory movements, and that he was concerned with the serious question whether model tenements intended for the very poor would really be occupied by them and not by people of superior means and less need who would be attracted by the low rents.[30] That the rents would almost inevitably be higher than the poor could afford seems not to have occurred to him at all. Like the reformers who crusaded for stronger laws and strict enforcement, he expected improvement in housing mainly from "wise ordinances so enforced that there are no rookeries, that there is nothing worse than this to which the poor can go."[31]

Limited though his perspective was, Robinson sensed the need for a new type of specialist to help other experts "to put before the community a vision of what its own town might be and should be."[32] He suggested a professional commission including not only an architect, a landscape architect, a sculptor, and an engineer, but also "one member who would stand not for engineering alone, nor for architecture alone, nor for landscape design alone, nor for sculpture alone, but for all these together and comprehensively, as one who has made a special study of the general science and art of city-building."[33] This call for a generalist capable of synthesizing the aesthetic and the technical foreshadowed by a quarter of a century the establishment of the first graduate school of city planning at Harvard University and came six years before that institution offered the first city planning course in the United States in its department of landscape architecture. Robinson himself, it should be noted, had no idea what to call the broadly qualified practitioner he described, nor were American cities yet ready to offer permanent employment to specialists in "the general science and art of city-building" or even to maintain permanent planning commissions. But the nation was rapidly accepting the idea that municipalities should attempt to coordinate improvements in every aspect of urban life.

Public Education at an Exposition

In 1904, the year after *Modern Civic Art* appeared, the city of St. Louis gave impetus to the social enlightenment bursting upon the country by presenting an exposition "based upon the conclusion that education is the source of all progress." The Louisiana Purchase Exposition, celebrating the centennial of Jefferson's acquisition of vast French territories in the midcontinent, for the first time in history featured a Palace of Education in which visitors could compare "the educational experience and methods of all the leading civilized countries."[34]

Almost as prominent as the school exhibitions in this structure was a section on "social economy," illustrating, among other things, the advances American cities were making in public health, housing, social work, protection of life and property, recreation, and municipal engineering. Here visitors could study displays of cooperative building companies and the Tenement House Commission of the City of New York, the boards of charities of many states and municipalities, the International Association of Chiefs of Police, the American Medical Association and various foreign and American boards of health, the school of social sciences of the Catholic University of America, and the United States Department of Labor, to name only a few. Model public health laboratories, a model jail, and a garbage crematory invited inspection. The exhibition of greatest interest to many of those concerned with civic betterment was not, however, inside the building at all.

The model street, first projected as an entire model city, and a central public square with a monument to Civic Pride suggested even more forcefully than the interior displays some of the good things to be sought in city-building. This street and the town hall facing the square were the work of Albert Kelsey, a Philadelphia architect who was to find himself, two years later, serving with Robinson on a temporary five-man city plan commission in Columbus, Ohio. Ranged along the street were buildings erected by the cities of New York, San Francisco, Kansas City, and the twin cities of Minneapolis and St. Paul, several restaurants, a drugstore, and a pavilion of the New Jersey Road Department. At intervals on both sides of the street stood ornamental streetlamps; combination streetlamps, letter boxes, and signposts; tree guards and trolley poles; several styles of drinking fountains and ornamental fountains; advertising

22. Model street, Louisiana Purchase Exposition, St. Louis, 1904 *(Missouri Historical Society)*

kiosks from Berlin and Dresden, Germany; and other examples of street furniture. The surface of the street itself was an exhibition of paving materials. Near the public square was a model playground occupying almost three-quarters of an acre, containing play apparatus, shelters, and special buildings for the care of smaller children and infants. The monument in the square, commemorating the young Charles Eliot, who was cut off in his prime, was inscribed with a quotation from T. Jefferson Coolidge: "In any city, town or village where men and women give jointly and freely of their wisdom, strength and substance to achieve and maintain appropriate beauty in the surroundings of public and private buildings, the visible perfection of a place whose ways are ways of pleasantness . . . bears witness to the enlightened civic pride of its inhabitants."[35]

Amid all the huge palaces, plazas, lagoons, fountains, and gardens on the 1,271-acre site of the exposition this rather modest piece of a city may have seemed relatively insignificant, yet it did not escape the attention of journalists and an increasing number of citizens who were eager to promote local improvements. The American Civic Association, which had sponsored Kelsey's project, not only urged the members of affiliated organizations to visit the model street but also worked with the influential Chautauqua Assembly to publicize it. But since it was, after all, only a single street rather than a model city, it stimulated more proposals for individual playgrounds or ornamental squares or fountains than for city-wide plans, as McFarland ruefully acknowledged some years later. Still, communities just awakening to the need for a better environment had to start with fairly simple projects that everyone could understand, and many that began with merely a playground or a small park progressed afterward to broader planning. The fair itself, almost as large as the earlier Philadelphia, Chicago, Omaha, and Buffalo expositions together, was such an impressive example of large-scale planning that it gave the whole City Beautiful movement another great thrust forward, as Olmsted, Robinson, Kelsey, Burnham, and a new young planner named John Nolen soon realized. All received invitations to prepare "improvement plans" for civic organizations or municipalities.

Efforts to Cope with Social and Physical Problems

Although Robinson and Burnham usually included recommendations for playgrounds in their reports, Olmsted and Nolen, both landscape architects, probably had stronger convictions about the need for such areas than other planners. They especially deplored the "vague way" in which most citizens approved of a large increase in the number of playgrounds and parks without understanding that public open spaces should be of great variety and should be carefully selected and designed to serve specific purposes.[36] As coauthors of a lengthy, well-illustrated article in

Charities and The Commons, the influential journal of social work, they attempted to educate an important segment of American society by describing six types of open areas representing "the normal requirements of large cities": streets, boulevards, and parkways; city squares, commons, and public gardens; playgrounds of three kinds—for little children, for children of school age, and for youths and young adults; small neighborhood parks; large in-city parks; and great outlying reservations like those acquired in the Boston metropolitan district.

Reflecting Theodore Roosevelt's enthusiasm for physical culture and outdoor life, as well as their own awareness that an increasing proportion of Americans was engaged in confining occupations, they called for systematic municipal action to provide "convenient provision for exercise in the open air."[37] For children of school age the playground should be preferably next to the school, so that it could be used during the recesses as well as after hours.[38] For adolescents and young adults the outdoor gymnasium or sports center should be "ample, accessible, thoroughly complete in . . . arrangement and well maintained."[39]

In suggesting that "the size, character and location of sites for each particular purpose must be carefully considered,"[40] Olmsted and Nolen were beginning to think of the whole city as a complex of interrelated systems, the arteries of circulation articulated with the larger parks and outlying reservations, the small playgrounds planned as adjuncts of the schools, the neighborhood parks and larger playgrounds distributed throughout the city as systematically as the schools. They were searching for a physical pattern to meet the social needs of the community, but they were perhaps not so advanced in thought as Jacob Riis and Jane Addams or certain citizen groups, such as one of the committees of the Civic League of St. Louis.

As early as 1902, or even before then, Riis envisaged every neighborhood or district of a city utilizing its public school as a social and educational center and having its own distinct civic life while cooperating with other neighborhoods. In 1907 the Committee on Civic Centers of the St. Louis league, interested not in monumental public buildings but in neighborhood centers, surpassed Riis in social vision by proposing that a public school, parochial school, branch library, park and playground, public bath, model tenement, settlement house, church, police station, fire-engine house, and homes of athletic and social organizations be grouped around a common center.[41] Not until a decade later would Clarence Arthur Perry, who is often credited with formulating the neighborhood unit concept, even begin to develop his ideas about physically and socially defined areas in cities; and not until the late twenties would he diagram and describe his model neighborhood of five or six thousand residents, with the elementary school as center.

There was a special reason why Riis and the St. Louis group were more alert to problems of social organization than men trained as designers or self-taught as planners. Riis, an immigrant himself, had a profound sympathy for the foreigner struggling to adjust to a new life in the tenement districts. The St. Louis committee, chosen from a representative cross section of citizens in a city with a large immigrant population, recalled a 1904 report proposing a civic center for the entire city and conceived the idea that a small civic center in each neighborhood would "tend toward the development of better citizenship."[42] But the more carefully the committee studied conditions in the crowded low-income areas of the city, the more alarmed it became and the more convinced that neighborhood centers were essential. "The indiscriminate herding together of large masses of human beings ignorant of the simplest laws of sanitation, the evils of child labor, the corruption in political life, and, above all, the weakening of the ties which bind together the home — these are dangers which strike at the very roots of society," the committe found. "To combat them the government must employ every resource in its power."[43]

Strongly imbued with Progressive ideals, the committee marshaled these arguments for developing a neighborhood center wherever one was needed:

> It would center the interests of the people in the neighborhood and would enable the different institutions to supplement one another. For example, it would enable many parents to use the various institutions in their only leisure hours, the evenings, by leaving their children in the playground or social settlement near by, whereas otherwise they would be unable to leave them alone at home; it would give a splendid opportunity for an harmonious architectural and landscape treatment of the various buildings, thus adding to the intrinsic beauty of each; it would foster civic pride in the neighborhood and would form a model for improvement work, the influence of which would extend to every home in the district; it would give to the immigrant — ignorant of our customs and institutions — a personal contact with the higher functions which the government exercises towards him, as manifested in the only municipal institution with which he is brought in contact — the police station — a feeling that the government is, after all, maintained for his individual well-being as well as for that of the native-born inhabitant. Lastly, it would develop a neighborhood feeling, which in these days of specialization has grown weak, with a resulting lack of interest in local politics and the consequent corruption and disregard of the best interests of the people by their representatives.[44]

In this proposal, originally inspired by a report illustrated with architectural drawings of the Washington and Cleveland malls, the City Beautiful concept became transformed into an instrument of social planning. Had the public officials and citizens of St. Louis had the foresight to make use of it liberally, the forces of disintegration always at work in our society might have been somewhat retarded. But the members of the Committee on Civic Centers were, unfortunately, far more enlightened than their contemporaries. Their hope of furthering "the unity of our civic life" by a combination of physical and social planning was not realized. Yet the report of this group must be remembered as one of the most significant in a period marked by increasing knowledge of urban needs and possibilities. Its recommendations give special distinction to a larger report that is itself an unusual document because it represents solely citizens' views, formed without the advice of any of the men then emerging as city planners.

A City Plan for St. Louis, issued by the Civic League in January, 1907, looked ahead to 1925 in the optimistic belief that a million and a quarter persons would then be living within a radius of ten miles from the City Hall.[45] To bring "civic orderliness and beauty" into the environment of this increased population, the league offered the coordinated recommendations of half-a-dozen committees. In addition to a group plan of municipal buildings and as many neighborhood centers as might be needed, it proposed the purchase and improvement of some five thousand acres of park land and the construction of more than forty miles of parkway in St. Louis County, varied street and riverfront improvements, the establishment of a municipal art commission to exercise general supervision over the design of public buildings, and legislation necessary to carry into effect the plans as outlined. Except for the proposal for neighborhood centers, the recommendations were typical of the City Beautiful era. But in describing conditions in residential areas, the league indicated that it was aware of the need for much more than its committees were suggesting—planning the uses of land in various sections of the city, particularly the residential areas, and regulating the uses under new statutes. The league pointed out that

> Building lines have not been observed [in the residential sections]; business blocks and livery stables have been permitted to encroach upon purely residence streets; flats have been jammed in between beautiful homes; the choicest paved streets have become main thoroughfares for heavy hauling; and only the "Places" [exclusive courts entered through ornamental gates] are protected from the encroachment of street cars, switch tracks and objectionable buildings. The average citizen, who is seeking a quiet home away from the noise and discomfort of traffic, is helpless in the face of this riot of conflicting and selfish interests—the direct results of a lack of plan and insufficient regulations.[46]

The neighborhood deterioration of which the league complained was becoming all too characteristic of residential sections in cities throughout the United States. The only protection these areas had against invasion

by corner grocery stores, apartment houses, and small factories and repair shops was private deed restrictions. Sometimes, however, such covenants proved legally defective, and even those that could be enforced
usually included termination dates. Thus entire areas, at the end of
twenty or twenty-five years, were at the mercy of speculators who wished
to erect apartment houses on vacant lots or convert large homes into
several cheap rental units, taking advantage of the quality of a good
neighborhood but immediately blighting it. The City Beautiful movement offered little to combat this serious problem—merely vague hopes
that tree-lined boulevards and parks would establish a neighborhood
"tone" which everyone would respect. Most planning reports issued up
to 1908 contained not the slightest suggestion that lack of regulation
of the use of land causes blight and initiates the process of decline.

The steps taken by cities to restrict the use of private property came
almost exclusively in response to the demands of housing reformers and
municipal fire and health departments. The former sought to make tenements more livable by limiting the number of stories, decreasing the
percentage of the lot covered, and banning laundries, bakeries, and
cleaning establishments from basements because of fire hazards. The
separation of these businesses from tenements was one of the earliest
attempts to segregate incompatible uses, if one excepts the many still
earlier prohibitions on the operation of slaughter houses, tanneries,
glue factories, and other offensive or nuisance establishments in built-
up areas and the somewhat later ordinances of some California cities
banning steam laundries (run by the Chinese) in the more exclusive
residential sections. One of these laws, enacted by the city of Modesto
in 1885, has been cited by some as the first example of a zoning ordinance
because it restricted certain kinds of uses to a particular area. Public
laundries or washhouses were relegated to a section situated on the west
or "wrong" side of the tracks.

Municipal departments occasionally attacked the problem of danger
to persons and property from fires by advocating limitations on the height
of buildings—limitations which also helped to reduce traffic congestion
and prevented high buildings on narrow streets from robbing lower structures of light and air. In 1904 Boston imposed height restrictions generally, limiting wooden buildings to 45 feet, structures in the business
district to a maximum of 125 feet, and buildings in other parts of the
city to 80 feet. But Congress had set an example in Washington in 1899
by adopting regulations specifying 60 feet as a maximum height for
nonfireproof residential structures, prohibiting any building exceeding
90 feet on a residential street, and limiting buildings on the widest streets
to 130 feet. There was an aesthetic aspect to this last height restriction;

it was designed to maintain the dominance of the dome of the Capitol in the District of Columbia.

The *use* of private land in American cities was almost everywhere controlled only in the most piecemeal fashion until, on December 28, 1909, Los Angeles adopted an ordinance creating seven industrial districts (later increased to twenty-seven) and two weeks afterward established almost all the rest of the city as a residential district. Within the latter businesses were permitted, subject to certain conditions, as "residence exceptions." Municipal authorities actually ejected a number of small businesses from the residential district, but even more drastic was another attempt to protect residential amenities. After an outlying area, in which a brick industry was situated, had been annexed to the city, another ordinance was enacted prohibiting brickyards in residential districts. The owner of course fought the municipality's effort to put him out of business, carrying his case (Hadacheck *v.* Sebastian) all the way to the United States Supreme Court and losing in 1915 in a sweeping decision which stated that the city had not acted arbitrarily in the exercise of its police power. But the Los Angeles ordinances were less well known to other American cities than the zoning regulations of German municipalities. It was these laws which planning enthusiasts presently began citing as inspiration for cities struggling to find ways to combat the deterioration of residential areas and the congestion of population.

The Need for Continuity of Control

The report of the Civic League of St. Louis was but one of several indications that the City Beautiful movement was beginning to be affected by social movements concerned with the living conditions of the working class and by a middle-class interest in something stronger than private deed restrictions to protect residential areas from invasion by inharmonious activities and uses. As the City Beautiful fervor reached its crest, these social and economic concerns were, however, generally obscured by the widespread passion for programs of beautification and civic improvement. Business groups, women's clubs, civic associations, and municipal art commissions in greater and greater numbers engaged consultants to produce the usual package of park, boulevard, and civic center proposals. Individual architects, groups of architects, unofficial commissions, and chambers of commerce all put forth their own schemes for groups of monumental buildings, riverfront drives, parks, and playgrounds. If there were social overtones to some of these proposals, they tended to be overwhelmed by the more dominant themes of local patriotism and booster-like promotion.

Yet the undeniable virtue of this movement was that it had an educational effect on many of those drawn into it, leading them to broader

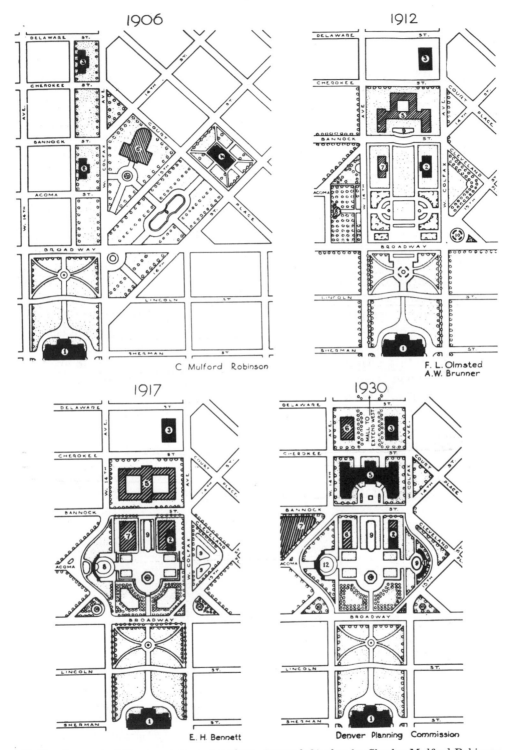

23. Development of Denver civic center plans: (upper left) plan by Charles Mulford Robinson, 1906; (upper right) plan by Frederick L. Olmsted, the younger, and Arnold W. Brunner, 1912; (lower left) plan by Edward H. Bennett, 1917; (lower right) plan by Denver City Planning Commission, 1930

civic involvement. Park commissioners who engaged Nolen or Olmsted or Kessler to prepare plans for park systems invariably became interested in other public improvements. Kessler's work in Cincinnati and Indianapolis as a park consultant undoubtedly laid the foundations for city planning in those cities in later years, as did Nolen's park work in Little Rock, Arkansas, and Olmsted's in Providence, Rhode Island. In Milwaukee the metropolitan park commission established in 1907 became in 1911 a city planning commission. Occasionally the necessity of selecting the site for a new federal building, as in Minneapolis, or a new city hall, as in Portland, Maine, raised the question of developing a civic center, and if the agitation was sufficiently strong, as it was in Minneapolis in 1908, an entire city plan eventually resulted — Edward H. Bennett's preliminary plan of 1911 and his comprehensive plan of 1917. The contagious enthusiasm of some one man could also inspire a whole community leadership to support planning, witness the success of George B. Dealey, vice president and general manager of the *Dallas News,* in inducing his fellow businessmen to invite Kessler to prepare a comprehensive plan for Dallas. If an entire organization had put its own brainpower into drafting a planning report, that organization could even put over a bond issue of $11,500,000 for public improvements a year later, convert itself into a city planning association the year after that, and in time hail the creation of an official city planning commission. Such was the record of the Civic League of St. Louis.

Still, not everyone was enchanted with the City Beautiful movement. From the beginning it had had its critics. In the early stages, when the municipal art commissions and art leagues proposed the embellishment of cities with statues, fountains, and memorial arches, the *Chicago Post*

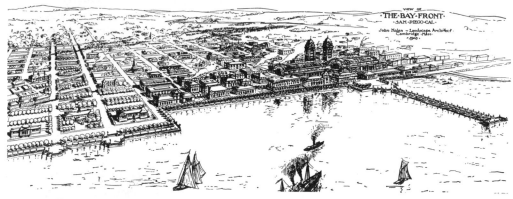

24. Perspective drawing showing John Nolen's proposed development of the bay front, San Diego, 1908

expressed the scorn of practical minds by asking, "What is the use of buying $1,000,000 worth of public works of art annually while our anti-smoke ordinances are violated every hour of the day and our streets are never even half cleaned?"[47]

In 1907 the millionaire plumber Richard T. Crane, a self-made man who had begun work at nine years of age in a textile mill, expressed disapproval of the movement for its seeming indifference to some of the more obvious social problems: "I have no quarrel with those who would make the city more beautiful than it is, but I would have all such schemes begin at the bottom. I would not put money into boulevards and statues and fine bridges and elaborate public buildings until the immediate surroundings of the poor are made better and decenter."[48]

Herbert Croly, a Progressive intellectual who might have been expected to echo Crane's sentiments, attacked the movement not for its lack of social objectives but for its failure to convert plans into reality, though charity—and his passion for reform—inclined him to blame

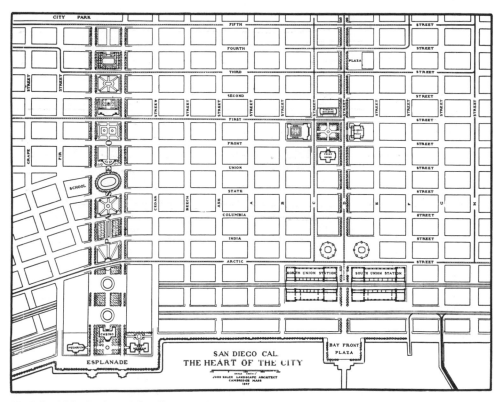

25. John Nolen's plan of San Diego, 1907

municipal misgovernment and his favorite whipping boys, the real estate speculators, for the inability of the City Beautiful enthusiasts to carry out their schemes. Why should citizens vote bonds for construction programs that would enrich grasping property owners and provide opportunities for politicians to graft? To Croly it seemed unlikely that many civic centers or grand boulevards would materialize until state legislatures strengthened city governments.

Horace McFarland, working closely with citizens' groups, found, on the other hand, that many Americans considered Burnham, Olmsted, Nolen, and other designer-planners dangerous believers in "centralized government" or paternalists who would give the people handsome buildings and plazas whether or not they could afford them. The situation demanded extensive public education, but McFarland was disappointed in the lack of interest shown by institutions of higher learning. "It is the layman, the 'crank,' the unsatisfied one, the golden-hearted woman seeking to see a bit of the heavenly city in advance, who move communities," he observed.[49] The universities, he thought, for the most part were neglecting broad civic needs.

All these criticisms foretold the eventual decline of the City Beautiful movement and its transformation into something more realistic and practical. In most cities it had produced few noteworthy changes. But it had nevertheless served the indispensable function of showing the need for permanent city planning commissions.

The first such official body was established at Hartford, Connecticut, in March, 1907. Mainly at the urging of the park department of the state capital, the state legislature amended the city charter to provide for "a commission on the city plan" consisting of the mayor, the city engineer, the presidents of the board of street commissioners and the board of park commissioners, a member of the board of aldermen, a member of the common council board, and two citizens, neither of whom should hold any other municipal office.

The participation of elected officials and heads of boards was far greater than had been authorized in any previous commission, public or private, and was indeed greater than would be sanctioned by most cities embarking on official planning programs in the next decade or two. There could be no doubt that the legislature wished the city administration to give deeper thought to the future of Hartford, or at least those parts of the city affected by public action.

Modeled in some respects after the bill defining the powers of the Group Plan Commission of the city of Cleveland, the amendment empowered the new commission to make a map or maps of the city showing locations proposed for new public buildings, streets, boulevards, esplanades, parkways, squares, and parks, as well as any proposed changes in the location of existing buildings, streets, squares, and parks. Further, the measure made mandatory the referral of questions concerning public buildings, avenues of circulation, and open spaces to the city plan commission before the common council could take action. That body was given permission to refer the construction or carrying out of public works not expressly within the province of other departments to the plan commission—an administrative responsibility with which an advisory agency would not nowadays be burdened. Altogether lacking was any authorization for broad control over the uses of private land. The only ways in which the new agency could affect private property were by establishing building and veranda lines and by approving or disapproving street locations and grades proposed by developers of new subdivisions.

Residents of Hartford witnessed no immediate or spectacular improvement in their city as a result of the creation of the commission. With the exception of the city engineer, Frederick L. Ford, who was actually an architect, the members pretended to no special expertise. More than a year passed before the commissioners received an appropriation of $2,800 to employ the New York firm of Carrère and Hastings as advisory architects, and not until 1911 was the commission in possession of the *Plan of the City of Hartford,* in the main the work of the architects.

Elsewhere more and more persons interested in city planning were also coming to the conclusion that the temporary commission no longer met the needs of the times, though these new champions of the permanent, official commission were not always aware of the significant step taken in Hartford. One who apparently did not know of the action of the Connecticut legislature was Robert W. de Forest, who as president of the Municipal Art Commission of the city of New York and president of the New York Charity Organization Society united in his own person both the aesthetic and the social interests in the city planning movement. Also vice-president of the recently established Russell Sage Foundation (1907), he was in a particularly strong position to influence the emerging social trend. Early in 1908 he wrote that "some central city authority should regulate and control the location of all parks and public buildings, and should forecast and control the laying out of streets and the location of possible future parks and public buildings in the undeveloped outlying districts."[50]

The weakness of American city development, as De Forest observed it, was not only the lack of "any single control over all related public improvements" but also the lack of any provision for continuity of control. "Our form of city government may be wisely adapted to carrying out the particular will of the people at the time of election, but efficient city planning involves looking to a longer future and to providing some means whereby city plans which require many years for their execution can be entrusted to those who can remain in control long enough to have those plans carried out."[51] Citing the recently created Rapid Transit Commission of New York City as an example of an agency with a tenure of office far beyond that of any elective officers, De Forest suggested a city planning commission of eight or ten members, two of whom would go out of office every year and each of whom would serve for four or five years. Two or three elective officials would be included as ex officio members. Such a body, while having sufficient continuity to carry its wise decisions into effect, would have "sufficient changeability to ensure a recognition of strong public opinion and the abandonment of any unwise conclusions."[52]

The very scope of the planning problem in a huge, expanding metropolis such as New York convinced Frederick Stymetz Lamb, former secretary of the Municipal Art Society of that city, that no temporary commission could hope to present a satisfactory plan. In a review of the final report of the City Improvement Commission he expressed his surprise at finding no recommendations for extensions of the subway system, or for new bridges, or for the development of the New Jersey shore of the Hudson River although "this area is just as important . . . to Greater New York as if it were contained within its boundaries." These shortcomings he attributed to the commission's acute awareness of its impermanence and its unwillingness to suggest projects that could not be immediately financed and executed. "The greater city of the future – the city of twenty years to come – has not been adequately realized in imagination," he charged, adding that "the work of this commission proves conclusively the necessity of a permanent commission . . . adequately remunerated to enable it to carry on its important work with efficiency."[53]

Another New Yorker who sounded a critical note, and who was equally certain that broad, long-range metropolitan planning was essential, was Benjamin C. Marsh, secretary of the Committee on Congestion of Population in New York. But Marsh had in mind a planning commission altogether different from any Lamb imagined. "The grouping of public buildings, and the installation of speedways, parks and drives, which affect only moderately the daily lives of the city's toilers, are important," Marsh conceded, "but vastly more so is the securing of decent home conditions for the countless thousands who otherwise can but occasionally escape from their squalid, confining surroundings to view the architectural perfection and to experience the aesthetic delights of the remote improvements."[54] Greater New York needed comprehensive planning not just because it would increase in population and expand physically but because it had become, in Cobbett's phrase, "a great wen," with bestial overcrowding in its tenements, deaths among children under five so numerous as to constitute "a Herodian slaughter," nearly three hundred thousand dark, interior bedrooms breeding tuberculosis and other communicable diseases, towering rents correlative with towering land values, imperial fortunes for the few and sweated wages for the multitudes, every vice and depravity known to Lucifer — and thousands of acres of land in outlying areas where the working classes could and should be living in single- or two-family houses, with their own gardens and ample opportunity to enjoy light, air, and sunshine. As Marsh saw it, only by distributing the population at relatively low densities throughout these sparsely settled districts and providing fast, convenient, low-cost transit to places of work could there be any real improvement in living conditions. To bring about this kind of organization in Greater New York, or in any other large metropolis, an agency similar to the Metropolitan Improvement Commission of Boston was required.

This areawide commission appealed to Marsh because the bill establishing it directed the governor of Massachusetts and the mayor of Boston to appoint not just architects but also "persons of recognized qualification and large experience" in such other fields as finance, commerce, industry, transportation, real estate, engineering, civic administration, and law — men who had some grasp of social and economic fundamentals. Further, the legislation empowered the commission to "investigate and report as to the advisability of any public needs . . . which in its opinion will tend to the convenience of the people, the development of local business, the beautifying of the district, or the improvement of the same as a place of residence."[55] That last phrase was particularly pleasing to Marsh, but not more so than the sentence saying that the commission "shall consider the establishment of a systematic method of internal communication by highways, the control or direction of traffic and transportation, and the location of such docks and terminals as the interests of the district may demand"[56] — matters generally neglected by the City Beautiful planners but vital to any scheme for decongesting population and industrial establishments. If New York could create a commission that would concern itself more with housing, transit, and the location of manufacturing plants than with monumental buildings and civic adornment, then indeed the goals of the Committee on Congestion of Population might be attained.

Formed in the winter of 1907 by such outstanding settlement leaders as Lillian Wald, Mary K. Simkhovitch, and the Reverend Gaylord S. White, together with their friends Florence Kelley, of the National Consumers League, and Dr. Herman C. Bumpus, director of the American Museum of Natural History, this committee united representatives of thirty-seven important civic and philanthropic organizations. Its program contemplated informing the public of the evils of the excessive massing of people in New York City, indicating current methods of dealing with the problems involved, and pointing out means of relieving congestion.

In Marsh the group found the ideal executive secretary. Unwittingly, it also found the man who would make the city planning movement more socially responsive and better known nationally.

"Cures" for Congestion of Population

Benjamin Marsh was a former fund-raiser for the Congregationalist Board of Commissioners for Foreign Missions and a disciple of Professor Simon Patten of the University of Pennsylvania, who maintained that the economy of scarcity was obsolete and that the future promised an economy of abundance as a new basis of civilization. "When poverty is gone, the last formidable obstacle to the upward movement of the race will have disappeared," Patten declared.[57] And Marsh reflected his mentor's faith by asserting, "The right of the citizen to leisure, to health, to care in sickness, to work under normal conditions, and to live under conditions which will not impair his health or his efficiency is coming to be recognized as fully as the right of the state to restrain the wrongdoer or its duty to protect property."[58] The single-tax theories of Henry George, too, had influenced the young Marsh, and so had the doctrines of the Fabian socialists of Britain. In fact, everything in his background and all his sensibilities and intellectual interests fitted him for the plunge into the initial activity of the Committee on Congestion of Population — a large exhibition designed to present in detail the wretched conditions in the nation's largest metropolis, the known causes, and the various categories of "cures."

In preparation for his work on this undertaking, Marsh spent the summer of 1907 in Europe, gathering material on city planning and housing mainly in Germany, France, and Britain and attending an international housing conference in London. The sights he saw, the speeches he heard,

26. Benjamin C. Marsh
(American City)

the people with whom he talked—all provided him with far more information than could be packed into a single exhibition. He returned home not exactly a different man, but certainly a man with new missions in life, not the least of which would be the production of one of the first American books on city planning and the organization of the first national conference on city planning. To these larger tasks the exhibition which opened at the American Museum of Natural History in New York City in March, 1908, was but a stepping stone.

Irreverently called the "Congestion Show" by Marsh and his associates, the exhibition presented a varied array of maps, diagrams, charts, statistics, models, photographs, and drawings depicting the social and economic costs of overcrowded land and buildings. Individual displays all contributed to the main purpose of starting an investigation of methods of spreading the population over wider areas. The Metropolitan Parks Association, for example, exhibited a large map upon which small shot, each representing one person, was scattered and piled to show the density of population. On the lower part of Manhattan the shot was heaped up and running over the fences used to hold it in place, whereas in great areas on the outskirts it was "scattered thin as flowers in meadows."[59] The City Club of New York entered a map showing how lower Manhattan, in which 70 per cent of the manufacturing of the metropolis was then carried on, could be relieved of congestion by relocating factories along waterfronts and transportation lines in other boroughs. To eliminate the journey to work for thousands of workmen, single- or double-family houses would be developed adjacent to each industrial belt. Still another display graphically suggested the construction of model villages around transplanted factories in the unsettled parts of the city where land was still relatively cheap. But the chief cures for congestion proposed by the exhibition were those Marsh now fervently espoused—adaptation of

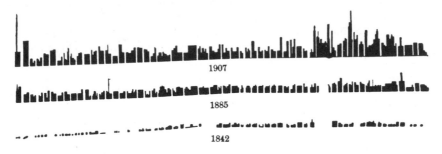

27. Changing skyline of Broadway, New York, from Twenty-fourth Street to the Battery: (bottom) 1842; (middle) 1885; (top) 1907, the year the Committee on Congestion of Population was formed

German town planning and zoning to American conditions, and extensions of the transit system, with a universal five-cent fare.

In an article published the month before the exhibition opened, Marsh formulated his ideas as a prescription of five somewhat novel functions that American municipal governments henceforth should perform:

> (1) The limitation of the area within which factories may be located (like fire lines) and the securing by the municipality of proper facilities for transportation of freight by canal, railroad, subway, etc. (2) The determination by the municipality of the districts or zones within which houses of a given height may be erected, the number of houses which may be erected per acre, the site to be covered and consequently the density of population per acre. (3) The securing by the municipality of the proper means of transportation of the people. (4) The provision of adequate streets, open spaces, parks and playgrounds in anticipation of the needs of the growing community. (5) The right of excess condemnation, i.e., the authority to condemn more than the area to be used for the immediate purposes contemplated by the condemnation, so that ultimately the city make no net expenditure for land to be used for public purposes.[60]

In 1908 any proposal to restrict factories that were not definitely in the nuisance category to designated locations undoubtedly sounded radical, but Marsh was ready with his arguments:

> We grant of course that men and women should not be required to spend two or three hours a day in going to and from their work. Are we yet equally honest in acknowledging that unless factories and places of employment afford proper habitation within a given limit of time and money, those who must work in them will herd within this time and money limit, no matter what inducements to lead a normal life may be offered them elsewhere?

> To limit the areas within which factories may be erected is to recognize the right of the workingman to leisure, and to a home life during the time when he is not employed. But it is essential, in order that factories may be able to compete with others, and that there may not be a waste in loading and unloading, that proper transportation facilities should be provided. It is futile to prohibit the location of a factory on Manhattan Island, for instance, in the midst of a population of 500 to the acre, but where it has the best of transportation facilities, and to order it to locate in a remote part of Queens, where land may be cheap and the population only five to the acre, but where there are absolutely no transportation facilities. The city should therefore have the right to say to the prospective employer of labor: "Before you locate your factory we must be assured that due regard is had to the welfare of those whom you will employ, and we stand ready to help you in securing the proper transportation facilities for your freight. . . ."[61]

As for establishing zones in which the number of persons per acre would be limited by law, such control would be "only an extension of the health and police regulations of most American cities, analogous in spirit to the regulations of boards of health . . . as to the number of cubic feet of air space required in rooms for each adult or minor."[62] Marsh was willing to acknowledge that in built-up sections of cities, where high prices had already been paid for land, severe restrictions on future construction might amount to confiscation of property rights, but he saw no reason to refrain from imposing strict controls on undeveloped land. "Where the maximum income is even approximately determined in advance, loss by speculation is prevented since anticipated use of land determines the price paid for it, and no one is injured but the owner who hoped, by 'cornering the market' on the health, income and privacy of prospective dwellers, to reap large profits where he had sown nothing, and to make a fortune by a transaction through which he had added nothing to the value of the land. . . ."[63] Further, Marsh, the advocate of large public investments in transit facilities, had no wish to see private landowners capitalizing on the public investment by raising the price of land near transit lines — and consequently the rents paid by those trying to escape the intolerable conditions of the congested areas.

"Who should be first in Brooklyn, with a density of less than thirty-five to the acre," he asked, "in the Bronx with a density of less than twenty to the acre, in Queens with its 82,000 acres and a density of about three, and in Richmond with a density of two to the acre — the land speculator or the grafting politician, concerned solely with his income, or the municipality with due regard to the interests of all concerned?"[64]

In the interests of the "whole population" Marsh of course favored proper provision of parks and open spaces. "When it is realized," he wrote, "that a city should ordinarily own for streets, parks, playgrounds, and public buildings about half of the territory within its limits, the importance of the business policy of plan instead of chance in its development is very apparent."[65]

Excess condemnation, or the right to take possession of a larger area than is needed for the immediate public purpose contemplated, seemed to Marsh, and to many other persons in the early years of this century, a promising way to acquire land for low-cost housing and other socially desirable schemes, though its constitutionality always appeared doubtful and Progressives realized that, even if legally permissible, it might offer untold possibilities for graft. Marsh was willing to risk that danger if excess condemnation would enable a city to buy at reasonable prices the land it "must ultimately own to secure the normal development of its citizenship."[66]

In pointing to the Metropolitan Improvement Commission of Boston as the kind of agency other communities, particularly New York, should create and empower to determine the location and size of industrial and residential areas, propose regulations therein, and plan all necessary public facilities, Marsh was more optimistic than realistic. The Boston group felt none of his keen concern for the working classes and gave most of its attention to the need for harbor development, terminal problems, belt lines, dock systems, passenger terminals, and financial considerations. Marsh and the members of the Committee on Congestion of Population exploited the public interest in their exhibition not by striving for the immediate establishment of a metropolitan planning commission — for which the community was far from ready — but by persuading Governor Charles E. Hughes to create a study commission that would enable them to carry on further educational work. Called the Commission on Distribution of Population, this temporary state organization, with Marsh as secretary (without salary), held hearings on methods of securing "a more efficient placement of people," investigated various housing projects, and submitted a report advocating more public control over the location of factories, state aid to resettle poor families on farms, and the shifting of taxation "from labor products to land values."[67]

Social Propagandists at Work

While serving as prime mover of the state commission, the indefatigable Marsh not only continued his work with the Committee on Congestion of Population but also assumed the position of unpaid secretary of a new Society to Lower Rents and Reduce Taxes on Homes in New York (which advocated transfer of taxes on buildings to land values), labored for the appointment of a City Commission on Congestion of Population, spoke at and arranged many public meetings and conferences, presented the congestion exhibition in Brooklyn and other boroughs, wrote *An Introduction to City Planning: Democracy's Challenge to the American City,* supervised the preparation of the first large exhibition on European and American city planning ever held in the United States, and organized the first national conference on city planning.

The small, paperback *Introduction* appeared in May, 1909, just before delegates assembled in Washington, D.C., for the national conference. Marsh modestly disclaimed that the 158-page work was anything more than its title indicated — a brief statement of the problems of cities, an outline of the achievements of foreign cities, especially Frankfurt, Germany, and a summary review of city planning in selected American cities. The heading of the first page of text — "A city without a plan is like a ship without a rudder" — revealed Marsh's intention that the book should be used as a manual for actionists. The skilled propagandist and organizer included a chapter entitled "Methods of Securing a City Plan in Some Cities," the amendment to the charter of Hartford, Connecticut, providing for a city plan commission, the bill introduced in the Wisconsin state legislature in 1909 to authorize planning commissions in cities of the second and third class, steps to take to get a city plan, and a list of "some good books on city planning," including early works of Patrick Geddes, Thomas Adams, Charles M. Robinson, and the most significant city planning and housing reports issued in the United States, Britain, and Germany between 1901 and 1908. Marsh's good friend George B. Ford, architect, contributed a chapter on the technical phases of city planning.

"No large American city has as yet adopted a comprehensive scheme for its development along economic, aesthetic, and hygienic lines," Marsh pointed out. "Several cities have worked out more or less definite schemes, but the public has not been trained to demand such farseeing outlook and plan for the city as a whole as is required in sections of the city. Public improvements, in the main, have been put in on the piecemeal and unrelated scheme, and after the city has paid the price of continued and needless speculation in land."[68]

The city Marsh cited as having most successfully discouraged speculation in land was, of course, Frankfurt-am-Main, where property was not only zoned as to use, maximum permissible height of structures, and maximum land coverage, but was also taxed on its increased value every time there was a transfer of title. The municipality itself, by consistently pursuing a policy of purchasing land for future development both inside and outside the city limits, had effectively removed vast areas from the speculative real estate market. In 1907 it owned approximately 49 per cent of the land within its boundaries, as well as 8,500 acres outside.

Marsh could point to no American city with similar policies, but he did include in his book a section on the English garden city of Letchworth, begun in 1903, and such earlier planned industrial towns as Port Sunlight and Bourneville, whose sites were originally entirely in corporate ownership and whose excellent development had been completely controlled from the beginning.

Letchworth, thirty-five miles from London, was the brainchild of *Ebenezer Howard* Ebenezer Howard, the socially-minded and inventive court stenographer whose slim volume *Tomorrow: The Peaceful Path to Real Reform*, first published in 1898 and reissued four years later as *Garden Cities of Tomorrow*, had started a worldwide garden city movement. The town included 3,800 acres owned by a corporation in which some of the most prominent English statesmen, intellectuals, and philanthropists were stockholders. Intended to embody the best features of both city and country and to be self-sustaining, it included residential, commercial, and industrial areas carefully planned by the architects Raymond Unwin and Barry Parker for a maximum population of some 30,000. Surrounding these areas was an agricultural and recreational greenbelt considered an integral part of the town and a permanent assurance against encroachment by other developments or the expansion of the town beyond its planned size. Howard thought of Letchworth as an evangelical demonstration of the way to deter the further sprawling growth of London and other large cities and to initiate the development of whole clusters of garden cities, which in the aggregate would offer all the economic, social, and cultural advantages of the vital but disorderly urban complexes of his day. Marsh especially admired Letchworth because its residential areas contained not more than twelve dwelling units to the acre and offered the inhabitants ample open space and amenities. Further, the garden city corporation held the entire town site in trust for the benefit of the residents, leased all parcels for long-term use, and passed on to the community any increment in the value of the land.

For some reason, Marsh omitted any reference to the Garden City Association of America, formed in 1906 by Howard and a group of American churchmen and financiers, among whom were Bishop Henry C. Potter of the Episcopal Church; August Belmont, the New York banker; Elgin R. L. Gould, president of the City and Suburban Homes Company; and William D. P. Bliss, an Episcopal minister and Christian Socialist. The association proposed to build no model towns itself but rather to advise industrialists how to plan new cities incorporating Howard's principles. "The very best thing that can be given a workingman is steady work with a good home in a country community," it proclaimed.[69]

In the spring of 1907 Dr. Bliss announced that companies investigated and approved by the association were planning to build towns on Long Island and in Connecticut, New Jersey, Pennsylvania, and Virginia. In all, the association hoped to see 375,000 families relocated in surroundings not only healthful but beautiful, each house with its own garden, each neighborhood with its parks, playgrounds, schools, churches, clubhouses, and a library. But the financial "panic" of 1907 and other vicissitudes blighted the great expectations of the association, and no garden cities as Howard conceived them came into being under the sponsorship of this well-intentioned group.

America nevertheless was to produce many developments influenced by Howard's ideas — garden suburbs and garden villages reflecting the residential environment of Letchworth but lacking supporting industrial areas — and invariably too expensive for most working-class families. One of the first of the garden suburbs was Forest Hills Gardens, a project of the Russell Sage Foundation, whose executive committee was interested in "investment for social betterment." The foundation purchased the site of 160 or more acres in the Borough of Queens in New York City about the time Marsh published his book, and later in the year formed the Sage Foundation Homes Company to build the project. In time Frederick Law Olmsted was engaged to prepare the site plan and Grosvenor Atterbury to design the houses. In the history of American city planning Forest

Hills Gardens assumes importance, however, not so much because it was one of the first garden suburbs but because Clarence Arthur Perry, while living there, developed ideas which eventually found expression in his neighborhood unit concept — a construct as widely adopted by city planners as the garden city ideal. Perry was, of course, indebted to Olmsted for some of the physical features of his model neighborhood.

Forest Hills Gardens was not a social experiment intended to benefit blue-collar workers. Only the middle class could afford its Tudor-style houses with spacious lawns. The Russell Sage Foundation announced that it had other plans for solving the housing problem of the factory hand and day laborer, but these economically more difficult schemes never materialized.

Many of the views Marsh expressed in his book formed the basis of the extensive city planning exhibition the Committee on Congestion of Population and the Municipal Art Society of New York presented jointly at the Twenty-second Regiment Armory early in May, 1909. A graphic review of American city planning "from Honolulu to Boston," as well as of town planning in Germany, England, Scotland, and even the Philippines, this exhibition served as a curtain-raiser for the first national conference on city planning, at which it was shown a week after it closed in New York.

28. Forest Hills Gardens, New York, as it had developed by 1930

In developing the numerous displays, Marsh succumbed to the temptation to indulge in heavy-handed propaganda. Not content, for instance, to let the public draw its own conclusions, Marsh placed above an installation depicting the land system of a large city two eye-catching cards. One stated, "Taxation Is Democracy's Most Effective Method of Securing Social Justice"; the other, "If the City Secured by Taxation a Large Part of the Increase in Land Values, Congestion Would Lose Most of Its Charm."[70]

Charles Mulford Robinson, an able propagandist in his own way, observed, "These immediately put the average man on the defensive. He feared he was getting into something socialistic, and, quite possibly having some interest in land and certainly in taxes, was on his guard. It was less easy after that to convince him."[71] Robinson furthermore questioned the wisdom of emphasizing the taxation problem when there were "a good many other things that could be accomplished more easily and promptly than changes in the tax laws."[72] He was, for instance, not averse to proposals for extensive municipal purchases of land for the two-fold purpose of restricting rents by "checking a rampant private speculation in outside lands" and recouping the cost of improvement by the resale of adjoining land at the enhanced values which the improvements themselves created.[73] "All this means, of course, that cities would embark in the real estate business," Robinson acknowledged. "But there is no necessary reason why, in its separate bureau, that business should not be honestly, sagaciously and justly managed; and if the exhibition showed anything, it showed that such municipal action was necessary to the welfare of the city, in a large sense, as for example, the municipality's embarking in the water business, or the lighting business."[74]

That Robinson, who had once looked to private effort and mere regulation to produce better living conditions for city dwellers, should now be willing to embrace the idea of municipal ownership of land was as significant as his finding the exhibition "epoch-marking." Like most intellectuals, to say nothing of millions of less cerebral citizens, he had been greatly affected by the general impatience with laissez-faire economics and by the search for more effective controls over private enterprise and private property. His acceptance of ideas that would have seemed radical a decade earlier was a tribute to the zeal of the more militant reformers and their allies the muckrakers, who had created a climate of public opinion in which all sorts of views, even the most heretical, at least could be openly discussed.

The sensational journalists and the more flamboyant crusaders had about had their day, however, and henceforth reform was to be based on somewhat more substantial revelations of weaknesses in the social and economic system than they purveyed. Marsh was not the man to provide the new factual knowledge needed, nor were the City Beautiful planners, but some of the social workers with whom Marsh was associated were. He and the Committee on Congestion of Population produced their city planning exhibition and called their national conference on city planning at a time when the nation was stirred by the first disclosures of the famous Pittsburgh Survey, a devastatingly factual analysis of a city whose industrial position was unique but whose social conditions were worse only in magnitude of wretchedness than those of scores of others. Here in initial form were the kinds of studies the social scientists of a later era would make in cities throughout the nation.

After Lincoln Steffens had stung the pride of the citizens of the steel center by his dissection of its politics, industry, and housing conditions, reform leaders had risen to power and appointed a civic commission to consider the entire range of community problems. At the suggestion of Robinson, this group had turned to landscape architect Frederick L. Olmsted, civil engineer John R. Freeman, and transportation expert Bion Arnold for a city plan. To the magazine *Charities and The Commons,* later renamed the *Survey,* it had appealed for help in studying social and living conditions. What might have been a limited investigation became an amazingly comprehensive examination of employment, wages, working conditions, industrial accidents, housing, and public and private community services when, in 1907, the Russell Sage Foundation provided an initial grant of $7,000 for fieldwork and within a year increased its total contribution to $27,000. By the latter part of 1908 and the early months of 1909 the magazines and newspapers of the nation were disseminating some of the preliminary findings of the survey, although the first of six volumes about this trail-blazing social investigation of a city

29. Shelby M. Harrison, under whose direction the maps, charts, and statistical tables of the Pittsburgh Survey were prepared *(Russell Sage Foundation)*

did not appear until somewhat later. *Charities* commented,

> Fort, trading-post, mill-town — the Pittsburgh district has become the greatest ganglion of steel producing furnaces and mills in the world — an industry which, save one, is the most completely organized as to administrative control and out-put efficiency. The energy and imagination of the men in that industry have been bent along lines of production — and as a consequence, in the conditions of the people brought together to do the work, many of the unsolved problems in social economy stand out boldly. The result is that in the leading industrial community in the country we have Painter's Rows, and Saw-mill Runs and Basin Alleys, which are a threat to the wholesome living of the whole town; we have the persistence of small administrative areas and old social institutions ill-fitted to meet the demands of a great urban and industrial district; we find the aldermen's court discredited, the schools in the grip of a vestry system of ward control, the charities unorganized, the hospitals uncorrelated; we find the absence of social records that would show what is the price to the general welfare of the stress and long hours and recklessness of life which its best

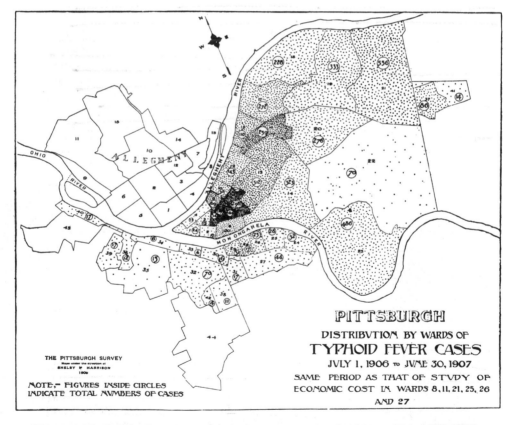

30. Map from the famous Pittsburgh Survey: Distribution of typhoid fever cases, 1906–1907

friends admit are part of steel production as at present carried on. The list could be lengthened indefinitely. It raises a great, grimed question mark as to whether this is the type of community which the leading industrial center of the country is to set. Or some other. What are American standards anyway?[75]

The First National Conference on City Planning

The same question, an ever-present challenge, confronted every leader who attended the First National Conference on City Planning and the Problems of Congestion, convened in Washington, D.C., on May 21 and 22, 1909. What should a nation as rich as the United States provide its citizens—in housing, schools, parks, playgrounds, hospitals, transportation facilities, and cultural institutions, in industrial plants, stores, and offices, in governmental services, in the physical environments of towns, cities, and entire metropolitan areas? Surely, something better than Pittsburgh or crowded Manhattan or smoke-blackened Chicago.

Herbert Croly, who came to the conference as the recent author of *The Promise of American Life,* looked back on American history and saw that the people had been promised "comfort, prosperity, and the oppor-

31. Outdoor privies and slums in Pittsburgh, 1907 *(Carnegie Library of Pittsburgh)*

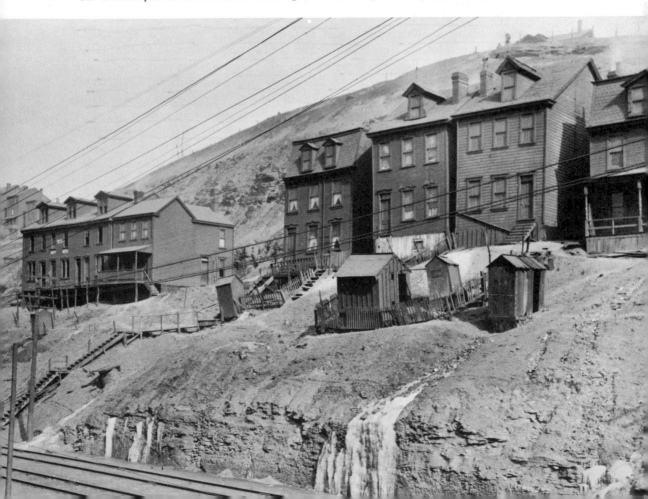

tunity for self-improvement," not "a morally and socially undesirable distribution of wealth."[76] His book warned that the promise could never be redeemed by "an indiscriminate individual scramble for wealth."[77] Like others attending the conference, he came ostensibly to hear about and to discuss city planning and the evils of congestion, but in reality he and everyone else — public officials, attorneys, economists, social workers, financiers, landscape architects, architects, public health officers, conservationists, engineers, newspaper men — had come to carry on the great struggle of the American people to define their national purpose, to make economic power socially responsible, and to evolve political institutions capable of guaranteeing a larger measure of individual fulfillment.

"We have had a moral awakening, and are ready and anxious to do our duty," financier Henry Morgenthau declared. "We are all proud of our country, its achievements, and the opportunities it has offered us and is offering others. We will not permit anything to mar its onward and upward progress, if we can help it. There is an evil [congestion] which is gnawing at the vitals of the country, to remedy which we have come together — an evil that breeds physical disease, moral depravity, discontent, and socialism — and all these must be cured and eradicated or else our great body politic will be weakened."[78]

Marsh and some others may have smiled at the financier's dread of socialism, yet Morgenthau was typically American in his pragmatic search for solutions to economic and social problems that would avoid extremism. His hearers were almost all representatives of the upper middle class, and a few, like himself, were men of wealth. This was to be a conference in the great tradition of American democracy, accepting that which had been found socially beneficial, rejecting that which had proved of little or no value, adapting, from whatever source, any new ideas that promised material and social betterment.

The City Beautiful, once a vision of the New Jerusalem to those in the vanguard of the city planning movement, no longer loomed as the goal of the national pilgrimage. Believers returning from the sacred precincts reported the discovery of slums similar to those Haussmann hid behind the uniform façades of the replanned Paris, and alley dwellings like those Henry B. F. Macfarland, Commissioner of the District of Columbia, described as a disgrace to the national capital. The new Zion toward which America marched was yet unfinished, but already it was even more radiant than the showy but disillusioning City Beautiful because it was being planned for social and economic ends, as landscape architect Robert Anderson Pope informed the delegates.[79]

Just as true happiness is the by-product of useful effort, so will be the aesthetic in city planning the by-product of doing what needs doing well. This means, then, that the purely aesthetic development of city planning must be of national growth. It must be the expression of a high national ideal . . . if it is to produce a permanently satisfying result. But, as Raymond Unwin, the English architect, has said, "it is only by conscious endeavor to satisfy these [economic and social] needs in the most beautiful manner which we know that we can expect to build up a tradition of beautiful city development," and it must not be inferred that it is necessary or desirable to suspend our efforts along aesthetic lines.[80]

In a sense, the participants in the conference were there to help fashion the new city. One who could not be present, the Honorable James Bryce, British ambassador to the United States, sent a letter suggesting that perhaps it should take the form of a garden city of thirty to fifty thousand population, to which would be transferred from the not distant great city all industries which could operate with economic advantage in the smaller town. The particular merits of this solution of the "terrible city problem in the United States" would be that it would end for many the "great and constantly growing economic waste" of daily commuting and would enable workers "to get into rural surroundings and have at least once or twice a week a certain possibility of being in touch with nature."[81]

Frederick Law Olmsted, recently returned from Europe, presented a detailed account of German and Swiss town planning, describing cities presumably far more orderly than any in America. "A city plan in Germany," he explained, "includes in one unified project not only a surveyor's plat for the layout of streets, and so forth, but the whole code of building regulations, health ordinances, police rules, and system of taxation in so far as they have a direct influence upon the physical development of the city."[82] Moreover, many of the cities, by owning large reserves of land, were in a position to control much of their future development exactly as they wished. But lest the delegates think that all this planning was somehow excessively bureaucratic, Olmsted pointed out that districting, or zoning, regulations were adopted for any particular area only after "full and repeated public hearings at which the views and wishes of the property owners are expressed and considered, and the endeavor is to give each district as nearly as possible just what it wants, to protect it from deterioration at the hands of a selfish minority, and to give stability to real estate values."[83]

Should American cities, then, be modeled after those of Germany? Perhaps Olmsted saw gleams in the eyes of certain delegates as they listened to him — "full and repeated public hearings . . . [protection from] deterioration at the hands of a selfish minority . . . stability to real estate values." Had imperial Germany found the panacea for the ills of American cities? Not altogether, Olmsted thought. "It would be very foolish for us to copy blindly what is being done there," he said. "Apart from the differences in climatic, economic, social, and political conditions between European countries and America, there is need for some caution lest we copy the mistakes."[84] But the appeal of German planning, especially zoning, was great, so great, indeed, that a large proportion of the participants in the conference doubtless ignored his admonitions in their enthusiasm for what seemed like *the* remedy for urban congestion and ruinous individualism. Moreover, several other speakers also urged the adoption of regulations such as those applied by German cities.

John Nolen was as much an admirer of European cities as Olmsted, but he, too, rejected the idea of imitation. The American city of the future should have, above all, individuality, as had the most beautiful European cities. "As our interest in human life is in the distinctly personal, so is it in towns and cities. We need a local concept, a love and pride in local traditions and local ideas. Civic art furnishes the most available means to express these local customs and local aspirations, and it should be remembered that only in expression do we truly possess them."[85]

But Nolen was not advocating a return to the City Beautiful. He realized that current methods of city development were "fatal" and that henceforth cities needed "an open-minded and skillful investigation of their problems, united and hearty cooperation . . . of various public authorities and private individuals in the solution of these problems," and finally, "prompt and courageous execution of the plan found to be best for all concerned."[86]

The plan best for all concerned, it appeared, must serve as a guide for the reconstruction of the congested areas and as an instrument for shaping the development of the sparsely settled outlying territories. Experience already suggested a host of measures for revamping the older parts of the city: widening the streets, providing diagonal thoroughfares, extensively rehabilitating housing, restricting the occupancy and use of private property, rerouting street railways, diverting traffic from heavily traveled streets at certain hours of the day, removing poles, wires, and unsightly advertising. Morgenthau, Pope, the architects Frederick L. Ford and George B. Ford, and many others believed that they knew what should be done, but what was done in the crowded districts depended considerably upon how the outlying areas developed.

Perhaps without realizing that he was actually proposing to alter the entire structure of urban areas, Pope put forth a suggestion for the peripheral sections that he borrowed from Germany. A more equitable distribution of land values could be effected, he said, by building a *ringstrasse* entirely around the built-up city, making it possible for traffic to move from point to point in the newly developing suburbs without first going to the center of the city. "The same principle," he continued, "can be applied to belt-line railroads, and by means of this provision, factories of all kinds can be attracted to the outskirts, and will eventually bring with them their employees from the city centers."[87] In short, Pope urged changing from a city in which all lines of movement focused on the center to one in which much of the circulation would be centrifugal, as in almost all large metropolitan areas today. But the prophetic implications of the suggestion escaped the participants in the conference. The image of the future city, in its totality, was indistinct; only certain parts appeared relatively clear.

Marsh's tools for comp. plans

Far from unclear, at least to Marsh, were the tools needed to prepare the comprehensive plan: a survey, publicity, and legislation authorizing cities to plan. The survey, of course, was a marshaling of "facts," and to Marsh facts were weapons "against which corporate interests cannot contend."[88] No less important than ascertaining the facts was "a campaign of vigorous publicity"—illustrated lectures, newspaper articles, exhibitions—"to make possible the awakening of the public interest."[89] If some delegates had the impression that city planning was for Marsh a holy war against predatory forces, especially real estate speculators, they were perhaps not mistaken, but he wanted his factual ammunition to come not alone from local sources.

Marsh proposed that there be "a civic census conducted by the Federal Government of those conditions in our cities which must be dealt with directly by a comprehensive city plan."[90] The propagandist in him told him, however, that the government would not act until a national city-planning committee pressed its demands for more detailed information about social conditions in cities. In the meantime, the committee should function as a clearinghouse of information about cities throughout the nation—a suggestion an advisory group rejected, though the members did recommend making the conference an annual event in which all organizations and persons contributing to the development of city planning might take part.

Others also believed that the federal government should assist planning efforts. Pope called for the appointment of a federal commission to study city planning abroad and apply its findings in making the District of Columbia an example to all municipalities throughout the land.[91] Mrs. Simkhovitch, of Greenwich House in New York City, urged the appointment of a national commission or bureau to consider and report upon the entire subject of city planning and development. Senator Francis G. Newlands of Nevada, who had mentioned the need for a permanent city planning commission in San Francisco soon after the Burnham plan for that city was completed, envisaged "a bureau of the arts" that should gradually be enlarged into a department or ministry of arts. "The Department of Agriculture," he noted, "has become a great educational force, operating in an auxiliary way in the various states and state universities and institutions in such a way as to develop a common knowledge upon all subjects relating to agriculture, forestry, good roads, and other matters of the kind; and the bureau or department of arts should take an educational lead on similar lines in everything that relates to city planning, city engineering, public buildings, and the artistic side of waterway development."[92]

Unfortunately, Senator Newlands was even too progressive for the Progressive era. More than half a century would pass before the Congress established a federal department to aid cities in their planning and development, though many other persons in the meantime would make suggestions similar to the senator's, invariably comparing the proposed department to the Department of Agriculture.

As the conference drew to a close, the participants could not but realize that the city planning movement had become, or would soon become, an integral part of American life. Frederick L. Ford, of Hartford, had told them that planning under the auspices of private groups would soon be a thing of the past and that "hereafter the work will be undertaken more by official commissions with ample authority to employ experts, and with sufficient appropriations at their disposal to make more exhaustive and detailed investigations and reports than most of those heretofore undertaken."[93] Pope had spoken of the need for "a profession equipped to make city planning the social and economic factor it ought to be."[94] Nor could anyone present be unaware that such men as Olmsted, Nolen, the two Fords, and some of those who had described planning in particular cities already constituted the nucleus of the new profession. The most compelling reason, however, for believing that city planning would become increasingly important was the rapidity with which American cities were growing and their problems multiplying. To avoid the mistakes of the past and to assure greater health and happiness to all citizens, municipalities would have to undertake planning far broader in scope than that attempted thus far by any of the private groups, art commissions, or temporary city plan commissions.

1909: Benchmark in the History of City Planning

This first national conference was but one of several events making the year 1909 a great benchmark in the history of city planning, not only in the United States but also in Great Britain. The British Parliament approved a town planning act permitting local authorities—cities, boroughs, urban districts, and rural districts—to prepare comprehensive schemes for land in course of development or likely to be used for building purposes. The University of Liverpool responded to this broad enactment by establishing the first academic department of city planning anywhere in the world, the School of Civic Design. In the United States the legislature of Wisconsin adopted the first state law granting broad authority to large and medium-size cities to create city planning commissions and prepare city plans. Significantly, the law authorized commissions to review subdivision layouts for areas within a mile and a half of cities as well as for areas inside city boundaries. At Harvard University Professor James Sturgis Pray inaugurated the first city planning course offered in any American university, "The Principles of City Planning," though twenty years were to pass before Harvard followed the example of the University of Liverpool and created a department of city planning. The United States Supreme Court indicated that in time it would probably approve broad use of the police power to establish different types of regulations for various areas of cities. It sustained a Massachusetts State Supreme Court decision upholding the constitutionality of the act creating height zones in Boston. But undoubtedly the publication of Burnham's impressive *Plan of Chicago* on the Fourth of July and the creation of the Chicago Plan Commission four months later did more to stimulate official city planning than any other developments in this landmark year.

From time to time in the early years of the decade both the Merchants Club and the Commercial Club of Chicago had considered sponsoring the preparation of a city plan, but nothing was done until three members of the former organization took personal interest in the project. They were Charles Dyer Norton, Charles H. Wacker, and Frederic A. Delano. Norton, an insurance executive, had evidenced his belief in long-range planning by persuading his fellow alumni of Amherst College to finance a plan for the future development of that institution. Delano, president of the Wabash Railroad, had worked out a proposal in 1904 for relocating railroad terminals in Chicago. Together with Wacker, a wealthy merchant, they persuaded Burnham to revive his lakefront scheme and expand it into a plan for the entire city, but there was a problem. He felt committed to proceed under the auspices of the Commercial Club. Finally the problem was solved when the two clubs merged in 1907. Norton became chairman of the general committee aiding Burnham's planning efforts. Wacker was vice-chairman and Delano secretary. All three were to have decisive influence on the course of American planning in later years.

Many months before the plan appeared, Professor Graham Romeyn Taylor of the Chicago Theological Seminary predicted that it would be as significant for the civic life of America as it would be epoch-making for Chicago. The earlier plans for Washington, Cleveland, and San Francisco were minor productions compared with this signal achievement, the greatest of the City Beautiful plans and the first plan of general scope for any of the half-dozen cities in the occidental world with a population of some two million or more. Burnham referred to it as the supreme effort of his life. He donated his own services to the Commercial Club, but even more than his labor and his talent went into the plan—his almost filial devotion to his native city and his faith that his fellow Chicagoans would match his contribution by carrying out the plan in every way possible. That they did so in the next fifteen years to an unprecedented extent, expending almost $300,000,000 for developments related to the plan, is still cause for wonder. Certainly, hardly another city in the nation can equal the record of Chicago in programming public improvements in accordance with a specific plan.

Published in a quarto volume containing 142 illustrations, some 50 of them by the world-renowed French artist Jules Guerin, the *Plan of Chicago* not only set a new standard of magnificence in city planning

32. Luncheon given by Daniel Hudson Burnham when the Plan of Chicago was completed in 1908. Burnham is first on the left in the upper row, Charles D. Norton second, and Edward H. Bennett fifth. Charles H. Wacker is on the far right in the lower row. Frederic A. Delano attended the historic meeting but is not shown in the photograph. *(Chicago Department of Development and Planning)*

reports; it also dramatized the importance of the urban region as the essential planning unit, though it was by no means the first plan containing regional elements. From their office atop the Railway Exchange Building Burnham and his chief assistant, Edward H. Bennett, and their five draftsmen could scan a vast fan-shaped agglomeration stretching far beyond the 190 square miles embraced by the municipality of Chicago. The metropolis portrayed in their handsome plates extends in a radius of sixty miles from the downtown Loop—as far north as Kenosha on the Wisconsin shore and as far south as Michigan City, Indiana. These limits, though taken arbitrarily, seemed wholly justified because the distance from the center to the circumference of the huge arclike region was "no greater than the present suburban electric lines extend, or the automobilist may cover in a drive of two hours."[95]

For the four thousand square miles encompassed within this planning area Burnham and Bennett outlined two regional systems, a network of highways and an outer chain of forest preserves and parkways. The planners found that if a few missing links in the country roadways were constructed, four concentric circuit routes could be completed which would traverse the region at distances of from ten to sixty miles from the

33. Regional scope of the Plan of Chicago as shown in a general diagram of highways

heart of Chicago. Radial routes running directly to the center of the metropolis likewise could be provided throughout the fan-shaped territory by adding other connections. Accessibility to many of the wooded reserves forming the proposed park system would be afforded by this web of highways and by additional parkways, some following natural watercourses.

In part, Burnham based the scheme of outlying reservations and pleasure drives on a report prepared by Dwight H. Perkins in 1904 for the Special Park Commission appointed to consider metropolitan needs. Perkins had recommended 37,000 acres of park lands. Burnham proposed from 40,000 to 50,000, so that the region would have a total of 60,000 acres, including the parks of Chicago proper.

A striking feature of the system of open spaces was the projected lakeshore development extending from Jackson Park to Wilmette, a distance of twenty-five miles. An elaboration of Burnham's earlier scheme for the South Shore Drive, this element of the plan indicated how wastes and excavated materials from the city, then sufficient to "make" twenty-seven to thirty acres of land each year in the lake, could be utilized to create parks, lagoons, and islands along the entire waterfront.

In Chicago itself the plan contemplated a revised street system with

34. Chicago lakefront today: in the foreground, Jackson Park, once the site of the World's Columbian Exposition; in the distance, Burnham Park, extending for several miles along the shore *(Chicago Park District)*

many diagonal routes, round points, and widened thoroughfares. A mile west of the lakefront several of the radial routes converged on a great civic center planned by Ferdinand Janin of Paris. Here the architect envisaged an immense city hall reminiscent of the Administration Building at the exposition of 1893. Congress Street, transformed into a broad boulevard, linked the group of municipal buildings surrounding the city hall with Michigan Avenue and a complex of cultural institutions in Grant Park, on the mid-waterfront.

In all these proposals for streets, parks, and public structures the plan of Chicago followed the traditions of the City Beautiful movement, though on an especially grand scale. It broke with those traditions in its suggestions for improving the transit and transportation of the metropolis. Aside from recommending a union terminal and the elimination of grade crossings, the typical City Beautiful plan ignored transportation, whereas the plan of Chicago included a system of freight handling for land and water transportation, a scheme for consolidating railroad facilities, and proposals for the creation of elevated, surface, and subway loops around an enlarged business district.

These elements of the plan reflected the interest of the members of the Commercial Club in the practical side of urban development. Burnham was probably indebted to the club's Committee on Railway Terminals for the proposal for a central clearing and warehousing yard in the southwestern part of the city, linked by underground lines with the freight stations of all the railroads and with harbors to be created at the mouths of the Chicago and Calumet rivers. He based his recommendations for relocating existing passenger terminals farther from the business district and adding others in a north–south line west of the Chicago River on the earlier plan of Frederic A. Delano, the man destined a quarter of a century later to head the only national planning agency the United States has ever had, in the administration of his nephew, Franklin Delano Roosevelt.

The text of the planning report, edited by Charles Moore, who had prepared the report of the McMillan Commission, revealed that Burnham and his associates hoped for the eventual creation of a metropolitan commission "for the treatment of the entire area."[96] Pending the establishment of such an agency, they suggested that the public officials or the improvement associations of each town confer with their neighbors and agree on the routes of connecting highways and the design of the planting spaces bordering them. Even better would be the formation of a public-improvement commission in every town "to bring about the most orderly conditions within the town itself, and especially to act in co-operation with similar bodies in neighboring towns so as to secure harmonious, connected, and continuous improvement."[97]

Foreseeing large population increases in the areas immediately west of Chicago, Burnham urged that the city itself prepare and adopt a plan for platting all lands reasonably certain to be annexed in the next few years. "The entire territory extending westward to the Des Plaines [River] should be laid out to meet future requirements, with the requisite area for residences, as well as wide thoroughfares for traffic, well-planned diagonals to gather and distribute the travel, and adequate park spaces," the report stated.[98]

Within Chicago itself the planners expected that the railroads and transit companies would voluntarily carry out the improvements proposed, concluding that these were to their advantage. The public projects embodied in the plan were for the most part to be undertaken by the municipality, which already had, according to a legal analysis prepared by attorney Walter L. Fisher, sufficient legislative authorization to act upon many of the recommendations. The state legislature, Fisher pointed out, had ample power to grant to the city or to other governmental agencies such additional authority as might be needed to carry out all the proposals "as fully and as rapidly as may be found wise."[99]

Fisher ended his analysis, which was included as an appendix to the report, with a discussion of the kind of official agency most desirable to translate the plan into reality:

> As a matter of theory, the best results could be achieved through a consolidation of the city and county governments, or by placing the entire metropolitan district, which constitutes the real city of Chicago, under a unified municipal administration, endowed with broad powers of local self-government, including the power to levy taxes and incur indebtedness. Practically, however, the enlargement of the powers of these two government bodies—the city and the county—within the limits permitted by the present constitution, is probably the most available method of attaining desirable results. As a means of coordinating the two it is respectfully suggested that a permanent Commission on City and County Plan should be created by joint resolution or ordinance of the city council and the county board. This commission should contain appropriate representation for each body, and it should be charged with the duty of reporting to each its recommendations as to all matters falling within the general scope of a city and county plan. It might well be ordained by the city council that no public buildings should be hereafter located or erected, and that no parks should be acquired and no streets or boulevards be opened, without a report from the commission or the city members thereof. The commission might be composed entirely of city and county officials, or might contain some representation of those who are not public officials but who are particularly interested in and particularly qualified for its work. The city board of local improvements and the present park boards or any future consolidated park board should be directly represented.[100]

Burham and Bennett, Moore, Fisher, and the members of the Commercial Club who offered consultation and encouragement undoubtedly believed that the *Plan of Chicago* was as complete and effective a document as could be presented to inspire an ambitious city to transfigure itself and become an ideal city, the quintessence of order and beauty, with the very best conditions of city life for all the people.[101] Holding primacy over a midcontinental domain "larger than Austria-Hungary, or Germany, or France," it might well be in fifty years "larger than London: that is, larger than any existing city."[102] Apparently no physical, political, or financial limitations impeded its progress; its opportunities were multitudinous. On page after page of the *Plan* they unfold. Burnham (or is it Moore?) elucidates, prophesies, persuades, and entices. Occasionally he praises his proposals as shamelessly as an auctioneer striving for a high bid. How can his fellow citizens *not* embrace these concepts so manifestly to their advantage? But there must be appeals to reason, and some practical questions must be asked: "How are we living? Are we in reality prosperous? Is the city a convenient place for business? Is it a good labor market in the sense that labor is sufficiently comfortable to be efficient and content? Will the coming generation be able to stand the nervous strain of city life? When a competence has been accumulated, must we go elsewhere to enjoy the fruits of independence? If the city does not become better as it becomes bigger, shall not the defect be remedied?"[103]

The questions betray the values of the businessman. The city must be convenient so that its enterprises can flourish. Its residential neighborhoods must be comfortable so that workers will be efficient and content. It must be beautiful so that wealthy people will not spend their money in New York or Paris. What is good for business is, of course, good for the people, and vice versa. Burnham is nothing if not sincere, but he is no Benjamin Marsh or Jacob Riis. In his way, he is an idealist, but his vision is a paradoxical blend of the unattainable past and the entirely possible future. This curious quality is nowhere more clearly seen than in Jules Guerin's lyrical evocations of various features of the great plan, which Burnham must have approved.

These muted illustrations, suggesting a city bathed in pale sunlight or suffused with opalescent twilight, depict an American Paris on the shores of Lake Michigan. The buildings rise to a uniform cornice height. Along certain boulevards they are as much as twelve or thirteen stories high, whereas the façades along Haussmann's grand avenues seldom exceed six stories. But a Frenchman would not necessarily be disturbed by the taller structures in this idealized metropolis. The classic serenity and dignity would be familiar. So, too, would be the forms of public structures, one vaguely like Garnier's Opéra, another an echo of the Invalides. Nowhere to be seen are the towering, big-windowed skyscrapers such as Burnham himself designed in his younger days. Nor are there any ugly factories and stockyards in this Haussmannized capital of the Middle West.

Some of Burnham's contemporaries objected. "A uniform sky-line is everywhere indicated for adjacent buildings, although the 'Chicago construction' not only contradicts in its anarchistic practice such uniformity, but makes stupendous architectural effects possible by a proper use of its variety of unparalleled altitudes," George Hooker, civic secretary of the City Club of Chicago, pointed out. "The report does not suggest the splendid and picturesque possibilities which might be realized through a harmonious use of such variety—with arched or corridor links perhaps across intervening streets—for the business fronts of Michigan Avenue, for example, or Congress Street, where there could be no objection to buildings of unusual heights."[104]

In many respects the Chicago of the Burnham plan is a city of a past that America never knew, notwithstanding the facilities for transportation and transit, the network of roadways for automobiles, and the generous provision of recreation areas for the people. It is an essentially aristocratic city, pleasing to the merchant princes who participated in its conception but not meeting some of the basic economic and human needs. In this metropolis for businessmen there are, with the exception of the central business district, no carefully designated areas for commercial enterprises, well distributed throughout the city. Nor are there any model tenements for workers, much less model neighborhoods. Not that Burnham, Bennett, and Moore were oblivious to the housing problem. Slums are mentioned, but only in one paragraph suggesting that "It is no attack on private property to argue that society has the inherent right to protect itself [against] gross evils and known perils" by imposing restrictions on overcrowding, enforcing sanitary regulations, and limiting lot coverage.[105] There is even an assertion that if private enterprise cannot rehouse persons forced out of congested quarters, the city itself may have to do so "in common justice to men and women so degraded by long life in the slums that they have lost all power of caring for themselves."[106] But this daring idea is tucked into the report almost surreptitiously, as if it were an irrelevancy to be overlooked in the contemplation of magnificent boulevards, imposing public structures, and splendid parks.

At the time Burnham and Bennett were preparing their plan hardly any of the so-called planning experts troubled themselves much about social data as a basis for planning. The only evidence that the Pittsburgh Survey may have influenced the Chicago planners slightly is a diagram of the general scheme of street circulation and parks imposed on a map showing various densities of population. These range from 0 to 25 persons per acre to 250 to 300 per acre. There is no specific discussion of the relation between densities and elements of the plan, though there is a recommendation that in crowded residential districts the paved area of streets should be reduced to provide a wide space between curb and sidewalk for trees and grass plots, "so that the smaller children may have playgrounds close at hand, and restful shade may prevail."[107] Hooker noted disapprovingly, "It [the plan] is not based upon any series of special statistical investigations made for the purpose, and no data are put forth with it save what appear in the popularly written text."[108]

With all its shortcomings, the plan of Chicago was a milestone. At its best, particularly in its proposals for regional roadways, forest preserves, and lakeshore parks and beaches, it was imaginative and far-sighted. At its worst, as in its baroque street pattern, it was patently grandiose and unrealistic. It unquestionably appealed to the civic pride of humble citizens as well as the members of the Commercial Club who paid $85,000 for its preparation and publication in a limited edition of 1,650 copies, priced at $25 each. The enthusiasm it generated made irresistible the demand for the appointment of the Chicago Plan Commission. Once that group was in operation under the leadership of Charles H. Wacker, other cities could hardly fail to follow the example of Chicago and establish official city-planning commissions. The story of the way in which Chicago carried out projects embodied in the Burnham plan belongs, however, in another context.

CHAPTER 3

SCIENCE AND
THE CITY FUNCTIONAL

A Noble Experiment in Boston

The "city problem" in the United States was, as President A. Lawrence Lowell of Harvard University said, like a jelly fish. You could not pick up a part here and a part there and succeed. You had to lift it altogether.

Edward A. Filene, Louis D. Brandeis, and half a dozen other Bostonians had reached the same conclusion when they set out in the spring of 1909 to organize a movement called "Boston—1915." In six years they hoped, by resolutely attacking every aspect of the city problem, to raise Boston to heights of democratic achievement so exemplary that the city itself could be put on display for all the world to study, admire, and emulate.

Visitors would go by automobile or streetcar to the parks, schools, factories, stores, residential areas, hospitals, charitable institutions, municipal buildings, and docks as they would to the various pavilions in a great exposition. They would marvel not just at the unity, convenience, and beauty of the city but at the prosperity of its industries, the enlightened labor policies of its employers, the efficiency of its city government, the progressiveness of its educational and recreational institutions, and the attractiveness and healthfulness of even its least costly housing.

To accomplish in one concerted effort the social regeneration, economic reconstruction, and physical rehabilitation and development of Boston, the directors of the 1915 movement proposed to enlist the services of every businessman capable of creative public endeavor and of every civic organization in the city. Their sixteen-point "plan for a Boston plan" outlined work for all and established target dates for the attainment of specific goals.

By 1910 Filene and his associates planned to have "an expert accounting of the financial conditions and resources of the city, present and prospective," so clearly stated, explained, and illustrated that the man in the street could understand the waste and other losses in the public finances and services.[1] This study suggesting how government could be made more efficient was to be paralleled by several undertakings designed to strengthen the economy of the area—an inventory of the skills of workers and the abilities of executives; an organized movement for the extension of existing industries and the introduction of new enterprises; and "a broad-minded consideration" of employer-employee relations, presumably leading to better wages and working conditions.[2] On the civic front a system of neighborhood centers was to be established, offering opportunities for city officials to "meet the people" and for community organizations to present courses of lectures on civil government, politics, city planning, recreation, health, and business.

The movement contemplated having collected by 1911 most of the information needed to organize a federation of cities and towns in the metropolitan district, as the directors were acutely aware that the real Boston was a community of a million and a half persons rather than just the 670,000 residents of the city proper. Economic studies were to be broadened to include detailed information on the agricultural and other natural resources of the Boston region and all New England.

The chief accomplishment in 1912 was to be the publication of a city plan showing how Boston would look physically when finished.[3] Embodying the best of European and American experience, this guide for future development would include "such features as help to make a city a place of healthy, happy homes—playgrounds and public buildings that are really for the people."

At the end of the six-year period of economic, social, and physical planning and development the directors of the 1915 movement hoped to have, in addition to everything achieved in the first few years. "the most complete organization possible for guarding the public health," so that the skill and energy employed in the past in curing diseases and healing bodies impaired by accidents would be utilized effectively in preventing sickness and injury.[4] The timetable also called for having in successful operation a system of public education for adults as well as children and youths. The health and education programs were to be reinforced by the general adoption of a comprehensive system of wage-earners' insurance and old age pensions, lessening the burden on the community of supporting the elderly, the handicapped, and the incapacitated. Finally, "an intelligent system of transportation for the city, state, and New England as a whole" was to be well along toward completion.[5]

The entire program sounded wildly utopian to the cynics, who quipped about Boston's attaining the "1915 Filennium."[6] The *Bean Pot* wrote amusingly of businessmen who wished to put salt on the tail of perfection.[7] Skeptics might well question whether the 1915 movement was so far-reaching and all-inclusive as to be unrealistic. Did the community have the financial resources, the energy, and the will to undertake so many constructive activities simultaneously? Even if desirable, was it practical to attempt to move forward in all fields at the same time? Could the varied studies and development programs be coordinated, and by whom?

35. Edward A. Filene
(Filene's, Boston)

Boston—1915 was not the dream child of naïve idealists or inexperienced visionaries. Filene was the eminently successful owner of one of the largest department stores in the country. Brandeis, destined eventually to wear the robes of a justice of the United States Supreme Court, was an attorney with an enviable reputation for solving labor problems and increasing the productivity of once strife-torn plants. Other directors of the movement were heads of large corporations, unions, social agencies, hospitals, and public commissions. All saw clearly that although Boston boasted outstanding cultural institutions and had park, water-supply, and sanitation systems unmatched in the entire nation, it shared with other communities the serious problems of crime, bad housing, high disease and mortality rates, inadequate wages, municipal corruption, and excessive expenditures for public services of less than superior quality. Religious and economic gulfs divided the population; the business of the port was not expanding; new construction in the downtown area was almost at a standstill; and some industries were falling behind in productivity or the development of new markets, or both. Boston—1915 was as much a rescue operation as a reform effort, but Filene and his associates shrewdly emphasized the opportunities beckoning to the community rather than the economic and social ills threatening its well-being.

These civic leaders also took into account the wealth of statistical information that had already been amassed on various aspects of community life. In the field of city administration the Boston Finance Commission, which had gone out of existence early in 1909, had collected a large body of revealing facts. Robert A. Wood, head of South End House and author of *The City Wilderness,* had voluminous material on housing conditions. Dr. Richard C. Cabot, who had developed the social work of Massachusetts General Hospital, knew as much about the deficiencies of charity services and the need for family counseling as Brandeis did about wages and hours, working conditions, and employment policies. Boston was not Pittsburgh, backward in civic achievement and starting almost from scratch to investigate its problems. To the directors of the 1915 movement it seemed not only possible to bring together the many kinds of data available but also to develop additional information with the cooperation of able men in numerous civic groups. Careful analysis of the facts would suggest ways to attain the broad goals of the movement.

Were Filene and his friends too optimistic? Not to be sanguine would be to deny their own collective record of accomplishment. Not to have faith in rational processes would be to repudiate the lessons of their own experience. The times, moreover, encouraged men of social vision to think large and to act boldly. Cautious Taft was in the White House, but America had had seven and a half years of strenuous Teddy, and the atmosphere of energetic liberalism persisted. The directors of Boston—1915 believed that thousands of ordinary citizens, as well as the leaders in business and civic work, shared their own enthusiasm for municipal progress and social reform.

For a time the movement forged ahead, though many of the Brahmins who had retreated to the suburbs remained aloof and some businessmen either shortsightedly or selfishly evidenced no interest. Thirteen conferences of "experts" representing twelve hundred organizations contributed suggestions for the program, which was revised to include only items considered worthy of being carried out at once. Cooperating groups issued bulletins, presented lectures, or staged civic pageants. Committees persuaded legislators to introduce bills to provide funds for varied studies, but few appropriations were forthcoming. Tenement-house conditions received a thorough investigation. A Public Playground League came into being to increase the use of playgrounds and further the development of additional facilities. The city council appropriated money for new convenience stations. The movement reached a high point in the late spring of 1911 when the state legislature authorized the governor to appoint a temporary commission charged with investigating the need for a metropolitan plan.

Governor Eugene N. Foss selected as members of the commission Filene, J. Randolph Coolidge, Jr., architect, and John Nolen. After six months of study they submitted a report to the legislature in January, 1912, recommending the creation of a permanent metropolitan planning board of five members, three to be appointed by the governor and two by the mayor of Boston. For the chairman of the board a salary of $10,000 was suggested—then a handsome sum indeed.

36. John Nolen
(John Nolen, Jr.)

The proposed board would develop for the district encompassing Boston and thirty-seven neighboring cities and towns a comprehensive plan embodying matters of metropolitan scope. The general scheme would indicate ways of preventing and relieving congestion both of population and of traffic; a distribution of areas for the several purposes of residence, manufacturing, trade, and transportation; and an extensive system of mass transit facilities. As Nolen explained the board's capabilities, it would have

> the knowledge and power . . . to consider the relation of traffic highways and traffic open spaces to transportation, of transportation to parks and playgrounds, of parks and playgrounds to the homes of the people, of the homes of the people to manufacturing districts, of manufacturing districts to transportation, and on and on, through that unending relationship and inter-relationship which stamps the character of modern life, and on the profitable and skilful provision for which depends, in many instances, the success or failure of a public improvement and the return or dividend on a public investment.[8]

Filene, Coolidge, and Nolen had in mind the kind of plan that would win the approbation of a Benjamin Marsh—the kind of long-term, adjustable guide that would go far beyond Burnham's Chicago plan by designating areas for particular activities and attempting to establish satisfactory spatial realtionships among them. The group knew the weaknesses of the earlier proposals of the Metropolitan Improvement Commission, which had neglected living arrangements in its concentration on transportation planning. The metropolitan plan prepared by the projected commission was to be socially desirable as well as economically realistic.

The commission would have the power to review all plans of local governments in the Boston region before they could be carried out, and to state in writing its reasons for approving or disapproving them. If it found that the plans of some city or town conflicted with the areawide plan, it would have the authority to stay the execution of the local plan for a year, to give opportunity for revisions that would bring it into conformity with the metropolitan scheme. Except for this suspensive veto, the metropolitan board would not abridge the powers of local jurisdictions.

Filene and his fellow members of the temporary investigatory group proposed to induce local cooperation with the metropolitan planning board by providing for state loans and contributions for projects classified as ordinary or as extraordinary metropolitan improvements, thereby overcoming problems of the debt limits of the cities and towns of the district. A local government would pay 65 per cent of the cost of an ordinary metropolitan improvement benefiting only part of the Boston district, while the entire district would pay 25 per cent and the state 10 per cent. In any one year the participation of the commonwealth would be limited, however, to $500,000. The distribution of the cost of an extraordinary metropolitan improvement unquestionably serving the whole district would be determined by a commission appointed by the supreme court of the state.

Not even financial incentives were sufficient to prevent the opposition of suburban communities to this proposal, which they suspected of threatening their freedom of action and local autonomy, as the directors of Boston—1915 soon discovered. Filene, Coolidge, and Nolen argued for coordination of effort, for ending the waste and inefficiency of piecemeal planning, for developing the metropolitan district as a unit. In vain! Amid roars of protest from the outlying cities and towns, the legislature declined to enact the bill providing for a metropolitan planning board, and in April, 1912, the 1915 movement dissolved.

Mayor John F. Fitzgerald of Boston, grandfather of President John F. Kennedy, castigated the upper-class towns such as Newton and Brookline for their parochial shortsightedness and lack of enlightenment. When the fourth national conference on city planning was held in Boston a few weeks later, he told the assembled delegates that "the environs of Boston afford an excellent missionary field for the labors of your association."[9]

Boston—1915 was what is known as a noble experiment. Specific accomplishments were few, disappointments many. The effect on the public was difficult to gauge, though perhaps even the most passive citizens learned something from the educational propaganda. Only a few supporting organizations sustained their participation, and some refused to cooperate with others and withdrew altogether. In the first place, Filene and his associates were clearly naïve in their assumption that everyone else shared their high-minded concern for the general welfare. They overlooked the possibility that selfish interests would actively or passively oppose their program, just as they disregarded the known antipathy of many of the suburbs toward Boston. But even if other citizens had been as idealistic and rational as these leaders were, there would have been formidable obstacles to the success of their undertaking. Filene and his associates were pioneering; for guidance they could turn to no other metropolitan community which had attempted to mobilize a wide variety of civic organizations and individuals in an areawide program of self-analysis and remedial action. Further, these public-spirited men were handicapped by the fledgling state of the social sciences and of the city planning movement. Research methods and techniques were rudimentary and for the most part untested. The statistical records of public and private agencies failed to provide many kinds of data needed in surveys. Specialists in the fields of social work, public health, medicine, and education dared not speak with ringing authority about standards for services and facilities; their co-workers might disagree with them. It was as difficult to formulate firm goals as it was to coordinate the activities of a multiplicity of well-meaning volunteers and maintain their enthusiasm for the overall endeavor.

Boston—1915 was nevertheless significant. It presented dramatically, albeit sketchily, the possibilities of linking planning in one field with planning in others. Had it been less instigative and more solidly productive, with its own central research staff, it might in time have effected important linkages among the social, economic, and physical programs with which it was concerned. In its comparatively brief existence the movement neither proved nor disproved the validity of the proposition that the city problem should be approached from all sides at once. The undertaking was inconclusive. It bequeathed to later generations the task of finding ways to carry out a total planning program, of which planning for physical improvement and development would necessarily be only one part.

City Planning as an Exact Science

Though concerned principally with improving the three-dimensional environment, the city planning movement in the period just before the outbreak of the First World War became aware of connections with many other fields and was greatly affected by the new interest in the collection and analysis of factual information and statistical data stimulated by the Pittsburgh Survey and various studies made by organizations cooperating in the Boston—1915 program. The movement was also influenced by the enthusiasm of leading businessmen and some of the more advanced public administrators for principles of scientific management. City planners, too, wanted to be "scientific" in their diagnosis of the ills of the city and to base their proposals on arrays of "facts" and sound deductions drawn therefrom. But since they had originally fixed their attention on the physical expression of social and economic needs, their pursuit of a more rational basis for planning or replanning the city tended to separate them more and more from groups attempting to improve social and economic conditions. An appreciation of the importance of decent housing linked them to tenement-house reformers and social workers for a time, but the newest instrument sought as a means of regulation—zoning or districting—eventually led planners further and further from their earlier allies, as well as further from the larger economic and social issues in housing. Yet in the years just after the first national conference on city planning, leading planners glimpsed broad relationships with other progressive movements, sought to be more practical or functional than aesthetic in their planning, and concentrated on institutionalizing city planning, professionally and administratively.

Speaking at the second national conference on city planning at Rochester, New York, in May, 1910, Olmsted, for one, was almost overwhelmed by "the complex unity, the appalling breadth and ramification, of real city planning."[10] He realized, not for the first time, that he and his fellow practitioners were "dealing . . . with the play of enormously complex forces which no one clearly understands and few pretend to."[11] He humbly acknowledged that "our efforts to control [these forces] so often lead to unexpected and deplorable results that sober-minded people are often tempted to give up trying to exercise a large control, and to confine themselves to the day's obvious duty and let these remoter matters take their course."[12] But Olmsted rejected the idea of letting things drift. The free interplay of economic forces and social impulses would only pile up unendurable evils. Difficult though the effort might be, planners must try to comprehend the intricate web of the city—all its diverse threads of cause and effect, the good and the bad, the ugly and the beautiful—and to intervene in the public interest, insofar as they could determine it.

Olmsted spoke, however, mainly of the physical city. Where did this city of sights and sounds and smells shade into the cultural city, the city of politics and government, the legal and the fiscal city? Olmsted did not say. He hoped to master the complexities of the visible city "through better knowledge of facts, clearer definition of purpose, and through improvements of technique."[13] The city was a chaos of conflicting purposes, of separate, fragmentary planning resulting in conditions in which people could not attain "the maximum of productive efficiency, of health, and of enjoyment of life."[14] Somehow the varied public and private purposes must be harmonized into a set of dominant social purposes. But Olmsted had less to say about the clarification of purposes and the planning of "physical results suitable to these purposes" than about the need for collecting and analyzing data and devising legal and administrative machinery to carry out city plans. He did not mention that he himself was particularly perplexed by the problem of interpreting facts and translating findings into sound plans.

In December, 1910, the New Haven Civic Improvement Commission issued a report that revealed Olmsted's failure to be as scientific as he wished. In 1907 the commission had employed him and the architect Cass Gilbert to prepare a city plan. Before beginning their labors, they had taken what was then an unusual step. They had employed a young man named Roland M. Byrnes, a member of the senior class of Yale University who was specializing in "social and statistical science," to compile a statistical picture of New Haven. This, they expected, would enable them "to discover what sort of things now lacking to the city would contribute most to the satisfaction of its citizens."[15] Olmsted listed a wide range of items on which he wanted data, such as population, tax rates, assessed valuations, industrial employment, freight shipments, street-railway patronage, counts of vehicular traffic, occupancy of housing, mortality rates, miles of paved and unpaved streets, area of districts used in tabulating population statistics and percentages occupied by streets, squares, railroad property, parks, public grounds, cemeteries, and water and marshes. He mentioned, however, that he was especially interested in "the human facts." Byrnes therefore submitted mostly social statistics, together with some information about property valuations, tax rates and levies, and the city debt. He would hardly have had time between November, 1907, when he began work, and February, 1908, when he turned in his report, to collect material on all the items on Olmsted's list, even if the statistics had been available. For many items they could not be obtained from any source in those days; and Byrnes lamented that "the chief difficulties were found in the inadequacy of the records kept by the city."[16]

Confronted with what they considered a vast amount of material, Olmsted and Gilbert apparently did not know how to make use of it. They included Byrne's compilation in their report as an appendix and made only the most general references to social conditions, as the architect George B. Ford noted somewhat scornfully when he wrote an article on "recent" city planning reports in 1912.[17] The one essay at forecasting on the basis of Byrnes's statistics was hesitant. A comparison of growth curves suggested "the probable doubling of the present population of New Haven in about the next twenty-five years, and a population of some 400,000 by the year 1950," whereas the actual population of the metropolitan area at midcentury was 244,836.[18] This prediction was followed by a reckless assertion that "it is more likely than not that the end of the twentieth century will find New Haven Green the center of a metropoli-

37. Frederick Law Olmsted, the younger, as he appeared in later life (*Prentiss French*)

tan population of about a million and a half."[19] The designer-planners were obviously uncomfortable in the attempt to utilize statistical data. Instinctively they fell back on their own humanist motivations and aesthetic judgments, appealing to conservative citizens to face the prospects of growth and change and to provide New Haven with better public facilities and services.

Once a pleasant little New England college town with a population of relatively independent, individualistic, and self-sufficing householders, New Haven was becoming a "widespread urban metropolis of the twentieth century, the citizens of which will be wholly dependent upon joint action for a very large proportion of the good things of civic life."[20] Olmsted frankly warned the upper crust that a laissez-faire policy applicable to New England Yankees would not suffice for a city with a large proportion of immigrants from southern and eastern Europe, not to mention the Irish, who still predominated among the foreign-born.[21] "People of the old New England stock still to a large extent control the city," he wrote, "and if they want New Haven to be a fit and worthy place for their descendants it behooves them to establish conditions about the lives of *all* the people that will make the best fellow-citizens of them and their children."[22] If his report lacked social analysis, it somewhat atoned for the deficiency by offering enlightened social philosophy. Its tone was admirably straightforward and democratic, as befitted a document appearing at the end of the decade in which the United States absorbed eight million immigrants—half the total population increase for the ten-year period and the largest number of foreigners admitted to the country at any time in its history.

The man who was most determined to make city planning a science was architect George B. Ford, author of the article criticizing Olmsted's none-too-successful encounter with statistical data. Ford had contributed a chapter to Marsh's book on city planning in 1909 and had spoken about housing and the arrangement of residential streets at the first national conference on city planning. A graduate of Harvard in 1899, he later earned Bachelor's and Master's degrees in science from the Massachusetts Institute of Technology (in mechanical engineering) and then studied at the Ecole des Beaux Arts in Paris. At that center of eclecticism his thesis problem was not the design of a monumental city hall or church but "A Tenement in a Large City"—a choice of subject no doubt reflecting the influence of his brother, Dr. James Ford, housing expert of Harvard University. George's interest in multifamily housing led him to investigate city planning and to become increasingly concerned with the economic and social aspects of the city. By 1912 he viewed it as a functional unit which, above all, should provide suitably for living, work, and play. Any city development which did not take due cognizance of the basic needs was not only unscientific; it was criminal, he declared in an address before the American Civic Association.[23] He was willing to concede that the City Beautiful was "a most desirable object, for we do crave beauty," but he asked, "Can we with equanimity stand by and help the city spend its money on . . . frills and furbelows when only a step away the hideous slum, reeking with filth and disease, rotten with crime, is sapping the very life-blood of the city?"[24]

To make the city itself more healthful, convenient, and pleasurable, Ford believed that city planning, the means to a better city, must be transformed from a "rather capricious procedure into that highly respectable thing known as an exact science."[25] Not that he wished to "administer a snub" to the aesthetic side of city planning, but the "things which foster . . . delight in the city" should always "follow the lines laid down by the practical interests of the community."[26] Determining the best plan for a city was solely a matter of proceeding logically from the known to the unknown—of gathering factual information, analyzing it, and discovering that in almost every case there was "one, and only one, logical and convincing solution of the problems involved."[27]

What facts needed to be collected? Ford listed twelve main headings under which various subclassifications of information should be gathered: streets; transportation of people; transportation of goods; factories and warehouses; food-supply markets; water supply and sanitation; housing; recreation; parks, boulevards, street planting; architecture; laws; and financing or methods of paying for improvements. The first ten categories indicated the content of the comprehensive plan as he understood it; the last two concerned implementation of the plan.

Ford illustrated his scientific method by discussing street widening and extension. Planners should determine the ideal street cross-section for each type of pedestrian and vehicular use and for various combinations of use. Highway engineers could provide them with standards to apply, so that they themselves would only need to have up-to-date surveys and maps, historical maps for the study of trends, detailed traffic counts, and maps showing the distribution of population in order to see at a glance whether any particular street was functioning efficiently. They could then study means of diverting traffic from heavily traveled streets to others less used, or could determine where streets should be widened or cut through.

Ford tried to make the whole process of planning sound facile, objective, and 99 per cent technical. He underemphasized the part personal judgment played in determining the kinds of data to be gathered, evaluating data, formulating standards, and selecting solutions. He was loathe to consider the values of the community, as he indicated by cautioning that "our best laid plans may be interfered with by some political or local prejudice,"[28] as if resistance to a planner's proposals might not stem from his own failure to appreciate local traditions or his blithe willingness to alter beyond recognition some cherished landmark or familiar row of buildings by a street widening. Genuinely concerned about human welfare though he was, Ford was so intent on creating respect for the planning process that he was in danger of losing sight of the importance of plumbing the desires, feelings, hopes, and aspirations of community and neighborhood—and of taking them into account in planning.

An unsigned article entitled "Efficiency in City Planning," either written by Ford for the *American City* magazine or based on his material, provided a clue to this myopia. Ford wanted to make the businessman— "who has to pay the bills"—a convert to city planning.[29] The businessman, at least the executive, was at that time greatly impressed by a little book by Frederick Winslow Taylor entitled *The Principles of Scientific Management,* or by popular articles and trade journal accounts of the efficacy of applying Taylor's principles to industrial production, one of which was the separation of the planning of work from its execution. Taylor, however, was only the most spectacular of dozens of men in the early 1900s who wrote about systematizing production. By the time his book appeared in 1911 the business world was well prepared to accept his "science of work" and to consider "Taylorizing" manufacturing plants by establishing planning departments to manage the entire process of production. The enthusiasm for scientific management was so widespread, in fact, that progressives in politics advocated its application to government, as had Taylor himself in his book. The Bureau of Municipal Research in New York City was especially influential in urging the need to "functionalize work" in municipal administrations and to separate politics from administration, though Woodrow Wilson and Professor Frank J. Goodnow had earlier proposed much the same thing. When Ford presented city planning as a systematic method of solving urban problems, he reflected both the reformer's passion for efficiency in municipal government and the alert businessman's interest in broader applications of the principles of scientific management.

The article in the *American City,* describing survey procedures that Ford and engineer E. P. Goodrich had developed while preparing plans for Newark and Jersey City, closed with a paragraph more expressive of Ford's hopes than of his success in making businessmen ardent supporters of city planning: "This method of work, systematized, standardized, 'Taylorized,' as it is, has most decidedly proved its worth. It appeals strongly to the businessman . . . and convinces everyone that the experts have real knowledge on which to base their recommendations, and are not presenting mere dreams, pretty but impracticable."[30]

The Newark City Planning Commission did not retain Ford after 1913 or Goodrich after March, 1914, except as an adviser on call. To their young assistant, Harland Bartholomew, who had wanted to be an engineer and who reluctantly became a city planner when Goodrich assigned him to work in Newark, fell the chief responsibility of developing the comprehensive plan the partners had outlined. Bartholomew helped to devise Ford's methodology, improved upon it in 1914 and 1915 when he was working entirely on his own, and in the long run spent a lifetime refining the techniques of city planning and the concept of the overall plan. The commission he served was perhaps the first in the nation to employ a full-time professional city planner.

Planning the City Functional

The emphasis on the City Efficient or the City Functional characterizing the city planning movement by 1912 was in some ways a logical outgrowth of the social impulses that had crept into the City Beautiful movement as it became concerned with playgrounds, transportation, and terminals. The playground movement, particularly, deepened the social undercurrents of the earlier park movement and gave a democratic coloration to city planning as it increasingly absorbed the park movement. Outdoor play space afforded such obvious relief to the wretchedness of life in the slums that even the most callous citizens acknowledged its necessity. In making provision for it, designer-planners and engineers contemplated the possibility of improving housing and decreasing densities. Consideration of transportation and freight-handling facilities in manufacturing districts evoked the thought that such districts required special planning and separation from other types of areas. Once the idea of protecting both residential and industrial areas from incompatible activities presented itself, the adaptation of German zoning to American purposes seemed all the more desirable. City planning thus became a matter of altering spatial relationships to achieve the practical ends of efficiency and convenience. In the evolution of the city planning movement the City Functional was a logical phase.

Even so aesthetic a planner as Robinson kept in step with the times and was as eager as his fellows to stress practicality. In two reports issued between the first and second national conferences on city planning—one on Fort Wayne, Indiana, and the other on Waterloo, Iowa—he proposed prohibiting manufacturing establishments in residential areas and restricting the heights of buildings in business districts to lessen the danger of generating intolerable traffic conditions. The report to the Civic Improvement Association of Fort Wayne also suggested private development of an industrial tract second to none in the United States in its convenience for manufacturers—a kind of forerunner of the planned industrial district. In an area adjacent to railroads "the land would be laid out not in the usual house lots, but in manufacturing plats; and to serve these at the minimum expenditure of time and effort the streets and sidings would be planned."[31] To create this new manufacturing section, Robinson urged the formation of a freight terminal company in which the railroads would be stockholders jointly with realty and industrial interests.

Invited to Dallas in 1910 to prepare a city plan for that city, George Kessler revealed that he, too, had expanded his conception of the comprehensive plan and wished to be eminently realistic in all his proposals. He foresaw the need for such problem-solving improvements as street openings and widenings in the downtown area, a central freight terminal, a belt railroad around the city, and the construction of levees along the Trinity River to make possible the reclamation of an area for manufacturing. He noted that the city had begun, "along natural lines," to segregate its lands for varying uses. [32] On the lower grounds were the railroads and industrial concerns, slightly higher than these the retail and wholesale houses near the center of the city, and on the surrounding elevations the residential areas. "Regard for the interests of the people at large," he observed, "means that a city should be divided into areas and zones, each devoted to its own particular purpose. The greatest possible accessibility for all should be provided in ample and direct connecting thoroughfares and all barriers, such as railroad grade crossings, narrow, congested streets and excessively long blocks, should be removed and corrected."[33]

In two sentences Kessler outlined almost exactly the kind of city planning program dozens of American cities would be engaged in, if not immediately, in the years after the First World War — a program of zoning and the improvement of circulation systems. It was the kind of "practical" program businessmen particularly approved, but Kessler was more than the businessman's planner. Having first become famous as a landscape architect, he never belittled the importance of natural beauty in the urban environment. Happily, Dallas has, in Turtle Creek Parkway, Lake Cliff Park, and the great park adjacent to White Rock Reservoir, evidence of his efforts to provide for both the body and the spirit. In the downtown area some broad arteries testify to his recognition of the need for improved traffic flow.

One of the special appeals of the City Efficient concept was inherited from Theodore Roosevelt's presidency: the promise to eliminate waste. "City planning is municipal conservation," the Pittsburgh Civic Commission stated in 1910 in a preface to a report by Olmsted on thoroughfares and public open spaces.[34] Olmsted bolstered this idea by suggesting the prompt establishment of new building lines along all main arteries requiring widening, so that in the future the city would be able to avoid costly condemnation suits. The drain on the municipal treasury would be reduced still further, he pointed out, if the city exercised wise control of the growing suburban districts, into which streets, sewers, and other public works were daily extended with no knowledge of how they could later be continued into areas still farther out.[35] The municipal Bureau of Surveys, whose "unprogressive mediaeval methods" he deplored, had no official surveys of "the complicated topography" of these undeveloped areas, but this lack was not entirely its fault.[36] It had insufficient funds. Olmsted advised the city to loosen its purse strings and establish an accurate framework of survey reference points, to tie existing local surveys and records into the framework, and as soon as possible to complete topographical maps for the entire municipality in accordance with a uniform system.

Neither in 1910 nor later did Olmsted become the narrow functionalist. The designer in him was always too strong. In his Pittsburgh report he could not refrain from attempting to educate the commission about the value of "civic comeliness." The "inefficient, primitive condition" of the riverfronts, with their railroads and hideous factories, pained him. "One of the deplorable consequences of the short-sighted and wasteful commercialism of the later nineteenth century lay in its disregard of what might have been the esthetic by-products of economic improvement; in the false impression spread abroad that economical and useful things were normally ugly; and in the vicious idea which followed, that beauty and the higher pleasures of civilized life were to be sought only in things otherwise useless," he complained. "Thus the pursuit of beauty was confounded with extravagance."[37] It would be no waste of money, he assured the commission, to create "ample wide water-front streets," with the outer sidewalks treated as tree-shaded promenades. Or to build some well-designed bridges in the world capital of the steel bridge industry. Pittsburgh, he observed, had not a single bridge over its rivers that was outstanding for its beauty or its perfect engineering adaptation to its purpose.

Though other planners might lose their sense of balance and overemphasize the functional at the expense of the aesthetic, Olmsted steadfastly maintained that both practicality and beauty were possible and that both should be sought in planning. "So far as the demands of beauty can be distinguished from those of economy," he had said at the conference in Rochester, "the kind of beauty most to be sought in the planning of cities is that which results from seizing instinctively with a keen and sensitive appreciation the limitless opportunities which present themselves in the course of the most rigorously practical solution of any problem for a choice between decisions of substantially equal economic merit but of widely differing aesthetic quality."[38] For a landscape architect-planner, however, the choices might be easier than for planners whose previous experience was in engineering or law. Such men were becoming interested in the practice of city planning. Would they have the "keen and sensitive appreciation" to choose with unerring aesthetic judgment between alternatives of "substantially equal economic merit"?

Virgil Bogue, who had spent a lifetime as a railroad engineer and consultant on the engineering problems of municipal development, was an example of the technically trained man attracted to the city planning field as efficiency and functionalism became dominant values. Among other things, Bogue had arranged the waterfront terminal facilities of railroads in Baltimore, San Francisco, Tacoma, and Seattle; and it was his work in the latter two cities which recommended him to the Municipal Plans Commission of Seattle in 1910.

Of 113 pages in his report to the commission in 1911, all but 16 concerned transportation, harbor improvements, and arterial highways. In the few pages not given over to detailed consideration of circulation and port facilities, Bogue proposed a civic center similar to those designed by architect-planners, suggested boulevards and esplanades in the traditional City Beautiful mode, and endorsed without criticism a plan for parks prepared by the Olmsted brothers in 1903. As a young man just graduated from Rensslaer Polytechnic Institute, Bogue had worked briefly on the engineering staff of Prospect Park, Brooklyn, under the elder Olmsted. It was natural for him to respect the work of the sons. He made suggestions only for additional parks that would be required beyond the city limits to serve the future "Greater Seattle." He also proposed more playgrounds as a means of assuring "a generation of useful, law-abiding, industrious citizens."[39]

Bogue outdid himself in specific suggestions for major streets and highways, seawalls and docks, ferry services, a coordinated railroad system, and rapid transit, interurban, and street railway lines, even proposing exact locations and providing measured preliminary drawings and construction details for some facilities. The form and location of the civic center, in fact, were determined by the solution of highway, transit, and railway problems.

The engineer's recommendations for rapid transit were particularly farsighted: "The city's growth will be retarded with a tendency to develop congested, undesirable and unhealthful districts unless rapid transit facilities are provided. Businessmen, and workers generally, cannot be served by a surface street railway system, over lines stretching out six or seven miles, with stops at every street crossing, consuming from thirty minutes to an hour twice each day. And the more the population increases in these suburban sections over which the city must expand, the more difficult the problem becomes."[40]

Bogue offered no population or economic studies, however, to justify the large investment in public works contemplated by his supposedly very practical plan. Nor did he suggest legislative or fiscal measures to carry it out. The temporary Municipal Plans Commission published ten thousand copies of his report and then disbanded, leaving such civic organizations as the Municipal League of Seattle and prominent architects and engineers to carry on a public educational campaign in behalf of the plan before it was submitted to the electorate in March, 1912, as required by the city charter.

Opposition soon came from many quarters, but particularly from downtown property owners who objected to shifting the civic center and the railroad depots. On election day the voters decisively defeated the plan by a vote of 24,996 to 14,506—a result the Municipal League attributed to a lack of general public understanding, to a feeling that the entire scheme was too rigid, and to the fear of many property owners that the plan would adversely affect their holdings or require the condemnation of their property.

Whether the voters would have approved the plan if they had known more about it, no one can say. More knowledge about this plan which purported to be sound because of its wealth of engineering detail might have convinced an even greater number of persons that Bogue had failed to justify his proposals. The fate of the plan perhaps indicated that "practical" planners had as far to go in winning public approval as those who espoused the City Beautiful.

Parenthetically, it must be noted, however, that notwithstanding the defeat of the plan, in later years Seattle based the development of its arterial highway network, park system, and part of its waterfront on Bogue's proposals. The projected civic center, central station, rapid-transit routes, and extensive port and industrial facilities were never constructed.

The Relationship of Housing to City Planning

To John Nolen, as to George Ford, the functional city was one in which the citizens enjoyed good housing and a healthful, pleasant residential environment as well as efficient transportation, well-planned streets, ample parks and playgrounds, and adequate facilities for business and industry. In a report submitted to the Madison [Wisconsin] Park and Pleasure Drive Association in 1910 Nolen boldly asserted, "The most important features of city planning are not the public buildings, not the railroad approaches, not even the parks and playgrounds. They are the location of streets, the establishment of block lines, the subdivision of property into lots, the regulations of buildings, and the housing of the people."[41] Madison, he was sorry to say, had failed to take advantage of its unusually picturesque site, but perhaps more deplorable was the fact that its housing was far from satisfactory.[42]

On at least three trips to Europe Nolen had been especially impressed by the cities in Germany and Switzerland, and particularly by the industrial city of Dusseldorf. It held in Germany an economic position comparable to that of Pittsburgh in the United States, yet it was a model of order and cleanliness achieved without waste or extravagance. Its districting or zoning system was one of the best in Germany. With it in mind, Nolen did not hesitate to recommend to citizens of Madison that public regulation and control be greatly widened and strengthened. "Even the so-called 'zone system' of the German cities, adapted, of course, to American conditions, is not too much to expect," he stated, adding that "such regulations must sooner or later prevail in American cities even if they interfere with property rights."[43] If that sounded radical, he had an eminent authority to cite—Theodore Roosevelt, who in a lecture at the Sorbonne in Paris had recently declared that "human rights and property rights are fundamentally and in the long run identical, but when it clearly appears that there is a real conflict between them, human rights must have the upper hand, for property belongs to man and not man to property."[44]

Although most American city planners recognized the importance of housing and the residential environment, they could not determine the most effective ways to improve the quality of dwellings and neighborhoods or how to increase the supply of accommodations for low-income families. Since the planning and development of housing was a private endeavor, the only judicially approved controls over it appeared to be building and health codes and tenement-house regulations imposing certain height and land-coverage restrictions, in addition to requirements concerning interior arrangement and sanitary facilities. The problems of effecting better site planning, reducing the cost of housing low-income families, clearing or renewing slum areas, and preventing good neighborhoods from being blighted by the invasion of stores and factories or streams of traffic loomed large and begged for solution. But would American courts ever regard as constitutional the types of control used in German cities? Would municipal governments ever be willing or financially able to build low-rent housing for poor families even if the courts upheld laws permitting them to do so? How could local governments persuade or require private builders to plan better houses and arrange them on the land in more livable and attractive ways?

Most planners preferred not to grapple with such questions, at least while carrying on busy practices. When Olmsted, Arnold Brunner, and Bion Arnold, the transportation expert, prepared a report for the Rochester Improvement Committee in 1911, they indicated that the whole question of establishing greater control over private property was too complex and too fraught with legal difficulties for them to investigate in the limited time at their disposal.[45] Olmsted offered "systematic adherence to the principle of distinction between thoroughfares and local streets" as one way of bringing about the separation of inharmonious activities by a process of natural selection.[46] Wide thoroughfares would attract through traffic, and business establishments would seek location on such routes in order to exploit the heavy travel. They would thus not encroach on intermediate streets, destroying the residential atmosphere and injuring property values. Plausible as the argument appeared, it took no account, of course, of the retarding effect of strip commercial developments on traffic movement. Automobiles were not then numerous—in the entire United States there were fewer than 650,000 registered motor vehicles—but horse-drawn conveyances could generate impressive traffic jams in commercial areas. The proposed solution of the problem of safeguarding residential precincts threatened to create other problems equally troublesome.

In their annual national conferences planners and housing reformers found the relationship between housing and city planning a bedeviling topic. At the conference in Rochester in 1910 Edward T. Hartman, secretary of the Massachusetts Civic League, took city planners to task because their "so-called plans ignore all this [problem of congestion of population] with premeditated connivance."[47] But Hartman could not have been more unfair, because some of those present had at least given a great deal of thought to housing, even if they had not come to any particularly helpful conclusions. For example, Grosvenor Atterbury, architect for the Forest Hills Gardens project of the Sage Foundation, especially wanted to make a distinction between congestion or overcrowding of population and concentration under desirable conditions but was unable to establish the "safe limit of centralization under various conditions and for various classes of population."[48] Taking into consideration "racial, climatic, and other fundamental conditions," at what point did concentration become "undue"? Similarly, Lawrence Veiller, who had written the New York tenement-house legislation of 1901 and founded the National Housing Association in the latter part of 1909, was at a loss to define undue concentration. "Frankly," he said, "I do not know. I doubt if anyone knows."[49] He strongly believed, however, that proper design of structures and careful site planning might permit a very considerable number of persons to be well housed in a small area:

> If, for instance, the area 200 feet by 400 feet [about two acres], now devoted to tenement house purposes in the ordinary New York City block, were so disposed as to produce three parallel rows of six-story tenements, each 25 feet in depth, and the full size of the block in length (400 feet), with two streets

each 60 feet wide between them, practically ideal conditions of city housing would be had. The buildings thus produced would each be but two rooms deep, thus ensuring "through" ventilation; every room would be an "outside room"; courts, shafts, yards and all similar devices to secure light and air would no longer be necessary, and the housing problem would cease to be an architectural one. With such a disposition of the land, over 1,500 persons to the acre could be thus housed . . . and this same city block would then house 2,592 persons under sanitary conditions.[50]

The proceedings of the conference do not record that participants rose in outrage at the thought of housing with densities of fifteen hundred persons per acre. Neither was there any enthusiasm for very high densities under conditions presumably affording ample light and air. Most conferees assumed that there must be some optimum density, scientifically determinable, though none expressed willingness to undertake the kind of research Atterbury outlined.

As in all previous discussions of the housing problem, there were several proposals for developing housing for workers in outlying areas. George Hooker, of Chicago, and Edward E. Pratt, of the New York School of Philanthropy, both described the migration of some leading industries to suburban locations. Pratt presented a study of the places of work and of residence of Italian workers showing that "not only do the employees tend to group themselves about the establishment, but when the establishment moves out of the center of the city to some near-by suburb, a large proportion of the workers retain their position in the new location and in the course of time a good proportion of them take up residence in the vicinity."[51] These findings led Pratt "irresistibly" to the conclusion that the regulation of the location of factories would in some measure prevent further increase of density in older areas.[52]

Pratt saw opportunities for private philanthropic agencies to cooperate in programs for the relocation of factories by developing suburban industrial centers at sites "chosen with relation to the economic advantages of the place, with regard to water and rail transportation, ease of communication with the city, and the cost of land."[53] He expected that factories could easily be attracted to these suburban centers. The function of the philanthropic agencies would be to provide decent housing for the workers and develop social activities for them.

Henry C. Wright, the New York architect who would some day be associated with Clarence S. Stein in planning the model town of Radburn, New Jersey, agreed that the removal of factories from central locations seemed to be the most hopeful method of relieving congestion of population, but he posed more than two dozen questions requiring "a great amount of detailed study" before anyone could say with certainty whether

[handwritten margin note: removal of factories to outlying areas would solve problem] it would be possible to effect planned dispersion.[54] Wright wondered what the attitude of the courts would be toward restricting the use of private property. He was assailed by doubts about the economic feasibility of operating factories in outlying locations. He questioned whether satisfactory housing could be provided for workers at rents or sale prices they could afford. And if workers had to continue to live in central areas, he was not even sure whether they could afford to pay a five-cent fare on rapid transit lines to the suburbs, or whether the city could finance the construction of new lines.

When the third national conference on city planning was held in Philadelphia in 1911, all the unresolved and frustrating questions raised by Wright and others at the previous conference again demanded attention. In comparison with the German city, the American municipality seemed to Frederick C. Howe, former member of the Cleveland City Council and the Ohio State Senate, almost helpless to control its growth and development. The courts so strictly construed the law that cities could hardly exercise the right of eminent domain. They were denied the use of excess condemnation as a means of recouping part of the cost of improvements. State legislatures not only limited the public purposes for which land could be acquired; they also carefully prescribed the use of special assessments to finance street improvements and related projects. In many states developers could lay out streets of any width they desired, install sewers and paving, and build cheap tenements or tall apartments regardless of municipal protests. Notwithstanding widespread knowledge of "the vice, crime, and disease which the tenement produces," old conditions in the larger cities were "reproducing themselves."[55]

Howe's gloomy portrait of the American city was all the more somber beside his rosy description of the German city, which planned its outlying areas far in advance of predicted growth, required landowners to dedicate a certain percentage of their holdings for streets and open spaces, and constructed all streets under the direction of its own engineers and landscape architects. The German city excited Howe's greatest admiration, however, because of its taxation of unearned increment, its municipal ownership of large tracts of land, and its housing programs. He cited the city of Ulm as having carried through the most comprehensive housing policy.

The German municipality had purchased fourteen hundred acres of land in the suburbs, built detached dwellings "of an attractive type," and sold them to workingmen under long-term contracts providing for payments "just sufficient to reimburse the city for its cost and interest charges." Contracts contained "a few simple and obviously necessary regulations" and required the assent of the city to any transfer. Under this program almost a third of the population of Ulm had acquired good housing.

The city also encouraged the construction of cooperative apartment houses, financed partly by contributions of private capital, partly by loans at a very low rate of interest from the state insurance funds, partly by subscriptions from the city, and partly by installment payments from workingmen. In addition to the houses themselves, the cooperative developments included libraries, restaurants, kindergartens, and inner playgrounds and rest places for the occupants. "Germany has decided that the housing question is too important a problem to be left to the free play of capitalistic exploitation," Howe concluded.[56]

To most of Howe's compatriots direct construction schemes such as those of the German municipalities probably seemed the remotest of possibilities in the United States. Even the mixed economic arrangements under which both national and local governments cooperated with private enterprise in financing housing were unacceptable to conservative housing reformers such as Veiller and De Forest. Only local government, Veiller maintained, should concern itself with housing, and then, at most, to enforce tenement-house regulations, restrict the height of buildings, lay out street systems conducive to the construction of multifamily structures two rooms deep, and control the use of land in various parts of the city. Up to 1911 but one federal agency, Roosevelt's Homes Commission of Washington, D.C., had recommended any form of financial assistance to private enterprise. In 1908 it had proposed that the Congress authorize low-interest loans to limited-dividend building associations, but nothing had come of the recommendation. In Massachusetts the legislature was about to approve the creation of the Massachusetts Homestead Commission, which would do much to stimulate city planning but would succeed in building no more than twelve homes for workers before its demise in 1919. Elsewhere in the nation progressives such as Howe could point to no proposals for governmental participation in the provision of housing for low-income families.

American planners desirous of improving housing could concentrate on trying to bring about better planning of suburban areas, as the British planner Thomas Adams suggested, and on adapting zoning to American conditions, but they could not expect, then or for many years to come, to find much support for governmental housing schemes. At the national conference in 1912 J. Randolph Coolidge, Jr., the Boston architect, acknowledged that municipal housing such as Germany and England had built was "looked on askance in this country as an unwarranted invasion of the field of private enterprise."[57] To call for recognition of the housing problem as a national economic issue, as young Carol Aronovici did in 1914, was to be suspected of being un-American. But whether or not it

≡ dr. E Wood.

was taboo to suggest that the federal government should do something about housing, Edith Elmer Wood, who decided in 1917 to become a professional in the field of housing, brought together every housing survey she could find and for the first time put the housing problem in national perspective. In a dissertation published in 1919 under the title *Housing of the Unskilled Wage Earner* she estimated that a third of the people of the United States were living under substandard housing conditions.[58] She also showed that only the wealthiest third of the population constituted the effective market for new private housing. But while she was crusading and conducting her studies, city planners came to regard zoning as the most practicable means of improving living conditions, mainly because there were some domestic precedents for it. It was related to tenement-house laws, could be used to prevent the construction of tenement houses in suburban areas, and offered hope of bettering conditions in the entire city, particularly the residential districts. To gain this one rather promising form of control over private property, most planners were resigned to abandoning, for the time being, the larger economic and social issues in housing. The long struggle to establish the constitutionality of comprehensive zoning was, however, part of a still broader effort to forge a variety of means of carrying out the city plan.

Carrying Out the City Plan

Olmsted realized as early as 1909 that if the city planning movement was ever to progress beyond the plan-making stage and decisively influence the growth and development of cities, it would have to overcome the resistance of the courts to broader regulation of the use of private property and municipal acquisition of land for newly recognized public needs. From his friend John Glenn, attorney and executive director of the Russell Sage Foundation, he obtained a promise of funds for an investigation of state and local laws that had withstood attack and for publication of a book describing them. He then appeared one morning at the office of a Boston law firm and asked to see a young attorney named Flavel Shurtleff, who he had been told was just the man to carry out the study.

"I want you to write a book about city planning," he informed Shurtleff, who immediately protested that he knew nothing whatsoever about the subject. But Olmsted was not a man to be talked down. He outlined the project as if Shurtleff had already agreed to undertake it and finally offered him $300 a month and payment of all expenses.

Shurtleff recalled at the age of eighty-five that he thought the proposal "sounded like a pretty good stunt";[59] so he accepted, little realizing that from time to time all the rest of his life he would serve the cause of city planning as writer, conference manager, publicist, teacher, consultant, and expert witness in zoning cases.

After talking with Olmsted for several weeks and reading everything about city planning on his bookshelves, Shurtleff set out to interview mayors, city planning commissions, heads of municipal departments, and city attorneys or their deputies in cities from coast to coast. In two years of travel, study, and diligent correspondence with legal authorities all over the United States, he discovered that, viewed nationally, the law of city planning was, if not chaotic, distressingly divergent from state to state. One city was not always aware of a procedure or legal mechanism used effectively by another municipality in the same state. Even neighboring states sometimes lacked information about one another's planning laws and court decisions affecting planning. The situation, in short, called for the speedy publication of a book showing how to break through the legal obstacles to the execution of plans, as well as how to develop new legal instruments for carrying on planning programs.

However urgent the need, Shurtleff soon learned that Olmsted could not be hurried when matters of quality were concerned. He made Shurtleff rewrite his manuscript at least three times, and each time went over it word by word and comma by comma, penciling searching comments in the margin and raising endless questions. At length, in desperation Shurtleff wrapped up his latest version and sent it to John Glenn, telling him that if he ever hoped to see *Carrying Out the City Plan* in print, he had better go ahead without further consulting "that perfectionist, Frederick Law Olmsted."[60]

38. Flavel Shurtleff

When the book appeared in 1914, some of the text had already become obsolete. The work nevertheless enjoyed a ready sale and offered encouragement to planning commissioners, city attorneys, and the various professions interested in the advancement of the planning movement. Generally, Shurtleff noted severe restrictions on the authority of cities to innovate, but he found some hopeful indications that the courts were beginning to sanction broader interpretations of the state and federal constitutions.

The growth of great centers of population, for instance, had already obliged state legislatures to recognize new public needs and permit cities to acquire land for such community facilities as playgrounds and natatoriums, which earlier would not have been considered essential. "It is not inconceivable," Shurtleff speculated, "that more radical needs will be recognized by legislatures and the courts in the next twenty years," until eventually American cities might even be able to act under as broad a conception of the term "public use" as that accepted in Germany, where the rights of the community usually took precedence over those of the individual.[61] Shurtleff found, however, that except in Pennsylvania, state supreme courts were not yet willing to uphold legislation requiring private property owners, without payment for damages, to comply with street plans prepared by municipal departments and recorded on official maps. Nor did he believe that in the long run cities could place much reliance on being permitted to practice excess condemnation. Most courts

39. John M. Glenn
(Russell Sage Foundation)

regarded the excess land as property not required for a public purpose.

From his examination of the use of the police power to regulate private property Shurtleff foresaw no difficulty in extending the legal principles invoked in limiting the height of buildings. "If the legislature can establish two building [height] districts, it certainly can establish three or even four," he wrote. "If its authority to delegate to a commission power to regulate the height of buildings in each district is sustained by the courts on the ground that it is a reasonable way of securing an adequate amount of light and air, it should follow that the power to regulate the amount of space that each building may occupy in a horizontal direction can also be delegated."[62] But the regulation of the use of land was altogether another matter. Shurtleff's book revealed that the courts validated measures restricting the location and operation of businesses deemed to be outright nuisances, whereas they usually declared unconstitutional the newer types of regulations excluding from residential areas industrial or commercial establishments which, though producing little or no smoke, noise, and odors, were nevertheless objectionable because of the size and appearance of the buildings or the large number of persons attracted. "It is not held to be within the scope of the police power to guard the amenities of life," Shurtleff observed.[63] Readers of the book understood that the big battle with the courts would be over the right of cities to designate zones for various kinds of uses or activities.

The last chapter disclosed the problems of city planning commissions in getting a toehold in municipal government. Some had no power even of suggestion unless called upon by the mayor and council. Long-established and powerful public works or park departments in some cities frankly ignored the planning commission and carried out projects without ever referring the plans to it for review. "If the plan commission is to be an intelligent correlating agency," Shurtleff admonished, "there must be provision for constant reference to it of new construction work of all municipal departments even at the risk of swamping the clerical force of the city plan commission by a mass of detail with little bearing on the city plan."[64]

Shurtleff conceived of the planning department as a research agency properly staffed to carry on long-range studies, in addition to performing its coordinating function. Thus it would be able to foresee changes in the economic and social life of the community necessitating new terminals, better access to commercial and industrial centers, and additional parks and playgrounds. "There is not a city of 100,000 in the United States which ought not today to widen streets or open new ones in order to give an adequate approach to travel centers," he pointed out. "If this widening or opening were done at the time when it could be done economically and when a planning board would advise it, if the problem were constantly studied by such a board, cities would be saved great outlays for recon- struction and great losses through failure to reconstruct."[65] In fact, Shurt- leff believed that the planning commission "should at all times be a propagandist body educating the citizens to see the economy of planning in general and to decide every specific question of the city's physical growth from the standpoint of city planning."[66]

Shurtleff failed to describe ways in which a planning agency could educate the public to appreciate the value of city planning and volun- tarily cooperate with it in carrying out a city plan; nor did he discuss long-range planning of municipal expenditures, to assure adequate funds year in and year out for constructing projects proposed in the overall plan. Apparently neither he nor Olmsted thought of these means of ex- ecuting the plan as appropriately within the legal context of Shurtleff's study. Indeed, until the late 1920s hardly anyone spoke of systematic budgeting of funds for capital improvements as one of the methods of implementing a plan, yet the architects Arnold Brunner and John Carrère had suggested the need for financial planning in a report to the Compre- hensive City Planning Commission of Grand Rapids, Michigan, in April, 1909. "It is . . . absolutely necessary," they urged, "that the same meth- ods should be adopted with regard to expenditures as with regard to im- provements; that is to say, they should be planned for years in advance on parallel lines with the improvements, so that you may know what your resources are and what you can undertake, and not load the city with obligations which will prevent it from undertaking in the future the things which are necessary and which require study in advance to decide."[67]

Two years before Shurtleff's book was off the press, John Nolen had also given serious consideration to the subject of financing public im- provements. In his book entitled *Replanning Small Cities,* based on his experience in preparing plans for cities such as Roanoke, Virginia, and Madison, Wisconsin, he asserted that "if American cities are to enter into large and far-sighted city planning schemes, a sounder policy of municipal finance must be adopted."[68] For one thing, most cities needed an increase in their borrowing capacity. "State regulations on this point appear to differ greatly," Nolen explained, "some cities (as in Massa- chusetts) being limited to $2\frac{1}{2}$ per cent of their assessed valuation, while others (as in New Jersey) may borrow as high as 25 per cent. The average, however, is low, from about 5 to 7 per cent, and the assessment is not usually full value. If American cities are to undertake great public im- provements in thoroughfares, transportation, docks, and harbors, public buildings and public grounds, housing, etc., a decided increase in city bond issues is essential."[69] Nolen also called for a nicer discrimination between improvements which are permanent and in the nature of investments and those which are not. Further, he pleaded for a more equitable distribution of current taxes.[70] With an eye to the future, he asked that there be "a much larger share for the community in increasing land values, a truer identification of the cost of public improvements and the benefits therefrom, and a wider use of the method of special assessment, as a means of meeting the cost of improvements."[71] "With a wiser, fairer and more businesslike system of city finance," he concluded, "it is not at all likely that the real burdens of city taxes would be heavier than at present. Indeed, they would probably be perceptibly lightened."[72]

Financing of the improvements embodied in the long-range plan increasingly occupied participants in the annual national conferences on city planning after Nolen, Shurtleff, Olmsted, and others directed attention to the importance of the subject. At the meeting in Boston in 1914 Andrew Wright Crawford, the Philadelphia attorney, exhorted planners not to be afraid to prepare plans which might seem to exceed the financial resources of the city. "Our present plans, if they are to be adequate when materialized in the future, must be correspondingly extensive, based on an understanding not only of what the needs of the future will be, but of what the financial ability of that future will be," he said.[73] Any plan for which the present fiscal capacity of a city was sufficient, he added, might be altogether inadequate by the time the improvements contemplated in the plan could be carried out, in, say, twenty-five years. Crawford's advice indicated that the makers of city plans had perhaps become unduly cautious, whereas only a few years earlier they had, as a group, been accused of concocting visionary schemes which would bankrupt cities.

At the same conference George McAneny, vice-mayor of New York City, suggested that if members of the embryonic planning profession really wished to see their plans translated into actual streets, parks, transit lines, and terminals, they should effect "the conversion of those who govern, and, for that matter, of the people who support those who govern."[74] The elected officials controlled the funds needed to carry out plans; to be effective, planners must influence the decision-makers. That, as Olmsted had realized six years earlier, was not playing politics but guiding policy. Educating the public about city planning was just another phase of creating the right political climate for planning. However, it was not McAneny's New York but Burnham's Chicago that provided the outstanding example of political receptivity to planning, as Shurtleff mentioned in his book. Burnham himself had died in 1912, but his spirit lived on in his plan, in the hearts of his friends, and in the tremendous educational effort they put forth in behalf of his plan.

Charles H. Wacker, the dedicated permanent chairman of the Chicago Plan Commission, had appeared at the annual conference in 1913 to describe progress made in carrying out the Burnham plan. As the summer of 1914 approached, he and his fellow commissioners and Walter D. Moody, the brilliant, hard-driving public relations man they had employed since 1911, were preparing to celebrate the fifth anniversary of the publication of the great plan. From all over the world they had gathered letters and published comments to include in a volume entitled *Chicago's World Wide Influence in City Planning*. In a few years the city had become internationally famous for its program of improvements based on the plan.

Chief among the projects being carried out in accordance with the plan were the widening of Twelfth Street from the crowded ghetto district to the lakefront, the widening of Michigan Avenue north to Lake Shore Drive, and the construction of new Pennsylvania Railroad passenger and freight stations costing from $40,000,000 to $50,000,000. Had the voters not approved bonds for the improvement of Twelfth Street at an election in November, 1912, Wacker and Moody would have believed that they had failed to convince the public of the practicality of the plan. This artery was the south base-line of the two-square-mile quadrangle forming the foundation of the street circulatory system of the plan. Wacker and Moody reasoned that if their fellow Chicagoans could not appreciate the importance of improving Twelfth Street and carrying it on a mile-long viaduct across the railroad yards south of the Loop, they would not support further efforts to put the plan into effect. In the crucial test of public acceptance of the plan, the voters had given the bonds a large majority, fortifying the plan commission for additional labors. The commission's latest triumph was an agreement under which the Pennsylvania Railroad abandoned schemes to build new stations at locations that would have interfered seriously with the execution of the Burnham plan. Instead, the railroad accepted almost a score of recommendations of the commission for locations shown on the plan and for streets, viaducts, bridges, and other improvements.

Behind the success of the commission was a story of Moody's ingenuity and indefatigability as a propagandist. No one has ever equaled him in promoting city planning, convincing an entire metropolis of its value, and winning support of a particular plan from voters and public officials alike. Persuaded by Wacker to leave his position as executive secretary of the Chicago Association of Commerce, Moody set to work to publicize the Burnham plan with the aggressiveness of a salesman and the fervor of a religious zealot. Finding that many persons considered the plan impractical and idealistic, he soon had Wacker and other influential members of the Commercial Club (which provided most of the funds for his promotional campaign) emphasizing the "city practical" at every opportunity. In preparation for the vote on the Twelfth Street bonds Moody wrote a ninety-three-page illustrated brochure called *Chicago's Greatest*

Issue—An Official Plan. He had 165,000 copies published at a cost of $18,000 and distributed them throughout the city to everyone paying a monthly rent of $25 or more. A month later the 328 members of the commission adopted the Burnham plan as the official general plan of Chicago. The impressive majority in favor of the bonds testified to the effectiveness of Moody's simple prose, as well as to his adroitness in cultivating the press. Similarly productive of support was an elementary school textbook which this evangelist of planning entitled *Wacker's Manual of the Plan of Chicago,* to identify the chairman of the commission with the plan. Adopted by the board of education in 1912 for use as an eighth-grade text, the manual was read not only by school children but also by their parents, as Moody had foreseen. (Eventually 50,000 copies were printed.)

As skillful with other media as he was with publications, Moody developed a splendid lantern slide collection illustrating the Burnham plan and examples of fine planning throughout the world. Speakers using this collection gave as many as ninety lectures in school auditoriums in a single winter season. Moody made sure that there were capacity audiences by distributing twice as many tickets for each lecture as there were seats. His tactics were the same for showings of a two-reel motion picture entitled "A Tale of One City," the first documentary film on city planning ever produced. More than 150,000 persons saw the film. Attendance at the slide lectures totaled approximately 175,000 in seven years.

In 1914, when Chicago had not yet begun to carry out the lakefront developments proposed in the Burnham plan, Moody had far from exhausted his resourcefulness as a promoter. Still to appear were three other highly effective publications: *Fifty Million Dollars for Nothing,* pointing out that the city could use waste material to create waterfront parks; *Economic Readjustment from a War to a Peace Basis,* urging additional projects as means of providing postwar employment; and *Seed Thoughts for Sermons,* which inspired ministers throughout the city to preach the value of comprehensive planning to their congregations.

Without the financial support of the Commercial Club, whose total investment in his activities was more than $200,000, Moody could not have done the spectacular job that brought him fame. But neither could Wacker, the commission, and the club have achieved as much as they did without the services of this unusual man. Together all of them created such a pervasive understanding of the Burnham plan that for at least fifteen years elected officials viewed it, as did Wacker, as a kind of civic bible.

"We are to make the Plan of Chicago our ideal and keep it before us — dare to recognize it—and to believe in it and build for it," began the creed adopted at a meeting of the Chicago Plan Commission in 1912. The commission, furthermore, was "to establish by the influence and work of a united citizenship the power of law necessary for Chicago's advancement, commensurate with her greatness."[75] What could mere politicians do but acquiesce to the demands of men who subscribed to and acted in accordance with such a creed?

The Appeal of Bureaucracy

Planning commissions lacking the dynamic leadership of men such as Wacker, the financial support and influential backing of organizations such as the Commercial Club, and the united cooperation of local newspapers faced governmental, legal, and staff problems which tended to be ignored in Chicago, yet the time would come when the Chicago Plan Commission no longer enjoyed a charmed life and had to surrender a certain independence for a closer relationship to the legislative and administrative agencies of municipal government. The leaders of the emerging city-planning profession who took a long view of urban problems and understood that there was much more to planning than carrying out a specific scheme, no matter how grand, very soon became concerned about integrating the planning function with other operations of local government because they believed that only insofar as comprehensive planning gained acceptance within the municipal bureaucracy could practitioners influence the many kinds of planning continually going on in the city hall.

As if he foresaw the course of planning activity in Chicago under Wacker and were warning against it, Olmsted declared in 1911 at the third national conference on city planning,

> We must disabuse the public mind of the idea that a city plan means a fixed record upon paper of a desire by some group of individuals prescribing, out of their wisdom and authority, where and how the more important changes and improvements in the physical layout of the city are to be made—a plan to be completed and put on file and followed more or less faithfully and mechanically, much as a contractor follows the architect's drawings for a house. We must cultivate in our own minds and in the mind of the people the conception of a city plan as a device or piece of administrative machinery for preparing, and keeping constantly up to date, a unified forecast and definition of all the important changes, additions and extensions of the physical equipment and arrangement of the city which a sound judgment holds likely to become desirable and practicable in the course of time, so as to avoid so far as possible both ignorantly wasteful action and ignorantly wasteful inaction in the control of the city's physical growth.[76]

Olmsted was not unappreciative of the public educational efforts of the Chicago Plan Commission, but he said in 1913, when the national conference was held in the Illinois metropolis, that he regarded the Burnham plan as a study for a city plan rather than as the authoritative document the commission took it to be.[77] The commission, he indicated, should perfect the plan by revising it again and again, continually broadening its scope and taking into consideration matters overlooked by Burnham and his cronies in the Commercial Club.

Looking ahead, Olmsted dared to dream of a time, perhaps fifty years in the future, when every well-conducted American city would have a "complex but humdrum human mechanism" guiding its growth and development—a city planning office with a well-organized staff.[78] This office, "fully established in the framework of municipal government, accepted and supported by public opinion as firmly as the public school system or the fire department," would have the defects as well as the advantages of any agency in a bureaucracy, though Olmsted clearly believed the advantages would outweigh the defects.[79] The staff would be permanently and exclusively dedicated to the job of recording, indexing, and interpreting the city survey and the city plan, adjusting conflicting or inconsistent proposals to harmonize with the plan, discovering the deficiencies of the scheme, and amending it as directed by "the deliberate authority in control of the office."[80]

Whether the authority controlling the staff was an individual official, a commission of citizens, an ex officio board composed of department heads, or some combination of citizens and department heads seemed to him immaterial for the time being.[81] The important thing was that the steering group's early educational efforts should be directed as much to city officials as to the public, so that when the propaganda phase of planning activity was over, there would be in city government many permanent officials who believed in long-range planning and would be willing to cooperate with the planning staff, regardless of the composition of the planning board.

Mayor William A. Magee of Pittsburgh agreed with Olmsted that the planning commission "must have the respect, and become essentially a part, of the bureaucracy."[82] Magee suggested having the commission assign to appropriate departments various elements of the city plan. The street department, for instance, would address itself to perfecting a scheme for a comprehensive thoroughfare system; the park department would prepare proposals for extending the park system; and so forth. The planning staff, providing the larger view, would then attempt to integrate these preliminary schemes in a comprehensive plan, consulting with the department heads about adjustments to be made in each element to harmonize it with an overall concept.

The mayor expressed the desire of a growing number of elected officials to give the planning commission and its staff a strategic position in municipal government. He wished, moreover, to make the planning group influential not only with other municipal departments but also with public service corporations and volunteer organizations. The commission, in short, should become "a grand clearing-house of effort" and "set the whole city to planning."[83]

Those who were struggling to institutionalize city planning doubtless heard Olmsted and Magee with mixed emotions. The goals they set forth—the well-organized staff, the catalytic agency inspiring the entire community to plan for a better future—seemed altogether desirable but well-nigh unattainable, or at least out of reach for a long time to come. Only a few states had authorized cities to appoint planning commissions, and most of the commissions thus far created did not even have appropriations to employ consulting architects, landscape architects, or engineers to prepare a preliminary city plan. The permanent staff was, however, a necessity if any commission was to discharge its advisory role effectively, reviewing all proposals affecting the physical environment and giving advice to the city council, operating departments, and private companies and agencies on the basis of a long-term plan.

A model enabling act submitted at the 1913 conference by the committee on legislation authorized the creation of "an additional executive department in the government of cities . . . to be known as the Department of City Planning." To staff the department, the planning commission was empowered to employ "engineers and other persons." Presumably on the advice of its employees the commission could make "any changes in the city plan . . . deemed advisable," could offer recommendations to the council concerning public features of the city, and could also advise "any public authorities . . . corporations, or individuals . . . with reference to the location of any buildings, structures, or works to be erected or constructed by them."[84]

The model act suggested only an advisory function for the planning commission, but men such as Dr. Matthew D. Mann, of Buffalo, believed that the commission, as guardian of the city plan, should have power to veto proposals not in harmony with it. He was willing to let the veto be overridden, but only by a two-thirds majority of the city council. There were others who, in their eagerness to make planning effective, wished to submit the city plan to a referendum, as had been done in Seattle, and if the plan were approved by the voters, to make adherence to the plan obligatory on both public and private interests. On this issue of the degree of authority to be accorded the commission and the plan there was to be disagreement for many years, as on many other matters, including the fundamental question whether states should make city planning mandatory for all municipal governments.

A questionnaire circulated to 246 individuals and city planning commissions before the seventh national conference was held in Detroit in 1915 elicited eighty responses and revealed some crystallization of opinion concerning the basic issues troubling the planning movement. Two-thirds of the respondents favored requiring cities to plan. The overwhelming majority wished to arm the planning commission with a veto yet not to make the rejection difficult for the city council to override.

Replies to questions about the planning commission itself disclosed that the old City Beautiful image of the commission as a civic art jury was still strong, notwithstanding the trend toward the practical and functional. Three out of every seven respondents approved giving the commission the power to review the design of public buildings and ornamental features of the city.

The increasing emphasis on the need for an Americanized form of districting or zoning, however, had convinced most of those answering the questionnaire that zoning for purposes of regulating the height, area, and use of buildings should be included as an element of the general plan, together with schemes for the street system, the park and playground system, the transit system, rail and water terminals, grouping of public buildings, and markets. No city had yet adopted a comprehensive zoning ordinance of the type suggested in the questionnaire, but already city planners thought of zoning as the equivalent of a scheme of land uses, thereby confusing precise, legally enforceable regulations under the police power with an element of the plan which, if it shared the characteristics of other parts of the plan, would show not so much presently permitted uses as future desirable allocations of the land resources of the city. This failure to distinguish clearly between the legally sanctioned use and the proposed or eventually desirable use was to cause endless difficulty for planning commissions for the next thirty years, but apparently no planner in 1915 realized the mistake being made in identifying an administrative device as a part of the plan itself.

The conflicting ideas of the purposes of planning and the most effective way to organize the planning function expressed by planning commissioners and practitioners tended to bewilder persons outside the planning movement. Such persons had little knowledge of city planning in the first place, and the divergent views they overheard or read from time to time perhaps added to their perplexity. This lamentable state of affairs became evident when representatives of fourteen professional and semiofficial organizations held a special meeting at the 1915 conference. "The delegates were rather afraid that comparatively few of their fellow members had any clear conception of what city planning meant or what local city planning bodies were really trying to do," George B. Ford's report of the meeting stated.[85] Yet these delegates were spokesmen of the very groups planners might expect to be most knowledgeable about their activities and aims: the Conference of American Mayors, the National Municipal League, the National Housing Association, the American Society of Park Superintendents, the American Society of Municipal Improvement, the National Association of Builders Exchanges, the professional engineering societies, the American Society of Landscape Architects, the American Federation of Arts, and several others. If such groups confessed ignorance of city planning and lack of understanding of the programs of local planning commissions, then talk of well-organized staffs, adequate budgetary appropriations for planning, and an enhanced status for the planning commission as an overall coordinating agency in the city hall was not only premature but also rather unrealistic. The formidable work of informing the public, and particularly civic leaders, city officials, and professional groups, needed to be undertaken on a larger scale than ever before. Concurrently the leaders of the planning movement needed to sharpen their own concepts, achieve greater agreement among themselves, and more skillfully interpret their ideas to the American people. The planning movement was still only a ripple in the broad stream of American urban development.

Efforts to Educate the Public

"There is an understanding between the city authorities and the Commission that no major public works not included in the Plan of Chicago shall be initiated by the city without having first referred the same to the Plan Commission," Walter D. Moody wrote in *The City Plan,* a new quarterly of the National Conference on City Planning published in March, 1915. "Under this established policy, scarcely a month passes that some Council committee or city department does not invoke the advice and assistance of the Commission."[86]

In striving to educate the public about the importance of city planning and the place it should hold in city government, the leaders of the city planning movement could find no better example of rapport between a planning commission and city officials than that which Chicago provided. The Chicago Plan Commission might have a less than dynamic conception of the city plan, but at least this agency had won respect for its endeavors and was earnestly trying to relate new proposals to the plan it was carrying out. If the leaders of the planning movement, as a result of their renewed educational efforts, could stimulate other cities to prepare general plans and institute the regular referral process followed in Chicago, there might be greater hope for systematic improvement of American cities. One of the goals of the public informational program was abundantly clear.

The National Municipal League, one of the fourteen organizations cooperating with the National Conference on City Planning in increasing public understanding of planning, promulgated a model city charter in 1916 with a planning provision designed to formalize the relationship Moody described as an "understanding" or "established policy." This provision stated that "all acts of the council or of any other branch of the city government affecting the city plan shall be submitted to the [planning] board for report and recommendations."[87] In another section the provision went even further by stating that no action by the council on any matter affecting the plan "shall be legal or binding until it has been referred to the board and until the recommendations of the board thereon have been accepted or rejected by the council."[88]

In an earlier model city charter the League had included no provision for exercise of the planning function. The four sections suggesting creation of a city planning board with authority to review all projects for their conformity with the city plan therefore indicated that this influential private organization had concluded that municipalities could no longer be regarded as well governed unless they undertook long-range planning.

Additional proof of the League's desire to aid planners in their educational program was a volume entitled *City Planning,* published as one of a series having to do with the problems of organization and administration in cities. Edited by John Nolen, who identified himself on the title page as a Fellow of the American Society of Landscape Architects, the book contained an introduction by Olmsted and seventeen papers about "the essential elements of a city plan" by such well-known authorities as Edward H. Bennett, J. Horace McFarland, E. P. Goodrich, George B. Ford and his brother James, Flavel Shurtleff and his distant cousin Arthur A. Shurtleff, and Charles M. Robinson, not to mention Frank Backus Williams, Arthur C. Comey, and others who were just becoming prominent in the planning field. A foreword by Clinton Rogers Woodruff, general editor of the League's governmental series, assured readers that these men *were* the city planning movement in America.

The contents clearly indicated the broadening scope of city planning. Besides papers about streets, public buildings, recreation facilities, and transportation, there were chapters discussing the subdivision of land, public control of private real estate, neighborhood centers, water supply, navigable waters, residential and industrial decentralization, fundamental data for city planning work, methods of financing improvements contemplated in the city plan, and city planning legislation. Bibliographies at the end of each paper and a general bibliography at the end of the book revealed what a wealth of books and articles about city planning had appeared since Benjamin Marsh issued his paperback *Introduction to City Planning* in 1909. Most of these publications, however, had not come to the attention of the general reader, as planners hoped this volume would.

With a few exceptions, the contributors to the book wrote of the city as a complex organism whose parts, like those of man or an animal, functioned interdependently, but the analogy to a living creature was not apt because the authors realized that human decisions affect the growth and development of the city and that the problem of the city planner is to discover how to make the most intelligent decisions. "We are learning," Olmsted explained, "how . . . anything we decide to do or leave undone may have important and inevitable consequences wholly foreign to the motive immediately controlling the decision, but seriously affecting the welfare of the future city; and with our recognition of this is a growing sense of social responsibility for estimating these remoter consequences and giving them due weight in reaching every decision."[89]

Olmsted, a sane man, realized that the planner's quest for data—and for certainty—could become a mania. "He relies upon his common sense to fix an arbitrary limit upon the factors which he will take the time to weigh before forming his judgment and proceeding to action in any particular case" Olmsted stated.[90] But could the common sense of a man, or a group of men, become the basis of a "science" of city planning? The question evidently did not trouble Olmsted, who had always been sure that planning must be as much an art as a science.

City Planning contained no chapter presenting a philosophy or theory of planning. The papers were wholly practical, summarizing what each author had learned from his own experience and that of others to be useful and progressive. In all but two or three the writers developed the idea that the city plan, like the city itself, must be modified from time to time. The volume reflected the aspirations of the emerging planning profession and highlighted the problems with which it was wrestling, particularly the legal and financial problems involving interpretation of the federal and state constitutional protections of private property. The perceptive reader perhaps could sense the mounting pressure for greater public control of suburban development, housing, properties fronting on heavily traveled streets, and areas especially desirable for residential or industrial purposes.

Nelson P. Lewis, Chief Engineer of the Board of Estimate and Apportionment of New York City, was the author of another noteworthy volume on city planning published in 1916. He entitled it *The Planning of the Modern City* and dedicated it to his fellow municipal engineers, "the first men on the ground in city planning as in city building, in the hope that it may help them to realize their responsibilities and opportunities in determining the manner in which our cities will develop."[91]

Lewis explained in his introduction that his book was "frankly written with the idea that the fundamental problems of city planning are, and from their very nature must be, engineering problems."[92] Since he was no less convinced than Olmsted, Nolen, and the architect-planners that the concern of city planning was the physical city, his professional bias readily enabled him to restrict his definition of the "real plan" to four controlling elements—the transportation system, the street system, the park and recreation facilities, and the location of public buildings – and to exclude broader considerations, though he was aware of other views:

> There are many who believe that the chief purposes of city planning are social, that the problems of housing, the provision of recreation and amusement for the people, the control and even the ownership and operation of all public utilities, the establishment and conduct of public markets, the collection and disposal of wastes, the protection of public health, the building of hospitals, the care of paupers, criminals and the insane, and all of the other activities of the modern city are all a part of city planning. All of these, however, are matters of administration rather than of planning in the sense that it will be considered in this volume. . . .[93]

His chief emphasis, he stated, would be placed "upon the initial work of planning which will make all of these [other matters] easier of attainment."[94] Lewis thus perhaps encouraged a profession already inclined to regard city planning as chiefly a technical problem to continue thinking of it somewhat narrowly, though his obvious intention was to provide his brother engineers the larger reference necessary to insure the enduring social utility of their often costly and ambitious projects.

Certainly, Lewis made no appeal to the vanity of his professional colleagues. "The creation of a proper plan," he said, "will require years of patient work, and the men who do it will be forgotten before it is finally carried out. It is no one-man job and it is never actually finished. However carefully and skillfully the first plan may have been made, unforeseen changes will take place, new methods of transportation will be developed, new inventions will powerfully affect the social life of the community, and the plan, where still susceptible of change, must be modified to meet

40. Nelson P. Lewis
(Olin Library, Cornell University)

these changed conditions." Comprehensive city planning should therefore be entrusted to a regularly employed technical staff including men familiar with the history and traditions of the community and capable of adapting the old to the new without destroying it. "The work should be directed by men who do not think the exercise of imagination an engineering crime; men who are enthusiasts without being doctrinaires; men who are content to do their work well without hope of popular applause. . . ."[95]

Lewis believed that far too much of city planning was merely the correction of past mistakes and that too little attention was being given to planning for future growth, especially in the environs of cities. He doubted, however, whether cities alone could exercise the sort of control needed to insure intelligent planning in areas including several municipalities and towns. "It [areawide planning] must be undertaken by the state," he wrote, "either through the medium of state laws or by the creation of metropolitan planning boards or commissions whose jurisdiction shall extend over large areas, including a group of populous communities and the intervening districts. . . ."[96] Lewis realized, though, that such boards or commissions would have no authority to impose restrictions on private property. He failed to point out that they would also be powerless to require municipalities to construct their public improvements in accordance with an areawide general plan. Without attempting to think out the problems of metropolitan planning in detail, he suggested that the state itself could play a part in shaping the development of metropolitan regions by designating widths and setbacks of main highways and carefully selecting sites for state institutions. Impressed by the land policies of German cities, he thought that the purely speculative, haphazard expansion of American cities could be prevented by the adoption of a "happy mean" between full municipal ownership and unregulated private action "which will give sufficient opportunity for private enterprise and yet will insure to the city, or to all the people of the city, a share in the values created by their presence and their labor."[97] Lewis did not even hint what the happy mean might be. Rich in factual information, his book again and again raised formidable issues without proposing solutions.

Not to be overlooked as an educational undertaking complementing Lewis's book and the volume edited by Nolen was a large exhibition of American and foreign city planning circulated by the American City Bureau. After thousands of persons in New York and Jersey City had seen this visual presentation, Charles Henry Cheney, a California architect, had it shipped across the continent in 1914 for showing in San Francisco, Oakland, and Los Angeles. Two years later it was being shown in Indiana cities in an effort to mobilize citizen support for legislation authorizing municipalities to engage in city planning, because one of the results achieved by Cheney in bringing the exhibition to the Pacific Coast had been the enactment in 1915 of a measure permitting all California cities to appoint city planning commissions, develop long-term plans, and regulate the subdivision of land. Civic groups in Indiana failed early in 1917 to obtain legislation similar to that passed in California but laid a foundation for later success. Indiana adopted enabling legislation in 1921.

The City as a State and National Problem

The earnest educational and informational activities of city planners seemed to George Hooker, secretary of the Chicago City Club, to be based on the assumption that urban problems required mainly local action, whereas he thought of them as national problems demanding the attention of the federal government. Looking about the world, he saw other countries actively promoting city planning, Germany fostering it as a national movement, England furthering it by passage of the Town Planning Act of 1909, Canada encouraging it by employing Thomas Adams, past president of the Town Planning Institute of Great Britian, as town planning advisor to the Commission of Conservation, and India recognizing its importance by summoning Professor Patrick Geddes to advise the government what should be done to plan better cities. Yet in the United States the national government was doing little or nothing to aid cities in their long-term development.

At the eighth national conference on city planning, in 1916, Hooker called for a federal commission of inquiry to do at least two things: suggest a desirable distribution of city planning powers among the local, state, and federal governments; and investigate and report on "some of the difficult and important technical and social questions which are involved in the city planning problem, but which are too intricate, difficult and far-reaching for the resources of individual experts or indeed of individual cities or states."[98] For example, were the centralizing tendencies that had demanded enormous investments in transit and office buildings in accord with the demands of the economic and social needs, or were radical modifications in the distribution of cities and their internal structure to be expected and planned for? Hooker suggested that "the problem of transportation in relation to city structure on the one hand and national economy on the other" was in urgent need of thorough scientific analysis.[99]

Some of the planners listening to Hooker were reminded of a similar proposal made in 1911 by attorney Philip Kates, of Tulsa, Oklahoma, for a federally supported Municipal Commission charged with the duty of compiling a general survey of the working and living conditions of city dwellers, revealing the relation of the industrial system to the "city problem," and disseminating knowledge of the operation of various theories of municipal government.[100] Kates, too, had regarded the city problem as a national problem and had stated some time later in an article in the *American City* that "If we would solve the problem for the future, the Federal Government must take up the work."[101]

Thomas Adams, a guest at the conference at which Hooker spoke, drew upon his British and Canadian experience to suggest an answer to one of the large questions the Midwesterner wanted an expert commission to investigate. Both state planning agencies and a federal bureau of planning, attached to a general bureau of municipal government, would be desirable, Adams said. The state agencies would be channels through which extensive information about public health, city and state planning, highways, housing and local improvements, municipal finance, municipal administration, unemployment, public utilities, water supply, sewerage, and the extension of city boundaries would be made available from the national bureau. Adams envisaged the state agencies as departments of municipal affairs, initially providing model ordinances, rules of procedure, and forms of municipal accounts for adoption by cities and later reviewing all municipal legislation before its enactment. He realized that his decidedly British proposals would raise the cry of interference with local home rule, but he stoutly defended them. "The present tendency to look to 'local home rule' as the cure for all the evil of unnecessary and unintelligent state interference with city government is a dangerous one," he cautioned; "it will inevitably succeed in lessening the power of the city in the state, as well as the state in the city. Cooperation between the state and city authorities under expert guidance in both cases, is the proper solution of the problem."[102]

John Nolen agreed on the need for a state planning board or department of municipal affairs, but only as an advisory agency attempting to encourage uniformly good city planning and adequate financing of public improvements:

> It would be a mistake not to recognize the objection that prevails just now on the part of those who advocate more home rule for cities, to state boards and commissions, even of an advisory nature. But, after all, the purpose of such a state board as is here suggested is not to check or limit local government, but to offer it aid and to help it to be efficient and economical. It should be recognized, however, that even with such a state board or department, good city planning could still depend largely upon the efficiency of the city government and the successful organization and utilization of the best forces of the community, both public and private.[103]

Nolen did not suggest and Adams only hinted that there was need for an altogether different kind of state planning agency—one which would prepare a plan showing areas suited for various types of agriculture and for industry, commerce, and residential development; a state park system; a state highway system related to rail and water transportation facilities; a scheme for the development and control of water resources; and sites for all state institutions. Arthur C. Comey, a member of the only state planning agency in the entire United States, the Massachusetts Homestead Commission, had proposed such a state plan in the first issue of the quarterly *The City Plan* in 1915, but he was as much ahead of the times in proposing a state plan to serve as a broad guide for the planning of individual cities and towns as Hooker, Adams, and Nolen were in advocating advisory federal and state planning agencies.

Zoning Without General Planning

While the leaders of the city planning movement were endeavoring to extend a broad knowledge of the purposes and principles of city planning to the American public, popular interest began to focus on one phase of city planning—zoning to protect single-family residential areas from invasion by factories, stores, and apartment houses. In response to the pleas of homeowners and real estate men, the legislatures of Wisconsin, Minnesota, and Illinois in 1913 empowered cities of certain classes to establish residential districts from which manufacturing and commercial establishments would be banned. As the legislation made no requirement that districting be preceded by the preparation of a city plan, cities in the first two of these states established residential zones upon petition of property owners. The governor of Illinois, however, vetoed the enabling act in his state upon advice of the attorney general, who held that residential zoning excluding other classes of buildings would be unconstitutional. In the state of New York the cities of Syracuse and Utica acted under authority of a Housing Law for Second Class Cities, enacted in 1913, to establish "residence districts" in which buildings other than single- or two-family dwellings were prohibited. Like similar laws in other states, the statute made no reference to a general plan and permitted city councils to designate residence districts no larger than one side of a city block.

To Frank Backus Williams, who had studied at the New York School of Philanthropy before deciding to specialize in the legal aspects of city planning, the whole trend toward the imposition of controls before any kind of overall plan had been prepared seemed deplorable. "So far," he said at the 1914 national conference on city planning, "what we have done along districting lines has been, practically, housing without city planning instead of housing as an element of city planning, so little has districting been a part of the planning of the city as a whole, so little has it been used to aid in the solution of more general city problems."[104]

Alfred Bettman, a Cincinnati lawyer, had even more cogent objections to zoning regulations unsupported by city planning considerations. "In the present stage of constitutional law in the United States," he told delegates to the 1914 conference, "it is . . . necessary to show that the particular residential-district ordinance or statute under discussion has behind it a motive other than an aesthetic motive, has a motive related to safety or comfort or order or health." It would therefore be wise, he suggested, to precede the enactment of zoning regulations by "some scientific study of the city's plan, so that the residential-district ordinance may bear a relation to the plan of the city, and the plan should be devised with a view to the health or the comfort or the safety of the people of the city."[105] For example, the promoters of a residential-district ordinance should first have some leading physicians make a study of the effect of noise upon the nervous system of human beings; and then, if the study showed that reducing "noises and turmoil and hurly-burly" tended to lessen nervous diseases in the city, there should be a systematic study of the distribution of residential and industrial districts which would, by directing the course of vehicular and pedestrian traffic, protect the residential districts from noise.[106] No court, Bettman contended, could then say that the ordinance was passed solely for the promotion of aesthetic satisfactions. Constitutionality, in short, probably depended, ultimately, upon comprehensive planning for the promotion of the common health, safety, and welfare, or so Bettman thought—and such was to be his reasoning in his famous defense of the zoning ordinance of the Village of Euclid, Ohio, a dozen years later.

But the city which gave the greatest stimulus to city-wide or comprehensive zoning in the United States—New York City—failed to proceed from scientific investigation to "a carefully wrought plan for the promotion of the health, safety, convenience, and welfare of the whole community"[107] and finally to the adoption of zoning regulations related thereto because the need to control the building of skyscrapers and halt the movement of factories into high-class retail areas seemed altogether more imperative than the need for a city plan. As early as 1911 the Commission on Congestion of Population struck the note of urgency. This body, which Mayor Gaynor had appointed in 1910 at the entreaty of Benjamin Marsh and his associates, brought out a voluminous report citing towering office buildings as breeders of congestion and traffic problems. The commission's committee on streets and highways recommended that height restrictions be imposed at once throughout the metropolis, even before a general plan of the city could be formulated, although the committee also advocated immediate preparation of such a plan. Not until almost three and a half years later, however, did the powerful Board of Estimate and Apportionment appoint a Committee on the City Plan, and by then the drive for curbs on skyscrapers had gathered so much momentum that the committee was merely another group supporting the demand for restrictions. Indeed, its chairman, George McAneny, had carried forward the movement for height limitations by pressing the Board of Estimate to create a Committee on the Height, Size, and Arrangement of

Buildings. The committee, in turn, appointed an advisory Heights of Buildings Commission, and from this group, headed by attorney Edward M. Bassett, formerly Public Service Commissioner, came the proposal in 1913 that the entire city be districted or zoned. A new body, the Commission on Building Districts and Restrictions, was therefore appointed, with Robert H. Whitten, the secretary of the Committee on City Plan, serving as secretary and George B. Ford as consultant.

While these men and a large staff were at work on overall zoning regulations, one segment of the business community of New York City experienced a crisis illustrating in intense form the distress felt by property owners when economic activities shifted unpredictably and migrating factories, garages, and other noisy establishments blighted previously stable areas. Early in the century garment factories and warehouses had begun invading Fifth Avenue. Exclusive department stores and shops had then moved farther up the avenue, only to find the manufacturing establishments following them, depreciating property values and causing traffic problems by the movement of their trucks. The loud complaints of the retailers contributed to the demand for zoning but did not stop the incursions of the manufacturers. Finally, several months before Bassett and his colleagues finished their labors, the embattled merchants took full-page advertisements in the daily newspapers threatening to boycott any garment manufacturers who did not remove their plants from an area extending from Thirty-third to Fifty-ninth Streets and from Third Avenue to Seventh Avenue by February 1, 1917.

"Shall We Save New York?" the advertisements asked. "Shall we save New York from what? Shall we save it from unnatural and unnecessary crowding, from depopulated sections, from being a city unbeautiful, from high rents, from excessive and illy distributed taxation? We can save it from all of these, so far at least as they are caused by one specified industrial evil—the erection of factories in the residential and famous retail section." The text explained that "the lower wholesale and retail districts are deserted, and there is now enough vacant space to accommodate many times over the manufacturing plants of the city. If new modern factory buildings are required, why not encourage the erection of such structures in that section instead of erecting factory buildings in the midst of our homes and fine retail sections?"[108]

The advertisements sought to convince all citizens that the plight of the large department stores and high-class shops was also their own problem. "Every man in the city pays taxes either as owner or tenant," the copy stated. "The wide area of vacant or depreciated property in the lower middle part of town means reduced taxes, leaving a deficit made up by extra assessment on other sections. Taxes have grown to startling figures and this affects all interests."

To check the "impending menace to all interests" and to "prevent a destruction similar to that which has occurred below Twenty-third Street," the advertisements asked the cooperation not only of the various garment manufacturers and unions but also of "every financial interest" and "every man who owns a home or rents an apartment."

Long before this combined ultimatum and request for cooperation appeared, the major real estate concerns, life insurance, title and trust companies, savings banks, and commercial and civic associations were, however, already allied with the beleaguered mercantile establishments. Bassett and his zoning team produced their intricate regulations in an atmosphere dominated by the financial and commercial interests of the city. Significantly, Lawrence Veiller refused to sign the final report of the special Commission on Building Districts and Restrictions because he thought its recommendations were too favorable to these interests. Many of his fellow housing reformers, social workers, civic organizations interested in public health and sanitation, and similar groups requested more stringent restrictions than those proposed but had to be content with what the business community wanted. The large corporations and financial interests, Bassett said, urged "that we use the greatest speed to put these restrictions into force, so that localities shall not be invaded with unsuitable uses before the law can go into effect."[109] Though he and his associates were two years evolving their overall scheme (after the state legislature amended the city charter in 1914 to permit the Board of Estimate to zone the city), and though "at least 150 public hearings or conferences of a formal character" were held while the work was in progress, the sense of pressure and crisis and expedient compromise pervaded the effort.[110]

For Bassett there was, moreover, one overriding consideration tending at all times to make his handiwork extremely conservative: that everything proposed should be able to withstand legal attacks on its constitutionality. Having determined to justify zoning as regulation in the public interest under the police power of the state and to reject the view that restrictions must be regarded as a taking of property rights requiring invocation of the power of eminent domain and the payment of compensation, Bassett designed every restriction to meet the narrowest and most legalistic interpretation of the phrases "public welfare" and "public health, safety, morals, and convenience." To his credit, the zoning resolution adopted by the Board of Estimate in July, 1916, proved invulnerable in every court test, but its provisions lacked the broader justification of farsighted planning to meet new and unforeseen conditions. Bassett was inclined to give legal sanction to the status quo, to prevent only gross disorder, and to ignore long-term changes that might be socially desirable. "We have gone at it block by block and in some cases a block will constitute a [zoning] district," he declared, indicating that the land uses and building heights already prevailing in various parts of the city were usually accepted and "frozen" by the zoning maps he and his colleagues prepared.[111]

The zoning resolution provided for three categories of use districts— residential, commercial, and unrestricted; for five kinds of height districts, in which building heights were limited in proportion to the width of the adjoining street; and for five kinds of area districts, regulating the size of yards and courts. The height and area, or bulk, regulations introduced a new concept in zoning that was a logical response to the need to restrict the intense scramble for light and air by recourse to height. The combination of bulk with use regulations throughout an entire city was, of course, unprecedented, as was the use of maps to designate the locations and limits of districts. The various types of use, height, and area restrictions were combined in so many ways, however, that the zoning resolution was extremely confusing, and some of the possible combinations were, as one authority has remarked, obviously absurd.[112] Strangest of all were the provisions dictating the shape and design of structures in the high-bulk areas, which forced architects to fit the building mass into an "envelope" resembling a Babylonian ziggurat, with the upper stories progressively set back above a certain height to allow sunlight to penetrate to the street. These architectural constraints, in large measure proposed by Ford, had regard neither for economy of construction nor for the developer's specific needs for his site and building. Frank Backus Williams, who worked closely with Bassett in drafting the text of the zoning resolution, foresaw, in fact, that almost none of the regulations pertaining to tall structures would be truly effective. On the eve of the adoption of the resolution by the Board of Estimate he wrote, "The result of our districting regulations, necessarily based on present conditions, allow in future buildings such extremes of height and area of buildings in proportion to the lots they are to occupy, and an amount of confusion of uses and types of buildings, as to permit a regrettable increase of congestion and maladjustment."[113]

Bassett and his associates assured some protection to residential and commercial areas, but in these areas also they were inhibited by existing conditions. Approximately two-fifths of Manhattan Island and almost two-thirds of the whole city were set aside for strictly residential use, but as Williams pointed out, "Our districting is altogether too much of the congested tenement-house type. If conditions here have made this a necessity for us, conditions do not necessitate it elsewhere."[114] The main thoroughfares, the transit streets, and all other streets that, as Ford said, might be appropriately used for stores or show rooms were zoned for business.[115] In the business districts any residential use was allowed

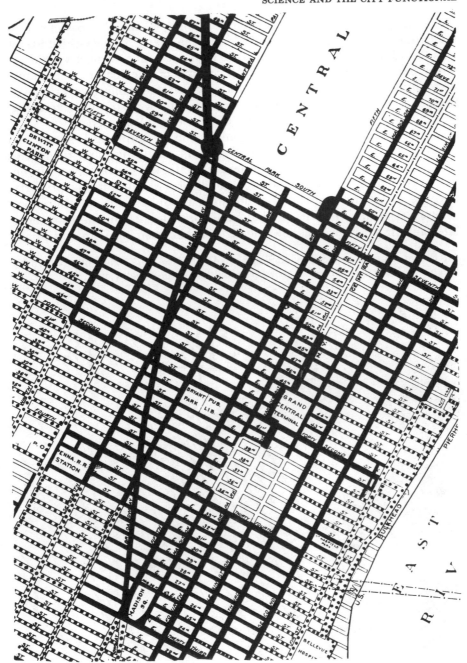

41. New York zoning plan of 1916, showing use zones in Manhattan south of Central Park: streets in black zoned for residence and business uses; streets in white restricted to residential use; streets marked by dots unrestricted in use and even a certain small proportion of "unobjectionable" types of manufacturing. All the central part of Manhattan above Twenty-third Street was forbidden to factories, though the law, not being retroactive, did not affect existing factory lofts. The ultimatum of the leading merchants accomplished what the zoning resolution could not: it effectively removed most of them. In the unrestricted districts any kind of manufacturing, warehousing operation, or open use of land was authorized.

Meticulous as the staff of the Commission on Building Districts and Restrictions was in investigating "existing conditions and tendencies with regard to all property and improvements, the character and intensity of their use, all natural physical conditions as they affected property, and the distribution of the use and effect of public utilities," the zoning scheme resulting from its prodigious labors was not, in the best sense, city planning, as Ford acknowledged.[116] "It has been borne in continually

42. Height restrictions in central Manhattan under the New York zoning plan of 1916: the height limitation in each zone is shown as a multiple of the street width

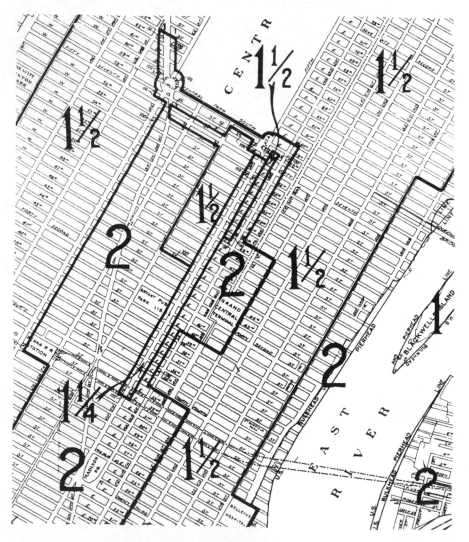

43. Setback architecture resulting from the 1916 zoning resolution, New York City; looking northeast from the Chrysler Building at Lexington Avenue and Forty-second Street in 1932 *(Gottscho-Schleisner, Inc.)*

upon the Commission [on Building Districts and Restrictions] that districting without comprehensive city planning left the job only half done and that as various new streets or parks were laid out, or new transit lines opened up, or terminal features planned, they would change the [zoning] districts in their neighborhoods. It was a matter of great regret that it was not feasible in this case to carry on both the general planning and districting at the same time."[117]

Under pretense of regulation the staff of the Commission on Building Districts and Restrictions devised a scheme little better than the piecemeal districting previously adopted by other cities. In the name of constitutionality it permitted the extension of conditions which actually provided little more protection than a nuisance ordinance. In many ways the zoning resolution was deceptive, sanctioning excessive overcrowding and permitting in commercial and unrestricted zones the very mixture of uses that had aroused the cry for regulation. Apparently no one attempted to determine what the total population of the city might be at various times in the future and to indicate some realistic distribution, at reasonable and desirable densities, throughout five boroughs. Apparently no one even calculated how many acres of land or millions of square feet of floor space might be required to accommodate the economic activities of the metropolis if it doubled or tripled in population. Bassett's preoccupation with property rights as he understood them led to a zoning scheme under which a population as great as that of the whole United States in 1900 could be lodged in New York City. As for work space, the resolution allowed enough for more than 300,000,000 employees inside the city limits. The wonder is that no one ever tried to overturn the resolution on the simple ground that it was absurd.

Both Ford and Williams were apprehensive lest other cities take it as a model. "Other cities can do better than we, and will be most culpable if they fail to do so," Williams warned.[118] And Ford cautioned, "It would be most unfortunate if the law were applied, as it stands, to other cities, for it is full of unduly liberal provisions in the way of height and size that tend strongly to defeat the object of the law but which were necessitated by the exceptional economic conditions of New York."[119] But citizens and officials of other cities, perhaps not realizing that the very absurdity of the resolution facilitated its adoption and acceptance as a pioneering experiment, disregarded the admonitions of some of its authors, especially since the legal underpinning withstood the onslaughts of opponents and impressed city officials, homeowners, and real estate men throughout the land. In fact, the New York zoning resolution was in some respects a setback to the city planning movement because it contributed to the widespread practice of zoning before planning and, in many cities, to the acceptance of zoning as a substitute for long-term planning. In the wake of this constitutionally defensible but socially defective regulatory instru-ment came all those equally unrealistic zoning ordinances spawned by city attorneys, engineers, realtors-turned-planning-commissioners, and planning consultants themselves in the 1920s and 1930s. The regulations became more varied, the legal substantiation more precise, but with few exceptions the allocations of the land resources of cities under these enactments were preposterous, often providing for population densities and uses beyond any reasonable prospect of growth. Most cities also con-tinued the New York practice of permitting so-called lesser economic land uses, such as residential developments, in zones of higher economic use, such as commercial and industrial districts, thereby perpetuating many of the frictions of earlier periods.

Berkeley, California, however, was an exception. Charles H. Cheney, consultant to the Civic Art Commission (which later changed its name to the City Planning Commission), reported at the ninth national confer-ence on city planning in 1917 that the Berkeley zoning ordinance sought to protect industry from residences as well as residences from industry. "Some manufacturers said to us," Cheney reported, " 'Why, if the city keeps factories out of residence districts, should not residences be kept out of factory districts? We find in most cities the most abject poverty and the worst tenements and bad housing conditions in the factory neigh-borhoods. When we want heavy traffic pavement for heavy hauling with spur tracks in the sidewalk areas, these . . . home owners appear before the City Council and holler so loud that the improvements are held up. So we have dejected housing and hampered industry.' "[120] In drafting the

44. Charles H. Cheney
(Warren Cheney)

zoning ordinance for Berkeley, Cheney therefore provided that no new residences might be constructed in factory districts.

Cheney's ordinance illustrated the beginnings of another trend in zoning—the rigid segregation of uses. The Berkeley ordinance provided for twenty-seven classes of districts, some of which Cheney thought might never actually be established. It authorized, for example, one type of district for single-family residences, another for two-family dwellings, and still others for group houses and for apartment houses. The intent to protect the single-family and duplex structures from being overshadowed by bulky apartment houses may have been admirable, but by its inflexibility the ordinance precluded the possibility of interesting combinations of dwelling types under appropriate controls. This particular kind of zoning orthodoxy, with its insistence on strict compartmentalization of uses, not only tended to make some residential areas monotonous; in many instances it also made cities less convenient by unduly separating services from residential areas. In 1916 and 1917, as later, there was nevertheless considerable demand by citizens for uncompromising segregation of residential development from other land uses.

Thomas Adams proposed at the 1917 conference that cities should make provision in their regulatory laws for agricultural as well as residential and industrial zones. Noting that suburban centers were beginning to spring up three, four, and five miles from the original business districts of urban areas of 800,000 or more, as in the St. Louis metropolitan area, he foresaw the possibility that in a good many cities much of the anticipated congestion and the expected increase in land values in central districts might never materialize. The new trend suggested to him that cities only half the size of St. Louis should maintain open land at the periphery and direct further growth to new towns beyond the greenbelt. Adams realized, however, that if land were to be zoned against any form of building development, the system of taxation would require adjustment to the use to which the land was actually put. Otherwise, agricultural zones might be taxed as potential urban land and forced onto the market even though the owners might prefer to continue using their holdings as estates or farms.

Adams's perception of problems that would trouble cities in the future and of the need for comprehensive urban land and development policy marked him as a much more farsighted and creative planner than some of the men who produced the New York zoning resolution. But even those planners who were least observant of new trends and least imaginative in foreseeing the opportunities of the future had by now achieved a certain public recognition as "experts," thanks to the kinds of legal and technical problems raised by zoning ordinances, even those of the piecemeal variety, and by the increasing volume of traffic on city streets. It was therefore perhaps not surprising that at the 1917 conference, in which Adams was but one of several speakers calling for metropolitan planning and foreshadowing a broader sphere of activity for planners, Frederick Law Olmsted should raise the issue of distinguishing the specialist in city planning from members of other professions, and that his associates in developing the city planning movement should agree that as a group they now possessed expertise warranting separate status.

Other planners may not have known, however, how Olmsted happened to broach the subject of forming a new professional organization.

The Birth of a Professional Institute

On the train taking them to Kansas City for the national meeting, Olmsted and Flavel Shurtleff fell into conversation about their feeling that the annual conclave was somehow not meeting the needs of the men regularly engaged in city planning. Held in a different city each year, the conference had brought planning directly and indirectly to the attention of thousands of citizens, but it no longer afforded those who were giving their full time to the practice of city planning sufficient opportunity to discuss technical problems and to learn from one another. Presently the two were selecting the name of a new fellowship that would meet several times a year for the presentation of carefully prepared papers on timely subjects, followed by intensive discussion and criticism. It would be called the American City Planning Institute (now the American Institute of Planners). To strengthen the national conference on city planning, the new institute would hold one meeting each year at the time of the conference. But just what the qualifications for membership should be, Olmsted and Shurtleff could not then decide.

With the approval of participants in the Kansas City conference, Olmsted and Shurtleff went about forming the new institute in the summer and fall of 1917. They finally determined that everyone asked to become a member should have at least two years of experience in some form of city planning activity. Shurtleff then wrote letters asking those chosen for membership for $10 in annual dues. The charter members numbered fifty-two and included fourteen landscape architects, thirteen engineers, six attorneys, five architects, four realtors, two publishers, two "housers," and an assorted group of writers, tax specialists, land economists, educators, and public officials. Though landscape architects and engineers constituted the largest groups, the membership represented a range of occupations and interests uncommon in a professional society. Did all these men have the same idea of city planning? Or would time reveal sharp disagreements among them about the purposes and methods of city planning? Collectively, they provided the new institute with a richness of experience certain to contribute to a breadth of understanding of urban problems and opportunities. But the very diversity of

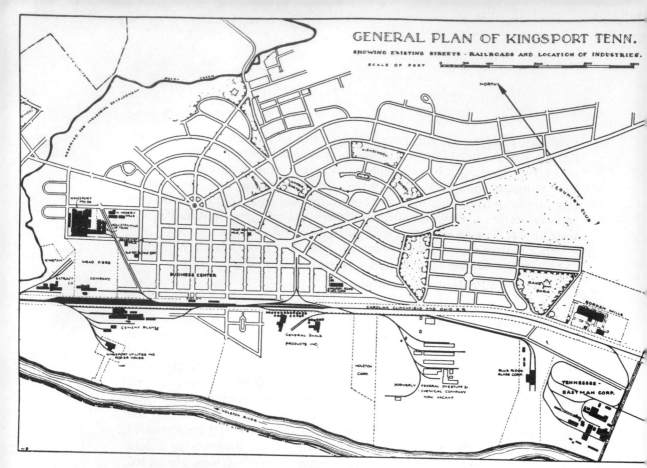

45. General plan of Kingsport, Tennessee, an industrial city planned by John Nolen for the Carolina, Clinchfield and Ohio Railroad

their backgrounds also indicated that this would be a professional organization in which consensus might be difficult to achieve, at least in the beginning and perhaps for a long time to come.

Among the more prominent charter members were Thomas Adams, Grosvenor Atterbury, Harland Bartholomew, Edward Bassett, Edward H. Bennett, Alfred Bettman, Charles Cheney, Arthur C. Comey, Stephen Child (landscape architect), Andrew Wright Crawford, George Dealey (publisher of the *Dallas News*), George Ford, E. P. Goodrich, B. A. Haldeman, George Hooker, Henry V. Hubbard, John Ihlder (housing expert), George Kessler, Nelson P. Lewis, Horace McFarland, Charles Moore, J. C. Nichols (Kansas City developer), John Nolen, Olmsted, Professor James S. Pray of Harvard University, Arthur and Flavel Shurtleff, Lawrence Veiller, Robert Whitten, and Frank B. Williams. Missing from the list are the names of Charles Mulford Robinson, who died at the age of forty-nine while the institute was being formed, and Benjamin Marsh, who had become interested in other causes.

46. Business district of Kingsport: (upper) airview taken in 1938; (lower) airview taken in 1963. Note that some buildings have been replaced by parking lots (*Richard H. Alvey, Wings over Kingsport*)

In this galaxy of pioneer planners were the men who had prepared most of the city plans commissioned by American municipalities and civic organizations since 1905. On the statute books of several states and many municipalities were city planning laws they had drafted or assisted in formulating. From their pens had come the textbooks used in university and college courses in city planning, not to mention countless newspaper and magazine articles explaining planning to laymen. Some of these men had led housing movements; others had shown how to design better residential areas. A surprising number had already foreseen the need for state and federal planning agencies that would not be created for fifteen or twenty years, and almost all were aware of controversial issues that would agitate their own ranks at various future times and deeply disturb American society. Theirs was a profession concerned, they thought, with physical change, but inevitably they would discover that its involvement was with the whole social order. Their discomfort would arise, from time to time, from attempting to divorce the "city problem" from national problems.

As yet there was no overwhelming demand for the services of members of the new profession. Harland Bartholomew, who had migrated from Newark to St. Louis as "city planning engineer" at the invitation of a committee of prominent citizens and members of the city planning commission, was one of the few with a planning position in municipal government—and the citizens' committee, not the city government, had provided the money for his department the first year he was on the job. New York has spent $65,000 for the preparation of its zoning regulations, but now that the work was completed, Cleveland was probably the only city in the country willing to spend as much as $20,000 a year for the employment of "planning experts." Boston, which had appointed a planning commission in 1914, provided only $7,500 annually for its activities. Such small Callifornia cities as San Jose, Pasadena, and Fresno, with populations ranging from 29,000 to 50,000, were unusual in appropriating $2,500 annually for city planning. In Bettman's Cincinnati the planning commission was merely an unofficial group appointed by the mayor, since the city council two years earlier had refused even to establish an official agency. Cities did not cease to create planning commissions during the war, but they were not inclined, under the circumstances, to provide them with more than token budgets.

Although the past six or seven years had witnessed great emphasis on "scientific" planning, including the making of surveys and the analysis of many kinds of statistical data, a publication of the American Institute of Architects entitled *City Planning Progress* revealed that the influence of the City Beautiful movement was still strong in many cities. Of 227 illustrations in this volume reviewing planning efforts in cities from coast to coast, more that half portrayed civic centers, state capitols, parks, waterfront developments, monumental bridges, city gates, great parkways, and imposing plazas which had been proposed in recent years, or were actually under construction, or were soon to be put to a vote of the citizens. Only 5 per cent of the illustrations depicted residential developments and low-cost housing.

As if to counteract the impression made by the large number of drawings and photographs of opulent projects, George B. Ford and Ralph F. Warner, editors of the publication, included a preface in which they stated:

> Throughout the book the Committee [on Town Planning of the A.I.A.] has laid particular stress on the economic and engineering side of city planning, because it believes that that is fundamental to progress, and while, as architects, the members of the Committee are necessarily strongly interested in the esthetic side of city planning, they are firmly convinced that city planning in America has been retarded because the first emphasis has been given to the "City Beautiful" instead of to the "City Practical." They insist with vigor that all city planning should start on a foundation of economic practicableness and good business; that it must be something which will appeal to the businessman, and to the manufacturer, as sane and reasonable.[121]

In an introduction entitled "Getting Started on City Planning," Ford and Warner outlined the whole process of initiating and carrying on city planning without suggesting that a planning commission should have its own permanent staff. They stressed that planning costs money, but ad-

47. Harland Bartholomew

vised that a commission's budget should be spent to employ consultants "who, from current practice, are thoroughly familiar with the experience of other cities and towns generally."[122] The role the editors envisaged for the commission after the consultants had done their work was that of "custodian, or watch-dog . . . of the comprehensive plans to see that all improvements . . . conform to them."[123] Apparently all the discussion in sessions of the national conference about the desirability of creating a planning department with close relations with other departments of city government had failed to impress Ford. He himself seemed to be content with the arrangements prevailing in the old City Beautiful days, though his views were perhaps no longer representative of progressive thought in the planning profession.

City Planning Progress was more a retrospect than a preview of developments which would occupy planners in the postwar years. It mentioned the extensive use of motor vehicles in France for the transport of troops and military supplies but barely hinted at the congestion and parking problems the automobile was already causing in some cities in the United States. The text noted that French cities expected to use military landing fields commercially after the war but failed to urge consideration of the future of the airplane in the American economy. With its handsome architectural renderings of proposed union stations and maps of improved transit systems, the publication saluted the age of steam and electric railway transportation, whereas in the San Francisco Bay Area, the Los Angeles metropolitan region, and many other places the automobile and bus had already curtailed the expansion of interurban electric railway lines and the extension of railroads. At the national planning conference in 1916 Werner Hegemann, the German city planner, had called attention to a proposal to build a high-speed toll road something like a present-day freeway along the banks of the Arroyo Seco between Los Angeles and Pasadena, and Nelson P. Lewis and others had forecast the need for routes bypassing congested districts, "subway parking stations under public open spaces" in downtown areas, and the widening and extension of streets to accommodate great volumes of motor traffic, yet Ford and his assistant editor included little to prepare readers for the tremendous changes cities would face as automobile registrations soared—from 5,118,000 in 1917 to 9,239,000 in 1920, and to more than 20,000,000 in 1925.

This survey of planning in 230 American cities did indicate, however, that zoning would receive much, indeed too much, attention in the future. Just before the Board of Estimate adopted zoning regulations in New York City, Lawrence Veiller had predicted that a wave of public sentiment for the adoption of similar regulations would spread throughout the entire land, even into the smaller cities.[124] No prediction was ever more accurate. Only a year later *City Planning Progress* stated that as a result of the success of the New York movement, zoning was either under way or being "agitated" in twenty-one cities, including such large municipalities as Baltimore, Chicago, Cleveland, Los Angeles, Milwaukee, Minneapolis, Philadelphia, St. Louis, San Francisco, Seattle, and Washington, D.C., and such small cities as East Orange, New Jersey; Elgin, Illinois; and Sacramento, California.[125] Although most of these cities met obstacles and delays in working out zoning ordinances, the immediate strength of the zoning movement suggested that the next few years and the 1920s would be marked by debates over ordinances, speculative pressures for commercial and industrial zoning of certain locations, court tests, invalidation of some ordinances and retrogression to chaotic prezoning conditions, and new efforts to draft constitutionally sound regulations. Nelson P. Lewis, who was already troubled about the rising number of automobiles and trucks, foresaw some measure of relief for traffic problems in the separation of commercial, industrial, and residential uses into distinct zones, because he observed that the most serious congestion developed in areas in which activities were indiscriminately mixed. Zoning therefore appealed not only to homeowners and realtors selling residential properties but also to city officials who were struggling to control mechanized transportation.

Perhaps no other new profession ever had to contend with so many rapid technological advances, so many startling changes in urban areas, and so many unfamiliar technical and legal problems as the city planning profession encountered just before and after its founding. The dispersal of population which Marsh had thought in 1909 would be brought about mainly by the extension of rapid transit lines now took place swiftly through the agency of the automobile. The year before the American City Planning Institute was formed Andrew W. Crawford became alarmed at the diffusion of population in an area from ten to twenty miles around Philadelphia and spoke of "several parks we have had in mind that we must get before they are taken up by private residences in the next five or six years."[126] Two years after the institute was organized, Secretary of the Interior Franklin K. Lane viewed the six hundred miles from Washington, D.C., to Boston as one vast industrial and urban complex (now described as the Atlantic seaboard megalopolis) and projected a comprehensive, interconnected power system serving the entire region. Not merely the metropolis and its environs but the multistate region was potentially the sphere of activity of the city planner, but his new professional fellowship was too small and too limited in experience to make much impact on the huge, restless, still none-too-well-governed cities. And while a war was being waged, his abilities were needed to assure his country of victory.

Lessons From Wartime Planning

One morning in the middle of May, 1917, Frederick Law Olmsted, George B. Ford, and E. P. Goodrich appeared at the office of the chairman of the General Munitions Board of the Council of National Defense to present two resolutions adopted a few days earlier at the Kansas City conference. Both documents called the attention of federal officials to the importance of utilizing the principles and methods of city planning in creating cantonments for troops and housing for workers in war industries, and both offered the services of members of the conference in planning and developing these two types of emergency facilities. The chairman of the board received his trio of callers politely but without enthusiasm and referred them to the board's committee on emergency construction.

The head of that committee, a New York architect who had recently donned the uniform of a major, quickly erased the bad impression made by his superior. A former vice-president of a large construction company, the major readily appreciated all that the planners wished to make available to their government: an understanding of the value of teamwork, a comprehensive view of the physical requirements of the military cities and industrial housing the government planned to build, and knowledge of minimum standards of facilities necessary to make the emergency projects reasonably healthful and efficient. Within three days he arranged for Olmsted to be appointed a member of the committee, which in the meantime had been made an advisory group to a new administrative division of the Quartermaster Corps of the Army. This division was to design and construct all the cantonments required for the training of soldiers.

In his new wartime position Olmsted helped to expand the division from fewer than a dozen men to an organization occupying four floors of the Adams Building in Washington, D.C. Under his direction the engineers, architects, and former contractors comprising the division began to develop a typical general plan for a cantonment, changing the scheme almost daily, sometimes hourly, because the general staff of the Army was still trying to decide on the best way to organize the military forces and kept altering the requirements. Olmsted and his group nevertheless succeeded in devising a reasonably satisfactory prototype plan. They then prepared a manual explaining how to adapt it to local conditions in various parts of the country and set about putting together teams of planning consultants, engineers, architects, contractors, and surveyors who could readjust all the essential features of a very large and complex plan economically and quickly to sites chosen by the Secretary of War.

Olmsted later said that his service in the planning division of the Quartermaster Corps sometimes was "like swimming in buffeting rapids."[127] But it may have been more satisfying than his efforts to expedite the planning and construction of housing for workers in war industries. From start to finish the story of official Washington's attempts to cope with the serious housing shortages in war production centers is a saga of delays, controversies, shortcomings, and waste, though some of the nation's best planners and architects managed, in spite of all obstacles, to produce a few residential developments far superior to most of those existing at the time. Unfortunately, none was completed before the war ended, perhaps a year sooner than the government had expected.

Problems of congestion and high turnover of labor showed up in many industrial centers as soon as plants began expanding to fill contracts for munitions, supplies, and ships for Britain and France, long before the United States was drawn into the global conflict. Not until early 1917, however, did a special housing subcommittee of the Council of National Defense investigate housing conditions, and it was August 30 of that year before a conference was held at Bridgeport, Connecticut, to discuss the findings. By that time the situation was so urgent that the conference sent a report directly to President Wilson. But further delays and studies held up action until March 1, 1918, when Congress appropriated $50,000,000 (later raised to $75,000,000) for the Emergency Fleet Corporation to lend to shipbuilders or their subsidiaries for the construction of war housing meeting the design standards and rental and management policies of the agency. By that time almost three hundred thousand war workers in more than seventy urban areas desperately needed housing. Three and a half months later the Secretary of Labor decided that the federal government itself should build, own, control, and rent some of the housing needed. A reluctant Congress authorized the Bureau of Industrial Housing and Transportation in his department to form the United States Housing Corporation and appropriated $100,000,000 for a program of direct governmental construction — just five months before the armistice.

The controversies over war housing raised anew all the ancient fears about government participation in the field of housing. Many senators and representatives suspected that war housing would be but the first step toward something almost as abhorrent as German imperialism — socialism. Long discussions revolved around whether war housing should be temporary or permanent. To some, "temporary" housing implied uncomfortable and unsatisfactory housing, even during the period for which it was designed to be used. Others feared that such buildings would not be destroyed at the end of the war but would be continued in use, like the alley dwellings built in the national capital during the Civil War, long after they had become dilapidated. The term "permanent," on the other hand, suggested "the whole nightmare of government participation in the business of civilian housing."[128] Congress finally resolved the quandary by approving permanent housing while stipulating that it should be designed for sale to private companies and individual buyers after the war.

The United States Housing Corporation contemplated building sixty-seven projects in forty-seven cities hard hit by housing shortages. At the time the armistice was agreed to, on November 11, 1918, the agency had awarded general contracts on sixty and had made expenditures on fifty-five. A month later Congress directed that work cease on all projects which were less than 75 per cent completed. Only twenty-seven, including some six thousand family units, were therefore carried out as planned, and, ironically, the first tenants did not move into any projects until January 1, 1919, more than a month and a half after the guns fell silent.

Sales at fair market value began in July, 1919, as directed by Congress, with prospective homeowners having first choice over speculative investors. Having spent $52,000,000 on the entire program, the government recovered in rents, sales, and payments for salvage only $27,000,000, but notwithstanding the losses, the nation benefited by such outstanding examples of planned residential developments as Yorkship Village at Camden, New Jersey; Atlantic Heights in Portsmouth, New Hampshire; Buchman in Chester, Pennsylvania; Union Gardens at Wilmington, Delaware; and several subcommunities in Bridgeport, Connecticut.

When Congress investigated the projects after the war, it complained that they were too good — a backhanded tribute to Olmsted and the city planners whom he selected to work with him. Olmsted headed the town planning section of the United States Housing Corporation, the staff of which was essentially the same as that of the Bureau of Industrial Housing and Transportation. This section, together with two others concerned with architecture and engineering, formed the Construction and Procedural Division of the corporation. Olmsted's grasp of the problems involved in creating new residential developments was evident in the leadership assumed by his section. Not only was it responsible for general coordination of all site planning and design; it also controlled and correlated decisions about the planning of each project by making a town planner the supervisory head of each design team in the field. In all there were thirty-five such teams or committees, each including a town planner, an architect, and an engineer. Among the planners entrusted with individual projects were John Nolen, Henry V. Hubbard, Arthur A. Shurtleff, and Stephen Child, whose technical skill, aesthetic sensitivity, and social consciousness were revealed in street systems following the contours of the land, the excellent spacing and placing of structures, the grouping of public and semipublic buildings, the preservation of attractive natural features, and the provision of recreational space wherever possible.

Frustrating, exhausting, and disappointing as much of the wartime planning effort was, Olmsted drew from it some valuable lessons for the future. For one thing, he gained a new appreciation of the importance of the systematic advance planning of "the few big things" which determine the general healthfulness, convenience, and social well-being of a city: the principal thoroughfares and transportation routes, main water supply lines, trunk sewers and storm drains, sites for schools, parks, and playgrounds, and "districting" or zoning, which to him and his contemporaries usually connoted a scheme of land uses.[129] Only in Philadelphia had he and his fellow planners in the United States Housing Corporation found municipal authorities equipped with plans indicating which proposed but not yet developed streets were intended to carry heavy traffic. Elsewhere plans failed to differentiate between local and through streets. Nor did most cities have plans for sewerage and storm drainage in outlying areas ripe for development. Olmsted and his project planners all

48. Fairview, Camden, New Jersey, formerly known as Yorkship Village, a planned community begun in the First World War *(National Resources Committee)*

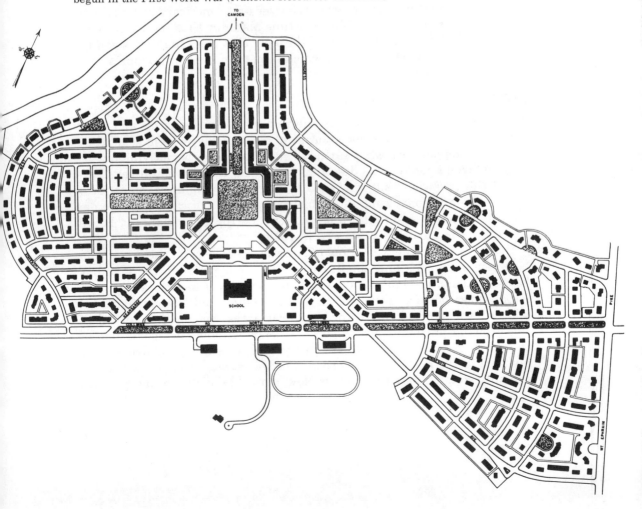

too often had to make decisions about major facilities that should have been made long before by city officials. In view of the rudimentary state of long-range planning in most municipalities, he concluded that wherever comprehensive city planning did gain a foothold, the planners should not "bite off more than they can chew" but should concentrate on planning the interrelationships of various kinds of city-wide systems and facilities and leave details to specialized departments, utility companies, and private developers.[130]

The wartime experience also taught him that the man with the best overall grasp of the complex problems of city development and the best executive head would emerge as the head of the planning team, regardless of his own specialty, provided he recognized his own limitations and had a proper respect for the points of view and capabilities of others.

As most of the housing subcommunities projected to meet the housing shortage were on the peripheries of cities, the planners engaged in designing them necessarily had to concern themselves with the larger urban environment and its future. If these permanent developments were to be of maximum long-term usefulness, they would undoubtedly have to function as parts of expanding cities, for all signs pointed to an outward movement once the war was over and Americans could satisfy the desire to own an automobile. Wartime planning thus served, in some respects, to focus the attention of the new city planning profession on metropolitan regional planning, which soon after the war became a serious concern of planners.

Prelude to Regional Planning

At no time after the 1880s were the relations between cities and their suburbs altogether amicable, nor is it particularly evident that they were harmonious somewhat earlier. The residents of the outlying towns, having for various reasons deserted the central community, always harbored the suspicion that it wished to engulf its neighbors, or at least reduce them to some kind of economic or political vassalage, as the defeat of the bill providing for a permanent metropolitan planning board in the Boston area clearly showed in 1912.

Even worse for the well-being of American democracy, the dissension between metropolis and satellites had its counterpart in the hostility between the cities and country districts. Scarcely a session of the state legislatures of New York, Pennsylvania, Ohio, and Illinois convened without the representatives of the rural areas voicing their dread of the growing predominance of large cities or without the spokesmen of the cities excoriating the despotism or rural legislators and demanding home rule. To E. J. Batten, writing in *The Public* in December, 1913, the only solution for cities such as New York, Philadelphia, and Chicago appeared to be "absolute divorce" from other parts of their states. "Turn the large cities into separate states," he suggested, "and these difficulties will disappear as if by magic."[131]

J. Horace McFarland, president of the American Civic Association, welcomed this proposal. "The adoption of any plan which would give entity, separation, and self-government to cities of over a million would be a great advantage to those cities," he agreed, but he wanted no half-way measures. If New York City or Philadelphia were to be made city-states, they should embrace all the populous territory round about, without regard to "arbitrary" geographical or state lines.[132]

Frederic C. Howe, a political liberal, could see only disaster in Batten's idea. "Remedial labor legislation, movements for improved taxation, for public ownership [of utilities], for improvement in the health and education of the state, have almost all emanated from the cities, rather than the country districts," he pointed out. "The city is the most forceful agency of democracy, and it is largely through the city that the democratic movement is being carried forward. To deprive the country districts of this democratic impulse would undoubtedly retard the state and also the nation. It would add but little to the freedom which our cities are beginning to and will ultimately enjoy."[133]

The controversy stirred up by Batten was trebly significant. It focused attention on the long struggle of cities to win the right of self-government; it bared representational imbalances requiring the reapportionment of state legislatures; and it highlighted the realities of metropolitan growth and the need, in all matters of areawide importance, for overall policy-making, administration, and long-range planning.

The metropolitan state perhaps was never regarded seriously as a means of achieving unified urban development, but the supercity of truly metropolitan proportions long fascinated officials of the big cities. Even while rising from the ashes of the catastrophic fire of 1906, San Francisco launched a Greater San Francisco movement with the hope of creating a metropolitan borough system similar to that formed earlier in New York; and though the transbay cities of Oakland, Berkeley, and Alameda decisively defeated a state constitutional amendment in 1912 which would have paved the way for such a federation, some San Francisco officeholders were still talking of annexing sister cities as late as the 1930s. In St. Louis, too, the thought of political sway over outlying towns beguiled city councilmen. At the time Filene, Nolen, and Coolidge were drafting their proposal for a metropolitan planning board in Boston, John H. Gundlach, president of the St. Louis City Council, spoke feelingly before the League of American Municipalities of his belief that "the political corporation should embrace a territory so large as to include all of the suburban population which is immediately identified with the central organization." Density of population, scientific sanitation, the telephone, rapid transit, and the automobile had created conditions making it impossible for the big city to regard only the problems within its own limits, he said. "The thought and energy of the city of tomorrow must be focused on a proper development of its suburbs that it may supplement the needs of the central city."[134]

The metropolitan perspective of the mayors and councilmen of the older centers seldom rose above self-interest. Invariably they viewed "the proper development" of the suburban belt as being primarily for the benefit of the parent city. Their brand of metropolitanism repelled the suburbs, but the suburbs themselves were incapable of intergovernmental cooperation, if one may judge by the history of the Suburban Metropolitan Planning Commission created in the environs of Philadelphia in 1913.

This agency was empowered to prepare "coordinated, comprehensive plans of highways and roads, parks and parkways, and all other means of inter-communication, water-supply, sewerage and sewage disposal, collection and disposal of garbage, housing, sanitation and health, playgrounds, civic centers, and other public improvements" for a district encompassing more than 130 local governmental units within a twenty-five-mile radius of Penn's city.[135] At first the fifteen commissioners attended meetings faithfully; then attendance diminished. Some townships questioned the validity of the act authorizing the commission, contending that the legislature should not have delegated to it the power to levy assessments upon them but should have provided the commission with state funds or should have required the political units in the district to contribute their own funds on some equitable basis. Other cities and towns complained that the commission did not even consult them. At length, on June 1, 1915, the legislature repealed the act creating the suburban planning district.

Notwithstanding the resistance to metropolitan planning in the Boston and Philadelphia areas, the failure of any metropolitan movement to develop in the Chicago region, and the general inability of large centers to win friends among their smaller neighbors, the appeal of areawide planning was perennial. In New York a former Chicagoan who was chairman of an Advisory Committee on City Plan which was never asked to give any advice drew up a proposed public statement in 1915 suggesting that the city needed a plan for "all the area in which all New Yorkers earn their livelihood and make their homes."[136] He was full of what he called "Dan Burnham notions," and his name was Charles Dyer Norton — the same who had joined Charles H. Wacker and Frederic A. Delano in persuading Burnham to undertake his plan of Chicago. A resident of

New York since 1911, Norton had thought for years that the city should have a plan and should take a vital interest in it.[137] By 1915 he was convinced that the plan should be in all respects a metropolitan regional plan. His proposed public statement described the area it should embrace: "From the City Hall a circle must be swung which will include the Atlantic Highlands and Princeton; the lovely Jersey hills back of Morristown and Tuxedo; the incomparable Hudson as far as Newburg; the Westchester lakes and ridges, to Bridgeport and beyond, and all of Long Island."[138]

Recalling the success of Chicago citizens in sponsoring, publicizing, and carrying out the Burnham plan, Norton suggested enlisting a hundred men and women as a supporting group, raising $200,000 by voluntary contributions, and carrying on a planning program for at least five years.[139] Once the plan was completed, he envisaged a triumphant repetition of the Chicago experience. The plan would be published "in permanent form for the use of experts and engineers," condensed into an attractive textbook for use in the public schools, and converted into lantern slides for public lectures.[140]

Alas, New York was not a larger Chicago. Not even fellow members of the Advisory Committee on City Plan and Norton's good friends fully shared his enthusiasm for a privately financed regional planning program. "It does not seem to me wise to include so wide an area in your city plan," one friend wrote, ending his letter with a warning about the danger of overplanning.[141] A fellow committee member rejected the suggestion that he become a vice-chairman of the sponsoring group because he did "not feel interested in the project as keenly as a responsible head should. . . ."[142]

Discouraging as these reactions were, even more disheartening were changes at the City Hall and the distractions of the war. In 1916 Norton's friend George McAneny, who had been the most prominent elected official favoring a city planning program, resigned from the presidency of the borough of Manhattan; and two years later a Tammany victory "swept into limbo" what little support for comprehensive city planning McAneny had built up through the years.[143] Upon the entrance of the United States into the war, many leading New Yorkers rushed to Washington to serve in government agencies, volunteered for Red Cross work, or worked overtime in their own businesses. The times were not propitious for promoting regional planning.

Norton's hopes brightened, however, when he became a trustee and the treasurer of the Russell Sage Foundation in 1918. The foundation was committed by the terms of its bequest to spend at least 25 per cent of its revenues for the benefit of the New York area. What could be of greater benefit to the community than the kind of plan he had in mind? Early in 1919, when future programs of the foundation were being discussed, Norton renewed his proposal for a regional plan, but Robert de Forest, the president, and other trustees regarded the project as too ambitious and too expensive, especially since Norton had now increased his estimate of the cost to $300,000. One of the trustees, Alfred White, was nevertheless "distinctly and actively interested," and was later to revive Norton's proposal.[144]

In the meantime, Nelson P. Lewis, long a friend of White's and for many years a proponent of the idea of planning the outlying areas of Greater New York, had become aware of widespread interest in metropolitan cooperation. The City Club of New York, at the suggestion of the Westchester County Planning Commission, had held a conference in 1917 at which representatives of fifty cities and towns in the New York area had discussed metropolitan programs and had contemplated forming an unofficial organization to meet monthly for an exchange of views. Lewis had been one of the speakers at the meeting. Though the declaration of war and ensuing events had soon disrupted plans for further meetings, he remembered the eagerness with which those attending the meeting had responded to the suggestion that they work together to solve regional problems.

Doubtless that meeting and White's interest in Norton's proposed regional plan were on Lewis's mind as he listened to the speakers at the eleventh national conference on city planning at Niagara Falls and Buffalo in May, 1919. The theme of one of the sessions was regional planning and the setting was particularly appropriate because many persons in the province of Ontario and in the cities and towns on the American side of the "Niagara frontier" were impressed by the possibility of united action to further the economic development of the area. Already the combination of cheap power, adequate transportation facilities, and reasonably priced land had stimulated considerable expansion in manufacturing. Thomas Adams, who was still the housing and town planning adviser of the Canadian Government, gave impetus to the establishment of a regional planning program in the area in a paper which he said might well have the descriptive title "The Regional Survey as the Basis for the Regional Plan, and the Regional Plan as the Basis for the Town Plan."[145]

Three years earlier at Cleveland, Adams had said that in order to plan that city, one should first prepare a plan for the state of Ohio and then fit the city plan into the state plan. Time had strengthened his conviction that city and country were interdependent. "Recent tendencies in industrial decentralization," he remarked, "have also shown the importance of one of the modern aspects of town planning, namely, the direction and control of the growth taking place within the rural and semi-rural districts where new industries are being established. The artificial boundaries of cities are becoming more and more meaningless."[146]

With persuasive logic Adams went on to say that "no city planning scheme can be satisfactory which is not prepared with due regard to the regional development surrounding the city, and no local plan of means of communication by rail or road can be adequate and efficient."[147] He declared that the skeleton plan of the region should come first, followed by a series of city and town planning schemes, and that both must be preceded by a regional survey.

For the survey various kinds of information would be required which would make possible the development of a plan indicating, among other things, the classification of land for industry, residences, and agriculture; minimum standards of housing for the entire region; the relation between main arterial highways and railways and between industries and all means of communication; the sources and distribution of power; water supply and waste disposal systems; and regional parks, scenic drives, and "general amenities."

Perhaps little realizing how soon he would be called upon to formulate just such a regional plan as he outlined, Adams told his fellow planners that "the nature of modern growth of communities, of the relation which exists between different elements in our community life, and the changes which are ever taking place in method and conditions, impose upon us the obligation to deal with the regulation of growth on elastic principles over wide areas, and at greater expense of time and money than we have hitherto given to it." Not only should planners prepare their schemes by gradual steps, he said, but also "in such a way that gradual fulfillment will be obtained."[148]

Members of the planning profession had been greatly concerned in previous years with the means of carrying out city plans, but this was the first conference at which they examined ways to put a regional plan into effect. Morris Knowles, consulting engineer with offices in Pittsburgh, Pennsylvania, spoke of the regional plan as "a kind of regional constitution" with which developments undertaken by local governments and private enterprise should not conflict.[149] Since he viewed the main features of such a plan as large-scale public works or essentially engineering projects, most of which would be constructed by governmental agencies, he was concerned to find the most effective political organization for carrying out areawide improvements. County government, he thought, would usually be "neither efficient enough or sufficiently representative in personnel" to develop and manage technically complicated projects even if the county jurisdiction should correspond to a natural physiographic region.[150] Nor did he think that much hope lay in the expansion of large cities into veritable regional cities by the process of consolidation and annexation—if the record of surburban jealousy of central cities was a trustworthy indicator. Contracts between municipalities were, of course, possible, but for Knowles the organization of large districts serving both incorporated and unincorporated areas seemed to be the best solution of the problem.[151] Districts could be formed for particular areas and for particular problems, he pointed out.

Although the sanitation, water supply, and park districts of the Boston area had recently been combined, Knowles did not mention the still more desirable possibility of a multipurpose district; nor did he suggest a regional federation of local governments to construct and operate regional facilities. In years to come planners would hear proposals for these and other forms of political organization designed to overcome the difficulties of depending entirely upon the voluntary cooperation of local governments and private corporations to carry out a regional plan. In 1919 the subject of regional cooperation was more novel to city planners than it would have been to an assembly of political scientists. So few planners had had occasion to prepare plans for areas larger than cities that most of them had given little consideration to the political implications of regional planning. W. J. Donald, secretary of the Niagara Falls Chamber of Commerce, may have been more perspicacious than any of them when he foresaw that the idea of municipal home rule might obstruct regional planning and said that communities should begin to talk about regional home rule and "the final provision of such legislation as might seem essential in the interests of the region as opposed to the narrowed interests of the individual municipalities."[152] Consolidation of city and county government appealed to him as one way to encourage areawide planning and development, though he acknowledged that this method would hardly suffice to solve the problem of the diffusion of power in regions composed of several counties.

Donald expressed anew the desire for a state department of municipal affairs to aid cities and regions in long-range planning, but others at the conference still hoped for "some kind of federal agency to deal with housing, town planning or community planning."[153] Olmsted, McFarland, and Lawson Purdy, president of the Department of Taxes and Assessments of New York City, together with Robert de Forest and Samuel Gompers, the labor leader, had met with Andrew Crawford in Philadelphia in February and had agreed to work for the establishment of an agency whose function would be chiefly research, experimentation, and dissemination of information. Its own technical investigations would be limited to fields not studied by other federal agencies, but it would bring together studies of other bureaus and divisions and would make many kinds of data about cities and their regions available to municipalities and state governments.

The goal of the group was modest indeed in comparison with a proposal put forth by Harlean James, executive secretary of the American Civic Association, for a new federal Department of Civic Economy, as she called it. Under this "cabinet department of service" she envisaged five bureaus performing many of the functions of the present Department of Housing and Urban Development and the Department of Health, Education and Welfare. The bureau of community planning and housing service in itself would be the equivalent of the first-named department since it would offer guidance in the renewal of cities, the planning of new subdivisions and towns, the development of low-cost housing, and the solution of problems of light and power, water supply, waste disposal, fire protection, and local transportation.

Miss James estimated that the proposed department would require "an initial appropriation of $15,000,000 or thereabouts, with progressive increases for a period of years." The cost to the nation would be "small in proportion to the returns bound to accrue in increased man and woman power during the trying years of readjustment to new international and industrial tasks set for us by world conditions."[154]

After years of anxiety, sacrifice, physical strain, patriotic fervor, and moral frenzy America had reached a period in which it was no longer receptive to progressive proposals such as Miss James and the leaders of the planning profession advanced. The reform movement had lost almost all its crusading drive by the time the United States entered the war. Now that that bloody struggle was over and an economic depression was gripping the country, particularly the industrial centers which had expanded to meet the need for ships, munitions, and supplies, the American people were in no mood to consider enlarging the federal bureaucracy. They had had more than enough of regulation, rationing, and red tape; they had seen prodigal waste resulting from governmental inefficiency, much of it unavoidable but nevertheless scandalous to a people brought up on notions of thrift; and they had expended, for the time being, too much of their capital of optimistic altruism. As the postwar disillusionment set in, taking its heavy toll of their idealism and their sense of responsibility for the welfare of others, they wanted to think — those of them who had jobs — only about their own affairs, about day-to-day living, getting a new car or a better job, going to the movies or a ball game, taking a vacation at the seashore. The city planning movement, which had been part of the great upsurge of reform, had forged its professionalism during years of crisis — a crisis which had weakened the liberal impulse needed to sustain the new profession in its growth and development. Now one of its critics saw it faltering.

Frederick L. Ackerman attacked the city planning movement in 1919 for no longer being concerned about "the causes which give rise to existing maladjustments." The entire planning movement, he charged, "is so based upon considerations of 'expediency' as to amount to inhibition or stultification." He saw the planners, in preparing zoning ordinances, becoming unduly concerned with what they termed normal tendencies of city growth. In his view, the term "normal tendencies" represented "the right of the individual to use the community as a machine for procuring individual profits and benefits, without regard to what happens to the community." That was why America had maladjusted communities, and it would continue to have them "so long as the spokesmen of city planning continue to proclaim that adjustment can be had without touching the sacred causes of maladjustment."[155]

If the city planner had ceased to be the reformer that Ackerman once thought he was, he had not yet become the effective molder of cities that John Nolen wanted him to be. "With the possible exception of Chicago, no large town or city in the United States has yet taken city planning very seriously," Nolen said wistfully. The city planner was not a professional publicity man and was not usually even a citizen of the city for which he prepared a plan. He had only his planning report, prepared "in as popular a form as possible," to arouse the community. For him to take part in a local educational campaign would be of doubtful expediency, Nolen thought.[156] And yet if the chamber of commerce, the women's clubs, the unions, churches, and other organizations did not champion his plan and see that it was carried out, how could he avoid having his handiwork filed away and forgotten?

The city planning movement was at another turning point. In the years since Benjamin C. Marsh had organized the first national conference, it had developed a new professional organization, had evolved new techniques and methods, had produced a sizable body of planning literature, and had come to understand that it should assume responsibility for planning entire metropolitan regions. Almost three hundred cities in the United States had planning commissions. Yet the general public still knew little about planning, and only a handful of commissions employed staffs. Popular enthusiasm for zoning threatened to overshadow comprehensive planning and to ally the new profession with dominant business interests. Attacked by disappointed liberals for abandoning its reform ideals and accused by some of its own members of having made little impact on American cities, the new profession of city planning entered a period in which altogether different social and economic conditions would test its ability to make significant contributions to American society.

CHAPTER 4

CITY PLANNING IN
THE AGE OF BUSINESS

The New Dimensions of Urban America

In November, 1920, the overwhelming majority of American voters stamped their ballots for electors pledged to a small-town presidential candidate—handsome, mediocre, poker-playing, platitudinous Warren Gamaliel Harding. They were weary of Wilsonian high-mindedness, world responsibilities, and the oppressive complexity of modern civilization. They voted for "normalcy" but not for small-townism in their national life, and by the millions they were soon in revolt against one of the conspicuous manifestations of small-townism: prohibition, which had gone into effect almost eleven months before the election. They flocked to speakeasies, bragged about their bootleggers, carried hip flasks to football games, made bathtub gin, and developed a morbid curiosity about gangsters and their molls. Hating prohibition, they hated the Gopher Prairies and Zeniths where the bluenoses ruled supreme. When Sinclair Lewis skewered the provincials of Main Street, they bought his novel by the thousands; and when Henry L. Mencken wrote about the *boobus Americanus,* they had no trouble identifying the chief habitat of the species. All the ignorant piety of which agrarian America had been proud suffered the ultimate in derision in 1926 when Clarence Darrow demolished William Jennings Bryan, the folk hero of the prairies and the Bible Belt, at the trial of young John Scopes on charges of teaching the theory of evolution in the backward state of Tennessee. Small-townism was not only nineteenth-centuryism; in its ugliest form it was the Ku Klux Klan and lynchings and character assassination. By the end of the twenties small-town America was in full retreat before the forces of urban America, vanquished as much by urban America's radios, electric refrigerators, and movies as by its satire and its pervasive propaganda. But urban America paid a price for its victory in the excesses to which it went in order to defeat small-townism. And urban America itself was not so truly urban as it pretended to be. Millions of Americans wanted something between the big city and the small town, as their preference for the suburbs indicated.

In 1920 the United States was officially a predominantly urban nation for the first time in its history. The census revealed that 51.4 per cent of the population lived in incorporated areas of 2,500 or more inhabitants, but in the larger scale of things a "city" of 2,500 or 5,000 or even 10,000 usually had all the attributes of a small town unless it was part of a metropolitan agglomeration. More than a third of the total population of the nation, however, now lived in cities of 100,000 or more and in the adjacent thickly settled territories, and these centers, like magnets with ever greater attractive power, were increasingly pulling people from the rural areas, villages, and small towns. In the Middle Atlantic states three out of five persons were considered urban dwellers, and in New England almost the same proportion; even in the Pacific Coast states 47 per cent of the population was urban. Since 1910 the movement from rural areas to the cities had caused a decrease in population in a third of the 3,000 counties in the nation. The thousand counties suffering population losses represented 900,000 square miles in all — a third of the total area of the continental United States.

War industries, of course, had attracted great numbers from the farms to the cities, but wartime conditions had merely accelerated long-term trends. Employment on farms had reached a peak even before the United States declared war on Germany. In the future the increasing mechanization of agricultural production would steadily reduce the proportion of workers required on the land. The technological advances of American industry that had expanded employment in the cities promised even more new jobs for city people—not only in factories but also in new kinds of retail outlets, in new types of service establishments catering to a more affluent society, in federal, state, and municipal agencies providing information and advice, regulatory services, and recreational opportunities that earlier generations would never have expected from government or would not even have thought proper for government to offer.

While luring energetic young people from the rural areas and small towns, the larger urban centers had also been generating a centrifugal movement resulting in the growth of surburbs and satellite cities. In all the metropolitan districts of the nation together the rate of growth in the central cities from 1910 to 1920 had been a little greater than in the outside areas, but in various places the seekers after more living space were giving the chamber of commerce in the central city a good deal to worry about. In the metropolitan districts of Atlanta, Buffalo, Cleveland, Pittsburgh, Philadelphia, and St. Louis the population of the outlying territories had increased twice as fast as that of the central city, in Chicago and Louisville three times as fast, and in Seattle four times as rapidly. In southern California the towns and unincorporated areas around Los Angeles had enjoyed a population gain of 108 per cent, the city itself an increase of 80 per cent. An overgrown town of a little more than 100,000 in 1900, Los Angeles now boasted, in the loudest chamber-of-commerce manner, 576,673 residents, more than a quarter of a million of whom had arrived since 1910. But unlike the peripheral growth in some other metropolitan districts, the settlement of the outlying territories in that sunlit land was no flight from congestion and bad housing. In substantial measure it was the work of promoters who enticed tourists to new tracts with free bus rides, free lunches, and evangelistic oratory. In a city that had swallowed first one and then another independent town and had become the largest in area in the entire nation (434 square miles), downtown merchants did not yet fear the growth of neighboring communities, but for businessmen in the older cities of the East and Middle West the accelerated development of the suburbs was a threat. If peripheral areas had attracted thousands of upper- and middle-class families and some blue-collar workers in a decade of political tensions and war, how much would they grow in an era of peace and prosperity?

For an indication the proprietors of downtown establishments had only to watch the sale of automobiles. The American people were in love with that essentially iconoclastic mechanism, the private passenger car. It released a man from dependence on the crowded transportation system of the city; it enabled him to live on the edge of the city, where larks sang in the fields and wild flowers bloomed in the spring; it invited him to explore rural lanes and quiet valleys on Sundays. It gave him more power for his personal enjoyment than the ordinary man had commanded in any previous age. Although the American scarcely thought of his car as an instrument for reshaping the city, it was to prove the most potent means of crippling central business districts and upbuilding outlying shopping areas that had ever been invented. It was the most effective device for spreading the city over a vast territory that history had ever seen. Its potential for destruction and for construction was, in short, awesome. But Americans in the mass were not awed at all; they simply yearned to get behind the steering wheel and go joyriding. No sooner was the postwar depression of 1919–1920 over than they bought automobiles by the millions—2,274,000 in 1922, more than 3,000,000 annually from 1923 to 1926, almost as many in 1927, 3,775,000 in 1928, and 4,455,000 in the climatic year 1929, when the stock market soared to dizzy heights and then collapsed. By that time millions of American families had forsaken the tenement, the upstairs flat, the row house, the attic apartment,

49. "What will it be in 1930?" a report of Harland Bartholomew and Associates asked in 1927

and the converted basement for the market version of a man's castle. It occupied a lot forty or fifty feet wide and a hundred to a hundred and twenty feet deep; and it was in the suburbs, in many instances in a new subdivision served neither by a bus line nor an electric railway. This haven supposedly represented freedom from all the evils of congestion associated with the central city, but since it was a tiny part of a metropolitan area, its occupants could escape none of the problems of the larger community. These problems emerged clearly in the 1920s and are the very ones with which urban areas struggle today.

The automobile contributed enormously to environmental and financial stress. It choked the streets of central business districts, causing merchants and city officials to clamor for major traffic street plans showing proposed street widenings, extensions, and openings. It put additional strains on municipal treasuries with its insatiable requirements: expensive traffic signals, directional and regulatory signs, new traffic bureaus, grade-crossing separations, municipal garages and parking lots, and emergency hospitals, ambulances, and doctors to care for the injured and dying. It deprived electric railway systems of so many patrons that by the middle of the decade some companies were in financial distress and city officials were faced with the prospect of taking over their operations and continuing service under mounting deficits. It created traffic jams on gravel roads miles from the center of the city, obliging county and state governments to initiate or greatly expand areawide highway programs. By encouraging families to move to outlying developments, it accelerated the incorporation of new cities and towns, added to the governmental complexity of metropolitan regions, and heightened the long-standing resentment between older and newer communities. This mechanical idol most shamelessly accepted the blandishments of highway billboards and strewed roadhouses, gas stations, and hamburger stands along once charming country roads. Even worse, it aided and abetted the premature subdividing of thousands of acres of fields and farmlands in a period of prosperity more bedazzling than real, piling up assessments for the installation of streets, sidewalks, and streetlamps that eventually, as in Los Angeles County, became burdens upon all the taxpayers.

Everywhere this technological problem-child went it caused staggering losses. It made profits for many, too, but the losses aroused more comment, particularly the deaths and injuries from accidents. By 1925 the toll from automobile accidents was approximately 24,000 lives annually. The injured numbered 600,000 or more each year. The annual economic loss to the whole country from the carnage was computed at $600,000,000 and for one city alone—St. Louis—at more than $5,000,000. In 1926 Secretary of Commerce Herbert Hoover estimated the national losses due to inadequate traffic facilities at $2,000,000,000 a year. The New York region, it was said, lost $1,000,000 a day from traffic congestion, Cincinnati (a city of some 400,000) $100,000 a day, and the smaller city of Worcester, Massachusetts, $35,000 a day. In Boston the annual loss in trucking costs alone was $6,000,000. But there were other types of losses as well. Des Moines, Iowa, for example, spent $2,000,000 in a seven-year period just to rectify defects in its street system resulting from poor subdividing—jogs, hazardous intersections, and dead-end streets.

The fatalities and injuries prompted some of the most constructive endeavors of the times. Secretary Hoover called national conferences on street and highway safety which did much to stimulate interest in city planning. The Studebaker Corporation provided an endowment to Harvard University for the establishment of the Erskine Bureau, which under the directorship of Miller McClintock investigated traffic problems in cities from coast to coast. The Policyholders' Service Bureau of the Metropolitan Life Insurance Company undertook a demonstration traffic survey of Albany, New York, to determine the best traffic-control measures and to show how great a reduction of deaths and injuries could be made by a concentrated attack on accidents. William E. Harmon, suburban developer and president of the Harmon Foundation, became something of a national hero when he announced that all his future subdivisions would include playgrounds and recreation fields because "automobile travel has made streets literally death traps for children."[1] It was a great pity, he thought, that mandatory legislation could not be passed to compel the dedication of a part of each subdivision for recreational purposes. Planning consultant Robert Whitten and Clarence Arthur Perry, a member of the staff of the Russell Sage Foundation, both made studies showing how residential areas could be planned so that they would be insulated from the noise, fumes, and hazards of floods of automobiles. And as the profligate and heady twenties drew to a close, the City Housing Corporation, a New York firm, built in the Fairlawn Borough of New Jersey a new town described as a city for the motor age: the famous Radburn, with superblocks of thirty to fifty acres in which there were interior parks where children could play without fear of falling under the wheels of the mechanical juggernaut.

In the big cities and in many of the smaller ones as well a considerable number of persons coupled the automobile with something else they regarded as a menace—the skyscraper. The taller the skyscraper, the more executives and junior executives were encouraged to drive to work. The rising skyline portended more inconvenience and frustration for everyone: more hours wasted in traffic jams, more nerves frayed trying to find parking space, more tardy arrivals for appointments, more engagements cancelled. Yet the rattle of the riveting gun deafened central business districts as steel frames rose higher and higher in New York, Chicago, Detroit, San Francisco, and even Miami. An ordinance limiting buildings to a maximum height of 150 feet because of the earthquake hazard kept them from soaring to twenty or thirty stories in Los Angeles, but the citizens voted for one exception—a twenty-seven-story city hall topped by an attenuated version of the mausoleum of Halicarnassus. Was the symbolism of death prophetic? In another twenty years the downtown area of Los Angeles would be doing not only a smaller proportion of the retail business of the metropolitan community but also a smaller actual dollar volume of business. But in the days of Harding's successor, "Silent Cal" Coolidge, who said that "the business of America is business," the skyscrapers everywhere but in Los Angeles soared optimistically into the blue, notwithstanding the warnings of those who foresaw that shoppers from the suburbs would become discouraged with clotted streets and would eventually do most of their purchasing in outlying shopping centers.

"Let us frankly admit that there is something to be said for skyscrapers," wrote Frederic A. Delano, president of the American Civic Association and chairman of the Regional Plan of New York and Its Environs, in 1926.[2] "There is great convenience incident to concentration."[3] He

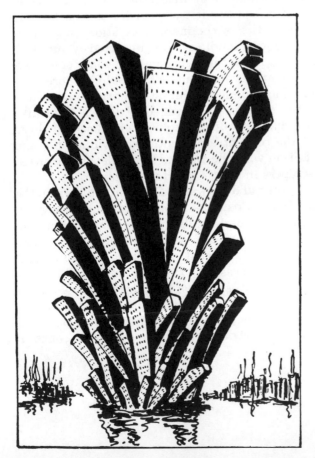

50. "Top-heavy," an illustration from *Story of America*, by Hendrik Willem van Loon *(Liveright Publishing Corporation)*

considered a single office building forty stories high on an acre of land no worse as a cause of congestion than four office buildings of similar floor area each ten stories high, though his argument of course required the further supposition that three acres adjacent to the forty-story building would remain vacant. But he acknowledged that without regulations the other three acres would sprout skyscrapers; and so he was "inevitably drawn to the conclusion that the average height cubage or population capacity of buildings must be limited to the feasible capacity of the arterial street system."[4]

Neither in New York nor in any other city, however, was the capacity of buildings adjusted to the load limit of the streets. City planners who were preparing zoning ordinances for municipalities pondered the problem, but they disagreed among themselves about restrictions. Meanwhile the artist Hugh Ferriss delighted architects and laymen alike with visions of great structures thrusting heavenward. Superhighways swooped among the lofty piles, some at ground level, others on the setbacks of buildings, and still others on bridges over the man-made canyons. The city-in-the-making was but a prelude to a future metropolis more exciting than all the Babylons and Alexandrias of history. With little thought of the congestion to which they contributed, architects accepted commissions to design ever more daring towers of commerce and finance. Traffic engineers came forth with proposals for two-level streets. And toward the end of the twenties, when the nation became fully awakened to the possibilities of commercial aviation, magazines published breathtaking drawings of landing fields supported by hundred-story skyscrapers or the pylons of enormous bridges or by lacy steel towers rising from ship piers along the waterfront. What could be more vital than business districts in which one looked up at construction workers balancing on steel beams two or three hundred feet above the sidewalk? What could be more certain than the supermetropolis of tomorrow? Hosts of Americans denied that the concentrated center was vulnerable and paid no heed to Thomas Edison when he warned them that they courted disaster by building skyscrapers in overcrowded districts.

Growing upward at the center and outward at the circumference, the urban complex was headed in all directions at once. But in the long run the growth at the periphery was bound to affect the center and diminish some of its functions, or at least duplicate certain functions in widely scattered locations. And now another agent of dispersal as significant as the automobile joined in the process of extending and transforming the urban accretion. The electric transmission line, drawing power from sources a hundred or two hundred miles distant and making it available to factories far removed from the congested industrial districts of earlier days, raised prospects of a new distribution of manufacturing zones in metropolitan regions—not just one or two in proximity to ports and railroad yards but many throughout the urban area, some in small municipalities, some in locations served only by industrial highways, and others in places favored by both rail and highway transportation. Men of broad social vision—such as Governor Gifford Pinchot of Pennsylvania and his adviser Morris L. Cooke and that small, farseeing confraternity called the Regional Planning Association of America, among whose members were Lewis Mumford, Benton MacKaye, Clarence Stein, and Henry Wright, envisaged whole states and groups of states, or at the very least the larger regions within states, as the beneficiaries of giant power—an integrated system of power plants (some at dams, others at coal mines) and transmission lines providing electrical energy to city, village, and farm. But whether a metropolitan region had giant power or superpower, which to the detriment of rural areas piled up power upon existing power in great centers of production, its expanding energy resources and facilities promised a new ordering of its productive and distributive activi-

51. "Speaking of Skyscrapers," a cartoon from the weekly bulletin of the Brooklyn Chamber of Commerce, 1926

ties — and these, in turn, a new configuration of the whole spatial environment.

The "Other End" of the Planning Problem

City planners acknowledged the dynamism of the urban area at the very beginning of the decade, before 9,000,000 automobiles had multiplied to 26,000,000, before the skyscrapers had shot up to new heights, before the transmission lines had interlaced city and suburb and village. Planning programs should broaden out and include areas over which urban development would spread in the future, a regional planning committee recommended at the annual national planning conference in 1920.[5] There should be state and national legislation creating regional planning organizations, but it would "not do . . . to suspend all thought of regional planning pending so uncertain a thing as favorable legislation."[6] Citizens' committees and committees of public officials representing neighboring communities might well initiate areawide planning without waiting for the tedious legislative process to provide new enabling legislation.

Speaking extemporaneously, Thomas Adams declared that to broaden city planning to take in regional planning seemed to him not only desirable; it also seemed inevitable, because the municipal boundary was no longer the proper boundary for planning purposes in an industrialized society.[7] Begin with the region, he urged, and the city plan, the village plan, and the plan for the rural areas would all follow logically. Then formulate the various elements of each plan, such as housing, industrial development, and, in due course, zoning. To begin with zoning, as he suspected many of his fellow planners might be willing to do, would be to start at the "other end," the wrong end, of the planning problem.[8]

But urban America was in something of a zoning crisis in the early 1920s. Like a patient who could endure his fever until he suddenly learned that there was a new remedy for it and who was then impatient to be cured, urban America was now sure that it would perish if it did not have zoning. Nothing appeared so destructive of urban order as garages and machine shops in residential areas, or loft buildings in exclusive shopping districts, or breweries amid small stores and light manufacturing establishments. Nothing caused an investor so much anguish as the sight of a grocery store being erected next door to a single-family residence on which he had lent money. Nothing made whole neighborhoods feel so outraged and helpless as the construction of apartment houses when the private deed restrictions expired and there was no zoning to prevent vacant lots from being used for multifamily structures. Zoning was the heaven-sent nostrum for sick cities, the wonder drug of the planners, the balm sought by lending institutions and householders alike. City after city worked itself into a state of acute apprehension until it could adopt a zoning ordinance.

Millions of ordinary citizens could understand the need for zoning if not for general planning. Relatively few could appreciate the need for metropolitan regional planning even though highways became congested, water supplies in many places began to prove inadequate, sewer systems became overloaded, rivers reeked with pollution, farmlands disappeared before the advance of subdivisions, and potential park lands passed into the hands of speculative developers. To the average man all these evidences of deterioration in the metropolitan environment were perhaps nothing more than growing pains; only to an intellectual elite were they indications of future emergencies and warnings that some of the interlocking systems of the urban complex were in danger of breakdown. City planners were members of this elite, but they often experienced difficulty in making city officials and civic leaders see the larger needs and opportunities—and frequently convinced themselves that the best way to lead people to an appreciation of the broader problems was to begin with something they did understand. Throughout the presidencies of Harding, Coolidge, and Hoover the order of procedure in most cities was zoning first, city-wide planning second—if at all. Some of the leading planning consultants endeavored to work out zoning schemes while preparing the comprehensive plan. Only in a few of the more populous metropolitan regions and predominantly urban counties was areawide planning undertaken, but these pioneering attempts to guide the development of entire urban clusters and the outlying areas into which they were expanding aroused so much interest that every city plan tended to become, in some respects, a regional plan. If nothing more, the local plan provided some suggestions for the extension of streets into the surrounding territory, designated natural areas that would be suitable for parks, and proposed standards for the design of subdivisions within a mile and a half or three miles of the city boundaries.

The drive for zoning was well under way before most of the regional planning programs were even contemplated. By 1919 at least ten states had authorized all or certain classes of cities to adopt zoning. In that year the Congress also instructed the commissioners of the District of Columbia to prepare comprehensive zoning regulations. The Texas legislature approved an amendment to the city charter of Dallas in 1920 to permit overall zoning, and the next year it sanctioned zoning for all cities in the state. In 1921 there was a flood of zoning legislation. Connecticut, Indiana, Kansas, Michigan, Missouri, Nebraska, Rhode Island, South Carolina, and Tennessee all granted cities the privilege of invoking the police power to regulate the use of land as well as the height and area of buildings. None had previously authorized use zoning.

In 1921 Herbert Hoover, who could have been Harding's Secretary of the Interior but chose instead to be his Secretary of Commerce, became so impressed with the importance of zoning that he appointed a special advisory committee to draft a model or standard state zoning enabling act under which municipalities could adopt zoning regulations. To the committee he named as chairman Edward M. Bassett, whom many called the father of zoning. Serving with him were Irving B. Hiett, former president of the American Association of Real Estate Boards, and such well-known members of the National City Planning Institute as Frederick Law Olmsted, Nelson P. Lewis, J. Horace McFarland, Lawrence Veiller, Morris Knowles, and John Ihlder.

Within a year the committee had a preliminary draft of its proposed standard act ready to circulate in mimeographed form; and by February, 1924, the Government Printing Office was issuing a final version with a foreword by Hoover. "The discovery that it is practical by city zoning to carry out reasonably neighborly agreements as to the use of land has made an almost instant appeal to the American people," the Secretary wrote.[9] He noted that when his advisory committee began its labors in September, 1921, only 48 cities and towns, with fewer than 11,000,000 inhabitants, had adopted zoning ordinances. By the end of 1923, he was happy to report, zoning was in effect in 218 municipalities, with more than 22,000,000 residents, and new zones were being added to the list each month.[10] Most satisfactory of all, within a year of the issuance of the final draft of the standard act, eleven states had passed enabling legislation modeled either wholly or partly after it, and four other states were considering similar acts.

The danger of attempting zoning without the sanction of the state legislature was nowhere better illustrated than in St. Louis. In 1918 that city was the second in the nation to adopt a comprehensive zoning ordinance, but it did so under a city charter provision giving the board of aldermen authority "to prescribe limits within which business, occupations and practices liable to be nuisances or detrimental to the . . . general welfare . . . may lawfully be established" rather than under a specific grant of power from the state legislature.[11] Five years later the Missouri Supreme Court, in a five-to-four decision, invalidated the ordinance because the city had used the police power to zone without having the proper authorization from the legislature. The overthrow of the ordinance was followed by a two-year hiatus in zoning in which approximately $10,000,000 was spent for buildings whose uses violated the districts established by the original ordinance. The large, older residential areas west of Grand Avenue were invaded by apartment houses; older residents fled; renters moved in who did not maintain the properties well; and entire neighborhoods deteriorated.

The standard zoning act was not, however, an unmixed blessing. A footnote advised that "it is highly desirable that all zoning schemes should be worked out as an integral part of the city plan," preferably by the city planning commission.[12] But the main text of the act stated merely that the regulations "shall be made in accordance with a comprehensive plan" without specifying what kind of comprehensive plan the authors had in mind.[13] Another footnote indicated that their intention was to prevent haphazard or piecemeal zoning rather than to insist upon a long-range, all-inclusive plan as a reasonable basis for city-wide zoning. The model act thus encouraged overall zoning unsupported by a thoughfully prepared general plan for the future development of the city.

One of the consequences of the failure of many cities to develop long-term plans before preparing zoning ordinances was that they zoned far more land for certain purposes than the community could use in the next fifty or one hundred years. Persons who prepared zoning ordinances usually lacked detailed information about the amount of land actually being used for various purposes and therefore could not make adequate projections about future needs. But not infrequently the allocation of excessive amounts of street frontage for apartment houses and for commercial establishments resulted from political pressures exerted by particular property owners, realtors, and special interests. "It should be noted that zoning is not intended to enhance the value of buildings but to conserve that value, i.e., to prevent depreciation of values such as come in 'blighted districts,' for instance; but it *is* to encourage the most appropriate use of land," a footnote to the text of the standard act stated.[14] Property owners quickly realized, however, that the designation of an apartment house zone or a commercial zone conferred a new speculative value on properties in that zone. They were invariably eager to reap the profits such a designation promised, as Louis Brownlow and Colonel Charles Kutz, the commissioners of the District of Columbia, discovered after they engaged Harland Bartholomew in 1920 to prepare a zoning ordinance for the national capital.

Washington real estate men put pressure on the two officials to permit the construction of apartment houses in the northwest section of the city, which contained most of the good single-family residential areas. But upon advice of their consultant, Brownlow and Kutz decided not to allow multifamily structures between Wisconsin and Massachusetts avenues, north and west of Rock Creek Park. By 1926, however, the agitation for a change of zone to authorize apartments was so great that the commissioners were almost persuaded to make some concessions. Bartholomew then suggested that a detailed study of land use in the entire city should be made, as well as a determination of how much land was absorbed each year by the construction of new apartment houses. The extensive land-use survey took more than a year to complete but enabled Brownlow and Kutz to stand firm against the real estate men. To the surprise of the commissioners and the consternation of those who wanted a zoning change, the survey revealed that less than one per cent of the city was actually used for apartment houses and that there was a considerable amount of vacant land zoned for such structures in other parts of the city.

Many planning consultants, city attorneys, city engineers, and others entrusted with the work of preparing zoning ordinances "guesstimated" the amounts of land needed for various purposes, or they yielded now and then to the clamor of property owners. In time, of course, the well-known consultants who served cities in different sections of the country developed fairly realistic ideas about land requirements, yet zoning in the 1920s could hardly be called scientific; nor was it usually economically sound.

The Chicago zoning ordinance of 1923, for instance, was typical in the generosity of its provisions for certain uses. Citing it as one of his "terrible examples" at a conference at Purdue University in 1938, Walter Blucher, then executive director of the American Society of Planning Officials, dissected it thus:

> At the time of the adoption of the ordinance there was in use for single-family dwellings 12 per cent of the city's area. But did they zone 12 per cent? They did not. They zoned 3 per cent. In 1923, 8 per cent of the area was used for two-family dwellings, but this was not enough. They zoned 19 per cent for two-family dwellings. Five per cent was in use for multiple dwellings or apartment houses, but that too was not enough; 13 per cent was zoned for multiple dwelling purposes. That was bad, but they did worse. Less than 5 per cent of the city's area was used, in 1923, for commercial purposes, but they zoned 14 per cent; and 12 per cent was in use for manufacturing, but they doubled it to 24 per cent.[15]

In the next thirteen years less than six-tenths of a square mile was occupied by new industry in Chicago.

Blucher also commented on the frequent changes in the Chicago ordinance in this same thirteen-year period. There were no fewer than 13,000. "Although I have been condemned for saying this," he told the Purdue University conference, "I maintain that the people of Chicago have been the worse for the zoning ordinance. In Chicago you are lulled under a false security. You think you have zoning when, in fact, you have not. I have called these 13,000 changes 13,000 violations."[16]

In some cities a record of an excessive number of amendments to the zoning ordinance attested to the corruption of public officials, in others to the inadequacy of the ordinance itself. A few municipalities suffered both from venal officials and from poorly drawn regulations. Citizens might well be suspicious of an ordinance like the second one adopted in St. Louis in 1925, under authority of a new state law similar to the standard zoning enabling act. An otherwise satisfactory statute, this second zoning ordinance denied the city planning commission the opportunity to review proposed changes. Members of the large board of aldermen introduced changes at will and did so with such frequency that the grand jury began an investiagtion. The mayor thereupon announced that he would sign no further amendments that did not have the approval of the city planning commission.

The troubles of St. Louis with zoning were far from ended, though. The Director of Public Safety, who was also the superior officer of the Building Commissioner, brought his considerable political prestige to bear to force the commissioner to issue building permits in violation of the zoning ordinance. In only a few instances did aggrieved property owners bring court action to prevent erection of the buildings illegally authorized. Still worse, the Director of Public Safety succeeded in having himself appointed chairman of the Board of Zoning Appeals, in which position he exercised his influence to overturn decisions of the planning commission. A zoning ordinance in itself was thus not necessarily insurance against poor municipal development; unsympathetic or corrupt officials could nullify its effectiveness, and in some cities frequent changes, reversal of planning commission decisions by the board of appeals, and deliberate evasions of the law created conditions little better than those obtaining before the enactment of any zoning regulations.

Particularly subject to abuse were the provisions of some state enabling laws and local zoning ordinances permitting city councils to grant variances in use in cases of undue hardship when recommended by boards of zoning appeals. Generally a change of use requires an amendment to the zoning ordinance and must apply to an area of some extent, so as not to confer special privileges on one or two property owners. Because of ignorance, softheartedness, or venality, however, some boards of appeals and councils so liberally sanctioned exceptions to authorized uses that they made a mockery of zoning, in effect creating "spot zones" throughout the city. In fact, municipalities in which spot zoning was common were more numerous than city planners liked to admit.

The planners themselves in the trying times of the early twenties were groping for effective means of controlling not only the use of land but also the density of population and the character of residential areas. At sessions of the annual national conference on city planning their debates about the best method of limiting density were often complicated by discussion of the ideal density and the maximum density that should be allowed. Was the ideal density twelve families to the acre, as the British thought? Or was it eight? Should the maximum be 140 families per acre? Or should it be eighty? There was no agreement on either the ideal or the maximum; nor was there agreement on the best method of regulating density. Some planners insisted that definite limits should be established by prescribing a certain number of square feet of lot area per family; for example, a requirement of 1,250 square feet per family in a multiple-dwelling zone in which the lots included 5,000 square feet would limit structures to four apartments. Others wished to avoid such prescriptions because they tended to invite maximum use of every lot and to concentrate population unduly. Let us have, they said, more refined height and area limitations, assuring plenty of light and air for occupants, but no arbitrary restrictions on density.

Even in those days the increasing separation of uses — nothing but single-family houses in one zone, only duplexes in another, apartment houses exclusively in still another — occasionally aroused the ire of some planner, but his fellows tended to regard him as a maverick. George H. Gray of New Haven, contended, for instance, that it would be perfectly possible to combine row houses, single-family dwellings, and apartment houses under ideal conditions. "If homes get the necessary air, light, and recreation space, they get what is necessary," he declared.[17] But the new orthodoxy was against mixture of any kind. Most planners also had a ready answer for the criticism that zoning tended toward undemocratic segregation of the various economic classes. "A reasonable segregation is normal, inevitable and desirable and cannot be greatly affected, one way or the other, by zoning," Robert Whitten asserted.[18]

Municipal engineers, utility corporations, and transit companies all accepted the rigid districting favored by the planners. "City engineers report that zoning is saving the city money in the design of sewers, paving, grading, and other public works, as it is now possible to calculate the kind and intensity of future growth without having to make a large allowance for contingencies," George B. Ford noted with great satisfaction in 1924. "Telephone, electric light, gas, and trolley companies report that zoning is making it possible for them to eliminate much of their guesswork as to what service they must provide ahead for."[19]

Urban America enthusiastically embraced the new order, and for the sake of economy, efficient administration, and reliable long-range planning straightjacketed its growth and development within highly restricted zones — except, of course, when it pleased politicians, speculators, and weak planning commissions to circumvent the regulations. Few planners would even admit that there might be a better system of control that would permit engineers and utility companies to calculate maximum future needs and yet would permit cities to develop with variety and greater convenience for their residents.

Regional Planning: The Rewards of Persistence

While the enthusiasm for zoning swept the nation and engaged the attention of some planners to the exclusion of all else, metropolitan regional planning slowly got under way in a few of the larger metropolitan areas, not always initiated by city planners. Would the New York area have embarked on a regional planning program if Charles Dyer Norton had not persisted in advocating one? Perhaps, though half the twenties might have passed before anyone else displayed the vision and courage he possessed. And who might that someone else have been? Not Nelson Lewis, whose thoughts were mostly of retirement; not Ford and Goodrich, whose consulting practice provided challenging work in many other cities; not Robert Whitten, though he thought much about the spatial organization of large urban areas; and probably no other member of the board of trustees of the Russell Sage Foundation, with the possible exception of Alfred White, but he lived only long enough to revive Norton's hope of such a program. In Chicago, Professor Graham R. Taylor and the members of the City Club provided the impetus for regional planning; in the St. Paul-Minneapolis area, the Northwest Section of the American Society of Civil Engineers; and in the San Francisco Bay Area, the members of the city planning section of the Commonwealth Club, among whose members was, however, one city planner — Russell Van Nest Black. In the Los Angeles area a man who was not originally a city planner, but who became one through his fascination with the possibilities of city planning, almost single-handedly launched an areawide planning effort, incidentally stimulating the regional planning endeavors in Chicago and the San Francisco Bay Area. His name was Gordon C. Whitnall and he worked for almost a decade before he succeeded in getting a county-wide planning program established.

Whitnall and Norton, on opposite sides of the continent, worked simultaneously in pursuit of their dreams of metropolitan planning, the former striving for an official planning agency, the latter for a well-financed private organization. Norton achieved his goal first and no doubt indirectly aided Whitnall in consummating his campaign for a county regional planning commission.

In early December, 1920, Norton and his fellow trustee White had a long talk, in the course of which White again expressed interest in his friend's regional planning project. Norton himself had almost decided to forget about the whole thing because it did not seem to appeal to Robert de Forest. But a few days later White invited De Forest, John Glenn, Nelson P. Lewis, and Norton to lunch to discuss it. With a smile, Norton pointed out that the scheme they had previously thought too big was now even bigger; whereupon he plunged into an argument for a comprehensive plan for the vast area he had earlier described as the true New York region. De Forest gasped, laughed, finally acknowledged that after a full discussion with White he was now willing to consider the employment of

Lewis, who had recently resigned from his position with the city of New York, to make at least a preliminary investigation of the project.

On Saturday morning, January 29, 1921, White called on Norton to discuss presentation of the project to the full board of trustees of the Russell Sage Foundation the following Monday. That very afternoon White was drowned while skating at the Harriman estate at Central Valley. His sudden death caused the trustees to postpone their meeting, but they must have been moved by memories of him when they appoved the employment of Lewis for a period not to exceed a year, at a salary of $1,000 a month. They also authorized the appointment of a committee — De Forest, Norton, and Glenn — with power to spend as much as $25,000 for preliminary inquiries designed to develop "basic facts and fundamental considerations" to guide future planning.[20]

At that point Norton's dream was all but realized. He knew the kinds of studies that should be commissioned, and he had in mind the men to make them. His tentative suggestions for a preliminary survey were all set down in a memorandum he read at a dinner to which he invited De Forest, Glenn, and some of the very men he wished the foundation to employ as consultants. Lewis, who had left on a previously planned trip to California, would "visit personally every municipality embraced within the plan area, mapping and recording existing local conditions and plans, and interviewing local officials and interested citizens who later might be organized into a larger group or advisory committee representing the whole area."[21] Shelby M. Harrison, who had edited the six volumes of the Pittsburgh Survey, would study and report on the social as-

52. Alfred T. White, a trustee of the Russell Sage Foundation who shared Charles Dyer Norton's dream of a regional plan for New York *(Russell Sage Foundation)*

pects of the proposed plan of New York.[22] Norton fervently hoped that
from the outset the five-man Committee on Plan of New York to be appointed by De Forest would be "alive to the needs of the masses of the
people—particularly of those in congested areas, who are less fortunately
housed and environed."[23] Norton's old friend Frederic A. Delano would
collect and analyze data on harbor and railroad terminal problems and
proposed solutions for such problems, as he had done in Chicago when
Burnham was preparing the plan sponsored by the Commerical Club.
E. P. Goodrich would make a study of local transportation, Bassett a report on zoning, Veiller a study of housing conditions and possible sources
of relief from congestion,[24] and Lawson Purdy an analysis of taxation
problems and needed reform legislation. For Olmsted two tasks were outlined: a study of park and recreation problems and a report on "whether
it is feasible to find within the [planning] area . . . locations for one or
more garden cities similar to Letchworth."[25] Norton proposed that attorney Frank B. Williams indicate the limitations which existing laws
imposed on the Committee on Plan of New York and that he suggest
desirable changes in the laws of New Jersey, New York, and Connecticut.[26] Norton also proposed to invite such other prominent men as Herbert Hoover, the sculptor Daniel Chester French, Arnold Brunner, and
Charles Moore to offer advice about methods the committee should adopt.

The planning program eventually shaped up rather differently from
the way Norton originally envisaged it, but his memorandum is interesting as a personal document revealing his human sympathies, his idealism, and his confidence in old friends and well-known leaders.

53. Charles Dyer Norton, first
chairman of the Committee on
the Regional Plan of New York
and Its Environs *(C. McKim
Norton)*

Three months later the trustees of the Sage Foundation formally appointed Norton chairman of what became known as the Committee on Regional Plan of New York and Its Environs. De Forest graciously relinquished the chairmanship because of his friend's passionate interest in the project. Two additional committee memberships authorized by the trustees were filled by Delano and Dwight Morrow, a partner of J. P. Morgan and later ambassador to Mexico. Delano was by then not only the head of several railroad lines but also vice-governor of the Federal Reserve Board. (Six other members, including George McAneny and Lawson Purdy, were added some time later when the project was converted to autonomous status.) The trustees also appropriated an additional $25,000 for the work of the committee and recognized that it might spend as much as $300,000 in a period of three or four years.[27]

Not until May 10, 1922, when survey work had been under way for fifteen months, was the ambitious undertaking announced to the general public. The meeting at which it was presented offered an imposing array of speakers: Elihu Root, Herbert Hoover, Lillian D. Wald, Charles Dana Gibson, John C. Carty, Mrs. August Belmont, and, of course, Norton and De Forest. Hoover, who had visions of a society dedicated to the principles of equality of opportunity and of service, spoke of "the enormous losses in human happiness and in money which have resulted from lack of city plans which take into account the conditions of modern life."[28] The scarcity of open space, the congestion of streets, and the misery of tenement life together constituted "an untold charge against our American life."[29] Elihu Root acknowledged that he and his fellow New Yorkers had "not quite succeeded in building a city"; it was "worth while to try to find out what the touble is."[30] Norton was, however, the hero of the occasion. In his simple, unaffected way he thrilled the participants with his description of the project that had been so long gestating in his mind. From this endeavor he expected "a plan which, with wide public participation and approval, shall embody and record the best thought of our engineers, our artists and architects, our public servants, our social workers and economists, and far-seeing business men." His committee would propose "no abnormal expansion of public expenditures" but rather the direction of tax revenues into projects of "permanent constructive value," conceived as parts of an areawide scheme of development. He had faith that "the public will welcome comprehensive planning, and will endeavor through the proper public authorities and citizen organizations to realize to the utmost, as the decades pass, the social, the industrial, the commerical and the artistic values of this great world capital and port."[31]

Less than a year later Norton was dead, his chairmanship taken over by his sorrowing friend Delano. But Norton had lived to see his great planning enterprise well launched. Some weeks after the public announcement of the project, he visited France, Belgium, Holland, and England with Frederick P. Keppel, secretary of the International Chamber of Commerce. Norton persuaded Keppel to leave Paris and come to New York as executive secretary of the regional plan committee, a post he held until he became president of the Carnegie Corporation in September, 1923. Flavel Shurtleff, who was eventually to become director of public relations, joined the staff as Keppel's assistant. Thomas Adams, who had left his position as town planning adviser to the Canadian Government in 1921 and was by 1922 head of a town planning firm in England as well as a visiting lecturer on town planning at the Massachusetts Institute of Technology, advised the committee on the organization of the regional plan. Here was the "Daniel Burnham" whom Norton sought to direct the regional survey and shape the plan. At a November meeting of the trustees of the foundation Norton had the pleasure of seeing an additional appropriation of $500,000 approved for the monumental endeavor. About that time Raymond Unwin, the British architect and town planner, came for conferences and discussed, among other things, Norton's hope of developing garden cities in the vicinity of New York. By the time Norton died, in March, 1923, Lewis, Harrison, Bassett, Williams, and others had gathered an enormous amount of data and had written several memoranda outlining the scope of various studies.

Adams assumed the position of general director of plans and surveys in 1923. The regional plan committee engaged the most prominent city planners in the United States to work with him on a preliminary pathfinding study of the region. They included Olmsted, Nolen, George Ford, Edward H. Bennett, and Harland Bartholomew. Olmsted was assisted by Henry V. Hubbard, Ford by Ernest P. Goodrich, and Bartholomew by L. Deming Tilton. Nolen and Bennett had as their associates Philip W. Foster and H. T. Frost, respectively. Each pair of planners prepared maps and reports on land uses and circulation in a major division of the region, Adams being responsible for the Westchester section and for overall guidance.

When Nelson P. Lewis died, in March, 1924, the regional plan committee was an independent organization with six special divisions, four advisory committees of architects, a large advisory engineering committee, an advisory legal committee, and dozens of special consultants. On its staff served men who later would hold important positions in the National Resources Planning Board, the National Capital Park and Planning Commission, the New York City Planning Commission, and countless other planning agencies. Some of the most distinguished attorneys, architects, and engineers in the nation graced its advisory committees. In every way this privately sponsored project promised to be the most significant planning venture in the twenties, as much because of the caliber of the planners and other experts participating in it as because of the scope of the undertaking.

Regional Planning versus Regional Growth

Three thousand miles away in southern California Whitnall meanwhile had achieved his goal of a county planning commission, but the accomplishment had been preceded by years of hard work to establish a city planning commission in Los Angeles—years in which Whitnall created so much public sentiment in favor of planning that the advent of both a city and a county planning commission became almost inevitable.

Whitnall began his campaign for a city planning commission in 1913. Just when he thought he had convinced the city council of the need for such an agency, a municipal election so changed the composition of the council that he had to start all over. Two years later, after further efforts to educate the council, another election again swept out of office so many members that he faced a third attempt to get planning officially accepted. This time he decided to develop an irresistible demand for a planning commission. As organizer and secretary of the Los Angeles City Planning Association, Whitnall persuaded such dissimilar groups as the Municipal League, the Socialist Party, the Los Angeles Chamber of Commerce, the Los Angeles Realty Board, the Native Sons and the Native Daughters of the Golden West, the labor unions, and the southern California chapter of the American Institute of Architects to endorse his proposal. To make sure that the momentum of support would continue after the establishment of a commission, he drafted a proposed ordinance providing for a broadly representative body of fifty-one members, with an executive committee of nine. Finally, in April, 1920, the council approved the ordinance. Five years later a new city charter reduced the number of commissioners to five, but the initial large membership served the purpose of assuring widespread interest in city planning.

Not surprisingly, Whitnall became director of the commission he had labored to create. As he had clearly foreseen, the members soon found that any plans they might further for the development of the city of Los Angeles would be inadequate because the city was but a small part of a complex of municipalities and towns occupying the valleys and the coastal plain between the lofty Sierra Madre Mountains and the Pacific Ocean. Seven years earlier unusually heavy runoff from the slopes above Pasadena had rushed down the Arroyo Seco, carrying away homes, bridges, railroad tracks, and entire embankments and depositing them in the channels of the harbors of Los Angeles and Long Beach, more than twenty miles away. That flood and others in subsequent years had convinced citizens of the several municipalities that they should form a county flood control district to plan areawide defenses against further disasters. But the flood menace was only one of several serious problems demanding regional planning and cooperative political solutions.

At a higher elevation than Los Angeles lies the city of Glendale, at the base of the Verdugo Hills. In the early 1920s Glendale was a city of 35,000 population—without a single foot of sewers. The entire city was built upon a honeycomb of cesspools which filled up during the rainy months, overflowed, and drained down the slopes into the Los Angeles River, from which the city of Los Angeles then obtained approximately a third of its domestic water supply. Whitnall realized that Los Angeles alone could not solve this problem, nor could Glendale, with its limited financial resources. The problem was regional, as were problems of zoning near city boundaries; the regulation of new subdivisions in unincorporated areas that would sooner or later be annexed to cities; the development of

54. Bird's-eye view of the Los Angeles County flood control program, 1922 *(Los Angeles Times)*

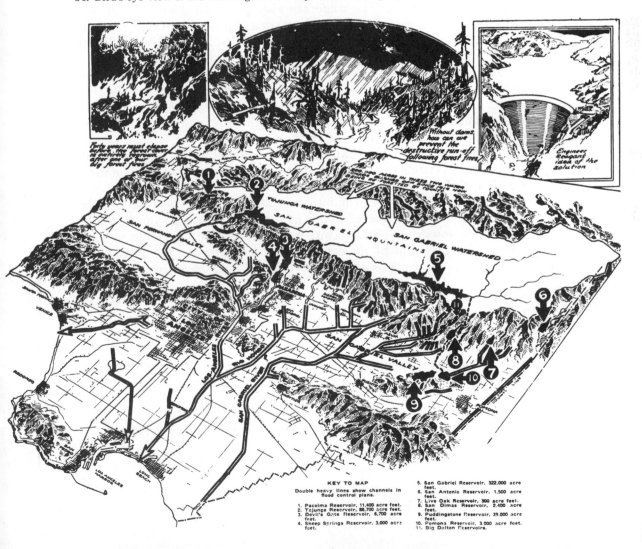

KEY TO MAP

Double heavy lines show channels in flood control plans.

1. Pacoima Reservoir, 11,400 acre feet.
2. Tejunga Reservoir, 88,700 acre feet.
3. Devil's Gate Reservoir, 6,700 acre feet.
4. Sheep Springs Reservoir, 3,000 acre feet.
5. San Gabriel Reservoir, 322,000 acre feet.
6. San Antonio Reservoir, 1,500 acre feet.
7. Live Oak Reservoir, 300 acre feet.
8. San Dimas Reservoir, 2,400 acre feet.
9. Puddingstone Reservoir, 39,000 acre feet.
10. Pomona Reservoir, 3,000 acre feet.
11. Big Dalton Reservoirs.

a highway network and additional transit facilities to serve all the cities in the Los Angeles basin; the provision of adequate public beaches, regional parks, and connecting parkways; the development of additional water supplies; the disposal of garbage and sewage; and the control of the devastating fires that sweep through the tinder-dry plant cover of the southern California hills and mountains in summer and early fall.

With authorization from the Los Angeles City Council and the Los Angeles County Board of Supervisors, Whitnall organized a regional planning conference to focus attention on the need for an agency empowered to take an overall view of the problems of the thirty-eight municipalities and fifty unincorporated towns in the metropolitan aggregation. Invitations were sent to officials of all the jurisdictions concerned, as well as to representatives of chambers of commerce, civic organizations, labor unions, electric railways, and automobile clubs. Whitnall opened the meeting at Pasadena on January 21, 1922, with a "Declaration of Interdependence" setting the tone for a thorough analysis of every physical problem of the region. The conferees also discussed, heatedly but constructively, general governmental matters and problems of finance, taxation, and overlapping special districts. By the fall of 1922 not only the public officials who had participated in the conference but also civic leaders and many members of the general public understood the necessity of an advisory planning agency in the county government. In December the board of supervisors adopted an ordinance, prepared by Whitnall, creating the Los Angeles County Regional Planning Commission, the first organization of its kind in the nation.

At the suggestion of the chairman of the board of supervisors, Whitnall selected five persons to be appointed to the new commission. Among them was Hugh R. Pomeroy, a member of the state legislature who had first evidenced great interest in planning while serving as secretary of the Redondo Beach Chamber of Commerce. Whitnall was so impressed by Pomeroy's integrity, enthusiasm, quick perception, forcefulness, and speaking ability that he indicated the young legislator not only should be named to the commission but also should later be appointed head of the staff.

In his new position Pomeroy was innately a public educator. In the first ten months after the formal inauguration of the work of the commission Pomeroy made no fewer than two hundred public addresses to chambers of commerce, realty boards, women's clubs, civic clubs, churches, colleges, and gatherings of public officials, always perspicaciously adapting his remarks to the particular audience when explaining the purposes of the new planning agency.

Generally, the commission's program developed from a document known as the "Interlocking Specifications for the Regional Plan of Los

Angeles County," a heritage from the conference of 1922. Any theoretical order of procedure that the commission might have contemplated had little likelihood of being followed in the mushrooming Los Angeles area of the 1920s. Population poured into the county from all over the United States, attracted by the benign climate, the opening of branch plants of large eastern corporations, and the reputation the area had gained in the postwar depression as the "white spot" of America, the one big metropolitan area in which there was little or no unemployment. Two overwhelming problems immediately engrossed the commission: the inadequacy of the highways and the urgency to establish standards for the design of subdivisions. In 1923, subdividers filed 1,434 maps of new tracts with the county recorder—half again as many as in 1922 and more than twice as many as in 1921.

In the first nine months after it opened its offices the regional planning commission was obliged to review more than eight hundred plans for new tracts in unincorporated territory directly under its jurisdiction. Directed by the board of supervisors to prepare a master plan of highways, the commission, with the cooperation of the municipalities, hastily evolved

55. One of Hugh R. Pomeroy's posters publicizing and explaining the services of the new Los Angeles County Regional Planning Commission

the broad outlines of a gridiron or checkerboard system of highways and attempted to make proposed subdivisions conform at least with the principal routes—major trafficways on the section lines, secondary highways on the half-section lines, and bypass highways on the quarter-section lines. All subdividers were put on notice that they must file tentative plats of their projects with the commission before accepting "reservations" for lots. The commission then referred the preliminary maps to the county road department, county surveyor, and the flood control district for their recommendations before it passed upon plats. Such specifications as the commission itself imposed were devised by the County Engineers' Association and were at the time more stringent than those adopted by municipalities in the county.

Los Angeles and the surrounding area experienced in the twenties the equivalent of all the booms California had gone through in the previous seventy years. During the decade the net immigration (entries minus departures) to Los Angeles County was greater than the total immigration since 1850. The population of the county increased 136 per cent (from 936,000 to 2,208,000), that of the city of Los Angeles 114.7 per cent (from 576,000 to 1,238,000). Downtown Los Angeles was filled with the chatter of rivet guns as workers speeded the construction of the steel frames of office buildings, department stores, theaters, and hotels. Wilshire Boulevard, which beyond Western Avenue had been only a two-lane road through open fields almost all the way to Santa Monica, swiftly became a leading thoroughfare, lined by handsome churches, clubs, apartment houses, and shops. Huge tire factories, automobile assembly plants, oil refineries, and motion picture studios, with "lots" resembling world's fairs in the variety of their sets, sprang up in bean fields and truck gardens. Planners, surveyors, engineers, and contractors worked feverishly to build highways, widen streets, connect arteries, extend thoroughfares, eliminate grade crossings, and build bridges. The cities spread out so rapidly that they coalesced into an amorphous agglomeration of stucco houses in every conceivable style, but at the end of the decade the erratic, leapfrogging development had left in its wake more than a quarter of a million vacant lots.

In this era of runaway growth the County Regional Planning Commission, the Los Angeles City Planning Commission, and the planning agencies of the smaller cities, all new and feeling their way, could barely keep pace with day-to-day demands. Planning consultants from other areas supplemented local staffs. The regional agency and the Los Angeles City Planning Commission jointly engaged the firm of Kelker and De Leuw to make a transportation survey. Pasadena contracted with Edward H. Bennett and H. T. Frost to plan its civic center. A private group known as the Southern California Development Association, formed at the suggestion of a special committee created by the Automobile Club of Southern California, sponsored a metropolitan highway plan prepared by the Olmsted brothers, Harland Bartholomew, and Charles Cheney. This association consisted of the editors of the three leading Los Angeles newspapers, who boldly proposed a "wheel tax" to carry out the plan, had the entire plan and the proposed tax submitted to the voters on a referendum, propagandized for the plan and the tax, and eventually witnessed the expenditure of more than $200,000,000 on street widenings and openings carried out in accordance with the plan. But a park and recreation plan prepared by Olmsted and Bartholomew suffered neglect, owing to the untimely death of the chief proponent, although many of the projects proposed in the plan were later carried out in some form.

In 1925 the regional agency took the lead in forming the Association of City Planners of Los Angeles County. That organization then held, between January and March, 1926, a series of conferences on zoning in which Bartholomew and Carol Aronovici served as discussion leaders. These conferences greatly influenced the zoning regulations of the smaller municipalities and gave definite direction to the work of the regional agency, which in 1927 adopted a county zoning ordinance.

In this formative period not the least of the accomplishments of the Los Angeles planning department and its counterpart in the county was persuading the federal authorities to resurvey the area and prepare accurate topographical maps, using a process in which aerial photography was employed. When Whitnall described this innovation in mapping at the national planning conference held in Los Angeles in 1924, he spoke of the way in which the aerial view enabled him to see where the reservoirs of population were and "where the great flow of population must occur." He had a sense of beholding a community in its inception and yet of having a "fair realization of what the future holds in store." He hoped that he and his fellow planners in the Los Angeles area could "prevent the recurrence of those mistakes which have happened in the growth of metropolitan areas in the east."[32]

But the combination of unprecedented immigration, excessive real estate speculation, and the necessity of expending enormous sums just to provide highways, sewers, storm drains, schools, and other essentials almost inevitably shattered the great expectations of the planners. Before they could prepare zoning ordinances, get-rich-quick developers opened residential subdivisions in some areas that might more appropriately have been used for manufacturing, and industrialists pounced on acreage that should have been given over to homes. Fields that should have been saved for parks were cut up into small lots and sold. Privately owned beach houses walled off the view of the Pacific for miles along Santa Monica Bay and the south coastal area. The whole coastal plain developed with such a low density of population that investors lost interest in a rail rapid transit system. Money for special industrial highways, scenic drives, and mountain parks was unavailable. The great opportunity of the Los Angeles region to set an example of superior planning and development for other metropolitan areas of the nation was irretrievably lost.

The Fruits of Political Realism

Perhaps no other metropolis was more immediately susceptible to the influence of the New York and Los Angeles regional planning efforts than Norton's former home city of Chicago, where civic leaders recalled his zeal in initiating the Burnham Plan. But even before the New York venture was publicly announced, a particularly articulate member of the Chicago City Plan Commission was asking why the official and voluntary agencies of Chicago and Cook County should not, like those in the city and the county of Los Angeles, organize "a regional-plan conference" to consider an overall approach to common problems. The commissioner was Graham R. Taylor, whom Whitnall had invited to address the regional conference at Pasadena. Returning to Chicago, Taylor wrote in the *Chicago Daily News* that he had just attended "one of the most significant county conferences that has ever taken preliminary initiative toward co-operative ends." It was all the more significant, especially to Chicago and Cook County, he observed, "because deadlocking issues had divided the people of these different communities [in the Los Angeles area] as they do in Illinois."[33]

Thirteen months later, on March 3, 1923, 250 persons representing almost every city and village in Cook County, several communities in Lake County, and cities in northern Indiana came together in a conference called by the Chicago City Club. To show what could be accomplished by concerted action, disregarding municipal boundary lines, speakers cited the Cook County Forest Preserve System, which had acquired more than 20,000 acres, in addition to the 5,000 acres of the Chicago park system, and was about to add 15,000 more. Thus encouraged, the participants authorized the president of the City Club to appoint a committee of twenty-one citizens, at least half of whom should reside outside Chicago, to consider a planning program for the entire metropolitan area.

At a second conference in the fall of the year, Frederic A. Delano, Norton's successor in the chairmanship of the New York regional planning committee, returned to the scene of his early activities as an instigator of the Burnham Plan and fired his listeners with an impressive account of the progress being made in his adopted city. The citizens and public officials present unanimously adopted the steering committee's recommendation that a Chicago Regional Planning Association be formed.

To head the new organization they chose Dwight H. Perkins, past president of the American Institute of Architects, but illness during most of the next year forced him to yield to a successor, Daniel H. Burnham, Jr., architect and third son of the man who advised, "Make no little plans."

Older Chicagoans perhaps expected their famous architect-planner's son to champion the preparation of a grand plan such as his father and Edward H. Bennett had fashioned sixteen years earlier or a comprehensive plan such as Thomas Adams and his associates were formulating in New York. But the younger Burnham had no enthusiasm for a planning program dominated by professional planners. He considered himself, above all, a political realist. He intended to invite public officials to participate to the utmost in solving areawide problems and developing a regional plan, especially since he was mindful that the Chicago Regional Planning Association was an organization of "sovereign municipal bodies" having "full legal authority to plan and build within their own jurisdiction." In a policy statement issued soon after he assumed the presidency of the association, he indicated that the kind of regional plan sought would be a composite of many local plans and of various regional schemes devised in response to particular regional problems. "We shall bring together, again and again," he declared, "the state, county, and municipal officials of the Region to expedite the accomplishment of street and highway plans across the dividing lines. Park and playground programs, zoning, sewerage and sewage treatment, water supplies, and many other plans should be fitted together." The regional planning association would aid local authorites to better their plans as they progressed.[34]

Burnham's strategy of encouraging local units of government to do their own planning, using basic studies and standards provided by the Chicago Regional Planning Association, began to pay dividends as the various jurisdictions attempted to harmonize their plans. Many quickly realized the need for some overall scheme to which to relate their individual plans. But it was Robert Kingery, secretary of the association, rather than Burnham who first suggested the desirability of this indirect or evolutionary approach to regional planning and who initially experimented with it in the field of highway planning.

Before becoming secretary of the association, Kingery had been assistant manager of the highway bureau of the Portland Cement Association. Aware that the boards or commissioners and supervisors of the counties in the region realized the need for adjusting their plans at county boundaries, he had written a booklet entitled *Highways of the Region of Chicago*, analyzing highway problems in maps and photographs and suggesting linkages to form a regional system. When Kingery presented this publication to the directors of the regional planning association, they immediately employed him. A few months later the Board of Cook County Commissioners adopted a resolution stating that "there is only one organization with the equipment and ability to serve as a coordinating agency for all counties and to prepare with their cooperation a comprehensive highway plan for the entire region, including parts of Wisconsin and Indiana as well as Illinois—the Chicago Regional Planning Association."[35]

From then on, Kingery and a committee of the association assumed the task of welding the various city, county, and state highway proposals into a tentative plan for a regional system. In the course of shaping this general scheme, Kingery and the committee effected an agreement under which the United States Bureau of Public Roads, the Illinois Division of Highways, the Cook County Department of Highways, and the Chicago Plan Commission pledged that no one of them would depart from the areawide framework without submitting proposed changes to the other three. As a result of this coordinating effort, in a ten-year period the disjointed highways of the three-state region were connected to form a reasonably well integrated circulation network.

Another field in which the Chicago Regional Planning Association achieved a considerable measure of success was park planning. Under its aegis the forest preserve districts of Cook, Du Page, Kane, and Will counties in Illinois adopted plans for forest protection and programs for land acquisition. The association also helped plan needed improvements in the Indiana Dunes State Park and assisted in developing plans for the expansion of Illinois state parks in the Chicago region. The 41,500 acres of state, county, and municipal park lands in the area in January, 1925, were augmented in the next thirty years by 26,500 additional acres.

Many municipalities in the environs of Chicago adopted zoning and subdivision regulations based on models offered by the association. Although some new tracts were better designed than they might otherwise have been, and although some subdividers planned streets to conform with the regional highway plan, none of the subdivision regulations promoted by the association was designed to prevent the greatest evil of the times—excessive conversion of cow pastures and cornfields into residential lots. No less a civic leader than Charles H. Wacker, whose name was synonymous with city planning to two generations of Chicagoans, contributed to the saturnalia of subdividing by estimating in 1924 that the metropolis would have a population of 18,000,000 in 1974; and even Professor J. Paul Goode, who had directed the preparation of a base map of the Chicago region for the association, was so carried away by the boom psychology of the Coolidge era that he predicted the city of Chicago alone would have 15,000,000 residents at some indeterminate future date when it might be the most populous center in the world. Disregarded by the speculators was the conservative forecast of Helen R. Jeter in a population study commissioned by the association: 5,100,000 in Chicago in

1960. But even this less optimistic figure was to prove wide of the mark. In 1960 Chicago had a population of 3,550,000, approximately 70,000 fewer than in 1950. The metropolis and its sister cities in Cook County were burdened with 894,000 unused lots at the end of the 1920s, a high proportion of which were destined to become tax-delinquent in the depression of the 1930s.

The Chicago Regional Planning Association's view of areawide planning as mainly a coordinating effort necessarily militated against its achieving the integration present-day planners would consider essential. Various regional systems and schemes evolved separately by different groups of officials cannot have the close relationship to one another that is desirable, even when a well-meaning association provides supervisory direction of the work and bases the planning on a common set of assumptions, forecasts, principles, and standards. The association's gradualist method was interesting, nevertheless, as a contrast to the centralized, professional approach adopted by Thomas Adams in the New York region.

Regional Planning from Coast to Coast

From New York in the East, Chicago in the Middle West, and Los Angeles in the West the enthusiasm for metropolitan regional planning spread rapidly to other large urban aggregations, stimulated by special talks and discussions about this broader form of planning at the national conferences on city planning in 1923 and in 1925. Several of the new regional organizations were county planning agencies, like that in the Los Angeles area; others were private, like the Committee on the Regional Plan of New York and its Environs, and the Chicago Regional Planning Association.

Of the county agencies, one had actually been in existence for four years as an unofficial body before it was legally constituted in the same year in which the Los Angeles County Regional Planning Commission began its work. This was the Allegheny County Planning Commission, serving the Pittsburgh area and functioning as part of the county department of public works. In 1924 two more county planning agencies were formed. The County Park Commission in Milwaukee County, Wisconsin, petitioned county officials to create the Milwaukee County Regional Planning Department, citing the confusion in the development of the areas between the cities of the county "incident to the rapid growth in population and commercial interests" and the desirability of providing recreational areas throughout the county "before the people arrive in great numbers."[36] The city planning commission of Toledo, Ohio, spearheaded the movement to establish the Lucas County Planning Commission. Of the eleven members appointed, four were chosen from the city body.

Santa Barbara County, California; Glynn County, Georgia; Onondaga and Monroe counties in New York; and Hamilton County, Ohio, created planning commissions in the latter part of the twenties, the first four chiefly to conserve and enhance their scenic and recreational resources. The enabling legislation under which Santa Barbara County established its planning commission in 1927 was revised in 1929 to make planning mandatory in all counties of California, but most of the other counties did not form commissions until the thirties.

Somewhat different from the other governmental agencies established in this period when the larger cities became acutely conscious of functional relationships with their environs was the National Capital Park and Planning Commission, created by act of Congress in 1926. Superseding the earlier National Capital Park Commission, this new agency was empowered to undertake regional planning in cooperation with such representatives or agencies as the states of Maryland and Virginia might designate, to carry on city planning within the limits of the District of Columbia, to assume the administrative duties of the former highway commission in connection with the street plan of Washington, and to purchase property for parks, parkways, and playgrounds. Charles Eliot II, nephew of the planner of the Boston metropolitan park system, headed the staff.

Noting the regional planning authorization of the new commission, the state legislature of Maryland in 1927 established the Maryland-National Capital Park and Planning Commission, embracing parts of Montgomery and Prince Georges counties, to coordinate its planning with that of the agency in the District of Columbia.

Like the District of Columbia and Maryland commissions, almost all the county planning agencies became concerned with highway and park planning because the increasing popularity of the automobile focused attention on the deficiencies of outlying roads and the inadequacy of regional recreational reserves. Inevitably, too, the county commissions and the Maryland-National Capital Park and Planning Commission encountered problems of urban expansion requiring consideration of zoning and subdivision regulation. The Milwaukee County Regional Planning Department, established as a branch of the highway commissioner's office, shared with the Los Angeles County Regional Planning Commission the distinction of being one of the first in the nation to adopt land-use controls for unincorporated areas. Other county agencies encouraged municipalities to form planning commissions to adopt zoning and subdivision regulations.

The tendency of several metropolitan regions to limit their areawide planning to park and highway systems, and the willingness of officials and voters to create new special districts and authorities to plan and develop water systems or port facilities, troubled some of the leaders in planning circles. Alfred Bettman, for instance, spoke against this trend at the national conference on city planning in 1925, pointing out that "if the planning of the park system of a region or any other single type of utility may be treated as independent of the planning of the other utilities and amenities, then there is no need for general regional planning."[37]

Several of the privately sponsored regional planning associations formed in the 1920s evidenced more interest in multipurpose planning than some of the metropolitan commissions and committees composed of public officials. Among these private groups were the Metropolitan Planning District Association of St. Paul-Minneapolis and Environs, the Regional Plan Association of the San Francisco Bay Counties, and the Regional Planning Federation of the Philadelphia Tri-State District.

The St. Paul-Minneapolis association concerned itself with regional zoning, recreation, transportation, and drainage and pollution problems, as well as with general public educational work and the preparation of a regional base map such as the Chicago Regional Planning Association commissioned. One of the first fruits of the activities of this Twin Cities organization was the establishment of an official Metropolitan Drainage Commission.

The Regional Plan Association of San Francisco Bay Counties, formed in 1925, had before it from the beginning a report prepared by Russell Van Nest Black proposing that it study a variety of areawide problems. In 1923 Gordon Whitnall had appeared before the section to describe the program of the Los Angeles County Regional Planning Commission, and in April, 1924, George B. Ford, Edward M. Bassett, Flavel Shurtleff, and Harland Bartholomew had spoken about various aspects of the regional planning program in New York. Black's prospectus reflected the broad conception of both these programs. When the association formally began work, it therefore engaged Bartholomew to make an initial survey of the whole range of physical problems confronting the nine-county region surrounding San Francisco Bay.

Bartholomew identified almost all the intercounty matters that were to trouble the region for the next forty years. In addition, he singled out "psychological obstacles of local pride and prejudice" as the most serious difficulties to be faced.[38] Unfortunately, the head of the association, a wealthy merchant named Fred Dohrmann, was less interested in governmental relationships than in the physical needs of the Bay area. He failed to cultivate the political leaders of the metropolitan region, but even if he had done so, he would have been plagued at that time by the suspicion that San Francisco wished to dominate other communities. The emergence in Oakland of an East Bay Regional Planning Association headed by

Fred E. Reed, an ambitious realtor, seriously weakened the influence of Dohrmann's association. It failed to generate the financial support necessary for sustained activity and ceased operations in 1928, leaving as a legacy several reports and studies which inspired later attempts to establish a regional planning agency in the politically divided Bay area.

Like other regional efforts in the twenties, Dohrmann's was handicapped by the lack of strong local planning. Few of the cities in the Bay area then had planning commissions, and outside the City and County of San Francisco there were no county planning commissions to cooperate with a regional organization and lend it moral support. Dohrmann, however, did little to stimulate the formation of new city planning commissions and took no part in a movement in 1927 to broaden California enabling legislation to authorize planning in nonchartered counties and in regions composed of two or more counties. By limiting his appeals for cooperation mainly to business and civic groups, he doomed his Regional Plan Association to an early demise.

The Regional Planning Federation of the Philadelphia Tri-State District was, in a sense, an offspring of the Committee on the Regional Plan of New York and Its Environs. The enthusiasm of Samuel Price Wetherill, Jr., paint manufacturer and scion of an old Philadelphia family, for the broad-scale program supported by the Russell Sage Foundation brought the federation into being in 1924 on a relatively modest budget. But a newspaper editor who had been chosen by Wetherill as one of the original members of the board of directors of the organization said of it later that he had never known anything which promised so much and came to so little.[39] The federation's program was, nevertheless, significant because of an initial concern with problems of metropolitan form discussed many years earlier at the first national conference on city planning.

Having left California for the region in which he had grown up, Russell Van Nest Black outlined for the Regional Planning Federation of the Philadelphia Tri-State District as comprehensive a program as he had proposed for the Regional Plan Association of the San Francisco Bay Counties. He saw his first task as director of plans and surveys for the federation as one of determining a theoretical or diagrammatic plan as a basis for a final regional plan, but he realistically assumed that "every regional plan for an established community must be in the nature of a compromise between the old form of growth and the new—between the inevitable and the ideal."[40] He therefore sought to find in the existing urban complex suggestions for "the form of development appearing to be most adaptable to the Philadelphia Region."[41]

Difficult as it was in those days to obtain even general information on land use, highways and transportation facilities, recreation areas and forest reserves, sanitation, and water supply systems in a region of 4,550 square miles, Black managed to assemble enough graphic material and historical statistical data to reveal what time and man had wrought in a great tri-state district with no physical obstructions to prevent expansion in any direction. Population had extended outward from Philadelphia in a fingerlike pattern along major lines of transportation and the river, leaving wedges of open land penetrating close into the densely populated areas of the central city. This natural development seemed to indicate a desirable relation between open space and urban settlements — one that should be perpetuated and encouraged by plan. Black assumed, however, that the "universal availability of electricity," improved highways, and the use of the motor truck called for "a widening distribution of industry with correspondingly wider spread of population." He regarded considerable growth of the central city as inevitable but foresaw a relatively much larger rate of increase in population in many of the outlying communities. The prospect gave him pause, for he was a man with strong natural feeling for the productivity and the beauty of the land. "A danger most to be avoided," he cautioned, was spoliation of the region by "too widely scattered and illogically distributed population; and on the other hand, by too great a concentration of population in existing already crowded centers." Like most planners, he hoped for the establishment of garden cities, one for Delaware and three or four each for Pennsylvania and New Jersey. He envisaged "remedying present deficiencies in circum-

56. Russell Van Nest Black

ferential highways and cross-country routes," providing "airway landing fields" in all the larger cities, coordinating railway terminals with air, water, and highway transportation, and acquiring such natural recreation places as streams, hilltops, and steep wooded hillsides to form an interrelated system of parks and public forests extending throughout the region. Although his diagrammatic scheme embodied many assumptions, Black was confident that it would serve as a basis for developing a comprehensive regional plan. He was not daunted by the "great dearth of exact knowledge concerning the social and economic laws which underlie urban growth." Only by plunging into formidable projects would planners develop the knowledge and methods needed to fashion a "planning science."[42]

Eager to proceed from his theoretical scheme to a more realistic one that could guide further development of the tri-state district, Black worked out and presented to the executive committee his program for preparing the final plan. But in the meantime a great change had taken place in the affairs of the federation. Professional fund-raisers had can-

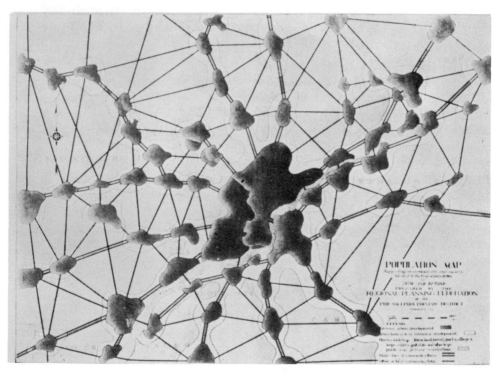

57. Russell Black's diagrammatic scheme for a theoretically desirable ultimate distribution of urban population and open space in the Philadelphia Tri-State District

vassed the region and obtained $600,000 from banks, railroads, utilities, the Duponts of Delaware, and other wealthy men; some of the older civic leaders on the board of directors had been dropped and had been replaced by representatives of large corporations; and a politically motivated former commissioner of state highways in Pennsylvania had been brought in as director. When Black proposed a detailed regional land use study, a telephone company executive immediately objected. "We'll have none of that," he said; "it sounds too much like zoning."[43] The company was opposed to any study that might even remotely interfere with its plan to put its central station in what it called the "wire center" of Philadelphia, even though the center was in a residential area from which such a major facility ordinarily would be excluded. If Black had remained with the association, he would have circumvented the objections of the company by making the study under another name, but this incident and others convinced him that the new director and the new board members would not be sympathetic to the far-reaching planning program he had in mind. He recalled that he had asked the heterodox historian Charles A. Beard to be a consultant to the association and had received the reply, "Your organization wouldn't want me."[44] Now Black understood that he, too, was the wrong man to develop a program for the association. The new director hastened his departure by denying him access to the executive committee.

Before its demise in the depression of the early 1930s, the Regional Planning Federation published several special reports and a final report presenting findings and proposals, but there was nothing in any of them to challenge the economic dominance of the financial contributors. The reports were not, however, without value in suggesting solutions to problems of river pollution, preservation of recreational resources, coordination of transportation services, and improvement of water supplies. Technical advisory committees composed of municipal and county department heads and well-known engineers, architects, and landscape architects provided most of the information on which the reports were based and devised most of the solutions advanced. Political realism and hardnosed practicality characterized many of the proposals. The final plan incorporated Black's proposals for stream-valley parks and parkways but deviated from his scheme of bypass routes and gave no hint of his suggestion for a fingerlike arrangement of urban areas along corridors of movement, with open country saved for agricultural, recreational, and scenic purposes.

The Regional Planning Federation had chiefly an educational influence on the tri-state district. Most of the specific improvements made in accordance with the final plan would have been carried out in any event, as they were in the works, so to speak, before being incorporated into the

220 CITY PLANNING IN THE AGE OF BUSINESS

plan. In its eight years of activity the federation implanted the idea of planning in the minds of many persons who might not otherwise have come to appreciate it, though only Mercer County, New Jersey, in which Trenton, the state capital, is situated, actually formed a planning commission as a result of the federation's efforts. Looking back on this private endeavor, Black concluded that a less lavish expenditure of money in the last few years and a more sustained, modest operation over a longer period of time probably would have benefitted the tri-state district far more than the "big organization" program undertaken between 1928 and 1931.

Black's frustration over the conservative course of the federation's program seems almost to have been foretold in an article that Charles Beard wrote about regional planning in 1926. The historian asked for "a deeper consideration of the economic forces which may be enlisted for or against the dreams and blue prints of artists and engineers, and the precise social and political modes in which those economic forces operate."[45] Beard explained that he was not advocating detailed industrial surveys or exhaustive studies of land values and assessments but was referring to subjects "not usually mentioned in polite society—to themes that are usually as tabu in academic circles as sex at a Boston tea party—to topics vulgarly known as special interests, private rights—acquired and potential—honest graft, and plain graft."[46] As he saw it, regional planners had the task of analyzing and exposing to public gaze, on the one hand, the various economic interests likely to profit by maintaining the status quo or forcing antisocial developments and, on the other hand, the economic groups that might be enlisted, by virtue of their practical interests, on the side of a comprehensive community scheme. Until such inquiry was made "in a scientific spirit and with meticulous attention to microscopic detail," Beard was firmly convinced that "our so-called social science, of which regional planning is merely one branch," would remain very much "in a state in which Harvey found medicine and Descartes and Cavalieri found mathematical science."[47] The social forces confronting the regional planner were "as real as those handled by the hydraulic engineer."[48] It was not likely that the planner, or the public "for whom he speaks," would advance very far in the conquest of urban chaos until he "applied his theodolite to the realities of his situation."[49]

A planner with the public interest at heart though employed by a private organization financed by powerful corporations was not, however, in a position to "apply his theodolite to the realities of his situation." Nor was the planner on the payroll of a government agency necessarily free to "expose to public gaze" the self-seeking interests that might obstruct the preparation or execution of a comprehensive plan, since such interests protect themselves, as often as they can, by contributing to the political campaigns of elected officials — the very men who make the final decisions concerning proposals of the planner and the recommendations of the planning commission. Presumably only an academician dedicated to the pursuit of truth, or the researcher engaged by a foundation with a reputation for being, like Caesar's wife, above suspicion, could undertake the disinterested inquiry suggested by Beard. But any investigator faces the problem of gaining a hearing in a society in which many of the media of communication are controlled by self-serving interests. Beard clearly perceived the political problem of the planner but was perhaps naïve in supposing that there could be any "scientific" solution to it in a pluralistic society enjoying the liberties guaranteed by the Constitution of the United States.

Conflicting Conceptions of Regionalism

Of all the regional plans conceived in the 1920s, Black's theoretical or diagrammatic plan was probably closest in spirit to the kind of regional plan envisaged by Henry Wright in a report issued by the New York State Commission of Housing and Regional Planning in 1926, the year Black joined the staff of the Regional Planning Federation of the Tri-State District as a "planning engineer." Wright maintained that "the conservation and the future development of the resources of a region to the end that an economic gain may not involve inevitable social loss, requires the preservation of all existing natural values both of the country and of the city."[50] He added, "This does not mean the complete subordination of country to urban influences," yet that is what most metropolitan regional plans of the decade contemplated, even those which made handsome provision for the recreational use of streams and forests. Seldom was there thought of preserving the distinctive character of rural areas and small settlements, but Wright held this as an ideal and quoted the views of his friend Lewis Mumford:

> Regional planning asks not how wide an area can be brought under the aegis of the metropolis, but how the population and civic facilities can be distributed so as to promote and stimulate a vivid, creative life throughout the whole region — a region being any geographic area that possesses a certain unity of climate, soil, vegetation, industry and culture. The regionalist attempts to plan such an area so that all its sites and resources, from forest to city, from highland to water level, may be soundly developed, and so that the population will be distributed so as to utilize, rather than to nullify or destroy its natural advantages. It sees people, industry and the land as a single unit.[51]

True regionalism, in the opinion of chairman Clarence Stein and his fellow members of the Commission of Housing and Regional Planning, necessitated releasing the state of New York from "centralizing pressures" and "the apparently insoluble problems — physical, economic and social—that are raised by the pyramiding city."[52] In their way, the commissioners were as much troubled by the drift of population to the big centers, and by the consequent impoverishment and cultural depletion of the rural areas of the state, as Ebenezer Howard had been by the same trends in the England of the aging Queen Victoria. They saw in long-distance transmission of electric power and motor transport new tools for rehabilitating declining areas and saving large cities from the economic wastes and loss of human values resulting from congestion. Hard-surfaced roads and the automobile would break down the isolation of the farm and would extend the area over which it could serve urban centers with perishable products. Cheap electric power would lighten the drudgery of farm life. Motor transport would enable factories once entirely dependent on railroads for the delivery of raw materials and the shipment of finished products to disperse to locations served only by highways. Workers formerly confined to crowded districts could live in suburban regions and drive their own cars or could go by bus to plants in outlying areas. By taking full economic and social advantage of the new technology, every region of the state could achieve a more effective utilization of its human and economic resources. A new state pattern would emerge, unlike the widely distributed development of the mid-nineteenth century or the concentration along main lines of transportation between 1880 and 1920. In the future each region, in concert with others, could serve its logical function in support of wholesome activity and good living. Regions with many hundreds of thousands of acres of substandard land still held in use for farming purposes could gradually be reforested and used for scientific lumbering, as sources of water supply, and as playgrounds for urban millions, while those with potentialities for increased agricultural and industrial development could be more carefully planned for a variety of economic activities.

The instrument for effecting the transformation of the state into a group of functionally interdependent regions was to be a state plan—a general scheme that would not seek to limit local action "with hard-and-fast outlines" but would "attempt to help the several regions solve their problems by bringing out the relationship of their special situations to outside conditions." The basis of the state plan would be "a complete 'land economic survey' such as that which is being undertaken in Michigan" and an industrial economic survey. Every important state department and many private interests as well would contribute to the development of the plan. The task of making the plan and using it to coordinate the decisions of both public agencies and private companies would be "intrusted to some State agency close to the central executive."[53]

"Up to now we have been too greatly at the mercy of blind chance and of our necessities," planning adviser Wright and the staff of the state commission noted. "We have been to a large extent the creatures of circumstances; we have permitted external forces to shape our lives, without making an effort to see how far these forces conformed to useful human purpose."[54] But now, by using nature and machinery intelligently, the people of the (then) most populous state in the Union could become the creators of their future instead of the passive creatures of circumstance. Two regional agencies—the Niagara Frontier Planning Board, serving the counties of Erie and Niagara, and the Albany Capital District Planning Commission—were brought into being to prepare plans that could be integrated into the overall state plan, but only the former succeeded in developing a program.

The vision of a replanned and revitalized state was not alone Wright's and the commission's but also that of the Regional Planning Association of America. Formed in 1923, the group included not only Stein, Wright, Mumford, and MacKaye but also Frederick Ackerman, Charles H. Whitaker, realtor Alexander Bing, economist Stuart Chase, and architects Robert D. Kohn, John Irwin Bright, and Frederick Bigger. Others associated with it later were Tracy Augur, Catherine Bauer, Clarence A. Perry, Robert Bruere, Joseph K. Hart, Russell Black, and Edith Elmer Wood. Never a formal organization with an office, a staff, regular publications, and a schedule of meetings and conferences, the association was really little more than a circle of friends held together by a broad conception of planning. This conception synthesized the ideas of various members of the group with those of the cultural regionalists of France, the Scottish biosociologist and planner Patrick Geddes, various American geographers, conservationists, and naturalists, and such English planners as Ebenezer Howard and Thomas Adams. Adams was particularly admired for his work in Canada, since it stressed the importance of linking the urban center with the agricultural district and controlling the use of natural resources, preventing speculation, and meeting social needs. Yet the kind of metropolitan regional planning which Adams espoused as general director of the staff of the Committee on the Regional Plan of New York and Its Environs seemed to the Regional Planning Association of America to be widely at variance with his own earlier practice and the regionalism of Wright and the state Commission of Housing and Regional Planning. Generally, the regionalism of Wright and the commission was that of the Regional Planning Association of America, though the latter group never formulated any precise credo.

In planning for Greater New York, Adams concerned himself with approximately the area originally defined by Charles Dyer Norton. It was, for the most part, the territory "within easy commuting distance" of Manhattan, though in one direction the outer limits of the planning area were 130 miles from the center. Within the 5,528 square miles of this urban region were more than 500 incorporated communities, and it was the political complexion of the area, more than anything else, which profoundly affected Adam's whole approach to the development of a comprehensive plan. "The Regional Plan Committee is a voluntary advisory body and cannot of course carry out any of the proposals contained in the plan being prepared by its staff," Adams pointed out at a meeting in 1926. "Nor is there any public authority—either existing or in prospect of being formed—that has the power to give effect to the Plan."[55] The realization of the plan would rest with the counties, cities, towns, and villages of the metropolitan region. Either they would find it practical and properly respectful of local sentiment, or they would disregard it and render the work of the planners useless. As Adams saw it, "a regional plan—and even a city plan in some respects—has to be elastic and capable of adjustment and readjustment to suit change and ever varying circumstances in community growth."[56] He was therefore intent on producing "a broad outline of proposals for guidance of public authorities and utility corporations," leaving the development of details to "the local authorities through their planning commissions, the county authorities through their highway and park commissions, the port authorities, and the railroad authorities."[57] His hope was for a general plan representing " a high degree of unanimity in regard to the general pattern and principles." To this end he instituted, from the beginning, a cooperative planning process in which local officials conferred with his staff.

"Every community," Adams said, "should have its planning commission, and the members of each planning commission should come to our office, sit down with us and look at these plans and consider them in relation to their community. If they have criticisms to offer we shall welcome them. The power to carry out our ideas rests with these local commissions and we want them to see that the Regional Plan is properly related to their own district. We want it endorsed by them after due criticism and discussion."[58]

Adam's political realism matched that of Daniel H. Burnham, Jr., in the Chicago region and Whitnall's in the Los Angeles area. With ample funds at his disposal, Adams could, however, provide a far more satisfactory background of factual information as a basis for his planning program than Burnham and Whitnall could for theirs. Yet Adams knew that he could not rely upon facts or the interpretation of facts to assure the success of the planning effort. He had as his political aid the energetic Flavel Shurtleff, to whom Norton had said in 1922, "What we want you to do is to keep your ears open and tell us what is said about us." When Shurtleff had replied, "Nothing is said about you," Norton had agreed that the Committee on the Regional Plan needed to "make a bigger splash," and from then on Shurtleff had "preached the gospel of planning" throughout the New York region, stimulating the formation of planning commissions, the adoption of zoning ordinances, and the co-operation of local officials with the staff of the committee.[59]

The regional plan which Adams described at public meetings in 1926 was even then evolving as a quasi-political document "dealing rather with the future than with the present, and with tendencies rather than with conditions."[60] Since he accepted the prediction that there would be from 15,000,000 to 20,000,000 people in the New York region in thirty to forty years, he and his staff were preparing a plan to provide for more than double the mid-twenties population of some 9,000,000. Adams was "impressed with the importance of bringing metropolitan New York and metropolitan New Jersey into closer collaboration," providing better means of communication between Long Island and New Jersey, without going through Manhattan, and improving connections between the Bronx and Queens.[61] If the daily migration of more than 2,800,000 people into Manhattan south of Fifty-ninth Street should increase, the "vital pulse of the region" might be strangled. Adams therefore sought more even development throughout the region and a reduction in the journey between home and place of work. The economic survey conducted by Dr. Robert M. Haig revealed a tendency toward the transference of heavy industries and some of the lighter industries from the center and certain movements toward the dispersal of retail business and amusement places to the boroughs of Brooklyn, the Bronx, and Queens. To Adams these trends indicated opportunities for creating subcenters and satellite communities and for strengthening circumferential means of transportation. But the achievement of "better balanced growth" necessarily assumed "more control of land development in the environs, greater stringency of zoning restrictions, and adequate measures to restrain the improper use of unhealthy or deteriorated structures in old sections of the City."[62] Without the cooperation of hundreds of communities, the regional plan would remain, in its larger aspects, a dream. Were Adams and the Committee on the Regional Plan wishful thinkers?

In the opinion of Thomas H. Reed, professor of government at the University of Michigan, they were not. Speaking at the national conference on city planning in 1925, Reed had said: "It is easy enough to understand why the directors of the 'Plan of New York and Its Environs' pin their faith to voluntary co-operation. They have nothing else to pin to. The proposal to unite in any formal way the parts of three states which fall within the metropolitan area of New York would arouse suspicions and antagonisms enough to lose the battle before it is begun." Under such circumstances it was clearly the part of wisdom to preach voluntary cooperation. Given an intelligently directed and adequately supported planning agency to stimulate the multitude of diverse authorities to action, great things might be thus accomplished. In general, however, to rely on voluntary cooperation was to surrender all hope of substantial success.[63]

Having dismissed the possibility of achieving some form of areawide government in the immensely complex New York region, Reed maintained that for other urban regions an overall unit of government was essential. City planners themselves, almost unwittingly, were laying the foundation of a new unit of local government by popularizing the idea of the region.[64] Indeed, without regional government the very fabric of their dreams would "fray out to tattered fragments" because "consistent and comprehensive results cannot ordinarily be expected from the mere voluntary co-operation of the authorities concerned."[65] Nor could the metropolitan problem any longer be solved by the annexation of small communities to the big city, or by direct state administration of metropolitan affairs — "It is too distinct a violation of the principle of home rule to be acceptable to the public" — or by the creation of various ad hoc authorities, since this would only diffuse further the public interest in metropolitan affairs, as well as result in lack of coordination among agencies.[66]

Reed proposed the creation of areawide governments in regions centering usually upon some relatively large urban community and including the territory socially and economically dependent on it. He could see no reason why small regions should not center on Albany, Syracuse, and Rochester as well as large ones on New York and Chicago. His suggestion of the region, he explained, was based upon "the commonly neglected fact that the question of metropolitan areas is curiously interrelated with that of efficient areas for rural local government." In recent years the cost of services expected of rural governments had mounted with such extraordinary rapidity that they could no longer meet the demands upon them. Even county governments exhibited financial incapacity to discharge their obligations adequately. If state subsidies to rural governments, "with accompanying state control," were to be avoided, the only avenue of escape was the creation of "large areas of local government centering upon and including the cities."[67]

But Reed advocated no wholesale extinction of municipal governments. His proposal, he emphasized, "would affect the existence, dignity, and essential independence of none of the existing units of government." The regional government, headed by a council elected at large by proportional representation, would be strictly limited to functions of areawide importance: "planning, including zoning and the preservation of suitable forest and shore reservations; transportation, including street railways, buses, and rapid transit lines; traffic, including highway construction and maintenance; water supply and electric energy; drainage; and certain aspects of police, health, and charity administration." Such a regional government would be financially competent, Reed believed, to "give ample relief to the overburdened rural treasuries," but it would not entirely obviate the necessity of some state contributions to equalize local burdens in such matters as education and highway construction.[68] For services not of direct benefit to the whole region, small assessment districts could be created.

The professor assumed that the prospect of relief from financial difficulties would naturally tend to reconcile rural areas and small cities to the surrender of a few functions to the regional government, but he made no promises. "No one dares promise what the popular response will be to any suggestion," he acknowledged, though he held out "reasonable hopes" that in time two-level government would be accepted as the chief means of solving metropolitan problems.[69]

Planning Consultants and the Comprehensive Plan

Although the problems of the large city and the metropolitan region occupied the spotlight in the twenties, most of the plans prepared in this decade were for cities whose residents were untroubled about tall buildings and crowded tenements. Of approximately a hundred plans completed between 1920 and the end of 1926, more than three-fourths were for municipalities with fewer than 100,000 inhabitants. Many of these small cities had only 30,000 to 40,000 citizens, yet planning consultants with wide experience, such as John Nolen, Harland Bartholomew, and Edward H. Bennett, were eager to guide their development. Bartholomew, the most active consultant, prepared comprehensive plans for thirty-two cities in the 1920s, including Pittsburgh, New Orleans, Kansas City, Memphis, and other important centers, but the greater part of his practice was in such small cities as Kenosha, Wisconsin (population 40,000), Hutchinson, Kansas (population 23,000), and Grand Haven, Michigan (population 7,000).

Only in some of the sparsely settled mountain states of the West and Southwest, a few of the southern states, and the upper New England states were cities unawakened to the need for some measure of control over their growth and development. John Nolen noted in 1927, however, that three times as many cities had adopted zoning ordinances as had equipped themselves with long-range plans. Throughout the decade planners talked earnestly at their conferences about the urgency of "selling" planning to the public and occasionally invited some chamber-of-commerce official to instruct them in the fine art of promotion, but they were not always successful in convincing a community that it should have an overall plan outlining interrelated aspects of its development. To a great many cities zoning was the be-all and end-all of planning. Some were satisfied with only a street plan or a plan of streets and parks. A few wanted a preliminary plan but would not enter into a contract for its completion.

The lack of planning staffs in many cities indicated that, in general, the country did not yet accept city planning as an indispensable, continuing function of government. Most of the larger cities maintained planning offices of their own and budgeted from $15,000 to $20,000 or more for the purpose, but smaller cities tended to depend upon their bureaus of engineering or departments of public works for such planning services as they received. Even in the larger centers a good deal of the work tended to be detailed concern with street improvements, zoning, and subdivision regulation rather than farsighted planning for city-wide development. Consultants still provided the larger vision needed in most planning programs.

In the mid-twenties there were twenty-three consultant firms available to planning commissions, citizens' groups, and private developers. Nolen, Bartholomew, Robert Whitten, and Ford and Goodrich, whose firm was known as the Technical Advisory Corporation, practiced in many states. Most of the other planners were active in only one or two states — Arthur A. Shurtleff in Massachusetts, H. S. Swan in New Jersey and Connecticut, Lawrence V. Sheridan in Indiana, B. A. Haldeman in Pennsylvania, M. W. West chiefly in Illinois and Wisconsin, and Charles Cheney and Carol Aronovici in California and Oregon.

These consultants all offered what was described as a comprehensive plan, though the degree of comprehensiveness varied widely. The typical plan consisted of only six elements: zoning (generally thought of as a land use scheme), streets, transit, rail and water transportation, public recreation, and civic art or civic appearance. Harland Bartholomew, who had been interested in housing ever since his early work with Ford in Newark, included a section on housing in a report on Wichita, Kansas, in 1923, but made no proposals for relieving the shortage of low-rent dwellings for poor families. In the business-dominated 1920s his other planning reports made no mention of housing, not because he had changed his ideas about the importance of the subject but because his clients were indifferent. Ford himself was one of the few other planners who attempted to discuss the housing problem. In the report he and Goodrich prepared for Cincinnati in 1925 he cited a study John Nolen had made for the Housing Betterment League of that city and described the housing situation of wage earners as more pressing than it had been at any time in the past. Ford saw no possibility, however, of building housing within the means of "the vast majority of colored families and a great many white wage earners." He could suggest only "the amelioration of living conditions in the older part of the town by zoning protection and by provision of parks, playgrounds, community centers and open spaces."[70]

The Ford-Goodrich plan for Cincinnati, costing the "unheard of" sum of $120,000, was something of a landmark in the twenties because its scope was far broader than that of most plans of the period. In addition to the familiar elements, it contained sections on the historical growth of the city and probable trends of future development, downtown traffic problems, subdivisions and housing, schools and play yards, garbage and refuse disposal, means of financing improvements, and a program for a citizens' city planning committee, included as one of the appendixes. Much more detailed than a general plan would be nowadays, this one reflected Goodrich's concern as an engineer with the specifics of street widening and extension and the interest of various city department heads in improving public areas under their jurisdiction. Illustrations of well-designed features of European cities, interspersed throughout the report as in City Beautiful plans, revealed that Ford had lost none of his enthusiasm for the aesthetic. Indeed, he had complained a few years earlier that

58. Aerial perspective from Harland Bartholomew's comprehensive plan of Wichita, Kansas: the view is toward the central business district and the Arkansas River; the plan included proposals for major streets, transit, transportation, recreation, housing and sanitation, civic art, and zoning

"the suppression of the beautiful in our planning [is] merely another
manifestation of that puritanical mask which so many of us have inherited."[71]

The chapter on zoning illustrated some of the pecularities and weaknesses of general plans of the times. Entitled "Building Zones," it would
appear today as a section on land use. It explained the zoning ordinance
and even included the text of the rules of procedure of the zoning board
of appeals. Ford and Goodrich pointed out that "at every stage the zoning
map was compared with the studies going on simultaneously on each
feature of the City Plan, so as to avoid 'surprises' and the necessity of
undoing the Zoning Plan later to conform with the rest of the City Plan."
They had, they stated, made calculations from field studies of the amount
of business space which would probably be needed for the next fifty years
in each part of the city to take care of local needs and had similarly calculated the amount of industrial space needed in proportion to the growing population.[72] Yet their planning "science" seems to have been affected
by the business optimism of the era, as was that of almost all of their
fellow planning consultants. They delineated commercial districts providing for the needs of five times the population of Cincinnati, then estimated at 415,000 and not expected, by their own projections, to exceed
675,000 by the year 2100. The industrial zones provided for at least ten
times as much industrial acreage as the community was then using.

The chapter on subdivisions and housing reflected the struggle throughout the twenties to raise standards for the design of new tracts, to extend
municipal control of platting well beyond city boundaries, and to curtail
premature subdividing. Even a very slow-growing city such as Cincinnati
witnessed a spurt in subdividing in its environs and officially shared the
general conviction that new tracts which might someday be annexed
should have streets properly related to proposed highways and major
thoroughfares and should make adequate provision for sanitation and
drainage. Ford and Goodrich reproduced in their chapter an Ohio law
of 1923—in the main the handiwork of Alfred Bettman and the Ohio
State Conference on City Planning—giving cities which had adopted a
long-range plan of streets and parks the right to regulate subdivisions
within three miles of their boundaries. The consultants also included the
innovative rules and regulations adopted by the city planning commission
requiring developers, at their own expense, to plant street trees and install streets and utilities under the watchful eye of a city inspector and
in accordance with specifications approved by the city engineer. These
significant deterrents to wholly speculative enterprise were matched by
other regulations, equally advanced, intended to enhance residential
amenity and reduce the amount of land used for roadways by encouraging
the design of narrower local streets, the elimination of alleys, and the

planning of longer blocks, in which lots were at least fifty feet wide.

The Ford-Goodrich plan attracted attention not only because of its broad scope but also because of a certain authoritative status conferred on it when the Cincinnati City Planning Commission officially endorsed it. The commission acted under a city charter of 1918 and a state law of 1923, both of which provided that once a plan was approved by the commission, any proposed departure from the scheme must first be submitted to the commission and if disapproved must be passed by a two-thirds vote of the city council.

"For the first time in the United States, a complete comprehensive city plan has become the law of the city," Ford boasted.[73] But Alfred Bettman, whose guiding hand could be seen in both the city charter and the state law, demurred. "In stating that the Cincinnati plan has the force of 'law,' Mr. Ford is using an expression which, from the point of view of lawyers, is inaccurate," he pointed out. The plan could not be enforced by the courts. The state statute, like the city charter provision, merely gave the planning commission "an influence somewhat analogous to the veto power of a mayor or other chief executive." The intent of the law was to "force council into . . . discussion with the planning commission," so that the governing group would "learn to realize the value of city planning and the merits of the plan." The compulsory controversy guaranteed by the law would also enable public opinion to be "aroused and mobilized and to express itself," Bettman believed, with the result that the plan would have "a force, prestige and power which it would not otherwise have."[74]

Bartholomew and many other city planners were far from convinced, however, that any city planning commission should have such powers as the Cincinnati City Planning Commission enjoyed. "I fear," he said, "that there may arise in Cincinnati official resentment against the plan and the plan commission which may seriously affect its success." As he saw it, there could never be 100 per cent accomplishment in city planning, but for even modest accomplishment there must be strong support by the public—"It is more important than legal checks and safeguards."[75]

Fortunately, the cause of city planning in Cincinnati had both public and official support. Throughout the three years in which Ford and Goodrich were at work on their plan they invited the collaboration of every municipal department and every public utility affected by their proposals. There was, moreover, such widespread public interest in the zoning ordinance developed while the plan was being prepared that the city council adopted this regulatory measure unanimously in 1924. The comprehensive plan therefore came before the planning commission and the city council with substantial popular and governmental backing not necessarily requiring the invocation of laws providing that the planning commission's disapproval of a proposed departure from the plan could be overridden only by a two-thirds vote of the council.

New Towns in the Boom Years

Preparing plans for older cities with many problems was a perennial challenge to the planning fraternity. What every consultant hoped for was more opportunities to create brand new environments with improved street patterns, novel arrangements of dwellings, and groupings of public and semipublic structures. The wartime experience of planning new residential developments had been exhilarating, in spite of the difficulties, because it afforded occasion for experimentation and innovation. The booming twenties offered another chance to advance the art of town planning, though not the expansive opportunities Ebenezer Howard envisaged when he appeared at the international planning conference in New York in 1925 and spoke of the "possibilities of creating not only new towns, but new regions, of creating a new civilization which shall surpass ours [in England] as the civilization of our times surpasses the old." The new additions to cities and the new towns of the period, all privately sponsored, lacked any relation to broad public policy for the distribution of population and the development of larger regions. With the exception of New York, the states had not even considered long-range development policy. But some of the suburban subdivisions and garden villages and one or two company towns of the 1920s exemplified good site planning and showed a creditable concern of the developers for the provision of community facilities and the preservation of such natural features as streams, waterfronts, forests, and views. At times, however, planners hoped for too much and were bitterly disappointed at the rejection of some of their best proposals, as in many of the undertakings in southern California and Florida.

Of several new towns begun in the decade, Mariemont, near Cincinnati, was one of the first to arouse great expectations. The sponsor was Mrs. T. J. Emery, widow of a wealthy industrialist, who was known for her many benefactions to Cincinnati. She purchased the 365-acre site overlooking the Little Miami River in the greatest secrecy, kept her meetings with her planning consultant, John Nolen, from public knowledge, and then announced the project with great showmanship at a large public dinner. Nolen's nationwide fame as the planner of the industrial city of Kingsport, Tennessee, and her advertisements of the town as "a National Exemplar" that would bring the good community life to "all classes of people" assured the venture national publicity.[76] But Mariemont was no sociological experiment in meeting the housing needs of a broad segment of the population. In Nolen's words, it was "a project . . . intended to justify itself along business lines followed with all efficiency."[77] Even the more moderate dwellings were comparatively costly, and the penchant of Mrs. Emery's estate executor, T. J. Livingood, for expensive construction greatly increased the overall investment. Mariemont turned out to be a beautiful suburb in which only high-income families could afford to live, whereas Nolen had hoped at one time to interest Mrs. Emery in a copartnership purchase-plan to attract "all classes" of working people. At heart she was a conservative with a desire for nothing more than a private housing program at low interest rates. Conceived as a community with an immediate population of 5,000 and an eventual population of 10,000, Mariemont was still only half developed a decade after Nolen's role in it ended in 1925.

Like most of Nolen's plans, the Mariemont scheme combined some rather formal, almost baroque, street arrangements with naturalistic parks and open spaces, the largest extending diagonally through the site. Conspicuous features of the town were a civic center with sites for public buildings, radiating streets and boulevards, a village green, and a concourse along the bluff, commanding a view. A federal study in the 1930s judged the engineering, landscape development, and the house groups exceptional. Installation of underground wiring cost a million dollars and added greatly to the attractive appearance of the town.

Palos Verdes Estates, designed by the landscape architectural firm of Olmsted Brothers with Charles H. Cheney as city planning consultant, was perhaps the most carefully planned and highly restricted garden suburb of the 1920s. This development on the coast some twenty miles from downtown Los Angeles was "predominantly for fairly prosperous people wanting detached houses with a garden setting but unwilling to burden themselves with the care of extensive grounds — predominantly people who would want lots ranging from 60 by 125 feet to an acre or so in extent."[78] Of the entire area of rolling hills and terraces, a fourth was reserved for community parks, playgrounds, seashore, a golf course, bridle paths, and other recreational features. In some places sites with especially fine views were selected first, regardless of street pattern, and the streets were then planned to provide access to them. The protective restrictions, at that time referred to as the most complete in America, numbered twenty or more and included comprehensive zoning regulations on use, height, and area, building setback lines, variation in setbacks, type of architecture, minimum cost of buildings, requirements for maintaining natural drainage, and even a ban on the burning of refuse without a permit. Architectural control of private improvements was placed in the hands of a permanent art jury of six members, three of whom were required to be chosen from a list of persons nominated by the southern California chapter of the American Institute of Architects and one from a list submitted by the American City Planning Institute.

Longview, Washington, and Chicopee, Georgia, were among the out-standing industrial towns of the period. Founded in 1922 by the Long-Bell Lumber Company, Longview was designed by the Kansas City firm of Hare and Hare, with George E. Kessler as planning consultant. Partly gridiron in plan, with radial streets slicing through the rectangular blocks and converging on a six-acre park and town center, and partly a system of curvilinear streets, Longview exhibited no innovations in layout but was thoughtfully planned so that moderate expansion of each separate type of land use would not necessitate early conversion of land from one use to another.

Chicopee, a mill town designed by Earle S. Draper for a subsidiary of the Johnson and Johnson Company, manufacturers of surgical and sanitary dressings, closely followed the original plan of its development. Draper's scheme separated the main mill from the residential areas and the town center by a park. Between the two residential areas, with their curvilinear streets conforming to the topography, he planned a park, recreation areas, and the town center. Surrounding the town was a green-belt of 4,000 acres, partly forested but mostly available for farming by the company. The small size of the town (population approximately 2,000) facilitated a design possessing great unity and focus.

In the early twenties no other area of the country seemed so promising for planning *de novo* as Florida, which Nolen called "the last frontier of the United States."[79] There, resourceful men did daring things and invested millions. Carl G. Fisher, for example, cut off the mangrove trees two feet above ground, leaving the stumps where they were, then pumped sand up from the bottom of Biscayne Bay until they were buried five feet deep, and marketed the new-made "land" for $40,000,000. In Tampa Bay another miracle-worker, D. P. Davis, pumped up a 900-acre island from the bottom of the sea, covered it with hotels, clubs, and residences, and sold the whole for $25,000,000. At Sarasota and on its outlying keys the Ringling brothers, John and Charles, created a playground for lotus-eaters and seekers after health. Henry Ford, Harvey Firestone, Marshall Field III, August Heckscher, Otto H. Kahn, and other millionaires bought huge holdings, built highways or short railroads, and cleared thousands of acres for small farms and home sites. Other rich men stripped doors, windows, tiles, fireplaces, and pavements from European and Latin American palaces, monasteries, and convents and sent them to Boca Raton and Coral Gables for Addison Mizner to incorporate into mansions more incredible than Hollywood sets. In the course of the treasure hunt all the roof tiles of the seventeenth century cathedral at Truxillo in Honduras suddenly vanished, then later reappeared on the roofs of houses in Miami. Florida was more circus and gamblers' carnival than the great "laboratory" of urban planning that the leading planning consultants at first thought it might be. Every excess in which the boom-crazed twenties indulged was there magnified, and there the great deflation began at least three years before it overtook the rest of the country.

By 1926, when Nolen became president of the national conference on city planning, he realized that if ever a state needed help in avoiding mistakes and profiting by the experience of areas with some history of planning, it was Florida, destined as a result of its speculative fever to have enough platted lots to house the population of the whole United States. His own branch office in Jacksonville, opened in 1925, was planning eight developments evidencing the best in current planning practice—Alturas, Belmont-on-the-Gulf, Clewiston, Tamiami City, Bay View and San Jose Estates near Jacksonville, Myakka River Tract at Venice, and University Park near Gainesville; but a few widely scattered examples of careful planning, such as these and the city of Homosassa that the Bartholomew firm was designing, hardly sufficed to influence the gamblers who were subdividing sand and swamps, hell-bent on profits and heedless of the amenities. Hoping to stimulate some interest in good

59. John Nolen's general plan of Venice, Florida, 1926 *(National Resources Committee)*

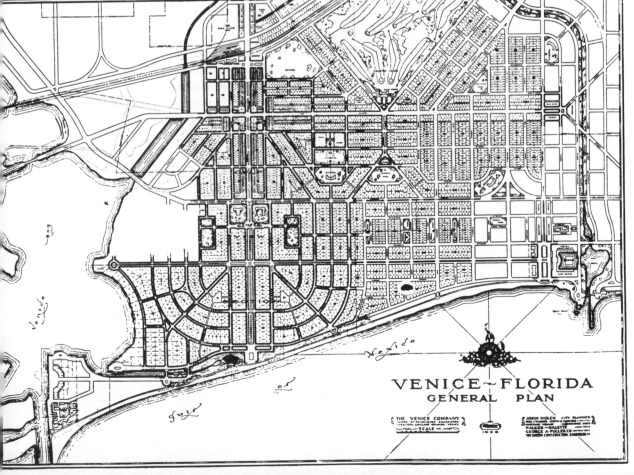

planning among the Florida chambers of commerce, real estate boards, and speculators, Nolen and Flavel Shurtleff arranged to hold the annual conference at St. Petersburg and Palm Beach. The chairman of the St. Petersburg City Planning Commission, which Nolen served as consultant, welcomed the participants to "this rose garden of brotherly love and affection" and expressed the hope that they would buy "one of our wonderful sand lots, teeming . . . with humus, nitrates, phosphates, and red bugs," but he did not even bother to wish them success in bringing the light to Florida.[80] Doubtless he did not believe in miracles.

Olmsted tried, nevertheless, to impart "the word," beginning with a facetious recipe for a modern American pleasure resort—"select firm, plump land that is neither bony or full of hard lumps nor too juicy—juiciness is a real danger in some parts of Florida"[81]—and ending with a sober assurance that resorts are "in general more urgently in need of deliberate planning for the maintenance of their pleasurable qualities and avoidance of growing disadvantages than any other kind of community, because their pleasantness is with them a prime asset, and because in proportion as their pleasantness brings rapid growth and change it is in constant danger of destroying itself."[82]

Robert Whitten, too, essayed to prescribe for boom-delirious Florida. It needed "a different sort of planning and zoning control" from that appropriate for older urban areas.[83] Detailed planning should not even be attempted initially. For broad areas of unsubdivided land the first essential was a general plan with perhaps only three basic elements: the main thoroughfares and parkways, the larger industrial and business zones, the areas suitable for large parks and for water supply and forest reservations. If the principal thoroughfares and parkways were laid out at half-mile intervals, the general pattern thus formed would separate the residential areas into 160-acre tracts, each surrounded by main traffic roads. Each of the 160-acre tracts could then be planned as a "complete neighborhood unit with provision for small parks and playgrounds, a public school, and a neighborhood shopping center."[84] The population of the unit would be from 3,000 to 6,000, the number of pupils in the school from 600 to 1,200. No child would have to walk much more than a quarter of a mile to school.

Whitten, like Clarence Arthur Perry, who is generally credited with having developed the neighborhood unit concept, had been making studies of an ideal residential area. If Florida had been planned as Whitten suggested, it would no doubt have become a model for other states, but he acknowledged that "the capital required for the complete development of a 160-acre tract is very large and the period of development during which carrying charges mount must necessarily extend over a considerable period of years."[85] As most Florida subdividers wanted to make a fast killing, small tracts, with some cheap sidewalks, gravel roadways, and fancy lamp-standards to lure the suckers, were preferable to big, costly, long-range undertakings. In the aftermath of the boom hundreds of these needless subdivisions, ill-planned and unrelated to surrounding areas, would lie abandoned on the outskirts of cities and in mutilated palm groves miles from any town, the weeds growing in their dreary streets and the lamp standards lying broken on the sidewalks. Yet some residents of Florida shared the views of Olmsted and Whitten, denounced exploiters for carving the land into "postage stamp lots," and even yearned to make the state a paradise of innovation and research, guided by a state plan that would induce cooperation among cities and end their greedy rivalry.

Vain hopes! The collapse of the boom not only doomed countless speculative subdivisions; it also shelved general plans of established cities and aborted the development of well-planned towns. One of the few to enjoy reasonably healthy growth was Clewiston, designed by Nolen for a Florida company and later taken over by the Celotex Company of Chicago. Described by the Urbanism Committee in 1939 as "perhaps the most interesting attempt to combine climatic attractions with business and industrial enterprise," Clewiston proved that something besides sunshine and promotion were essential for survival.[86]

City planners who got caught up in the Florida town planning and subdividing spree usually looked back on it with mixed feelings of amusement, chagrin, and frustration. They knew that the speculative madness was almost universal at the time and that Florida was only the extreme example of promotional insanity. Was it really any worse than the town on the south shore of Long Island in which subdividers laid out 9,000 lots in 1925 and 1926 although there were in the vicinity more than 20,000 lots on which no taxes had been paid for several years? Still, men inspired by the ideal of service, as most planners were, could not help feeling a bit apologetic about some of the commissions they undertook in the southern state for get-rich-quick schemers. When the boom ended, many a planner left Florida with an intensified desire for stable planning commissions, well-managed municipal governments, and the strongest possible zoning and subdivision ordinances.

A Momentous Decision of the Supreme Court

In a decade characterized by frenetic activity, runaway urban growth that seemed impossible to control, wild fluctuations in municipal expenditures for public improvements, and considerable uncertainty about the constitutionality of regulating the use of land, there were times when city planners almost despaired of finding solid ground on which to build for the future. The year 1926, when the fate of all American zoning hung in the balance, was perhaps one of the most trying.

For years zoning cases had been coming before courts of first instance, appellate courts, and state supreme courts. By the end of 1925 the highest tribunals of California, New York, Louisiana, Wisconsin, Massachusetts, Ohio, Minnesota, and Kansas had all upheld the constitutionality of zoning. The supreme court of Maine had rendered an advisory opinion supporting the validity of a zoning enabling act. Lower courts in Pennsylvania, Tennessee, and the District of Columbia had also ruled in favor of zoning. Adverse decisions in zoning cases before the supreme courts of Missouri, Maryland, and New Jersey were perhaps to be expected because these states had not yet enacted zoning enabling laws. But no case involving comprehensive use zoning had ever been adjudicated by the United States Supreme Court, and now the auguries for eventual approval of city-wide use zoning by that court of last resort did not appear encouraging. The United States District Court in northern Ohio had granted an injunction against the enforcement of the zoning ordinance of the village of Euclid, a suburb of Cleveland, and in doing so had held that zoning ordinances were necessarily unconstitutional because they "took" property without compensation, in violation of the Fourteenth Amendment to the federal constitution.

To more than four hundred municipalities with comprehensive zoning ordinances, this opinion of the district court was highly disconcerting. Nor was there any comfort in it for hundreds of other municipalities then engaged in drafting zoning ordinances. It raised the prospect that the 27,000,000 Americans living in cities with zoning regulations, and millions of other city dwellers who were looking forward to the prevention of some of the worst forms of development, might not be much better off in the long run than earlier generations had been.

The village of Euclid took its case to Washington on appeal, but it was not at all sure that it had a good case because the judge of the district court had also held that the municipal ordinance unreasonably affected the land of the plaintiff, the Ambler Realty Company. Boulevard frontage that the company had hoped to market as commercial property and land that it had expected to sell for industrial development had been placed in residential zones, with resulting loss in value, the company contended. If the company could satisfy the Supreme Court justices that the ordinance was inherently weak and provided as well for an unlawful exercise of authority, then zoning would indeed fall.

Alfred Bettman had long been waiting for a zoning case to come before the nation's highest bench. In fact, he had asked the clerk of the court to notify him when hearings on the Euclid case were to be held, so that he might appear as a friend of the court on behalf of the National Conference of City Planning, the Ohio State Conference on City Planning, and other organizations. To his consternation he learned one day that the court had already heard arguments in the case and was pondering a verdict. The clerk had forgotten to notify him. Bettman thereupon took the extraordinary step of asking his friend Chief Justice Taft, a fellow Cincinnatian, to reopen the case. In view of the crucial nature of the matter, the request was granted. Bettman then filed with the court his masterful brief *amici curiae* recounting the history of zoning and citing expressions of the state and federal courts upon the relationship of zoning to the public health, safety, and general welfare.

The sole issue in the case, Bettman contended, was the constitutionality of comprehensive land use regulation, since earlier United States Supreme Court decisions had already sustained height and area restrictions. The plea of the company that it was entitled to direct money compensation for an assumed loss in the value of some of its land was "wholly beside the point" because the Euclid ordinance was "frankly and expressly an exercise of the police power and not of the power of eminent domain."[87] The community was not taking or destroying any property or property rights for public use but was invoking a general power over private property which is necessary for the orderly existence of all governments. The "overwhelming weight of authority," as expressed in judicial decisions, was in favor of the constitutionality of zoning. The judge of the district court, though citing numerous cases, had included only two which involved "true zoning ordinances" rather than block or residential district or other types of ordinances. Meanwhile, eleven state supreme courts had upheld zoning "in clear-cut cases and with decisive opinions." Any con-

60. Alfred Bettman
*(Keller Studio and
Cincinnati City
Planning Commission)*

tentions in the arguments before the district court that the constitutional issue was in an uncertain, conflicting, or indecisive stage had "ceased to have any basis."[88]

Bettman's brief saved the day for zoning. One justice who had previously been persuaded that use zoning was unconstitutional changed his mind, and on November 22, 1926, the high court upheld this form of regulation in a momentous four-to-three decision. If there really had been "ample ground" for the suspicion that the Ambler Realty Company, while genuinely the party plaintiff, represented "a larger group seeking to destroy the zoning movement,"[89] as Bettman thought, it was now possible for planners and their cohorts to shift from the defense of zoning to its improvement as a means of carrying out planned development. Bettman himself had always regretted the emphasis on its negative or restrictive aspects.

States in which the courts had struck down zoning ordinances because of inadequate enabling legislation or constitutional authorization or because judges were unconvinced that zoning had any demonstrable relation to the public welfare soon adjusted to the dictum of the nation's highest tribunal. Pennsylvania, which until then had been doubtful, joined the commonwealths already on record as approving land use regulation under the police power. The state legislature of Texas passed a legally sound zoning enabling act. The voters of New Jersey in September, 1927, approved a zoning amendment to the state constitution, silencing the bitter complaints of planners that the courts "rule that in our city building we may not even be intelligent."[90] Many courts in other states declared that so long as zoning ordinances were reasonably related to the community health, safety, morals, and general welfare, the judges would not attempt to scrutinize the details of zoning but would leave them entirely to the discretion of city councils. Arbitrary or discriminatory zoning would, of course, always be subject to litigation.

City planners themselves began to be highly critical of zoning practice. Land economists, real estate men, and attorneys joined them in pointing the way to regulations based on much more careful analysis of factual data. One of the most significant studies was initiated, in fact, before the United States Supreme Court removed doubts about the constitutionality of use zoning. Knowing that many zoning ordinances allocated excessive amounts of land for commercial purposes, the Committee on Subdivision Plats and Zoning of the Chicago Regional Planning Association began an investigation of retail business frontages in cities within a fifty-mile radius of Chicago in the summer of 1926 and continued it in the summer and fall of 1927. The study of forty cities revealed that although the most common size of retail business district in outlying municipalities was from 45 to 55 front feet per 100 persons of the city population, the farther a city was from the metropolitan center, the greater its ratio of business frontage to population tended to be. For example, cities fifty to sixty minutes from Chicago had almost eleven feet more business frontage per 100 population than cities in the forty-to-fifty-minute zone. The size and general character of a city seemed to have no clear effect on the relative size of the business district, but the investigators nevertheless warned that "economic analysis and conversely economic planning or forecasting must not neglect individual variations." Coleman Woodbury, a participant in this pioneer effort, expressed the hope that it would "aid the more economic proportioning of urban land within metropolitan areas." He also thought that if the study were later repeated in the same manner, it might disclose "interesting facts on the extent and character of the movement of retail business."[91] Similar studies in other regions might provide some basis for comparisons of the economic organization of metropolitan areas.

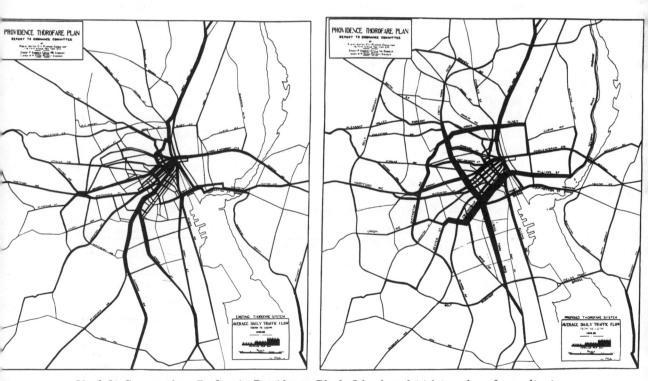

61. (left) Congested traffic flow in Providence, Rhode Island, and (right) a plan of consultants Robert Whitten and E. P. Goodrich for improving circulation: street and highway plans of the 1920s revealed the powerful influence of the automobile in reshaping cities

With all the talk of decentralization, no one in the late 1920s had a clear idea how the automobile, the assembly line, and other agents of change were reshaping urban complexes. To any observer it was obvious, however, that the automobile was encouraging the development of shoe-string business streets and that the zoning of long arteries for business could hardly be defended as being necessary for the public health, safety, morals, and general welfare. George H. Coffin, Jr., president of the Los Angeles Realty Board, viewed this kind of zoning as a particular evil because he knew how some of it came about: "Certain realtors and professional promoters seek the zoning of residential property for business in order to exploit it, pocket the false value created by the establishment of a business zone and depart, leaving a trail of depleted residential value in their wake."[92] Coffin indicated that "such a practice is in conflict with the Realtor's Code of Ethics, and the man who profits by such practice should be dealt with accordingly." His positive suggestion for correcting abuses and developing better cities was to "reform" zoning by centralizing business in "compact districts," in downtown areas as well as outlying sections. The long stretches of frontage between compact business districts on principal arteries would then "naturally develop with the type of apartment or hotel which the territory justifies."[93] Greater values would attach both to commercial properties and to residential lots, and the principle of taxation according to permitted usage could be generally applied.

Coffin's proposal for compact business districts was not, of course, novel. All the better developments of the time, from Palos Verdes Estates to Mariemont, had specially planned, concentrated commercial areas, but it was unusual to have a prominent real estate man endorsing a better kind of business zoning and by implication exposing some of the mythology associated with land use regulation.

Progress and Confusion in a Model Act

All those who hoped for zoning based on more realistic estimates of the amount of land needed for various purposes and for a closer relationship between long-range planning and zoning expected that a new Standard City Planning Enabling Act distributed by Secretary of Commerce Herbert Hoover would have a beneficial influence. The earlier Standard State Zoning Enabling Act, which had encouraged states to enact laws permitting cities to establish a zoning commission even before they had a planning commission, had resulted in adoption of zoning regulations wholly unrelated to any long-range city plan. The Standard City Planning Act issued in a preliminary edition in March, 1927, emphasized, above all, the importance of the city planning commission and the preparation and adoption of a master plan. The model statute suggested that all powers previously granted to the zoning commission be transferred to the city planning commission as soon as one was created. If a zoning commission was nearing completion of a zoning ordinance, the transfer of its powers might be postponed, but no longer than six months. If a new planning commission was undertaking to produce a master plan, the model act provided that the plan should include, among other things, "a zoning plan for the control of the height, area, bulk, location, and use of buildings and premises."[94] Clearly, the authors wished to entrust zoning to an agency which would consider the long-term implications of proposed allocations of the land resources of the community.

Secretary Hoover's advisory committee nevertheless tended to defeat its own laudable aim, as many planners later realized. Immediately enforceable restrictions necessarily must sanction, for a reasonable period of time, some uses which it might be desirable to terminate eventually. There is thus a difference between the detailed, legally permissible uses of the present and the new uses and spatial relationships which the community might hope to achieve in the future. But the Standard City Planning Enabling Act failed to make this distinction and encouraged cities to portray in long-range plans the conditions of the present rather than the changes required to improve the order, efficiency, and amenity of the city. Worse, the act confused a precise administrative device with an instrument which most planners thought of as a graphic statement of goals and a coordinating mechanism, not as an exact blueprint for the development of the city.

Other confusing and contradictory features of the act perhaps also resulted from its multiple authorship or from irreconcilable differences of opinion among strong-minded men. Edward M. Bassett and Alfred Bettman, both attorneys, and Frederick Law Olmsted unquestionably played particularly important roles in shaping this second model law, though the other six committeemen were also old hands at drafting legislation. In any event, notwithstanding all their good intentions, the nine produced an act which tended to perpetuate the rather narrow scope of city plans and to encourage city planning commissions to develop piecemeal plans rather than a thoroughly integrated, overall plan.

An important provision of the act avoided an express definition of the term "master plan" but illustrated its contents by enumerating five broad classifications of subject matter: streets, other types of public grounds, public buildings, public utilities, and zoning. Bassett, who later wrote a book expressing the view that the master plan should be limited to just seven elements, including zoning, may well have wished to restrict the scope of the plan, whereas Bettman and Olmsted may have insisted on adding several sentences indicating that a city planning commission could make the plan as inclusive as it wished. Two footnotes, in which

Bettman and Olmsted may have collaborated, also sought to convey the idea that there were no limitations on the subject matter of the master plan, so long as its focus was on physical development. But the classifications listed in the standard act were repeated later in many state laws, and the explanatory footnotes were forgotten, with the result that for many years planners as well as citizen planning commissioners labored under the impression that a master plan should include little more.

The failure of the advisory committee to state what it considered the fundamental or indispensable elements of a general plan also had unfortunate consequences. Countless cities produced lopsided plans omitting some of the essential community facilities and almost none included the full complement of utilities.

Two sections of the standard act could be erroneously interpreted to sanction a piecemeal planning procedure, though truly careful study of the text and the footnotes would disabuse most readers of the idea that Bettman and Olmsted, for instance, favored anything but the preparation of a well-rounded, tightly knit plan. This sentence, repeated or adapted in many state laws based on the model act, furthered the lamentable tendency of all too many planning commissions to develop elements of the city plan one at a time, with almost inevitable lack of coordination among elements: "As the work of making the whole master plan progresses, the commission may from time to time adopt and publish a part or parts thereof, any such part to cover one or more of the aforesaid or other functional matters to be included in the plan."[95] Some committeeman, perhaps Bettman or Olmsted, appended a footnote explaining that "the city plan is an organic whole, every part of which, whether considered territorially or as to subject matter, is organically interrelated with every other part,"[96] but neither in the text of the act nor in the footnotes is it specifically suggested that a planning consultant or planning staff would first do well to work out a general scheme relating all essential elements. From this weakness of the act stemmed all those single-function plans of later years labeled "master plar of streets and highways" or "master plan of parks," though no comprehensive plan of which they were parts could be brought forth for inspection.

Some writers have sought to exonerate the advisory committee for providing for successive adoptions of various parts of the master plan by pointing out that this expedient probably seemed advisable because of the small size of planning staffs in the 1920s or because planning consultants were often under pressure to produce certain functional schemes well ahead of a comprehensive plan. Years later, however, when some planning departments had large staffs that would have been capable of developing the "organic whole," the practice of preparing single-element plans and calling them "master plans" was still in vogue.

A section of the standard act reflected the origins of the planning movement in the days of municipal reform, when city councils were distrusted as corrupt. It provided for adoption of the master plan by the planning commission and transmission of a certified copy to the local governing group, but not a word implied that the city fathers themselves should adopt the plan. The model act, like the Cincinnati city charter and the Ohio planning act of 1923, provided, furthermore, that commission disapproval of the location, character, and extent of a proposed public improvement could be overridden only by a two-thirds vote of the council. Bettman was almost unmistakably the author of these features of the act, for he had argued for the two-thirds vote from the days when he first started attending the annual national conferences on city planning. The planning commission was thus, as in the City Beautiful days, the guardian of the plan and the nonpolitical champion of the people's interests, from time to time putting thoughtless or rascally politicians on the spot. It is little wonder that as one state legislature after another patterned its planning law on this standard act, city councils continued to regard city planning as something less than their direct concern and to grant none-too-generous budgets to planning departments.

On the other hand, Bettman's chief purpose was to make sure that the planning commission would have an opportunity to review proposed public improvements and zoning changes, so that it could point out deficiencies or conflicts with the goals expressed in the long-range plan. Some planners regard the provision for mandatory referral of matters affecting the development of the city as marking the beginning of a long, gradual shift of emphasis from the plan as an ideal but actually unattainable end-state to the process of directing environmental change in accordance with well-established policies, bringing expertise to bear on all the little day-to-day decisions which mold and remold the city. Had the standard act provided that the city council should also adopt the long-term plan, by resolution, and take an active interest in it as an expression of public policy, the shift from a certain preoccupation of planning commissions with the distant future to close collaboration with the council in effecting desirable change might have been hastened. Paradoxically, Bettman encouraged the shift but protracted it.

Only in the first title or part of the act, concerning municipal planning, did the authors profess to be on familiar ground. They were less sure about the other three titles, although they believed that they had worked out provisions on subdivision control, mapped streets, and regional planning representing the best prevailing thought on these subjects. Since legislation concerning these matters was still in the trial and error stage, undergoing modification in the light of judicial decisions, no one could be "dogmatic about the best or final form of legislation on these subjects."[97]

The committee's guideline act suggested that planning commissions should adopt clear-cut rules and regulations for the subdivision of land, should have power to enforce such regulation in unincorporated territory within five miles of the municipality except where another municipality might exercise similar jurisdiction, and should work out with the subdivider the zoning to apply in his tract, in no instance authorizing a violation of the effective zoning ordinance. A primary object of subdivision control, the act made clear, was to preserve the integrity of the master plan as it applied to newly developing areas.

In the title pertaining to mapped streets the advisory committee provided for the reservation of future rights-of-way for a stated period and their acquisition under eminent domain proceedings, but for states in which the use of the police power to protect mapped streets might be feasible, a footnote outlined an alternative method.

The final title of the model act outlined a permissive procedure under which the planning commission of any municipality or the county commissioners of any county or any group of one hundred citizens could petition the governor to establish a region for planning purposes and appoint a regional planning commission. But a footnote suggested that enabling legislation might also provide for cooperative regional planning commissions formed upon the initiative of neighboring municipalities or a group of counties. Such an association of governmental units would decide for itself what should constitute a region, whereas the authors of the model act assumed that a region designated by a governor would be determined upon the advice of the petitioners. However a regional commission might be established, its chief duty would be to "make, adopt, amend, extend, and add to a master regional plan for the physical development of its region."[98] The plan would include streets, parks and open spaces, public buildings, and public utilities affecting the development of the region as a whole or large parts of it, as well as forests, agricultural and open development areas, water supply, sanitary and drainage facilities, and "a zoning plan for the control of the height and area, or bulk, location, and use of buildings and premises, and of the density of population."[99] Upon its adoption by the regional commission, the plan would be sent to municipalities and counties and if adopted by these units would have the force and effect of their own properly adopted plans.[100] In unincorporated territory of the region, no type of development contemplated in the plan could proceed until approved by the regional commission, but this agency would have no control over subdivisions lying within the regulatory jurisdiction of municipal planning commissions.

The authors of the standard act frankly confessed their own perplexity over the inclusion of a zoning plan in the regional plan. Here they were concerned, as in a city plan, not merely with a long-term, desirable scheme of land uses but with specific, current regulations — and they did not know whether the power to enact the zoning plan into legislation should be reposed in the state legislature or in the county commissioners, or whether zoning regulation of nonmunicipal territory should "wait until a regional legislative organ is created."[101] They wondered whether a system of building permits should be created as a method of enforcing zoning legislation in unincorporated areas. Such problems would have to be solved in the near future.

Just what the advisory committee thought of as "a regional legislative organ" is not clear, but probably the members did not have in mind multipurpose areawide government, because one of their footnotes mentions as the logical and intelligent order of events "first the regional planning commission, second the regional plan, and then the creation of the regional and metropolitan boards for the actual execution of the regional or metropolitan public works and development."[102] Even if some of the committeemen had favored genuine metropolitan government, they might have thought it unwise to imply that regional planning was the first step toward such government. The suspicion with which this kind of government is generally regarded even today indicates that forty years ago any group seriously furthering regional planning was perhaps well advised not to complicate the issue.

The standard act not only ignored the problem of areawide government; it also dodged the matter of state planning. A footnote presented an optional section providing for the creation of a state bureau of regional planning, the functions of which would be to advise the governor on the establishment of regions for planning purposes and to make available to regional planning commissions information and data that would be helpful in preparing and carrying out regional plans. If some of the authors of the act believed that in time such a bureau might develop into a state planning agency, they did not say so. Nothing indicated that any of them thought regional plans should be related to a state development plan, such as the Commission of Housing and Regional Planning had proposed for the state of New York.

In the light of all that has happened in the past forty years, it is perhaps difficult to understand why city planners of the later 1920s considered the Standard City Planning Enabling Act a great milestone. The handiwork of Hoover's advisory committee now seems in many respects confused, contradictory, tentative, and cautious, yet in its time it answered many legal questions troubling planning commissioners and legislators and served as a basis for establishing greater uniformity among state enabling acts authorizing city and regional planning. Merely as an educational document, the model act was of considerable value; with its copious explanatory footnotes, it was in a sense a treatise on city planning. It went far toward clarifying the major emphases of regional planning and the relationship of municipal planning to this broader form of planning. In a few of its suggestions, such as the proposal for the maintenance of agricultural belts and other types of open development in rapidly growing metropolitan regions, it was even ahead of its time. Not the least that the authors accomplished by drafting this guide for planning legislation was further stimulation of thought about city planning among civic groups, city officials, allied professions, and state officials. The standard act set off a chain reaction that kept going well into the 1930s and resulted in the revision of many state laws and local ordinances providing for exercise of the planning function.

An Anniversary Conference: Retrospect and Prospect

City planners shared a feeling of assurance as they gathered in the national capital in May, 1927, for the nineteenth annual conference on city planning. They had more to be thankful for than at any previous convocation of their fellowship. The United States Supreme Court's decision in the Euclid Village case had strengthened their efforts to create more orderly cities, and now Secretary Hoover's sponsorship of a second standard act and his urging the states to place city and regional planning on a firmer legal foundation seemed tantamount to federal recognition of the importance of city planning in national life. Moreover, the year marked the twentieth anniversary of the establishment of the first official city planning commission at Hartford, Connecticut, in 1907. Conference president John Nolen appropriately grasped the opportunity for a "bird's eye or aeroplane view" of the progress city planning had made in the past two decades.

Looking back over a period in which the world had "leaped forward especially in the mechanization of life," Nolen found that city planning itself had come a long way. Prior to the creation of the Hartford commission there had been no comprehensive city plans or master plans as the planning fraternity now thought of them, with the possible exception of the McMillan Commission's plan of Washington, D.C., and Burnham's plan of San Francisco; ". . . the idea of the civic survey was unknown, as was regional planning also; no zoning ordinances restricting heights *and* [emphasis added] use of buildings had been passed; there was no National Conference on City Planning and no American City Planning Institute; no teaching of city planning in technical schools or colleges; and virtually no books or other publications of note on this subject." Among the people generally, the only discernible interest in city planning was the enthusiasm of certain civic groups for the City Beautiful.[103]

Measured statistically, the progress of city planning had been substantial. One hundred and seventy-six cities, with a total population of more than 25,000,000, had been "broadly replanned."[104] Thirty-five or more new towns and garden suburbs distinguished for the high quality of their planning had come into being. City planning commissions had been established in 390 cities. In six states—Massachusetts, Pennsylvania, Ohio, California, Indiana, and Kansas—commissions were so numerous that statewide federations had been formed to support and advance city planning. Five hundred and twenty-five cities had adopted zoning ordinances. Twenty-nine colleges, universities, and technical schools had inaugurated courses or lectures in city planning. But little of all this could have been accomplished, Nolen generously conceded, without the cooperation of other professional societies, a large proportion of the 350 city managers in the United States, the National Municipal League, the American Civic Association, the National Association of Real Estate Boards, the National Automobile Chamber of Commerce, Secretary Hoover, and five departed leaders who deserved exceptional honors—Burnham, Robinson, Kessler, Nelson P. Lewis, and Charles Dyer Norton.

The recital of numbers, names, and events nevertheless left unanswered the searching questions: Had Nolen and his fellow planners enhanced the fitness of cities as environments for new generations? Had they shown a mastery of new conditions by adopting new methods of replanning and reconstructing cities? Were cities better not merely for a favored few but for all city dwellers?

Nolen himself was only too well aware of unsolved problems—how to relieve traffic congestion and increase safety in city streets, how to relieve congested working and living conditions, how to reduce what Stuart Chase called "the tragedy of waste," how to control and regulate the size of cities and provide a wiser method for the distribution of population, and how to combine a new, modern, and appropriate beauty with American ideas of efficiency.

"Let us be honest," Nolen urged. "There is no easy solution to these grave municipal problems, no cheap solution, no complete solution, and no permanent solution." True progress demanded much more not only of city planners but also of other citizens: "better and still better city government and administration, combined with regional government and administration"; more planning commissions, with better financial backing and official support; "comprehensive city plans combined with comprehensive financing"; far greater sums for the replanning and extension of cities; an increase in technical knowledge of planning and broad design; and "long-range planning of public works as a prosperity reserve to stabilize industry and insure economy." Nolen foresaw, too, the necessity for deeper consideration of "the related social, economic and governmental conditions which influence and color all that is now being done or attempted." He described the task ahead as "the gradual creation of an environment . . . so different from the present that without exaggeration it could be called new."[105] To fashion such an environment, city planners would need new methods and new ideas; they would have, indeed, to form new habits.

Lewis Mumford, whom Nolen introduced as the author of *Sticks and Stones,* essayed to provide a vision of the environment that might replace the megalopolitan growth encouraged by existing financial, industrial, and political institutions. "If so little genuine improvement has been effected in our cities, in spite of all the efforts during the last twenty years that Mr. Nolen has enumerated," Mumford declared, "it is perhaps simply for the reason that our dominant desire for quantitative growth and large speculative profits and much conspicuous expenditure, personal and civic, has produced its own kind of physical image in crowded sky-scrapers, packed subways, and endless miles of semi-respectable, semi-sanitary, semi-habitable urban slums. . . ."[106]

Challenging his audience to reject "the premise that city planning is merely a way of providing the physical means for a continuous expansion and congestion of our cities," the young author posed the problem of the planner during the next twenty years as that of defining an intelligent attitude toward urban development.[107] He must "systematically aid those forces which are working against the domination of purely financial values" and must make use of modern technology—the auto, the radio, giant power, standardized production—along with the human desire for a finer and more enjoyable life, to build up "a more satisfactory layout, region by region, with countryside and city developed together for the purpose of promoting and enhancing the good life."[108] Mumford offered no precise description of the "humanized environment" needed in the future, though he left no doubt that every element of it—the school, the factory, the university, the city—had its limit of growth, set by its functions. Qualitative achievement should be the sole criterion for determining the size of any unit, and growth which threatened quality should be prevented by the production of new cities, new colleges, and new manufacturing plants in other areas. He evoked "the great city" mainly by stating the ends it would serve: " . . . it is the place where the arts and sciences come together for the promotion of an interesting life; it is that form of the community in which man can enter most fully into his social heritage; it is the place where the physical means of living are so arranged that men can pass through the crises of animal existence, birth and death, and pursue their work and mate and become the parents of children, and be neighbors and companions in work with the smallest amount of frustration and waste, and the largest enjoyment and exuberance of life."[109]

Mumford's talk announced the theme of many of his later writings, including *The Culture of Cities* and the still larger book embodying the greater part of that work, *The City in History*. His plea to the planners to "execute a flank movement" to head off further megalopolitan growth perhaps found favor with most of them in much the same way that a fine sermon pleases a congregation rutted in its worldly ways. "The city we have in mind is a city to live in," John Ihlder said for them, but could it be as desirable as they hoped if it were as large as the forecasts indicated?[110] The predictions were that almost every large center would double or treble its population in a generation or two and that the United States by the end of the century, if not long before, would be the homeland of more than 200,000,000 people, at least 70 per cent of whom would be urban. Thomas Adams, with whom Mumford would clash later over the basic assumptions of the New York regional plan, asserted that there was space within twenty-five miles of downtown Manhattan to house the 20,000,000 people of the 1960s "at the rate of thirty people or six houses to the acre of land which is adaptable for building purposes."[111] There was, moreover, no reason why ample areas should not be provided for parks and parkways. But Adams did not say anything to indicate that he accepted the idea of limiting the growth of urban accretions, nor did other speakers who discussed superhighways, rapid transit, subdivision planning, and recreation areas. The extended metropolis, with fatiguing distances and enormous problems of supply, waste disposal, and adjustment to change, was already aborning. Mumford's hope for "renewal" of the larger region, embracing farmland and forest as well as village and city, seemingly was hardly shared, though in another decade city planners would be more receptive to his views. The garden city and the greenbelt were still among their articles of faith, even if they succumbed to the wiles of megalopolis.

Accent on the Practical: The Capital Budget

The still-young profession of city planning (which some older professions did yet regard as a profession) was, understandably, so preoccupied with the struggle to improve essential legislation, develop techniques, and forge additional means of carrying out the master plan that its members tended to work within the context of existing institutions and to indulge only occasionally in the kind of wide-ranging, critical thought for which Mumford had already become well known in intellectual circles. The waste and inefficiency of cities greatly troubled planners, and they prided themselves on reducing it by almost everything they did, but perhaps most of them regarded utopian thought as a luxury, and bold schemes for the reorganization of urban areas as futile. Did not many businessmen, politicians, and civic leaders still speak of planners as visionaries?

Would not proposals expressing or implying deep dissatisfaction with the present order invite further disparagement or even outright attacks? As long as plans promised reasonable progress in adjusting streets to to the requirements of the automobile, providing additional parks and playgrounds, facilitating the shift of industry to outlying locations, and protecting residential areas from unwanted traffic and stores and factories, city planners could gradually win a more secure place for themselves in American life. But let them march too far ahead of the public and they risked losing much that they had gained by hard work and personal sacrifice.

To extend the city was easier than to conceive new forms for urban areas and try to persuade people to accept them; to perceive what appeared to be strong trends, such as the opening of branches of downtown stores in suburban shopping areas, and to move with the trends was less arduous than the crusade for government sponsorship of wholly new cities. There was resistance enough to the very idea of drastically restricting the cubage in skyscrapers and eliminating parking on some heavily traveled streets. Why choose more difficult issues to arouse the wrath of vested interests and ordinary citizens? If planners had become less adventurous in thought, more complacent about slums and social injustices, and more engrossed in the details of traffic analysis, street planning, zoning, and subdivision control, it was because the materialism of the times was inimical to philosophic probing and because the rapidity of urban growth demanded "practical" plans and immediate decisions. The members of the profession perhaps did not acknowledge, even to themselves, that they had submerged broader issues in order to concentrate on day-to-day problems and professional gains.

One of the new tools they needed to assure the success of their work — long-term financial planning for carrying out the master plan — would, of course, benefit society as much as it would bolster city planning. Fortunately for the planning profession, a movement had been developing throughout the United States to systematize expenditures for planned improvements. By the mid-twenties this movement began to support the efforts of city planning commissions and the planning profession to find dependable financing for effecting the comprehensive plan. For the strength of this movement and the widespread interest it attracted, planners could thank the municipal reformation which had resulted in the employment of city managers and the establishment of municipal bureaus of research, sometimes called bureaus of budget and efficiency, as in Los Angeles. In the late 1920s these agencies and their privately supported counterparts were making presentations before the American Society for Municipal Improvements explaining procedures for the simultaneous preparation of a capital improvement program and a plan of financing.

Probably the first long-term financial plan for any governmental unit in the United States was that announced by the Minneapolis Board of Education in 1916. Entitled "A Million a Year," the plan presented a "carefully analyzed and comprehensive program of permanent improvements and extensions of the school plan required to serve the educational needs of the city during the next five years in accordance with standards that the people generally appear to approve and demand."[112] Three years later the city of Newark outlined a five-year civic program, and about the same time Kalamazoo, Michigan, adopted an improvement program to be financed under a pay-as-you-go policy. In 1924 the Bureau of Governmental Research in San Francisco and the chamber of commerce formulated a tentative ten-year development program for the city, but the proposal was not submitted to city officials and was in no way related to a long-range, general plan, since the city then had none. The Detroit Bureau of Governmental Research, a private organization, the next year worked with a Mayor's Committee on Finances in estimating future increases in municipal revenues and the amounts that would be available for capital expenditures under various tax rates. Every department of city government submitted projects for inclusion in a ten-year schedule, which was revised in 1927 and again in 1929 and was finally submitted as a $340,000,000 program, exclusive of $200,000,000 for rapid transit. Cincinnati, however, was the first large city to devise a long-range programming procedure definitely related to a comprehensive city plan.

In 1926 the mayor of the Ohio city called together representatives of civic organizations to consider various proposals for bond issues to finance community improvements, some to be constructed by the city and others by the county and the school district. The participants appointed a subcommittee to suggest a plan of procedure for coordinating the bond proposals of these governmental units. Its members, the city manager and the chairman of the finance committee of the city council, immediately requested the engineer of the city planning commission and the director of the Bureau of Municipal Research to cooperate with them in outlining an improvement program and a plan of financing. This group drew up a scheme showing the complete capital requirements of the city, the school district, and the county for five years, assigned priorities to the projects, and determined the amounts needed to finance them. After the civic committee approved the scheme, the legislative bodies of the governmental units adopted it, and at a subsequent election the voters, who had not been in the habit of authorizing bonds, marked their ballots affirmatively.

Although the Cincinnati Plan, as the procedure came to be known, was initially developed for a program to be financed by bonds, its general principles were applicable to programs financed by a combination of taxes, departmental revenues, special assessments, bonds, state subventions, and other monies. After the first successful experience with the procedure, the Cincinnati City Council worked out a municipal ordinance modifying it somewhat and instituting it on a formal basis. The ordinance established a City Committee composed of the city manager, a member of the council (usually the chairman of the finance committee), and a member of the city planning commission. It designated the city auditor as the secretary of the committee. Thus the planning, operating, financial, and legislative points of view were directly brought to bear upon the selection of a tentative five-year improvement program from lists of projects proposed by the various departments and individuals and assembled by the manager as agent of the council. The ordinance provided that the program, arranged according to the urgency of projects, should not exceed the financial resources of the municipality as shown in a financial analysis prepared by the Bureau of Municipal Research. Authorization for annual revision of the program and its extension for another five-year period as the projects having highest priority were completed or put under construction assured continuity of financial planning and progress in carrying out the comprehensive city plan. As the city wished to continue to coordinate its own capital expenditures with those of other governmental units, the ordinance also required that the program formulated by the City Committee be submitted to a city-wide Joint Improvement Committee for review and coordination with the programs of the county and the school district. So well did this procedure function that fourteen years after its inauguration those concerned with its administration could report that none of the governing bodies had once deviated from the adjusted programs recommended by the Joint Committee.

The contribution of the Cincinnati City Planning Commission and of the entire governmental leadership of Cincinnati and Hamilton County to the development of what has now become a standardized programming procedure in well-governed municipalities can be all the more appreciated by comparing the Cincinnati effort with an attempt at long-range financial planning in Dallas. In 1927 the mayor, the chairman of the city planning commission, the president of the Kessler Plan Association, and the president of the chamber of commerce selected a group known as the Ulrickson Committee to correlate the various improvement plans presented to the city from time to time but laid aside because of insufficient funds. This committee after much study proposed a program of eighty-one projects to be financed by bond issues totaling $23,900,000 and to be consummated in nine years or less, with no more than $4,000,000 in bonds to be issued in any one year, since municipal bond issues had actually not much exceeded that amount annually for the past nine years without any plan. Included in the program were schools, parks, streets, sewers, storm drains, additions to the water system, hospitals and other public buildings, and a municipal airport. Many of these capital items conformed with the 1919 revision of the Kessler Plan. The committee suggested, however, that a charter amendment be submitted requiring the proceeds of the bonds to be spent only for projects consistent with the general plan. Although the entire program was approved by the voters in December, 1927, no permanent procedure for scheduling and financing public works resulted from this well-intentioned effort.

The national conference on city planning formally approved long-range programming in 1928 by adopting a resolution commending "thorough budgeting of capital expenditures on the basis of a progressive period of years sufficiently long to spread adequately the resources of communities so as to attain the greatest results and advantages from such necessary expenditures."[113] That same year the League of California Municipalities took similar action. And in 1929 the city of White Plains, New York, set some kind of record by issuing a city plan (prepared by Ernest Goodrich and Robert Whitten) containing a fifty-year capital budget showing the cost of each improvement recommended in the plan, probable future total assessed valuations, probable future costs of government, and estimated future annual tax rates for the whole period. The enthusiastic city commissioner of finance had developed the elaborate program.

Had not a depression overtaken the nation just as the movement for long-range financing of planned public improvements was beginning to bear fruit, innumerable cities might have emulated the example of Cincinnati. After this first flurry of interest in capital budgeting, almost a decade was to pass before cities again began to consider long-term programming of public works.

The Troublesome Problem of Housing

Problems of municipal finance challenged some businessmen in the 1920s because they realized that many features of an improved public plant would benefit them personally. Their willingness to serve on citizens' committees to work out procedures for long-term budgeting of public works was not matched, however, by any readiness to consider the problem of financing an important category of private additions to the city—houses for lower-income groups. Throughout the decade most chambers of commerce and other business associations, though supposedly fascinated by the problem of eliminating waste and inefficiency, paid little heed to the excessive cost of providing municipal services to slums and blighted areas, and were hostile to suggestions that government aid should be made available to enable wage earners to buy or build homes. Congress enacted no measures to assist the lower-paid half of the population who needed good dwellings the most, and only New York and California attempted to increase home ownership, the former by exempting approved limited-dividend companies from state taxes or fees and the latter by using state bond monies to purchase homes and farms for resale to war veterans under a twenty-year payment plan.

The times were so discouraging to persons concerned with housing that even the National Housing Association held only three national conferences in the twenties, one in 1920 when the country was suffering from a postwar housing shortage, a second in 1923, and no others until 1929. After hearing a plea from Lawrence Veiller in 1920 for a slumless America, city planners hardly mentioned housing at their annual national conferences thereafter, or did so only when discussing zoning or subdivision regulation or decentralization. Not that they wished to sweep the subject under the rug; most of them could see no way to solve the difficult problem of providing dwellings for the lower-income groups, and all sensed that the country was in no mood for a crusade to eradicate slums and build decent low-cost housing.

The Detroit City Planning Commission, which Walter Blucher served as city planner and secretary, was one of the few planning agencies in the country to investigate local housing conditions. In 1927 it cooperated with the Michigan Housing Association in a series of surveys of Detroit and found "what was to be expected"—that juvenile delinquency, deaths from tuberculosis and pneumonia, infant mortality, crime, and dependency were more prevalent in the blighted areas than they were in other parts of the city.[114] "It is not going beyond the truth to say that housing conditions in some sections of our city are almost intolerable," Blucher wrote in the planning commission's annual report in 1928. "We cannot continue to disregard the housing of our small-income citizens. Poor housing conditions result in the creation of criminal hot-beds."[115]

On the assumption that sooner or later the municipality would be asked to cooperate in housing reform, Blucher had begun to gather "much information . . . with regard to housing conditions and housing remedies in other cities."[116] But other cities had few remedies to tell about. A brave Milwaukee effort to have city and county help finance cooperative housing "folded its wings," as Dr. Edith Elmer Wood said, "after producing 105 little houses, partly because the Chamber of Commerce did not fancy it and partly because the tenants did not really want cooperative ownership."[117] August Heckscher, the multimillionaire, returned from a study of European housing in 1926 to lay before Mayor James

N.Y. schemes

Walker of New York a plan to "get 500 wealthy and public-spirited citizens in New York to promise a contribution of $100,000 each annually for five years as a nucleus toward eliminating the slums once and for all,"[118] but other wealthy men displayed no enthusiasm for the scheme, even though some matching funds from state and city were suggested. In 1927 the municipality did, however, take advantage of the state housing law of the previous year and exempted from taxation for twenty years the buildings and improvements of limited-dividend companies whose projects received state approval. By 1928 two cooperatives and one civic group had developments under way, and soon another cooperative and two commerical companies planned to start construction, but in a city of 9,000,000 people only 1,700 families would find accommodations in the new apartments. American municipal governments generally were not disturbed by the housing problem.

The 1929 conference of the National Housing Association, held in Philadelphia, attempted to put issues in perspective and to survey a broad range of topics from the advent of the steel-frame house and the "scientific kitchen" to slum clearance and the relation of housing to city planning. Although many city planners were on the program, the speaker who succinctly defined the problem was knowledgeable Dr. Wood. "The housing problem, here as elsewhere, is fundamentally economic," she declared. "The distribution of income and cost of building are such that only a third of the population can afford to buy or rent a new home."[119] The construction industry served mainly the top third, the families having incomes of $2,000 or more annually. The middle third, with incomes from $1,200 to $2,000, were housed only fairly, and the lowest third, with yearly earnings of less than $1,200, badly. The United States was "at the point where Great Britain was 78 years ago, where Belgium and Germany were 40 years ago, France 35 years ago, and Holland 28 years ago, debating whether or not nation, state and city should provide housing credits, on an at-cost basis, to cut down the price of wholesome housing to be within the reach of lower-income groups that cannot otherwise attain it."[120]

Dr. Wood favored state-controlled loans to "those below the income groups which can use the machinery of the building and loan associations." She was not advocating government subsidies, only government aid in the form of housing credits. Whether this kind of aid would prove sufficient by itself to solve housing problems could be told only after a full and fair trial. She pointed out that it did not prove enough in Europe. The industrialized nations there had had to adopt municipal housing and slum clearance programs. But the financial status of American workers might be "enough better . . . so that loans will suffice." If not, then there were "the steps beyond" that would have to be taken.[121]

258 CITY PLANNING IN THE AGE OF BUSINESS

The steps beyond were the "abominations" that even Dr. Wood's well-informed and presumably humane audience dreaded. Lawrence Veiller as passionately urged clearing slums as he ever had—"it must be done because the public interest indicates that their demolition is required"—but the government should not rehouse the displaced families, for that would be "foreign to American practice and principles."[122] Let limited-dividend companies build on part of every cleared site and let the city take over the rest for a park or recreation ground. Harold S. Buttenheim, publisher of the *American City* magazine, similarly believed that "all—or almost all—of us would draw [the line] this side of government housing."[123] Americans did not favor subsidies, though state loans for housing, without ultimate cost to the public, or reduced taxes on buildings (which he evidently did not consider a form of subsidy) would be acceptable. In the meantime, would it not be worthwhile to hasten the reconditioning of houses worth saving and to speed the demolition of "uncontrovertible slums" by vigorous enforcement of building and sanitary codes "more drastic than now exist in most states and cities"?[124] And should there not be greater civic effort "to the end that hard-headed complacency and capital seeking investment and philanthropy seeking a constructive outlet may come to realize—more generally than at present—that improvements in the housing of the lower-income groups of our cities are economically possible and of fundamental social importance?"[125]

In January, 1929, all the old and unsuccessful formulas for producing safe and sanitary housing for those who needed it most still seemed promising. In December, after the collapse of the stock market and the onset of an ever deepening depression, they would appear increasingly impractical.

The participants in the conference moved on to evidences of progress in the creation of a better environment. Clarence A. Perry's scheme for a self-contained neighborhood unit—an area bounded by arterial thoroughfares, with a school at the center and shops at the traffic intersections on the periphery—appealed to Robert Whitten as an economical and eminently satisfactory way to organize residential communities. Applying it to a 160-acre tract in the Borough of Queens that had been tentatively platted with a rectangular street system, he had devised an interior circulation system reducing the percentage of land in streets and consequently the requirements for sewers, paving, curbs, and sidewalks. By effecting other economies, he calculated that he would be able "to secure savings amounting to about $371 a lot, as compared with the ordinary standardized subdivision."[126] But this neighborhood of predominantly single-family homes would be only for families with incomes of $1,800 to $2,500 a year—the same economic groups for whom speculative builders put up monotonous rows of flimsy houses elsewhere in Queens. Whitten was as far from solving the housing problems of lower-income families as everyone else.

A development described by Louis Brownlow, now municipal consultant of the City Housing Corporation, probably was no answer to the low-cost housing riddle either, though it was undoubtedly a provocative synthesis of excellent ideas in residential-site planning, old and new. This was Radburn, near Paterson, New Jersey. Designed by Clarence Stein and Henry Wright, the same architects who had striven nobly, though unsuccessfully, to reduce building costs at Sunnyside in Queens, Radburn was to be a city for 25,000 people. Although only 180 houses were then under construction, the plans for the project excited more

62. Radburn, New Jersey, established by the City Housing Corporation in 1929; site and housing planned by Henry Wright and Clarence Stein (*National Resources Committee*)

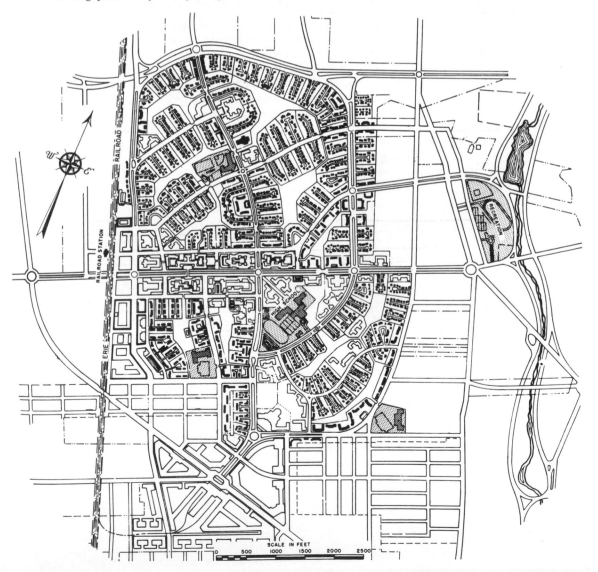

interest than those for any other new community of the decade. Stein and Wright did boldly what other designers attempted timidly: arranged the houses in superblocks penetrated only by cul-de-sacs, separated pedestrian and vehicular traffic, faced the houses toward gardens, reserved the interiors of the superblocks for parks, and connected the superblocks by a system of walks with underpasses under the motorways. "Within three or four months it will be possible at Radburn to walk a mile on sidewalks without stepping down from a curb, or being where a motor vehicle can possibly attack one," Brownlow proclaimed.[127]

John Nolen was impressed by the fact that "a client has been found willing to trust to the lead of designers who are proposing new ways of doing things."[128] He lauded the faith and imagination of Alexander Bing, president of the City Housing Corporation. Radburn was particularly significant to Nolen because of all the important questions it raised. After hearing Brownlow describe the town again at the national conference on city planning four months later, Nolen asked:

> If we are going to build new towns as a part of our regional planning and development, where are they to be and how are they to be located? Can we take, by eminent domain, land for new towns on the theory that it is taken for a public purpose? How can large funds be secured from great corporations like insurance companies for the building of Radburns? Can the very difficult problem of the housing of the very poor be solved in developments like Radburn? Can we find other groups of practical idealists willing to put into community planning, for a return of 6 per cent, such an amount of not only money but of effort, skill, even genius, and take a risk which, in other fields of investment, would yield far greater returns? Can Radburn be repeated not only in the environs of Philadelphia, Chicago, Boston, Buffalo, but even outside of smaller cities like Niagara Falls?[129]

In effect, Nolen asked whether America was yet ready to devise and follow a public policy for the planning and development of urban areas, envisaging some kind of partnership or cooperation between private enterprise and government that would permit each to contribute in the best way possible to the solution of the problems of housing, industrial location, transportation, and land use. Generally, the country was wholly unprepared to entertain the question, even though it had heard much discussion of urban growth for several years. Not even the regional planning associations and county planning commissions in the more populous areas had faced some of the specific questions Nolen posed. Most city planning and such regional planning as was being done was mainly rather short-range problem-solving. Larger questions of the most advantageous long-term arrangement of urban regions rarely aroused interest, if, indeed, they were phrased at all.

A Gift to the People of the New York Region

On May 27, 1929, a few days after the conference at which Nolen had propounded his searching questions, national interest focused on a public meeting in New York City at which the Committee on the Regional Plan presented the first volume of its plan to the people of the New York region as a gift from the Russell Sage Foundation. The meeting also launched a new Regional Plan Association to carry on educational work and guide the development of the region in accordance with the plan. The Sage Foundation again played the role of benefactor by contributing $25,000 to the association "to enable it to get a proper start and secure contributions from other sources."[130]

The volume brought before the public was entitled *The Graphic Regional Plan* and did not in itself represent all that the distinguished staff of the Committee on the Regional Plan had to say about the future development of the New York region. From time to time since 1927 the committee had issued various survey volumes containing the factual information and analyses used in preparing the plan. These reports had included findings about major economic factors in metropolitan growth and arrangement, population, highway traffic, transit and transportation, public recreation, neighborhood and community planning, and public services. Together with the volume on the graphic plan, they re-

63. Airview of Radburn, 1940 *(Daniel E. Ryan, courtesy of Clarence Stein)*

vealed the chief directions in which Thomas Adams and his fellow planners thought metropolitan regional growth should be channeled, but a still more explanatory volume, *The Building of the City*, and another survey publication, *Buildings: Their Uses and the Spaces About Them*, were not to appear until 1931. The public and persons intensely interested in this monumental planning effort could not yet fully estimate its value, nor could critics pronounce final judgement on it.

A discussion of the object and scope of the plan disclosed that Adams and his staff had sought a middle ground between visionary schemes and shortsighted practicality:

> In considering what proposals to include in the Plan for securing the object of a better balanced system of growth, the staff has had to have regard to existing methods of growth, habits and wants. These it could not ignore. Nor could it assume that there would be any revolutionary change on the part of the public in favor of a more ideal system of city development. And yet the staff has acted on the principle of looking at the problems of the city on the basis of what should be, qualified by what is and can be, rather than on that of projecting present conditions and methods into the future merely because they have the wide assent of public opinon.[131]

That such an approach exposed them to attack by "either the practical man who thinks mainly of the immediate present or the idealist who dreams of a perfect future" the planners readily acknowledged.[132] Their choice nevertheless had been to seek "an ideal based on realities" and to "present a picture of possibilities within the limits of reasonable anticipation of what the collective intelligence of the community will accept and promote."[133]

On the assumption that what was needed was to prevent concentration from reaching "an undesirable degree or quality" in any industrial, business, or residential district, Adams and his associates proposed three major directions of development:

> First—Diffused re-centralization of industry with the objects of lessening the density of congested centers and of creating new centers.
> Second—Diffusion of residence into compact residential neighborhoods throughout the whole urban region integrated with the industrial sections so as to reduce distances between homes and places of work.
> Third—Sub-centralization of business so arranged as to provide the maximum of convenience to residents.[134]

A plan contemplating the emergence of many new commercial centers in outlying areas and the widespread dispersal of industries along waterways and in areas served by rail and highway systems necessarily emphasized the development and coordination of all types of facilities for movement. Indeed, Adams and his colleagues have been credited with offering "the first product of a 'systems approach' to urban transportation planning in the United States."[135] Like other urban regions in the 1920s, the New York region had only begun to meet the insatiable requirements of the automobile. It was especially deficient in river crossings and express highways, not to mention parkways and boulevards. The greater part of the first volume of the regional plan not surprisingly presented proposals for a metropolitan loop highway, inner routes, radial routes,

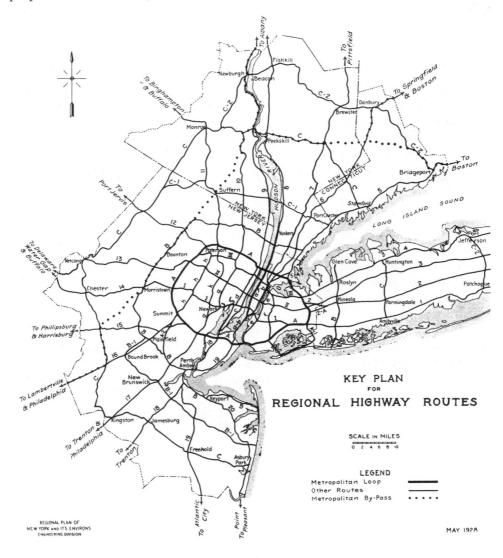

64. Plan of regional highway routes, Regional Plan of New York and Its Environs, 1929

outer circumferential routes, a metropolitan bypass, and numerous minor highways, as well as proposals for new rail and waterway projects, airports, and a suburban rapid transit system. Lest all these additional circulation facilities lead to further congestion, however, the plan advocated stronger land use controls and limitations on the bulk of buildings. As the planners foresaw the possibility of providing ample living space for additional millions in well-organized suburban areas, they proposed the maintenance of three-fourths of the whole region as open development — public parks, water-supply reservations, institutional properties and golf courses, military reservations, landing fields, water areas, and extensive areas for farming.

A monograph by Adams, Bassett, and Whitten in the survey volume on neighborhood and community planning hailed Radburn as probably the most forward step in town planning in America and contended that "some such scheme is necessary as an object lesson before effective solutions can be obtained for the problems of congestion, of unbalanced distribution and of overcrowded housing conditions in the New York region."[136] The authors noted that there would almost certainly be a considerable movement of industries from older production areas if the manufacturers had any assurance that their workers would be provided with housing accommodations. But industrialists had no such assurance — for the simple reason that builders and financial institutions did not find it profitable to construct housing for the wage-earning class, though Adams and his fellow planners did not state this obvious fact. They acknowledged that it would be clearly impracticable to clear and rebuild large areas of deteriorated housing and obsolescent factories in crowded centers.[137] The only practicable things to do were to build satellite cities and to prevent overcrowded conditions from developing in suburban areas. Bassett, of course, had faith that the adoption of adequate zoning ordinances would protect the suburbs from repeating the mistakes of the older centers, but apparently neither he nor Adams and Whitten fully realized in 1929 that building costs were the roadblock to the creation of satellite cities. Adams and Wayne D. Heydecker were to investigate the entire subject further and to give special attention to one of Nolen's important questions: Could land for new towns be taken by eminent domain? If it could be, what kind of public agency should exercise this power?

The regional plan projected a multicentered urban complex of vast proportions and held out the hope that densities in the newly developing areas would be neither unduly low and wasteful of land resources nor too high and inimical to good living conditions. Its strong emphasis on the desirability of making open space accessible throughout the region was particularly exemplary. The various survey volumes disclosed, however, that the economic analyses on which the plan was based were inconclusive and that many crucial questions of public policy, law, and finance required additional study. The new Regional Plan Association had a two-fold opportunity to conduct further surveys and research and to encourage local governments in the region to cooperate in carrying out the plan.

The "Rapidly Growing Mass of Knowledge"

As nothing else had before, the preparation of the New York regional plan revealed the strengths and deficiencies of the men who called themselves city planners. Educated as engineers, architects, and landscape architects or as attorneys, they had worked in this endeavor with experts in social welfare and economics, transit and transportation, political science and public administration, industrial management, and public health. From these authorities they had acquired a wealth of new knowledge and had surpassed their previous performances in synthesizing it with what they already knew; and yet the experience had made them realize anew that as men self-taught in the field of city planning, they were in many respects ill equipped for the work they did. Surely, younger men entering the field should be more broadly educated and should begin their labors with a greater competence. To Adams, Nolen, Olmsted, and others it was therefore a special satisfaction to know that one of the by-products of their struggles to develop a plan for the New York region was a new School of City Planning at Harvard University, opened in 1929.

A year before the Committee on the Regional Plan submitted the first volume of the plan to the public, its members had joined with President Nicholas Murray Butler of Columbia University in calling a Conference on Research and Instruction in City and Regional Planning. Frederic Delano had presided, and among the participants had been Adams, Shelby Harrison, Professor Henry V. Hubbard of Harvard, Professor Charles E. Merriam of the University of Chicago, Nolen, Flavel Shurtleff, and Delano's fellow committeemen Henry James and Lawson Purdy. From this conference had come a general statement forecasting that the next twenty-five years would witness an "unprecedented amount of city building in this country" and that the increasing demand for city planners might call forth many men of "poor training and narrow outlook" to pilot the development of cities. A further danger was that there would not be "sufficient body of digested experience and doctrine to guide planners." Everything considered, the time had come when "more ample provision should be made for fundamental research, for the development of the profession, and for the training of younger men entering it."[138]

The conference was less concerned with whether an existing institution should be expanded or a new one founded than with indicating the scope of research and instruction. City planning, it held, was "not merely a special field for the application of the skill of any single profession," such as engineering or landscape architecture, but must draw upon the several arts and sciences, including architecture, political economy, the science of government, sociology, sanitary science, physical geography, and "publicity, public movements and organizations."[139] Even though it might be impracticable for any one man to be a master of all aspects of city planning, he should be "a master of one, at least, which provides training in design" and, in addition, should "possess a sufficient understanding of the manner in which others impinge upon his total problem to be able to coordinate the efforts of other specialists in any project of research, teaching, or practice."[140]

That Harvard University would be the first of the thirty-three American universities and colleges offering courses in city planning to accept the challenge of the conference was perhaps to be expected. It had presented the first instruction in city planning and had consistently exercised leadership in the field. Since 1923 it had been awarding a degree of Master of Landscape Architecture in City Planning, and through the years its library had built up the most extensive collection of city planning literature in the nation. The establishment of a separate graduate School of City Planning was the next logical step, made possible by a grant from the Rockefeller Foundation for a limited period and by the endowment of the Charles Dyer Norton Chair of Regional Planning by alumnus James F. Curtis, a friend of Norton's.

First to occupy the newly endowed chair and to direct the school was Professor Hubbard, who edited the quarterly *City Planning,* official organ of the American City Planning Institute and the National Conference on City Planning. With his wife, Theodora Kimball Hubbard, he had been engaged in a two-year survey and analysis of progress in city planning and zoning in the United States, published in 1929 under the title *Our Cities To-Day and To-Morrow.* As an educator, he had thought long and searchingly about city planning as a profession.

Knowing that many persons did not think that there was such a thing as a profession of city planning distinct from architecture, engineering, law, or some other already recognized profession, Hubbard had written in 1927, "It seems to the editor [of *City Planning*] that there does exist a very important and rapidly growing mass of knowledge which is not engineering, which is not architecture, which is not law, which is not medicine, but which furthers certain general goods toward which, each in its specific way, all these specialized professions and a good many more are also contributing." If a man could grasp and apply enough of this general knowledge and combine it with knowledge of some specialized subject having a bearing upon the long-term improvement of "the surroundings of civilized humanity," he might justifiably be called a professional city planner. But Hubbard also expressed the belief that "by far the greatest bulk of city planning accomplishment has been done in the past and will always be done in the future by socially-minded people, each person working his own work and knowing necessarily only enough of the generalities to be able to cooperate with all kinds of other people towards a common end."[141] The "generalities" presumably embraced "laws" and theories explaining the growth and development of cities and the endeavors of men to better them. Hubbard used such terms with no more attempt to elucidate them than to indicate the nature of the "growing mass of knowledge" a prospective city planner should master.

It was hardly to be expected in 1929 that anyone could offer a definition of city planning or a curriculum that would not be decidedly controversial. The hopeful aspect of the establishment of a graduate school of city planning at Harvard was that new men entering the field would bring to it a broader perspective and a deeper knowledge of some of the many disciplines contributing to its development.

The year 1929 also saw the leaders of the planning movement allied with some prominent industrialists in an attempt to raise funds for a central national clearinghouse of planning information. Never having succeeded in inducing the Congress to create such an agency in the federal government, the directors of the National Conference on City Planning had voted in 1928 to incorporate the Planning Foundation of America, so that it might organize and support the desired research, informational, and promotional program. Ninety-four per cent of the communities of 2,500 or more inhabitants were unplanned for future growth, they observed; 84 per cent were unprotected by zoning ordinances; and 86 per cent had no planning commissions. The recital of planning accomplishments made by Nolen in 1927 and other morale-boosting efforts at stocktaking could not obscure the fact that as yet professional endeavor had "only scratched the surface of the city planning problem in America."[142] In the hope of stimulating the formation of more planning agencies and guiding public opinion in support of city planning, the planners had turned to the business world and now had among the members of the advisory council of the new foundation Harry Chandler, publisher of the *Los Angeles Times;* George B. Dealey, president of the *Dallas News;* Walter A. Draper, president of the Cincinnati Street Railway Company; Howard Heinz, the Pittsburgh food manufacturer; Paul G. Hoffman, of the Studebaker Corporation; and Bancroft Gheradi, chief engineer and vice-president of the American Telephone and Telegraph Company.

In the late summer of 1929 Russell Van Nest Black set out on a trip to promote the foundation, taking with him a brochure entitled *New Cities for the New Age.* It traced the growth and development of cities in the United States and warned that the old, familiar urban problems had now become "menaces which must be faced and conquered."[143] The foundation needed $50,000 a year for its program, a fifth of which would be spent on research, a fifth on education, and three-fifths on promotion and publicity. If prospective donors would contribute liberally, it would be able to relieve the National Conference on City Planning of the burden of trying to provide advice and information to cities throughout the country on a budget of only $6,000 a year. But Black was on the road only two and a half months when a wildly inflated stock market suffered its first drastic break. For the next three weeks prices plunged, steadied momentarily, nose-dived again, and yet again and again until in mid-November the losses on paper amounted to $26,000,000,000, and the false front of prosperity lay in ruins. Crushed in the wreckage was the Planning Foundation of America, its pledges of financial support worthless and its hope of obtaining others all but destroyed.

Cracks in the rococo façade had begun to appear some months before the crash. Unemployment had risen, consumer spending had slackened, industrial production had fallen, and building contracts had declined sharply. The debacle in Wall Street was the dramatic and inevitable result of the failure of corporate America to reduce its prices to consumers and to augment the wages of its workers. When their incomes no longer were large enough in the aggregate to purchase the increased flood of goods made possible by scientific management and laborsaving technology, it was impossible to sustain the fictitious stock market values based on the expectation of an ever higher rate of spending. Herbert Hoover, the Great Engineer who had campaigned for the presidency with predictions that the people were "in sight of the day when poverty will be banished from this nation,"[144] now surveyed an economic structure that was in danger of falling in. The planners who had been grateful to him throughout the decade for his support of city planning apprehensively watched his efforts to stave off disaster by shoring up the walls and putting scaffolding under the roof.

The truth was that few of them had really understood Hoover, who seemed to be their friend, or the very process in which they were engaged. As they saw it, they were reducing the inefficiencies of the city and saving money for the taxpayers. But perspicacious Charles A. Beard discerned that in a pluralistic society, with its real estate interest, public utility interests, various manufacturing interests, commercial interests, shipping and carrying interests, banking interests, an organized labor interest, and office-holding and many lesser interests, the city planners actually were redistributing, or helping to redistribute, wealth from some groups to other groups. The business interests approved of such redistribution schemes as street improvements and utilities but opposed slum clearance and housing and related measures to better the congested districts. These programs, so far as the hardheaded tycoons could see, benefited the masses but not them personally. Such a view made the planner suspect, at least when he was advocating slum clearance, as a genteel revolutionary, whereas the planner was an innocent who scarcely thought of himself as a revolutionary at all. He was soon to discover, however, that he must more knowingly essay the role of social and economic revisionist — or fail of his larger mission. Many of his proposals, to his chagrin, raised the value of land so much that poor people could not afford to live in areas showing the effect of his handiwork; and many of his street-widening schemes so increased traffic that property values rose, encouraging landowners to put up bigger buildings. The large structures attracted more people, thereby still further congesting traffic and adding to the cost of municipal administration. If his planning were to confer genuine social benefits, it would have to be allied to policies consciously devised to effect desirable shifts in the distribution of wealth. Worsening economic conditions under Hoover made many city planners aware, some of them for the first time, of the need to use planning more deliberately as an instrument of social change.

CHAPTER 5

A NEW PERSPECTIVE: THE URBAN COMMUNITY IN NATIONAL LIFE

A Climate for National Planning

In 1927 Frederic A. Delano could hardly have imagined that in only six years he would be chairman of a national planning board. Yet he had begun to face the problems that such a board would consider. As president of the Federated Societies on Planning and Parks he had been persuaded to chair a Joint Committee on Bases of Sound Land Policy, which sought answers to two mind-stretching questions: Will our land area in the United States meet the demands of our future population? How are we to determine the best use of our land resources? Inherent in the ques-

270

tions was the idea of national planning, as the members of the various organizations composing the Federated Societies no doubt understood. These groups were the American Civic Association, National Conference on City Planning, American Institute of Park Executives, American Park Society, and the National Conference on State Parks.

From practical experience in the federal government several members of the Joint Committee knew the shocking consequences of the lack of any long-term, comprehensive plan or policy for the development and use of natural resources. While Congress tried to solve the problem of agricultural surpluses, it made appropriations for the reclamation of more land. While one branch of the government grappled with the problem of overproduction of oil, another canceled leases on federally owned oil lands because wells were not drilled by a specified time. While there were strikes, unemployment, and bankruptcies in the coal industry, the government continued to lease more coal lands and to insist on a minimum yearly production. Such inconsistencies deeply disturbed Dr. L. C. Gray, chief of the Division of Land Economics of the U.S. Department of Agriculture; Dr. Elwood Mead, Commissioner of Reclamation of the Department of the Interior and a director-at-large of the National Bureau of Economic Research; and Horace M. Albright, director of the National Park Service. Their concern was shared by various other members of the committee who were perhaps not directly affected by the vagaries of federal action but believed that the time had come to think about national planning. All had influential connections which assured that the group's suggestions for a national land policy would be widely disseminated.

The Joint Committee's first question about whether the land area of the United States would meet the demands of the future population of course raised questions about how many people there would be to feed, clothe, and house in fifty or a hundred years. Two widely respected teams of population experts, Raymond Pearl and L. J. Reed of Johns Hopkins University, and Warren S. Thompson and P. K. Whelpton of the Scripps Foundation for Research in Population Problems, had already convinced the intellectual elite of America that population growth was slowing up and that the nation would probably have a stable population by the last quarter of the century or soon after the year 2000. These two pairs of demographers differed in their estimates of the ultimate population and the time at which it might be expected, but they were certain from their studies of birth rates and death rates in the last several decades in various parts of the United States that a permanent decline in the national rate of growth had set in. As relatively fewer children were born, the proportion of middle-aged and elderly persons in the population would gradually increase. The country would become more conservative in business and politics, but people would develop greater interest in the quality of their environment. Planning, perhaps, would be more palatable than it had been in a society which equated bigger with better and developed its enterprises on the assumption of an ever increasing population. From time to time both Pearl and Reed and Thompson and Whelpton revised their estimates, especially after the census of 1930 was available, but no changes undermined the widespread acceptance of their conclusions about eventual stabilization of the population. In the last years of the 1920s, all during the 1930s, and in the early 1940s their miscalculations formed the basis for many types of long-range planning. Not surprisingly, therefore, the Joint Committee issued a report in 1929 assuming that the population of the United States would be not in excess of 200,000,000 by the year 2000, or possibly even below that figure — say, 180,000,000.[1]

What About the Year 2000?, as the committee's publication was entitled, answered affirmatively the question about resources to meet long-term needs. An area not much greater than what was then under cultivation might be sufficient to support the future population. The agricultural crisis seemed to be due mainly to overproduction caused by the cultivation of more land than was necessary, under modern agricultural techniques, to meet market demands. Crop lands should be restricted by retiring unprofitable or submarginal areas to reduce the volume of production; and any further public expenditures to reclaim lands by drainage or irrigation should be authorized *only* after "careful studies . . . to show economic and social justification for specific lands in specific crops. . . ."[2] Forests, wilderness areas, and water resources in the aggregate appeared to be adequate to meet future construction, recreational, and water supply requirements, but what particularly worried the committee were the conflicting claims for land use. Demands for habitation, commerce, industry, farms, grazing, forests, mineral deposits, parks, highways, scenic drives, railway routes, inland navigation ways, power reservoirs, storage sites for metropolitan water supplies and irrigation of dry farming lands, and countless other uses frequently fell upon identical or overlapping areas. Unless the nation adopted intelligent land-planning policies, there was every indication that these difficulties would become more acute with the passing years. The committee report stated,

We have developed to some extent a national point of view for public forests, for national parks, for arterial highways, and for a few other uses of land, but we now need to find a way to reconcile these various uses with each other. Just as progressive cities have been forced to abandon piecemeal planning, there are indications that the Nation will ultimately abandon piecemeal planning in favor of comprehensive land-planning, that is, there will be a conscious effort to establish control, through planning in advance, of the use of public and private land and its resources in the interests of the country, state, or region as a whole.[3]

How national planning might influence city and metropolitan regional planning, the report did not make clear, though it indicated that a national planning program might help to illumine many questions about urban development then unanswered. "Only slight progress has been made in solving the problems of the relation of one urban center to other centers, or to the surrounding rural territory or to the nation as a whole," the report observed. "This is not surprising because no one knows the best relationships between different cities or between cities and the whole country."[4] The only knowledge anyone had was of trends of urban development. These the committee discussed in some detail, noting in particular the spread of urban population over larger and larger areas and calling attention to the prediction that the strip of land along the Atlantic seaboard from Portland, Maine, to Washington, D.C., would become an almost continuous urban settlement. In this and other emerging megalopolitan complexes it might be necessary "to decide conflicting claims for water supplies for the various sections of the population."[5] Thus urban growth and development assumed the proportions of a national problem and was significantly related to the compelling problem of planning for the use of natural resources for varied purposes.

By the time *What About the Year 2000?* came off the press something of a climate for consideration of a more coordinated attack on national problems had been created. It probably affected only limited segments of the business community, though it undoubtedly could be felt in a good many governmental agencies, universities, scientific and professional societies, and editorial offices. Herbert Hoover, in particular, had contributed to the development of this climate by establishing a Conference on Unemployment in the postwar depression of 1921, when he was Secretary of Commerce, and by keeping this organization going with the assistance of the National Bureau of Economic Research and many governmental and private agencies. In January, 1928, shortly before he took office as President, he significantly stimulated interest in this new atmosphere of forethought by appointing the Committee on Recent Economic Changes as an arm of the conference. Business and labor leaders served on the committee, and distinguished professors, manufacturers, and professional men wrote the report it issued in February, 1929, reviewing economic changes since the First World War and pointing to the need of developing "a technique of balance" to keep the complex and intricate national economic machine producing continuously.[6]

"With certain natural resources still wastefully exploited, with great industries, such as agriculture and coal mining, still below the general level of prosperity, with certain regions retarded, there remains much to do," the committee observed.[7] The most pointed comments in its published volumes were written by Wesley C. Mitchell, professor of economics at Columbia University and one of the co-directors of the research staff of the National Bureau of Economic Research. He noted that "we are leaving 1921 well behind, and there are signs that the caution inspired by that disastrous year is wearing thin."[8] If business prosperity were to be maintained, it would have to be earned "month after month and year after year by intelligent effort." The incomes disbursed to consumers, and to wage earners in particular, would have to be increased "on a scale sufficient to pay for the swelling volume of consumers' goods sent to market."[9] The credit structure would have to be kept in due adjustment to the earnings of business enterprises, commodity stocks held in line with current sales, and overcommitments of all sorts avoided. Mitchell's warning indicated that he personally, and doubtless some other members of the committee, realized the dangers of another economic catastrophe, but millions of other Americans firmly believed the popular fiction that cyclical fluctuations in the economy had been permanently ironed out. The climate for national planning then expanding in intellectual circles touched them not at all.

How much Herbert Hoover understood or accepted the more serious implications of the report of his Committee on Recent Economic Changes would be difficult to say. At least, he agreed that there remained much to do. In September, 1929, some weeks before the stock market went into a tailspin, he summoned Mitchell and five other social scientists "to examine and to report upon recent social trends in the United States with a view to providing such a review as might supply a basis for the formulation of large national policies looking to the next phase in the nation's development."[10] Whatever Hoover had in mind as the next phase in the nation's development, he appealed for further guidance to a group whose members breathed the new rarefied atmosphere of policy planning, or, more accurately, research for policy planning. Although Mitchell was the only one who had participated in the study of economic changes, the others—Charles E. Merriam, William F. Ogburn, Howard W. Odum, Alice Hamilton, and Shelby M. Harrison—all knew about that undertaking and were also acquainted with the inquiry of the Joint Committee on Bases of Sound Land Policy. Merriam had learned about the latter endeavor from his brother John, vice-chairman of the National Research Council and president of the Carnegie Institution, as well as from Frederick Law Olmsted, who also had been a member of the Joint Committee, representing the National Conference on City Planning. Ogburn, who was a colleague of Merriam's at the University of Chicago, and Odum, a University of North Carolina professor who had many friends in the U.S. Department of Agriculture, were familiar with the project, as of course were Alice Hamilton and Harrison. In a way, both studies served as background for the ambitious investigation launched in December, 1929, by Hoover's formal appointment of Mitchell, Merriam, and the other four as the President's Research Committee on Social Trends.

The collapse of the stock market between the time Hoover first discussed the undertaking with them and the time he publicly announced their appointment changed the entire aspect of their research, although this did not become apparent until later. The President, by his repeated assurances that national recovery was "just around the corner," indicated that he believed the country was suffering only a temporary setback. Unfortunately, he had not participated in final sessions of his Committee on Recent Economic Changes and perhaps did not share the deep misgivings that Mitchell had expressed in its report. Certainly, as an official who had earlier professed to be much concerned about unemployment, Hoover had done little to gain support in 1928 for a counter-depression public works reserve scheme introduced at a Governor's Conference in New Orleans as the "Hoover plan," perhaps because after giving it nominal support he had concluded that it was really not urgent. His campaign speeches and his utterances in the first several months of his presidency all disclosed that he saw the path of national progress leading ever upward to new heights of achievement. He evidently conceived of the study of the momentous social changes since the First World War as the basis for some great constructive endeavor to be initiated later in his term and doubtless continued in a second term. The cruel turn of events, not unforeseen to economists other than Mitchell, necessarily gradually converted the investigation into an illumination of the strains and flaws in the American scheme of things, as Hoover himself noted in a foreword to the published volumes by mentioning the "emphasis on elements of instability rather than stability in our social structure."[11] Ironically, the massive report of his committee was to be of more value to his successor in the presidency than to Hoover, as were the findings and recommendations of several conferences he called during his unhappy term of office. For both Mitchell and Merriam the Research Committtee on Social Trends provided background for their service with Delano on the kind of agency the Joint Committee of the Federated Societies on Planning and Parks had hoped for — a national planning board.

Such an agency was more than three years in the future when Hoover's research committee began outlining the scope of its investigations and looking about for authorities to undertake specific studies. Ogburn became director of research and Odum the assistant director. For an executive secretary Mitchell turned to Edward Eyre Hunt, who was known as Hoover's "idea man" and had held the same position with the Committee on Recent Economic Changes. Thus it became clear that some of the same experts who had participated in the previous investigation would be asked to contribute to the new one. Economists Edward F. Gay of Harvard University and Leo Wolman of Columbia University, both of whom had written chapters for the report of the Committee on Recent Economic Changes, were engaged to collaborate on a study of trends in economic organization. Wolman also undertook research on labor groups in the social structure. O. E. Baker, one of the agricultural economists who had reviewed the manuscript of *What About the Year 2000?* and had made suggestions that were incorporated in the final publication, discussed the utilization of agricultural and forest land. The team of Thompson and Whelpton prepared a detailed analysis of the population of the nation. Charles E. Merriam contributed a chapter on government and society, Odum one on public welfare activities, Ogburn one on the family and its functions and another on the influence of invention and discovery. Five other colleagues of Merriam's and Ogburn's at the University of Chicago, associates of Odum's at the University of North Carolina and of Mitchell's at Columbia University, and professors in eight other universities prepared studies for the committee. In addition, experts in several foundations and private institutes contributed chapters for the final report of the group.

But since all these authorities sought information and suggestions from hundreds of other professors, government officials, industrialists, publishers, and executives of civic, professional, welfare, financial, and cultural associations, the committee succeeded in making its activities truly nationwide. In so doing, it doubtless sharpened the knife of criticism that cut deeper and deeper into the beleaguered champion of rugged individualism in the White House. Still more significantly, it paved the way for the wholesale enlistment of the brainpower of the nation in governmental endeavor in Franklin D. Roosevelt's administration. Among those whose help the Research Committee on Social Trends acknowledged receiving were dozens of persons who later worked in or with New Deal agencies, including two men who were destined to serve on the National Resources Committee and its successor, the National Resources Planning Board — Henry S. Dennison, manufacturer, and Beardsley Ruml, executive of the Spelman Fund.

The monographs and reports of Hoover's research group provided a substantial foundation for later studies, including the study of the role of cities in the national economy undertaken by the Urbanism Committee of the National Resources Committee in 1937. As a task force concerned with national trends, Hoover's committee, however, perhaps did not sufficiently focus attention on the urban area as the locus of significant social change and the breeding ground of social problems. Only one of the monographs specially commissioned by the committee specifically dealt with the city. This was R. D. McKenzie's *The Metropolitan Community,* which included chapters by various other authorities, among whom were the coauthors of a chapter on city and regional planning, Flavel Shurtleff and Shelby M. Harrison. The latter, besides being a member of the Hoover committee, was general director of the Russell Sage Foundation and the former director of social studies of the Regional Plan of New York and Its Environs. A condensation of the monograph appeared in the two-volume report of the committee as a chapter entitled "The Rise of the Metropolitan Community."

In linking the development of city and regional planning to the ascendency of large urban areas in our national life, McKenzie placed the planning function in the proper perspective, but the discussion of the subject by Shurtleff and Harrison, a dry recital of historical facts and statistics about the number of planning commissions and zoning ordinances, scarcely explained the reasons for the emergence of city planning as a new activity of urban government and gave no hint of the probable course of planning in the future. McKenzie himself somewhat compensated for the deficiencies of their presentation by pointing out in his summary and conclusions that the recent outward movement of population and industrial enterprises, business outlets, and service institutions confronted every large city with the problem of revitalizing extensive blighted areas. He observed that such areas were rarely rehabilitated by private enterprise and were, moreover, in competition with newer subdivisions which offered a more inviting field for capital investment. But McKenzie noted the "unprecedented speculative development of subdivision platting" in outlying territories in the twenties and commented on the "present municipal tax burdens and transportation difficulties."[12] The reliance of widely scattered suburban residents on the private automobile necessitated huge expenditures for street and highway construction and raised "a host of related problems of taxation and special assessments." He found that almost every one of the new problems of great cities "comes home sooner or later to the governmental agencies," of which there had been a rapid increase in the past thirty years, with the result that one of the most serious difficulties of the metropolitan community was the multiplicity of separate governments. Regional planning on a scale commensurate with actual needs was thwarted by the large number of politically independent units. Drawing upon the studies of his colleague at the University of Michigan, political scientist Thomas H. Reed, McKenzie suggested "the need of some sort of supermetropolitan government."[13] He was hopeful that as regional communities became more conscious of their common interests, they would support an increasing amount of purposeful planning, not entirely restricted to "the mere physical aspects of community structure and municipal functions" but including "an increasing range of economic and social activities."[14]

The pressures of the time indeed indicated that city planners would increasingly be forced to pay greater attention to the economic and social aspects of the city even though their professional inclination might be to continue to regard the physical plant as their chief concern. The development of metropolitan regional planning had already broadened their knowledge of the economic functions of urban areas. Some talk of state planning had perhaps spread the impression that the formulation of economic policies was as important as, or more important than, the preparation of schemes for physical improvement. The worsening of the depression throughout the three years the Research Committee on Social Trends was at work—unemployment increased from 3,000,000 to more than 15,000,000—emphasized the economic aspects of life as had few other events in the history of the nation, with the exception of wars. The social ills accompanying the chaos into which the depression plunged the country seemed more the reflection of economic conditions than maladjustments of distinguishable nature. The lack of adequate housing for low-income families, for example, at last began to appear as an unsolved economic problem related to the technological backwardness of the building industry and to rigid notions about further government participation in an already mixed economy. The racial problems associated with bad housing, the higher incidence of disease, crime, and dependency in slums, and the divisive effects of deteriorating older areas on metropolitan social structure all now seemed peculiarly part of the larger problem of restoring a sick economy and then making it function more satisfactorily than ever before. National planning of some sort, supported by state planning or river basin planning and more effective local planning, loomed as an imperative need the more the country drifted toward economic disintegration.

City Planning: Target of "Economy" Groups

The onset of the depression found some city planners concerned not with large economic and social issues but with the question whether miniature golf courses were commercial or recreational uses of land. "Peewee golf," as it was popularly called, was one of the lighter manifestations of an otherwise dark era. Suddenly this version of a noble Scottish sport became the national craze, as much because thousands of enterprising souls thought that opening a miniature golf course was the way to "lick" the depression as because millions of others welcomed a new pastime that would take their minds off their troubles. Vacant lots all over cities presently were converted into tiny golf courses on which players putted under the glare of electric lights far into the night. These amusement parks-in-little caused no problems in commercial areas, but those in residential neighborhoods brought outcries from residents whose sleep was disturbed by the illumination and by the loud conversation and laughter of patrons. Eventually planners agreed that miniature golf was a commercial form of recreation inappropriate in residential zones, though by the time some communities settled the issue the popular interest in the game had waned. Thousands of operators went broke and some joined the unemployed sitting on park benches or standing in breadlines. The diminutive lakes went dry; the Lilliputian bridges fell in; weeds again flourished in the vacant lots.

Unfortunately, the zoning problems associated with miniature golf were not unique in depression days. Property owners who thought they saw an opportunity to make a little money by turning vacant lots into midget golf courses were part of a much larger group who wished desperately to circumvent or change zoning ordinances in order to solve their personal financial problems. In 1931 the Cleveland Board of Zoning Appeals reported a wide variety of requests for permission to do things in residential districts which would be contrary to the zoning regulations:

> There were twenty-five owners who wanted to add to the number of families already on the premises by dividing existing suites, by adding a room on the

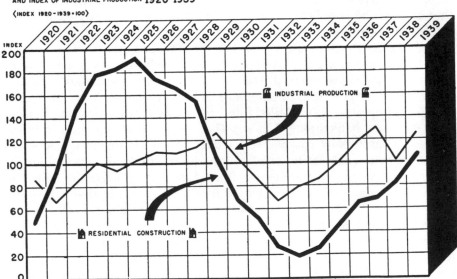

INDEX OF THE NUMBER OF NON-FARM DWELLING UNITS STARTED
AND INDEX OF INDUSTRIAL PRODUCTION 1920-1939

⟨INDEX 1920-1939=100⟩

★Index of Physical Volume of Industrial Production.

65. The sharp decline in residential construction and industrial production in the great depression of the 1930s *(National Housing Agency)*

rear or by remodeling the attic, on the plea that the demand now is for smaller suites and that they needed the income to pay the taxes—(not an uncommon need at any time). There were sixty-four cases where the bread winner was out of work and wanted to start a small store or a beauty shop in the front of the house, or an ice station, a shoe shop, a bake shop, a paint shop, a repair shop, a welding shop, a plating shop or some other kind of enterprise in the garage in the rear in order to earn a living. There was the jobless man who wanted to raise chickens, pigeons or rabbits at home, or wanted to start a parking lot in his yard.[15]

Numerous, too, were the homeowners in cities throughout the nation who had suffered losses, wanted to sell their houses, and petitioned to have the zoning in their neighborhoods changed to multifamily residential or commercial because they believed that zoning that permitted more intensive use would increase the value of their properties.

In some cities the board of zoning appeals pointed out, as did the Cleveland board, that it had no power to grant what amounted to changes in the regulations. In other cities the board of appeals or the planning commission or the city council could not withstand the pressures of distressed petitioners and their sympathizers. Spot zones were created to permit the use of corner lots in residential areas for service stations; "variances" were granted sanctioning the use of basement rooms or back rooms on the first floor of apartment houses for small shops; or entire areas were rezoned to satisfy the demands of householders who failed to realize that it would be as difficult to sell property for apartment houses or stores as for single-family residential use.

The dramas enacted before boards of appeals and city councils by citizens who hoped to stave off impoverishment reflected the general hardships of a period in which real estate values suffered widespread deflation, some of the largest skyscraper office buildings, hotels, and apartment houses in important cities failed financially, and many cities experienced near or actual bankruptcy. Usually these were cities that had over extended themselves for costly street widening and extension projects and for services to speculative subdivisions in the flush twenties. John E. Surratt, secretary of the Kessler Plan Association of Dallas, saw the depression as having been sent by a kind Providence to save cities and counties from further spending sprees.[16] He might have been less smug if his own city had lacked funds to continue its public works program. Thanks, however, to the Ulrickson plan approved in happier days, Dallas had ample bond monies to carry out needed projects and put unemployed men to work. Cincinnati, St. Paul, and Springfield, Massachusetts, were other cities whose foresighted budgeting made possible continued progress in developing public features of the long-range city plan. Kenosha, Wisconsin, pursued a pay-as-you-go policy enabling it to complete almost all important features of a comprehensive plan prepared by Harland Bartholomew, including an eight-block civic center replacing a blighted district, a central parkway, five neighborhood parks, four school sites, a trackless trolley system, eleven street-widening projects, and some developments in a waterfront park embracing 60 per cent of the shoreline of Lake Michigan within the city limits. But many cities drastically curtailed expenditures for public improvements, or they wastefully spent what capital funds they could scrape together on quickly improvised projects wholly unrelated to any long-range city plan — projects whose only merit was that they provided work for men who would otherwise be out of a job or who were already unemployed.

Among planning commission, the Los Angeles County Regional Planning Commission was one of the few benefiting by the depression, but only briefly. The county employees had created a fund for the relief of unemployment, in southern California by giving 2 per cent of their salaries. Utilizing this fund, the commission employed 165 highly qualified engineers, landscape architects, draftsmen, and others for four months in making traffic studies, surveying community business centers and industries, and preparing plans for park projects to be put into construction to relieve unemployment. Many commissions, however, had their appropriations severely cut and had to reduce their staffs. Some were abolished. Statistics showing an increase in the number of official local planning agencies from 786 in 1930 to 828 in 1931 and then a slight decrease in 1932 to 806 tended to disguise the true state of affairs. Flavel Shurtleff pointed out that at least thirty of the commissions in the larger cities (those with populations of 100,000 or more) were inactive. He estimated that half of the commissions in the 168 cities of 25,000 to 100,000 population were similarly moribund. He had no way of knowing how many of the 577 cities under 25,000 had active planning agencies. The Division of Building and Housing in the Department of Commerce recorded a loss of 67 official municipal planning agencies in 1932, but since it had discovered 45 others of whose existence it previously had been unaware, its annual totals failed to reveal the attrition among commissions. Shurtleff observed,

> Many of the planning commissions . . . never had a fair chance. They were appointed by a complaisant mayor who saw no harm in them, or, for that matter, saw no particular good in them. They were hardly more than pleasant gestures. Appointments to the commission were quite often political henchmen who never really found out what their job was. Other commissions started off under happy auspices and did creditable work until political changes brought in an unsympathetic administration. Still others with records of from five to ten years of plan administration have suffered from the recent wave of almost hysterical municipal economy attendant on the depression.[17]

The Detroit City Planning Commission was one of those having to fight for its life. The automobile center had been especially hard hit by the depression. In 1932 one "economy" group attacked the commission as an unnecessary frill; another contended that the commission's work could as well be done by one of the other municipal departments. At a hearing before the city council the commission showed that it had saved the taxpayers millions of dollars by obtaining the dedication of twenty-five miles of outer drive and a new diagonal thoroughfare within Wayne County, at no cost to the city. As for the contention that some other department could take over its work, the commission reminded the council of a project that a large committee composed of several department heads (including the head of the department that was to do the commission's work), engineers, and representatives of prominent manufacturers had approved but which the commission had opposed. Forced to reconsider

66. Occupancy of lots in a slum area in Detroit

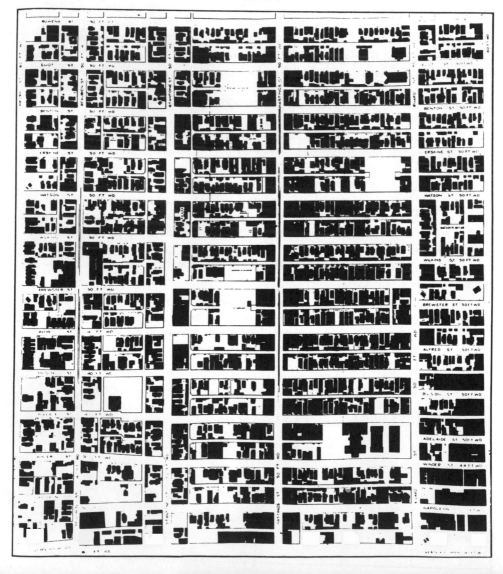

the proposal, the committee had admitted making a mistake. Though the commission survived, it had to carry on with a skeleton staff. The few planners who were left began making studies of housing and plans for the rehabilitation of blighted districts.

The Emergence of Housing Issues

Events of the previous year explained why Detroit's planning director, Walter Blucher, believed that it was worthwhile for his staff to concentrate on replanning the obsolete areas of the city. Dr. Edith Elmer Wood published a book entitled *Recent Trends in American Housing,* in which she noted that there was "persistent talk of slum clearance which may some time produce action."[18] She also mentioned the increasing interest

67. Plan of the Detroit City Plan Commission for municipal housing in the same neighborhood, 1933

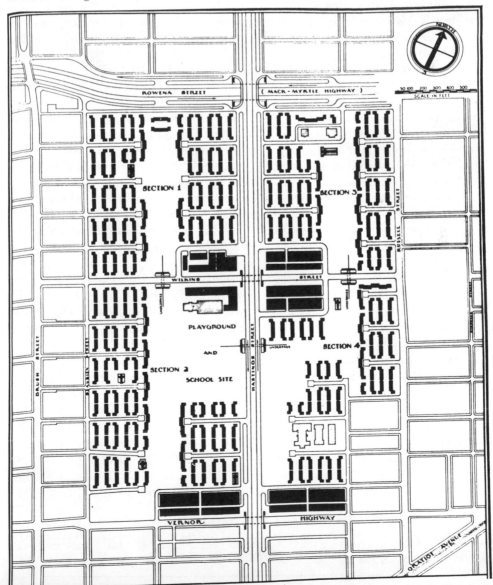

in municipal housing as "a thing not desired, but perhaps offering the only way out."[19] Some of the discussion of slum clearance had been stimulated by conferences of the American Construction Council in New York and Chicago in the spring of 1930. At both meetings the delegates had suggested the possibility of launching a national movement for the rebuilding of slum districts, though the majority had cautiously stated their preference for limited-dividend corporations as the instrumentalities for rebuilding and had declared that the municipal authorities should restrict themselves to offering cordial cooperation. However the task of replacing the slums might be undertaken, Dr. Wood realized that it would be an enormous job. By her own rough calculations nine million American homes were "bad enough to be demolished."[20] Building that many new ones would cost $40,000,000,000, she estimated, but how much, she asked, did obsolete dwellings cost America yearly in preventable deaths, sickness, and crime? She again extolled European housing for working-class families and indicated that she, for one, thought governmental financial assistance was necessary for any solution of the housing problem.

Dr. Wood's book appeared while twenty-five fact-finding committees were preparing for a national Conference on Home Building and Home Ownership called by President Hoover. When the 3,700 persons invited to the sessions gathered in December, 1931, to begin their deliberations, the Chief Executive informed them that the main question before them was how to "make a home available for installment purchase on terms that dignify the name credit."[21] Although the conference had before it "also some phases of that other great segment of housing," the standards of tenement and apartment dwellings, the President indicated that slum clearance and related matters were not of immediate concern by expressing the hope that at some future time the question of blighted areas and slums might be subjected to "more definitely organized national intelligence."[22] The conference, he made clear, was "not to set up government in the building of homes but to stimulate individual endeavor and make community conditions propitious."[23] Specifically, he broadly hinted, the assembled delegates were to endorse his own proposal for the creation of a system of home loan banks — a proposal altogether consistent with Hoover's belief that the way to revive the anemic economy was to extend help principally to business institutions.

In due course the participants adopted a resolution favoring the President's scheme, but the conference was memorable not so much for this action foreshadowing the enactment of the Federal Home Loan Bank Act in the next session of the Congress as for various conclusions and recommendations looking to much broader governmental action in the fields of housing and finance. None other than the chairman of the conference, Secretary of the Interior Ray Lyman Wilbur, stated that "unless business men and business groups accept the challenge [of providing an adequate supply of good housing at moderate prices], housing by public authority is inevitable."[24] The committee on blighted areas and slums foresaw "irresistible demand for governmental action" unless private enterprise undertook complete demolition and rebuilding of slum areas that could not be salvaged by piecemeal demolition and reconditioning.[25] The committee on city planning and zoning proposed, among other things, that in every city "a legislative program be made for the redemption of blighted areas, including replanning, clearance of slum sites, establishment of zoning control, reconstruction on a large scale protected by building regulations."[26] Various other committees made recommendations presaging the reform of mortgage lending practices, the establishment of the Federal Housing Administration, and the passage of state laws granting the use of the right of eminent domain to private corporations that built housing for middle-income families. Somehow, though, the carefully managed conference sidestepped a challenging issue that a large group of the delegates really wanted to get their teeth into: direct federal participation in housing. By avoiding this issue, Herbert Hoover merely aided in making it politically appealing to a growing number of persons familiar with the European concept of housing as a public utility.

The indictment of private enterprise for its failure to alleviate housing problems was particularly strong in a collection of articles published in 1932 by the editors of *Fortune* under the title *Housing America*. The principal author, Coleman Woodbury later learned, was the holder of a law degree, a keen analyst of public affairs, and a poet — Archibald MacLeish. The housing situation, he wrote, was the disgrace of American industry.[27] Less than half the homes in the country measured up to minimum standards of health and decency; private enterprise had "signally and magnificently muffed" its opportunities to reach a market of 14,500,000 to 15,000,000 nonfarm families who could afford to own homes; and many segments of society shared the blame for the enormous shortage of adequate housing — the building industry for the inefficiency and disorder of its management, labor for its obstructive tactics, speculative real estate dealers for inflating the price of land, financial interests for charging exorbitant rates, public officials for maintaining antiquated building codes and tax laws. Worrisome as these conditions were, MacLeish and the editors found something new to alarm them. They believed that "important interests" would soon manufacture an inexpensive, mass-produced house in such numbers that a new kind of urban chaos would ensue. They made the case for workable cooperation of private industry and government in which the latter would assure a well-planned environment and would aid in making land available "at the proper prices." [28] But what the role of government should be in the event there was no breakthrough in low-cost production of houses, they did not say. By default they left to actionists the discussion of the need for creating governmental housing agencies, using government loans and subsidies to provide housing for families unable to afford home ownership, and for expanding the legal powers of government to replan and renew the urban environment.

Orrin C. Lester, a vice-president of the Bowery Savings Bank of New York City, brought the question of subsidies straightforwardly before the annual national city planning conference at Pittsburgh in November, 1932, by pointing out that if the entire lower East Side of Manhattan Island could be reconstructed at one time, probably less than a tenth of the residents could afford to occupy the new structures. In the twenty years from 1910 to 1930 that part of New York had lost three-fifths of its population—a decrease from 531,000 to 249,000. The better paid and more able inhabitants had joined the migration to the suburbs, leaving those whose incomes required very low rent still occupying the slums in the area. "It would seem clear," said Lester, "that if we undertook . . . to provide houses in accordance with modern standards for the people who now live there, it would have to be done through great public subsidies." A fundamental decision for the American people was whether it would be desirable for the federal government "to get into the housing and slum clearance business as an independent public duty standing on its own merits."[29]

But Lester was not content merely to state the issue that several other speakers had skirted; he wanted detailed study of the whole problem of rebuilding slum areas before the federal government and localities rushed into low-cost housing and slum clearance mainly to provide work for the unemployed. He spoke as a conservative banker fearful of further upsetting an already demoralized housing market, yet much that he recommended would be included in any sound planning for the reconstruction of deteriorated areas inhabited by economically disadvantaged families: "We should determine by our investigation how many of the existing tenements in local areas can profitably be remodelled, how many must be torn down, what community planning and municipal support is needed, what design and character of construction is best suited to the needs, and at what rate we may reasonably create and absorb new construction in order not to overstock the market."[30]

Few, if any, municipalities had made the kinds of housing surveys and planning studies needed for an intelligent program of clearance and renewal, much less grappled with alternatives to the illusory hope that limited-dividend companies could transform decaying areas and rehouse the poverty-stricken families living in them. Lester rather doubted whether it would be "sound economic policy to attempt to house very poor people on as expensive land as we have in these central urban areas,"[31] and other speakers wisely urged not jumping to the conclusion that such areas should be replanned for residential purposes, but first determining their best use in the light of city-wide needs and opportunities.

Architect Robert D. Kohn foresaw the possibility of making one of the great mistakes of government-sponsored clearance programs in Europe: "We must not build great areas of our cities for just one class of person," he warned. "We must get diversity. Every great scheme of large-scale replanning and housing should work toward providing within a particular area accommodations for a variety of [household] units at a great number of different economic levels. Those principles of democracy which some of us still believe valid and which have been so sadly lost during our boom period must at least find a realistic expression in our attack on the housing problem."[32]

If housing issues were not yet well defined, they were at least much clearer as a result of the Pittsburgh conference than they had been for many years. Not since the days before the first World War had city planners talked so earnestly about blighted areas and slums, low-cost dwellings for the poor, and the relation of housing to city planning.

Contributions to the Future

Disappointed by one false hope after another, the American people watched their country slide deeper and deeper into the depression. The 8,000,000 unemployed in 1931 were joined by 4,000,000 more in 1932. Mortgage foreclosures rose from approximately 194,000 in 1931 to almost 248,000 in 1932. Most people were so distressed by their own problems that they failed to speculate on the significance of the inability of the League of Nations to halt the Japanese conquest of Manchuria and the establishment of the puppet state of Manchukuo. But they understood that the closing of the Kreditanstalt in Vienna and the financial collapse of Central Europe reflected the ordeal of America and was a further blow to its recovery. In the spring of 1932 United States Steel slashed wages for the second time, and more wage cuts followed in other industries. Nothing the Hoover Administration did broke the downward spiral of the economy more than temporarily. And everywhere the feeling of helplessness, the sense of waiting for something decisive to happen, the despair, resentment, and desperation increased.

In such times it was difficult for men in the city planning profession to sustain their faith in the future, to believe that the expertise they had gained in a period of intense activity would again be in demand and that the knowledge they had acquired would be applicable under changed conditions. Yet they had to look forward, to assess what had been done, to see what might be done better, to prepare for new, perhaps greater opportunities. In 1931 Karl B. Lohmann, professor of landscape architecture at the University of Illinois, published a new textbook entitled *Principles of City Planning,* a volume welcomed by professors in many other universities and colleges offering courses in city planning. Harvard University began bringing out various studies initiated under its program of

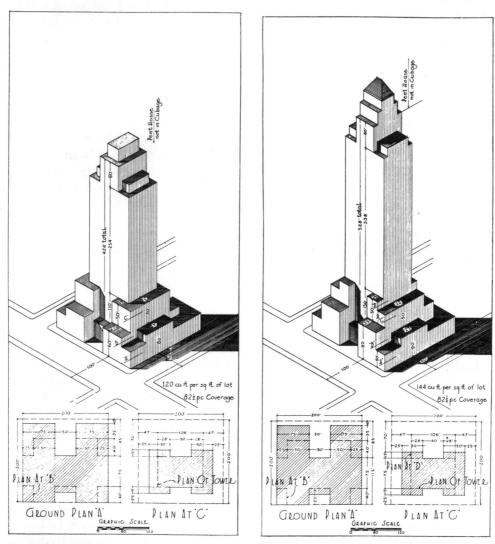

68. Recommendations of the Regional Plan of New York for increasing light and air around tall buildings *(Committee on Regional Plan of New York and Its Environs)*

research, including Harland Bartholomew's *Urban Land Uses,* analyzing the amounts of land used and needed for various purposes in typical American cities. The Committee on the Regional Plan of New York and Its Environs issued *The Building of the City,* Thomas Adams's final volume of the great plan begun a decade earlier. On hand for the presentation was Governor Franklin D. Roosevelt of New York, who had been reelected in 1930 with a plurality of more than 750,000 votes and was regarded by astute politicians as the most promising Democratic presidential possibility. The governor was reminded of the day, twenty years past, when Charles Dyer Norton had first talked to him about the plan of Chicago. From that very moment he had been interested in "not the mere planning of a single city but in the larger aspects of planning"; and now he thought that "perhaps the day is not far distant when planning will become a part of the national policy of this country."[33]

In *The Building of the City* Thomas Adams essayed to vivify the two-dimensional graphic plan of 1929 with three-dimensional possibilities. Here, for all to see, but particularly the leaders of the metropolitan community, were "envelopes" of types of buildings recommended for business centers, architects' conceptions of elevated waterfront boulevards, bridge approaches, airports, and railroad terminals, "suggestions" for new streets and plazas on the lower East Side, bird's-eye views of proposed watergates and palisades parks, "glimpses" of industrial sections, plans and perspective drawings of proposed civic centers in Brooklyn, Newark, and smaller cities, aerial photographs with planned developments drawn in, "architectural possibilities" of second-level pedestrian walks and arcades, and sketch studies of architectural treatments for the Manhattan waterfronts. Some of the drawings—the handiwork of advisory committees of architects—suggested that the City Beautiful had been disinterred, if indeed it had ever been buried, as most city planners seemed to think. But Adams himself was not resurrecting visions of the past; rather, he was striving to stimulate lethargic imaginations—and to do much more. Taking the scope and character of opportunities as his subject, he sought to show how civic art might be created in solving some of the most important problems of the region—how the ground plan, structures, open spaces, and the quality of design might together express the spirit of the metropolis and produce visual satisfaction, even magnificence. Though his hopes were high and his appeal was to individual citizens to raise their standards, he acknowledged that, after all, the city of the future would be "a picture of free citizenship," beautiful only to the degree that the inhabitants were "awakened to apply true art."[34] The regional plan was but a beginning; the next step was education. "We can only hope," he wrote, "that education will develop foresight, that the greatness of the need will develop a passion for improvement, and that both these things will lead to unity of action so that the New York-New Jersey metropolitan region shall achieve unique distinction among great city-regions for the order and true economy, the balance and true dignity of its building."[35]

Assuming that the outline plan of communications and land uses presented in the graphic plan would be followed, in principle at least, Adams visualized "the spreading of urban growth outwards over the great open spaces in the environs rather than the adding in an unhealthy degree to its intensity in a few centers."[36] Because he believed that in time the city would find its salvation as a place of residence as well as of business in doing more to lessen its congestion by expansion outwards, he could accept "with equanimity the erection of some tower buildings of unlimited height, on very limited areas of land, so long as adquate steps are taken to secure as much space as is practicable about all buildings for light, ventilation and movement."[37] In the region as a whole he concluded that there should be at least 60 per cent of combined public and private open area to 40 per cent or less actually occupied by buildings. In the central areas, however, the proportion of street and other traffic space would be much greater than in residential districts, but on the other hand, the latter would require a much greater proportion of parks, playgrounds, and private yards than the former.

Pursuing his earlier proposal for new model towns and neighborhood communities as object lessons in good planning, Adams suggested public purchase of raw land, construction of the local improvements, and then disposition of the improved land for development by private enterprise under zoning and building regulations that would prevent undesirable changes in density or other conditions and by doing so would restrain private speculation. He could not convince himself that public authorities should actually build low-cost houses, but he could accept the idea that preparing land for use by private companies would not be "fundamentally different" from municipal installation of streets, sewers, water mains, and other essential facilities. Public enterprise of this kind would "give the benefit of great savings in cost to prospective home owners," Adams believed.[38] He did not answer the question whether it would be possible to house any low-income families in the model towns and planned neighborhoods.

Dr. Edith Elmer Wood accused Adams and his fellow planners of being less than courageous about housing. "There was never a more perfect opportunity to relate slum clearance to a comprehensive city — and re-gional — plan than was open to the Committee on the Regional Plan of New York and Its Environs, which, however, successfully sidestepped the whole issue," she charged. "The Regional Plan Association is now calling for a general housing survey preliminary to such a step. But that does

69. (upper) Crowded Manhattan and (lower) the skyline of the future, with skyscrapers regulated in accordance with the recommendations of the Regional Plan of New York *(Committee on Regional Plan of New York and Its Environs)*

not answer the question why it was not done by the Sage organization while the staff and the funds were in being."[39]

Lewis Mumford was another member of the Regional Plan Association of America who, after a "painstaking examination" of the completed plan, found it a disappointment. "One must finally judge the Regional Plan not by its separate details," he decided, "but by its *drift*." And to Mumford its drift was toward further metropolitan centralization even though it talked of garden cities, toward "present chaotic methods" of subdividing land and building houses even though it talked of neighborhood planning and better housing, toward overintensive uses of even suburban areas although it talked of objective standards of light and air for buildings. "The net result of this Pauline effort to be all things to all men is to neutralize the effect of any particular proposal," Mumford scoffed.[40] In the first place, the New York region, as described in the plan, was "a purely arbitrary concept, based upon future possibilities of transportation and past facts of city growth."[41] Adams and his fellow planners assumed that growth would continue automatically in the future under the same conditions prevailing in the past, and while they provided a plan for a period of at least thirty-five years, they cast its solutions as far as possible into terms which would admit of their immediate fulfillment. By creating a plan for immediate adoption, they had made a plan that was "not worth adopting," a plan that was, indeed, "a monumental failure." Not only had their methodology and their investigations been inadequate, they had also been working for the wrong sponsors — for financial rulers whose aim was "as much human welfare and amentiy as could be obtained without altering any of the political or business institutions which have made the city precisely what it is."[42]

"Genuine regional planning, as distinguished from the superficial metropolitan planning to which the Russell Sage planners are committed," Mumford asserted, "is not content to accept any of the factors in city growth as outside human foresight and control. If we cannot create better urban conditions without changing our present methods and institutions and controls, we must be prepared to change them: to hold that the present means are sacred and untouchable is to succumb to a superstitious capitalistic taboo."[43]

Adams struck back in a "Defense of the Regional Plan" which accused Mumford of many specific inaccuracies and misinterpretations but attacked him principally as "an esthete-sociologist, who has a religion that is based on high ideals, but is unworkable." Mumford's main quarrel was with the plan's drift — "It drifts away from his ideal conception of what a plan should be, and he is intolerant toward any other conception." Adams saw Mumford as "an apostle of economic changes that would require the combined power of the President, Congress and state legislatures to bring about." The regional plan went far in proposing restrictions on property rights, but not further than it was reasonable to expect public opinion to go or government to authorize in the future. "It would have been folly to have attempted to make it a charter for rebuilding the social state in tri-state regions, as Mr. Mumford implies it should have been," Adams countered. "Moreover, if planning were done in the way he conceives it should be done, it would require a despotic government to carry it out. I would rather have the evils that go with freedom than have a perfect physical order achieved at the price of freedom."[44]

To a man who had taken a prominent part in selecting the site for the first garden city in England in 1903, who had been admired by the Regional Planning Association of America for his planning in Canada, and who had known Mumford's chief idol, the ecologist-planner Sir Patrick Geddes, "probably before Mr. Mumford was born," the wholesale indictment of the regional plan seemed as unfair as it was personally grievous. If Mumford was in some measure misleading in his criticism, there was validity to his complaint that Adams and his associates had not sufficiently considered, or at least had not presented, alternative schemes for organizing the metropolitan region. Certainly, the plan was in many respects conservative, and in none more so than in its treatment of the housing problem. Adams, advised by Bassett, was unwilling to go beyond public purchase of land to lower housing costs. The plan entirely avoided any serious analysis of the problem of providing suitable housing for the lowest income groups and included the indefensible statement that "all housing should be economic, in the respect that it should yield a fair return on the investment in building and land."[45] As an undertaking which Adams knew would be regarded as an example for other urban areas, the plan missed opportunities to come to grips with some fundamental economic and social issues. Adams, moreover, could not plead that such issues were beyond the scope of a physical plan. He mentioned them but refused to face them. His conservatism kept him from being a truly great planner. He was incapable of being ahead of his time. Most of his proposals were already orthodox.

The Committee on the Regional Plan of New York and Its Environs disbanded soon after the publication of *The Building of the City,* and the Regional Plan Association that had been formed to mount an educational program and obtain the cooperation of local governments in gradually carrying out the 470 projects included in the plan stepped up its activities. The association first organized unofficial local planning councils and brought about their affiliation with county planning councils, beginning initially in Bergen and Essex counties in New Jersey and Rockland County in New York and later undertaking organization work in Westchester County, New York, and Middlesex and Union counties in New Jersey.

For each county the association prepared a booklet of approximately twenty-four pages, briefly describing the regional plan and presenting those parts of the plan applying to the particular county. County-wide meetings were then called at which booklets were formally presented to county officials, together with sets of the regional plan volumes. Thus began the long and tireless endeavor by which much of the plan was translated into reality, with initial successes greatest in highway and railroad improvements and in the expansion of the regional park system.

State Planning: Conservation, Parks, and Surveys

Not since the mid-twenties, when Henry Wright produced his brilliant state plan for the Commission of Housing and Regional Planning in New York State, had there been much discussion of state planning, but in the last two years of Hoover's presidency interest in this broader form of planning began to revive, stimulated in the main by the activities of some of the midwestern and eastern states. In 1929 Wisconsin had organized a State Regional Planning Committee, composed of representatives of several state departments, to assist local planning agencies and to co-operate with the state conservation commission in preparing a statewide recreation plan and with the state board of health in controlling pollution of lakes and streams. Michigan had conducted land economic surveys under a state conservation commission seeking, in particular, to find new uses for cutover northern areas. In 1931 the state legislature of New Jersey authorized a state park commission to begin developing a state park system, and in the rural state of Vermont a commission on country life issued a report inventorying the physical, social, and historical resources of the commonwealth and suggesting their future development. The report, however, was a diagnosis rather than a prescription for action. City planners who reviewed it hoped that the commission would take the next important step and sponsor a statewide plan.

The two states most clearly showing the way for others were Illinois and Iowa, although the preliminary planning effort in the former state was an unofficial one initiated in 1930 by the Civic Development Department of the Illinois Chamber of Commerce to show the need for state planning, whereas the Iowa project was supported by the governor and authorized by the state legislature in 1931. The report of the Illinois Chamber of Commerce committee led, however, to the establishment of a state planning commission of twenty-five members, appointed by the governor in 1932.

By analyzing population movements, changes in land use, and trends in important industries, the state chamber's planning consultant, Jacob L. Crane, Jr., rather quickly discovered serious problems suggesting the kind of state planning program that should be undertaken in Illinois.

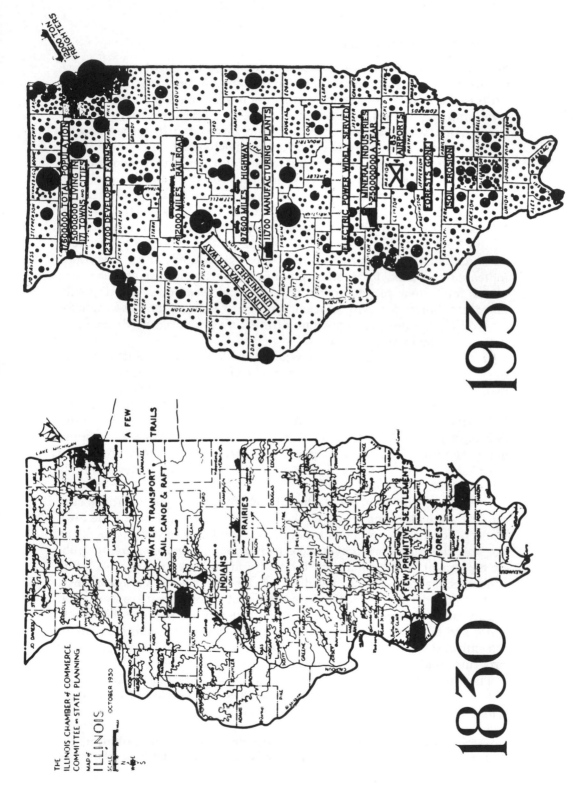

70. A century of development in Illinois: maps prepared by planner Jacob L. Crane, Jr., for the Illinois Chamber of Commerce

For several decades there had been a tendency for population to move toward the Chicago industrial area and to the larger towns, leaving the little towns and rural districts with a relatively small proportion of the total state population. Of the 102 counties in Illinois, seventy-two were losing population. Accompanying these changes and in large measure accounting for them were the accelerated mechanization of agriculture, the abandonment of farming in submarginal areas, the development of cooperative management, and the concentration of trading, school, and recreational activities in centers accessible by the better roads. Half or even two-thirds of the land in the state was subject to destructive soil erosion. In the better farming areas of the northern part of the state and in the heavily industrialized areas, underground water supplies were being exhausted and surface waters grossly polluted. These conditions indicated the need for a state planning program aimed at allocating larger land areas for watershed purposes and reservoirs; utilizing submarginal lands for reforestation, parks, preserves, and watersheds; controlling soil erosion to prevent silting; and providing new parkways, river ways, and trade routes.

To the new state planning commission made up of manufacturers and businessmen, publicists, legislators, and conservationists, Crane recommended a program beginning with land utilization surveys and further studies of industrial migration. The commission had wide investigative authority but as yet no directive from the legislature to guide the state's development. The data obtained from the surveys would be useful, Crane believed, to private as well as public agencies. He foresaw in Illinois the emergence of a continuous planning process rather than a movement for a "specific, fixed state plan."[46]

In Iowa, on the other hand, the aim of private and public groups supporting state planning was from the beginning a definite plan—the Iowa Conservation Plan, intended to serve as a guide for recovering as far as possible the state's original outdoor recreation resources for greater public enjoyment, and for making "the best and highest economic use" of its lands and waters.[47] Crane, who directed the employees of various county, state, and federal agencies and volunteers of many private conservation organizations in preparing the plan, regarded it as "perhaps the underlying and most important phase of comprehensive state planning" in an agricultural state such as Iowa, but he realized that a full-scale planning program would include much more.[48]

The wastefulness of unplanned conservation work and the steady deterioration of once abundant natural resources gave rise to the drive for a long-term conservation plan. Crane explained,

A great loss of soil is going on through erosion, which in turn is silting up the streams and lakes, destroying fish life, and causing floods and other difficulties.

In addition to the silting, Iowa's fine streams and lakes are now heavily polluted. The people are robbed of these original assets for water supply, for recreation, and for fishing. The wooded areas have been mostly cut off, until probably no similar area in America is so devoid of native growth and of cover for game and wild life. Lakes have been drained, in some cases with no advantage to agriculture, but taking out of use water areas valuable for recreation, for hunting and fishing, and for landscape enjoyment.[49]

The state planning program envisaged the production of a three-part plan, one section of which would concern economic resources such as agriculture, forestry, water supplies, and water power, another the recreational resources of the state, and a third various scientific assets, including sites of botanic and historical interest. Proposals for highways, parkways, and riverways were to be included. This undertaking, scheduled for completion in 1933, was destined, however, to become part of a much broader state planning effort than its sponsors had contemplated. Iowa, though a state with no city larger than 150,000 population, had many needs related to its urban areas that could not be met by a conservation plan alone, and as the times became increasingly difficult, the limitations of the project became apparent.

The severity of the depression moved Governor Gifford Pinchot of Pennsylvania to attempt a more wide-ranging attack on the problems of his state by appointing a Greater Pennsylvania Council to collaborate with planning, civic, industrial, agricultural, and other agencies in preparing studies to promote the economic and social welfare of the commonwealth. "The migration of capital from our state and the great trends and shifts in our population indicate the need for realistic planning," he told this advisory group of 150 members when it convened in January, 1932. "By sound planning you may assist in creating increased demands for our industrial and agricultural products, you may enhance the advantages of our recreational areas, and you may aid in bringing new industry within our borders. . . ."[50]

State planning, these early examples indicated, would become something of a cross between the conservation and development of natural resources and economic promotion, with a good measure of public works planning added. Since this type of planning required analysis of population trends, studies of land use (in the broadest sense), and the planning of public facilities, it offered a new field for city planners, but it also demanded a far more detailed knowledge of economics, industrial operations, resources management, and welfare programs than most city planners possessed. That some groups concerned with state and national planning would tend to regard them as interlopers was perhaps foretold by events associated with a nationwide land utilization conference called by Secretary of Agriculture Arthur M. Hyde in Chicago in November, 1931.

Planned with the cooperation of the Association of Land Grant Colleges and Universities, the conference was attended by approximately three hundred persons widely representative of organizations interested in land and rural problems. The delegates criticized federal and state land policies as having, in the main, "encouraged the rapid transfer of public lands to private ownership with little regard given to the uses to which the land was best adapted or to the demand for its products." They called for the formulation of new policies "which shall be actively addressed, through adequate and unified organization and co-ordination, to the intelligent use of all publicly and privately owned land and whether or not it be sub-marginal or super-marginal."[51] Various committees proposed inventories of land resources and classification of soils, federal and state programs for the utilization of idle or misused lands, soil conservation and watershed protection, and federal acquisition of lands for forests, game refuges, national parks, and other purposes. At the close of the conference two important committees were authorized, a National Land Use Planning Committee and a National Advisory and Legislative Committee on Land Use, but among the public and private agencies requested to make appointments to the committees were none identified with city planning; and when Harold S. Buttenheim read reports of the committees ten months later, he failed to find the National Conference on City Planning included in the list of cooperating organizations. Nor did he note the names of other organizations with which many city planners were affiliated, such as the American Society of Landscape Architects, the American Society of Civil Engineers, and the National Recreation Association.

Although Buttenheim thought it strange that the planning profession had been overlooked by public agencies and private groups exercising substantial influence in the growing movement for state and national land use planning, he took comfort from this sentence in a statement of organization and objectives: "In the long run the determination of most effective [land] use becomes a matter of regional or local planning which will take account of important public considerations and necessary adjustments."[52] As men whose professional ethic demanded that they give primary emphasis to the public welfare in determining allocations of land and selecting areas for various purposes, city planners had significant contributions to make to the larger planning programs then looming on the horizon, but the actions of the agricultural groups participating in the Chicago conference suggested that the planners needed to develop new alliances and to broaden the scope of their interests before they could become truly effective on the national scene. The cities and metropolitan regions for which they prepared plans were, to a far greater extent than they appreciated, reflections of the economies of multistate regions and the nation. If the planners could demonstrate a new capacity for state, river basin, and national planning, they would become even more skillful in the field they understood best—city and metropolitan planning.

"The reorganization of our cities remains an essential element of the whole planning movement, not to be replaced, but rather to be aided, by state planning," Jacob Crane assured planners at their annual national meeting in 1932. State planning, he explained, tended to establish a larger conception of the physical environment and of the city in that greater milieu; it suggested new methods of studying and forecasting and perhaps guiding population distribution; it determined the desirable utilization of major land divisions and the effect of such determinations upon all elements of local planning; it gave "a hand-hold on the great puzzle of industrial localization in relation to urban development"; and it dealt with broad problems of water sources, power supply, and transport, and with their influence on city building. In short, it promised to become "a new and sounder background for city and regional planning."[53] But even more important than the value of state planning to local planning was its value to national planning. In Crane's view the state planning programs under way in Illinois, Iowa, Wisconsin, and Michigan were, in a sense, "getting us ready for national economic planning" and would "fit neatly into that job" when it was undertaken.[54]

Throughout Hoover's last year in office the widespread discussions of the need for national planning almost certainly foretold that various forms of it would be attempted in the not distant future. Business leaders such as Gerard Swope, president of the General Electric Company, and members of the Committee on Continuity of Business and Employment of the Chamber of Commerce of the United States advocated a "National Economic Council" responsible not to the federal government but to the Chamber of Commerce. Professor Rexford G. Tugwell of Columbia University, on the other hand, contended that competitive industry operating under the profit motive was inherently unstable and would have to be transformed into a completely planned economy to save America's mechanized civilization from utter disaster. Less dogmatic analysts of the national predicament discarded both industrial self-regulation and detailed economic control by government in favor of some middle way minimizing unsocial speculative profit as distinguished from profit obtained by serving public needs. The land use planning desired by agricultural groups could not but be a combination of physical and economic planning. In addition, it would inevitably necessitate administrative and budgetary planning by the national government because no effective program of conservation and development of resources could be undertaken without the construction of large-scale public works by innumerable governmental agencies.

While the debates on national planning proceeded, with frequent references to the Soviet Gosplan and to the myopia of those who had not understood the implications of Frederick W. Taylor's *Shop Management*, Hoover's Research Committee on Social Trends issued its two-volume report prophesying "a larger measure of public control to promote the common welfare" and suggesting various approaches to the "major emerging problem . . . of closer coordination and more effective integration of the swiftly changing elements in American social life."[55] After its exhaustive scrutiny of almost every form of social change, it concluded: ". . . it is clear that the type of planning now most urgently required is neither economic planning alone, nor governmental planning alone. The new synthesis must include the scientific, the educational, as well as the economic (including here the industrial and the agricultural) and also the governmental. All these factors are inextricably intertwined in modern life, and it is impossible to make rapid progress under present conditions without drawing them all together."[56]

Careful reading of the committee's report revealed, however, that the group thought chiefly of the need for continuing research to illuminate "fundamental questions of the social order" rather than of some mechanism for carrying out well-related programs. The committee suggested, for instance, that "there might in time emerge a National Advisory Council, including scientific, educational, governmental, economic (industrial, agricultural and labor) points of contact, or other appropriate elements, able to contribute to the consideration of the basic social problems of the nation."[57] That such a council might assist federal officials to make more circumspect decisions there could be no doubt, but it would be in the main an agency planning for planning rather than one directly influencing and coordinating the programs of the federal establishment and through these programs the economic and social life of the nation. The conception of the advisory council was, however, to have its effect on the national planning effort soon to be initiated under the man whom the American people had chosen in November, 1932, to succeed Herbert Hoover.

City Planners and the National Planning Board

Franklin D. Roosevelt brought to the presidency a conviction of the need for planning and some ideas so farsighted that they amazed even persons whose business it was to take the long view. As a country squire who had reforested an estate damaged by erosion, as a distant cousin of an earlier president who had launched the conservation movement, as a public official who had first begun struggling with problems of natural resources while serving as chairman of the Forest, Fish and Game Committee of the New York State Senate, the new Chief Executive had a passionate interest in the land and everything pertaining to it. In the months between election day and his inauguration he spent long hours discussing conservation, reclamation, reforestation, flood control, public ownership of power, and public works with his closest advisers. On a visit to Muscle Shoals with Senator George Norris he outlined a program for multipurpose development of the Tennessee Valley so broad that it left the elderly champion of public power almost overcome with admiration. In the Presidential vision there were other river valleys, too, in which the development of agriculture and industry should be linked with flood control, the generation of power, forestry, and soil conservation—the Ohio, the Missouri, the Arkansas, and the Columbia. For all these areas the instrumentality proposed for the Tennessee Valley, an authority "clothed with the power of government but possessed of the flexibility and initiative of a private enterprise,"[58] might be the means of restoring misused land, harnessing wasted water, and revitalizing despondent human beings. But for other areas of the country and for the nation in its entirety the mechanism or mechanisms for planning were far from clear; and in the meantime there were all the scores of agencies that had always done piecemeal planning. Each was jealous of its prerogatives and its political influence, and some were ambitious to absorb others or were afraid of being gobbled up by more powerful rivals. Whether even a President who believed strongly in certain policies and the implementation of them by coordinated action could realize his hopes was a question.

In the first hundred days of Roosevelt's administration a hard-driven Congress enacted legislation to make possible some of the planning desired: the Agricultural Adjustment Act, the Tennessee Valley Authority Act, the act establishing the Civilian Conservation Corps, the Railroad Coordination Act, various monetary and fiscal measures designed to rebuild a shattered economy, and a National Industrial Recovery Act providing, among other things, for a $3,300,000,000 public works program. But no congressional act authorized comprehensive national planning of the kind Soviet Russia was believed to practice or of the sort that ultra conservatives thought Tugwell was working to institute. Title II of the National Industrial Recovery Act, however, established the Public Works Administration to carry out and stimulate work relief projects, and it was in this agency that Secretary of the Interior Harold L. Ickes, with the blessing of the President, created the National Planning Board soon after becoming administrator of the huge public works program.

Although Ickes' immediate need was a planning group to advise him on the selection and scheduling of federal projects and to assist state and local governments in getting construction under way, this sometime Bull Moose Republican and ardent conservationist was looking far into the future. "We hope," he told city planners and members of the American Civic Association in the fall of 1933, "that long after the necessity for stimulating industry and creating new buying power by a comprehensive system of public works shall be a thing of the past, national planning will go on as a permanent Government institution."⁵⁹ If the American people were now definitely committed to the testing of new social values, if they had turned their backs "for all time on the dreadful implications in the expression 'rugged individualism,'" and if they had given over feeding themselves and their women and children to "the gluttony of ruthless industrialism," then national planning would become a major governmental activity.⁶⁰

To aid him in demonstrating the value of planning, Ickes chose a board composed of the President's uncle, seventy-year-old Frederic A. Delano, and professors Charles E. Merriam and Wesley C. Mitchell. Charles W. Eliot II, director of the National Capital Park and Planning Commission in Washington, became executive director of the new agency.

The board represented, Eliot explained to his fellow planners, three main types of planning.

> Doctor Wesley C. Mitchell, of the National Bureau of Economic Research, represents [economic] "*charting*," and through his previous work on "Recent Economic Changes" and on the "Committee on Social Trends" is obviously qualified to lead in the "charting" movement. Doctor Charles E. Merriam, Political Science Professor of the University of Chicago, through his practical political experience [as a Chicago city councilman], and as Vice Chairman of the Committee on Social Trends, is the obvious man to lead in the "*organizing*" field or planning work. And Mr. Frederic A. Delano, who did so much to start the Chicago Plan, carried through the New York Plan, and who still heads the Washington planning organization, is the natural representative of the physical planning movement, including "*purposing*," "*projecting*" and all its other aspects.⁶¹

Eliot's description of the members indicated that the National Planning Board some day might be capable of a heady combination of economic, administrative, and physical planning. Its initial activities, however, appeared more specific and restricted: the planning and programming of public works, a research program for development of the social and economic aspects of public policy, coordination of federal planning activities, and stimulation of regional, state, and local planning. But Ickes, like Eliot, envisaged almost limitless endeavor for this new agency. "We believe that at last we realize the importance of looking at problems in their entirety," he said.⁶² Accordingly, the board had appointed a Mississippi Valley Committee of various experts and, to cooperate with them, a Missouri Valley Committee, a Red River Valley Committee, and an Arkansas River Valley Committee. "All problems now affecting the vast combined watersheds of these rivers will be studied as a whole and no future Federal development with respect to any of these individual watersheds will be undertaken until its relationship to the whole is understood," the Public Works Administrator proclaimed.[63] He saw the board concerning itself with a transcontinental arterial highway, with questions of transportation and the distribution and cost of electric current, the redistribution of population, the necessity and practicability of reclamation projects, harbor improvements, public buildings, the correction of soil erosion, and many other things. "In fact," he concluded, "it is difficult to think of any domestic interest or activity in which the National Government is concerned which might not first be submitted to the careful scrutiny of the National Planning Board."[64]

"Honest Harold," as sharpshooters dubbed him because his incorruptibility was even more celebrated than his pugnacity, perhaps then

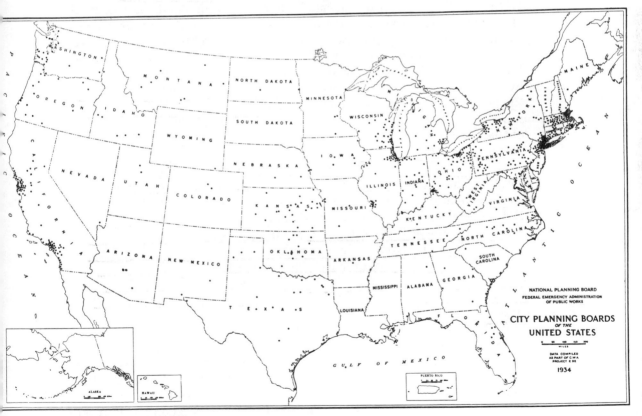

71. City planning boards in the United States, 1934 *(National Planning Board)*

little realized, since he was a newcomer to federal government, how resentfully old-line agencies viewed the prospect of having to permit a johnny-come-lately New Deal organization to weigh the merits of their proposals. One in particular, there is reason to suspect, was inimical to the whole idea from the very beginning and long waited its opportunity to end such interference. But perhaps Ickes did not fully appreciate all the implications of the fact that before Charles Eliot became the executive director of the National Planning Board, he worsted the Army Corps of Engineers in a lengthy battle to prevent the construction of dams on the Potomac River.

While the new board made its way in the federal jungle, where emergency alphabetical agencies sprang up in bewildering variety, regional advisers of the Public Works Administration, acting as the field representatives of the board, offered its assistance to governors who would appoint unpaid state planning boards, develop a planning program, and outline specific studies to be undertaken in the next six months. The National Planning Board suggested that state boards should be composed of, say, four department heads and three citizens, including an official of the state university or some other institution of higher education. As a condition for receiving the help of consultants who would be paid by the Public Works Administration and of staff members who would be assigned by the Civil Works Administration, the board requested assurances of the governors that they would sponsor legislation to make the state planning board permanent and would appoint the chief planner or chairman of the state board as the state representative on a regional or interstate planning committee if one were organized.

The National Planning Board hoped that perhaps as many as ten states would set up planning boards. To its astonishment, governors — and a few state legislatures — acted so expeditiously that by the end of February, 1934, there were thirty-six boards and a year later forty-five. By 1936 every state except Delaware had a planning board cooperating with the national planning agency. In accordance with its suggestions, most of the state boards initially prepared long-range programs of public works, conducted statewide land use studies, and investigated ways to integrate transportation systems, or at least attempted to "tool up" for such activities.

Among the appointees to these boards were some citizens and officials long identified with city and metropolitan planning. George McAneny, president of the Regional Plan Association of New York, served on the New York State Planning Board, Daniel H. Burnham, Jr., on the Illinois board, Alfred Bettman on the Ohio board, and Gordon Whitnall on the California board, together with William J. Fox, chief engineer of the Los Angeles County Regional Planning Commission. Howard Odum, who had been a member of Hoover's Research Committee on Social Trends, was a member of the North Carolina board. In Connecticut, Wisconsin, and other states members of citizens' planning associations, chairmen of county planning commissions, and city planning directors participated in decisions with state department heads, university officials, and other prominent citizens.

As its "ambassadors of planning" to these newly created agencies, the National Planning Board selected some of the leading city planners of the day. John Nolen and his associates, Justin Hartzog and Geoffrey Platt, became consultants to the state planning board of New Hampshire, and Nolen also served the Vermont board. Russell Van Nest Black was consultant to the boards in New York, Pennsylvania, and Virginia and consultant-director of the New Jersey board. Ladislas Segoe was appointed consultant to the planning boards of Ohio and Kentucky. Later Lawrence V. Sheridan, who was consultant to the Indiana board, replaced Segoe as consultant to the Kentucky board. Earl O. Mills was assigned to the boards in Arkansas and Oklahoma, and S. R. DeBoer to the boards in Utah and New Mexico. Jacob Crane continued to advise the board in Illinois and also became consultant to the board in Wisconsin. He and Walter Blucher both provided services to the Michigan State Planning Board. Harland Bartholomew and S. Herbert Hare were consultants to the Missouri State Planning Board, and Hare also advised the board in Kansas. L. Deming Tilton, once a planner in Bartholomew's office, was assigned to the California board.

Black observed, years later, that "these multiple assignments came about, of course, because there were so few of us who had even a minimal background in large-scale and broad-based planning." The national board was obliged to employ many consultants without comparable experience, such as secretaries of chambers of commerce, civil engineers, landscape architects, architects, economists, and newspaper men. Because of their lack of adequate preparation for their new work, some of them "got hung up on surveys and never did get around to planning," Black noted.[65] The land planning consultants assigned to each state were, however, almost all well-qualified men with backgrounds in agriculture and conservation.

Each state planning effort was in a sense a unique laboratory experiment since no two states had exactly the same problems, resources, laws, governmental organization, and traditions. States with conservation commissions perhaps had some advantage over others which had not attempted to do much long-range planning. But all had enormous deficiencies of information about their soils, forests, mineral deposits, water resources, population and industries, educational systems, state institutions and facilities, and financial structures. In varying degrees all lacked up-to-date maps and had insufficient geological and meteorological data. In some states important department heads had never sat down together to consider overall state needs and the desirability of coordinating projects until the governor appointed them to the state planning board; nor did department heads always find it possible to work cooperatively. Personality clashes developed. Some officials were so busy that they seldom attended meetings, and planning consultants in several states recommended that boards be reconstituted entirely with citizen members who could give unstintingly of their time. Rare was the state that knew in detail how many or what kinds of public works its various departments had planned or could suggest as elements of statewide programs. The states, in short, were willing to embark on the relatively novel activity of long-range planning but were generally woefully inexperienced and ill equipped for the endeavor.

The city planning consultants assigned to help them had their shortcomings, too, but at least they brought to the work a well-tried method of procedure. They were skilled at collecting information and analyzing it to identify problems, needs, and opportunities, at formulating a tentative plan and studying the advantages and disadvantages of the various proposals incorporated in it, at submitting the scheme for criticism and explaining its purposes, revising it, and finally suggesting means of carrying it out. Many consultants had participated in preparing capital improvement programs—experience doubly valuable in view of the federal government's emphasis on relating public works to long-range plans and scheduling construction according to the urgency of needs. Perhaps to a man the city planners among the consultants appreciated the need for preventing the misuse and waste of land, having seen speculative subdivisions destroy good farming acreage and invade scenic areas especially desirable for recreational use. Those with experience in county planning, particularly those who had prepared county zoning ordinances, were well qualified to coordinate their efforts with the land planning consultants engaged in devising plans for the use of rural areas and submarginal lands. And since one of the aims of the National Planning Board in encouraging state planning was to strengthen city planning and stimulate the formation of new city and county planning commissions, the city planning consultants enjoyed a new field for the educational, not to say missionary, activities that were second nature to most of them.

Planners working with state boards in the eastern and north central states discovered problems related to density of population and the development of large urban areas: river pollution, inadequate sewage treatment facilities, accumulations of obsolete housing, an insufficiency of regional recreation areas, antiquated taxation systems, and an excessive number of small, meagerly financed governmental units (Black, for

instance, found one small county in New Jersey with seventy-two municipalities averaging only 3.4 square miles in area). Planners in the western,
corn belt, and southern states found themselves concerned with the less
familiar problems of poor farming practices, soil erosion, waste of precious
water resources, inadequate highway systems (because of political log-
rolling), and underdevelopment of industries using locally available raw
materials. In the South and West, particularly, the establishment of the
Tennessee Valley Authority and its multipurpose program for the conservation, use, and development of land and water resources had great
impact on state planning programs, but the significance of the TVA was
not lost on the older eastern and midwestern states.

Throughout the country the inauguration of the Civilian Conservation
Corps, making the labor of 300,000 youths available for the development
of state and metropolitan parks, forest conservation, and related projects,
stimulated state planning boards to prepare statewide recreation plans,
many of which logically dovetailed with programs for the development

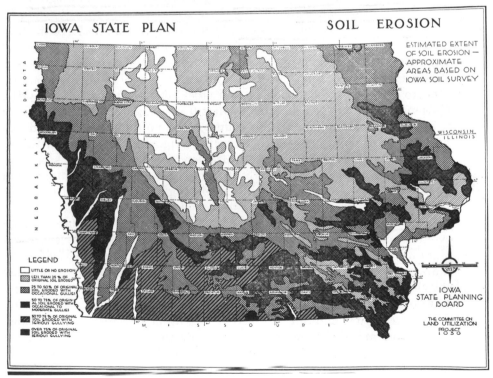

72. Soil erosion in Iowa: survey findings presented graphically by the Iowa State Planning Board,
1935

and use of water resources and the further construction of state highway systems. Disastrous floods on the Mississippi River in the late spring of 1934 and catastrophic dust storms and drought in the midwestern and central states as far south as Texas and as far east as the Alleghenies in the summer of that year dramatized for every state planning board the dangers of continued abuse of the land. Never had Nature taken such terrible vengeance on man for violating her fundamental arrangements. Swirling waters inundated thousands of acres along the great river. Choking clouds of wind-scourged topsoil blackened the sky from the Dakotas to Oklahoma and Arkansas, sending the human victims of the mighty upheaval westward to California, where John Steinbeck immortalized their sufferings in *The Grapes of Wrath*.

In their search for information on which to base state planning programs, the consultants and staff of the new planning agencies went first to various state offices, the universities, state chambers of commerce, private foundations and research bureaus, utility companies, and large manufacturing corporations—every organization that might already have useful records. Many boards set up special committees whose members, drawn from all walks of life, had access to authoritative data or knew how they could be developed. In Iowa, for instance, 175 of the best technical men in the state gave their services and "never failed to respond to a call for advice on any occasion," according to the director-consultant, Philip H. Elwood.[66] City and county planning commissions also contributed to the statewide surveying and stocktaking set in motion by the National Planning Board. After a careful investigation of the status of urban planning throughout the country, the national board found two hundred local planning agencies eager to augment their staffs with unemployed engineers, architects, draftsmen, statisticians, and stenographers made available by the Civil Works Administration. More than 10,000 of these workers aided in correlating information and filling in the gaps in data revealed by the state and local planning efforts.

Some of the consultants assigned by the national board contemplated eventual preparation of a comprehensive state plan as a guide for project planning by state departments and localities. Lawrence Sheridan, in Indiana, envisaged a plan whose purpose would be "coordination of the activities of the state";[67] and L. Deming Tilton, in California, spoke of a state plan as a goal but emphasized that making it would take time and that a premature plan might discredit planning.[68] In many states, however, plans and programs of various kinds rather than *a* plan seemed much more reasonable expectations. Most of the planners were so conscious of pioneering that they could think only of general goals, a few tangible accomplishments to convince legislatures that state planning was worthwhile, and some broad schemes for developing particular resources or industries.

A report of the New York State Planning Board mentioned the desirability of a "broad framework of national planning to insure wise state planning,"[69] and several other state boards expressed the hope that the national planning agency would at least lay down the main lines of a coordinated national transportation system—rail, highway, water, and air—and guidelines for the use of land and water resources. Delano from time to time spoke of a national plan, as did Eliot. By dividing the nation into interstate regions and encouraging the formation of regional planning commissions, the national board indicated that any national plan eventually formulated would be in the main an integration of regional plans, all reflecting certain overall policies.

The first regional commission was formed in the Pacific Northwest in January, 1934, by representatives of the planning boards of Washington, Oregon, Idaho, and Montana. The second came into being in March, 1934, in New England, where several attempts had previously been made to organize a New England planning association. In both these regions interstate river problems were of immediate concern. Pollution, floods, and erosion in the Connecticut, Merrimack, and Blackstone river drainage basins had long been a problem in the New England states. In the Pacific Northwest the federal government's plans to invest almost $200,000,000 in power, reclamation, and navigation projects at Bonneville and Grand Coulee on the Columbia River and at Fork Peck on the Missouri River pointed directly to the need for planning for new agricultural and industrial development, but the effect of these huge projects on urban areas was readily foreseen by the Pacific Northwest Regional Planning Commission, which stimulated the formation of 226 local planning commissions. Ironically, the more the national agency supported the New England states in investigating interstate compacts to control their rivers, and the more it urged the state planning boards and the regional commission in the Pacific Northwest to express their own ideas about long-range planning, the more it incurred the enmity of the powerful Army Engineers, whose proprietary attitude toward navigable waters seemed to be challenged.

As the national board realized the importance of urban planning in the context of state and interstate planning, it early gave its blessing to a metropolitan planning project that it hoped would inspire other metropolitan efforts throughout the nation. No sooner had the board been created than a revived planning federation in St. Louis applied for funds for the preparation of a metropolitan plan. At the suggestion of the board, the federation was converted into a St. Louis Regional Planning Commission composed of representatives appointed by the governing authorities of St. Louis and of each of the seven counties in the bistate area. Under the auspices of this commission, planning consultant Harland Bartholomew and a planning staff provided by emergency relief agencies developed a preliminary report of such promise that a more detailed report was authorized in 1935. The final report, completed in 1936, recommended a five-member interstate agency to advise and cooperate in the development of the St. Louis region in Missouri and Illinois. The commission proposed that the agency be established by acts of the two state legislatures "with Federal participation and Federal consent to an interstate compact."[70] One of the tasks envisaged for such an agency was the preparation and adoption of a metropolitan plan "with particular emphasis on sanitation, highway, transportation, and recreation problems involving the two States and the Federal Government."[71]

Of far more significance that this one report on a metropolitan region was an ambitious undertaking of the national planning agency itself, revealing that two years of intensive promotion of state and regional planning had brought it to a new appreciation of national and regional influences on urban development. In 1935, after the agency had undergone two changes in name, becoming in 1934 the National Resources Board and the following year the National Resources Committee, and had been reconstituted by presidential order as an interdepartmental organization including five Cabinet officers and the Federal Emergency Relief Administrator, as well as the Delano group, it announced the appointment of a Research Committee on Urbanism. This group, headed by Clarence A. Dykstra, former city manager of Cincinnati, would make, the agency said, the first major national study of cities in the United States.

Eliot had hinted that such a study was contemplated when he had pointed out in a speech at Cincinnati that city planners often came "smack up against" social and economic conditions or "governmental tangles" which made their physical planning programs impossible or fruitless. "Is it not time," he had asked, "to look at the whole problem the other way around, to examine more closely, more intensively the social-economic limitations and the governmental procedures and methods which limit and influence the kind of plans which are both desirable and practicable?"[72]

The announcement of the formation of the committee was notice to city planners throughout the country that at long last important federal officials realized that physical planning should be more realistically based on economic, social, and political considerations. The membership of the Urbanism Committee indicated that few if any of the forces shaping cities would be ignored. It included, besides Dykstra, Louis Brownlow, of the Public Adminstration Clearing House; Arthur C. Comey, of the Harvard School of City Planning; Harold D. Smith, of the Michigan Municipal League; Dr. M. L. Wilson, Undersecretary of Agriculture; Louis Wirth, University of Chicago sociologist; and Eliot. Ladislas Segoe headed the research staff.

Some months after the study was under way Segoe explained that the objectives were "to determine what the role of the urban community is in national life; what the social and economic functions are which can best be performed in urban communities; and what can be done to enable these communities better to perform such functions and, at the same time, to remedy and combat the evils and problems which appear to be associated with intensive urbanization."[73]

"At least a few of us," he said, had felt for some time that city planning was deficient in two respects: city plans framed by the corporate limits or at the most by a border a few miles distant were integrated neither with their immediate environs nor with the broader plans for large regions and states; and planning practice "stayed too close to the surface" because its approach was not fundamental enough and it lacked adequate tools with which to make a more basic plan effective.[74]

"The possibility of remedying the first of these major deficiencies—integration with the plans of region and State—appears now to be in sight with the state and regional planning movement in full swing," Segoe declared. "Assistance in a new approach to urban planning and finding new means for making it more effective should emerge from the Urbanism Study."[75]

Planning in the Tennessee Valley

The regional planning program that was watched with keenest interest in the early New Deal days was not, of course, under the aegis of the National Planning Board and its successors. In the 42,000 square miles of the Tennessee Valley the work of harnessing rivers, reforesting eroded slopes, restoring fertility to depleted acres, fostering agricultural development, building towns and highways, and providing hydroelectric power to industries, farms, and households went forward under the general direction of a three-man board established by the Tennessee Valley Authority Act. Its members were the chairman, Arthur E. Morgan, distinguished engineer and president of Antioch College; Harcourt A. Morgan (no relation), agricultural scientist and president of the University of Tennessee; and David Lilienthal, a Harvard protégé of Felix Frankfurter and chairman of the Wisconsin Public Service Commission. Together these three brilliant men brought into being a whole new regional government, with departments and divisions for the control of rivers, the utilization of power, the conservation and use of water on the land, long-range planning, and the economic and social improvement of the entire area.

To head the regional planning and housing activities of the authority, Arthur Morgan turned to a member of the American City Planning Institute, just as chairmen of state planning boards sought the help of men identified with city and metropolitan planning. A few days after his appointment by President Roosevelt, Morgan put in a call from his hotel in Washington, D.C., to Earle S. Draper in Charlotte, North Carolina. The chairman recalled hearing of the company-owned textile towns that Draper had planned with singular success in various parts of the South. Such a man, he believed, would understand the requirements of the new towns to be constructed under the TVA program and of older towns that would undergo adjustments and perhaps expansion. Draper's office reported that he also was in the national capital, at the Cosmos Club, a block from Morgan's hotel. The two men met later in the morning, and Draper agreed to leave his practice in the hands of an associate and take charge of the regional planning activities of the nation's boldest experiment in regional development.

Needing an experienced planner to assist him, Draper offered a position to Tracy B. Augur, who had recently gone into private practice in Detroit, only to find that in a time of depression most consultants had much privacy and no practice. Fresh in his mind, moreover, was a conversation he had just had with Dexter M. Ferry, head of the nationally known seed company: "The businessmen of Detroit are interested in only two things—money and golf. They'll never do anything big for the town. If you want worthwhile work, you'd better go somewhere else."[76] Augur took his friend's advice, accepted Draper's offer, and headed south.

One of the first jobs to be done was to provide housing for the thousands of workers employed in building the great dams that were to regulate the flow of the Tennessee River, generate power, and improve navigation. Draper had quickly decided that there was one thing he would not do if he could possibly avoid it—"throw together long ranges of barracks with a cook-shack and commissary stuck in somewhere, and call it a construction camp."[77] Even the flimsiest, crudest camps would cost considerable money. If even rudimentary precautions were taken to prevent discomfort, dissatisfaction, and disease among workers, it would be necessary to install adequate water supply and sewerage systems, construct good temporary living quarters, and make some provision for the spare-time activities of the workers. With the investment of a little more money, buildings and improvements of permanent value could be created, and the original cost would not be "sacrificed within a few years."[78]

Morgan and his fellow board members were sympathetic to the idea that, within reasonable limits, the new communities should be conceived as permanent settlements with as many modern conveniences as possible rather than as temporary shack-towns, even though barracks-like dormitories would have to be provided for a good many of the workers. But the legal staff of the authority raised objections, contending that Congress would not sanction the expenditure of more money than ordinarily would be required to develop construction camps. Draper fought for some financial concessions but in the long run had to work within severe cost limitations.

Under the circumstances, the new towns for workers on the dams could not be models of town development. They could, however, demonstrate that "the unduly congested, insanitary, matter-of-fact ugliness and the usual haphazard growth of a small rural community" could be avoided inexpensively.[79] After the completion of the dams, these settlements, if planned with proper forethought, could serve adequately to house the permanent forces employed in the operation of the dams and their adjuncts, in reforestation and erosion control, and in management of

73. Plan of Norris, one of the first towns developed by the Tennessee Valley Authority *(Tennessee Valley Authority)*

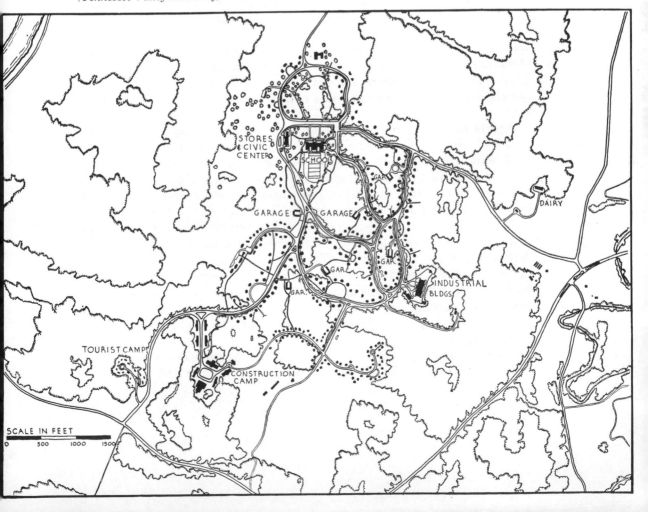

nearby TVA properties. They could also accommodate workers engaged in various small industries that might be expected to spring up as a result of the authority's program of economic development.

Draper and Augur began by reviewing the plans of two of the most famous planned towns in America—the industrial town of Kingsport, Tennessee, which Draper, as a young planner working with John Nolen, had helped to plan during the first World War, and Radburn, New Jersey. Neither, they concluded, should serve as a prototype for the first of their communities, the town of Norris, to be built on a high, rugged plateau four miles from the site of the Norris Dam. The topography of the locale ruled out superblocks of the sort used at Radburn and the more expansive street layouts found in Kingsport. Instead, the terrain suggested roadways molded into the natural contours of the ground, sweeping into broad curves and dividing the land into irregularly shaped plots. Cul-de-sacs could be introduced wherever practicable to provide access to lots on the spurs of hills and to prevent through traffic on residential streets.

From his knowledge of southern preferences, Draper also decided that row houses would be unsuitable even if they made possible some savings in construction costs. R. A. Wank, head of the Section of Architecture, and his staff devised more than thirty basic types of house plans, ranging from completely electrified, fully insulated, steel-casemented two-story houses of six or seven rooms to compact three-room cottages of very simple but durable construction. In a southern architectural vernacular, the structures had shake roofs and elicited some criticism, though not from Eliel Saarinen, who spent several days with Draper while the town of Norris was being planned and was highly complimentary about what he saw.

Norris and two other towns built in the early days of TVA, Wheeler and Pickwick Landing, were not conceived as garden cities, though they had some aspects of Ebenezer Howard's ideal community, thanks to Draper's desire to protect them from uncontrolled growth around the outskirts. At Norris, for instance, Draper planned a protective belt of 2,000 acres similar to the greenbelts of Letchworth and Welwyn. Much of this ground consists of steep declivities along river and creek valleys, but some of it provides space for recreational areas and for four-acre subsistence farm plots. Like the English garden cities, Norris also has a town center in which there is a fourteen-acre common, a school and community auditorium, and a business group containing stores, a post office, a telephone exchange, and other establishments.

Although Norris was planned for a thousand houses, it had only 294 single-family dwellings and some thirty duplex and apartment units in 1940 because of the legal counsel's insistance that no more be spent on it than would be spent on a construction camp. Sold outright to a private purchaser in 1946, it was the only town built in the 1930s by the federal government that brought a price greater than its total cost.

Draper and Augur and their associates had realized that even to plan a small town such as Norris, many of the wider aspects of regional development needed to be taken into account. Norris, for instance, was conceived as part of a metropolitan complex centering on Knoxville and linked to it by a rapidly expanding network of roads, some of interstate importance. To a degree, the requirements of regional transportation and communication determined the location of the town. But regional needs and prospects also influenced the entire planning program and forced the planning staff to assume a coordinating function, relating the activities of such federal agencies as the Forest Service and the Civilian Conservation Corps to TVA programs and harmonizing the plans of state highway commissions and state planning boards with the authority's plans for relocating populations, building dams and creating huge new reservoirs, developing new diversified farming areas, and establishing permanent forest and recreation reserves. The National Resources Committee considered Draper's role so pivotal in the whole scheme of things that it appointed him its unpaid southern regional coordinator, to act as liaison with the TVA departments and the state planning boards in the seven states having a stake in the rehabilitation and development of the

74. Town center, Norris *(Tennessee Valley Authority)*

Tennessee Valley. The boards of Tennessee and Alabama were particularly cooperative in furthering programs for the development of natural resources, and the Tennessee board extensively assisted local planning agencies affected by the broad-scale activities of the authority.

Facilitated by an ample legislative mandate and by strong administrative controls, the TVA program differed from other regional programs of the 1930s in the breadth and intensity of its attack on persistent problems. It gave men who spoke of themselves as physical planners opportunities to become in some measure social and economic planners. They participated in studies looking to the establishment of production forests on a sustained-yield basis. They studied the economic and social aspects of agriculture and particularly the possibility of diversifying land uses in order to bring higher returns to small farmers. They investigated the possibility of cooperatives of residents to operate recreational areas. They reviewed proposals to protect reservoirs from silting by terracing slopes, growing new cover crops, instituting better fertilizer programs, and improving grazing practice. They analyzed the effects that the widespread use of low-cost electricity would have on agriculture, on industrial development, and cities. In short, TVA planners learned that town and city growth are the result of such a vast interplay of forces that physical planning must be regarded as only one of the tools for shaping the destiny of an area.

Housing: A New Governmental Responsibility

New Deal efforts in the field of housing altogether lacked the attempted comprehensiveness of the TVA planning program and some of the endeavors launched by the National Planning Board. Reviewing the events of Roosevelt's first year in office, Harold Buttenheim said that candor compelled him to state that the impetus for slum clearance and low-cost housing came more from a desire to provide jobs than to provide houses.[80] The sad truth was that the Roosevelt Administration had no well-conceived housing program, only some good intentions, a knowledge that building trades workers were desperately in need of employment, a realization that something decisive should be done to stop foreclosures on homes, and hope that private enterprise, with some government aid, could be spurred to demolish ancient tenements and rebuild for the low-income families living in them.

Among the major laws enacted in the legendary Hundred Days at the beginning of Roosevelt's first term was the Home Owners Loan Act, a bold measure to save the roofs over the heads of hundreds of thousands of families who were in arrears on mortgage payments. A large proportion of these middle-class Americans probably should not have attempted to become homeowners in the first place, in view of their restricted incomes, the high rates of interest charged in the halcyon days of the 1920s, and the comparatively short terms for which loans were made. These families were, in a sense, victims of the own-your-own-home movement that Herbert Hoover had encouraged but had not supported with an effort to reduce interest charges or seriously reform mortgage lending practices. The rescue operation undertaken by the Home Owners Loan Corporation created under the emergency legislation refinanced mortgages on more than a million homes in a two-year period, but 252,000 families neverthe-

75. Boat dock near Norris Dam in the Tennessee Valley *(Tennessee Valley Authority)*

less lost their homes in 1933 and more than a million others suffered similar losses between 1934 and 1939.

The New Deal's other initial housing effort was also authorized in the flood of bills approved by Congress in the Hundred Days. The same National Industrial Recovery Act which provided for a $3,300,000,000 public works program included a provision for the "construction under public regulation or control of low-cost housing and slum clearance projects."[81] In addition to the authority to make loans, the act conferred power on the Public Works Administrator "to make grants to States, municipalities, or other public bodies for the construction, repair, or improvement of any such projects," provided the grant did not exceed 30 per cent of the cost of the labor and material employed upon a project.

Administrator Ickes quickly set up a Housing Division to receive applications from private and semipublic groups for limited-dividend projects. With the single exception of the Knickerbocker Village project on the site of the notorious "lung block" on the lower East Side of Manhattan, all the housing projects taken under consideration by the Reconstruction Finance Corporation set up in Hoover's presidency were turned over to the new division. In a few weeks it had more than five hundred applications for loans on projects whose total estimated cost exceeded $2,000,000,000, but careful scrutiny of these requests for loans revealed only eighteen projects worthy of tentative allotments of funds, and of these eighteen only seven finally met conditions that seemed necessary and reasonable to the division.

"It is not possible without a subsidy to produce housing for the lower income groups," Ickes said bluntly as he prepared to shift his course. "American cities cannot produce a single instance in which slums have been cleared and new dwellings built to rehouse the dispossessed occupants by private enterprise operating on a commercial basis." Indeed, private enterprise had "left the slums of America's cities to stew in their own unhealthy juice," and now the cities were paying the price of its failure in higher taxes for municipal services, in increased fire risk, and in increased health problems.[82]

In October, 1933, Ickes announced that he had formed the Public Works Emergency Housing Corporation to "engage in low-cost housing and slum clearance projects which otherwise would not be undertaken." The corporation would lend "every assistance" to states, municipalities, and public housing authorities in the development of worthy projects, and it might finance projects outright "as a demonstration to the country of what can be done." Lest private enterprise become alarmed, the PWA administrator stated that "the policy of the Public Works Administration is not to interfere with or enter into competition against legitimate private businesses, but to supplement and stimulate these businesses in a field of vital social importance."[83] His use of the word "legitimate," however, implied a threat to the owners of rookeries and other rundown properties and left no doubt in the minds of many persons that Ickes favored "socialistic" experiments in housing.

The administrator's reference to public housing authorities indicated that he expected other states to follow the lead of Ohio in enacting legislation authorizing localities to establish separate housing agencies comparable in some ways to the Port of New York Authority. The Ohio statute, permitting the creation of metropolitan housing authorities, had been drafted by Councilman Ernest J. Bohn of Cleveland and adopted by the state legislature on August 30, 1933. But it was based on principles formulated by a committee of attorneys and housing experts whom Bohn had appointed at a National Conference on Slum Clearance held at Cleveland early in July—a conference proposed by Bohn in the first place and convened at the invitation of Mayor Ray T. Miller of Cleveland and Bohn's fellow councilmen. The alert Bohn had noted that under the National Industrial Recovery Act the Federal Emergency Administration of Public Works could lend funds and make grants to *public* corporations for housing as well as make loans to private limited-dividend housing corporations; but since most cities lacked suitable public agencies to clear slums and rehouse the occupants of slum areas, he had realized at once that legislation would be needed to encourage their creation.

The committee appointed at the Cleveland conference favored authorities to engage in a subsidized housing program because it concluded that such agencies would have a much better chance of acting quickly and efficiently than departments or divisions of municipal government.[84] In view of the criticism of housing authorities by city planners in later years, it is interesting to note that among those proposing the establishment of such independent agencies were Alfred Bettman, then president of the National Conference on City Planning as well as chairman (since 1930) of the Cincinnati City Planning Commission, California planner Hugh Pomeroy, and Walter Blucher. Other members of the committee were Edith Elmer Wood; Coleman Woodbury, executive secretary of the temporary Illinois Housing Commission created in 1931 to investigate housing conditions and recommend needed legislation to the state legislature; and Charles S. Ascher, executive secretary of the Public Administration Clearing House.

The planners in the group foresaw the possibility that autonomous authorities might disregard broader city planning considerations and fail to consult local planning agencies. The principles drawn up to guide legislators and proponents of enabling legislation therefore stated that "a clause should be inserted requiring submission of any plans to the local planning authority, with veto power within a fixed time."[85]

The precedent-setting Ohio statute drafted by Bohn with particular help from Bettman required referral to the planning commission of all proposed streets, parks, and other public space in low-rent housing projects, thereby actually assuring full review of the plans of housing authorities.

Ickes' expectation that other states would enact legislation similar to that passed in Ohio was soon fulfilled. In December the legislature of New Jersey approved a measure providing for a statewide housing authority, and in January, 1934, Michigan and New York adopted laws authorizing the establishment of local housing authorities. Illinois, Kentucky, and West Virginia followed their example in March, and Delaware in April. Among these early laws that of Kentucky closely resembled the Ohio statute, especially in its provisions for referral of the plans of public housing projects to the local city planning commission.

In the meantime, the Public Administration Clearing House took steps to bring into being a new organization to assist those who would be pioneering in the new field of public housing. At its invitation federal, state, and local officials directly concerned with housing activities met in Chicago on November 25, 1933, but conspicuously absent was any representative of the conservative National Housing Association founded by Lawrence Veiller. The participants unanimously agreed to form the National Association of Housing Officials. Ernest Bohn was elected president, and Charles Ascher, who had spearheaded an earlier drive for legislation authorizing the creation of state boards to supervise the activities of limited-dividend housing corporations, became executive director with the understanding that Coleman Woodbury, the associate director, would succeed him in six months. Beardsley Ruml, executive of the Spelman Fund, and his board of directors provided a supporting grant for the new association, just as they had for the Public Administration Clearing House when Louis Brownlow founded it in 1930 with the aid of Charles Merriam, Luther Gulick, John Gaus, and others interested in improving the quality of American governmental services.

The new organization opened its offices near the University of Chicago on January 2, 1934. No association was ever more needed. The initial activities of the Housing Division of the PWA had disclosed enormous ignorance of the entire field of low-rent housing. Comparatively few Americans had studied the great public housing programs carried on in England, the Netherlands, and Germany since the First World War and even fewer had participated in planning, financing, or constructing large-scale projects sponsored by unions, philanthropic trusts, and similar groups in this country. As the new housing authorities and commissions began sending in applications for funds and tentative designs for projects, the Housing Division discovered that public agencies were no better prepared to undertake low-rent housing programs than most limited-dividend housing corporations had been. Few applications were accompanied by adequate surveys and basic information showing how many people were to be housed, how many persons in an area had jobs, what rents could be paid, how accessible employment centers were, or what transportation facilities existed. The proposed projects were frequently poorly designed, inexpertly assembled, and were entirely inharmonious with the principles of low-cost housing. Colonel Horatio B. Hackett, who succeeded architect Robert Kohn as director of the Housing Division, wrote in dismay, "Our cities wanted housing and didn't know what to do about it. Consequently most of them did little or nothing, but they still wanted their housing."[86]

The National Association of Housing Officials set to work at once to develop administrative standards for public housing agencies and sound procedures for the initiation, construction, and operation of low-cost housing under public auspices. It published three pamphlets designed to give practical assistance on various phases of the housing problem: State Laws for Public Housing, Public Housing Surveys, and The Demolition of Unsafe and Insanitary Housing. Most important of all, it sent technically qualified field consultants to cities needing help.

Foreseeing delays in local programs, the Housing Division of the PWA decided to move ahead by organizing for direct building in some of the larger cities of the country. (The division assumed the functions of the Public Works Emergency Housing Corporation, whose dissolution the Controller General had forced because he questioned its legal status.) Through trial and error the division worked out a land acquisition technique and began taking title to land in the slum sections of Atlanta, Indianapolis, Cleveland, Chicago, New York, and a dozen other cities.

While these activities of the National Association of Housing Officials and the Housing Division of PWA were going on, the Federal Civil Works Administration, at the urging of Harold Ickes and with the cooperation of the Department of Commerce, launched a project designed to disperse the clouds of darkness enveloping urban housing conditions. This was the Real Property Inventory conducted in the first several months of 1934 — a general survey of residential properties in sixty-four cities selected to give a reasonably good geographic and industrial representation of the urban areas of the nation, plus a sample survey of the financial capacity of a smaller percentage of households. In city after city whose more fortunate residents boasted that there were no slums, the enumerators recorded incontrovertible facts about congested "packingtowns" and gashouse districts, muddy "back of the yards," and "railroad avenues."

When the tabulation of data about 3,000,000 residential units was completed, it showed that 15 per cent of the total were overcrowded, 17 per cent lacked private indoor toilets, 23 per cent were without either bathtub or shower, 8 per cent were without running water, and that slightly more than that proportion had no electricity or gas for lighting. For the first time, cities and the federal government had reliable information to use as a basis for planning low-rent housing, and sociologists had a new gold mine of factual data to study. Financial institutions used the information as a guide for the control of the flow of credit into housing; the construction industry studied it in planning private projects; and businessmen analyzed it to gauge the market for household appliances and furnishings.

To the overwhelming evidence of a nationwide substandard housing problem was soon added factual information from many sources indicating how slums drained municipal treasuries. The temporary Illinois Housing Commission had been the first to investigate the disparity between municipal expenditures and revenues in slum areas. Its final report in April, 1933, had pointed out that in a sample area of one square mile approximately three miles from downtown Chicago "the expenditures made by the city . . . for ordinary municipal services were more

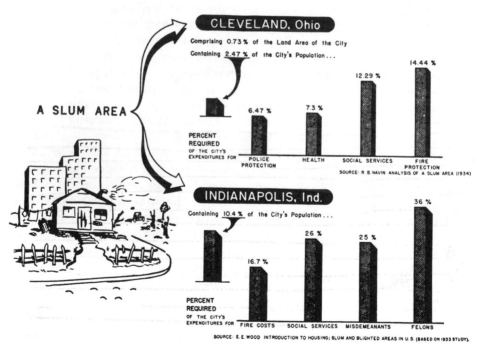

76. The high cost of slums as shown in studies of the 1930s *(National Housing Agency)*

than two and a half times the revenues levied."[87] But this study did not receive the wide attention given to an analysis of the cost to the city of Cleveland of allowing a 333-acre central area to remain a slum. In a dissertation published by the Catholic University of America, a young priest named Robert Bernard Navin showed that the community expenses in this section in 1932 for police and fire protection, public health, sanitary services, and relief were $1,972,000, whereas the area returned in taxes only $225,000, leaving the city with a deficit of $1,747,000. Neither the Reverend Mr. Navin's study nor that of the Illinois commission — both of which inspired similar cost studies in Indianapolis, Newark, and many other cities — implied that great reductions in the cost of welfare work and social service could be expected to result from the rehousing of the tenants of slum areas, but they did hold out the hope that fire, police, and health costs might be considerably diminished. Such studies and the real property inventories tended to shift the approach to the housing problem from exclusively sociological or humanitarian arguments to economic considerations more likely to impress city councilmen and businessmen — and to justify governmental subsidies.

Ickes' plans for slum-clearance projects and various local efforts to form public housing authorities did not at first arouse opposition from private enterprise, nor did the proponents of public housing hesitate to make common cause with the champions of private enterprise in seeking enactment of the National Housing Act of 1934, which provided insurance protection for savings in insured savings and loan associations and established the Federal Housing Administration to insure small loans for home modernization and improvement and mortgages for homes and rental housing projects. Like other housing measures of the times, this one was designed to relieve unemployment and revive the construction industry and allied enterprises. Foreshadowed by Hoover's conference on home building and home ownership, it was welcomed by almost everyone as a long-overdue reformation of mortgage lending practices and as a serious attempt to establish minimum physical property standards for the protection of lender and borrower. Bohn, Woodbury, Louis Brownlow, and others with a large view of housing needs served on the first FHA advisory council. But there were a few militant proponents of low-rent public housing, such as architect Albert Mayer, who denounced the National Housing Act as the "Anti-Housing Act," contending that it would encourage continuance, on a larger scale than ever, of the hit-or-miss speculative development of urban communities and would saddle municipalities with excessive costs for services to new subdivisions.[88]

In comparison with the large sums potentially available for investment in new private housing schemes under the mortgage insurance programs of the FHA, the allotment of only $150,000,000 for PWA slum clearance and low-rent housing projects seemed altogether inadequate to Mayer and his friends Henry Wright and Lewis Mumford. Their hope for a massive program to meet the needs of the income groups affected by bad housing appeared to be frustrated, and the three were, in addition, unhappy about what they considered an inherent defect of Ickes' direct building program: its commitment to slum clearance. Land costs in slum areas would probably be too high to make possible low rents; dislocated families would be forced into even worse quarters; new projects would be built in some areas better suited for commerical or industrial develop-ment and when completed would be isolated amid acres of decaying structures. The trio advocated, instead, the construction of low-rent housing on cheap land (vacant land not necessarily far from centers of employment), slum clearance only after families had been removed to the new units or other adequate housing, and rescue or rehabilitation of large areas in danger of becoming slums. The use of cheap land, they believed, would eliminate the danger of developing projects with high densities and curtailing recreation spaces and other amenities.[89]

Amid arguments in intellectual circles about federal housing programs and Ickes' slashing attacks on "those who clear slums between courses at conference luncheons,"[90] an important book came off the press, observing that although housing had become a public issue, there was as yet nothing in the United States which could properly be called a housing movement. In *Modern Housing* Catherine Bauer attributed the lack of any real drive for low-rent housing, such as the more advanced European countries had built in the past fifteen years, to the failure of liberal intellectuals, trade unions, social workers, consumers' organizations, and church groups to unite for political action. Between the lines of her volume describing the futility of American housing reform and the accomplishments of govern-ment housing programs abroad, the discerning reader could perhaps per-ceive the determination of the strong-minded young author to create an effective political demand for something more than a token low-rent housing program.

Miss Bauer had allies in the National Association of Housing Officials. Recognizing that the extensive European experience in housing, if intel-ligently applied, would be of value to this country, the association organ-ized an "international housing commission" to tour the United States and develop greater support for public housing. Its members were Sir Ray-mond Unwin, the eminent British planner; Ernst Kahn, economist, banker, and formerly manager of public housing projects at Frankfurt-am-Main; and Miss Alice J. Samuel, manager of the housing estates of the Bebington Urban District Council and member of the council of the (British) Society of Women Housing Estate Managers. Accompanied by Henry Wright and Ernest Bohn, these experts appeared in fourteen major cities of the East, Midwest, and South under auspices of local sponsoring committees. In Cincinnati Unwin told a crowded meeting, "I know that many persons over here believe that private enterprise is going to be interfered with by this work [public housing]. Don't believe it for a moment. You will see that although we have built 800,000 houses in England by public credit and through municipal enterprise, private enterprise has had the era of its life in the last year."[91] At the end of the seven-weeks tour Unwin, Louis Brownlow, Bohn, Wright, and Woodbury drafted some memorandums presenting the main outlines of a low-rent housing program for the United States.

The time had come at last for leading architects, city planners, housing officials, welfare executives, and spokesmen for citizens' housing organizations to adopt such a program. The National Association of Housing Officials brought eighty deeply concerned men and women together in Baltimore early in October, 1934, to meet with Unwin, Kahn, and Miss Samuel. It was one of the most distinguished gatherings in the history of American planning and housing endeavor. From New York came Mrs. Mary K. Simkhovitch, who had been a member of the Committee on Congestion of Population in the first decade of the century and was now president of the National Public Housing Conference that had been formed in New York in 1931. John Nolen attended as the president of the International Federation for Housing and Town Planning, and Alfred Bettman as president of the National Conference on City Planning. Jacob Crane was there as president of the American City Planning Institute. The executive directors of the United States Conference of Mayors, American Public Welfare Association, Public Administration Clearing House, Municipal Finance Officers' Association, International City Managers' Association, American Society of Municipal Engineers, and the American Legislators' Association were all participants. Dr. Edith Elmer Wood was on hand as a member of the New Jersey State Housing Authority, and Catherine Bauer as executive director of the Labor Housing Conference. Men well known for their interest in housing even then and destined to become national authorities in the field were included in the group— Abraham Goldfeld, Miles L. Colean, Langdon W. Post, Allan A. Twichell, Bleecker Marquette, Bohn, and Woodbury. No one could fail to notice that city planners formed a substantial corps. Among them, in addition to those already mentioned, were Tracy Augur, Harland Bartholomew, Charles B. Bennett, Frederick Bigger, Walter Blucher, Myron Downs, Earle Draper, and Ladislas Segoe.

Resolutely the conference transformed the memorandums of Unwin, Brownlow, Bohn, Wright, and Woodbury into a proposed national housing program and then patiently reviewed a summary of the program, paragraph by paragraph, criticizing it and modifying it until it represented the consensus of the group. The opening statement envisaged "a standard of housing not below the minimum needed for decent family life . . . for all the citizens."[92] This minimum standard, the program suggested, should be secured and maintained by a concert of governmental agencies in much the same way that various governmental agencies, acting on behalf of the community, assume responsibility for seeing that the quality of education does not fall below a certain socially acceptable standard. For the federal government a permanent housing agency, under which would be grouped all housing activities, would act to maintain the standard in all housing enterprises, public and private, aided by the government. In the states similar coordinating agencies would assist local housing activities and cooperate with the federal government in upholding the quality of housing. And in the cities and counties the local authorities, "on whom should rest ultimately the responsibility for seeing that an adequate standard of housing is maintained in their areas," would be equipped with "suitable powers" to work effectively with state and federal housing agencies.[93] The proposal for a hierarchy of federal, state, and local agencies did not imply, however, that a basic standard would be applied so rigidly that there would be no opportunity to adapt it to local climatic and economic conditions.

Farsighted in its advocacy of a single federal housing agency, the program was equally advanced in recognizing that "housing is essentially a local matter," even though the authors granted that Ickes' direct building program would provide some exemplary low-rent housing projects and was initially desirable. "Federal and state powers, credit and financial aid may properly be used to promote the needed [housing] activity," the program stated, "but the aim should be to inspire a local sense of responsibility, and to stimulate local cooperation both in the economical execution of work, and in the finance and expense."[94] The lengthy document on which the summary was based explained why the participants in the conference looked forward to local control of housing: "The very intimate dependence of housing on city development and planning, and on all other activities of local governments, suggests the need for securing close and harmonious relations between such authorities and any planning or housing agencies created."[95]

Although the conference, concerned principally with the need for subsidized public housing, endorsed the use of capital grants and annual grants in aid of rent, the summary statement also favored the use of a wide range of governmental aids to increase the supply of low-cost nonsubsidized housing and reduce to a minimum the number of families requiring subsidized accommodations.[96] It pointed out that slum clearance and the reconditioning of blighted areas were as essential as the provision of additional low-cost dwellings but warned against coupling the public housing program with clearance activities, lest the costs of town improvement or of bailing out mortgage holders in decaying areas be charged against subsidized projects, increasing the rents or dissipating the housing funds. Housing projects might with advantage be built in outlying areas in which industries had already relocated and in "the satellite-town type of development," the summary suggested.[97]

A final section, which described commercial enterprise and publicly controlled and assisted housing agencies as "partners in providing adequate housing accommodations for the whole of the population," concluded that "in their more physical aspects . . . housing activities and projects need to be co-ordinated with regional and city planning so that they form part of and contribute to the building up of the city plan."[98] Such a view of the relationship between housing and city planning Nolen had always held, as had Bartholomew and others, even if the commerical temper of the twenties had been inimical to most attempts to produce communities in which housing was a functional element articulated with the entire planning scheme. But the program adopted in Baltimore expressed the convictions of leaders and in its breadth surpassed the understanding of housing found among most city councilmen and municipal department heads, architects, social workers, and union officials. Moreover, since many city planning agencies had withered or folded, the immediate likelihood of close coordination between housing activities and city planning throughout the nation was not great. Indeed, a good many city planners were as lacking in knowledge of the essentials of large-scale, low-rent housing developments as were some of the architects who tried their hand at designing projects.

Only a few weeks after the Baltimore conference approved "A Housing Program for the United States," the Federal District Court for the Western District of Kentucky handed down a decision hastening the advent of the decentralized housing program proposed by the eighty leaders. In January, 1935, Judge Charles I. Dawson blocked the efforts of the Housing Division of the PWA to acquire by condemnation a slum site for a public housing project in Louisville, holding that housing is not a federal purpose and that the division could not therefore exercise the power of eminent domain. On appeal to the United States Circuit Court of Appeals for the Sixth Circuit the government again suffered defeat, at Cincinnati on July 12, 1935. Ickes then announced, "We are fully prepared to continue our low-rent housing program within the limits set by the decision. We have laid the groundwork for proceeding without condemnation, and in a good many cities we have already selected alternate vacant land sites, where ownership usually is confined to one or to a few persons. We are not going to stop this work merely because of restriction of condemnation power."[99]

The adverse decision nevertheless added to the conviction held by advocates of local initiative in housing that in the long run the only solution was to cast the federal government in the role of principal financier and entrust the planning and construction of projects to local authorities empowered by their state governments to resort, if necessary, to condemnation in assembling sites. The Housing Division of the PWA eventually completed fifty-one projects, twenty-seven of which were built on sites previously occupied by slums, but even before the Circuit Court of Appeals rendered its 2 to 1 decision against the federal agency, and more than a year before construction was started on most of the PWA projects, Senator Robert F. Wagner of New York introduced a bill of the National Public Housing Conference providing for the initiation of low-rent projects by local authorities and for financing by the federal government. Representatives Wood of Missouri and Henry Ellenbogen of Pennsylvania also submitted bills contemplating a decentralized housing program, but Congress adjourned without holding hearings on their bills, and the Senate Committee on Education and Labor failed to issue a report on Wagner's bill.

Hearings on the senator's bill in April, 1936, revealed that Catherine Bauer, Ernest Bohn, Coleman Woodbury, and their many friends had begun to develop the national housing movement lacking at the time Miss Bauer published her book. The dynamic executive director of the Labor Housing Conference had herself generated much of its force by touring the country in 1935 and addressing central labor councils, with the result that there were American Federation of Labor housing committees in seventy-five cities in thirty-one states. But the movement ramified far beyond the ranks of labor and embraced groups of every description, as the parade of witnesses before the Senate Committee on Education and Labor disclosed. Speaking in favor of Senator Wagner's bill, which incorporated most of the provisions of the program adopted at Baltimore, were mayors, bankers, investment underwriters, rabbis, priests, Protestant ministers, chairmen and executives of local housing agencies, social workers, a representative of the National Association for the Advancement of Colored People, publishers, architects, and Secretary of Labor Frances Perkins. Real estate men, developers, heads of construction leagues, and savings and loan associations generally opposed the measure, objecting particularly to any federal subsidy and contending that localities could themselves solve their housing problems, notwithstanding Miss Bauer's testimony that "many of the local governments are in very bad shape financially."[100]

In June the Senate passed the Wagner bill by a vote of 42 to 24, but the companion bill was not brought to a vote in the House. President Roosevelt, campaigning in the fall of the year for reelection to a second term, declared at the dedication of one of the PWA housing projects in New York City (Williamsburg Houses) that the consideration given the bill would ease its passage at the next session, and his prediction was correct. Against the opposition of the same groups that had previously fought the measure, the Congress enacted the United States Housing Act of 1937, "to provide financial assistance to the States and political subdivisions thereof . . . for the provision of decent, safe, and sanitary dwellings for families of low income . . . and to create a United States Housing Authority."

The statute defined families of low income as those "who cannot afford to pay enough to cause private enterprise in their locality . . . to build an adequate supply of decent, safe, and sanitary dwellings for their use."[101] Financial provisions of the act, very different from those in the earlier bill, authorized the new federal agency to lend as much as 90 per cent of the total cost of a project at a low interest rate for a period up to sixty years and to enter into contracts with local housing authorities for annual contributions or subsidies to bridge the gap between economic rents and the amounts low-income families could afford to pay. But the total amount specified for loans, at first $500,000,000, later $800,000,000, obviously

77. Santa Rita low-rent, public housing project in Austin, Texas, one of the first federally aided projects approved by President Franklin D. Roosevelt (*U.S. Department of Housing and Urban Development*)

would not go far in a country as large as the United States, and in the next four years the 21,600 low-rent dwellings built by the Housing Division of the PWA were to be augmented by only 168,000 USHA-aided units — a mere beginning in a nation said to need from eight to ten million good dwellings for its less fortunate families.

A Comprehensive Approach to Housing

The inauguration of even a comparatively small decentralized housing program presented a serious challenge to city planners. Russell Van Nest Black observed that, "to put it mildly," the PWA program undertaken in only thirty-seven cities had produced "much friendly conflict" between housing officials and city planners. Planners were offended when zealous housers from Washington attempted to determine the location and character of a project "upon the basis of a three-day investigation . . . in a strange land."[102] Housers were angered when city planners, after insisting on the value of their city plans, showed them data and schemes that seemed to be obstacles rather than aids to good decisions. Nor were all planners enlightened about low-rent housing. Coleman Woodbury complained bitterly that some of them thought of it as "something to sandwich in between the new superhighway and the sewage disposal plant."[103] The omission from the Housing Act of 1937 of any provision requiring local housing agencies to seek the advice of the city planning commission, if any, or to submit project plans for review before forwarding them to Washington with an application for a loan only threatened to increase strained relations.

In states striving to enact legislation authorizing the creation of local housing agencies, city planners worked with legislators and persons interested in housing to include provisions for referral of proposed projects to city planning commisssions. Twenty-four states passed statutes making housing projects subject to the local planning and zoning laws, though some state laws were vague, requiring merely that housing authorities should cooperate with planning commissions or should take any city plan into account. A Wisconsin law enacted in November, 1937, was stronger than most. It required local housing agencies to seek the advice of the city planning commission, if there was one, before sending project applications to the United States Housing Authority. A Massachusetts statute enjoined housing authorities to encourage the creation of planning boards!

Sad to say, many city planning commissions were wholly incapable of providing the guidance the new housing agencies needed. A few months after passage of the federal act, Walter Blucher wrote that the majority of the 1,200 city planning commissions in the United States had become moribund, were "serving no useful purpose," had "failed to function satisfactorily for many years," and had "made no contribution to community development."[104] Never robust and in recent years starved for funds, the city planning movement was all too ineffective at the very moment its leaders wished to embrace opportunities to cooperate with eager new local housing authorities, of which there were more than a hundred by the end of 1937 and 221 at the beginning of 1939.

Not that these leaders were guilty of failing to do all that they could to strengthen the movement. Blucher was executive director of a new organization formed in the fall of 1934 especially to increase communication among professional planners, to bring planning commissioners, city managers, and other public officials more actively into the planning movement, and to serve as a clearinghouse of information about city planning. Called the American Society of Planning officials, the organization was at first tentatively named the National Association of Planning Officials and was thought of as a companion to the National Association of Housing Officials. ASPO, as it was popularly known, was one of several independent associations affiliated with the Public Administration Clearing House and helped to round out the influential Louis Brownlow's dream of a galaxy of interacting organizations of public officials. Brownlow himself had persuaded Blucher to accept the executive directorship of the new association.

After a first joint conference in 1935 with such older organizations as the American City Planning Institute, the National Conference on City Planning, and the American Civic Association, the new planning society moved with determination to attract policy-making officials and administrators as well as professional planners, while the National Conference on City Planning and the American Civic Association, merging as the American Planning and Civic Association, endeavored to develop as a forceful citizens' organization. By 1936 the American Society of Planning Officials had 700 members, including more from California than from any other state, but Blucher and Alfred Bettman, the president, discovered that breathing new life into almost stillborn planning commissions and reviving others afflicted with incipient rigor mortis was no easy task; nor could ASPO alone give public administrators and citizens serving on planning commissions the understanding of the relationship between housing and planning that they should have.

First of all, city planners and housing officials had to make sure that they themselves fully comprehended the integral importance of housing in urban planning and development. For years the planners had touched upon the matter, but only since the advent of the PWA low-rent projects had they really faced some of the larger issues associated with housing, such as the formulation of municipal land policies, the relation of social and economic planning to so-called physical planning, the need for future land use plans distinct from zoning maps and ordinances, the renewal not merely of the worst residential areas but of the more extensive blighted districts of which slums were often but segments, and the development of governmental machinery for preventing and arresting urban decay. At the height of the controversies over the selection of sites for PWA housing projects Black had asserted that "if a comprehensive city plan is really good enough to serve the other purposes for which it is intended, it is quite likely to serve equally well the needs of the housing officials," but he had had to admit that "in few cities has there been either the money or the interest to do the real planning job." [105] In fact, he ventured to say that more money had been expended in the making of any one of several real property inventories than had been available for city planning in the whole country in any given year since American cities began creating planning commissions. But Black had warned that housing officials could jeopardize the long-term value of their projects by ignoring the broader aspects of urban development: "If behind public housing . . . there is no breadth of vision, if public housing accepts perpetuation of the old social and economic evils of the present outmoded form of American city structure, then public housing carries within itself the seeds of its own destruction and promises too little of permanent good to be worth serious effort." [106] Upon planners fell the obligation of assisting housing agencies by doing "the real and the difficult job"— devising a future land use plan, not only for housing but for all planning purposes, that would both determine and be determined by the structural form of a city as shaped by transportation arteries, underground utilities, parks and other public properties, and natural features such as mountains and rivers. "The structural form of the city as represented by . . . public facilities *can* be fixed by law," Black insisted. "God is not likely to change His mind very much about most mountains and rivers. Private building enterprise and the use of land can be controlled in some degree through zoning. Much of guidance can be exercised through land subdivision control. Public housing enterprise certainly can be established quite in conformity with the land use plan." [107]

The plan for future uses of the land, in the sense that Black spoke of it, was of course a general scheme envisaging the urban area as it might be in two or three decades. Preparing such a plan required foreseeing as clearly as possible the major technological, economic, social, and political changes likely to affect the area, as well as some of the ways in which various kinds of change might manifest themselves. Had city planners the knowledge and the prescience to undertake so formidable a task? They had always assumed, perhaps presumptuously, that they had, or at least that their practice of studying many facets of a problem in the light of long-term trends and community aspirations enabled

them as well as or better than most city engineers, transportation executives, or utilities managers to determine the routes of highways and
transit lines, the locations of terminals and important buildings, the
size and location of parks and other open spaces, and the relationship
of residential, commercial, and industrial areas to one another. Certainly, as cities grew or declined someone had to plan and to make decisions, whether the planning was piecemeal and shortsighted or long-
range and imaginative. If time had proved that many earlier city plans
were based on poor estimates of future population growth, or failed to
gauge the impact of new technology, or ignored the competitive economic position of other urban regions, none of these shortcomings invalidated planning as a necessary function of government. The remedy for
inferior planning was better planning. Public housing, a political issue
as well as a tangible concern of city officials, real estate men, architects,
contractors, and low-income families, confronted planners anew with
gnawing questions about the purpose of their activities, the quality of
their performances, the adequacy of the means upon which they relied
to translate their plans into reality. As in the past, they resolved to improve techniques, to broaden the scope of plans, and to lift their sights.

In 1938 a committee composed of Charles B. Bennett, city planner of
Milwaukee; Jacob Crane, then assistant to the Administrator of the
United Stated Housing Authority; and John Ihlder, executive officer of
the Alley Dwelling Authority of the District of Columbia, presented a report at the annual joint conference of the American City Planning Institute, the American Planning and Civic Association, and the American
Society of Planning Officials proposing a comprehensive approach to housing. They suggested that planning commissions henceforth should prepare a "desirable and practical" residential land use pattern as an element
of the general plan of the entire urban region, showing thereon areas in
which housing should be conserved, areas in which the development of
housing should be discouraged, and areas which should be cleared and
either rebuilt for housing or reserved for other uses.[108] Such a plan, the
three planners pointed out, would have to be predicated on "a comprehensive understanding of local conditions," including specific knowledge
of present and future housing needs, the quantity, quality, and structural
condition of the present supply of housing, and the probable amount of
future housing to be supplied by private enterprise.[109] To obtain the required information, planning departments would inevitably have to carry
on extensive surveys seeking data not available through real property inventories or previous housing studies. Even house-to-house canvasses
might be necessary to provide certain kinds of information not to be
found in other municipal departments or among the records of private
institutions. The first "essential" of the long-range housing program,

however, was a land use map showing the actual use of every piece of property in the city—"a rather big undertaking in any large city," but an indispensable tool in any efficient planning program and a prerequisite for determining the locations of various kinds of housing developments, public and private.[110]

The committee not only outlined in detail a substantial technical operation to be conducted by the planning department but also foreshadowed the urban renewal programs of the 1950s and 1960s by indicating that a planned housing program should include delimitation of the respective fields of public and private housing, a progressive scheme for the timing and location of public housing projects, coordination of demolition with the provision of housing, control of private housing through strict enforcement of zoning and housing codes, condemnation of unfit buildings, detailed planning studies for neighborhood conservation or rehabilitation, and provision of various kinds of public improvements to serve housing developments.

Concerning the immediate problem of friction between housing authorities and planning agencies, the committee observed in conciliatory fashion that "very often, without the aid of extensive research, public officials intimately familiar with local conditions can determine the size, type, and location of a public housing project for low-wage earners and do as good a job of 'guessing' as the 'experts' could 'researching.'" But the committee hoped that in the future, housing agencies would respect the planning commission's "wider familiarity with community problems" and rely upon it to make the surveys and analyses used as a basis for selecting sites. The housing agency could then confidently perform its rightful functions—"the establishment of policies, the actual design of the houses, the plan for financing the program, the supervision of construction, and the ultimate management of the project." [111]

Bennett and his fellow committeemen proposed tasks greater than any planning department had the budget and staff to undertake then or might conceivably be able to undertake for years to come. Yet their recommendations were, in fact, no broader than those which Coleman Woodbury had made some months earlier in *Planning for Low-rent Housing*, issued by the National Association of Housing Officials. The leaders in both planning and housing were years ahead of most of their countrymen in realizing the need for the enlargement of planning concepts, the improvement of the data-gathering and analytical techniques of city planning, and the expansion of local code enforcement and public works programs. Even then Robert B. Mitchell, who had been engaged in a study of the possibility of rehabilitating the Woodlawn area of Chicago, pointed out that the funds available for public housing could reclaim only a small part of the blighted areas of cities and that "some eminent authorities" advocated the establishment of other agencies similar to housing authorities to acquire land in these areas, replan and replat it, and sell or lease it for private use, perhaps at such a reduced value that federal grants to municipalities would be necessary to make up the difference between the acquisition cost and a realistic resale price or ground rental.[112] Albert Mayer, too, concluded that "a large area, much larger than the single project, must be constituted with adequate planning and, above all, land control, with well-placed parks and playgrounds possibly as the periphery of this inner community, so that the inner city itself may be efficiently built." He spoke of the changing functions of the central city in the spreading urban region and of the urgency of considering the emerging areawide pattern of economic activities when replanning deteriorated districts, but action to salvage the blighted areas necessarily would have to include measures to prevent further weakening of the older city by "the indiscriminate spawning of new suburbs." Uncontrolled suburban growth would not only "increase the strain on utilities and transportation" but would also "erode and displace more and more of the countryside," whereas growth concentrated in one or two satellite towns surrounded by greenbelts would assure "the advantages of the inevitable decentralization without the present disadvantages." [113]

From the controversies about public housing thus emerged a new concern with regional relationships, evidenced by much discussion of the desirability of reorganizing older cities into systems of neighborhood units such as Clarence Arthur Perry had described and by various proposals for the creation of publicly owned land reserves, both inside cities and in outlying areas. The concept of the municipal land reserve, to be used for middle- and low-income housing or for an entire new town, enjoyed great popularity because Americans had witnessed or read about the construction of greenbelt towns on the outskirts of three of their own cities, Washington, Cincinnati, and Milwaukee. No projects of the federal government, in fact, had aroused so much curiosity or attracted such hordes of visitors as these three towns and the TVA town of Norris. Above all else, foreigners wanted to see Norris, and above all else, Americans wanted to damn or praise the greenbelt towns. In New Deal days almost no one was neutral. As for city planners, all those who had any part in designing or developing these communities are still starry-eyed at the very mention of them.

Greenbelt Villages and Lessons for the Future

In the experimental, reform atmosphere of Roosevelt's first term of office it would have been strange if the federal government had not embarked on some town-building projects designed to show how living conditions in metropolitan areas could be improved. Many senators, representatives, and presidential advisers had come forth in the Hundred Days of 1933 with proposals for creating new rural communities pointing the way to a better life for farmers and for workers who had lost their jobs in industrial areas. In consequence, the Federal Emergency Relief Administration was no sooner in operation than it was urging states to establish relief corporations to build agricultural and industrial satellite communities, using federal funds and the planning, architectural, and engineering services of the Rural Rehabilitation Division of the Department of Agriculture. The Division of Subsistence Homesteads, established under a rider attached to the National Industrial Recovery Act by Senator John Bankhead of Alabama, immediately was given $25,000,000 to develop small-farm villages; but not until 1935, when the Resettlement Administration was suddenly brought into being by executive order in the crisis occasioned by the Supreme Court's nullification of the National Industrial Recovery Act, was much thought given to suburban towns to rehouse low-income families living in city slums. Rexford G. Tugwell, administrator of the new agency, had long been interested, however, in the idea of satellite cities.

Tugwell began organizing his new-towns program just when a good many persons were suggesting alternatives to the rebuilding of slums and the establishment of isolated colonies of small farms. Jacob Crane, then president of the American City Planning Institute, asserted that "we can most nearly effect the economies we desire, most nearly provide a combination of urban living and country-side opportunities, and most nearly meet the deep-seated impulses of American life, through the semidecentralization of industry and population mainly within the regions immediately surrounding our hundred-odd metropolitan cities." [114] The suburban garden city, based on the English models but adapted to "the American situation," appealed to him as "the solution for a sizable proportion of the American people." Frank Lloyd Wright envisaged an even more daring departure from the traditional city in his scheme for "Broadacre City"—a four-square-mile, self-contained community of approximately fourteen hundred families, with small farms, small electric-powered factories, small schools, and homes on one-acre lots. Described in an article in *The Architectural Record* and exhibited in model form at Rockefeller Center in April, 1935, under the auspices of the National Alliance of Art and Industry, Wright's visionary amalgam of country and town impressed the defenders of the concentrated urban center as unrealistic, but both it and the English garden city were probably closer to the heart's desire of a large number of Americans than the environments exemplified in typical cities and suburbs.

By a curious coincidence the London County Council, the county borough councils in Greater London, and the London Regional Planning Committee at this time began discussing the preservation of a permanent greenbelt around London. And British leaders also began contemplating the creation of a national planning agency to develop general plans for urban regions, for although Britain had originated the garden city and had built hundreds of low-rent housing estates, no attempt had been made to weave the threads of change into a coherent pattern of social life, and the metropolitan region of London was, in the opinion of the eminent political scientist William A. Robson, a "mess." [115]

Sensitive to all these currents of planning thought and by temperament the eternal reformer, Tugwell upon becoming administrator of the Resettlement Administration seized his opportunity "to put houses and land and people together in such a way that the props under our economic and social structure will be permanently strengthened." [116] His idea, he said, was "to go just outside centers of population, pick up cheap land, build a whole community and entice people into it. Then go back into the cities and tear down whole slums and make parks of them." [117] Although the Suburban Resettlement Division that he set up in his new agency was destined never to replace any slums with parks or in any grand manner to reconstitute the amorphous urban areas of America, its greenbelt towns were to indicate how millions of Americans would prefer to live if they had the chance.

In the late spring and summer of 1935 Warren Jay Vinton, chief economist of the Resettlement Administration and, some say, the prime mover behind the scenes in the planning of the greenbelt communities, directed studies of the hundred largest cities in the United States, seeking to discover those with records of steady growth without booms or serious cyclical slumps, good labor policies, progressive civic attitudes, and high standards of local government. Eight metropolitan areas were selected within which greenbelt towns should be built, but the limitation of funds necessitated narrowing the choice of five. The Milwaukee area was among these five because of its high employment rate, its economic stability resulting from diversity of industry, and its housing shortage. The Cincinnati area was another, not only because it offered a town site with excellent topography and accessibility to employment but also because the city of Cincinnati had a fine tradition of city planning and a cooperative planning department commanding a wide range of factual information about metropolitan trends. The national capital area, the St. Louis area, and Franklin Township in New Jersey (near New Brunswick) were the other areas within which sites for suburban towns were selected.

Tugwell's agency, a hasty combination of divisions and sections from several other relief administrations, had inherited seventy rural villages and farm labor communities in process of development or only in the planning stage. Some of the engineers engaged in this work were at first assigned to design the proposed greenbelt towns, but Vinton suspected that their efforts were less than imaginative. When he suggested that he would like some of his planner friends to see their handiwork, they refused to let anyone inspect their plans. Vinton therefore sneaked Jacob Crane in at night to look over the drawings and was immediately told that they were "lousy." The street layouts bore no relation to the topography, and the proposed groupings of houses were dull. Tracy Augur, also conducted into the drafting room at night, pronounced the schemes "awful." [118] Vinton then appealed to John S. Lansill, director of the Suburban Resettlement Division, to employ some qualified planners.

After firing the engineers and scrapping their plans, Lansill asked four persons whose judgment he respected to draw up lists of experienced planners and architects. From the lists he chose an advisory planning group composed of Augur (whose name appeared on all four lists), Earle Draper, Russell Van Nest Black, Henry Wright, and Clarence Stein. With the help of this distinguished group, he selected planners and architects to design the proposed towns. Frederick Bigger was appointed chief of planning. Hale J. Walker, a member of the American City Planning Institute, and architects T. P. Ellington and R. J. Wadsworth were commissioned to design Greenbelt, Maryland. Justin Hartzog and William Strong were put in charge of planning Greenhills, the town to be built near Cincinnati. Jacob Crane and architect Elbert Peets were appointed to plan Greendale, several miles southwest of Milwaukee. The team selected to plan Greenbrook, the New Jersey town, included Henry Wright, Albert Mayer, and Henry Churchill, with Black as consultant. The town that was to have been built near St. Louis, however, was eleminated because of disagreement with the St. Louis Plan Commission.

Opposition to the New Jersey town for a time threatened to bring the planning and development of all the others to a halt. Under the influence of a hosiery manufacturer whose estate adjoined the Greenbrook site, real estate interests and the township officials loudly protested against the project, contending that it would require increased provision of local governmental services and would impose undue tax burdens on local property owners. In a suit against Tugwell as an official of the federal government the township challenged the whole suburban resettlement program on the ground that the grant of power given the President in the Emergency Relief Appropriation Act of 1935 was so broad that it was an unconstitutional delegation of legislative authority and that Congress, moreover, lacked the power to authorize the building of model communities. The Circuit Court of the District of Columbia decided both questions against the government, even holding that Congress lacked the power under the general welfare clause to authorize the resettlement program. The United States Attorney General, however, saved the other three greenbelt towns by announcing that the effect of the decision would be limited to the New Jersey venture. An appeal to the Supreme Court was dropped, and there were no legal challenges to the other projects.

Though Tugwell spoke of the greenbelt towns as "rural-industrial communities," they lacked sites for industries (except for ten acres of unutilized land in Greenbelt) and were not comparable to the self-contained English garden cities. Rather, they were small, well-planned garden suburbs that housed, in all, only a few more than 2,100 families when the resettlement program ended—Greenbelt, 885; Greenhills, 667; and Greendale, 572. The distinctive feature of all three, the greenbelt, served the same purpose as in Sir Ebenezer Howard's two towns, protecting the urban section from undesirable encroachment from the outside while providing forests and farmlands for field crops, fruit, dairy products, and, as Tugwell said, "such meat as can be raised in the particular climate." For this idealist the whole combination of surrounding open space, residential area, and town center comprised an almost utopian, functional scheme: "the farmer exchanging the fruits of his labor directly for the wages of industry [the planners hoped that light industries would be attracted to nearby areas]. The industrial worker, living in an environment far superior to that he normally is used to and provided with a partial anchor to windward through the opportunity to grow some of his own food. Costs reduced for both. Both sharing common recreation areas and community facilities. The old line between town and country virtually wiped out."[119]

Tugwell's emphasis on the opportunities for the town dwellers to raise some of their own food showed how much these federal enterprises were products of hard times in which 2,000,000 Americans joined a back-to-the-farm movement. Further, the towns would not have been built at all if there had not been an imperative need to provide employment for men on relief. And it was the use of relief labor, some of it none too efficient, which increased construction costs and caused criticism, though the most violent attacks on the projects, citing dwelling costs ranging from $15,000 to $16,500 or more, were unreasonable, as Coleman Woodbury noted indignantly. "The highly publicized cost figures, by themselves, mean absolutely nothing," he wrote. "The method of determining them, which consisted of taking all costs to date, including land purchased for future expansion, the greenbelt itself, all business and community facilities, roads, streets, water plant, etc., dividing it by the number of housed in the *first* units built, and comparing the resulting figures with private construction costs for individual structures alone, is a sophomoric performance, even if the results do appear in the Congressional Record."[120]

Of far more significance than the partial subsistence aspects of the towns — important mainly in the depression — was the high quality of the planning, which influenced residential development not only in this country but also abroad. Greenbelt exhibited a wedding of plan to site, almost an evolution of plan *from* site, and a careful consideration of the requirements of community life. On one of Tracy Augur's early visits to the site a system of superblocks was agreed upon, provided a sufficient area of suitable land could be found for such a scheme. Further study then revealed a crescent-shape plateau admirably adapted to the creation of five superblocks, with a large valley below the plateau that would lend itself to development as a recreational area. The vehicular trafficways follow the crescent shape of the plateau, with minor streets forming the superblocks. For pedestrian traffic Walker and his associates devised circumferential ways providing communication between the blocks and radial ways leading to the recreational valley and to the store center and community building situated at the head of the valley.

Greenhills, Ohio, and Greendale, Wisconsin, were equally exemplary of skillful site planning and appropriate housing. Under "the moulding influences of the land forms," Hartzog designed the former town to give "the effect of a quiet rural village."[121] A circuit road penetrates all sections of the original settlement. Off this road are minor streets and cul-de-sacs extending into fingers of level and of gently sloping land. Intervening wooded ravines and low lands provide an attractive outlook for the dwellings, mostly group houses and two-story flats, with a few detached and semidetached structures to lend variety, all ranged along the curving roadways. At Greendale, Crane and Peets displayed the same appreciation of the natural features of a 3,500-acre property bounded on one side by the county park system and graced with woods, meadows, lakes, and streams. Here, too, the aim was to achieve the form of a village, but Greendale seems more typically suburban than either Greenhills or Greenbelt.

Had Greenbrook been built, it might have been the most interesting of the resettlement towns. Henry Churchill recalled in 1960 that "Wright did not repeat that Radburn plan." He used superblocks and he carefully separated main traffic streets from secondaries; but there were fewer cul-de-sacs, and the large interior block parks and particularly the walkways — which, he felt, invaded privacy at Radburn — were more carefully located. The overpasses and underpasses were omitted, too; schools and neighborhood shopping were accessible without crossing main streets. "Yet the town was not 'conventional,'" Churchhill commented; "there was great care to develop pedestrian courts, variety of grouping, arrangements of charm, and changes of pace."[122]

The Suburban Resettlement Division contemplated the eventual expansion of the three towns that were built to accommodate approximately 3,000 families each, and there were even to be two other towns of similar size to the south of Greenbelt; but a Congress antipathetic to experimental planning abolished the agency in June, 1938, when the first cells of the towns were about completed. The only other important construction until after the federal government liquidated its interests in these communities (between 1948 and 1954) was an addition of 1,000 units of defense housing at Greenbelt just before the United States entered the Second World War.

To Lansill and Crane the greenbelts themselves were the most significant features of these federally planned and developed communities. These open acres were examples of the kind of land reserves all metropolitan areas should have. They wrote,

> With such large reserves of land in the possession or control of the agencies working on the housing problem, the actual construction of the houses and villages may be carried out by any one of a number of procedures. Private builders may be engaged to build houses. Cooperative societies can utilize available sites in the land reserve, and obviate many of the most serious difficulties inherent in floating a cooperative housing project. And in the metropolitan land reserves public agencies can initiate housing projects, particularly for families of lower income.

All types of development would be assured of an appropriate place in a broadly planned scheme, would be provided with essential services, and would enjoy "the green, open setting essential to suburban life."[123]

Not only to Lansill and Crane but also to many other people the greenbelt towns suggested an alternative to the haphazard, speculative growth-by-accretion that had long characterized American urban areas. At the time the Suburban Resettlement Division was building its greenbelt communities, Oslo owned a suburban area twice the size of the city proper, and Copenhagen held more than a third of the total urban and suburban land available for building. Stockholm had in reserve 20,000 acres, Helsingfors 13,000 acres, and Manchester 3,500 acres in the Wythenshawe ward. The Hague owned 45 per cent of the municipal area or approximately 4,400 acres. The adoption by American cities of the practice of purchasing open land long in advance of need and preplanning its development would, Lansill and Crane believe, "go a long way toward the solution of problems of housing, land utilization, highway development, recreation, public and private finance, and community life in the great metropolitan regions."

Frederic A. Delano proposed that the federal government provide some of the funds that metropolitan housing authorities would need to acquire outlying lands. But in Roosevelt's second term of office all proposals for public ownership and control of extensive amounts of land began to sound socialistic, if not communistic, to an increasingly conservative Congress. The Housing Act of 1937, under which local public housing authorities could at least use federal loans to purchase peripheral sites for low-rent housing projects, received approval because of the adroit political tactics of the proponents, but the struggle for passage revealed that real estate interests, private developers, most financial institutions, and a large segment of the general public looked with deep suspicion upon any broadening of governmental activities in the field of housing and land development. Had the greenbelt communities been created in partnership with private enterprise and not wholly by a federal agency, Lansill and Crane might have been able to present a more acceptable argument for public ownership of land reserves and governmental control of development. The very thoroughness with which Tugwell's Suburban Resettlement Division undertook its task probably defeated the hopes of planners that the three greenbelt towns would stimulate interest in comprehensive municipal land policies. Yet the towns undoubtedly were powerful demonstration projects, contributing to the public demand for better planning in residential areas and to the popularity of the idea of the planned community.

The Report of the Urbanism Committee

Although the Roosevelt Administration, in its various attempts to provide emergency employment, initiated many programs designed to alleviate urban problems, it had no clearly enunciated policy concerning the cities in which more than 56 per cent of the American people lived. "In comparison with the attention given the rural areas, the city remains the neglected child of the national family," Ladislas Segoe declared in presenting a preview of the report of the Urbanism Committee of the National Resources Committee at the national planning conference in Detroit in June, 1937.[124] On Capitol Hill and in state capitols throughout the land the rise of the city to a dominant position in the national scene had been accompanied by no adequate recognition of its assumption of the primary role in national life. Congressmen gave more thought to agricultural programs, dams, interstate highways, mining, national forests and national parks, and land-grant colleges than to the steady accumulation of obsolete and deteriorated structures in cities, the growth of Negro ghettos in northern industrial centers, the increasing pollution of rivers upon which urban populations depended for water supply, the decline of mass transit systems and the mounting traffic congestion, the chaotic proliferation of governmental units in metropolitan regions, the fiscal inadequacy of municipalities, and the still generally unplanned expansion of urban areas. State legislators, representing mainly the rural areas whose concerns were of paramount importance in an earlier, agrarian period, similarly ignored the dangerous intensification of urban mal-adjustments and the emergence of new urban needs.

The report which Segoe and an exceptionally capable staff had pro-duced, *Our Cities: Their Role in the National Economy,* was the first fed-eral document clearly describing the momentous transformation of the United States from a predominantly rural to an urban society, analyzing the problems facing urban America, proposing a federal policy of assist-ance to cities, and recommending specific measures to carry out such a policy. In the foreword to the report the National Resources Committee observed,

> It is not the business of the United States Government to assume responsibility for the solution of purely local problems any more than it is the business of local governments to assume primary responsibility for the settlement of na-tional problems. Yet, the United States Government cannot properly remain indifferent to the common life of American citizens simply because they happen to be found in what we call "cities." The sanitation, the education, the housing, the working and living conditions, the economic security — in brief, the general welfare of all its citizens — are American concerns, insofar as they are within the range of Federal power and responsibility under the Constitution.[125]

Actually, the national government had not turned a deaf ear to appeals of the cities for more and more help. In Washington some seventy fed-eral agencies, bureaus, and divisions provided various urban services, but their activities were scarcely coordinated and did not relate to any overall program for the reconstruction and development of cities. And while these centers had been growing in population and their problems had been increasing in complexity, the available information about them had become even less varied and detailed than in 1890. "In consequence," the National Resources Committee pointed out, "we know comparatively little about cities at a time when the need for accurate, complete, and fully analyzed data is most urgent. Not only is this true of elementary financial data but in marked degree there is a dearth of essential facts regarding many other urban questions."[126]

The committee's recommendations for a clearinghouse of urban in-formation in the Bureau of the Census, for a division of urban research "in some suitable Federal agency," and for closer coordination of federal activities in urban communities stemmed logically from the findings of its Urbanism Committee, but were not startling to city planners and di-rectors of municipal research bureaus. For almost four decades one group or another had been making similar proposals, though perhaps never at a time when the gradually developing urban crisis was more apparent. The committee's suggestions, however, embraced much more than the need for thorough study of urban communities. They included proposals, above all, for further efforts by government, industry, and labor to raise the level of family income and increase economic security, since the fundamental cause of many problems was inadequate and uncertain income. The committee realized, furthermore, that "it is no more possible to solve the national problem by looking at the city alone than by looking at the country alone, for the economic and political basis of America lies in the balance between the two elements in our national life, in their harmonious adjustment and happy interrelation."[127] It recommended that any permanent national planning board should continue to support state and regional planning as well as city and metropolitan planning, and that it improve the long-range programming of public works in cooperation with state, regional and local planning agencies.

All this a committee functioning in a time of trouble might have been expected to urge. Its other proposals, some relating to needs unmet even today and all contemplating deeper commitment of the federal government to safeguarding the welfare of urban areas, prefigured developments of the early 1960s and present-day demands for still more extensive aid to cities. Perhaps in the belief that eventual economic recovery would ease the financial plight of cities, the committee recommended the creation, "primarily for periods of economic distress," of a federal credit agency to make loans and grants to local governments for the construction of public works (including housing), acquisition or construction of public utilities, land purchases, and similar outlays.[128] The committee also proposed a permanent federal public works authority, the adoption of a national policy for rehousing low-income groups at acceptable minimum standards, a "thorough-going inquiry . . . of the entire subject of conflicting fiscal policies and taxation in local, State, and Federal Governments,"[129] programs directed toward crime prevention, federal action to improve the competence and prestige of urban public service, and federal legislation laying down conditions for the adoption of interstate compacts under which communities in metropolitan regions straddling state lines (there were then twenty-two) might jointly solve common problems.

Even if the federal government acted upon these well-considered recommendations, the greater part of the task of improving cities devolved upon the cities themselves. Segoe warned that the cities would have to abandon the worship of bigness and the disregard of quality fostered by their extremely rapid growth. "In the race to advance their position in the census volumes, our cities competed with one another, using every available means at their disposal, and thereby not infrequently laid the foundations of many of their present difficulties," he told his fellow planners.[130] Cities built or helped to finance often unnecessary competing transport facilities; they prematurely annexed outlying areas; they competed for industries without discrimination, offering free land, tax exemptions, free rent, payroll subsidies, low utility rates, and other

inducements, thus encouraging the selection of unsound industrial locations and the building of a weak and unstable industrial structure. In
the mistaken belief that whatever serves best the interest of the individual, serves best the community, they abetted speculation in urban
land, sometimes even selling municipal lands to finance improvements in
tracts marketed by glib promoters. The fruits of this passion for growth
could be seen almost everywhere in handicapped industries, fluctuations
in employment and low annual family income, heavy tax burdens, and
a low standard of urban living.

Had city planning benefited cities or in any way ameliorated the worst
aspects of their headlong development? "Although there are many individual instances in which planning has definitely improved and even
governed the physical development of communities," Segoe said, "it is
difficult, even impossible, to appraise the total effect of city planning by
itself as a preventive or remedy for the physical defects and social ills
against which it is directed." Case studies by Arthur C. Comey and Max
S. Wehrly of 144 planned towns, garden suburbs, and residential areas
showed, however, that as a result of planning, these communities were
comparatively free of the physical defects and deficiencies common in
unplanned urban areas. "They offer their inhabitants not only a more
satisfactory environment, but, in a great measure, a more attractive
existence," Segoe maintained.[131]

What form, then, did the Urbanism Committee believe would be
compatible with the effective performance of the economic and cultural
role of the urban community in the life of the nation? Not wholesale
decentralization, as some advocated, because undue dispersion would be
as wasteful of resources, time, and energy as extreme concentration.
Widespread diffusion of activity would probably increase the cost of production and distribution and the cost of providing public facilities and
services, thus rendering the attainment of a higher standard of material
and cultural well-being more difficult for the whole population. Provided
an urban community had a fundamentally sound economic base and a
site the disadvantages of which were not too costly to overcome, it might
well undertake "judicious reshaping" of its environment by systematic
development and redevelopment in accordance with a forward-looking
plan, gradually loosening up the central areas of congestion and creating
a moderately decentralized and yet integrated urban structure. Segoe
and his staff envisaged the whole urban area organized into neighborhoods and satellite communities, each providing for a maximum of opportunity to care for the daily activities and needs of its inhabitants,
each effectively performing its specialized function in the metropolitan
region, each possessing a social and political coherence capable of arousing community loyalty and participation and inspiring civic leadership.

But the attainment of such an urban community would require, as the report of the Urbanism Committee stated, "much better appreciation and understanding of the city and its distinctive problems, greatly improved governmental organization and wider powers, and far more fundamental and much more effective planning on all levels of government." [132]

In the years since 1929 the most capable city planners had indeed been struggling to deepen their knowledge of the city, to relate planning more closely to legislative and administrative functions, and to link local planning with state and national planning. Rather painfully they had come to realize that their characteristic emphasis upon land and the physical structures superimposed upon it tended to blind them to the web of social life generated in the course of historical development and sometimes to render their proposals politically unacceptable. "It is not that the land is no longer important," sociologist Louis Wirth told them, "but rather . . . that we can no longer effectively deal with it [at] all or if we would use it as an instrument in the enhancement of human welfare, we must not overlook the complex technological and social superstructure through which it has been modified and which limits and conditions our use of it." [133]

After two decades of intensive analysis of the human resources of the city, Wirth and his fellow social scientists knew the ways in which urban life differed from that of the village and rural areas; they could explain the social pathologies associated with urban work and living; and they could be sure that the city, notwithstanding all its poverty, crime, tensions, loneliness, and brutal exploitation, was an indispensable creative force, daily giving birth to new inventions, products, laws, works of art, communal services, and scientific advances. But neither Wirth nor any other sociologist could say with certainty how cities should be organized, how the findings of scholarship should be applied in the development and redevelopment of urban areas. "Many of the problems of urban living still remain unsolved and some of them are just looming on the horizon of national awareness," Wirth conceded. "They cannot be solved single-handed by any one group of specialists even if they call themselves planners."[134]

In addition to paying too little attention to the social fabric of the city, many planners had also slighted its political life and its governmental organization. Chiefly this was because city planning had its birth in a period of widespread municipal corruption, when the commercial clubs and chambers of commerce of the times wanted citizens with no ties to "the machine" to guide the preparation of the city plan; but the very detachment of the lay commission from the activities of city hall usually nullified its effectiveness—and that of the consultants who served it. In the meantime, revolutionary changes had come about in municipal government that planning commissioners did not always fully appreciate or city planners capitalize upon. "The irresponsible urban boss of the previous generation is extinct today except in a handful of cities," political scientist Albert Lepawsky reminded the planners.[135] For years experts had been displacing untrained amateurs in important positions in the city hall, and the organization of city government had grown more unified and coordinated through the concentration of executive responsibility in a single municipal executive, either the traditional mayor or the now ubiquitous city manager. In fact, structurally and technically, urban government had witnessed a development comparable to, though less heralded than, the growth of the nation's private corporate system and industrial machine, Lepawsky thought. Certainly, its reliance on the executive budget, central purchasing, and skilled personnel administration, and its ready adoption of scientific techniques and devices made it in significant respects similar to corporate enterprise. But the work of municipal reconstruction was far from finished, and only by a thoroughly planned system of administration would urban America achieve what city planners themselves sought: a coordinated administration of local services and a well-rounded municipal life. "Only by planning to administer are we going to be able to administer our plans," Lepawsky declared.[136]

Though city planners could influence municipal administrative reorganization if they were sufficiently knowledgeable and politically astute, and though they could profit by the ecological analyses of the sociologists, they understood least how they could relate physical planning to economic planning. Warren Vinton firmly believed that in the sphere reserved to private initiative, the business world, they could not effectively plan at all. "*Laissez faire* and the price system are still in effective control of commerce, industry, finance, and credit," he maintained.[137] In a second sphere or "intermediate zone" of enterprises greatly affected with a public interest, and therefore regulated by government or supported by government loans and subsidies, "negative planning," in the form of price regulation, zoning, and building restrictions, could be exercised. This kind of planning, applicable mainly to privately owned public utilities, such as electricity, gas, telephone, telegraph, and radio companies, had elements of both physical and economic planning and required the imposition of certain kinds of controls familiar to city planners. Only in a third sphere of wholly public initiative, lately broadened by the public low-rent housing program, could planners do effective positive planning, and here the planning was "primarily physical." Warning that economic and social planning must content itself with seeing that "our legislative rules of the game make economic sense," Vinton pleaded for "more physical planning imbued with social and economic validity."[138]

Russell Black expressed the typical city planner's view when he said that "broad social and economic planning is highly important to physical planning accomplishment but is not necessarily a part of the physical planning process." As he saw it, "coupling the social and economic planning job with that of proper physical planning, in the same planning program, would seem to be almost too much for a single body of men whether comprising a state or a national planning board."[139]

With these views the city planning profession generally agreed. Physical planning imbued with social and economic validity was now more certainly than ever its special province. And thanks to the varied experience of the depression years, many planners brought a new sophistication to their work. Those who had served as consultants to state planning boards or had held staff positions in such agencies had engaged in many studies seemingly tangential to physical planning but actually directly related to it—studies of industrial employment and production, public education, county government, health services, welfare programs, taxation, trade and market problems, rural electrification, fuel resources. Planners had a new appreciation of the ways in which such investigations yielded information bearing on the allocation of land for various purposes, the selection of sites for public institutions and facilities, the future distribution of population, the conservation and use of natural resources, and other important concerns of the profession. Men who had directed surveys of land use and housing in urban planning agencies making use of WPA workers had a broader understanding not only of physical conditions in cities but also of urban economies and social structures, since much of the statistical information obtained provided insight into trends in various industries, problems of low-income groups, minorities, the socially dependent, and the "technologically unemployed," who for the first time were of particular concern to American society in the 1930s.

Because similar studies were carried on in state and local planning agencies throughout the United States, comparative data previously unavailable provided a new source of enlightenment for planners. For the entire profession there was great value in the realization that the planning function suffered least in cities in which the planning commission and its staff had prepared a long-range plan and had used it advantageously to recommend emergency public works projects or had previously instituted a sound capital-budgeting procedure assuring funds for worthwhile improvements. The importance of allying the planning function closely with policy-making and administration did not escape those who led the profession—or those who, because of failure to master the intricacies of political structure and administrative organization, had seen planning budgets slashed or eliminated altogether.

The Resurgence of City and Regional Planning

As economic conditions began to improve in 1938, after a recession the year before, planning agencies throughout the nation applied some of the knowledge gained from all the studies and surveys undertaken as emergency projects. But their staffs were aware of many questions they could not answer and of many national and regional influences on urban areas that were difficult to assess. As Walter Blucher noted at a state-wide planning conference in Indiana, four principal problem areas were affecting cities hundreds of miles distant. From the old southern cotton belt, from the depleted agricultural and mining districts of Appalachia, from the cutover areas of Michigan, Wisconsin, and Minnesota, and from the Great Plains drought area impoverished families were migrating to cities, often forcing out of employment some of the older people, as in the automobile industry in Detroit, and creating a surplus population which could not be absorbed. Could a city planner accurately forecast how many people there would be in a city in five, ten, or fifteen years, what kinds of people they would be, or how many would be on relief? Could he predict how many would need public housing or how many would become homeowners? "Anybody who thinks you can answer these questions by merely adopting a zoning ordinance is very naïve," Blucher observed. He was not sure that even with the best kind of planning all the baffling questions could be answered, but like a seasoned professional, he thought one could come closer to the answers "through proper planning and consideration of the facts" than by not applying planning procedures at all.[140]

Time—and recent studies—had revealed that many of the zoning ordinances drafted ten or fifteen years earlier were scarcely based on "consideration of the facts," or certainly not the right facts. Even if it was difficult to make correct assumptions about the future and to forecast population changes accurately, these ordinances required drastic revision. In June, 1938, the American Society of Planning Officials reported that several hundred ordinances were in process of being "modernized." Planners were not only reducing the size of commercial, industrial, and multifamily residential zones to accord more closely with community needs but were also introducing new provisions excluding residences from industrial areas, restricting trailer camps—a relatively new manifestation of American interest in mobility—to commercial or industrial districts, and requiring off-street parking for private automobiles and adequate off-street loading and unloading space in commercial districts.

Marin County (situated across the Golden Gate from San Francisco) became the first county in California to adopt a comprehensive zoning ordinance under a new California Planning Act that did *not* include zoning as a part of the master or general plan. Having realized the inconsistency of treating a detailed legal instrument as an element of a scheme essentially general in character and intended to be used chiefly as the basis for policy-making, the California planners had revised their planning act of 1929 to distinguish between a plan of proposed land use and an ordinance devised as a means of accomplishing its objectives. Hugh Pomeroy, consultant to the Marin County Planning Commission, first outlined a land use plan for the entire county, showing desirable utilization based on studies of existing uses, tendencies of development, and regional influences. He then drafted an ordinance "vastly broader in scope than . . . if it had been developed as an aggregation of regulations for a series of local communities, based solely on conditions in those communities," and this ordinance the county supervisors enacted.[141]

As planners in other states took note of the distinction made in California between the long-term plan of desirable land use and the zoning ordinance, they were inclined to greet Edward M. Bassett's new book, *The Master Plan,* as a dated volume. The man who liked to be known as "the father of zoning" maintained that there were only seven elements of a master plan, of which zoning was one. The others he listed were streets, parks, sites for public buildings, public reservations, routes for public utilities, and pierhead and bulkhead lines. Bassett's horizon had been broadened hardly at all by the housing movement, the intense discussions of economic and social planning, the great attention given natural resources, and a groundswell of interest in "reclaiming" blighted areas.

Some months after his book appeared, a judge of the Superior Court in California handed down a ruling in a zoning case that extended the application of the police power in ways the conservative Bassett probably never thought possible. In a precedent-setting decision Judge Maurice T. Dooling, Jr., upheld a Monterey County zoning ordinance imposing certain building regulations upon the owners of property along the scenic Carmel–San Simeon coast highway for the purpose of protecting its natural beauties. Holding that roadside beauty is an economic as well as an aesthetic asset, the justice sustained the constitutionality of the restrictions. He remarked that a higher court might decide that he had attempted "to force the hands of the clock forward too rapidly," but he was nevertheless confident that time would ultimately justify his judgment.[142] He need not have feared. No higher court reversed his decision, and the Carmel–San Simeon highway, dedicated as a national scenic route in 1966, remains one of the world's most spectacular drives.

The land use surveys which led to the overhaul of outdated and unrealistic zoning regulations also contributed to better understanding of the need for preventing or at least deterring repetitions of the unrestrained subdividing of the 1920s, though most city and county governments throughout the United States merely relied upon requirements for a high quality of improvements to discourage promoters from prematurely subdividing and marketing land—a stratagem somewhat productive of the desired results in bad times but generally ineffective in periods of prosperity.

Efforts to better the design of subdivisions were more successful than attempts to limit the quantity. The Federal Housing Administration, for instance, placed land consultants in five regional offices in the spring of 1938 to cooperate with planning agencies and civic groups in improving subdivision layouts. As the men selected were city planners with

78. Examples of good and bad subdivision plans in the Federal Housing Administration's booklet *Planning Profitable Neighborhoods,* 1938

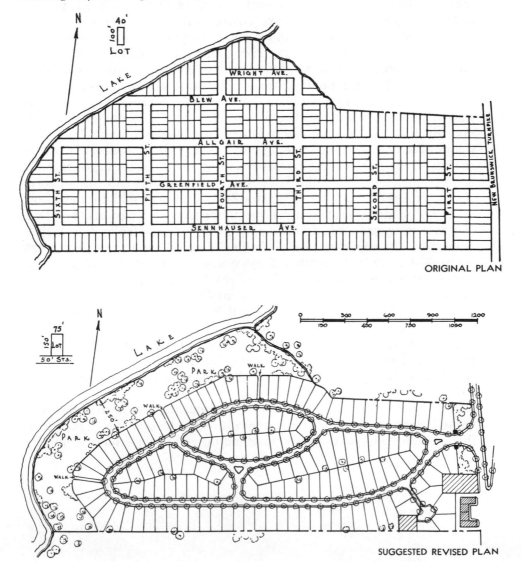

years of experience in public agencies or private practice, they gradually convinced the more skeptical real estate interests and developers that careful planning would make properties more salable as well as more convenient, attractive, and economically beneficial to purchasers. In 1939 these consultants reviewed and analyzed 2,615 residential subdivisions containing, in all, almost 283,000 separate lots. Frequently the review process resulted in revisions considerably enhancing the quality of the tract.

At their national conference in Boston that year planners agreed that no planning agency could adequately review proposed subdivisions unless it had prepared at least outline plans of undeveloped areas, preferably related to the comprehensive plan of the city and its surroundings. In order merely to know whether the main streets in a subdivision would conform to an areawide circulation system, a planning agency would need a long-range plan, Alfred Bettman pointed out. Yet many planning offices continued to be without a basic plan to indicate how newly platted areas should be fitted into the expanding community pattern.

The same deficiency handicapped some cities as they strove to improve capital budgeting and long-range programming of public works. Without a comprehensive plan to guide future growth and development, they could not well determine what kinds of facilities would be required, how many persons the improvements should serve, or where they should be constructed, much less decide which projects should be undertaken first and which should be scheduled in later years — as the National Resources Committee had suggested throughout the depression years, and as its successor, the National Resources Planning Board, again urged in 1939 when it appointed a Public Works Committee to assist in the preparation of a federal six-year program of public works and to encourage state and local governments to formulate similar programs. For lack of a long-range plan and detailed plans of projects related to it, countless cities had lost opportunities to obtain federal funds in the lean years from 1933 to 1938, had suffered more unemployment than was necessary, and had retarded operation of the federally aided public works program as a stabilizing mechanism in the national economy. In fact, as late as 1939 many cities were still losing federal funds because of their failure to support local planning.

To develop a workable methodology for programming municipal public works, the National Resources Planning Board decided to initiate demonstration studies in seven cities in various parts of the country: Winchester, Massachusetts; Nashville, Tennessee; Kalamazoo, Michigan; Dallas, Texas; Fargo, North Dakota; Sacramento, California; and Spokane, Washington. These were cities with some history of city planning, though none was particularly outstanding at the time for the quality or consistency of its planning; but all were interested in developing a public works program that could be adequately financed year after year, whether on a pay-as-you-go basis or chiefly by borrowing.

For experience on which to base the procedure to be tested in these cities the national agency went to the municipalities with a reputation for orderly programming of public works: Cincinnati, Milwaukee, San Diego, New York City, and Richmond, Virginia. Their methods of selecting and financing public improvements suggested a general pattern of programming that would necessarily require modifications to suit the particular needs and form of government of each of the seven cities chosen for the demonstration studies. Notwithstanding individual adjustments, a certain uniformity of procedure emerged from the tests. It included five steps: detailed analysis of financial resources; listing of all public improvements needed for a dozen or more years; scheduling of the most urgent projects for the ensuing fiscal year and of others throughout the next five years in the order of importance, with perhaps a third group to be undertaken in a subsequent six-year period; public hearings on the proposed program; and adoption by the local governing body of a capital budget (as part of the regular annual budget) appropriating funds for construction of the projects to be begun in the next fiscal year. Annual revisions of the program would advance a new group of projects for budgeting and would add others to the five-year reserve of improvements for which construction plans might be started.

The publication of the National Resources Planning Board describing the procedure (not issued until 1941) pointed out that the task of listing needed projects is appropriately a function of the local planning agency, though in Dallas the assistant director of finance and in Spokane the city engineer assembled lists of proposed improvements from department heads.[143] The national board implied that the city planning agency should also evaluate proposals and assign priorities to them — the most difficult and controversial of all the steps in the programming process. The board offered fourteen criteria for determining the relative importance of proposals but acknowledged that "each community will have its own ideas of what purposes should be served first in providing public improvements."[144] Experience in hundreds of cities since the board issued its report indicates that there probably can never be any final word on the matter of determining priorities.

In the late 1930s, when the National Resources Planning Board stimulated long-range programming as, among other things, a way to further city planning, not many persons perceived that federal grants to cities for public works and federal loans and subsidies to local public housing authorities were forging a new direct relationship of the national government to municipalities. Earle Draper was one who commented on this development and pointed out that it was strengthening, or would eventually strengthen, the local planning function:

> Direct federal grants to municipalities make Uncle Sam play an increasingly important role in the municipal government. And where our beneficent Uncle opens his money bags for the handling of city problems, he brings with him a system of checks and balances of involved contractual, long-time relationships that place the burden on the city to find out where the city is headed. Where the solution of local problems is of national significance, the Federal Government may give financial assistance, but in so doing the national government usually presupposes or requires a plan in the working out of the problem.

The federal insistence on long-range, comprehensive planning, Draper thought, would force administrators to become "plan-minded" and would reduce the "distance" between city planners and department heads, the city manager, and the city council.[145]

Even though federal pressures may not always have been contributory, there were some signs that city planning was staging a comeback, occasionally with the support of an enlightened administration, as in Los Angeles. Fletcher Bowron, who replaced a corrupt mayor in the only successful recall election in the history of that city, added seven new positions to the staff of the city planning department and declared that he believed it should be one of the most important departments of city government.[146] He deplored the high incidence of spot zoning during the tenure of his predecessor, called for the preparation of a master plan, and asked that it be used as the basis for rezoning the entire city. In Baltimore the voters approved a charter amendment establishing a new planning commission with authority to study all plans and proposals for the construction of public improvements and report to the board of estimate whether the projects were desirable. In Philadelphia a charter commission noted that "lack of proper authoritative city planning has led to untold loss, extravagance, and waste" and suggested the creation of a strong planning board "to provide for the considered future development of the city and its capital improvements. . . ."[147] After entrusting city planning for thirty years to a 300-member commission created only by resolution, Chicago in 1939 established the commission by ordinance for the first time, reducing its membership to 22 persons, 8 of whom were appointed by the mayor from an advisory board of 200. The mayor himself, heads of city departments, and chairmen of city council committees were included in the commission, making it a much more authoritative group — and also a more political one. County planning agencies in the vicinity of many large cities increased their activities, and in the New York region several counties created new planning agencies.

In the latter years of the decade there was also something of a revival of regional planning. The twenty-year-old Municipal Planning Association of Pittsburgh took the new name of Pittsburgh Regional Planning Association and enumerated twelve problems on which it hoped to make progress, including regional recreation and the spread of blight. The new Regional Association of Cleveland carried out a metropolitan land use survey with the help of WPA workers, thus laying a foundation for most of the city planning done in the area in subsequent years. The study was one of the first concerned with densities of population as well as with patterns of land use and quantities of land used for various purposes. Another new areawide organization, the Denver Regional Planning Association, embarked on a program of assisting communities in the region with the preparation of zoning ordinances and working out recreation, highway, water, and sewer plans. A special objective of this association was the removal and prevention of rural slums. A group in Tucson, Arizona, known as the Regional Plan, Inc., announced that it would develop land-use programs and sponsor legislation enabling the metropolitan community to carry out plans. The Regional Planning Committee of the Municipal League of Harrisburg, Pennsylvania, issued a report prepared by Malcolm H. Dill recommending the formation of a regional planning commission. The unusual thing about the report was that it was first published in its entirety in two local newspapers as fifty-two articles in three series. Impressed by this method of publicizing planning, the American Society of Planning Officials distributed copies of the complete report to all its members.

Perhaps none of these new regional endeavors, however successful, could hope to rival the still vital Regional Plan Association of the New York area. Of a total of 2,548 miles of major routes in the regional highway system shown in the plan of 1929, 789 miles had been constructed by 1937, particular progress having been made since 1933 on routes in the central part of the region. The regional park system had expanded by 30,447 acres (47.5 square miles) since 1928, though only a fifth of this gain could be credited to recent years. New York City had, however, witnessed exceptional expansion and development of its parks since 1933. Especially gratifying to the association was the increase in planning boards in the region—twenty-nine new municipal boards since 1932, and several new county planning agencies, making a total of seven in the seventeen suburban counties of the region. The Regional Plan Association acknowledged that "actual accomplishment has, of course, been made by the official agencies under whose jurisdiction the various projects fall," but much of the credit for seeing that the projects conformed to an areawide plan belonged to the association itself. The other significant factor in the record of achievement was "the availability of Federal funds for emergency appropriations" after the coming of the New Deal.[148]

The Status of State and National Planning

State planning, which in the early years of the Roosevelt Administration had been mainly in the hands of boards created by order of the governor, by 1938 had been entrusted in most states to boards authorized by the legislature. Only six states still had boards not sanctioned by statute, and only Delaware, Maine, and Kentucky were without any planning board. Even the territories of Hawaii and Alaska had planning agencies. The National Resources Committee, however, candidly acknowledged that not more than a third of these planning boards were "accepted as an integral part of the [state] governmental structure." Another third were in a "precarious condition," and the others were relatively inactive.[149] As if to confirm the committee's assessment of the tenuous position of some of the boards, the governors of the Dakotas, Texas, Iowa, and Oregon abolished their boards the very next year.

The national planning agency watched the fortunes of state planning boards with almost parental concern. Unless these agencies became strong and permanent, its hopes for the development of federal planning could hardly be realized, because it looked to the state boards to create better understanding of federal programs and to interpret state and local needs to the national government. It also depended upon these agencies to encourage city, county, and metropolitan planning and to coordinate local planning with that of the state. But the enthusiasm for state planning among state legislatures was apt to wax or wane according to the amount of assistance the federal government could provide in the form of consultants and workers from various relief programs. When the expenditures of emergency agencies for assistance to state planning projects dropped from $2,412,000 in 1936 to $1,800,000 in 1937 and then to $1,000,000 in 1938, state legislatures and governors did not boost the budgets of state planning boards proportionately. Many of the initial inventories and surveys had been completed, but there were dozens of additional studies needed, and the amounts appropriated or allocated to state planning boards were all too small, considering the assignments given them in some of the statutes. With an annual appropriation of $62,500, plus some supplementary federal aid, the Pennsylvania State Planning Board, for example, was directed to prepare a state master plan, advise state departments and bureaus, local authorities, and individuals "with a view to the coordinating of all physical development plans," prepare and keep up-to-date a long-term program of state improvement projects, encourage state agencies to prepare detailed plans for public works, review preliminary plans for projects, and cooperate with local and regional planning boards.[150] Other state boards were expected to undertake similar programs with far less financial support. Twenty-one of the state boards and the two territorial boards received less than $25,000 from their legislatures, and only three others besides Pennsylvania (Massachusetts, New York, and Wisconsin) obtained $40,000 or more in state funds. Theoretically, other state departments were eager to collaborate with state boards, either lending personnel for certain projects or contributing data, but in reality there was profound skepticism about state planning in some of the state governments and little actual cooperation. State planning, in short, was uneven in quality and provided a none too solid foundation for national planning.

"State boards have not, on the whole, arrived at the plan-making stage," the National Resources Committee reported in 1938. They had spent most of their time gathering basic information about land and water resources. In 1939 only a third were carrying on some type of industrial study. Even fewer had begun to investigate housing, health, education, and other subjects of a distinctly social nature. The National Resources Committee emphasized "certain achievements of an intangible character."[151] The state planning boards had hammered home the notion that for the conservation of our resources, natural and human, and their best utilization it is essential to take a long view ahead and develop a systematic and orderly program for land use, transportation development, public works, water use, and other governmental activities. The resulting popular education had been beneficial. So, too, had been the interchange among state officials and the cooperation between federal and state officials.

But had state planning strengthened city and county planning? Not more than a third of the state boards had been zealous in stimulating planning among municipalities and counties. Chief among those which had been were the boards of Massachusetts, New Jersey, New York, Pennsylvania, Virginia, Florida, Montana, and Kansas. The New Jersey and New York boards had sponsored conferences of local planning officials. The Florida board had helped in organizing county planning councils, the Montana board in promoting planning in districts and counties. Yet some of these boards were convinced that local planning would retrogress without state encouragement.

In the federal government the National Resources Committee itself enjoyed little more security than many of the state planning boards. Its friends in Congress were not sufficiently numerous to enact a bill giving it permanent status, though efforts were made year after year. The idea of national planning was repugnant to a good many conservative legislators. Others believed that if any agency should carry on such planning, it should be a long-established organization such as the Army Corps of Engineers, as the struggle over the President's proposal to create seven regional authorities similar to the Tennessee Valley Authority revealed.

In 1937 Roosevelt sent a message to Capitol Hill urging the establishment of an Atlantic seaboard authority, a second for the Great Lakes and the Ohio Valley, a third for the drainage basin of the Tennessee and Cumberland rivers, a fourth embracing the drainage basin of the Missouri River and the Red River of the North, a fifth embracing the drainage basins of the Arkansas, Red, and Rio Grande rivers, a sixth for the basins of the Colorado River and rivers flowing into the Pacific south of the California-Oregon line, and a seventh for the Columbia River Basin. The President mentioned that "when the national planning board is established [by act of Congress], I should expect to use that agency to coordinate the development of regional planning to ensure conformity to national policy, but not to give the proposed national planning board any executive authority over the construction of public works or over management of completed works. . . ."[152] This statement was intended, of course, to assure the old-line agencies and their supporters in Congress that there would be no infringement on time-honored prerogatives, but it had no mollifying effect on the Corps of Engineers.

Stoutly defending the status quo, the friends of the Corps and of other entrenched agencies appeared before committees of the Senate and the House in opposition to the regional authority bill. There were spokesmen for the Mississippi Valley Association, the Ohio Valley Conservation and Flood Control Congress, the National Coal Association, the Cincinnati Chamber of Commerce, the Lake Carriers Association, the Union Barge Line of Pittsburgh, and similar groups. All testified that the Army engineers were doing a fine job of flood control and that the work would be delayed if any conflicting authorities were established. The National Coal Association expressed its fear of any further stimulation of hydroelectric power. The lake carriers declared that there was no flood problem on the Great Lakes and no need for an authority in that area. In short, regional planning coordinated by a national planning agency was wholly unacceptable. Regional planning by the Corps of Engineers, however, might be considered.

In both the Senate and the House the bills proposing regional authorities were bottled up in committee. From the Senate emerged Joint Resolution No. 57, "to authorize the submission to Congress of a comprehensive national plan for the prevention and control of floods of all the major rivers of the United States, development of hydro-electric power resources, water and soil conservation, and other purposes."[153]

The President lost no time vetoing this authorization. With evident indignation, he wrote,

> By this resolution the War Department would become the national planning agency, not alone for flood control, but for all the other multiple uses of water. Although the Department of Agriculture would prepare reports on run-off

retardation and soil erosion prevention, and the Department of the Interior be consulted on reclamation projects, the War Department would report for these coordinate agencies directly to Congress instead of to the Chief Executive. The local and regional basis of planning would be ignored, and there would be no review of the whole program, prior to its presentation to Congress, from the standpoint of national budgetary considerations and national conservation policies.

Roosevelt acknowledged that the Army Corps of Engineers had had wide experience in the building of flood control projects and had executed them with great skill and ability, but he did not consider its experience and background sufficient for the planning of a comprehensive program for the development of the vast water and related resources of the nation. The planning of the use and control of water and other resources, moreover, was distributed by law among many federal agencies. The joint resolution encroached upon the functions of these agencies and ignored and duplicated the coordinated planning work already in progress under the general guidance of the National Resources Committee. He therefore found it impossible to subscribe to the proposal embodied in the resolution, though there was still a need for legislation to attain the objectives of the resolution. The Congress could expect "a comprehensive national plan for flood control and prevention and for the development of water and soil conservation" from him in the coming year—a plan that would be prepared "by all of the many Government agencies concerned."[154]

The Corps of Engineers had suffered a defeat, but its guerrilla war with the President's planning agency was far from over. It was merely suspended until circumstances presented some favorable opportunity to renew the attack. The proposal for regional authorities was, however, as much as dead.

In June, 1939, the Congress approved a reorganization plan under which the planning agency was renamed the National Resources Planning Board and was made an arm of the Executive Office of the President. Roosevelt had asked for an appropriation of $990,000 for the board but received only $750,000. The agency acquired the functions of the old Economic Stabilization Board of Hoover's administration and became responsible for preparing a six-year program of federal public works as well as for reporting economic trends to the President, so that action might be initiated to ward off recessions. The reorganization did not appear to affect the work of the agency's committees on land, science, transportation, water, and energy resources, composed of representatives from the staffs of departments of the federal government and leading professional men. In the past five years these committees and the staff had produced a valuable series of reports on technological trends, the problems of a changing population, research as a national resource, consumer incomes and expenditures, the structure of the American economy, energy resources and national policy, housing, regional planning, drainage basin problems, and farm tenancy and land planning. Since 1938, however, the President had been requesting studies of energy resources and transportation which indicated that he was increasingly troubled by the threatening course of events in Europe and was thinking of America's needs if war should come. And come it did, in September, 1939, when Hitler's troops, tanks, and planes swarmed into Poland in a blitzkrieg that wiped out all resistance in three weeks and left the country prostrate. Though the United States was not immediately involved as a combatant, the President must have known that it would be, sooner or later.

79. A freeway interchange in the "Futurama" at the New York World's Fair, 1939 *(General Motors)*

In November he instructed the National Resources Planning Board to concentrate on postwar planning, lest the conflict be followed by another depression, as after the First World War.

Visions of Things to Come

Little imagining how greatly the new upheaval would affect their lives for years to come, hundreds of thousands of Americans flocked to a world's fair in Flushing Meadows in New York City to marvel at the art and technology of nations already at war and to stand in long lines awaiting admission to the General Motors exhibit known as the "Futurama." Once inside the portals, they viewed the America of 1960 as designer Norman Bel Geddes depicted it in a model covering almost an acre and as traffic expert Miller McClintock had described it to the American City Planning Institute and other planning organizations at their annual conference in 1937. The seemingly fantastic urban region spread out before them, with its seven-lane, one-direction highways, its four-level streets and bridge approaches, its quarter-mile-high, glass-sheathed skyscrapers, and its green parkways, was the solution of the traffic researchers to the "basic maladjustments in automotive transportation" — maladjustments accounting for an annual toll of 36,000 lives and more than a million injuries and for the failure of rules and regulations backed up by punitive sanctions.[155]

In this automotive city of tomorrow, said a voice synchronized for each spectator with the section of the display before which he was passing, traffic moved at designated speeds of fifty, seventy-five, and a hundred miles an hour along highway surfaces automatically light at night by means of continuous tubing in the highway safety curbing. Cars from the farm roads and feeder lanes joined the motorway traffic at the same speed as cars traveling from city to city. By means of ramped loops, cars made right and left turns at speeds up to fifty miles an hour. In the distance gleamed the future city, its skyscrapers spaced far apart, the base of each one occupying a full city block. On the roofs of some were landing places for airplanes and autogyros, as helicopters were then called. Parks occupied a third of the total city area. It was a utopia of abundant sunshine, fresh air, and recreational opportunity. It seemed to be a flight of sheer fancy, yet when McClintock had given city planners a preview of it, he had reminded them that the counterparts of some of its features already could be seen: a cloverleaf intersection in New Jersey, the "traffic sorter" of the Triborough Bridge of New York City, the Outer Drive in Chicago, the West Side elevated highway in Manhattan, the "cathedral-like" tower of Radio City and the "prophetic form" of the Empire State Building.

For at least a decade there would be little money, materials, and manpower to build freeways, bridges, and skyscrapers like those in Bel Geddes' model, but in time they would materialize — all except the evenly illuminated road surfaces. Just then everything in the display appeared all the more incredible because cities were still struggling with what McClintock called "palliatives" for the frictions and inefficiencies of the street and highway system: accident prevention bureaus, new overhead street lighting, guard rails, mechanical control devices, and municipal parking lots. Merchants in Detroit and other large cities were loud in their complaints that traffic congestion was ruining their business. Flint, Michigan, had caused a stir with a planning report proposing parking areas on the periphery of the business district. In their conferences, however, many city planners declared that there should be a de-emphasis on transportation facilities for the individual and a concentration of attention on public transit which would carry masses of persons short distances cheaply, or on combined automobile and rapid transit ways providing for fast mass travel in electric trains and individual automobile travel chiefly between the central city and outlying communities. But the long-term trend was against increased patronage of mass transit and toward greater use of the automobile. The total number of passengers on public transit had declined from 15,567,000,000 in 1930 to 12,645,-000,000 in 1938, while motor vehicle registrations had climbed from some 24,000,000 in the grim year 1933 to more than 31,000,000 in 1939 — several millions higher than in the last year of Republican prosperity.

In another building of the fair the public saw the city as planners themselves would fashion it — and as it had developed haphazardly, wastefully, and inconveniently for decades before they arrived on the scene to try to remedy its worst defects and guide its expansion rationally. In a new kind of film known as the "documentary" the American Institute of Planners (formerly the American City Planning Institute) presented the story of American urban life from charming New England village to jerry-built factory town to congested metropolis, and then to planned community. Entitled *The City,* this forty-four-minute motion picture was the product of a nonprofit company organized by the Institute when it received a grant of $50,000 from the Carnegie Foundation to portray visually the goals to be sought not only in building new communities but also in remolding existing cities. The scenario and commentary were by Lewis Mumford, Henwar Rodakeiwicz, and Pare Lorentz, who was hailed as the wizard of the documentary form. The musical score was by Aaron Copland and Max Goverman, the photography by Willard Van Dyke and Ralph H. Steiner.

The City enthralled with its dramatic contrasts. Scenes of smoke belching from mills and locomotives in squalid industrial towns followed nostalgic glimpses of New England villagers haying or grinding corn to make johnnycake. The camera lens turned from the hectic lunch hour in the financial district to a forsaken Wall Street on a Sunday morning, with the bells of Trinity Church tolling forlornly, and then to a suburban two-lane highway jammed for miles with honking, exasperated motorists. After the photographic indictment of the unplanned city came the green city of forethought, a composite of Radburn and Greenbelt and other well-designed developments, but somehow the closing shots of children riding their bicycles along tree-shaded paths and of parents smiling at gurgling babies were anticlimactic after the brilliant sequence of urban horrors. The planned community was as dull as it was healthful and peaceful, whereas the strident, frenetic, materialistic metropolis was pulsing with life and fascinating in its anarchistic display of energy. The migration to the suburbs apparently left no doubt that a

80. Detail of the "Futurama": freeways and gigantic skyscrapers in the heart of the metropolis *(General Motors)*

large proportion of city dwellers would select the green city if they had a choice. Could city planners endow it with a little more urbanity, some variety, even a few irritants to spice its blandness?

The leaders of the National Association of Real Estate Boards agreed with some planners that the green city did not necessarily have to be on the urban fringe. It could be created right in the old city of creeping blight, where its residents would be close to bright lights, places of employment, many kinds of stores, and cultural institutions. Whole neighborhoods of festering slums could be demolished and rebuilt, or carefully rehabilitated. As consultant to the national association, Harland Bartholomew in 1938 had drafted a model "Neighborhood Improvement Act" under which property owners in a deteriorating area could form an improvement association and have it approved by the city council as a planning group. The improvement association could then prepare a neighborhood development plan, submit it to the city planning commission and council for approval, and year after year cooperate with the city in carrying it out. The model act required the planning commission to divide "all or part of the city into neighborhood areas in conformity with the official city plan," to hold hearings on the proposed division, and present it to the council for adoption.[156]

"Our cities are faced with economic collapse unless large numbers of people become persuaded that areas within the city can be made fully as attractive as the suburbs—and that taxes can be kept to levels as low as in suburban communities," Bartholomew contended. By extending planning for the whole city to the detailed planning of neighborhoods, municipal officials could achieve economy and stability "where there is now waste and deterioration."[157] Bartholomew suggested the repair of buildings, the cleaning of vacant lots, the elimination of nonconforming uses or the total removal of inharmonious uses of land and buildings, the provision of additional open spaces, the closing of certain streets, the use of schools as community centers, and other measures now regularly included in municipal plans for the upgrading of neighborhoods not requiring extensive clearance and rebuilding.

The National Association of Real Estate Boards, however, soon proposed something more unusual than a neighborhood improvement association functioning as a municipally approved planning and rehabilitation group. Herbert U. Nelson, its executive vice-president, advocated the chartering of "city rebuilding companies" to undertake "a planned rebuilding of deficit areas in such a way as to make the most of their possibilities economically and socially." These enterprises would be quasi-public, quasi-private agencies, working under a definite city plan and under carefully outlined conditions to achieve the public purpose of eliminating the urban blight viewed as "destroying billions of dollars in real estate values," causing the "rapid ballooning of city areas," and resulting in "immense unnecessary waste of human energy and man-hours entailed in shuttling over miles of blighted areas from home to daily work." Operating as public utilities, the chartered companies would perhaps obtain equity capital from the federal government and the bulk of their funds from the issue of securities that the FHA might be authorized to insure. Under legislative safeguards, the companies would exercise the power of eminent domain to acquire properties in blighted areas. They would be authorized to lease or sell reconstructed or new improvements in the redevelopment area to private individuals or companies, accompanying the leases and deeds with covenants providing for the maintenance of the neighborhood amenities for a long period of years. Nelson thought that the companies should not be limited to the production of low-income housing but should be free to "create what would best fit local conditions and needs," including the essential neighborhood stores and service establishments.[158]

Here were the tentative outlines of the urban redevelopment statutes to be enacted in several states in the 1940s and the salient features of Title I of the Housing Act of 1949. Nelson foresaw under his proposal an annual building program of "at least three billions of dollars, one that would employ perhaps three million men"—a program comparable to the building of the railroads in the nineteenth century and the construction of automobile highways in the twentieth. Some of the suggestions traced their lineage to Hoover's Conference on Home Building and Home Ownership, and all indirectly expressed the general distaste of the real estate fraternity for the public housing program. The mixed economic activities envisaged by Nelson would give private enterprise a new lease on life, perhaps would restrict the growth of the public housing program, though little was said about that.

The Diversity of Instruction in Planning

The vision of cities replanned and extensively rebuilt indicated the need for an expansion of the planning profession, and this need in turn suggested that other institutions of higher education besides Harvard, the Massachusetts Institute of Technology, Cornell, and Columbia University should ready themselves to offer graduate programs in city planning. "We are convinced that the country needs many men to carry on our job—many more and (we hope) much better men," a committee appointed by the American City Planning Institute to consider professional education had pointed out in 1936. "It needs them bitterly and it needs them now."[159]

Did the words of the committee have the ring of crisis because American universities and colleges were reluctant to develop new courses in planning or to establish new graduate schools of planning? Hardly. Instruction in planning was widespread. There were few sections of the country in which planning had not become "a regular part of the curriculum of most important educational institutions," still another committee of planners and educators had found in 1938.[160]

Whatever difficulties there were perhaps could be traced to the very word "planning." What did it mean? "Planning is a 'portmanteau' word of the worst sort which holds too many ideas," Professor Carl Feiss of Columbia University complained. "The limits of its meaning are fuzzy."[161] Consequently, no two institutions approached the subject in the same way. At Harvard, Cornell, and the University of Illinois instruction in planning reflected its beginnings in departments of landscape architecture. The Massachusetts Institute of Technology emphasized the "large-scale planning aspects of the field." Columbia University stressed urban replanning and housing. The University of Nebraska and Kansas State College taught planning in their schools of engineering and tended to treat it as a branch of engineering. In many of the rural agricultural schools of the South and Middle West instruction in planning was influenced by the conservation policies of the federal and state governments, and particularly by the planning program of the Tennessee Valley Authority and the work of the National Resources Planning Board. Because of the diversity of courses and curricula and the many conceptions of planning held by the scores of professors interested in the subject, Feiss believed that the teaching of planning lacked both organization and direction and badly needed "the stabilizing influence" of a central organization specializing in problems of the field.

Far from being dismayed, other planners insisted that the great variety of approaches was "a sign of youth and growth, demonstrating the fact that here is a new field of education for which definite methods and traditions of teaching have not yet been developed."[162] Indeed, nothing would be more detrimental to the cause of planning than to cast instruction into a fixed pattern. Yet many could agree that certain disciplines, such as sociology, economics, political science, and law, should contribute heavily to the education of future planners and that interdepartmental cooperation in colleges and universities was essential if students of planning were to be properly educated. The vigor of the struggles to define the core of knowledge the planner should encompass and to state precisely the process of analysis and synthesis he should master augured well for the initiation of new educational ventures.

A vast increase in the literature of planning almost demanded revisions in old courses and innovations in curricula. The creative reexamination of national and urban problems stimulated by the economic and social crises of the decade had resulted in a flood of books, pamphlets, reports, and articles on urban and regional economies, internal migration, housing, social welfare, conservation, recreation, traffic and transportation, aviation, shopping centers, government, taxation, and planning in foreign nations. Besides the numerous reports of the National Resources Committee and the state planning boards, which together constituted a whole new division of literature on planning, there were hundreds of reports by city, county, and metropolitan planning agencies, many of them presenting analyses of types of data unavailable to planners in the 1920's. Books on housing voluminously augmented the resources of students and professors. Thomas Adams converted some of the lectures he had given at the Massachusetts Institute of Technology over a period of eleven years into an *Outline of Town and City Planning,* showing "how change in the scope and art of city planning has responded to change in the character and size of cities."[163] Lewis Mumford in *The Culture of Cities,* a volume complementing his *Technics and Civilization,* provided a new view of the city as the complex expression of technical and social forces and eloquently pleaded for the creation of a new social order transcending the mechanization that was everywhere in danger of brutalizing human life. Werner Hegemann's monumental *City Planning and Housing* was in reality a work on civic art and architecture—a reminder in an era dominated by economic and social considerations that the aesthetic aspects of the city should never be disregarded. For everyone who sought better understanding of the larger environment of his city or metropolis there were two impressive volumes: *American Regionalism,* by Howard Odum and Harry Estill Moore, and Odum's *Southern Regions of the United States.* No previous decade had produced a comparable wealth of material on urban areas and natural regions and their potentialities for meeting a greater range of human needs.

If the prospect of utilizing all this new knowledge as readily outside the classroom as in it now seemed somewhat dim because of the outbreak of another war, in time all of it would surely be of inestimable value. In the aggregate it testified to the capacity of men and women in many professions and businesses to unlearn fallacious beliefs and accept new ideas, new goals, new techniques. Embedded in it was an agenda for the postwar years if not for the immediate future. The city planning movement had come through the ordeal of depression and recession with an enlarged outlook and broader opportunities for public service.

CHAPTER 6

DEFENSE, WAR, AND THE
STRUGGLE AGAINST BLIGHT

The City Vulnerable

Until the spring of 1940, when Nazi armies quickly occupied Denmark and Norway, overran the Netherlands, Belgium, and Luxemburg, and imposed a humiliating armistice on the French, millions of Americans clung to the hope of not being drawn into the war. Marked by the scars of the great depression, haunted by the follies of the twenties, the United States had problems of its own. More than 8,000,000 Americans were still unemployed. Thousands of migrants from the midcontinental Dust Bowl lived in roadside squatter camps or cheap auto and trailer camps or at best in one-room shacks on the outskirts of Los Angeles, Oakland, Fresno, and other California cities. Not much low-rent public housing had yet replaced the slums and blighted areas surveyed by relief workers in cities throughout the nation in the early years of the New Deal. And chambers of commerce in metropolitan centers feared, as well they might, that the suburbs were gaining at the expense of the parent city.

In April, the very month in which the Bureau of the Census began the nationwide enumeration that was to confirm these apprehensions, the Urban Land Institute, a new and autonomous offshoot of the National Association of Real Estate Boards, published a small pamphlet summarizing the causes of "decentralization" in 221 cities and warning that if the trend continued, cities would face financial ruin. The Institute viewed the close-knit center of the typical city as a nexus without which "much of what we now prize as civilization" could not survive. The downtown areas contained "all the institutions which hold the savings of the public" and much of the retail business structure of the nation. Let these centers erode and cities would become not only less efficient but even less livable. "The cure for the ills of the city is not escape from the city," the Institute asserted, but "new conceptions in community building and city planning"—new conceptions acknowledging that "the social and sociological requirements of people are quite as important as economic considerations."[1]

In various localities there were signs of a growing desire to meet the challenge of dispersion vigorously and imaginatively. In Cincinnati the staff of the city planning commission proposed alternative plans for relocating railroad tracks and yards of the central riverfront and generally improving this old area in which land values had declined from 50 to 65 per cent in less than twenty years. The leaders of the City Planning Association in Buffalo sketched a picture of a central business district rejuvenated with new stores and freed of traffic congestion by arterial bypasses. With the right kind of advertising and a program for better housing, neighborhood rehabilitation, and other public improvements, people might even be encouraged to live in Buffalo instead of the suburbs. In Atlanta, where more than half the dwellings were substandard or unfit for decent living, the public housing authority looked forward to a fifteen-year effort to rehouse families living in hovels. Its president, Charles F. Palmer, urged the city to enact and enforce a modern housing code and to "get going with better planning, so as to ease traffic flow, open up tightly congested centers, and relieve the drab appearance of large segments of our city."[2]

But the shattering events abroad raised doubts about the development of forward-looking community programs. Could the increasing threat to American safety be ignored? And if it were acknowledged, could domestic issues any longer receive chief consideration? Even as France fell, the president of the National Conference of Social Work, Grace L. Coyle, told her fellow social workers that "the most serious fifth column which has penetrated within our gates is the malnutrition of our population, the frustration and despair of our unemployed, the racial inequalities and antagonisms heightened by economic tensions, and the inhuman cynicism of those among us who can realize these conditions without attempting to remedy them."[3] So much cried to be done to create a better America that civic leaders and liberals could scarcely accept the thought of foresaking the battle against social injustices, giving up the struggle against decentralization and blight, and focusing their attention on "the emergency of national defense."

Must they, indeed, shift course? The National Defense Advisory Commission announced that the nation must train and equip an army of 2,000,000 men, build a two-ocean navy, and create an air force of 25,000 planes (later 50,000). If the very figures did not sound the death knell of familiar civic endeavor, then what did they portend?

"We can plan for peace as well as for war," Charles E. Merriam, vice-chairman of the National Resources Planning Board, assured the city planners of the nation when they gathered in San Francisco on July 8 for their annual national conference. "We can solve the basic problem of national production, the problem of unemployment, the problem of social security, if we have the will and vision to make a common effort worthy of the emergency in which we find ourselves." He reminded his audience that the American economy was not a closed one, that the people could increase their collective income of seventy to eighty billion dollars or some higher figure, "within the framework of free industry and free government." He foresaw the United States coming "triumphant through this the greatest ordeal of modern times—triumphant not merely in a material or in a military sense, but triumphant in the higher and finer values. . . ."[4]

Most of the participants in the conference so strongly shared Merriam's faith in America's ability to survive all tests that they did not even allude to the war. They spoke of county planning in California, the use of zoning as an instrument of planning, the development of industry in the Pacific Northwest, the use of tax-abandoned land, public education for planning, highways and transportation, and architectural control. Noting that "our cities have, to put it bluntly, almost stopped growing," Rexford G. Tugwell, chairman of the New York City Planning Commission, declared that in the future "either we are going to have to bring the population back from the suburbs or we are going to have to allow the city itself to be ruined."[5] He challenged his hearers to "create suburbs within the city instead of outside."[6] But Tracy Augur, mindful of the bombing of European cities, suggested that "the sheer vulnerability of great cities may force us as a matter of public policy to decentralize into communities of less tempting bulk."[7] If, to parry the threat of conflagrations, it should become necessary to build fire-resisting houses and arrange them in neighborhood cells with belts of open space in between, there was some comfort in the thought that the low building density would promote a better organization of peacetime life. "And if perchance," Augur said, "the very horror of the thought of New York, Chicago or San Francisco subjected to a rain of shells impels us to a redistribution of these over-grown metropolises on some saner pattern, let not the tears that we may shed over the loss of long cherished bigness wholly blot our vision to the fact that war will thus have served at least one constructive purpose."[8]

Augur's main point, however, was that whether the cities of the United States were faced with the unaccustomed blight of war or the customary blights of peace, the nation could not afford to leave the determination of its urban structure to the "hit-or-miss processes of individual enter-prise." The future of cities was the public's business. Unfortunately, the nation did not have the necessary federal, state, or even local govern-mental machinery to meet the challenge of urban reorganization. Still, only seven years earlier, it had had little governmental machinery for tackling the housing problem, whereas now it had a great deal. Though the machinery of government was not so readily fabricated as the ma-chinery of industrial production, its creation was not a hopeless task. Augur expected that a still young nation could fashion it, and like most liberals, he discounted all the "grave talk" about mortgaging the country's future to pay for housing and urban rehabilitation as "pure bunk." "Sup-pose," he asked, "that it should cost twenty billion dollars to provide public housing for the families that need it, as our [United States] Chamber of Commerce committee estimates with such obvious alarm? What if it should cost a hundred billions more of private funds to complete the process and really put the nation's cities on a more modern footing?"[9] The only thing that need concern Americans, he concluded, was that they must get their money's worth.

These were brave words, but they revealed that it was as difficult for Augur to face the realities of the new defense program as for others who were accustomed to planning in a peaceful world. He and his fellow planners had scarcely left San Francisco when the preliminary phase of the Battle of Britain began — intermittent attacks on coastal targets and convoys. In mid-August the German air assault reached furious in-tensity, evoking from Winston Churchill his memorable praise of the Royal Air Force: "Never in the field of human conflict was so much owed by so many to so few."[10] London became the chief target in September, and as American planners listened to the news broadcasts and read the front pages, they could not but wonder whether decentralization, unguided as it had been, might not prove a blessing if Britain succumbed and Hitler hurled his Luftwaffe at this country.

Ordeals in the Arsenals of Democracy

Now no longer emotionally neutral, though still officially not at war with Germany and her ally Italy, the United States rapidly stepped up defense activities. Into Washington poured petitions from cities all over the country for airplane factories, munitions plants, and training centers, sometimes on the theory that any establishment which would reduce local unemployment would be a boon. But older men who remembered the crippling effects of housing shortages in many production areas in the First World War warned against industrial expansion in areas with limited housing vacancies. Some city engineers foresaw at once that new defense housing would increase municipal expenses for the installation of sewers, water mains, street paving, and storm drains. Walter Blucher, executive director of the American Society of Planning Officials, wondered whether the planners were thinking about such things. "Planners should know to what extent a housing development will interfere with a highway program or vice versa, or whether particular areas are suited for industrial expansion or development," he advised. "They should also have some knowledge of resources available in the area, both physical and human."[11] Especially, they should know whether projects proposed for emergency use would be of value in the years of peace. If planning meant anything at all, it meant determining what information would be needed, what assistance could be given, and taking an active part in planning defense projects.

Among the first city planning agencies to cooperate with a local committee on national defense was the Board of Public Land Commissioners in Milwaukee. Charles B. Bennett, director of planning, and his staff prepared a report listing all local industries and providing detailed information on labor supply, housing vacancies and rentals, vacant lots available for residential and industrial purposes, and vacant industrial plants and the rail and water transportation serving them. Other planning departments, drawing upon data acquired in the course of various studies or supplementing readily available information with new investigations, hastened to assist municipal officials and federal representatives in selecting sites for defense plants, housing projects, and airports.

At the suggestion of the National Defense Council, governors of many states designated state planning boards as the fact-finding agencies of state defense councils. Particularly active immediately were the planning boards in New York, California, Kansas, Arkansas, Tennessee, and Virginia. The New York and Kansas boards made surveys of idle plant facilities and production capacity, in addition to compiling directories of manufacturing establishments willing to aid the defense effort. The California, Tennessee, and Virginia planning agencies conducted special research for the state defense councils, while the Arkansas State Planning Board set up special defense committees to examine manpower, manufacturing plants, transportation facilities, and agricultural, forest, and mineral resources.

Some communities in which there had never been any planning, and in which huge new industrial plants were suddenly constructed, endured conditions as chaotic as if they had suffered enemy attack. Charlestown, Indiana, was an example. A sleepy town of 936 inhabitants before the Battle of Britain began, it presently accommodated 2,500 persons, not to mention hundreds of families living in trailers. Instead of one modest beanery, it soon had fourteen cafes and restaurants. Served by a single drugstore in July, it had three by December. This burgeoning of enterprise resulted from the establishment of a $74,000,000 smokeless powder plant of the E. I. du Pont de Nemours and Company and the construction of an $18,000,000 bag-loading plant by a subsidiary of the Goodyear Tire and Rubber Company. Overwhelmed by the growth thrust upon it, Charlestown appealed to the State Defense Council of Indiana for assistance. The first step taken by James E. Zachary, the man sent to help the town board, was to engage Ladislas Segoe, of Cincinnati, to draft a zoning ordinance to regulate the location of the many new structures being built. Next a building code was adopted, ending the conversion of garages into living quarters. Then traffic regulations were put into effect, and in due time provisions were made for collecting garbage and rubbish, instituting mail delivery, offering a recreation program, expanding educational services, and in other ways transforming a village into a city.

Not even a long-time planning program and a city plan based on earlier plans prepared by John Nolen could save San Diego from the disruptions feared by cities called upon to become the "arsenals of democracy." For many years a West Coast naval base, San Diego in the late thirties had also begun to develop as an aircraft center. A few months after the United States inaugurated its defense program, San Diego's four aircraft companies had contracts totaling $332,000,000—more than twice the total assessed valuation of the city—and were employing more than 15,000 workers. Postal authorities, the San Diego Chamber of Commerce, and the city planning commission variously estimated the population increase from April to October, 1940, at 15,000 to 30,000 persons, but looked upon these newcomers as merely the vanguard of still larger numbers yet to arrive. Expansion plans of the Army, the Navy, and the aircraft companies indicated that the community would have to absorb and house 45,500 persons in the next eight months, in addition to some 16,000 men who would be housed in barracks and camps. So great was the alarm of ultraconservative citizens over this mushrooming growth that they prophesied that San Diego in later years would become a ghost town, with the vast aircraft plants standing empty and the sea breezes whistling through their broken windows. Optimists, on the other hand, predicted that San Diego would surpass Los Angeles and become the leading city of the Pacific Coast. Glenn A. Rick, then "planning engineer" of the city, soberly hoped that the huge emergency appropriations being spent in the area could be turned into permanent good for the city.[12] He advised the city planning commission to request the National Resources Planning Board, through the California State Planning Board, for the assistance of planning consultants. He and his staff set to work at once to fit new housing projects, street improvements, and industrial plants into the long-range development plan of the municipality, though not always with success.

Far from satisfactory were the planning commission's relations with the Public Buildings Administration and the Federal Works Agency, two of the several agencies entrusted with building defense projects. After Rick left to become director of planning for Los Angeles, the former agency selected a site for 3,000 homes in an area as yet undeveloped, to the north on Linda Vista Mesa. The area was served by a single ten-inch water main whose entire capacity was to be made available to an Army camp. There were no other facilities, and the nearest subcenter was at least five miles from the property. Had city planners and other officials been consulted, Lottie L. Crawford, the president of the planning commission, testified later before a Congressional investigating committee, the development could have been placed where all facilities were already available. "A new water main must be run to this property," she pointed out, "a complete sewer system must be installed, schools must be built, police and fire arrangements, garbage collection and all such facilities must be built for this property; so the original cost of the land is a very small proportion of what [the total] will be when these necessary facilities are added. . . ."[13]

Visiting the project after it had come into being, Walter Blucher found that the only approach to it was by way of an inadequate street. He saw no stores, no sidewalks, not a single developed recreational area, no schools. Children studied in 120 dwelling units used for school purposes and played in the streets. Garbage and rubbish collection were inadequate. But the Linda Vista project was only one of several that caused problems for the city. Mrs. Crawford mentioned that the Public Buildings

Administration also built dormitories near Old Town with disregard for the city plan and that the Federal Works Agency, brushing aside a request of the city council, selected a site for a thousand demountable homes in an area not approved by the city.

The tribulations of San Diego and Charlestown were matched in more than a hundred other communities as America euphemistically cloaked its preparations for war under the term "defense." Almost none of the coastal cities in which there were naval establishments, supply depots, and shipyards had sufficient housing to accommodate the hordes of workers and enlisted men converging upon them. Inland cities selected as the sites for new munitions plants, aircraft factories, and Army training centers were similarly short of housing. Appointed Defense Housing Coordinator by the Advisory Commission to the Council of National Defense, Charles F. Palmer, of Atlanta, moved quickly to obtain federal funds for scores of new projects: $10,000,000 from the President's Emergency Funds in August, 1940; $100,000,000 from the Congress in September for housing to be constructed for the Army, Navy, and Maritime Commission; $150,000,000 from the Congress in October under the Lanham Act for public defense-housing. By the end of January, 1941, funds had been allocated for the construction of some 68,000 family units in 125 localities, yet the emergency housing program had barely begun. Under later amendments to the Lanham Act and related laws, more than 900,000 public war-housing accommodations would be built, and each project would pose innumerable problems for the city in which it was situated.

The ordeal of shifting from a peacetime to a defense economy revealed alarming deficiencies in the nation's physical facilities. Although most of the strategic network of highways serving normal commerce and travel was suited for defense purposes, Federal Works Commissioner John M. Carmody estimated that approximately every thirty-five miles along all major routes there was a bridge too weak to carry the standard truck loading—a gross weight of fifteen tons. Eighteen hundred such bridges constituted hazards to the movement of raw materials, troops, and war supplies. Assistant Secretary of Commerce Robert H. Hinkley reported that fifty-three cities had airports so inadequate that transport planes could not use them. Instead of the 185 airports then capable of accommodating large planes, the nation needed dozens more, planned to serve military as well as civilian needs and to fit into a comprehensive plan of the Civil Aeronautics Authority for new construction or improvement of almost 4,000 airports. So little were the requirements of aviation understood that there was little uniformity among airport protective regulations, and even some great metropolitan centers had regulations that did not meet the requirements for instrument landings specified by the CAA. Many cities still attempted to protect the approaches to their airports with special building-height regulations of a type declared unconstitutional by a Maryland court. The Los Angeles County Regional Planning Commission pointed out that the needs of aviation could be satisfied only if airports were planned as integral parts of the urban area and protected by comprehensive zoning.

Besides disclosing the inadequacies of housing, highways, and airports, the defense effort exposed the general lack of foresight in city after city—the failure to think ahead and plan, to provide good public transportation and adequate water supply and sewer systems, to budget municipal expenditures systematically, to ally all departments of local government in the process of guiding development. The stringencies of a decade of depression could not always be offered as a sufficient excuse for poor performance. In a volume entitled *The Planning Function in Urban Government*, Robert A. Walker attributed the general ineffectiveness of city planning to the character of planning commissions as autonomous boards. Regarded by city officials either as groups of well-meaning amateurs or as holier-than-thou critics intent on embarrassing politicians, most commissions limped along with inadequate funds to do the long-range planning job expected of them. Few even utilized the advisory powers they possessed. Citing the suggestion of the Urbanism Committee that city planning "must gain for itself a place in the structure of government where it will be closer to the local legislative body, the chief executive and the administrative departments,"[14] Walker contended that the planning agency would be most likely to perform its function satisfactorily if it were made immediately responsible to the chief executive, the one official preeminently charged with taking an overall view of urban government, with coordinating its various activities, and with planning an integrated future program.

Even though many members of the planning profession did not accept Walker's view of city planning as exclusively an administrative function, a shift of opinion was taking place which foreshadowed less dependence of planning agencies upon consultants for the preparation of the long-range plan, the cultivation of closer working relations with administrators and policy makers, and greater influence of planning staffs and planning commissioners on decisions affecting urban development. The prospect of war and the drafting of men for military service, however, clouded hopes that planning agencies could appreciably increase their staffs in the near future and win a stronger position in city or county government. An indication that planning eventually would probably gain greater respect in administrative and legislative circles was a textbook published by the International City Managers' Association six months after the appearance of Walker's book. *Local Planning Administration,* destined to become a classic in planning literature and to be issued in revised editions in 1948, 1959, and 1968, went part way toward embracing Walker's thesis. A chapter on the organization of city planning stated:

> While a very large segment of the field of the planning agency is on the administrative level of planning, a large and perhaps even more important segment lies on the policy-making level. If local planning is to be fully and beneficially effective, it must have influence on both policy and administrative decisions. Under the form of local government where the administrative and policy-determining or legislative functions are separated, as under a council-manager form, the planning staff agency should be so placed, it seems, that its advice on the overall and long-term community developmental aspects of matters under consideration be directly available to, and may be taken fully into account by, both the chief administrator and the council. Under such a form of government, the planning staff agency should desirably be so placed as to be responsible to both.[15]

The authors of the chapter—Walter Blucher wrote the original draft and Ladislas Segoe revised and edited the entire volume—believed that this arrangement would result in closer collaboration between the chief administrator and his departments and the planning agency and would minimize, if not obviate, possible friction and antagonism. The planning agency, however, would still be able to submit its advice directly to the legislative group, so that long-term, overall considerations would be more adequately available to it than if transmitted by the chief administrator.

Conceding that there was little experience to substantiate the "correctness" of various arrangements, the authors expressed their belief in the desirability of "experimentation at this stage in the evolution of local planning." If the history of the development of other municipal functions was an indication, "the more integrated form of planning organization and its appropriate place under various forms of local government may be expected gradually to evolve with further advances in local planning and of local government organization."[16]

Proposals for Curing the Ills of the City

Cities caught up in the defense program either attempted to make use of such planning as had been done or they tried spur-of-the-moment planning—or they made no pretense of planning at all and reaped a harvest of mistakes. Another class of cities, not yet hard pressed by the demands of defense or still able, because of large size, to take the defense build-up in stride, suffered a different kind of municipal anxiety known as "census jitters." When, toward the end of August, 1940, the Bureau of the Census began releasing preliminary figures of the enumeration made in the spring, 62 of 274 cities included in one of the first reports learned that they had lost population in the past decade. Among them were such prominent cities as Akron, Cleveland, Newark, Philadelphia, Pittsburgh, St. Louis, San Francisco, Schenectady, Toledo, Wheeling, and Youngstown. Another report in September, listing 58 cities, showed 15 with losses. In a city with a slight decrease the usual reaction of the local chamber of commerce was to demand a recount or to insist that the census takers had failed to count everyone. In Schenectady, for instance, the municipality and a committee of the chamber of commerce enlisted the aid of newspapers and local radio stations in a drive to register all families who had been missed by the enumerators. The campaign disclosed 635 families, representing approximately 2,500 persons, who had been overlooked, and though these residents reduced the reported loss from 9,466 to less than 7,000, Schenectady felt that it was slipping. A final tally removed San Francisco from the list of declining cities and gave it a token gain of 634 persons, but its pride was nevertheless wounded and its leading citizens realized that steps must be taken to combat the lure of the suburbs. Like all unhappy cities that had exported population to outlying communities, San Francisco had blighted areas that sapped its municipal treasury and victimized many of its citizens. The census figures intensified interest in redeveloping these areas.

Complacency was also shattered in cities whose population gains were only a few thousand in comparison with gains of many thousands in the surrounding metropolitan district. Urban growth in the United States as a whole had been only 7.9 per cent in the 1930s, and the proportion of Americans living in cities had increased only three-tenths of one per cent (from 56.2 per cent to 56.5 per cent), but metropolitan areas outside some central cities had enjoyed substantial or even spectacular increases. Detroit had a gain within the city of 3.5 per cent, whereas the outlying area grew 25.4 per cent. Portland, Oregon, increased 1.2 per cent, the enveloping ring of communities 31.3 per cent. Milwaukee augmented its population by 1.6 per cent, but the newer municipalities beyond its borders together gained 22.8 per cent. The area outside Chicago increased 11.5 per cent, the city itself only 0.6 per cent. Even Los Angeles, one of the fastest growing big cities, gained proportionately less than the district outside the city—21.5 per cent compared with 29.6 per cent. The message of the census was clear to mayors and councilmen in all these centers that had developed civic patriotism on the expectation of large increases: plan, conserve, redevelop. But the defense program threatened not only to aggravate housing shortages and multiply substandard units but also to halt slum clearance and public housing.

At the annual meeting of the United States Conference of Mayors, held in New York in the latter part of September, 1940, the political spokesmen of the cities acclaimed the program of the United States Housing Authority, urged its immediate expansion, and favored the construction of defense projects by municipal housing authorities as the best means of integrating emergency housing with permanent community development.

Though the attack on urban decay was to be blunted by defense activities and later by war, officials of central cities now realized that remedial action had become a permanent item on the municipal agenda. Three methods of approaching the problem of slums and blight had emerged, only one of which — public housing — had received wide legislative sanction and had produced results. A second contemplated providing incentives for limited-dividend corporations to undertake redevelopment in badly deteriorated areas, whereas the third envisaged concerted public and private action to stem the ravages of time and neglect in declining but not hopelessly rundown neighborhoods. Public and private interests in the state of New York were attempting to work out satisfactory legislation to encourage private redevelopment. The principal proponent of cooperative programs to rescue shabby but still sound middle-class neighborhoods was the Federal Home Loan Bank Board, which had conducted a pilot study in the Waverly area of Baltimore with the assistance of several other federal agencies, the Housing Authority of the City of Baltimore, a neighborhood conservation league, and an advisory committee.

These collaborating agencies prescribed "a simple, preventive remedy" called "organized neighborhood housekeeping" to arrest the almost imperceptible but relentless downward trend in typical older residential areas. The proposed treatment of Waverly, for example, was compounded of "conservation," street adjustments, and "concerted and continued community effort."[17] It included the structural rehabilitation of all depreciated buildings, the development of interior play areas in nine blocks to compensate for a marked deficiency in public recreational space, the improvement of street lighting, the reduction of areas zoned for commercial purposes, the eventual elimination of nonconforming land utilization, and some street widenings as well as the opening and closing of a few streets.

The recommended program had one outstanding shortcoming: it was not dramatic. Only one building in the whole Waverly area warranted demolition. How could interest in a very gradual upgrading of such an area be sustained? The Home Loan Bank Board and its allies hoped that "a more complete understanding of the direct cost of neighborhood decay and a clearer conception of the economic value of neighborhood conservation, in terms of the taxpayer's dollar, may one day inspire the establishment, in every large city, of a 'Department of Conservation' whose sole function will be, by precept, example, and inspirational activity, to promote community stabilization projects in potentially and partially depreciated sections throughout the city."[18]

This proposal was, however, too farsighted for the time. Because the problem of incipient blight seemed much less critical than the economic stagnation, leprous decay, and human disorganization associated with badly blighted areas, most public and private groups concerned with the urban environment concentrated their attention on providing the legislative and financial means of clearing and rebuilding the focal points of urban deterioration, especially after New York State succeeded in enacting a redevelopment law that suggested a promising line of attack.

In 1941 the New York legislature revised a vetoed measure of the previous year to permit private urban redevelopment corporations to exercise the power of condemnation after they had acquired 51 per cent (rather than 60 per cent) of the properties, by area and value, in a project site. In addition, the lawmakers offered a special inducement to private enterprise to undertake redevelopment schemes—a freeze of the assessed value of a blighted area for ten years at a figure not above that prior to reconstruction; in other words, a subsidy amounting to the difference between what the community might expect in taxes on a new development and the revenues it had been receiving from obsolete and dilapidated structures. This enticement was offset somewhat by a limitation of annual profit to 5 per cent of the development cost and by various regulations designed to protect the public interest. A redevelopment corporation, for instance, was required to obtain the approval of its rebuilding plan by the local planning agency, as well as to submit its proposed financing, fees, sales or leases, and personnel to the scrutiny of a local supervising agency. Compliance with the building and planning standards prescribed by the planning or supervisory agency was mandatory. The corporation had, moreover, to show that adequate rehousing would be available for persons displaced by clearance operations. And unless it proceeded with dispatch and won approval of its plan within a year after being established, all the special rights granted by the legislation terminated.

Other state legislatures meanwhile had also been considering bills to aid private redevelopment corporations. Michigan lawmakers approved a statute with substantially the same provisions as the New York law but limited its applicability to Detroit. In Utah and California bills resembling both the New York and Michigan laws failed of passage. Redevelopment legislation adopted in Illinois differed in several respects from the New York act, particularly in a more stringent requirement that private corporations acquire 60 per cent of an area before being permitted to exercise the power of eminent domain. Nor did the Illinois legislators sugar their statute with tax concessions or public financial assistance, though they refrained from limiting corporate profits. Supervisory functions were vested in a five-man redevelopment commission appointed by the municipality, but the commission could not approve a redevelopment scheme unless the local planning agency had first certified it for conformity with the long-range city plan.

These state enactments quickly stimulated city planning departments to launch exploratory studies indicating how blighted areas could be replanned and developed anew. *Rebuilding Old Chicago,* for example, presented illustrative schemes of the Chicago Plan Commission for reorganizing and reconstructing degenerating neighborhoods relatively close to the Loop on the north, west, and south sides of the city. But Theodore T. McCrosky, executive director of the commission, appreciated the complexity of the problem of urban blight too much to expect any miracles as a result of the passage of the Illinois Neighborhood Redevelopment Corporation Law. He also realized that the system of priorities of building materials necessitated by the defense program probably excluded any possibility of rebuilding until after the war, though he acknowledged that the city should be ready with plans for the postwar era. In itself, however, the new legislation did not promise to improve the housing conditions of the people who would be most affected by redevelopment—those living in the deteriorated areas. The planning director observed,

> The rents which must be charged for new housing built by private enterprise are higher than a large part of the people living in blighted areas can afford. Only very low income families are eligible for public housing projects, and there remains an in-between group for which the only homes now available are in existing structures. If this group is to be provided with better dwellings, there would have to be either extensive remodeling of old structures or new homes built through some type of governmental collaboration with private enterprise, which has still to be explored and given legislative form.[19]

Suggestions for meeting this knotty problem appeared in *A Handbook on Urban Redevelopment for Cities in the United States,* issued by the Federal Housing Administration a month after *Rebuilding Old Chicago* was published. Although the handbook did not propose specific legislation, it did state that most municipalities lacked the financial resources to undertake rehabilitation and redevelopment and that three kinds of federal aid might be extended to them: aid in acquiring land and existing structures for rehabilitation and redevelopment; aid in financing public improvements in areas designated for reconditioning or rebuilding; and aid in the form of mortgage insurance designed to assist private redevelopment corporations in obtaining credit on favorable terms. Prepared under the direction of Earle S. Draper, assistant administrator of FHA, and written mainly by Frederick Bigger, chairman of the Pittsburgh City Planning Commission, the handbook outlined a metropolitan approach to the problem of urban deterioration, emphasizing the importance of modernizing neighborhoods in the vicinity of redevelopment projects as well as the importance of providing suitable accommodations for families in every income group.

In a pamphlet published by the National Planning Association, Guy Greer, the senior economist of the board of governors of the Federal Reserve System, and Alvin H. Hansen, professor of economics at Harvard University, not only endorsed the idea of federal aid but also proposed the establishment of a federal agency "charged with the direction (or at any rate the supervision) of all activities of the Government having to do with the structure of urban communities."[20] Here again was the conception of a department that would be to the urban economy what the Department of Agriculture had long been to the rural economy — essentially today's Department of Housing and Urban Development. Greer and Hansen thought of the urban agency as a consolidation of numerous housing agencies and other branches of the federal government concerned mainly with urban problems. It would, they indicated, work closely with a central agency of the Executive Office of the President whose chief function would be to outline "the broad framework, both national and regional, within which the urban planning itself would be done."[21] The proper agency appeared to be the National Resources Planning Board, perhaps reorganized and developed to meet future needs. In addition to making loans or grants of federal funds for the elimination of slums and blighted areas, the new urban organization would extend technical aid to the planning agencies of the urban communities. Further, it would approve such plans as were worked out in a satisfactory manner — a proposal similar to an FHA suggestion that any federal legislation authorizing financial aid for redevelopment should provide for "review of local master plans . . . with respect to conformance to general standards and scope."[22] Greer and Hansen emphasized, however, that the initial and principal responsibility for urban planning should lie with the urban communities themselves rather than the federal government.

Assuming that properly constituted federal and local agencies could be created, the two authors proposed a three-sided attack on the housing problem, including research and experimentation leading to drastic reform of the backward residential construction industry ("a small-scale handicraft business which hardly deserves to be called an industry at all");[23] continuance of federal aids to home ownership and special stimulation of the production, by private enterprise, of housing for rent to families of moderate-to-low income; and reexamination and revival of the public housing program, which since late 1940 had been almost at a stand still because of the refusal of Congress to appropriate any additional funds.

Among other things, the economists suggested that large investors in rental housing—life insurance companies, savings banks, trust estates, and foundations—should be protected against loss and should be guaranteed even a very low return of, say, 2 per cent for a period of "something like thirty years."[24] Such yield insurance, they believed, would be an incentive for repair and modernization of structures in partially blighted neighborhoods as well as for construction of new dwellings in clearance areas. They were not afraid to face the prospect that the federal government might be compelled to shoulder the greater part of the heavy financial burden of acquiring over-valued properties in deteriorated areas, in order that locatlities might make them available for new uses at ground rents or sales prices sufficiently favorable to attract private enterprise, or perhaps public agencies such as housing authorities. This federal contribution would be the public cost of "a job of civic sanitation—of cleaning up the social and economic mess left by past generations, for which only society as a whole can be held mainly to blame."[25]

As Hansen was consultant to the National Resources Planning Board at the time he and Greer were writing their pamphlet, some of the proposals it contained found their way, in almost indentical language, into the board's annual report on national resources development, transmitted to the President in December, 1941. Thus for the first time a federal agency put its stamp of approval on the idea that the threescore federal agencies offering significant aid to cities for housing, highways, recreation, and public works should be brought together in an urban affairs agency. On the touchier issue of federal financial contributions to "free" the land in redevelopment areas from the inflated assessed values rending it "sterile," the board's report discreetly stated that "Federal intervention is necessary, and its terms and conditions should be propounded."[26] Foreseeing that advances in agriculture would release at least 3,000,000 farm people to become urban dwellers, and that metropolitan areas, already crowded with almost half the national population, would become still larger, the board, too, called for comprehensive metropolitan planning and large-scale rebuilding of cities. "Post-war demands to put men and materials to work to rebuild cities cannot find us seeking postponement because master plans are not ready; on the other hand, it would be tragic to plunge into a series of unplanned public and private works. We must be in a position to bring to bear at the earliest possible date the available facts and the judgments of those who know their communities—officials, civic and social agencies, citizens— to produce at least rough sketches of the directions and forms which community development should take." Yet only 128 American cities of more than 30,000 population had "authorized this elaborate and time-consuming process."[27]

The board's long report said in detail some of the things a pamphlet entitled *After Defense — What?* said with brevity and urgency. Issued in August, 1941, when the German armies were overrunning the Ukraine and battering Smolensk in Hitler's long-planned invasion of Russia, this first of a series of popular tracts on postwar planning predicted that at the end of the war, perhaps in 1944, the United States would face the problem of transferring from 23,000,000 to 26,000,000 workers in war industries and 3,500,000 men in the armed services to peacetime activities. It challenged Americans to move from full employment for defense to full employment for peace without going through a low-employment slump, to establish new forms of social security, and to upbuild their country. In achieving full employment and adding to the national estate, local programs of public works would be closely related to programs for new housing and the redevelopment of blighted areas and for the rebuilding of "terminal facilities adapted to modern requirements for interchange among rail, highway, waterway, and air carriers, and between terminals and markets."[28]

"A great and continuing volume of economic activity and employment" after the war was also the goal espoused by the Urban Land Institute in formulating yet another important group of proposals for rebuilding cities. As much discussed as the FHA handbook and the Greer-Hansen pamphlet, the Institute's legislative program for reshaping urban areas embraced ideas that had been considered by the Committee on Housing and Blighted Areas of the National Association of Real Estate Boards for many months. Set forth in a booklet published in February, 1942, and later in an outline, the program called for the establishment of local metropolitan land commissions which would receive from a Federal Urban Land Commission long-term loans at low interest rates for the acquisition of land. The local land commission would be empowered not only to make a master plan for the entire metropolitan area but also to do almost everything necessary to carry out the plan except actually erect buildings. That would be mainly the work of private enterprise. The commission would have the right to "buy, lease, rent, condemn, and sell land in blighted areas and other areas." It would set aside areas for public use and for the use of various local governments, as well as hold land in reserve. It would "enact specific regulations for zoning all land, regardless of existing zoning ordinances." It would replan land, approve the installation of public improvements, and "set aside areas for recreation which it might condemn and turn over to the local park boards or administration." Most astonishing of all, this powerful commission would even "acquire by purchase, lease, or condemnation lands now held by local units of government as may be made necessary for the carrying out of the master plan."[29]

The Federal Urban Land Commission would "have the right to make outright grants to local land commissions for the purpose of making master plans for their metropolitan areas," but a condition of the grants would be that plans must meet certain criteria.[30]

As evidence of its desire to prevent further blight and to arrest the wasteful spread of metropolitan areas, the Institute proposed to have the master plan itself embrace "minimum construction requirements and property standards for all construction within the metropolitan area" and a land acquisition plan that would indicate not only lands for redevelopment and for public use but also "land to be acquired as a reserve against premature urban development for ultimate disposal to either public or private use."[31]

It would be difficult to imagine a program for rebuilding cities that would arouse more opposition among local governments in metropolitan areas than this one, yet the Urban Land Institute's proposals were symptomatic of the innovative thought aroused by the plight of urban areas. Probably many realtors regarded the Institute's ideas as somewhat alarming, particularly the notion that a metropolitan commission might acquire peripheral land for the express purpose of prohibiting speculative development. Even among stauch believers in a free hand for private initiative, however, old ideas about the role of government were changing. The precedent of federal loans and grants for public housing, for example, had started a train of reasoning which enabled even conservatives to conceive of the national government as a redistributor of wealth (the Institute suggested "federal grants for public improvements which the local government could not wholly finance"[32]), a generous lender, the supporter of needed research, the upholder of standards, and the promoter of "civic sanitation" ventures that would have made a McKinley blanch. In ten years, ideas about federal intervention that had seemed radical when mentioned at Herbert Hoover's Conference on Home Building and Home Ownership had gained respectability. Greer and Hansen had no monopoly on the controversial recommendation that slum properties acquired at high prices should be leased or sold for new uses at far less, with the federal government absorbing the greater part of the loss. The shift in attitudes that had taken place foretold the enactment, if not while the war raged, then afterward, of legislation bringing the government at Washington into partnership with cities for the replanning and rebuilding of deteriorated areas and the redevelopment of even partially vacant districts blighted by faulty street patterns or poor drainage.

The Greer-Hansen pamphlet, the FHA handbook, the Urban Land

Institute's outline, and every other publication projecting a nationwide housing and redevelopment effort based on competent metropolitan planning posed the need for a large corps of city planners. Greer and Hansen pointed out, however, that "the number of technicians in the country capable of doing the job is limited."[33] They urged that the federal government assist in initiating a training program for city planners, possibly by financing institutes of urbanism in ten or a dozen universities at once. Periods of study might be supplemented by "actual work with neighboring city planning bodies, thus making use of the principle of 'in-service' training."[34]

American universities were becoming more aware of the growing demand for persons with degrees in city planning, but they had not yet felt any strong pressure to expand professional education. The year 1941 witnessed the inauguration of three new graduate programs in city planning, at the University of Michigan, the Illinois Institute of Technology, and the University of Washington. Seven institutions of higher education were now offering master's degrees in planning, though the newest in the field, unlike Harvard, Cornell, and the Massachusetts Institute of Technology, did not entrust instruction to a distinct department of city and regional planning. At the University of Michigan and the Illinois Institute of Technology the departments of architecture administered the new programs, while the program of the University of Michigan was under the direction of an interdepartmental committee. The launching of the three new programs hardly promised a substantial increase in the number of qualified city planners. Other universities also needed to establish graduate curricula in the next few years, but the war, casting a more ominous shadow over domestic concerns month by month and drawing an ever greater number of young men into the armed forces, deterred plans for new courses and new departments.

From Defense to A Shooting War

By the fall of 1941 the defense program had been under way less than a year and a half, yet in that brief time the number of Americans who had left their homes in search of new jobs or had been displaced by defense activities was greater than the entire migration from the Old World to American shores from the time of the voyage of the Mayflower to the outbreak of the Revolution. Almost 1,300,000 had left the farms, but so many more city dwellers had also joined treks to the 275 defense areas of the nation that rural folk were in the minority among mobile Americans.

Wherever the call had gone out for defense workers, there were housing shortages. Statistics on the number of recent arrivals added to payrolls in various cities indicated the magnitude of the problem. At Indianapolis there were 20,000 newcomers, at Wichita 15,000, in the Louisville area 5,500 production workers and 35,000 construction workers, in the Philadelphia metropolitan area 150,000 industrial workers, at Pittsburgh 30,000 workers, at Tacoma 10,000 building tradesmen and shipyard workers. People lived in anything they could find. At Gadsden, Alabama, newly arrived steel-workers occupied garages, barns, old store buildings, and shacks with dirt floors. At Abilene and Mineral Wells, Texas, men paid three dollars a day to rent cots in crowded tarpaper shacks with no sanitary facilities. In Jacksonville, Florida, some workers

81. Map of Pentagon and environs: in 1941 the appropriation of funds for constructing this building outside the District of Columbia brought protests from many groups and officials who feared that Congress was abandoning the long-range plan of Washington *(Architectural Record)*

took up shelter under palmetto leaves spread over rude frames. And at Corpus Christi, Texas, a crew of temporary workers slept in the open.

"This housing shortage hits almost exlusively people in the low-income groups," William Green, president of the American Federation of Labor, testified bitterly at a congressional hearing on internal migration.[35] In his opinon, the country was suffering in the defense emergency because it had underbuilt for more than a decade. But no peacetime housing program could have prevented shortages in cities and rural areas chosen as the locations of new munitions plants or training camps. Nor did shortages, even in large cities, affect only those needing a place to live. In its ramifications the housing crisis seemed to touch every aspect of urban development. Cities equipped with a general plan and reasonably good zoning and subdivision regulations were far better prepared to cope with it than those which had neglected long-range planning and had become bogged down in the details of zoning administration; but even commissions with capable staffs and city-wide plans encountered entirely unforeseen difficulties and were subjected to well-nigh irresistible pressures to sanction expedient solutions to problems with serious, long-term implications.

The defense effort set off, for instance, an extensive campaign to remodel or convert large, single-family residences into multiple dwellings for defense workers in congested centers. But the American Society of Planning Officials immediately recognized this expedient for alleviating the housing shortage as still another threat to the stability of cities. In an editorial in its monthly newsletter, executive director Blucher warned that most cities already had excessive areas zoned for two-family and multiple-family use. "To break down single-residence zoning, therefore, in order to permit the reconstrubtion of a few dwellings that might be used for defense workers is illogical, and such a movement should be resisted," he maintained. If any rezoning were to take place, there should be careful determination of the areas suitable for conversion, and the needs of the community should govern any alterations in the zoning ordinance. Probably the districts selected should be small, to prevent committing large areas to different patterns of use at the outset. "Everybody is for all-out defense," Blucher acknowledged, but he thought it made no sense to use defense as an excuse for causing "further degeneration of our cities." He suggested that federal agencies concerned with remodeling programs should provide their own standards to protect communities and neighborhoods from irreparable damage.[36]

Many federal representatives, however, were far more intent on expediting the defense program than on conserving cities. Their arguments for relaxation of regulations and alteration of long-accepted plans sometimes carried the implication, moveover, that local officials were wanting in patriotism if they did not yield. A city planner who tried to hold the line risked getting a reputation for being uncooperative and recalcitrant, but if he needed courage to resist pressures during the defense period, he needed the fortitude of a hero after the Japanese bombed Pearl Harbor.

From millions of radios rose President Roosevelt's voice, solemnly declaring, "We are now in this war. We are all in it all the way. Every single man, woman, and child is a partner in the most tremendous undertaking of our American history. We must share together the bad news and the good news, the defeats and the victories—the changing fortunes of war."[37] The chief executive called for the production of 60,000 planes, 45,000 tanks, 20,000 antiaircraft guns, and 8,000,000 tons of ships in 1942.

Swiftly the nation learned what it meant to be at war. After January, 1942, the automobile industry would manufacture no more passenger cars and would convert its largest plants to the production of aircraft, tanks, and guns. Tires and tubes would be rationed, because the country had in reserve only a year's supply of rubber and expected the Japanese to conquer southeast Asian territories from which it obtained 98 per cent of its rubber. There would be sharp curtailments of most civilian goods. But as yet the country had only begun to absorb the shocks of total mobilization for war. Each month brought new pronouncements calling for further sacrifices and saw the imposition of new restrictions, further cutbacks in consumer goods, the placement of larger and larger orders for bombers, ships, and tanks, and the intensification of military demands for faster retooling of plants and speedups in production.

In this hectic atmosphere Huber E. Smutz, the zoning administrator for Los Angeles, felt at times as if he were waging a war within a war, not against foreign enemies but against a special breed of Americans who scorned the law. Smutz functioned in somewhat the same capacity as a board of zoning appeals or adjustment, granting variances under certain limitations and procedures prescribed by the municipal code; but now he was besieged by applicants who had little understanding of the prerequisities for variances and were, in fact, seeking permission to carry on businesses clearly prohibited in particular zones. Smutz later told a meeting of the League of California Cities,

> Most of these applicants insisted that their matter was absolutely essential to winning the war—that they had to have their building permit, power connection permit or license right now without any foolishness about silly zoning requirements—that they could get letters from the Army, Navy, Air Corps or even in some cases from the President himself to show the importance of their proposal, and, anyway, what the heck good was our zoning going to be if the Japs started bombing our city or we lost the war, as we probably would if their plant couldn't expand or be established.[38]

Angered by Smutz's refusal to circumvent procedures established by ordinance, some of the unsuccessful applicants complained to city councilmen, and because one or two truly important matters had been delayed, a few of the councilmen concluded that zoning should be suspended for the duration. The city attorney and the more judicious councilmen, however, pointed out that if it were desirable for the zoning administrator to have more extensive jurisdiction and authority, the zoning regulations should be amended. The council therefore adopted an emergency ordinance permitting the administrator to grant variances, valid until six months after the war emergency, for businesses engaged in the manufacture of material essential to the war effort or providing services related to the war.

The solution of wartime zoning controversies worked out in Los Angeles served as an example to many municipalities, though there were others in which officials stretched the law by interpretation rather than amendment, endangering respect for regulations and weakening measures designed to safeguard the community against undesirable development and deterioration. Like the Los Angeles council, the city council of Portland, Oregon, a year later chose the wiser policy of taking official action to relax local zoning, housing, and construction ordinances, but also by resolution put everyone on notice that when the exigencies of the war program ceased, the council would "repeal said ordinance provision relaxing ordinary code requirements, establish the various city codes and ordinances to their normal provisions and exact strict compliance therewith."[39]

The revamping of zoning to facilitate activities essential to the war effort or to speed the conversion of older houses for multiple occupancy probably placed less strain on most city planning departments than the working out of transportation programs to insure the maintenance of war production schedules with the least possible diminution of the nation's limited rubber supply. Throughout the United States the long-term decline in mass transit services had left many of the larger centers with obsolescent equipment, infrequent schedules, and a curtailed force of transport workers. Then there were all the smaller towns and cities in which the situation was perhaps equally critical. In the summer of 1941 the Automobile Manufacturers Association, in cooperation with the Bureau of Public Roads and state highway departments, had made a survey which revealed that twenty-one hundred communities with populations ranging from 2,500 to 50,000 had dispensed with or had grown up without interurban mass-transportation systems of their own and were almost entirely dependent upon private cars for daily travel. In these communities lived 12,000,000 Americans, many employed in industries vital to the war effort. Now, as Nazi submarines lurked along the Atlantic shipping lanes, frequently sinking tankers and freighters within sight of coastal cities, scarcities of gasoline as well as of rubber threatened to impede transport and industrial operations, especially in the East. How to plan for maximum use of inadequate transit systems and for drastic reduction of travel by private automobile was a problem most planning departments found difficult in the extreme, because for years they had tended to concentrate on improving highways and had neglected plans for renewing mass transit.

For Seattle the rubber and gasoline shortages posed the ultimate in perplexities, ironically because the city *had* "modernized" its municipally owned transit system. The transportation commission had removed the last streetcars in 1941 and converted the entire system to rubber-tired trolley and motor coaches! If citizens progressively laid up their private automobiles, public transit with an average weekday capacity of 250,000 passengers would probably be called upon to transport an average daily load of 590,000 riders by October, 1942, and 790,000 by October, 1943. The airplane and shipbuilding industries had already attracted 140,000 newcomers to the city since 1940 and doubtless would require still more workers as the war effort accelerated. Unless federal authorities granted the commission priorities for more coaches and tires, Seattle would be severely handicapped as a major war-production center. At midyear of 1942 its officials had already tried all the emergency transportation measures suggested in a flood of reports from Washington, from state highway departments and state planning boards, and from private foundations, insurance companies, and transit agencies.

This torrent of publications outlined procedures for making transportation surveys, described proposals for staggering working hours to ease the congestion on highways and transit vehicles, discussed schemes for diverting car-riders to public carriers, and listed ways to promote group-riding programs. In effect, every report urged local war-transportation committees to analyze the total problem of movement—something that many planning commissions and city planners working with such committees had not actually done before. But now, under the necessity of making every tire, automobile, bus, and streetcar last as long as possible and serve the utmost number of people, planners who had not previously done so began to form an integrated conception of urban circulation and to consider using every means of locomotion, including walking, in the most efficient manner. Into their calculations entered with particular insistence the desirability of building additional housing within short distances of industrial plants and other centers of activity, and of locating new plants close to developed areas.

Mainly, however, their eyes were opened to new opportunities to improve street and highway systems, transit services, traffic control, and law enforcement. As they analyzed the data from questionnaries and traffic counts, and as they prepared new maps and plans, they perceived ways to develop more rational street patterns, eliminate traffic bottle-necks, open alternate routes to relieve congestion on heavily traveled highways, and create district parking lots from which riders could either join car pools or board busses or trains to work—a wartime expedient that was potent with suggestions for increasing the use of mass transit in the postwar era. From the transit officials with whom they cooperated, city planners gained greater appreciation of the importance of eliminating duplicate runs, improving methods of collecting fares, using skip stops, instituting express service, and developing adequate feeder routes. Though many of the plans they helped to devise embodied measures more appropriate to the emergency than to long-term situations, the wartime experience provided a new understanding of the possibilities of improving the movement of people and goods in urban areas. Even the best emergency plans failed, however, to solve some of the most serious problems, and had federal agencies not made available more tires and vehicles, as in Seattle, and aided cities in restoring old streetcars to service, large numbers of war workers would have had no means of getting to work. In the San Francisco Bay Area, for instance, the cities of Oakland, Berkeley, and Richmond eventually obtained old elevated-railway cars from New York City to transport workers to the Kaiser shipyards in Richmond.

Planners in coastal cities and in many inland cities as well discovered that the wartime transportation problem was closely related to civilian defense programs, particularly to plans for evacuating citizens from danger zones. Cleveland, Ohio, was one of the first metropolitan areas in the country to prepare a plan for removing people from districts considered prime targets in the event of air raids or other forms of attack. With the assistance of the staff of the Regional Association, the Cuyahoga County Council for Civilian Defense completed a map showing all "unsafe areas" of Greater Cleveland—areas within a mile of plants producing war materials, important railroad yards, utility plants, bridges, and certain residential sections of close-standing frame structures. But Walter Blucher pointed out in a newsletter of the American Society of Planning Officials that transporting evacuees was only part of the problem of protecting civilians. He urged that defense councils make inventories showing all available housing and public and semipublic facilities outside industrial centers, as well as studies indicating sites for new facilities, some of which, if actually built, might be used for recreation after the war. "If there are no attacks, if there is no evacuation and no need for additional facilities, our foresight will have lost us nothing," Blucher concluded.[40]

Elizabeth M. Herlihy, chairman of the Massachusetts State Planning Board, believed enemy attack so distinct a possibility that she cooperated fully with a Committee on Post-War Readjustment, headed by Professor Melvin T. Copeland of Harvard University, in developing recommendations for legislation providing for the reconstruction of areas devastated by heavy raids. The group proposed that the governor be authorized to issue an emergency order prohibiting any rebuilding in bombed sections for ninety days. He would then appoint a rehabilitation committee composed of public officials (one of whom would be the chairman of the state planning board) to determine at once the areas to which the order should apply, to fix the dates when local authorities would be allowed to grant building permits, to decide which plan for the use of the land should be used if conflicting plans were presented, and to prepare plans for acquiring any land needed for arterial routes or other public purposes. For-

82. Kaiser Shipyards at Richmond, California, in the Second World War
(Kaiser Industries Corporation)

tunately, the United States experienced no crises in which such proposed legislation would have been desirable, nor did most citizens, after the first month or two, fear air attacks or enemy landings even though few communities failed to organize civilian protection crops.

If, however, Japanese of German bombers had rained their "eggs" on some American war-production centers, they could hardly have caused more disruption in operations than resulted from certain initial miscalculations and lack of overall planning and coordination. Behind many of the so-called miracles of technological performance were appalling records of turnover in labor, ceaseless recruiting of new workers, inefficiency caused by low morale, absenteeism, and sickness, and social tensions destructive of individual and family welfare. Invariably, much of the human breakdown and friction was attributable to failure to provide adequate housing or transportation or both, and nowhere was this failure more glaring than at Willow Run in southeastern Michigan, which one federal housing official described as "the worst mess in the whole United States."[41] Yet in spite of the "mess," this mammoth plant of the Ford Motor Company—the assembly line was 5,450 feet long— produced 8,685 B-24 bombers in a little more than three and a half years. With better planning in Washington and on the local scene, though, it might have manufactured planes more rapidly and in even greater numbers.

Willow Run, twenty-eight miles from downtown Detroit and three miles from the small city of Ypsilanti, was planned as a defense industry which would employ from 50,000 to 100,000 workers. Both the federal government, which awarded the contract to the Ford Motor Company to produce bombers, and the company itself assumed that workers would live within a radius of thirty or forty miles from the plant and drive to work. But one week after the company began hiring production workers, the Japanese perpetrated their sneak attack on Pearl Harbor—and immediately the shortage of rubber loomed as a threat to all personal automobile travel. The State Highway Department of Michigan, nevertheless, rushed work on a superhighway from Detroit to the bomber plant, though this link with the big city was not completed and dedicated until September, 1942. Long before that, of course, every dwelling in Detroit, Ypsilanti, and towns for miles around Willow Run was occupied by war workers, and additional thousands of in-migrants from nearby states and regions as far away as the West Coast were living in trailers, tarpaper shanties, made-over chicken coops, and tents. As if the Twentieth Century Fund had never issued Miles Colean's review of the federal government's inept handling of the housing situation in the First World war—*Housing for Defense*—and had not warned of the consequences of failure to coordinate housing with war production, no federal contract for shelter for workers at the bomber plant was let until late 1942, and then only for dormitories to house 3,000 to 4,500 single men and women. The first of these structures was not opened until February, 1943, by which time 36,000 persons were employed in the plant. A month later the first of 960 trailers for married couples were brought in. Not until July, 1943, a month after Willow Run had reached its peak employment of more than 42,000, were the first units of the much-publicized "Bomber City" of Willow Village opened for occupancy; and in the meantime this dream town that was to have provided 6,000 permanent homes within walking distance of the plant had been whittled down to 2,500 temporary dwellings. It is still more incredible that not until February, 1944, were stores in the community service center of the village opened for business.

The sordid story of housing at Willow Run is made up of company disavowal of responsibility for what happens to workers off the job, the opposition of local builders and real estate men to federal housing, the fear of townspeople and local officeholders that newcomers might become permanent residents and upset the political status quo, the myopia of unions, and the temporizing of federal officials. In some other war-

83. Willow Run bomber plant of the Ford Motor Company *(Ford Motor Company)*

production centers housing and transportation needs were more realistically anticipated, but elsewhere, too, there was antipathy between established residents and newcomers—in the Willow Run area they were all called "hillbillies"—and dread that temporary housing might linger long after the war, blighting the townscape and depressing property values. Not even the unification, early in 1942, of sixteen federal housing agencies in a single National Housing Agency, with John B. Blanford, Jr., as administrator, did much to hasten the resolution of difficulties at Willow Run, perhaps because the government had handicapped its housing program from the very beginning with a policy of relying as much as possible upon private enterprise to build homes for war workers, though private enterprise traditionally had served only the better-paid workers with long-term security of employment. Apparently, however, some lessons were learned at Willow Run, because Blanford's agency provided substantial amounts of temporary housing near shipyards and factories established after the spring and summer of 1942.

Except where the government assumed complete control, as in the supersecret towns built by the Atomic Energy Commission at Oak Ridge, Tennessee, Richland, Washington, and Los Alamos, New Mexico, city planners were rarely able to do more than advise local officials or prepare plans for particular housing developments. John Merrill, Tracy B. Augur, and Leon Zach served as planning consultants on Oak Ridge, which was designed by the architectural firm of Skidmore, Owings, and Merrill. Lawrence Sheridan developed the original scheme for Los Alamos, later expanded by W. S. Kruger and Associates. The plan for Richland was the product of the firm of Graham, Anderson, Probst, and White in association with S. Gordon Turnbull. Generally, however, wartime planning stopped short of whole towns and was more in the nature of expert site planning. Had Willow Village been built as planned, it would have included five neighborhood units arranged in a radial pattern around a town center containing the administrative buildings, stores, service establishments, the high school, and other community structures. But only an abbreviated version of the carefully conceived plan was carried out—with flimsy, frame buildings painted pale blue, ochre, and catsup red to relieve the dreariness of the place. Throughout the war most production centers presented a spectacle of innumerable federal agencies, the military, state and local governments, voluntary organizations, and private enterprise struggling against tremendous odds to achieve a reasonable degree of coordination. That ships slid down ways ahead of schedule and plants exceeded their production quotas seemed at times inexplicable. Certainly, no comprehensive planning accounted for America's prodigious wartime accomplishments.

A Nationwide Renaissance of City Planning

In a period when the popular cry "Don't you know there's a war on?" usually greeted any undertaking not considered contributory to the ultimate defeat of the Axis, civic leaders and city planners who took the long view sometimes obtained little cooperation. In several of the larger cities there were, nevertheless, stalwarts who refused to be intimidated by shortsighted criticism of their insistence on preparation for the postwar years or to be discouraged by the preoccupation of most people with the war effort. In the tense year 1942, citizens' planning associations in Rochester, Buffalo, Philadelphia, Los Angeles, and San Francisco called attention to the need for plans to guide future development. In 1943, similar groups formed in Denver, Milwaukee, Pittsburgh, and Syracuse to urge areawide or metropolitan planning, while the cities of Dallas and Portland, Oregon, engaged consultants to formulate city plans. But perhaps in no other urban center was long-range, general planning given the vigorous, understanding support that it received in Cleveland.

Under Mayor Frank J. Lausche the Ohio city adopted a city charter amendment in November, 1942, overhauling the planning function and making possible, as an advisory committee said, a program of general planning conceived as "a continual process of looking ahead rather than as a single or sporadic act of designing a plan or plans."[42] Whereas formerly the city planning commission had had only the right to be consulted on matters affecting city development, the charter amendment required that proposals relating to the city plan be referred to the city planning commission for its review and recommendations. The city council, moreover, could override the disapproval of the commission only by a twothirds vote — a provision adapted from Ohio law pertaining to non-charter cities. The commission was also authorized to "take the initiative in planning for the city and surrounding area"[43] and was empowered to recommend a capital improvement budget to the mayor each year, together with a comprehensive five-year capital improvement program.

The reorganized planning commission promptly nominated and the mayor appointed John T. Howard, who was city planner of the Regional Association, to head the staff. In 1943 his departmental work force numbered eleven, the following year twenty-one, thanks to a budget increase from $55,000 to more than $100,000. Howard set out to prepare a general plan, but because he appreciated the importance of making planning effective, he and his staff spent the greater part of their time advising municipal departments and other governmental agencies, reviewing matters referred to the commission for its recommendations, preparing the capital improvement program, providing information to the public about planning, and administering the zoning and subdivision ordinances. Perhaps only a fourth of staff time went into general planning, yet in due time Howard presented Cleveland with the comprehensive plan of which he had dreamed. Much of it, however, had already become reality by the day-to-day process of influencing public and private decisions — a pattern of activities that was to be widely instituted in American city planning departments as emphasis shifted from the plan itself to the means of putting it into effect.

In Cleveland, as in other cities in which citizens' groups and municipal administrations joined together to launch long-range planning programs, the dread of a postwar renewal of the struggle with the cyclical economic forces that had plunged the nation into the depression of the 1930s was perhaps an even stronger spur to action than the desire to meet the rapidly changing conditions of urban life or prevent further losses of population, trade, and industry caused by the spread of blight. President Roosevelt had declared, "We are going to win the war and we are going to win the peace that follows." His fellow citizens did not doubt that they could vanquish the Axis powers, but many of them were frankly gloomy about achieving a peacetime economy free of large-scale unemployment and widespread deprivation in the midst of abundant resources and productive capacity. Had not a depression followed the First World War, and was not the concentration of workers in war industries this time so great that mass idleness would inevitably mark the transition from war to peace? Only the demands of war had put millions of disheartened men back to work. Would not persistent unemployment again become a sad fact of American life? And would not cities compete more grimly with one another for economic advantage than ever in the past?

Clearly, the city planners of the nation thought so, for the new or expanded planning programs developed from 1942 to 1945 emphasized economic studies as never before. The tenor of planning reflected the anxiety of the business community, and from the mayor's office to the city engineering department and the city planning commission the urgency attached to preparing a backlog of public works as a means of providing jobs evidenced the prevalent feeling that mobilization for postwar economic resurgence was second in importance only to winning the war itself. The broad goals of decent housing for everyone, varied educational and recreational opportunities for all, and a more functional organization of the environment assumed the hue of economic objectives. In the flush of wartime prosperity, when both workers and municipal governments presently had financial surpluses, the specter of want was a powerful incentive to probe deep for the bedrock of future stability and to establish impregnable priorities for the undertakings deemed essential to community well-being.

The National Resources Planning Board took the lead in proclaiming the necessity of being well prepared for the period of demobilization and reconversion to peacetime production, as the President had directed it to do in November, 1940. Its pamphlets on postwar planning were read by mayors and councilmen, engineers and city planners, chamber-of-commerce managers, industrialists, bank presidents, heads of social agencies, educators, labor leaders, and people in every segment of society. *After the War—Full Employment* followed the initial essay in the series, *After Defense—What?* In April, 1942, came *Better Cities,* in which Charles S. Ascher wrote, "The end of the war will offer the people of the United States the chance to rebuild American cities."[44] Though discounting none of the difficulties of remaking the haphazardly developed and partially deteriorated cities of the nation, Ascher urged readers to bear in mind that "we shall be left after victory with the greatest industrial capacity we have ever had, with more skilled workers and better mobilized technicians."[45] If Americans thought through their problems, adopted an urban land policy recognizing the welfare of the community, prepared plans, and framed the right kind of organization, they could seize a unique opportunity to remold cities "by the square mile, rather than by the block." Closely related to Ascher's pamplet was another by Miles Colean entitled *The Role of the Housebuilding Industry.* In this succinct appraisal of the prospects for postwar building, Colean estimated that the country could absorb "anywhere from 900,000 to 1,200,000 new dwellings a year, for the decade after the war, and still be in need of a very large volume of repairs during the same period."[46]

In September of that same year the board issued three more publications in the popular series: *Post-War Planning, After the War—Toward Security,* and *The Future of Transportation.* The tone of all three was one of tempered optimism. *Post-War Planning* stressed the goals of full employment, security, and building America. Its message, appealing to American pride in wartime accomplishments, held forth the possibility of an economy surpassing anything known before: "The full employment and prosperity which comes [sic] with the war effort prove [sic] that we can have a full employment system and balanced production-consumption budget at a high level if we are determined to have it so, because we have the necessary manpower, resources, productive plant, and organizing ability."[47] To the board, and especially to its Committee on Long-range Work and Relief Policies, a necessary corollary of full employment and high levels of production and consumption was a system of social security removing fear of old age, want, dependency, sickness, unemployment, and accident, but many Americans who thought a vastly expanded economy attainable were not yet ready to agree that the United States could afford the far-reaching social measures advocated by the board. Its championship of a rounded and integrated program of minimum security for all increased the enmity of congressmen who considered it tinged with socialism and awaited the opportune moment to liquidate it. Its suggestion in *The Future of Transportation* that a national transportation agency should "be responsible for the unification of the Federal Government's planning, development, and administrative functions in the field of transportation"[48] impressed some of these same legislators as further proof of the board's passion for Big Government and tighter control over private enterprise.

While the National Resources Planning Board thus labored under an increasing burden of congressional distrust, local governments from coast to coast more and more fervently embraced its gospel of postwar planning and initiated preparations for the period of reconversion. Starting with a staff of fifteen in the spring of 1942, the Detroit city planning department in the next two years employed twenty additional persons to work on a comprehensive plan of community development needed to evaluate the desirability and validity of improvement projects. In the meantime, the municipality, fearing that unemployment might exceed 200,000 during the transition era, had more than 150 technicians engaged in making working drawings for forty unquestionably essential projects. At the urging of community leaders in Louisville, the Kentucky General Assembly passed legislation in the 1942 session creating the Louisville and Jefferson County Planning and Zoning Commission, in effect extending the jurisdiction of the city planning commission to a county area including approximately 400 square miles. This agency, immediately after its organization in December of that year, hastened to complete a master plan and zoning regulations for the unincorporated territory in the county. The plan, adopted in May, 1943, served, like the Detroit plan, as a means of appraising the merits of city and county projects proposed in a large public works reserve program.

The year 1943 witnessed the expansion of the city planning program in Los Angeles, the revival of the city planning commission in Kansas City, Missouri, the establishment of a city planning commision in Philadelphia, and the authorization of eleven new positions on the staff of the Milwaukee Board of Public Land Commissioners, the planning agency for the Wisconsin metropolis. The enlarged program in Los Angeles, made possible by a budget increase from $77,000 to $133,000, included not only the preparation of various city-wide plans but also the processing of a $707,000,000 list of proposed public works projects to determine which ones should have priority on the basis of need and the city's ability to finance them with local funds. Planning director Charles B. Bennett, who had come to Los Angeles from Milwaukee in 1940, acted as chairman of a coordinating board composed of principal department heads and exercised strategic influence in relating suggested projects to the plans his staff was shaping. The Kansas City planning program resulted from the city council's realization of the importance of an over-all plan and city manager L. P. Cookingham's suspicion that some of the 117 projects included in a tentative postwar construction program "did not stack up well." "One costly error avoided might pay for planning for several years," he noted.[49]

In Philadelphia the city fathers appropriated more than $149,000 for city planning and temporarily placed in the planning budget a fund of almost $700,000 for the design of public improvements. This arrangement seemed expedient to the councilmen because the ordinance creating the planning commission required that group annually to submit a six-year advance program of public works to the council as well as to carry on the comprehensive planning function. As planning director Robert B. Mitchell and his staff of some thirty persons recommended projects to the councilmen, they transferred funds from the $700,000 design budget to various departments charged with preparing plans and specifications for particular types of improvements. The reorganization of planning in Milwaukee, stimulated by a new Milwaukee Metropolitan Plan Association, also reflected the widespread desire to undertake in the post-war era only public projects conforming to a long-range plan.

Instead of expanding their planning departments or inaugurating new planning programs, some cities engaged consultants to assist them in getting ready for the years after victory. Dallas, for example, employed the firm of Harland Bartholomew and Associates to prepare a master plan looking forward to 1970. From September, 1943, to January 1, 1945, the plan appeared in a series of fifteen reports, one of the first of which recalled the city's good fortune in being able to carry out the $24,000,000 Ulrickson Plan of capital expenditures in the early days of the depression. The same report also cited public improvements made in the past three decades — mostly park and street projects — in accordance with the first city plan prepared by George E. Kessler in 1911. Postwar under-takings, the report suggested, should be fully coordinated with the new master plan. Like John Howard in Cleveland, the planners in Bar-tholomew's organization indicated that their scheme would not propose the kind of public improvements which might lead to unwise extension of the urbanized area. Indeed, their report singled out the Federal Housing Administration for special criticism for pursuing a policy of promoting the construction of "nearly all housing" in suburban areas. "This policy has hastened the process of urban decentralization immeas-urably," they observed. "The federal government, through its influence over housing policies and programs, is not encouraging comprehensive planning in cities, but on the contrary, is making more difficult its achievement."[50] If this criticism overlooked FHA's new interest in urban redevelopment and overall planning, it nevertheless stated the truth about the agency's past performance—and perhaps warned of the continuance of earlier attitudes.

In the fall of 1943 five local agencies in Portland, Oregon, pooled their funds to bring Robert Moses, the vocal and controversial park commissioner of New York City, to their city to diagnose its postwar prospects and recommend a program of public improvements. The city council had

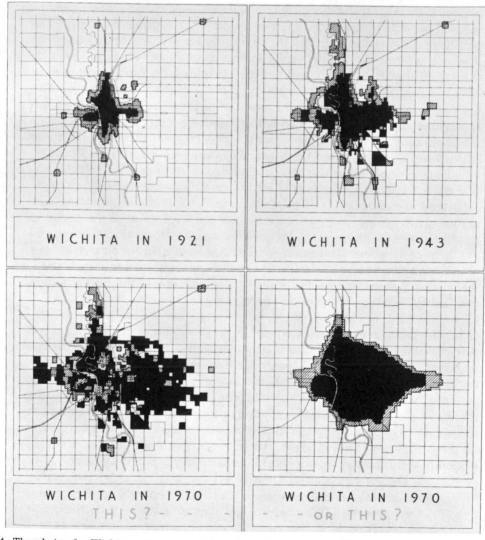

WICHITA IN 1921

WICHITA IN 1943

WICHITA IN 1970
THIS? - - - - -

WICHITA IN 1970
- - OR THIS?

84. The choice for Wichita: urban sprawl or compact development *(Harland Bartholomew and Associates)*

already revived the city planning commission and had given it a larger budget than it had ever had before, but a Portland Area Post-war Development Committee, appointed by the commissioner of public works at the urging of some of the leading citizens, was not satisfied that local talent, unaided, could steer Portland through the reefs and breakers of postwar readjustment. Wartime expansion of shipbuilding and other industries had increased the population approximately one and a half times what it had been in 1940 and had added almost 90,000 to the total labor pool. Since the city had had 25,000 unemployed prior to the war boom, the worried members of the postwar committee feared still greater unemployment when the shipyards closed down. These establishments alone had 92,000 employees on their payrolls in the summer of 1943.

Moses arrived in September with a group of engineers on whom he had relied in the past: Madigan-Hyland, W. Earle Andrews, Gilmore D. Clarke, and Waddell and Hardesty. In November he completed his report, having meantime consulted half a score of other engineers and park executives in his home state, not to mention several attorneys. He recommended a $75,000,000 program of public works which he estimated would employ perhaps 20,000 persons in the first two years after the war. It included proposals for a ring street system around the congested area of the city, a new bridge, a sewage disposal system to eliminate pollution of the Willamette River, public buildings and schools, improvement of the docks and airport, development of existing parks, and acquistion of additional park sites. Moses also suggested that "the present zoning ordinance must be abandoned in favor of a new ordinance," but he did not state that the new regulations should be based on a carefully studied general plan.[51]

Long at war with those who believed in comprehensive planning, the New York commissioner anticipated criticism for recommending a miscellany of projects rather than a program related to a long-range planning effort, as a paragraph in his report revealed: "Among ivory-tower planners who will accept nothing short of a revolution in urban life, this report is bound to be disappointing because, in accordance with our instructions, we are recommending only limited public improvements in the urgent class which this community, with help from the state and federal governments, can afford to compress and expedite in order to help meet the postwar emergency."[52]

But others besides "ivory-tower planners" were disappointed. The *New York Herald-Tribune* reported that public reaction to the Moses report was apathetic,[53] perhaps because, as the commissioner himself acknowledged, many of his recommendations merely traversed "ground already broken by competent local public officials, engineers and technicians."[54] Christopher Tunnard believed, however, that there might be another reason for the lack of enthusiasm about the report: "The public knows, as Mr. Moses clearly does not, that Portland needs something more than a plan with 'limited objectives' for the post-war period — a plan in which housing, health and community facilities, business, industrial and other needs can be integrated so that any section of it, including that of public works, can be carried out with some chance of being useful. Portland could probably get such a plan as cheaply, and certainly one that was better informed."[55]

The Portland procedure of calling in a man with a big name to warm over plans and proposals with which community leaders were familiar necessarily lacked the dynamism of postwar planning programs generated by the people themselves. Addicted to organizations, as Alexis de Tocqueville had observed as long ago as the 1830s, Americans liked nothing better than to participate as members of groups in movements for the improvement of their towns and cities. When the year 1943 brought victory more and more certainly into view, and employment in war industries attained magnitudes thoroughly frightening to everyone who contemplated reconversion, community organizations almost clamored to take part in planning for the period of readjustment. In fact, so popular was postwar planning that the *New Yorker* magazine included a cartoon of a curbside vendor holding aloft booklets entitled *Peace — What Then?* and exhorting passersby, "Don't get caught by changing times, men! Make your plans now for the postwar world!" But the cartoonist should have entitled the booklets *Action for Cities: A Guide for Community Planning,* for this was truly the publication of the hour. Distributed by the Public Administration Service and published under the sponsorship of the American Municipal Association, the American Society of Planning Officials, and the International City Managers' Association, this timely paperback offered exactly the kind of help interested and intelligent citizens and officials needed to develop planned programs for their communities. It had, moreover, the special virtue of embodying the experience of three cities in which many groups of residents representing a broad cross section of the entire citizenry had participated in formulating plans for the future.

These three cities were Corpus Christi, Salt Lake City, and Tacoma, selected by the National Resources Planning Board (NRPB) in 1942 to experiment with a planning technique devised by Robert B. Mitchell while he was chief of its Urban Section. For each of these cities the board provided a planning consultant and various services, but the local government in each city directed the planning effort and drafted the resulting recommendations.

In Corpus Christi the city planning commission, the mayor and city council, the chamber of commerce, and the Corpus Christi *Caller-Times* joined together in asking the board to let the city demonstrate the new technique of drawing an outline plan for overall development in progressive stages but in as short a time as possible. The national planning agency acceded to the request because of the city's rapid wartime expansion and the probability that it would retain its growth after the war. Sam B. Zisman was assigned as resident representative of the board and was soon working with almost every city and county department as well as with many private organizations. Above all, the city-wide program stressed the importance of sound economic and industrial development. With the aid of an industrial consultant from the NRPB, the chamber of commerce and other groups endeavored to establish realistic employment and production goals up to 1950. Subcommittees analyzed the resources of the area, studied industrial training programs, and considered problems of marketing. The local real estate board undertook a study of industrial sites, developed a method of land assembly, and reviewed the tax structure. A transportation committee of the chamber of commerce, the city engineer, and the navigation engineer investigated transportation problems and met at various times with an NRPB specialist on future trends in transportation, officials of the Civil Aeronautics Administration, and state highway engineers. But Corpus Christi was equally assiduous in planning for the social development of the community, even using school children to prepare maps for a study of the problem of redistrictng the elementary schools. The library board, local public housing authority, Council of Community Agencies, and the architectural school of the Texas Agricultural and Mechanical College were all drawn into the community-wide program. Although some studies could not be completed without outside technical aid, local citizens were amazed at the wealth of information they themselves were able to bring together and analyze. The sketch plan representing their collective labors was symbolic of a new understanding of community needs, problems, and prospects.

Action for Cities, containing many references to procedures and methods used in Salt Lake City and Tacoma as well as in Corpus Christi, did not suggest that do-it-yourself planning was any substitute for a well-staffed city planning department. Its point was that "the time is short and technicians are scarce," what with the draft taking younger planners into the armed forces, and municipal governments competing strenuously for the older planners who were available. If cities were to be even reasonably well prepared to face the tremendous problems of the postwar era, they would have to utilize every local source of knowledge and assistance, calling upon colleges and universities to help with population studies, businesses and industries to provide information on employment, trade, and production, local offices of state and federal agencies to work with community groups and city and county departments, and informed individuals to contribute their services where most needed. Even before *Action for Cities* appeared, a group of civic leaders in San Jose, California, formed a Citizens' Planning Council to carry on a program similar to that outlined in the pamphlet. As a result of their efforts, there were improvements in youth services, the schools, the public health program, and the public library system; a family service agency was established; and a movement for a reorganization of county government under a county charter was started, though it was not crowned with success until some years later. But little improvement of the physical environment could be credited to this council, whereas the National Resources Planning Board devised a technique which it hoped would indicate how broad economic and social planning could be combined with land use planning to produce better physical development.

Written in simple, nontechnical language, *Action for Cities* presented the steps to take in making a quick reconnaissance of the community, then outlined essential population studies, economic analyses, studies of the community as a place in which to live, a procedure for developing a ground plan of the urban area, and a program for putting plans into effect. It concluded with a section stating that planning should be a continuing activity: "Both official and citizen organization are needed to carry planning forward successfully. Planning must be a regular part of municipal operations. A citizens' council also should be organized to present the public's point of view and to keep the public fully informed. The public must study plans in order to create the widest understanding and to build support for the most effective program possible."[57]

The process of community participation set forth in this guide was, of course, appropriate mainly for small and medium-size cities. Salt Lake City, the largest of the communities in which the National Resources Planning Board experimented with the sketch plan technique, had a population of approximately 238,000 in February, 1943. Although Howard and other planners found citizens' committees and advisory groups of great assistance at times, municipal administrations in large cities such as Cleveland and Los Angeles realized more than ever, as they prepared for the transition from war to peace, that nothing could take the place of a competent planning staff.

The wartime renaissance of city planning in the United States was accompanied, however, by the rise of postwar planning organizations of indescribable variety. In 1942, when planning for the years after victory was only beginning, the Twentieth Century Fund published a report by George B. Galloway listing forty-five governmental agencies and more than three-score private organizations of national or regional importance that already had postwar planning committees. By 1943 dozens of other federal commissions and bureaus, as well as many more private associations and councils, had appointed similar groups.

Among the new nationwide organizations was the Committee for Economic Development, fostered by the Department of Commerce and supported by private corporations and businesses. When Beardsley Ruml, treasurer of R. H. Macy & Company and adviser to the National Resources Planning Board, described the CED, as it was popularly known, to the annual conference of the American Society of Planning Officials in May, 1943, it already had 11 regional chairmen, 68 district chairmen, and 130 community chairmen. Setting out to organize local committees in a thousand cities and towns, the national committee exerted enormous influence and created a receptivity to the whole concept of planning that perhaps no governmental agency or foundation could have effected. The CED's purpose, of course, was to stimulate postwar economic planning, but many of its local committees quickly understood that public improvements and land use planning directly affect the welfare of business and industry.

The Abolition of the National Resources Planning Board

To the dismay of city planners and many officials of state planning boards, the federal agency that had done the most to encourage planning for the period of demobilization and reconversion succumbed to the hostility of Congress just when enthusiasm for such foresighted activity was reaching a crescendo. Never fully accepted as an essential arm of government or given appropriations commensurate with the important functions the President assigned to it, the National Resources Planning Board almost from its beginning as the National Planning Board had struggled to gain a secure place in the federal establishment. In the 1930s many congressmen resented the fact that the board had been created not by legislative act but by executive order, although most of these same congressmen repeatedly opposed bills that would have given the agency permanent status as a kind of general staff to the chief executive.

In 1940, a year after the board had become an instrument of the Executive Office of the President and had acquired the functions of the old Economic Stabilization Board created under the Employment Stabilization Act of 1931, the Senate grudgingly agreed that the board had a proper inheritance of legislative authority; but in approving an appropriation for it, the Senate adopted an amendment providing that the agency should not acquire any greater powers than had been given to the old Stabilization Board. Though presumably restricted by this amendment to the narrow function of reviewing and analyzing public works proposed by numerous federal agencies, the board continued nevertheless to study economic trends, to maintain its committees on land, water, minerals, power, industry, science, transportation, urbanism, and work and relief, and to promote planning by municipalities and state governments. It justified its varied activities by pointing out that it was impossible to review federal projects without having extensive knowledge in many fields, yet Congress was suspicious of it. To the more conservative members the last straw was the report of the board's Committee on Long-range Work and Relief Policies, suggesting a broad national program of education, health, old age insurance and assistance, and unemployment insurance. Critics of this report denounced it as an "American Beveridge Plan" patterned after the cradle-to-grave social security system proposed by Sir William Beveridge in Great Britain, although economist Eveline M. Burns and her committee had undertaken their work in 1939, long before Beveridge had begun to prepare his report. In fact, the English economist had had access to the proposals of Mrs. Burns's committee, but since his report appeared first, the American group was accused of adapting a foreign socialistic scheme.

The furor over the publication of the Burns report offered Congress an excuse for doing what it had long wanted to do — abolish the National Resources Planning Board. The reasons for its elimination, however, were legion. Old-line agencies such as the Army Corps of Engineers and the Bureau of Reclamation had always chafed under its attempts to coordinate their projects; and its sponsorship of drainage basin planning and its recurrent suggestions that authorities similar to the Tennessee Valley Authority should be created for other great river systems particularly irked the Corps, which feared loss of its prerogatives and prestige. Individual congressmen disliked certain members of the staff of the board, or held grudges against the President and sought petty revenge by voting to liquidate the agency headed by his uncle. Charles Eliot II, executive director, attributed the demise of the organization to the belief of Republican Senator Robert Taft that the board was fashioning a powerful program of medical care, aid to education, and social security for the Democrats to use in the next presidential campaign.[58] Walter Blucher was equally sure that the NRPB was consigned to oblivion because many congressmen "could not point to a single thing the agency had ever done for their districts."[59] But, as planner George S. Duggar observed in a postmortem examination of the board,

> It was not its enemies but its lack of friends which really killed it. Year after year it was the President, the Budget Bureau, and Secretary Ickes, together with the faithful, dogged work in Congress by Senator [James F.] Byrnes, who preserved it. They had gotten less and less help from it; it had gone its own way. The Board was not helping much in the war, and certain personalities among the members and high on the staff had antagonized potential friends.

Its support moved away, and mild opposition could now wreak havoc. In a week marked by sharp criticism in Congress of the Office of Price Administration and the Office of War Information, NRPB was also taken to task. The other two survived.[60]

Undefended in its hour of need, the National Resources Planning Board was widely mourned outside the national capital, though in few editorial columns. The lamentation was all the more dolorous because the bill abolishing the board effective August 31, 1943, specified that "the functions exercised by such Board shall not be transferred to any other agency and shall not be performed after such date except as hereafter provided by law. . . ." The latter stipulation, reflecting congressional pique at Roosevelt's having fathered the board by executive order, left little hope that the legislators themselves would authorize a new national planning agency. To persons only generally familiar with it, the NRPB had appeared to fill a vital role, but its effectiveness had been weakened by internal conflicts and it had never, as one analyst has pointed out, "fully resolved whether it wanted to be primarily a research, propagandizing, operating, or advisory agency."[61] Charles Merriam, the dominant member of the board, favored research and emphasis on economic and social policy but had little enthusiasm for technical assistance to state planning agencies, whereas executive director Eliot believed ardently in furthering state planning, for one reason because "you could talk to Congressmen about what consultant help the NRPB was giving their state."[62]

From the eleven field offices through which the agency channeled its aid to states, the Washington staff in later years brought together reports on economic trends, but the NRPB was only one of several federal agencies reporting to the President on this subject, never the central fiscal and economic adviser. Roosevelt, in fact, made a practice of obtaining advice from many sources. From the board he sought mainly far-ranging contributions to the development of public policy and coordination of the activities of federal agencies. The coordinating function, carried on through technical committees composed of assistant secretaries and bureau chiefs and some members from private life, was more successful within particular fields, such as the formulation of policy for developing water resources, than on an overall basis. As Eliot wrote after the demise of the board, there were "problems of relationship among committees and between committees and the Board."[63] An effective committee, moving ahead on its own steam, sometimes ran afoul of its neighbors or encroached on the prerogatives of the board itself. Not acquainted with the internal strains and difficulties of the NRPB, citizens sympathetic to the idea of planning saw only that the one federal planning agency ever created had been eliminated, and they deplored the loss.

With all its shortcomings, the National Resources Planning Board left valuable legacies: closer relations between state and federal agencies operating in some fields; a greater respect for interagency planning within the federal government; a desire for state planning in most of the states of the Union; and several dozen authoritative publications on trends in population, income and spending habits of consumers, river basin development, urban government, city planning, urban and rural land policy, technology and research, energy resources, patterns of industry, housing, and transportation. Some of these reports contained proposals that have been accepted only in recent years, such as the suggestions for federal departments of urban affairs and transportation. The report on *Security, Work, and Relief Policies,* immediately contributory to the board's demise, has long since been translated into an ever widening system of social security. The reports of the Urbanism Committee continue to be milestones in the literature of city planning. Probably most effective of all the board's publications were the pamphlets on postwar planning, issued when the board was fighting for its life. As it went down, unrescued by a President who was absorbed in the problems of war, its members and advisers and its staff at least had the satisfaction of knowing that planning for the advent of peace had caught on in many federal agencies, in the realm of business and industry, and in the cities and towns of America.

The President, by executive order, quickly assigned to the Bureau of the Budget the board's responsibility for compiling a six-year program of federal public works, since the bureau annually reviewed all projects included in the President's budget. Some of the other functions of the NRPB were taken over by the Federal Works Agency, the War Production Board, Office of Economic Stabilization, and, later, by a newly created office of Demobilization and Conversion. In a final report on the work of the board, dated December 31, 1943, Eliot noted, "Those who are familiar with the Board's operations will recall that many of the activities of the Board were carried on in cooperation and association with other agencies. Those agencies have continued to exercise their 'functions' in these fields."[64] Planning, then, went on throughout the executive branch of government, but in more diffuse fashion. Still, some unofficial and informal interagency committees met to review proposals.

Repeatedly the National Resources Planning Board had urged the establishment of congressional committees on planning; but only in mid-March, 1943, after the President had transmitted the board's report on *Security, Work, and Relief Policies* to Capitol Hill, had the Senate authorized a Committee on Post-War Economic Policy and Planning, headed by Senator Walter F. George of Georgia. Somewhat later the

House set up a similar committee chaired by Representative William F. Colmer of Mississippi. These actions, too late to bring about joint consideration of planning by the executive and legislative branches of government, moved Charles Merriam to comment ruefully, "When there was a presidential board, there was no corresponding agency in Congress; and now when there is a congressional agency, there is no executive counterpart."[65] To Merriam it must have been ironical that in 1945, after two years of activity, the Colmer Committee brought in a proposal for a Construction Policy Board, to be set up under the executive, to determine "over-all construction policy at the top level, as is done in fiscal matters."[66] That, among other things, was precisely what the NRPB had done.

Changes in State Planning Programs

The termination of the national planning agency coincided with a significant change in state planning programs, resulting in part from the NRPB's own emphasis on providing new employment after the war for returning veterans and workers made jobless by the closing of war industries. Alabama, California, Georgia, Illinois, Indiana, and Missouri abolished their state planning boards and replaced them with postwar planning agencies specifically concerned with problems of employment and economic expansion. The National Resources Planning Board had consistently urged that planning for the period of readjustment should be related to an ongoing effort in each state to achieve a comprehensive plan, but even in those states in which the functions of the planning board supposedly were assumed by the new agency, broad planning tended to be slighted for the attainment of narrower economic goals.

In 1944 Nebraska, Kentucky, and New Jersey also established development commissions or departments as more state planning boards were eliminated or were made divisions of the new agencies, as in New Jersey. The following year Arkansas, South Carolina, and Washington were among the states creating economic organizations and abolishing their state planning boards. By the end of 1945 only twenty-eight states had typical state planning boards dating from the 1930s or more recent creations in the same pattern, whereas there were forty-five or more of the newer agencies with titles denoting their legislative mandate to improve the state economy, such as the Missouri Department of Resources and Development and the Agricultural and Industrial Development Board of Georgia.

As the statistics indicated, some states not only retained their planning boards but also created new agencies to give attention exclusively to problems of readjustment. In Maryland, for example, the legislature added a Commission on Post-War Reconstruction and Development, and in New Hampshire the governor appointed a Council on Post-War Planning and Rehabilitation. Massachusetts, either from unusual foresight or from excessive dread of a new crisis, by 1943 had no less than five agencies preparing for the transition from war to peace: its well-established state planning board; a Committee on Post-War Readjustment appointed by the governor a month before the Japanese attack on Pearl Harbor; an Emergency Public Works Commission originally created in 1933 and given a new authorization in 1943 to prepare a program of public projects for the postwar period; a Post-War Rehabilitation Commission of state senators, representatives, and gubernatorial appointees to study economic development; and a Veterans Rehabilitation and Reemployment Commission to provide information to returning soldiers about jobs, medical care, education, and state and federal aid.

Louis Wirth, planning director of the Illinois Post-War Planning Commission, successor to the Illinois State Planning Board, saw in the liquidation of the National Resources Planning Board a resurgence of states' rights resting upon "a blind provincialism which fails to recognize the facts of modern technology and economics which have made this nation one closely knit interdependent unit and which calls for a thoroughgoing reexamination of the proper function of state government."[67] Inevitably, states would be at a disadvantage in attempting postwar planning without guidance from Washington regarding national policies on industrial demobilization and reconversion, foreign trade, tariffs, taxation, debt, credit, public works, and related matters. His own commission, for example, could not "treat the state of Illinois as if it were a closed, autonomous economic unit,"[68] yet Wirth feared that some states might naïvely proceed to estimate their capacity to produce and to consume irrespective of neighboring states and of the nation and the world at large. Nor were his fears unconfirmed. In the absence of the regional offices that had enabled the National Resources Planning Board to establish a degree of coordination among state governments, or at least to effect helpful exchanges of information, some states were inclined to ignore regional or national conditions limiting their ability to execute ambitious programs. The New England states and the commonwealths of the Pacific Northwest, which had participated in regional planning commissions formed under the auspices of the NRPB, continued, however, to maintain the tradition of regional cooperation. Five governors organized the Northwest States Development Association to formulate plans for developing the Columbia River drainage basin. In New England the state planning boards maintained relationships on an informal basis.

With the aid and encouragement of the National Resources Planning Board, some of the state planning boards had prepared highly important reports on their natural resources, manufacturing industries, urban economies, and population trends. Many of these publications had been especially useful to the military and to war agencies and were now valuable to the new economic development commissions and councils. Carrying further the studies of the California State Planning Board and the Pacific Southwest regional office of the National Resources Planning Board, the California State Reconstruction and Reemployment Commission under the guidance of its chief of technical staff, Van Buren Stanbery, did special research designed to expand service enterprises, which even before the war had provided a high proportion of jobs in the Pacific Coast state. The Illinois Post-War Planning Commission investigated the possibility of broadening health, educational, and recreational services. Among the older state planning agencies, the Michigan Planning Commission studied ways to develop agricultural and tourist resources.

Almost without exception, the new postwar planning agencies and the surviving state planning boards regarded the programming of public works as one of their main functions. Besides spurring other state departments to crystallize their plans for desirable public projects, the planning boards and development agencies also urged local governments to consider construction programs. The California Reconstruction and Reemployment Commission, for example, employed Ross Miller, who had promoted public works planning among city and county governments for the Pacific Southwest regional office of the National Resources Planning Board, to continue his advisory work with local officials. The state legislature in 1944 gave a boost to his efforts by appropriating $10,000,000 of state funds on a matching basis for city and county postwar improvement projects, $7,000,000 of which was for the preparation of plans and specifications and $3,000,000 for the acquisition of sites. The Michigan legislature made $5,000,000 available to cities and towns for similar purposes, and Maryland and New Jersey each established funds of $500,000 to aid local governments in making construction drawings. But as the states and localities shaped up their programs, it became increasingly apparent that public works could provide employment for only a relatively small percentage of all those who would need new jobs after victory. To many professional planners one of the most disturbing aspects of the nationwide haste to decide on projects and get blueprints ready was the paucity of state and local comprehensive plans by which to judge the long-term utility of proposed new buildings, roads, bridges, and sewers. Many governments seemed destined to repeat some of the mistakes of the depression era and to waste money on projects improperly located or of inadequate or too great capacity.

If the states which had been assisting cities and towns with the preparation of their long-range plans had all continued to do so, some of the local public works programming would have been more realistic; but the replacement of a state planning board by an economic development agency sometimes meant that state aid for local planning was dropped, as in Arkansas and in California, too, until the State Reconstruction and Reemployment Commission realized the need to restore the program of assistance to municipal and county planning departments. The state planning boards in Louisiana, Michigan, New York, Rhode Island, Tennessee, Virginia, and Wisconsin, having discovered the benefits of services to cities and towns, continued to stimulate and assist local general planning.

Even in these states, however, the need among public officials for knowledge of planning and planning procedures was far greater than state boards, with their limited budgets and staffs, could meet. Knowing how welcome some guidance would be, the American Society of Planning Officials held special institutes on planning for city councilmen, mayors, city managers, and city engineers in California, Illinois, Michigan, Minnesota, Missouri, and Pennsylvania, and would have held others if its resources had permitted, but the demands for further institutes were more than it could fill. At each of these meetings Walter Blucher and his aids spent the first two of four and a half days discussing the need for population studies and the importance of understanding the relationship of a community to the state, the nation, and the international scene. Then, using a syllabus-notebook of some hundred pages, the instructors got down to particulars about transit and transportation, schools, parks and playgrounds, and all the other things that go into the making of a community—and only after showing how much essential information must be collected and analyzed in the planning process did they discuss the preparation of a public works program. But, unfortunately, hundreds rather than thousands received the benefit of these presentations, and local administrations in many other states compiled lists of proposed public improvements without knowing whether, in the long run, all of them would really be worth financing and carrying out.

The proliferation of postwar planning organizations of all kinds, public and private, confronted states and localities with crises of coordination. Most state planning boards already had various advisory committees and subcommittees assisting them. The new economic development agencies also quickly appointed committees and subcommittees to study salient problems. The Illinois Post-War Planning Commission, for instance, had fifteen committees, some of which had as many as six or seven subcommittees. New Hampshire had—in addition to its well-established Planning and Development Commission, dating from 1935, and its Council on Post-War Planning and Rehabilitation—interim commissions on soil erosion, timber taxation and conservation of forestry products, field services of the state, retirement, and other matters. Local communities in this state had CED (Council for Economic Development) committees and other private groups making surveys and plans in bewildering number. To avoid conflicts and chaos, the Council on Post-War Planning and Rehabilitation turned to the older Planning and Development Commission to act as a central integrating and coordinating agency for the multiplicity of well-meaning but not always well-directed state and local organizations, while the commission requested regional associations with paid secretaries to stimulate both postwar and long-range planning in their areas. In most cities, states, and larger regions of the United States, however, the sheer number of official agencies, citizens' committees, business groups, and professional societies attempting to chart courses for the future resulted in much duplication of effort, overlapping surveys, and the production of plans opposed to one another in basic assumptions, goals, and proposed solutions. Generally, the expectation of severe unemployment and financial stringency in the period of readjustment imbued the planning with an earnestness and a desire to be practical that had sometimes been lacking in the past; what was needed more than ever in most states and local communities was the synthesizing force of genuine long-range, comprehensive planning, but the shortage of experienced planners deprived many wartime planning efforts of the integrative touch.

Controversy Over Housing and Redevelopment

The American people had arrived at another of those periods in their history in which change and uncertainty produce a ferment of creative thought. They accepted full employment as a national goal, yet they disagreed widely about how to achieve it. Most believed that private enterprise should assume the responsibility or be given the opportunity of creating the greater proportion of postwar jobs. Controversy arose, however, over the roles of government and private enterprise in a field that potentially could offer an enormous amount of needed employment — housing. In the years 1943–1945, when the ultimate victory of the United States and its allies was no longer in question and Americans could confidently renew interest in proposed federal participation in urban redevelopment, the still inflammatory issue of public housing glowed at the center of all discussions of the problem of ridding urban areas of slums and blight.

At a conference on postwar housing held by the National Committee on Housing at Chicago in the spring of 1944, John B. Blanford, Jr., the Administrator of the National Housing Agency, declared that there was nothing inconsistent between the proposition that private enterprise should serve as much of the housing need as it possibly could and the proposition that public housing should serve the housing need that private enterprise did not serve. To reject either of these propositions was to reject either the goal of decent housing for all Americans or the principle of maintaining the system of private enterprise and utilizing it to the maximum extent. The current talk about urban redevelopment was "really a proposal that some of the methods employed by public housing, and some of the methods employed by private enterprise, be linked together to expand the potential field of profitable housing."[69]

Yet Herbert U. Nelson, executive vice president of the National Association of Real Estate Boards and secretary of the Urban Land Institute, personally rejected public housing. Denouncing "the new slavery of our cities to Washington," he demanded freedom for cities to handle their own affairs, including being permitted to tax the income from local real estate.[70] Nelson wanted private investment in long-term bonds of redevelopment agencies and remission of all federal taxes upon income from such bonds; and he proposed that low-rent housing be built with "capital which would also be deductible from current taxable federal income." Such housing would be "public housing under private ownership, private management, private control."[71] The public housing constructed under the Housing Act of 1937 was "segregated housing" in which every family was "marked as a special ward of the state through rents given at less than cost."[72]

Nelson sat down amid applause from some of the participants as Hugh Pomeroy, executive director of the National Association of Housing Officials, rose to defend public housing. Housing authorities in thirty-nine states were increasingly seeking to collaborate with private enterprise in studies of local housing needs and in the development of sound local community development and housing programs, he said, and now the opportunity for such collaboration was being impaired and the preparation of redevelopment programs was being thwarted "by the attitude of a miscellaneous group that seeks to abolish all existing public housing and to prohibit further public housing."[73] Its members maintained, "with hopeful promises but no proof or demonstration," that private enterprise could provide decent housing for all but physically or mentally disabled families or those temporarily in economic distress. A qualification of this claim was that low-income families could be provided with decent housing by building excess amounts of housing for higher-income families and letting this housing "filter down" to low-income families as it deteriorated in quality or desirability. "The 'filtering down' process has had full opportunity to work for the past hundred years," Pomeroy declared scornfully. "It has produced all our slums and blighted areas. There is no magic whereby there can be any other result."[74]

Like other public-housers of the era, Pomeroy was also vigorously opposed to a form of subsidy dear to the advocates of the filtering down process — rent certificates to enable low-income families to pay the higher rents charged by private enterprise for acceptable housing. It was part of the orthodoxy of housers in those days that the rent certificate scheme would perpetuate obsolescent structures and retard urban redevelopment and, furthermore, that it would be so difficult to administer that it would inevitably subsidize unfit dwellings. As for subsidies in the form of tax exemptions on private capital and other tax-incentive proposals, Pomeroy informed Nelson that public-housers had no intention of abandoning their program for "some mystic legerdemain that would be more hugely costly to the taxpayers than public housing could ever be, that could provide very little housing that low-income families could afford, and that thereby could never get very far toward the accomplishment of its avowed primary purpose of urban redevelopment."[75]

The verbal bout between Nelson and Pomeroy all too clearly foretold a struggle over the public housing issue in the halls of Congress. In the meantime, ten states were considering redevelopment bills, and ten had already enacted laws authorizing redevelopment companies or corporations to undertake the rebuilding of blighted areas with the assistance of certain public powers (including eminent domain), privileges, and exemptions. In Illinois, Indiana, New Jersey, New York, and Wisconsin the redevelopment legislation applied to any city in the state; in Kansas, Kentucky, Maryland, Michigan, and Missouri, only to the largest cities. This growing interest in slum clearance and the revitalization of economically stagnant areas was reflected in the creation of a subcommittee on housing and urban redevelopment of Senator Walter F. George's Special Committee on Post-war Economic Policy and Planning, which not three months after the Chicago conference on postwar housing held hearings on almost every aspect of the housing problem, including redevelopment.

Among the large number of informed persons appearing before the subcommittee, whose chairman was Senator Robert A. Taft of Ohio, was Seward H. Mott, director of the Urban Land Institute. Mott reported that opinion surveys conducted by the organization indicated that citizens and officials in cities throughout the country expected the dispersion which took place before the war to continue afterward, with perhaps three-fourths of postwar housing being built on new, undeveloped acreage. Obviously, the plight of older central areas would only become worse unless some concerted effort were made to revive them. Mott favored federal redevelopment legislation, but was not specific about forms of financial aid. He was, however, against viewing redevelopment bills as housing legislation since their purpose "should be to secure the highest and best use for the redeveloped area" rather than to rehouse displaced families.[76] He told of considerable opposition to public housing in most areas because of "bad location, excessive cost, and method of selecting tenants" as well as because of "what was called Federal interference in local affairs."[77] As public housing authorities were associated with a trend toward "centralization of authority in Washington," he recommended that local redevelopment programs be administered not by these agencies but by a well-balanced redevelopment agency, appointed by the city fathers and given wide power for land acquisition not only in inner-city areas but also in partially vacant and blighted subdivisions.[78]

Thanking Mott for his "very interesting survey," subcommittee chairman Taft welcomed to the stand his fellow townsman Alfred Bettman, who described himself as having been for many years chairman of the American Bar Association's committee on planning law and legislation as well as chairman of the legislative committee of the American Institute of Planners. In his exchanges with the senator it soon became apparent, perhaps to the chagrin of Mott, that conservative Republican Taft held strong convictions about the value of public housing, mainly because of humanitarian sensibility. But Bettman was no doubt surprised to find Taft saying that urban blight was a local concern and that he could not "see how it affects the national economy in any way."[79] Here, indeed, was formidable opposition to redevelopment legislation. Summoning all his powers of logic and persuasion and his considerable knowledge of conditions in blighted areas, Bettman pleaded for the elimination of the physical and economic sickness afflicting cities. He must have been further dismayed when Senator Allen J. Ellender of Louisiana observed that he, too, was "inclined to the belief of Senator Taft that the Federal Government should not step in and try to remedy the situation that you just described."[80] "No," said Bettman, "but just to aid it." Aid, perhaps, was something more reasonable. The interrogation continued, and presently Taft understood that Bettman made a clear distinction between the purposes of redevelopment and those of public housing. The one aimed chiefly at eliminating blight and reusing land for commercial or industrial structures or for purely private housing, whereas the other sought primarily to provide low-rent dwellings for low-income families.[81] Taft remarked that he would approve of redevelopment if it would "eliminate a comparatively large amount of slum housing," but he did not wish to have the cost of redevelopment "tacked on to low-cost housing" because he had heard testimony the previous day that the reuse of blighted areas for public housing sometimes added as much as $500 per unit to the cost.[82] Thus began to emerge in Taft's mind "the sound principle that the cost of slum clearance be kept separate from the cost of new housing."[83]

In his report to Senator George's committee Taft concluded that the same degree of assistance for land assembly and clearance should be provided regardless of the particular type of housing with which the land might be redeveloped. Because of the "accepted national interest in housing conditions," however, federal aid for redevelopment should be provided only "where the area in question is to be redeveloped primarily for residential use or where the area is now predominantly residential in character and the clearance of the area would in itself serve a public purpose through the removal of unsafe and unsanitary dwelling structures."[84] Taft believed that under the latter circumstance federal aid should be available for any use deemed appropriate by the city planning commission. What he did oppose, in his determination to have federal aid used to wipe out slums, was assistance for projects in which new commercial or industrial buildings would replace obsolete stores and factories. By insisting on tying redevelopment, one way or another, to the eradication of slums, he was perhaps not so much helping the cause of housing as limiting the effectiveness of a new tool for the economic revitalization of cities.

When Taft, Ellender, and Senator Robert F. Wagner of New York introduced their General Housing Act of 1945, the measure provided for both redevelopment and public housing, but the bill went far beyond these two subjects and proposed a broad housing program embodying many ideas of Greer and Hansen, Bettman, Draper and Bigger, the Urban Land Institute, and other organizations interested in the problems of cities. The first title, as each main division of the bill was called, provided for a permanent National Housing Agency. The second authorized the agency to conduct research on housing and community development and to give financial aid for local planning. A third title extended existing aid to privately financed housing. Two others offered special mortgage insurance for families of moderate income. Title VI provided federal aid for "land assembly for participation by private enterprise in development or redevelopment programs." Title VII continued the public housing program and expanded it by authorizing the rehabilitation of older buildings for the use of low-income families. Other titles concerned housing on farms and in rural areas, the disposition of war housing, and a periodic inventory of housing needs and programs. After many hearings, revisions, debates in Congress, and countless political maneuvers, this omnibus bill would finally become law as the Housing Act of 1949. The various titles contemplated making the federal government a participant in almost every form of housing enterprise and giving city planning more importance than it had ever had before. Such a bill was bound to be the target of all kinds of attacks.

In opening hearings on the bill late in 1945, Senator Wagner said,

I have heard some comment that all of these proposals to stimulate private enterprise are merely a camouflage for the public housing title of the bill. I do not think that any member of this committee will be able to draw that conclusion, upon studying the bill and hearing all the testimony that will be brought before us. I think this committee may conclude that the camouflage is in another quarter. The camouflage is on the part of those who are perfectly willing to advocate and favor governmental assistance in the accomplishment of their own objective, but who look with disfavor upon governmental assistance to ill-housed families of very low income, including veterans.[85]

As the senator expected, the public housing title of the bill drew particularly heavy fire; furthermore, representatives of financial institutions, associations of home builders, real estate groups, and business associations with few exceptions termed the entire bill dangerously inflationary in a period of scarcities of building materials and skilled labor. Some questioned the objective of encouraging the construction of 12,600,000 new dwelling units in the next ten years, saying that perhaps half that number would be sufficient. Others believed that urban redevelopment should be financially aided only by state and local governments. Still others regarded the bill as threatening ultimate federal ownership and control of all housing. Newton C. Farr, speaking for the National Association of Real Estate Boards, testified that his group would be very much happier about the bill if the public housing provisions were eliminated, giving private enterprise the opportunity to meet all housing needs.[86] "In other words," replied Senator Ellender, "you would want to set the bill aside and give you a chance to try to do it for another forty years, and maybe fail."[87]

Robert C. Weaver, then director of community services of the American Council on Race Relations, favored the bill but found its proposed housing authorization both inadequate and a potential impediment to an urban redevelopment program. He pointed out that the National Housing Agency itself estimated a need of 360,000 units annually for families of low income, yet the bill contemplated annual contributions or subsidies for only 125,000 units annually.

This not only sets an arbitrary limitation upon the extent to which the need of the lowest-income groups might be met, but also constitutes a menace to the excellent provisions in the land-assembly and urban-redevelopment section. It is obvious that the majority of the residents in the deteriorated areas subject to urban redevelopment are in the lowest-income group. The land-assembly provisions justly require that these residents be assured adequate, standard housing as a mandatory condition; yet the complementary program of public housing is limited in such a way as to impede the provison of housing to accommodate these site residents.[88]

Weaver had put his finger on a serious weakness of the bill. As finally passed, it would authorize 135,000 units of public housing annually for a six-year period, but at no time would the public housing program adequately complement the urban redevelopment program. By opposing public housing, conservative groups were laying up difficulties for the very program of redevelopment that some of them supported.

Redevelopment, however, was in its way almost as controversial as public housing. It, too, raised important constitutional questions, required public subsidies, confronted elected officials with troublesome issues of public policy, and challenged city planners to reexamine their long-range programs. Nothing served so well to dramatize the new problems posed by redevelopment as the huge Stuyvesant Town project of the Metropolitan Life Insurance Company, scheduled to be built as soon as the postwar shortage of building materials eased. Announced in April, 1943, the very month that the first redevelopment bill was introduced on Capitol Hill, this project depended only on types of aid authorized by the Urban Redevelopment Corporation Act of the State of New York; but as an initial venture by private enterprise into the field of urban redevelopment, the Metropolitan scheme brought to national attention most of the issues debated by state legislators and members of Congress as they considered redevelopment legislation in the period 1943–1949.

The postwar planning pamphlets of the National Resources Planning Board had urged large-scale rebuilding of cities. The Metropolitan project amply satisfied this criterion. It included eighteen blocks in the old "gashouse district" of Manhattan, from First Avenue to the East River between Fourteenth and Twentieth streets. At one time 27,000 persons had occupied the tenements in the area, but only 11,000 were living there at the time the life insurance company submitted its project plan to the city planning commission for approval. Architects, planners, and many others immediately criticized the scheme because the company proposed to house more than 24,000 persons on the 61-acre site, at an overall density of more than 390 persons per acre. (The original area of the tract was almost 67 acres, but 5 acres were ceded to the city for widening two bordering streets.) Even though the thirteen-story buildings in the development would cover only a fourth of the land, this density was called "shocking" by architect Simon Breines, "inhuman, anti-social, and uneconomic" by a group of Columbia University students, and "excessive" by any number of other protestants;[89] yet planning commissioner Robert Moses defended it because it was lower than the densities in most of the blocks in the vicinity, lower than those in some public housing projects, and lower than those in many new apartment neighborhoods. The company itself maintained that the high land costs, notwithstanding the twenty-five-year tax freeze on the site, necessitated this density. Was

85. (upper) Stuyvesant Town in foreground, Peter Cooper Village in background; (lower) Stuyvesant Town area before redevelopment *(Thomas Airviews, courtesy of Metropolitan Life Insurance Company)*

redevelopment, then, going to result in very high densities in other cities, whereas most proponents of redevelopment talked of decreasing the population in blighted areas and reducing congestion?

Architect Henry S. Churchill and many others deplored the omission of public schools in the plan of Stuyvesant Town, but this was perhaps less serious than the prospect of a discriminatory rental policy, which discussion of the lack of schools brought to light. When Frederick H. Ecker, chairman of the board of the Metropolitan Life Insurance Company, met with a special committee of the Citizens' Housing Council of New York, he explained that no provision had been made for a public school because if there were one, it would permit some children, including Negroes, to attend from outside the area. A week later at a public hearing before the city planning commission a reporter asked Ecker whether Negroes would be admitted to Stuyvesant Town. The board chairman replied that they would not be because "Negroes and whites don't mix."[90] Was a project that would benefit by the city's contribution of valuable street and school lands, partial tax exemption, and the building nearby of new city facilities, which the project would require, to be allowed to exclude applicants for apartments because of the color of their skins? A taxpayer's lawsuit to prevent the city from completing its contract with Metropolitan was dismissed by the courts as premature, since there was as yet no definite tenant-selection policy and hence no actual discrimination.[91] But the constitutional question of the right of a private company receiving public aid to discriminate against some of the taxpayers making possible that aid remained unsettled. Would the racial issue deter other large insurance companies and many financial institutions from investing in redevelopment? Would it dampen the interest of city councils and state legislatures in ridding urban areas of blight?

In his testimony before the Senate Committee on Banking and Currency Robert Weaver pointed out that approximately a million Negroes had moved during the war, some from rural to urban southern areas, others from the South to the urban North and West. "For the first time," he said, "many of them [Negroes] have the money to pay for satisfactory housing; our economy promises all equal access to consumer goods in a free market; but for minorities the housing market has not been and is not free. We must take steps to make it so."[92] He offered amendments to the Wagner-Ellender-Taft bill to prevent discrimination in publicly assisted housing, but was a majority of congressmen willing to prohibit unfair practices? Weaver spoke of the "suffering, despair, disillusionment, and frustration" common in restricted areas where high rents were charged for inferior accommodations, and he mentioned the possibility of a repitition of the race riots after the First World War.[93] Would redevelopment contribute to racial tensions, perhaps to explosive outbreaks?

At the behest of the Metropolitan Life Insurance Company the state legislature had amended the original urban redevelopment law in 1943 so that it did not require provision of housing for displaced families, whereas the Wagner-Ellender-Taft bill required "a feasible method for the temporary relocation of families living in the redevelopment area who are to be rehoused in new dwelling units built in the redevelopment" and a guarantee that "decent, safe, and sanitary dwellings" would be available for families forced to move elsewhere, at rents or prices within their means and "in areas not less desirable in regard to public utilities and public and commercial facilities."[94] The life insurance company later, however, established a tenant relocation bureau to assist families in the Stuyvesant Town area in finding new quarters. But before this was done, a survey of the Committee on Housing of the Community Service Society of New York revealed that not more than 3 per cent of the families living on the site could reasonably expect to be rehoused in the project itself and that only a little more than a fifth would be eligible for public housing. Late in 1945 an official of the relocation bureau reported that 90 per cent of the families had moved into better quarters than those they left and at equivalent rents, but few managed to escape old, overcrowded neighborhoods. The building of Stuyvesant Town suggested that redevelopment might cause the spread of congestion rather than its elimination, not only in New York City but also in many other cities. And what effect did removal have on the social relations of evicted families? Half the households occupying the blocks acquired by the Metropolitan had lived there for twenty years or more. How greatly were their friendships and their neighborhood ties disrupted?

Stuyvesant Town, in short, posed the fundamental question whether redevelopment projects were really in the public interest. A year before hearings on the General Housing Act of 1945 were held, the New York Court of Appeals had held that the Metropolitan project was justified on the grounds that it would result in the clearance and rehabilitation of substandard and insanitary areas—an opinion later upheld by the United States Supreme Court. Tracy Augur commented, "A public subsidy is being granted not to get something that the public wants so much as to get rid of something that the public considers disadvantageous. Will the public get the riddance that it pays for?"[95] Or would it get a whole new set of problems as vexing as any associated with blight? Until Stuyvesant Town was completed and in operation no one could know for sure. Augur thought the project would be "worth the price" if for no other reason than to induce and keep alive the kind of argument that had been generated by it, "argument that makes it the excuse for probing the imponderables of urbanism." Americans would continue to have "rotten cities" until they began to take them seriously and got at the underlying facts on which their rottenness was based. Burnham had warned against approaching their renovation with little plans because little plans have no magic to stir men's blood. Stuyvesant Town had already demonstrated its ability to stir men's blood and that in itself was a very useful function, Augur concluded.[96]

Although other cities noted the heated controversies generated by this nationally publicized project, they were not deterred from initiating urban redevelopment studies, supporting campaigns for state enabling legislation, and generally proceeding on the assumption that sooner or later the Congress would provide federal aid for redevelopment. State legislatures encouraged the movement to eradicate blight by broadening earlier legislation or enacting redevelopment measures for the first time. In 1945 Minnesota and Massachusetts followed the example of the states that had already authorized redevelopment companies or corporations to exercise the power of eminent domain in assembling land for redevelopment projects, and in the following year Virginia also enacted similar legislation. But since Senator Taft's report of the Subcommittee on Housing and Urban Redevelopment indicated that federal redevelopment legislation, when finally enacted, would probably provide financial assistance only to local public instrumentalities, eleven states took the further step in 1945 of adopting statutes that designated public housing authorities, municipal departments, or special redevelopment agencies as vehicles for acquiring land and clearing redevelopment sites. These states were California, Colorado, Connecticut, Illinois, Indiana, Maryland, Michigan, Missouri, New York, Pennsylvania, and Wisconsin. In 1946 Rhode Island and New Jersey also authorized public agencies to assemble land for redevelopment. Nine states, including Arkansas, Florida, Georgia, South Carolina, and Tennessee as well as some of those previously mentioned, permitted local housing authorities to be designated as redevelopment agencies. Other states, such as California, Pennsylvania, and Rhode Island, created a new quasi-independent redevelopment agency in each community, to become operative upon the appointment of commissioners by the local legislative group. Colorado and Indiana were among the states providing for new municipal departments to assemble land and prepare sites for rebuilding. Under the newer laws only two states sanctioned partial tax exemption of private projects in redevelopment areas.

Illinois alone appropriated state funds ($10,000,000) for grants to local housing authorities and land clearance commissions for urban redevelopment, but Indiana created a special taxing district in the Indianapolis area with power to levy a general tax for a redevelopment fund to be spent on a pay-as-you-go basis. The tax, with a millage limit on it, was estimated to produce $500,000 a year for the first few years and $250,000 a year thereafter. Skeptics doubted, however, whether such yields would be sufficient to finance much land acquisition. Most states indicated that they were awaiting federal aid by expressly stating that redevelopment agencies might receive federal loans or grants.

Of the score or more of states having redevelopment legislation by 1946, at least two-thirds required review of proposed projects by the local planning commission. The statutes of Indiana, Kansas, and Wisconsin expressly stated that the planning commission must approve any project before it could be carried out. Not all redevelopment laws specified, however, that the planning commission must have a general plan as a guide for judging whether a project would be of long-term benefit to the community. The California and Rhode Island laws, patterned after a model redevelopment law prepared by Alfred Bettman, required cities to have both a planning commission and a master plan before undertaking redevelopment. Both statutes listed the essential elements of such a plan. Though generally indicative of the acceptance of city planning, redevelopment legislation revealed that in some states and among many proponents of redevelopment there was as yet no great understanding of the planning function or of the importance of rebuilding blighted areas in accordance with a well-conceived comprehensive plan of community development.

Without state or federal financial assistance, or both, municipalities could actually do little to start the clearance and reconstruction of deteriorated sections. In 1945 the city council of Kansas City, Missouri, adopted an ordinance providing that any person or corporation desiring the aid of the city in furthering a redevelopment plan might petition the city council for approval of its plan. But in this and other cities which took action to invite life insurance companies and financial institutions to invest their funds in redevelopment, there were few firm proposals for projects. Meanwhile, studies by various planning commissions and private groups tended mainly to illuminate the difficulties of removing blight. A report prepared by the Los Angeles City Planning Commission indicated that 70 per cent of the families in residential areas requiring redevelopment were paying smaller rents than would have to be charged in projects built by private enterprise on cleared land. A booklet issued by the Manhattan Development Committee maintained that urban redevelopment projects offered large financial institutions an opportunity to make a stable profit, but the illustrative study of a square mile in East Harlem showed that even with the tax exemption available under the New York law, the land costs and construction costs would be so great that a density of almost 400 persons per acre would· be an economic necessity. And as in the Stuyvesant Town area, only a

LOS ANGELES

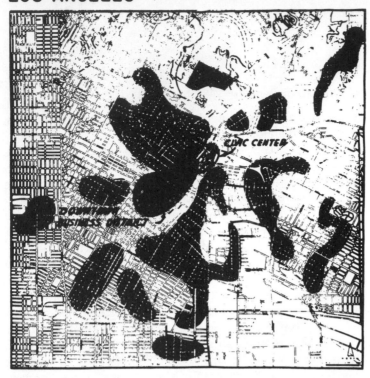

86. Areas of worst blight in Los Angeles and New York, 1945 *(National Housing Agency)*

NEW YORK

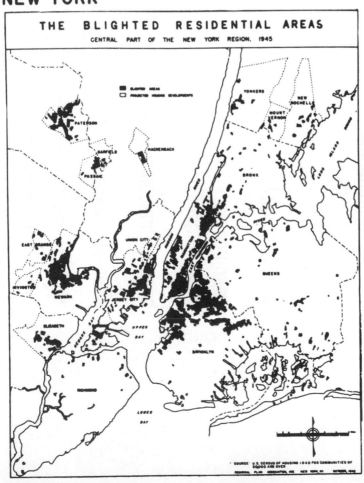

fifth of the persons living in the neighborhood could afford to become tenants in a new private development.

Worried merchants, city councilmen, and planning commissioners who had looked forward for years to the postwar rebuilding of the blighted areas surrounding central business districts had not foreseen that the return of peace would present a complex of conditions blocking redevelopment, the most serious of which was an acute housing shortage. Already severe at the end of the war because of the deficiencies in production during the thirties and the curtailments of wartime, the shortage became even more alarming as millions of servicemen were demobilized. By the end of 1945 approximately 6,500,000 had returned to civilian life, and in the following six months at least 3,300,000 more came home from garrisons in Europe and Asia. Most of those reunited with wives, or with families who had been living with relatives, sought to establish their own households; many others married and went house-hunting. In May, 1946, the Congress appropriated more than $250,000,000 to convert barracks, wartime housing, and trailers into temporary homes for veterans and their families, but these structures provided for only a small percentage of home seekers. The pressures on the existing supply of

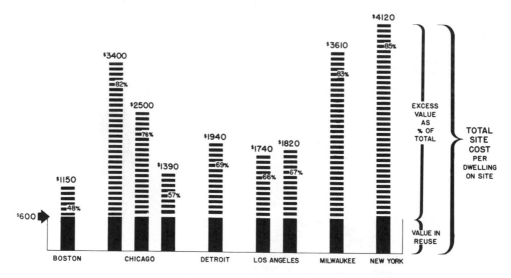

COST OF CENTRAL SLUM SITES PER DWELLING ON SITE COMPARED WITH REUSE VALUE FOR REDEVELOPMENT AT EXISTING DENSITIES–BASED ON LOCAL STUDIES IN 6 LARGE CITIES

87. The high cost of slum sites compared with the reuse value for redevelopment (*National Housing Agency*)

housing were so intense that families occupied even the most unsanitary
and deteriorated dwellings.

Although there was a back-to-the-farm movement in the two years
immediately following the war, which temporarily increased the farm
population by more than 2,000,000, another vast reshuffling of the population mainly added to the numbers in urban areas, particularly in the
West, the North Central States, and the East. Attempts of the Truman
Administration to stimulate the rapid construction of 1,200,000 homes
in 1946 were frustrated by the refusal of Congress to provide large subsidies to lower the cost of building materials, by the removal of price
controls and an immediate upward surge in costs, and by the shelving
of the Wagner-Ellender-Taft bill, which had been designed to generate
postwar employment in all segments of the construction industry. By
fall less than a third of the desired number of new dwellings had been
built, and the President's Housing Expediter, Wilson Wyatt, former
mayor of Louisville, resigned in disgust. Under such circumstances,
demolition of any but the most unsafe structures was unthinkable; nor
could redevelopment proceed without substantial federal aid to reduce
land costs in blighted areas.

The rejection of the Wagner-Ellender-Taft bill in some ways testified
to the success of all the postwar planning the federal government, state
and local governments, and private industry had done, poorly coordinated
as it was. Instead of experiencing a depression in which unemployment
idled 8,000,000 or more, the nation quickly reconverted to peacetime
production and had only 2,270,000 unemployed in 1946 and even fewer
jobless persons in 1947. Contributing to the relative ease with which
American industry and business readjusted to peacetime operations was
the huge backlog of consumer demands, supported by wartime savings
of approximately $140,000,000,000. Though the construction industry
did not share with other segments of the economy in the reestablishment of familiar patterns of activity, the senators and representatives on Capitol Hill felt no urgency about enacting an omnibus housing
statute as a counter-depression measure. The expected opposition to
the public housing title of the bill developed, but this alone did not cause
its defeat. Rather, the inflation unleashed by the termination of price
controls, the scarcity of materials and goods, and the rise in the value
of slum properties as well as everything else combined to make congressmen fear that 1946 was not the year to encourage redevelopment, especially in view of the necessity of making use of every available dwelling. Many powerful interests, moreover, were still lukewarm about the
rebuilding of blighted areas because the proponents of redevelopment
seemed to want to impose numerous planning, financial, and social controls on companies undertaking reconstruction projects.

The Metropolitan Problem: A New Quest for Solutions

An early emphasis on relating central redevelopment to metropolitan planning had impressed planners and leading citizens in many cities with the importance of being ready in the postwar era not just to rebuild blighted areas but to guide the development of the entire urban area. All the discussion of what was then called "decentralization" had, however, made civic leaders in the central cities painfully aware of the multiplicity of governmental units in metropolitan areas and the difficulties of carrying out areawide plans. The appearance in 1942 of Victor Jones's *Metropolitan Government* had revived interest in various solutions to the problem of fragmented political authority, but it had also convinced some persons that the attainment of multipurpose metropolitan government was a rather remote possibility. Some kind of regional council, composed either of officials or citizens, or both, might, on the other hand, achieve a certain degree of coordination and cooperation and lead eventually to the establishment of a viable areawide government, perhaps limited to particular functions.

To discover what might be the best form of council, A. P. Greensfelder, a planning commissioner of University City, a suburb of St. Louis, gave funds to the American Society of Planning Officials for a nationwide contest for the best proposal for the organization and operation of a regional council in a metropolitan area. The presentation of the prize-winning essays in New York in May, 1943, and their publication later in the year contributed to enthusiasm for regional planning, led to special competitions to solve the problems of "disintegrated metropolitan government" (a phrase used by Jones) in the Boston and Chicago areas, and generally gave impetus to the long-term search for some way to unite areawide planning with areawide decision-making and effective action in metropolitan communities.

Contributing to this heightened concern with the future of the larger urban areas was widespread admiration of two proposals for the replanning of the much-bombed British capital. The first to appear was the County of London Plan, contemplating the removal of 500,000 to 600,000 people from the 116-square-mile area at the heart of the metropolitan complex, not on the assumption that there would be further danger of air attacks but simply to decongest overcrowded areas and create more open space and amenity. This scheme, prepared in 1943 by J. H. Forshaw and Patrick Abercrombie, necessarily called for another indicating where the thousands removed from the central county could be resettled. In 1944 Abercrombie produced his Greater London Plan for an area of approximately 2,600 square miles. This fifty-year plan showed an outer country ring beyond the metropolitan greenbelt that would be suitable for the establishment of new satellites and the expansion of some small existing towns. The two plans together constituted an exciting model for metropolitan plans in other highly industrialized nations and marked the triumph of the garden city idea, long cherished by influential British planners. Americans also noted the use of the neighborhood unit as the basis for much of the planning, not only of the older sections of London but also of the proposed new towns. Coming from a people who had suffered long and intensely from the fury of the enemy but who were sanguine about the future, these plans had an authority commanding respect even among those inclined to denigrate planning. American civic leaders and planners who were already convinced of the need for metropolitan planning found additional inspiration in them for the formation of metropolitan planning associations and the organization of areawide planning programs.

In creating new associations and councils, as well as in establishing official metropolitan planning agencies, these leaders for the most part favored conservative approaches similar to some advanced in the prize-winning essays in the competition sponsored by the American Society of Planning Officials. The less daring proposals for regional councils were especially appealing because they provided for a great deal of citizen participation and appeared to be highly democratic. O'Brien Boldt's essay, for example, described a regional council representing government, private enterprise, and labor and functioning through committees on the problems confronting the metropolis. To make the organization broadly effective, Boldt, a member of the public relations staff of the New York Regional Plan Association, suggested that the regional council should be "rounded out" by the formation of district councils, each with its own committees on local problems.[97] C. McKim Norton and Frederick P. Clark, executive vice-president and planning director, respectively, of the New York Regional Plan Association, outlined a form of regional council that was also readily acceptable to civic-minded Americans because it was not very different from organizations with which they were familiar. Norton and Clark suggested a membership association open to "any individual, government agency, or private organization sufficiently interested to pay dues."[98] The executive board would be composed of some members representing geographical sectors of the urban area and some chosen at large because of their economic and social interests. Like Boldt's council, this one would analyze problems and projects affecting the metropolitan area, develop and coordinate plans and programs for meeting community needs, and secure action by proper public authorities and private interests. Norton and Clark conceded that eventually "some form of metropolitan government may have to be established" to cope with the problem of diffused political authority,[99] but in the meantime a regional council would be a means of getting citizens and important governmental agencies to work together.

Norman J. Gordon, a graduate student at the Massachusetts Institute of Technology, went a step further by describing a regional council that could be immediately organized within the political structure of the typical metropolitan area and later "imbedded in a metropolitan government."[100] His "first stage" council would be directed by a seven-member planning commission appointed by the chief executives of the central city and surrounding cities. The commission would have a professional staff and would be aided by two advisory councils, one composed of officials chosen by the legislatures of the various municipalities in the area, the other made up of citizens appointed by the chairman of the commission. Gordon's "final goal" regional council was also a seven-man group, one of whom would be appointed by the legislature of the metropolitan government and the others by the chief executive with the confirmation of the legislature. He saw no need for continuing the official advisory council, but he retained the citizen group.

The proposals of Boldt, Norton and Clark, and Gordon all served, in various degrees, as patterns for planning organizations created in the next few years. But no metropolitan area modeled a regional council after that outlined by first-prize winner Harvey F. Pinney, principal administrative analyst in the organization planning division of the Office of Price Administration. This fact is in itself a revealing commentary on the novelty of Pinney's ideas and the contemporary development of political thought in American urban communities. Pinney assumed that the federal government would exercise proportionately more influence over local government after the war than before, particularly through grant-in-aid programs, and that federal taxing, spending, and credit activities would play a much larger role in the national economy. He believed, too, that state governments would play a greater part in shaping urban areas. He therefore proposed a regional council—essentially a planning agency—made up entirely of experts, three of whom would be appointed by the federal government, three by the state government, three by the central municipality of the metropolitan area, but none by the suburban areas. Pinney suggested, however, a local-government advisory council and subordinate local-government councils on which suburban areas would be represented, not to mention various other councils designed to represent a wide variety of interests. But he was ahead of his time in wishing to accord the federal and state governments substantial participation in metropolitan planning and development; and he certainly did not understand the jealousy with which suburban areas regard central cities.

The first of the new regional councils came into being in the fall of

1943, and though they reflected the seminal influence of the competition sponsored by the American Society of Planning Officials, the impetus for their formation antedated the contest and stemmed in large measure from the general interest in postwar planning. In the Pittsburgh area the long-continued and impartial research of the University of Pittsburgh led to the organization of the Allegheny Conference on Community Development by leaders in business, labor, and government—the very groups that Boldt had proposed be represented in a regional council. The Allegheny Conference was from the beginning, however, an association of individuals rather than official spokesmen of organizations; and its annual budget of $50,000 was supplied by a central fund-raising agency, the Pittsburgh Civic-Business Council. It therefore enjoyed a certain freedom of action not vouchsafed to official agencies. Its aims were to study areawide needs, propose plans and programs to meet them, and coordinate the many kinds of planning being undertaken by public and private organizations. Essentially these were the purposes described by Norton and Clark in their proposal for a regional council, except that the New York Regional Plan Association with which they were affiliated and which they used as a model had as a reference for most of its actions the long-range plan prepared in the 1920s and frequently modified in the meantime. The Allegheny Conference, on the other hand, relied upon the privately financed and well-established Pittsburgh Regional Planning Association for research on areawide development, studies of mass transportation, and other aspects of so-called physical planning, since the directors had early decided to work whenever possible through existing agencies.

After making a wide range of initial studies through various committees, the conference displayed its strength as an action agency. It formulated and pushed to enactment legislation giving Allegheny County additional powers to control air and stream pollution, review plans of subdivisions in township areas, and dispose of garbage and refuse. The legislative program also enabled cities to create parking and redevelopment authorities and to broaden their tax base. Destined to be a force in the Pittsburgh area for the next quarter of a century and perhaps longer, the Allegheny Conference accomplished much because from the outset it insisted on the personal participation of the heads, not subordinates, of corporations, civic associations, institutions, and governmental units. At least, such was the explanation of its success given by David Lawrence, for many years mayor of Pittsburgh and later governor of Pennsylvania, in 1965 to the San Francisco Bay Area Council, an organization formed a year later than the Allegheny Conference and in many ways similar to it.

The Michigan Planning Commission encouraged community leaders and public officials in the Detroit area to form a regional planning council at about the same time that the Pittsburgh area organized for an attack on its metropolitan problems. As a result of the activities of the Detroit council, the Michigan state legislature in 1945 passed legislation authorizing the state commission to create a Detroit Metropolitan Area Regional Planning Commission. This the state agency did in June, 1947, just before it was superseded by a Department of Economic Development. Upon the recommendation of an advisory committee, the state commission by resolution established a metropolitan commission of forty-six members, half chosen from public officials in the 2,000-square-mile Detroit metropolitan region (the counties of Macomb, Oakland, and Wayne, and the four eastern townships of Washtenaw County) and half from civic, economic, and social fields. Larger than the "first stage" regional commission proposed by Gordon, this one was something of a cross between an official agency and a citizens' council. It had a planning staff too small to be organized in the six specialized divisions suggested by Gordon, but like all the ideal councils outlined by the contestants in the nationwide competition, it appointed technical committees of experts, some from official agencies, others from private businesses and educational institutions, to study problems of land use, transportation, water supply, drainage, pollution, and community services. The staff conducted research on the population, economy, and physical development of the region as a basis for the preparation of a long-term plan. But this commission labored under two serious handicaps: it depended entirely upon the voluntary contributions of local governments and private corporations to finance its operations, and like other metropolitan planning agencies, public as well as private, it could rely only on voluntary cooperation to carry out its plans.

A large regional council resembling the one described by Boldt initiated activities in the Kansas City area in 1944. The mayors of the three municipalities of Kansas City, North Kansas City, and Independence, Missouri, and the mayor of Kansas City, Kansas, in association with the presidents of the chambers of commerce of these four cities, formed the Citizens Regional Planning Council "to fashion and guide the reaction of citizens toward intelligent, long-distance planning through actual citizen participation in local and area problems and projects."[101] This presumably independent and autonomous organization, financed mainly by some two hundred business firms, soon fostered the creation of local planning councils in the three Kansas Cities and the smaller cities of Independence and Excelsior Springs. As all these local groups were affiliated with the regional council, almost 3,900 persons were studying and analyzing local and areawide problems by the fall of 1946, and the board of governors of the regional council was looking forward to an eventual regional membership of 10,000. Local councils had as many as fifteen committees on local problems, the regional council seven major committees concerned with such areawide matters as flood control, trade and manufacturing, railroads, legislation and taxation, and surveys and research. This elaborate committee structure, the founders believed, would assure coordination of regional development and provide support for city and county planning agencies. As late as 1949, therefore, no effort had been made to bring into being an official metropolitan planning agency.

The regional council proved its worth to public officials in the area when, in 1946, it formed a Citizens Bond Committee to determine needed public improvements and make recommendations to the city council of Kansas City, Missouri, and the county court of Jackson County, Missouri. The committee proposed sixteen projects costing $41,000,000, the various local councils supported bond issues for the projects, and at a special election in 1947 all the bond issues received the requisite two-thirds majority. Later the council successfully supported other multi-million-dollar bond issues. All in all, its record suggested that it was what its heads protested it was not — a project promotion organization. Though it focused on specific, well-recognized community needs, its failure to press for an official areawide planning agency understandably raised questions about the degree of coordination the metropolitan region actually achieved as it grew and developed.

The intellectual elite and many of the businessmen of the Boston area probably yearned more intensely for metropolitan planning and metropolitan government than community leaders anywhere else in the United States, partly from a sense of frustration. The region's earlier efforts to achieve some kind of confederation had failed; and since 1941 the Metropolitan District Commission had been without a planning division, though the loss was not, in truth, great because the planning division had had jurisdiction only over transportation matters and its absorption by the Massachusetts State Planning Board had not deprived Greater Boston of a full range of areawide planning services. Stimulated by the nationwide upsurge of interest in metropolitan planning, the Boston Society of Architects decided in 1944 to challenge citizens to outline policies that might be developed to solve the problems of the region. At the society's request, Boston University agreed to administer what was known as the Boston Contest. Among the sponsors were Governor Leverett Saltonstall, Mayor Maurice J. Tobin of Boston, the Boston Chamber of Commerce, Harvard University, and the Massachusetts Institute of Technology.

No fewer than ninety teams and individuals submitted master programs in this competition. The record number of entries indicated that though the Boston area might be politically chaotic, it had lost none of its intellectual capability. But there was nothing unusual about the proposal of the winning team, headed by Carl J. Friedrich, professor of government at Harvard University. Friedrich and his colleagues suggested "a Metropolitan Authority to exercise those joint functions which are clearly metropolitan in nature." It would be governed by a representative council, "possibly elected on the basis of proportional representation, with the pre-existing communities as electoral units." One agency of this federated government would be a planning commission, whose plans would be referred to the council. That body would have "the authority to enact ordinances, to make appropriations, and to enact comprehensive plans for metropolitan development."[102]

Alas, neither this nor any other proposal even hinting at further extension of metropolitan jurisdiction appealed to the suburban communities. As in the past, they distrusted and disliked Boston—its politics, its lower-class elements, its slums, and its high taxes. In a discussion conference held by the American Society of Planning Officials in the summer of 1945, Elizabeth Herlihy, the durable chairman of the Massachusetts State Planning Board, related that an attempt of Governor Saltonstall to bring together the mayors, chairmen of boards of selectmen, and one or two representative citizens from each of forty cities and towns in the Boston metropolitan region to discuss areawide health problems met with the same suspicion that had wrecked other attempts at regional cooperation. "We had to sit down at the telephone and personally contact every community," she said, "and in about 70 per cent of the communities we got back, 'This is another approach to annexation and we don't want to be annexed to Boston.' I don't know how you are going to overcome that feeling."[103]

A group of private citizens had already decided that perhaps they could overcome it by organizing the Greater Boston Development Committee, Incorporated. The committee, according to Theodore T. McCrosky, its executive director, was not an outgrowth of the Boston Contest but was "formed as a parallel expression of the civic consciousness."[104] Organized in March, 1944, as a private coordinating agency, the committee hoped eventually to produce "an over-all physical plan for the long-term needs of the Boston Region" but in the meantime intended to concentrate on such specific problems as the regional highway system, port development, extension of sewer and water systems, and the expansion of parks and parkways. As optimistic as other private regional groups, it buoyed itself with the belief that gradually there would be "progressive consolidation of separate administrative agencies" and some day—no telling when—a genuine desire for limited regional government.[105]

The Greater Boston Development Committee was, however, a disappointment. One of the participants in a metropolitan planning symposium at Harvard University some years later referred to it as having "gotten off the rails,"[106] and Catherine Bauer lamented that "the Boston problem is a puzzle to which the key apparently has been lost." Was it because, as she said, no one had a "defensible hypothesis about the dynamics of 'decentralization' under present and future conditions"? Real metropolitan planning, in her opinion, depended upon "over-all control of key factors in the nature and location of new development," but the winners of the first and second prizes in the Boston Contest had assumed an almost fixed pattern of homes, work places, and activities and had not tackled "the much tougher political problem" of determining "whether central areas should in the future have more or less population and industry, where any 'overspill' might go, and whether this suburban area should be developed as a 'balanced' community and that one prevented from further expansion."[107] Nor had the planners of the Greater Boston Development Committee determined, above all, to forgo concern with functional elements of the metropolis for an initial effort to comprehend the social, economic, and technological forces compelling a new configuration of the whole. Abercrombie and other British planners, time would show, had not fully understood such forces when they prepared the Greater London Plan, but they at least had ideas of urban livability to pilot their efforts, and they looked at the entire metropolitan region rather than at its various functional components one by one.

If the logical point of beginning for any attempt at metropolitan cooperation and eventual confederation was the preparation of a metropolitan plan assuming certain technological advances and an inevitable redistribution of population and economic activities, then Cincinnati perhaps pursued an ideal course. Its Citizens Planning Association was formed for the express purpose of promoting the development and use of a master plan for the bistate Cincinnati region, which includes most of Hamilton County in Ohio and the northerly parts of Kenton and Campbell counties across the Ohio River in Kentucky. The Cincinnati City Planning Commission had already decided, however, that the city plan of 1925 should be brought up to date or recast in its entirety, if need be, before the association was organized in the spring of 1944. The citizens' group was initially helpful in supporting the commission's request for an appropriation from the city council to start the work.

The amount granted—$100,000 rather than the $250,000 originally discussed—provided for the establishment of a new Division of City and Metropolitan Master Planning, which at the peak of activity numbered thirty-one persons besides planning consultants Ladislas Segoe and Tracy B. Augur and several specialists. Both state law and the city charter gave the commission the right to plan with respect to "any land out-side the city which in the opinion of the Commission bears a relation to the planning of the city," but since governmental units outside the bound-aries of Cincinnati might not make use of a metropolitan plan prepared without their participation, the commission itself set up a Metropolitan Planning Committee composed of thirty-six official representatives from all cities and counties in the metropolitan area. Five members of this group, three from Ohio and two from Kentucky, sat with the commis-sion in all its meetings on the plan, though the larger committee was not so active as had been hoped.

As the planning program progressed, the citizens' association published a newsletter which it distributed to approximately 8,000 citizens in the metropolitan area. It also sponsored a weekly radio program on various aspects of the master plan and provided speakers for community organi-zations. Still another educational effort was a specially prepared plan-ning leaflet distributed to school children in the upper grades, together with a folio of background material for the use of teachers. Exhibits created jointly by the association and the planning commission attracted large numbers of viewers.

The master plan that emerged as the product of all this official and unofficial activity was, like the earlier Cincinnati plan, a pacesetter, even though Sherwood L. Reeder, administrative head of the long-range planning staff, complained that "the heavy hand of a dead line" some-times curtailed research.[108] As Segoe explained at the annual meeting of the American Society of Planning Officials in 1947, the plan was based on "a complete diagnosis of existing conditions, needs and future require-ments of the whole [metropolitan] area and of each part, and the loca-tion of necessary facilities—for housing, shopping, industry, motorways, schools, recreation areas, etc.—where these were found to be most ap-propriate, regardless of municipal boundaries and in some instances even state boundaries."[109] The consultants and the staff viewed the funda-mental problem as that of refashioning a structural form "essentially of the last century" to fit the highly mechanized mode of living of the twentieth century—a problem common to most of the older cities of the United States and particularly challenging in Cincinnati, which had attained comparatively large size and distinction as the "Queen City of the West" in the decade before the Civil War. Like all venerable urban areas, this one exhibited "serious conflicts between the city as a produc-ing machine and the city as a place of residence" and had many sections in which factories, stores, and homes were indiscriminately mixed.[110] The master plan proposed to correct these defects by assembling indus-tries, railroad lines and other rail facilities, and the trunk-line motor-ways into belts or corridors and by organizing existing residential sections, as well as future ones, in nucleated communities equivalent to "self-contained cities of medium size."[111]

Both the topography and the historic growth of the Cincinnati area suggested the felicity of such a scheme. The metropolis lies in a basin formed by the recession of the hills on both sides of the Ohio River. Valleys lead into this natural place of settlement from the north and the south, along the courses of Mill Creek, the Little Miami River, and the Licking River. As Cincinnati grew, the terrain limited the choice of locations for railroads and industries mainly to the valleys. The residential areas developed first in the basin, later on the hilltops, which were actually sections of a plateau cut by the river valleys. In the process of urban growth some natural separation of land uses thus took place, and rather distinct communities developed, some originating as commuter villages, others as new additions to the metropolis. The master planning division and its consultants identified twenty-five of these communities, varying from 15,000 to 70,000 in population but generally corresponding to junior high school districts. Many had time-honored names and social traditions. It was therefore easy to visualize each one as a cluster of neighborhoods served by a junior high school, a central shopping district, and, wherever possible, a "community civic center" consisting of a branch library, recreation center, health center, post office, and appropriate semipublic buildings. The shopping area, a secondary business district in relation to downtown Cincinnati, would be the counterpart of Main Street in a medium-size city. Each of the neighborhoods would embrace from 400 to 800 acres, have a population of 4,000 to 10,000, and include an elementary public school with a children's playground, one or more small parks, a neighborhood shopping center, and perhaps additional local groups of stores. The various residential communities would be buffered from the industrial belts by recreational open spaces, steep hillsides, landscaped expressways, and industrial parking areas.

Segoe believed that the Cincinnati area "would capitalize to the fullest extent on all the advantages that an urban society can offer to the average family" if it were reorganized in accordance with the plan, since the area would then regain, in the system of internally cohesive communities, "the desirable environmental and social conditions" characteristic of cities of 50,000 to 100,000 population, yet would continue to have ready access to "those institutions to be had only in a great metropolitan city — such as the university, art museum, great library, symphony orchestra — things a town of 100,000 population can rarely afford."[112]

Segoe proposed a similar structural form for Detroit, San Fransisco, and other cities engaging his services as a consultant. In San Francisco, with its hills and valleys and its strong sectional interests, the new concept of the community area had particular applicability, but in the spread-out Michigan city it had less significance as an organizing principle. In Cincinnati the components of the community area, the neighborhood units, were, however, more difficult to shape than in either Detroit or San Francisco. "The theoretical ideal neighborhood is bounded but not entered by major traffic streets," Malcolm H. Dill, chief of planning and design in the Master Plan Division of the Cincinnati City Planning Department, pointed out. "In the Cincinnati area, however, the highly irregular street pattern and spacial limitations induced by rough topography make it almost impossible to develop even a single neighborhood that is not crossed by at least one fairly important thoroughfare."[113]

Another new element in the Cincinnati plan was the system of expressways, or as they would be called today, freeways. But it was new only in the sense that by then almost all metropolitan plans projected a network of these limited-access, grade-separated routes. The Los Angeles County Regional Planning Commission had presented an areawide freeway scheme in 1943. Similar proposals for the Cleveland and Denver areas had appeared in 1944, and for Atlanta in 1946. The Cincinnati web was designed to incorporate two links of the federal interregional highway system, one a north–south route running from Detroit to Florida, the other a northeast–southwest route from Cleveland to the Gulf States. The plan showed these routes joining on the south border of the central business district in an "expressway distributor" and continuing across the Ohio River into Kentucky as a single route. The blighted riverfront area where they came together, potentially the most accessible spot in the entire metropolitan region, was designated for redevelopment as a regional convention and recreation center, with an exposition hall-arena, auditorium, interregional bus terminal, heliport, riverview restaurant and garden cafe, high-rise apartments, waterside parks, and a floating harbor for small pleasure craft. This imaginative proposal, seizing upon the opportunities to revive an obsolescent commercial-industrial area provided by new means of circulation, central location, recreational possibilities, and recognized community needs, was in many ways the prototype of redevelopment plans for similar areas in Detroit, Pittsburgh, San Francisco, St. Louis, and other cities.

In several ways the Cincinnati metropolitan plan revealed a heightened awareness of city planning as a process. The motorways element, for instance, indicated the stages in which the freeway system might be developed. The report on residential areas (the plan first came before the public in a series of fifteen technical studies) designated some neighborhoods for complete clearance and redevelopment, others for extensive rehabilitation, still others for municipally guided conservation efforts,

and yet another group for protective action to keep them in good condition. The plan thus envisaged a variety of governmental activities
over a long period and presented "things to be done" in the fields of legislation, planning, and administration, but it pointed out that in the Ohio
city, as in cities throughout the nation, local action depended greatly
upon what the federal government eventually might do to assist urban
areas.

Until the Congress did more to stimulate the private housing industry
and to provide financial aid for clearing blighted areas, all master or
general plans would represent a certain frustration of city planners and
of the city councils and citizens who received them. Planners were beginning to realize that although they could sharpen the familiar instruments for carrying out plans—such as zoning, subdivision regulation,
the capital improvement program, mandatory referral of proposed projects to the planning commission for its review and recommendations,
the public information program, and public housing—much larger and
more varied programs of state and federal aid would be necessary to
effect any broad reshaping of cities. With few exceptions, the metropolitan planning efforts in the latter half of the 1940s were predicated on
federal assistance for the development of airports, interstate freeways,
flood control works, housing, and redevelopment projects—though not
as yet on the expectation of grants-in-aid for mass transportation, sewers,
water supply systems, neighborhood centers, open-space land, and urban
beautification, as in recent years.

Since the Cincinnati plan was a long-term guide for a metropolitan
area, what was lacking in the conception of planning as a process was
some program for creating a partnership of federal, state, and local governments to carry out the plan, perhaps including a limited regional
government to which the federal and state governments might make
grants-in-aid or with which they might negotiate agreements concerning projects to be constructed by their own agencies. W. R. Kellogg, city
manager of Cincinnati, held out the hope that Cincinnati itself would
make good use of the plan because "the function of city planning is closely
allied with the operating departments and legislative branches." But
would neighboring communities respect the plan? Kellogg noted how
the interests of the whole metropolitan area were inextricably woven
together, but the governmental, taxing, and planning functions were
"still hopelessly divided among a multiplicity of agencies," and people
did not seem as yet to recognize that " 'in union there is strength' in
metropolitan government as in national government."[114] Was the Cincinnati area, with a master plan but no prospect of metropolitan government, really any better off, then, than if it had no plan at all? City planners regarded the plan as a gain, but, as usual, they pinned their hopes

on the frail reed of voluntary cooperation among the local governments in the area—and prayed for the best.

Wrestling with the whole problem of making planning in metropolitan areas effective, political scientist Victor Jones suggested that the federal government itself should encourage the integration of local government in metropolitan areas. "One of the conditions for grants-in-aid in such fields as public health, education, public housing, urban redevelopment, highways, and other public works should be the justification of particular projects in terms of metropolitan needs and the effect of the project on other governmental programs in the metropolitan area," he wrote. The sidetracked Wagner-Ellender-Taft bill, for instance, required that federally aided redevelopment projects "shall conform to the locally approved redevelopment plan and be consistent with the interests of the locality as a whole." Jones believed that the term "locality" should be defined in the bill to include the entire metropolitan area.[115] Thus the federal government could oblige any metropolitan area to prepare an areawide plan if it hoped to justify its requests for federal funds for the construction of important projects; and thus metropolitan planning agencies might be summoned into being, and eventually perhaps also metropolitan governments with taxing powers and authority to guide the development of large urbanized territories.

Thomas H. Reed, another political scientist who believed strongly in metropolitan planning, had the satisfaction of knowing that he contributed to the formation of a metropolitan planning commission that enjoyed the favor of several local governments if not of a formal alliance of such governments. Called to Atlanta, Georgia, in 1937 to make a survey of the governmental problems of the area, he had left a report recommending, among other things, the establishment of a metropolitan planning commission. "Unless a master plan for the whole area is adopted, irreparable injury will be done," he had warned.[116] And though he may have thought that in subsequent years the community was indifferent to his suggestion, some members of the Atlanta Chamber of Commerce had not forgotten it. In 1947 they rallied their fellow members to urge the enactment of state legislation authorizing the creation of a metropolitan planning commission for a district including "all of the territorial area of Fulton and DeKalb Counties." The new agency, financed by annual voluntary appropriations from the City of Atlanta (55 per cent), Fulton County (37 per cent), and DeKalb County (8 per cent), had the distinction of being the first official metropolitan planning organization supported from the beginning entirely by public funds (if one excepts county planning commissions functioning as "regional" agencies).

No one knew more precisely than Reed the frustrations likely to attend the efforts of an advisory agency unattached to any regional authority, multipurpose district, or federation of local governments. Yet there was always the hope that the very gravity of metropolitan problems would induce city and county officials to respect a master plan prepared by the metropolitan planning agency, especially if some of them were members of it. In this instance, the mayors of Atlanta and Decatur, the two county seats in the metropolitan district, were ex officio members of the commission. The chairmen of the planning commissions of Fulton and DeKalb counties were also members. These and other commissioners realized only too well that the problems Reed had mentioned—haphazard suburban growth, slums and blight, snarled traffic, inadequate public transportation, and a deplorable insufficiency of recreation areas—had become more serious in the intervening years. If the governments these men represented invested their funds in devising a well-researched metropolitan plan, presumably they would find it useful—all the more so because the businessmen of the community expected results from the planning activity.

The new commission "tooled up" to produce, first, a land use scheme for a "primary planning area" of 300 urbanized square miles, then a plan for water and sewer systems, rail and truck facilities, schools, parks, and other community service areas. By 1952 a preliminary master plan would appear and by 1954 a revised plan reflecting community reactions and changing conditions, but so rapidly was the Atlanta area destined to grow that a few years later the need for a plan embracing five counties would become apparent and a new commission would replace the one formed in 1947.

Even more complex than the problems of the Atlanta area were those of the St. Louis metropolitan region, which, like the Cincinnati and Kansas City areas, was a bistate territory. But whereas citizens and officials in those two bisected urban areas contented themselves with programs of coordination or metropolitan planning efforts designed to induce cooperative action, the civic leaders and public officials in the St. Louis area had in mind something more substantial. They had not forgotten the final report of the St. Louis Regional Planning Commission of the mid-thirties, recommending an interstate agency to develop as well as plan the metropolitan region. When, in 1944, the widespread interest in postwar planning and metropolitan planning inspired the organization of a new voluntary citizens' group, the Metropolitan Plan Association, many of the leaders believed that they knew the direction in which its activities should lead—toward a bistate development commission.

The association carefully prepared the way for a revival of the earlier recommendation by appointing the usual study committees on metropolitan problems and making sure that citizens in all three counties of the metropolitan region participated. There were fourteen committees concerned with major aspects of regional development, planning groups in each of the counties and in the city of St. Louis, and representatives of each of the smaller planning groups on each of the fourteen functional committees. After a year's study these committees and groups unanimously agreed that some kind of Missouri-Illinois governmental agency was required to cope effectively with the critical, interrelated metropolitan development problems. Accordingly, the association set to work to draft bills to be introduced in the legislatures of Missouri and Illinois.

In 1947 the association was successful in having legislation passed by both states authorizing the appointment of temporary or interim commissioners to "prepare a program of organization and administration whereby the affected communities of the area may most effectively plan and guide the development of the area in matters which are of concern to the area as a whole."[117] The commissioners were directed to "give specific attention to and make recommendations as to the advisability of establishing a permanent bi-state administrative body." Their report was to be submitted to the legislatures of Missouri and Illinois in 1949, and for their work they were given an appropriation of $50,000.

The Metropolitan Plan Association then continued to exercise a controlling influence by engaging the firm of Harland Bartholomew and Associates to prepare a preliminary guide plan to serve as a starting-point for the deliberations of the commissioners and to give them "a reliable and comprehensive view of the metropolitan situation, which would be difficult to secure in any other way without large expenditures."[118] Bartholomew was, of course, a logical choice to prepare the plan because he had prepared the report of 1936 recommending that "a governmental agency be created by interstate compact or other legislative action to prepare unified plans within the St. Louis Region." That report, as has been pointed out, was developed with the cooperation of the National Resources Committee.

The metropolitan guide plan issued in 1948 presented a "new horizon" for the consideration of the interim committee. "What was once a single city has now become a multiplicity of governmental units," the Bartholomew report stated. "Plans for a great city cannot be prepared by a convention of communities. The vision and perspective required for planning the modern metropolitan city cannot be expected at the small community level. We need a new approach — big plans for the new big city. And then, if those plans are to be carried out successfully, certain administrative authority must be established at the metropolitan level."[119]

Was the new horizon as broad as it should be? There seemed to be a basic assumption in the guide plan that giving the St. Louis region "orderly form," preventing it from becoming "a vast heterogeneous sprawl," and improving its transportation facilities, housing, sewerage and drainage systems, and park and recreation areas would enable it to compete with other metropolitan communities for a fair share of national commercial and industrial growth. Bartholomew suggested that "a metropolitan agency" should conduct "a continuous economic survey whereby significant needs are promptly disclosed and correctives proposed,"[120] but the correctives mentioned were mainly public improvements to facilitate production and distribution. Were not some other forms of planning needed? If so, the report did not allude to them. Like most reports by city planners, it assumed that public investment in desirable projects and public planning and regulation of land uses would create the right conditions for the expansion of the regional economy; but in a nation making rapid technological and scientific advances and witnessing great shifts in population and an increasing tendency of people to choose places of residence with benign climate and urban amenities, this assumption was blithe and perilous. Unless a metropolitan region planned in the economic sphere, in education, and in social services, and unless it related all these other forms of planning to its program of physical development, it might not make the gains it expected, might become relatively less important among the populous centers of the nation. To a degree, the suggestions in the guide plan implied the need for planning in the fields of public health, transportation, industry, utilities, and recreation, and certainly in the realm of government, yet the plan in its entirety conveyed the impression that proper attention to major problems of the physical environment would assure metropolitan well-being.

The guide plan found much for a metropolitan agency to do. In addition to conducting a continuous economic survey, it should prepare detailed population studies from time to time and foster a well-balanced distribution of population, as well as maintain a comprehensive land inventory and make periodic analyses of trends within the entire metropolitan region. It should assist public agencies and private enterprise by sponsoring sound urban redevelopment, the enactment of minimum standards of housing, good subdivision regulations, modernized building codes, and adequate local planning and zoning throughout the area. The plan pointed out that a comprehensive transit study of the entire area and a comprehensive highway plan were seriously needed, not to mention studies of the desirability of combining certain rail, water, and truck terminals. It suggested that a metropolitan agency should develop and operate "a system of airfields adequate for the air transportation needs of the future."[121] It proposed complete control and operation of large parks and conservation areas by a metropolitan agency.[122] And it envisaged such an agency studying problems of water supply, recommending the interconnection of public water supplies serving adjacent districts, and sponsoring legislation to allow municipalities, sewer districts, and drainage districts to extend their boundaries and to maintain tax rates sufficient to construct and operate the sewerage and drainage facilities necessary for the protection of public health. In short, the guide plan projected a metropolitan agency that would serve both as a regional planning commission and as a public corporation similar to the Port of New York Authority. "Large-scale operations in any field of human endeavor whether in business, in war, or in government require centralized planning and direction," the plan concluded. "The alternative is chaos and waste, if not failure and defeat."[123]

Would the temporary bistate commission hesitate to propose so powerful an agency? Not at all, provided there was popular support for the idea. The commissioners enlisted the cooperation of the Metropolitan Plan Association to determine whether community leaders would endorse legislation creating a permanent bistate agency with authority to plan and operate airports, union freight terminals, highways and bridges, mass transportation, sewerage and drainage facilities, railroads, and parks and conservation areas. Without exception, committees concerned with each type of facility agreed that a bistate agency could help to solve the problems discussed in the guide plan. But before the commission drafted bills to submit to the Missouri and Illinois legislatures and filed its final report, there were more meetings in the counties, more committee reports, and an areawide conference. The proposal for a permanent metropolitan agency established under an interstate compact came before the lawmakers of the two states with the overwhelming weight of public opinion behind it.

Legislators, however, are usually more cautious than citizens, and a great deal more respectful of established political machinery. The Missouri and Illinois solons made sure that they were approving a "service organization" for the city of St. Louis and the six surrounding counties, not a supergovernment. They reworked the bills submitted to them, to maintain unimpaired the sanctities of municipal home rule and private enterprise. They authorized an agency that would be supported by income from the facilities operated and the services rendered but would have no taxing powers. It could make a comprehensive plan for the region and could construct and operate transportation facilities, bridges, tunnels, airports, and terminals; it could plan and establish policies for sewage and drainage facilities; and it could make plans for submission to the communities in the area for coordination of streets, highways, parkways, parking areas, terminals, water supply and sewage disposal works, and recreational and conservation facilities and projects. The Bi-State Development Agency created under the compact between Missouri and Illinois was a composite of a limited authority and a truncated metropolitan planning commission. Certainly, it was not the instrumentality Harland Bartholomew had conceived, nor did it meet the need for a broad-scale, areawide planning agency. On paper, at least, it was something more than many other metropolitan areas had achieved and much less than most urban areas desired, including the one it was to serve.

In 1950 the Congress approved the compact between the two states, specifying terms to protect the federal interest and stipulating that any additional grant of powers to the bistate agency must be submitted to Congress for approval before such further powers could become effective. Within three years it was apparent that there were deficiencies in the legislation and that the agency was hampered by limitations on its power to finance projects through the sale of revenue bonds. It managed to build a large river, rail, and highway terminal, to conduct a sewer survey which led to the establishment of the Metropolitan St. Louis Sewer District, and to make a study of Mississippi River pollution, but these were accomplishments far short of what had been expected. Throughout the greater part of its first ten years the agency sought additional powers, first from the state legislatures and finally from the Congress.

In Greater New York the bistate port authority which had served as the model for the Missouri-Illinois Bi-State Development Agency had never been expected to solve more than a few of the many interstate problems affecting that metropolitan region. Though the authority assumed additional functions from time to time, its general field was transportation. Even in this field its scope was limited, and some of the terminals and crossings it built created additional problems. The privately financed Regional Plan Association formed in 1929 continued to provide the three-state region with the only areawide guidance it received. After the 1930s, however, the association had lost much of its momentum, not only because many of the proposals of the regional plan prepared under the direction of Thomas Adams had been adopted but also because the latter years of the war had deprived the organization of its executive vice-president and its director of planning. Upon returning to the association in the fall of 1945, Norton and Clark had realized that the widespread use of the automobile—far exceeding anything imagined by the makers of the original plan—had caused the region to spread out in a kind of urban rash. Because public officials had spent money on highways rather than on extensions of the rapid transit system, new developments did not cluster around nodes of a region-wide rail transportation network but overran vast outlying areas. In the fifteen-year period from 1925 to 1940 the population of the region had increased 26 per cent while the build-up area had grown 56 per cent. Gone were many open spaces that might have provided scenic and recreational relief in the urban mosaic, and built into the diffuse pattern were enormous problems of communication and travel, governmental inefficiency, and excessive costs. The very failure of the metropolitan region to develop as the earlier planners had hoped suggested a new program to the leaders of the Regional Plan Association.

In a speech at the national Citizens Conference on Planning, held at Newark in the middle of May, 1948, Paul Windels, president of the Regional Plan Association, proposed that the New York region profit by the example of London and embark on a similar policy of planned decentralization. "The New York metropolitan area is today at the crossroads," Windels declared. "This may be the best, it may also be the last opportunity for an effective decision as to our future." Building, held back for years because of depression, war, and inflation, was at last under way again. In the next quarter of a century at least 2,000,000 more people would probably be added to the 13,500,000 already living in the area, and more than 500 square miles of new housing, stores, factories, and institutions of all kinds would be created to accommodate them — the equivalent of forty new cities the size of Stamford, Connecticut, or White Plains, New York. All this additional development would either help to achieve a better metropolitan region or would increase problems of congestion, traffic, parking, transportation, municipal services, and recreation. "Is this metropolitan region," Windels asked, "to become finally and permanently a massive and monolithic structure keyed largely to a few centers with a daily ebb and flow of millions of people to those relatively small areas, or is it to develop as a metropolitan region of many centers of housing, trade, industry and recreation, each clearly defined with its own distinctive identity, with people living closer to places of work and possessing greater opportunities for intimate participation in home community life?"[124]

Like many Americans, Windels viewed "the conglomerate urban mass" as the breeder of antisocial mass emotions, the destroyer of human individuality and dignity, the arch enemy of social responsibility. Influenced by F. J. Osborn of England, a highly articulate champion of the garden city, he urged channeling new growth into "fifty or more intelligently planned and developed centers throughout the region — some of them new towns."[125]

Windels was not prepared to have government appropriate all development rights in land, as the British were doing in creating new satellites and greenbelts. America would have to work out, in its own way and under its own system of government and constitutional powers, the legal mechanisms for controlling growth. But first America needed a policy and a purpose. "To date, there has been no policy of metropolitan development behind state or Federal housing and redevelopment legislation," Windels charged.[126] Every federal law affecting urban development and every state housing and redevelopment corporation law would have to be tested for its application to a new policy aimed at the reestablishment of neighborhood life in cities, the preservation of small regional communities, the creation of new towns, and the wider distribution of employment throughout metropolitan areas. Greater New York, with its twenty-six square miles of blight and its millions questing for more living space, was but the largest of 140 metropolitan areas searching for a more human urban pattern. If it could show the way, almost half the population of the entire country, resident in these areas, eventually might enjoy "infinitely pleasanter lives."

A few months later a federal agency, the National Security Resources Board, gave impetus to the very policy Windels advocated. Estimating that $12,000,000,000 to $14,000,000,000 were being spent annually in the United States for new industrial plants and equipment, the board found that too many of these structures were being built in highly concentrated areas that would be the most attractive targets in the event of atomic war. It issued a statement in which it said, "Studies made to date indicate that areas of industry concentration of less than five square miles, or urban concentrations of less than 50,000 people, separated by about ten miles of relatively open country, will be reasonably secure from attack under all circumstances expected to prevail."[127]

In those days the United States still had a monopoly of the atomic bomb but feared a Soviet scientific breakthrough at any time, after which the possibility of a sneak attack would be a constant threat. The National Security Resources Board discounted the likelihood of a super bomb, such as the hydrogen bomb, as "too remote to warrant serious consideration." The agency therefore set out to persuade American industry to disperse its plants throughout the country, particularly in small cities, because "the prohibitive expense of any enemy attempt to destroy this country's ability to defend itself" would contribute significantly toward outlawing war.[128] But persuasion alone was an almost ineffective power, though for a time the National Security Resources Board found some vocal allies in its campaign to deter further concentration of production facilities in big cities.

Tracy Augur, who had been haunted from the earliest days of the Second World War by the devastation visited upon congested European and British cities by air attacks, fully espoused the federal board's efforts to obtain voluntary consent to a national program of dispersal. "It is a most fortunate coincidence," he told delegates to the annual conference of the American Society of Planning Officials, "that a city of forty to fifty thousand, which the National Security Resources Board considers generally too small to present an attractive target for atom bomb attack, is a rather good size for effective social, economic and political organization."[129] If the United States could achieve a pattern of dispersed small cities located singly, in small clusters, and in large metropolitan agglomerations giving people all the advantages of a highly developed urban civilization, it could "reduce to the point of elimination" the two greatest dangers to its security—that the urban structure on which its economy was built would collapse of its own weight by producing constantly decreasing returns in goods and satisfactions at a constantly increasing cost in money and effort, and that, on the other hand, the urban structure would be put out of action by enemy attack.

For some reason, Windels had not capitalized on the possibility of atomic war as an argument for metropolitan dispersal, contenting himself merely with presenting the self-contained town as the alternative to urban sprawl. But Hans Blumenfeld, then on the staff of the Philadelphia City Planning Commission, was impressed neither by the supposed military necessity of dispersal nor by the assumed virtues of the small town, especially the garden city. All factors which had worked for concentration since the beginning of the industrial revolution were still in force, he noted. Nearness to raw materials or nearness to sources of energy were no longer the principal determinants of industrial location. Proximity to markets and ready availability of labor had grown in relative importance in influencing the selection of sites for industrial plants, and both worked in favor of the big metropolis, reinforcing each other. The basic trends were toward "concentration and decentralization"— concentration from the country into metropolitan areas, and decentralization within these areas—whereas the advocates of new towns wanted dispersal and recentralization into completely new and independent towns that would be prohibited from spreading beyond a preplanned limit.[130] Both the "modern King Canutes," who wanted to reverse the trend toward decentralization by pouring money into redevelopment, and the Windelses, who believed that government could prescribe the growth of satellite towns, even those whose industries and services were highly successful and needed to expand, were wholly unrealistic.

What did make sense was a metropolitan region developed on the principle of "mutual accessibility." This principle required "a combination of minimum need for commuting with maximum opportunity for commuting."[131] Taken alone, these basic requirements for a metropolitan area suited for *making a living* would result in a compact city with an even distribution of places of employment, but the requirements of *living* demanded that the compact city be interspersed with green and open spaces ranging from the domestic yard and the neighborhood park or playground to large parks and open country. Blumenfeld was personally inclined to visualize a city not unlike many that had developed without benefit of planning, with built-up areas radiating from a center, interlocking with green wedges extending from the open country into the heart of the city. But perhaps other urban forms should also be studied; for example, a gigantic grid of mile-wide strips of developed land at distances of, say, five miles, shocking as such a proposed arrangement might seem at first blush. In any event, Americans should approach the problem of the overall shape of the metropolitan region with "more critical analysis of its actual functions and with less emotional reaction to the visual appeal of the plan."[132]

The discussion of the relation of urban structure to urban function was all too rare in American planning circles. The regional planning movement of the 1920s had elicited some consideration of the matter, but there had been almost none during the 1930s and not much in the 1940s until the dangers of renewed sprawl and atomic attack brought the subject to the fore again. With their general distaste for theory and their disinclination to formulate and abide by policy, most Americans in public life, city planners as well as city officials and civic leaders, tended to dodge the whole issue of metropolitan form. Culturally conditioned to problem-solving and socially rewarded for displaying short-term practicality, they felt more at ease adapting to well-recognized trends and working cautiously within the context of a business-dominated economy. Neither the appeals of the National Security Resources Board for planned dispersal nor the Cassandra-like warnings of the more thoughtful planners against uncontrolled urbanization were heeded. Windels and some of his associates in the Regional Plan Association continued until 1950 to call for the development of a federal urban policy and to advocate the creation of satellite cities. Windels himself saw the need for the states of New York, New Jersey, and Connecticut to set up metropolitan district commissions for areas included in Greater New York, so that these three agencies could cooperate almost as one in developing a new areawide plan for the 7,500 square miles by then regarded as comprising the metropolitan region. But none of his proposals met with sufficient response to deflect the trend toward further expansion of peripheral areas. Nor were other metropolitan associations or official commissions any more successful in stemming the outward tide of development. It had continued even during the war as manufacturers chose outlying sites for war plants and contractors and government agencies slapped up housing in areas where cows had grazed. In the closing years of the decade it resumed with more dynamism than ever before, propelled by the pent-up demand for homes, a rising birth rate, large investments in new, spread-out factories, and well-financed highway and freeway programs.

The New Suburbia: Planned and Unplanned

The first seven years of the decade had seen more migration in the United States than in any other period of its history. The Bureau of the Census reported that 60,000,000 persons, or almost half the population, had moved to new homes from 1940 to 1947. Twelve million crossed state lines, and 13,000,000 changed counties within the same state. The West gained 2,000,000 new residents, while the South lost 1,500,000 persons. In this great reshuffling of the American people the farming areas, as usual, contributed to the growth of the cities. Although there was an increase of farm population in 1945 and 1946, when men in the armed forces were being demobilized and industry was converting for peacetime production, by 1948 the number of persons living on farms had begun to decline and was 10 per cent less than in 1940. In the urban areas the prewar trend of more rapid growth in the suburbs than in the central cities continued. The thirteen largest cities increased in population by 10.6 per cent from 1940 to 1947, but their suburbs showed an increase of 19.2 per cent; and in the latter years of the decade almost three-fifths of the new housing was built in the suburbs.

This boom in the outlying areas was just what officials of most central cities had feared. They had been warned to take what measures they could to prevent it, but they were somewhat like generals preparing for the next war by planning to refight the last one. The newsletter of the Municipal Finance Officers Association, for instance, admonished local governments in August, 1944, not to make the mistakes of the 1920s and expend large sums installing public improvements "for the benefit of subdividers." These land merchandisers, in effect subsidized by the taxpayers, would then sell lots to people of moderate or small incomes at relatively high prices, and if the economy should go into a tailspin, sooner or later there would be defaults on payments, mounting tax delinquencies, and more financial troubles such as municipalities experienced from 1929 to 1935. The newsletter pointed out that in most cities there was "a sufficient number of satisfactory building lots inside the city limits with all or some of the public improvements already available" and that construction outside the city limits would tend to further decrease the population and assessed valuation of property inside the city.[133]

The publication advised that the broadest control would be exercised by requiring all subdividers to record their plats and install all necessary public improvements before the plats were accepted and the lots offered for sale (as had been done in Cincinnati since the late twenties and in many other communities since the latter half of the thirties). It suggested that all plats should be approved by legally constituted planning authorities, in unincorporated areas of counties as well as in cities—something that planning commissions in most California cities and counties, for example, had been doing for at least fifteen years, and a few even longer. The newsletter also recommended that state enabling legislation should be enacted or revised to permit municipalities to control subdividing and building "within a reasonable distance outside the city limits." Some states, of course, already authorized cities to regulate developments within a mile and half, three miles, or even five miles of their boundaries; others gave municipal planning commissions at least the right to review proposed outlying subdivisions. And there was nothing novel about the newsletter's suggestion that "construction of undesirable homes in the suburban and rural areas might be prevented by a state building code requiring minimum standards of housing construction and minimum facilities in those areas where municipal building codes are not effective."[134] These and other proposals for forestalling the dreaded "urban explosion" were all measures that well-run states and localities had long ago adopted as sound and essential forms of regulation—but had not found particularly effective as deterrents to urban expansion.

Two years later, when the war was over and the home-building industry was getting back into production, the Public Administration Clearing House realized that there was a new "emergency" demanding new approaches. Under its auspices housing officials, city planners, directors of public works, and persons interested in recreation met for three days at an off-the-record conference in Chicago to discuss "land planning and community protection." They made some of the same suggestions the Municipal Finance Officers Association had put forth earlier and added a few of their own, such as that developers of subdivisions be required not only to install necessary improvements but also to reserve appropriate areas for schools, parks, and playgrounds; or that local governments at least "take timely action" to acquire sites for public purposes themselves.[135] The anxious participants proposed that state planning boards hold meetings of state and municipal authorities to work out a common approach to the problem of controlling new developments and that state boards provide a greater number of consultants to aid local governments. Local meetings between private builders and city officials were also suggested. The members of the conference thought, too, that the National Housing Agency and national organizations of public officials should "do their utmost to impress on local governments the dangers of unplanned development."[136] But there was a note of desperation in the recommendations of the conference—and more than a hint that the members were aware of the inadequacy of existing laws and procedures to head off further scattered, poorly planned development.

Looking beyond the immediate unhappy situation, the participants observed that "the provision of housing at moderate cost in newly developed and adequately planned subdivisions is so complex a task that a greater degree of public management and enterprise is required to supplement the traditional type of police power regulation."[137] This was tantamount to admitting that regulation alone would never produce well-organized residential areas, with schools and parks in appropriate locations and housing sufficiently varied to meet a range of needs. It was highly doubtful, for instance, whether the constitutions of most states would even permit local governments to require subdividers to reserve sites for schools and parks, or to hold them for a specified length of time, so that municipalities and school districts could consider bond issues or other kinds of financing.

A second long-range proposal indicated what the public officials had in mind. It was "that the powers and techniques adopted for urban redevelopment be also applied to the development of new neighborhoods, whether inside present municipal boundaries or not, in order to clear the land of legal and financial encumbrances and insure its orderly development by private or public construction." Going further, the conferees thought that there should be created in each municipality "a department or unit of land management, with adequate powers of condemnation and assembly of land, either by enlarging the functions and powers of an existing housing authority, or by the creation of a new agency."[138] The land could then be properly planned, the public improvements installed by public agencies, and the land sold to private enterprise—and perhaps, in part, to governmental agencies—to develop in accordance with the plan. Others, too, had dreamed of such governmental action to make possible socially desirable neighborhoods in outlying areas; and additional proponents of the idea would appear on the scene for the next two decades or more, always meeting resistance from most developers and real estate men. In 1946, when half the state legislatures and the Congress had not yet accepted the idea of using the power of eminent domain to assemble land in blighted areas, the thought of employing it to bring land in unbuilt areas under single control was frightening. It would "put the government into the real estate business."

The participants in the Chicago conference shared with other planners and with most students of government the desire for "unified," or at least coordinated, planning and development of land in metropolitan regions. They did not go so far as to mention metropolitan government, but they did say that steps should be taken to consolidate governmental units, or to annex fringe areas to municipalities, or to consolidate certain functions of areawide importance, or to grant cities the power to control the planning and use of lands beyond their boundaries. Although there would be many annexations in the coming years, particularly of unincorporated areas, hoped-for consolidations of governmental units and of areawide districts would be few. The vogue for metropolitan planning promised a certain amount of cooperation among governments in urban areas, but the long history of conflicts between central municipalities and suburban communities indicated that learning to work together even in planning would probably be a somewhat painful process and that agreement on programs to carry out plans might come still more slowly, if at all. Certainly, since the members of the conference placed the recommendations for governmental consolidation in the long-range category, they did not foresee early action that would affect the postwar building boom.

That many public officials were particularly blind to the character of the boom was revealed in their proposals for directing new building to older areas already provided with essential streets and utilities. Custom-building for the individual family was well-nigh over except in the upper·income ranges. Large-scale production of identical units or a few standardized models in tracts of twenty, fifty, a hundred, or several hundred acres was now the common practice. Nor was the "package deal" of house and lot really new. The annual report of the Los Angeles City Planning Commission for 1939 had observed that "very few subdivisions are now being created for the purpose of selling lots, but in a large number of new subdivisions the subdividers are actually building homes and selling the home rather than the vacant lots."[139] The merchant builders who had continued operations during the war, erecting small homes in war production areas, had made many innovations resulting in the elimination of laborious, costly methods of single-unit construction. By 1948, small operators could hardly compete with the big developers in most of the fast-growing metropolitan areas of the nation. These entrepreneurs cut costs and saved time by planning entire tracts, purchasing in carload lots, maintaining large inventories, and erecting and finishing many units at a time. They tended to buy acreage near the city limits or in unincorporated areas beyond municipal boundary lines, leaving to individual purchasers the vacant lots in older districts. Their invasion of truck farms, orchards, and dairy lands created new problems in the urban fringe and caught many counties and small cities without adequate laws to control their activities. The immediate postwar years were therefore marked by a flurry of investigations of conditions in the newly developing periphery, the passage of many local subdivision

ordinances and the revision of older ordinances, and the hasty enactment of county zoning measures or the rezoning of agricultural areas to
permit residential development.

An example of the tract providing the "package deal" of house and lot
was developer David D. Bohannon's San Lorenzo Village, near San
Leandro in the San Francisco Bay Area. Begun in 1944 as a wartime
housing project of 1,500 units, it was expanded toward the end of the
decade with an equal number of dwellings on lots measuring 55 by 110
feet. By 1955 it included more than 4,600 houses and had a community
center, a shopping center, schools, churches, and recreation areas.

Much larger was the "planned community" of Park Forest, Illinois,
on which construction began in 1947 on a 2,400-acre site thirty miles
south of the Chicago Loop. Designed for an ultimate population of more
than 30,000, this highly publicized model of the "new suburbia" had
row houses as well as single-family homes, rental units as well as

88. San Lorenzo Village, 1946 *(Gabriel Moulin Studios)*

owner-occupied dwellings. Some three thousand rental units, in row houses grouped around large open courts, were the first opened, together with a section of the main shopping center. Later approximately 950 acres of the site were developed with single-family houses on curvilinear streets adapted to the rolling land. The long-range plan indicated sites for schools, parks, churches, two secondary shopping centers, and public buildings, for Park Forest was conceived as a full-fledged suburb and, in fact, became incorporated under the laws of Illinois on February 1, 1949 — with Dennis O'Harrow, then assistant director of the American Society of Planning Officials, as the first president of the town. There was something particularly appropriate about his election as head of a new community which was the product of considerable planning skill and building know-how. Among those entrusted with the design of the town were H. Evert Kincaid, former director of planning in Chicago, Elbert Peets, who had had a hand in planning Greendale, Wisconsin, and architect Henry Churchill. Phillip M. Klutznick, who had been Commissioner of Public Housing during the war years, was president of the developing company, American Community Builders.

Even more populous than Park Forest was the much-discussed development of Levittown in Nassau County (Long Island) in the metropolitan area of New York. Started in 1947, the community had 51,000 residents living in some 15,000 identical houses at the end of 1950. Levitt & Sons, the builders, constructed the first 6,000 homes for rental purposes, then in 1949 began building homes for outright sale at a price of $8,000, later raised to $9,000. The developers set aside land for school buildings and provided ten neighborhood parks (each with a playground), nine swimming pools, and a community hall. Generally well planned, the project invited criticism because of the single house type, the lack of accommodations for anyone other than young adults with small children, and the governmental, transportation, and traffic problems it created by increasing the population of Nassau County approximately 25 per cent in three years.

San Lorenzo Village, Park Forest, and Levittown were, however, exceptional examples of the efforts of the operative builder. More typical of the postwar years were tracts of a hundred or two hundred houses and a small shopping center — the long-term money-maker for the developer. These developments were merely further additions to the amorphous urban mass, without identification other than the architecture of the houses, if dwellings with more popular appeal than distinction can be said to have any "architecture." Since many of these tracts were smaller than neighborhood size, as city planners familiar with the ideal concept of Clarence Arthur Perry thought of neighborhoods, they made no provision for schools, parks, and churches. The developers, intending to sell to veterans or buyers purchasing under terms of FHA-insured mortgages, usually endeavored to meet FHA standards in street layout and lot design if not compelled to adhere to the standards of local subdivision ordinances. But they added few if any amenities, and accretions of tracts bore no resemblance to well-planned communities. Indeed, the ubiquitous urban sprawl in itself constituted a persuasive argument for a public department of land management such as the participants in the conference of the Public Administration Clearing House had envisaged — a department with power to reserve sites for necessary public buildings and open uses and to acquire certain properties for development under leases or covenants requiring the provision of housing for a wide range of households. The typical tract, designed to attract the "average" middle-class family, was a phenomenon significantly lacking in diversity and urbanity. Most sociologists and many city planners would soon be condemning it as a one-class, antidemocratic, socially repressive environment.

But the monotony of the greater part of the new suburbia could not always be attributed to the developers or to the planners they employed. The older residents of some outlying areas were hostile to proposals seeking to introduce variety in the suburban scene. Consider the fate of a project designed by architect Vernon DeMars and some of his friends. Called Fort Drive Gardens and situated in Maryland just outside the District of Columbia, it was to include a combination of detached and semidetached houses, row houses, raised row houses, and a few high-rise structures on hilltops, but the householders of nearby suburban areas objected so strenuously to the very idea of having "apartment dwellers" in the vicinity that the development had to be redesigned as an area of single-family homes.

Frederick H. Allen, of the planning firm of Harrison, Ballard, and Allen, reported similar opposition in 1946 to the proposal of a group of prominent savings banks in New York City to develop garden apartments and a shopping center in Westchester County, New York. The banks wished to build on an old golf course, to save as many of the trees as possible, and to adapt a variable, open, and interesting site plan to the gently rolling topography, in direct contrast to the gridiron pattern of streets in adjoining residential areas. But again neighboring property owners protested. Apartments were apartments, no matter how well designed, and apartment tenants were necessarily inferior to homeowners. Rezoning of the area was defeated, and by 1950 it had been covered with a hodgepodge of nondescript, speculative single-family dwellings.

The New York Life Insurance Company succeeded in building a project in an outlying section of the Borough of Queens in New York City exemplifying the diversity that could be achieved in a large-scale development not hampered by the prejudiced or snobbish opposition of individual householders. Having purchased the Fresh Meadows Country Club, the company created what was known in city planning circles as a "life-cycle" neighborhood — a residential complex providing a variety of units suited to changing family requirements, from the early years of marriage to old age. It included two- and three-story buildings disposed in small groups and two thirteen-story buildings in which most of the small apartments were concentrated. An open, central park area, a six-acre stand of tall oaks, and spacious lawns beside the high-rise structures suggested the relatively low density of the 174-acre project, averaging only seventeen families per acre. For the convenience of the 11,000 residents of the area the company architect, G. Harmon Gurney, and the commissioned architects, Voorhees, Walker, Foley & Smith, designed two groups of service stores in parklike surroundings and a larger shopping center with branches of well-known department stores, restaurants, a theater, and a bowling alley.

The branches of Manhattan stores at Fresh Meadows showed the trend of the times. Merchants with a keen awareness of the population movements and industrial shifts that were remolding urban areas had been establishing new outlets in the suburbs ever since the mid-thirties, but now the big, regional shopping center serving a population of 100,000 to 125,000 or more began to make its appearance. Surrounded by acres of parking space, dominated by a branch department store almost as large as the parent emporium downtown, and boasting a pedestrian mall lined on both sides by carefully selected specialty shops, the new merchandising center was often the only visual relief amid the acres and acres of look-alike houses of the typical suburbia. Together with the freeway, this retail magnet symbolized the increasing detachment of the newer areas.

One of the most expertly planned of the regional centers, the mammoth Shoppers World at Framingham, north of Boston, was under construction toward the end of the decade, after more than two years of detailed market analysis and consideration of many problems of site selection, zoning, financing, architectural design, and coordination with the regional highway system. It represented an effort by the developers, a group known as National Suburban Centers, to "recentralize and re-create a complete pulling power" in the suburbs,[140] but with a somewhat more limited range of goods, styles, and prices than would be found in a central business district serving an entire metropolitan region. In its architectural unity, its calculated grouping of types of stores, its easy accessibility and convenience for customers, its peripheral parking for 4,000 cars, and its inclusion of space for expansion, Shoppers World exhibited all the distinquishing characteristics of a new form of commercial area in which nothing was left to chance. Indicative of the desire of the developers to overlook no important regional aspect of planning such a center was their employment of Professors Frederick J. Adams and John T. Howard, of the Department of City and Regional Planning at the Massachusetts Institute of Technology, as consultants on the project.

In the coming decade city planners would increasingly be sought as members of the teams engaged to do the research and analysis necessary for successful launching of one of these multimillion-dollar ventures. Their collaboration with economists, architects, engineers, landscape architects, financiers, and merchandising experts signified the growing interdependence of professions and businesses in a complex national economy undergoing rapid expansion and restructuring.

The regional shopping center eloquently testified to the growing importance of the consumer in this economy, yet one segment of the economy—

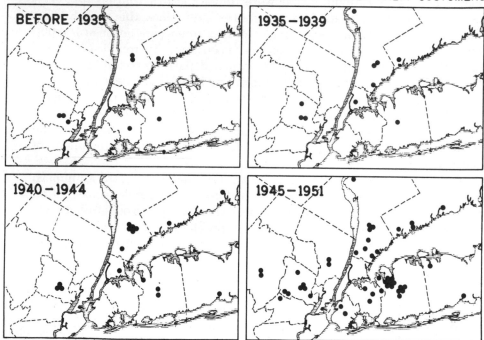

89. Increase in suburban branches of central stores, New York metropolitan area (*Regional Plan Association of New York*)

the home-building industry — lagged behind others in meeting the needs of consumers. Although estimates of the quantity of housing required to replace deteriorated structures and to keep abreast of the population increase varied from 1,000,000 to 1,500,000 annually, the building industry was unable until 1949 to construct as many as a million nonfarm dwellings per year. The Bureau of Labor Statistics reported 662,500 "starts" of private dwellings in 1946, 845,600 in 1947, and more than 913,000 in 1948, but the acute housing shortage persisted and, in relation to need, became even worse. Special housing surveys conducted in 108 selected localities by the Bureau of the Census in 1947 revealed that more than 6,000,000 low-income urban families were living in slums and other housing hazardous to safety, health, and character, and that the number of couples who were living "doubled up" was almost a million more than in 1940. In part, the shortage was aggravated by the extraordinary number of marriages in the first two years after the war—

90. Shoppers World, Framingham, Massachusetts, one of the first regional shopping centers *(Jordan Marsh Company and Arber-French & Company)*

2,300,000 in 1946 and 1,900,000 in 1947, whereas the normal number was said to be approximately 1,400,000 annually. But, more than anything else, the failure of the Congress to adopt a comprehensive housing policy and to provide a variety of financial aids to encourage increased production of housing accounted for the misery of those who were without adequate accommodations. Meanwhile, the mayors of central cities watched the bulk of new homes going up in suburban areas and the number of substandard dwellings in blighted districts increasing. The more suburbia expanded, the more the older cities seemed to lose ground. The political pressures for some decisive congressional action mounted and became irresistible.

The Housing Act of 1949

On Capitol Hill the chamber of the House of Representatives had become the graveyard of the Wagner-Ellender-Taft bill. In the Seventy-ninth Congress and again in the Eightieth Congress the Senate had passed the bill, but the House had allowed substantially similar legislation to expire. Of the seven important recommendations on housing made by the Subcommittee on Housing and Urban Redevelopment of the Senate Committee on Postwar Economic Policy and Planning in August, 1945, only two had been acted upon. In the summer of 1947 the Senate had approved the President's Reorganization Plan No. 3, establishing a permanent national housing agency—the Housing and Home Finance Agency—to succeed the temporary National Housing Agency created during the war. This action, bringing the Home Loan Bank Board, the Federal Housing Administration, and the Public Housing Administration under the supervision of a single administrator, promised coordination of the principal nonfarm housing functions of the federal government and raised expectations that in the not distant future the agency would be given still greater responsibilities for meeting the housing needs of the nation. In 1948 both houses of the Congress had agreed on an act liberalizing the Federal Housing Administration's mortgage insurance programs, instituting a new program for guaranteeing a minimum yield on direct investments in moderate rental housing, and authorizing a program of limited technical research. But this had been the only outcome of the extensive investigations of a Joint Committee on Housing that had held hearings in thirty-three cities from coast to coast in the fall of 1947, had adduced volumes of testimony, and had turned in a report little different from that of the Subcommittee on Housing and Urban Redevelopment in 1945, except that the new report indicated more strongly than ever the need for a declaration of national housing policy and a program to "reach and maintain housing production at a rate of 1,250,000 to 1,500,000 dwellings per year" for a decade or more.[141] In the

House all efforts to provide aid for slum clearance and the redevelopment of blighted areas, low-rent public housing, farm housing, and a comprehensive program of housing research were blocked.

President Harry S. Truman, who had won reelection in November, 1948, after a whistlestop campaign in which he jubilantly castigated "that notorious do-nothing Republican Eightieth Congress," was determined to extract a major housing statute from the Eighty-first Congress. On January 5, 1949, his administration's bill was introduced in the Senate by Senators Ellender, Wagner, and six other Democrats. Senator Taft and fifteen other Republicans, including ultraconservative William Knowland and ultraliberal Wayne Morse, introduced a similar bill. Both were new versions of the old Wagner-Ellender-Taft bill. Both provided $1,000,000,000 in loans and $500,000,000 in capital grants for redevelopment, and both proposed a renewed public housing program, though the administration bill provided for 900,000 new low-rent units and the Republican bill for only 600,000. Both also included aids for farm housing and broadened the housing research program authorized in 1948.

Various other housing bills fell into the legislative hopper, all signifying that the year 1949 would be a year of decision on the housing issue. Some sought to separate redevelopment from public housing, but the Truman Administration and eminent Republicans insisted that the two programs were complementary. Mayors of central cities had emphasized at the hearings of the Joint Committee on Housing in 1947 that without additional low-rent housing for the low-income families who would be displaced by the clearance of blighted areas, redevelopment projects could not be undertaken. After committee hearings, a new bill embodying the best features of the numerous bills was drafted and introduced with biparitsan support.

Two weeks before the Senate approved this bill, a committee of the House began hearings on a similar bill. As in previous years and at recent hearings before the Senate Committee on Banking and Currency, realtors and home builders attacked the public housing title of the bill, charging that the wishes of a local community would not be consulted and that "government housing" would be imposed.[142] "Nothing could be further from the truth," President Truman stated in a letter to Speaker of the House Sam Rayburn. "The role of the Federal Government is very carefully restricted by this bill to furnishing technical advice and financial assistance, and assuring that the requirements of the law as written are faithfully observed."[143] By the last week in June the opposition had been overcome and the House version of the bill was passed and sent to conference. On July 8 both the Senate and the House adopted the report of the conference recommending approval of the Senate bill with certain amendments proposed by the House. The bill authorized 810,000 new units of public housing over a six-year period and empowered the government to make loans and capital grants for redevelopment in the amounts specified in the administration's original bill. A week later the chief executive signed the measure known as the Housing Act of 1949, the first comprehensive housing legislation in the history of the United States and the first to set forth a national housing policy:

> The Congress hereby declares that the general welfare and security of the Nation and the health and living standards of its people require housing production and related community development sufficient to remedy the serious housing shortage, the elimination of substandard and other inadequate housing through the clearance of slums and blighted areas, and the realization as soon as feasible of the goal of a decent home and a suitable living environment for every American family, thus contributing to the development and redevelopment of communities and to the advancement of the growth, wealth, and security of the Nation.[144]

"The adoption of the Housing Act of 1949 is the most significant event in the development of city planning in the recent history of the United States," William L. C. Wheaton, then associate professor of regional planning at Harvard University, wrote in the *Journal of the American Institute of Planners.*[145] The Congress had at last recognized the importance of cities to the national welfare and the necessity for comprehensive planning, witness the provision that the governing body of a locality must find that the plan of a redevelopment project "conforms to a general plan for the development of the locality as a whole."

"The planners have been challenged!" G. Holmes Perkins, the editor of the *Journal*, asserted. With the passage of the Housing Act of 1949, planning in America had come of age, and legislative aids were now available to transform into achievements all the brave words that had been uttered at planning conferences since 1909. But the plans of even the most advanced cities were "puny in scope beside the breadth of the federal aids authorized." There was danger that broad opportunities for urban replanning would be lost in a scramble for isolated and unrelated projects. The legislation, moreover, raised formidable issues that most local governments and city planners had avoided. Were the centrifugal forces pulling cities out into the country to be checked or encouraged? Would cities yield to the temptation to increase the density of population in central areas, even while suburban building went on at an accelerated rate? Could central cities any longer avoid "the head-on impact of the issue of race segregation" if they undertook redevelopment on any widespread scale?[146]

The legislation itself provided no answers to the kinds of questions Perkins posed. It committed the federal government to no policy of metropolitan development; instead, it made available a variety of aids to serve any particular local policy. It offered opportunities for unwise as well as sound urban planning and development. Although it sought the attainment of a national goal of a decent home and a suitable living environment for every American family, it placed upon local communities the primary responsibility for determining what constituted a suitable environment and for making the decisions necessary to achieve one. A careful reading of the act nevertheless disclosed possibilities of conflict between the Housing and Home Finance Agency and cities that might attempt to evade the spirit and general intent of the law. It was, first and foremost, a housing act, and its fundamental purpose was to improve the living conditions of the American people. Nathaniel S. Keith, who had the distinction of being appointed Director of Slum Clearance and Urban Redevelopment in the Housing and Home Finance Agency (HHFA), told the annual conference of the American Society of Planning Officials that the Congress would measure the success or failure of local redevelopment programs by the degree to which they actually bettered living conditions in general "and particularly of the families now forced to live in an environment of slums, blight and congestion."[147] He gave the impression that the federal agency, however much it might endeavor to leave the initiative with local communities, had obligations of its own to see that federal money was spent for programs that would truly help to achieve the stated national goal.

To city planners one of the most significant provisions of the act was that which directed the administrator of HHFA to encourage the operation of local public agencies which could "contribute effectively toward the solution of community development or redevelopment problems on a State, or regional (within a State), or unified metropolitan basis."[148] This language of the act suggested that what communities needed was not just agencies empowered to assemble and clear land in blighted areas but agencies also authorized to initiate new developments on vacant sites either within the city limits of central cities or in territories outside their boundaries — perhaps even satellite cities. But how many states had enabling legislation permitting the creation of *metropolitan* development and redevelopment agencies? How many cities had public agencies, other than housing authorities, authorized to assemble either undeveloped sites or areas encumbered with deteriorated structures? Unquestionably the act enjoined the administrator of HHFA to encourage the formation of advisory metropolitan planning agencies, and since there was already nationwide interest in such agencies, gradually more and more of them would be created. But the act was many years ahead of its time in foreshadowing operating agencies of metropolitan or regional jurisdiction. And a score of states did not yet have legislation providing for urban redevelopment, notwithstanding all the years the subject had been under discussion.

The Housing Act of 1949 sanctioned contracts with a local public agency only if the local governing body found that a redevelopment plan conformed to "a general plan for the development of the locality as a whole."[149] The act had not been amended, as Victor Jones had hoped, specifically to define the term "locality" to mean the metropolitan area, but the injunction to the administrator to encourage local public agencies capable of contributing to the solution of community problems on a "unified metropolitan basis" indicated that the Housing and Home Finance Agency probably would interpret the word "locality" to mean the entire metropolitan or urban area. But how many cities had general plans fashioned on realistic assumptions concerning the growth and development of the entire urban area, projecting land uses and circulation systems based on detailed economic studies of the whole urban complex, and embodying certain proposals of areawide importance that might be reasonably acceptable to neighboring municipalities? Indeed, all too few. And should the federal agency accept the word of a city council that what it considered a general plan actually was one? The housing act did not define the term "general plan," as Bettman would have desired.[150] It did, however, state that a plan for the development or redevelopment of any area must be sufficiently complete "to indicate its relationship to definite local objectives as to appropriate land uses and improved traffic, public transportation, public utilities, recreational and community facilities, and other public improvements."[151] Clearly, the administrator would be justified in issuing regulations requiring that a general plan include as essential elements a scheme of proposed land uses, a plan for circulation, a plan for public utilities, and a plan for community facilities, all closely related to one another as parts of a whole. Clearly, too, the administrator or his deputies would have to judge the quality both of project plans and of the general plan to which they related. And though the Division of Slum Clearance and Urban Redevelopment might say much about local determination of goals and policies and local responsibility for preparing plans, the federal government inevitably would exercise a certain pressure to improve the techniques of planning and the content of local plans.

Title IV of the housing act, providing for a broadened research program, in fact authorized the administrator to "encourage localities to make studies of their own housing needs and markets, along with surveys and plans for housing, urban land use and related community development, and provide, where requested and needed by the localities, technical advice and guidance in the making of such studies, surveys, and plans."[152] Thus the administrator, while exacting higher standards in planning, could assist localities in meeting them.

The act opened infinite opportunities for the federal government to exercise leadership in promoting city and metropolitan planning, improving the quality of planning, stimulating the enactment of new state legislation authorizing metropolitan or regional development agencies, and effecting closer relations between public housing authorities and planning and redevelopment agencies. The solid inducement for local communities to respond to such leadership was the program of financial aids authorized in the various titles. Where redevelopment plans required that the land be sold at less than the cost of acquisition and preparation for reuse by private enterprise, the federal government would make a capital grant amounting to two-thirds of the net loss. The local government would be required to contribute only a third of any such loss, but its contribution might take the form of public works or public contributions of land or services necessary for the project. As the act made obligatory the rehousing of families displaced by clearance, both temporarily and permanently, it provided financial aids to increase the number of low-rent dwellings for low-income families: the backing of federal credit for the bonds of local housing authorities, and annual contributions of as much as $4\frac{1}{2}$ per cent of the capital housing cost of public housing projects for a forty-year period, to enable housing authorities to establish rents that low-income families could afford. The total amount of such contributions authorized was $308,000,000 annually. Related to these aids for public housing was a provision of importance in a time of housing shortage. New public housing projects could be built on open sites as well as on cleared slum sites. Thus additional low-rent dwellings could be built in advance to receive families who would have to be moved from sites marked for clearance and rebuilding. The federal law eliminated as many of the roadblocks to coordinated community action as any precedent-shattering statute perhaps could in its initial form. The rest was up to the cities and the state governments. If the law needed revision and expansion, theirs was the task of showing, on the basis of their experience with it, wherein it should be amended.

Members of the American Institute of Planners had foreseen that passage of this act would greatly increase the demand for qualified city planners, not only to prepare the general plans prerequisite to federal financial aid but also to staff redevelopment agencies and make plans for the reconstruction of blighted areas. Their profession was still small, numbering a few more than 600 members in 1949, but it had been growing rapidly since the end of the war, when the total national membership was only 240. As the planning departments of cities with populations of 250,000 or more employed at least 650 persons, and as many smaller municipalities also had one or more full-time employees engaged in city planning, the number of persons carrying on the planning function in urban government was considerably larger than the roster of the professional organization. Some were engineers, architects, landscape architects, economists, and public administration experts who had found opportunities to work in municipal and county planning offices or with planning consultants and were, so to speak, becoming city planners by learning on the job, under the supervision of older men who were members of the institute. But the profession realized that in the future its ranks should be swelled by men and women especially educated for the field, even though for many years it might be necessary to expand planning staffs by employing some promising applicants without academic degrees in city planning. The most hopeful augury for proper development of the profession and reasonable success in meeting the demand for competent planners was the increase in the number of graduate schools of planning since the end of the war.

After the establishment of planning programs at the University of Michigan, the Illinois Institute of Technology, and the University of Washington in 1941, only one other graduate curriculum in city planning had been inaugurated during the war, at the University of Wisconsin in 1944. That program, however, was offered not in a separate department but by a committee composed of sixteen members from twelve departments, whereas the graduate program in planning launched at the University of North Carolina in 1946 was the first to be established from the beginning as an independent department. This development came about as a result of several joint conferences between representatives of the university, the Tennessee Valley Authority, and state and local planning agencies in the area. The new program stressed urban rather than regional planning, notwithstanding the interest of officials of the authority and state planning agencies in its initiation.

That same year Michigan State College authorized a four-year undergraduate curriculum in urban planning—the first to be sponsored by a department of landscape architecture since Harvard University offered the degree of Master of Landscape Architecture in City Planning in 1923. In 1949 the college inaugurated a graduate program, although undergraduates continued to predominate in courses in planning.

In 1947 Rexford G. Tugwell was appointed chairman of an executive committee to administer a graduate curriculum in planning begun at the University of Chicago in 1945. Since this institution had contributed to significant advances in the study of the urban community through the research of eminent social scientists—for example, sociologists Robert E. Park and E. W. Burgess, geographer Charles C. Colby, and political scientist Charles E. Merriam—its planning program not unexpectedly emphasized social sciences, research, and regional studies. The curriculum was more closely allied in spirit with the program at the University of Wisconsin, which also was based on the social sciences, than with the older planning programs rooted in the disciplines of architecture and landscape architecture.

Other planning programs were begun in 1947 at the University of Illinois, Rutgers University, and the University of Texas. The department of landscape architecture at the University of Illinois had offered city planning courses since the time of Charles Mulford Robinson and proudly estimated that almost 40 per cent of its alumni held positions in the planning field, but it was not until that year that a program leading to a master's degree in city planning was authorized. Rutgers established a four-year undergraduate curriculum in city planning, and the University of Texas, through its school of architecture, a five-year undergraduate course leading to the degree of Bachelor of Architecture in Regional and City Planning.

In 1948 three more institutions of higher education recognized the need for special curricula in planning. The University of California at Berkeley and the University of Oklahoma enrolled their first students in two-year graduate programs, and the University of Florida inaugurated a graduate major in community planning as part of a six-year program leading to the degree of Master of Arts in Architecture. The program at Berkeley was under the direction of Professor Thomas J. Kent, Jr., who two years earlier had become director of planning in San Francisco at the age of twenty-nine and had distinguished himself by reorganizing the staff, launching a comprehensive planning program, initiating a pilot redevelopment study, and undertaking revision of an antiquated zoning ordinance. A graduate of the planning program at the Massachusetts Institute of Technology, Kent patterned the curriculum at Berkeley after that of the Cambridge institution. The program at the University of Oklahoma was administered by an advisory committee composed of members of the social and technical science departments, with Professor Leonard M. Logan, Director of the Institute of Community Development, serving as coordinator. This institute aided students in obtaining practical experience on a part-time basis and also provided opportunities for research work.

The department of landscape architecture at Iowa State College, like its counterpart at the University of Illinois, had long included courses in city planning in its regular curriculum before it organized a one-year graduate program in city planning in 1949. Almost a fourth of the alumni of the department had by that time found their way into planning work; hence, the new program leading to the degree of Master of Science, Major in Town and Regional Planning, was a logical development at this institution.

Varied as these postwar ventures in professional education were, they had in common an effort to broaden the background of the man who wished to be a city planner. He must necessarily be a generalist rather than a specialist, the Committee on Planning Education of the American Institute of Planners asserted in an influential report on the content of professional curricula in planning, adopted by the institute in the fall of 1947. Whatever differences of opinion there were concerning the meaning of planning—and the committee found that there were many—through them all ran a strong thread of agreement, namely, that "planning is primarily concerned with integration and hence with the relationships of things to each other."[153] Though this thought seemed to suggest that the planner should, godlike, know everything about everything, committee chairman John T. Howard and his colleagues, Edwin S. Burdell, Mark Fortune, Howard K. Menhinick, and Lawrence M. Orton, sensibly tried to designate the areas of knowledge that would enable the planner to "manipulate the environment" with adequate realization of the probable consequences of his acts. After painful years of practice supported by too little familiarity with some of the newer branches of knowledge, the profession had come to understand that when any of its members made a land use plan of a city or proposed even a single housing project, he was "tampering with the subject matter of all the social sciences." If young men entering the profession were not to labor in ignorance of "the issues at stake," they must have "a general acquaintance with the structures and operation of our modern economic society" and a grasp of the essential subject matter of sociology, economics, political science, law, and geography, as well as detailed knowledge of the techniques of planning, the history of cities and of city planning, the elements of the physical city, and the legal, financial, and educational means of "effectuating" plans.[154]

Examining the apparatus of higher education, the committee found most of it particularly unsuited for the preparation of generalists and integrators. Universities and colleges increasingly had abandoned the liberal educational curricula of the nineteenth century for highly specialized courses of study. The beginning courses in most fields, far from giving a broad view of the subject, were "shaped primarily to aid and encourage the student to go more deeply into that single field." The survey courses by means of which the student might generally acquaint himself with a subject without spending more time than he could afford were no longer available at many universities. Finally, there was the increasing departmentalism of the colleges to contend with. The competitiveness of departments and the passion of their professors for specialized research disqualified them for providing "the fare needed by the student with interests as broad as those of the planner must be."[155]

But the committee believed that it detected a movement against excessive and premature specialization and greater recognition of the need for better general education for the great body of students. Some institutions had diminished the number of electives and were requiring "a larger common core of the fundamentals for all students." If this were indeed the trend, it led to "the belief that selected and persistent students in the most progressive institutions may now actually achieve in their earlier years much of the broad educational background which is essential to a proper approach to the field of planning; and that therefore their later years may be employed effectively in the universities which undertake to provide broad-gauge training in planning."[156]

The committee undoubtedly deceived itself in thinking that there was any noteworthy reversal of the tide of academic specialization. Its report was significant because it heralded greater emphasis on the social sciences in planning curricula and evidenced the increasing sophistication of the planning profession. The members of the committee were, however, perhaps too much in awe of the social sciences, whose high priests often were more preoccupied with methodology than with the application of findings to problems demanding decisions and action. The genuflections to these still evolving branches of knowledge nevertheless indicated a deepening concern with the human element in planning—a concern which in time would lead some planners into closer collaboration with agencies attempting to solve problems of poverty, unemployment, lack of educational opportunity, racial segregation, and social disorganization.

The public housing program begun in the 1930s had brought some of these problems to the fore. The broader development and redevelopment program contemplated under the Housing Act of 1949 inevitably would confront planners with them in all their complexity and explosiveness, because the blighted areas were the repositories of all the dangerous and neglected issues a materialistic society dreaded but knew it could no longer sweep under the rug. It hoped somehow to transform the physical blight without becoming involved with the social blight. This was the most illusory of hopes, as the more thoughtful planners realized. The new breed of planners whom the planning schools were preparing to guide the growth and development of urban areas would indeed need all the knowledge of human behavior and social and economic conditions they could acquire before going to work in the city hall or the county courthouse.

CHAPTER 7

INQUIRY AND INNOVATION: RESPONSES TO URBAN FLUX

City Planning at Midcentury

At midcentury Americans were in a mood for retrospection and prediction. Those who had been born in the days of William McKinley had lived through two world wars and a depression almost as devastating to morale as a military defeat would have been. Now the whole world shuddered at the thought of a seemingly permanent threat—an atomic holocaust. In 1949 the Soviet Union had broken the American monopoly

of the A-bomb, and currently both the United States and her chief antago-
nist in the cold war were secretly at work on the ultimate horror, the
hydrogen bomb. All prognostications concerning the next half-century
began with an agonizing *if—if* there were no sudden annihilation of
the ninety-two American cities specifically identified as potential targets, *if* the political leaders of the two most powerful nations could find
some way to maintain diplomatic relations, *if* huge military expenditures
and foreign aid did not hinder domestic progress.

Assuming that there *was* a future for America, what would it be like?
Most of the executives of national associations dedicated to the improvement of cities foresaw a continuation of the trends that had shifted an
ever larger proportion of the total population to urban areas. These leaders almost without exception also viewed further outward growth of
urban agglomerations as inevitable, especially since all earlier forecasts of a gradual stabilization of the population appeared to have been
upset by the wartime and postwar "baby booms." And if the spread of
urban areas seemed a certainty, so too did many other things: more
children and young people in the schools; more old people retired and
living on pensions; increasing mechanization of all processes; more people with leisure because of shorter hours, curtailment of the working
week, and longer vacations; more wealth per capita; continually rising
demand for professional and governmental services as well as for automobiles, freeways and scenic highways, parks and playgrounds, recreation centers, and resort hotels and motels; and a need for additional supplies of water and power, larger sewerage systems, bigger airports, and
enlarged harbors.

Growth and change would also augment the problems of populous
areas. The struggle to modernize obsolete downtown centers and to redevelop slums would become more intense. Except for the upper- and
middle-income groups, the shortage of decent housing would probably
continue, notwithstanding the construction of more public housing. Air
and water pollution would increase. As new municipalities and special
districts were created, the problem of local governmental coordination
and of overlapping debts and taxes would get steadily worse. "By 1960,"
wrote Luther Gulick, president of the Institute of Public Administration,
"the vital, ungovernable, sprawling conurbations which will be our cities
will cry out for governmental reconstruction."[1]

Within the city planning profession there were various responses to
the phenomenal outward surge of development and the cancerous deterioration of older centers, but generally two points of view prevailed,
neither necessarily wholly exclusive of the other. Among planning directors, consultants, and heads of federal and state agencies concerned
with urban programs there was a conviction that stronger governmental

action should be taken to remedy the obvious defects in city structure and create a physical environment capable of meeting modern social and economic needs. This group tended to believe that city planning could be made more effective by greater use of available knowledge, concepts, and standards, by improvements in administrative techniques, and by closer relations between planners and policy makers. Among professors of city planning, directors of academic research institutes, heads of foundations interested in urban problems, and writers and critics in the field of human environment there was a realization that most or all of the assumptions on which planners had been proceeding needed to be reexamined. Old urban patterns were breaking up, but what was the model (or models) for the future? How much did anyone really know about human motivations, consumer desires, and the market forces reshaping urban regions? Were not city planners urgently in need of some theory to guide their efforts, new factual knowledge to support — or shatter — their hypotheses, deeper understanding of the society they were attempting to help, and clarification of their role in the political structure? The very questions, propounded in speeches at conferences, in articles in journals, and in proposals for research projects, created tensions within the professional ranks and goaded planners of almost every persuasion to reevaluate fundamental tenets and seek new knowledge with which to face a challenging future. From the beginning, the decade of the 1950s was for city planners a period of self-critical adjustment to the dynamism of the suburban boom, the growing intensity of social and environmental problems in the central cities, and the imperatives of important new federal programs affecting urban areas. Notwithstanding some resistance to pressures for reorientation of thought, professional inventiveness increased and the quality of planning improved.

The views of the "actionists" who placed their faith mainly in governmental measures and familiar constructs were represented in a statement of policy on urban development and expansion adopted by the American Institute of Planners at its annual meeting only a month before the census of 1950 was taken. This statement regarded suburban growth as "a move away from excessive congestion" but noted that most new development, in central areas as well as on the outskirts of cities, increased the unwieldiness of metropolitan concentrations and made them less and less able to operate effectively and economically. The ends of efficiency and economy would be met, the statement indicated, by distributing the population in three types of areas. The first would be large urban centers progressively redeveloped into clusters of communities and neighborhoods, each planned for its particular function in the metropolitan city. The second would be cities of "moderate size" developed from existing small towns and physically separated from other cities;

and the third type would be "well-planned new cities of limited size, both in suburban and rural locations."[2]

The statement pointed out that urban structure equivalent to that of a city of 3,500,000 residents was being built in the United States each year and that capital investments amounting to billions of dollars were represented in this annual "plant" expansion and replacement. The important thing, then, was to insure that new construction and rebuilding were in accordance with comprehensive or areawide planning. The federal government, whose agencies seldom coordinated their activities, should adopt a strong national policy "insuring that Federal funds and other aids extended to housing, urban redevelopment, highways, airports, and other facilities in urban areas be made available only in accordance with comprehensive plans prepared by those areas for their development and growth."[3] To make possible the creation of new towns, the states should authorize "new community corporations similar in character to those now operating in the rebuilding of deteriorated central city districts," and either state governments or the federal government, or both, should assist the community corporations financially.[4] Finally, the states should establish "urban districts" to insure "unified planning for urban areas already spread or spreading over municipal boundaries."[5] Such districts might even be vested with the planning and zoning powers previously delegated to municipalities.

In general, the group desirous of taking a fresh look at planning found these proposals acceptable, even stimulating, but many of its members were impatient with a certain orthodoxy among the city planners who regarded the statement as an "advanced" document. These practitioners, mostly the staff men in city and county planning offices, were much too inclined to pay obeisance to canons of zoning instituted in earlier days, to exhibit an almost pious belief in the desirability of the neighborhood unit, and to take as revealed truth the idea that cities should by physically separated by greenbelts. Theirs was the sin of faith or, to say the least, too little healthy skepticism. Itching with intellectual curiosity and questing for new worlds of research to conquer, the academicians and critics confronted their more pragmatic brethren with probing questions. Why, after all, should grocery stores and inoffensive light industries be banned from residential areas? Just how large should a new town be? How did advocates of cities of moderate size define the word "moderate"? Precisely what value was there in giving a community physical identity by surrounding it with a greenbelt? What functions were appropriate or possible for central cities now that urban areas embraced hundreds of square miles?

Catherine Bauer, who liked nothing better than to appear before city planners as an "amateur" and needle them about the limitations of their expertise, was not only the actionist par excellence but also the outstanding spokesman of the wing of the planning profession intent on bringing about reform through research. Addressing planners at their annual meeting in 1950 on "The Increasing Social Responsibility of the City Planner," she figuratively brushed aside the rules of thumb, time-honored regulations, and traditional attitudes and habits of planners, builders, architects, lending institutions, and bureaucrats and applied the scalpel to the very legislation on which they built their fondest hopes — the Housing Act of 1949. Among its stated objectives were "housing of sound standards of design, construction, livability, and size for adequate family life" and "well-planned, integrated residential neighborhoods." What, she asked, are "sound" standards for family living? What is an "integrated" neighborhood? Did anyone really know much about consumer preferences in housing or the kind of city people want? No. Yet day-to-day decisions by dozens of so-called experts were providing millions of people with environments which in the long run might be inimical to their welfare, or at least restrictive and inconvenient. Clearly, planners and their confreres needed help.

"Modern methods of intensive social research could be employed to give us more objective knowledge about how people live, how they want to live, and the social effects of different types of man-made environment," Miss Bauer maintained.[6] In the interrelated fields of sociology, cultural anthropology, and social psychology some very refined techniques for investigating human behavior and attitudes and for under-

91. Catherine Bauer (Mrs. William Wurster) *(Carol Baldwin)*

standing social institutions and human relations were gradually being developed. These techniques had been successfully used by military and industrial agencies but hardly at all by persons working in the fields of housing and city planning. At the Massachusetts Institute of Technology, Columbia University, and New York University some pioneering social studies were under way, but these initial investigations would provide no "answers" to complex social questions. A much larger body of documentation would be necessary, "geared much more closely to the actual decisions that housers and planners are called upon to make." But such refined and intensive analysis would be slow and expensive, and to be really useful would have to be carried out by social scientists working in partnership with housing and planning people. Miss Bauer called upon the planners to display determination and initiative in obtaining adequate resources for research and in establishing the machinery for effective teamwork.

Indeed, members of the American Institute of Planners who realized the inadequacy of contemporary knowledge of cities and political processes had already submitted a statement on the need for "Basic Research on the Urban Environment" to the Ford Foundation. Miss Bauer herself had participated in formulating it, some ten months before she spoke to the planners. It foreshadowed much of the important research undertaken in the next few years if not in the next fifteen or sixteen years; and it was especially indicative of the powerful influence institutions of higher education were beginning to exert on the entire planning field.

The suggested program of research included proposals for small, exploratory studies and for larger research efforts. Among the smaller projects outlined were studies of the influence of town size upon the costs of providing services, doing business, and living, and of the efficiency of towns of various sizes in providing the amenities of life. The scattered and unorganized growth of suburban areas suggested the urgency of detailed study of the economic, social, and legal considerations affecting the selection and planning of new tracts, as well as analysis of the adequacy of such public means of control as zoning and subdivision regulations and the provision of public utilities and other public improvements. The poor and often wasteful layout of many new subdivisions, which not only increased original capital costs but also permanently increased the city taxes necessary to service and maintain such areas, pointed to the need for studies leading to improved design and engineering. The many new residential areas and group developments being opened daily offered excellent opportunities to study social organization in the making—to observe and analyze the effect of house design, site plan, amenities, location, family income, education, and occupation upon the development of social relationships, shared values and attitudes, and group activities. Related to these studies would be another aimed at understanding the implications for cities of the economic, social, and geographic mobility of American families. In a society in which families moved from neighborhood to neighborhood, from city to city, and from one state to another at a rate unprecedented in human history, how could cities contend with the instability of neighborhoods, rapid shifts in land values, and changes in demand for services and goods? The planning of additional streets, highways, and transit services raised questions about the relation of traffic to land use. How little, in fact, was known about the traffic-generating effects of particular land uses and combinations of uses! The research prospectus suggested studies of the interrelations between land use and traffic that would yield new knowledge to guide both planners and transportation specialists.

The seven large research projects described in the proposed program similarly illustrated the critical need to probe current trends and to devise new tools for meeting new conditions. Technological changes in industry had altered the land requirements of manufacturing plants and had caused thousands of companies to seek new outlying sites, yet knowledge of the shifts in location and of the many reasons for the choices made was, at best, fragmentary. A proposed study of industrial dispersion and its effects on urban areas called for two years of intensive fact-finding and analysis, undoubtedly to be followed by further effort. Another study had as its purpose the discovery of the urban functions and activities which are intrinsically central in character and thus require space at a central location within a metropolitan area. Two other suggested studies were also concerned with the perturbing shifts taking place in urban areas, one an examination of the possibility of preventing further deterioration of areas threatened by blight, the other a broad investigation of general trends in the use of land in as many as thirty-five cities.

To fill a large gap in financial knowledge and to throw light on changes in the characteristics of areas, the research prospectus proposed the compiling of a dependable record of the operating and investment experience in major types of urban real estate. Such a record, the American Institute of Planners indicated, would influence taxation and land-development policies of cities, and federal and state aids for housing and urban redevelopment, not to mention the investment practices of financial institutions, real estate organizations, and many property owners.

Only two of the larger studies suggested were not concerned with gaining more insight into the little-understood mechanisms of the private market. One was a comprehensive and critical but impartial analysis of the public housing program, needed because "current discussions . . . are emotional rather than enlightening, dogmatic rather than analytical, and provocative rather than conciliatory."[7] The other was a general study of several metropolitan areas to discover why planning agencies were not more effective and what attitudes, economic and political relationships, interest groups, and governmental policies impeded the solution of areawide problems and prevented or weakened metropolitan planning.

The suggested research program exposed only the most glaring deficiencies in knowledge of urban and regional economies, urban structure, and urban society. To it were appended statements of proposed research prepared by half a dozen universities, the Regional Plan Association of New York, and the Urban Redevelopment Study instituted in 1948 with Coleman Woodbury as director. Together, the various statements constituted an indictment of previous studies of urban life. Many disciplines had contributed to knowledge of cities, but since most studies had been conducted from the special point of view of the researcher and had not taken adequate cognizance of the relevant knowledge provided by other disciplines, the academic world had failed to develop "a comprehensive and integrated theory of city growth and structure or a fully rounded understanding of any particular aspect of the problem."[8] The authors of the statement to the Ford Foundation hoped for an approach to problems of the urban environment that would bring together the knowledge and techniques of all the physical and social sciences. Rather than a highly centralized research effort, they proposed a coordinated utilization of institutions throughout the nation whose varied professional and technical resources could be brought into focus on urban problems on a continuing basis. "A high premium should be placed upon the development of new ideas, new hypotheses, and upon the stimulation of original thinking and approaches," the statement to the foundation emphasized.[9]

The authors were perhaps more sanguine about breaking down the rigidities of disciplines and removing the barriers among the social sciences than they should have been, but at least the suggested program of research marked the beginning of a movement to enlist a larger number of intellectuals in the struggle for enlightenment on the complex economic and social issues raised by the urban "explosion." Unfortunately, in the early 1950s there was no one in the Ford Foundation particularly interested in the kinds of urban problems with which the more thoughtful planners and professors of city planning were concerned. Not until 1955 did the foundation establish an urban and regional program to assist universities and civic groups in research, in the training of personnel, and in public educational activities. But in the meantime the universities themselves, other foundations, and civic organizations gradually recognized the need for a broader attack on urban problems and

inaugurated some of the investigations outlined in the statement submitted by the American Institute of Planners. The University of Pennsylvania, for instance, in 1951 established an Institute of Urban Studies
to conduct "basic and continuing studies of the urban community gen-
erically" and of the Philadelphia region particularly. Individual planners and scholars also undertook urban research on their own initiative.

As schools of planning enlarged their faculties (in response to the cry
for more trained planners) and from time to time persuaded experienced
planners to accept professorships, academic communities learned directly about the seriousness of urban problems and became more deeply
interested in urban studies. Yet there was no massive, coordinated program of urban research such as some of the more thoughtful members
of the planning profession had hoped for. And planners in public agencies
often complained that the new developments in research offered much
more promise than practical results of value in city planning. Researchers struggling to formulate theory and principles countered that there
should not necessarily be any attempt to produce immediately useful
"results." A problem common in other fields appeared: the difficulty of
communication. "How can researchers communicate to planners?" someone asked at the annual meeting of the American Institute of Planners
in 1952. Another planner put the question this way: "How can planners
learn to pick the brains of researchers?"[10] Thus was recognized a problem
that has not yet been solved, though the entire planning profession has
meanwhile become considerably more knowledgeable about the social
sciences and much better able to understand the purposes, methodologies, and findings of sophisticated research.

Disagreements About the Scope of City Planning

To many planners it was especially ironic that at the very time when
they themselves were examining their shortcomings and seeking to
close some of the numerous gaps in their knowledge, a public which had
previously often received their plans and recommendations with skepticism or indifference began to demand guidance on every aspect of urban
development. Even more perturbing was the presence in their own ranks
of men who used that much abused word "comprehensive" in a frighten-
ingly broad context and called upon their fellows to assume command
in fields of planning hitherto regarded as outside the scope of city planning although related to it.

"City planning, regional planning, fiscal planning, economic and social planning, they all are our subject matters, they all concern all of
us," declared Rafael Picó, president of the American Society of Planning
Officials and chairman of the Puerto Rico Planning Board.[11] In his view,
planners, to be effective, should "influence all stages of the creative proc-

ess, from the idea to reality," from the master or general plan to the construction and operation stages, and not merely in urban government but at all levels of government.[12] Economic and developmental planning should not be left mainly to the state planning and development agencies. Cities and counties, in order to do "realistic planning," should also "take into account the resources of the community and the industries that utilize them and provide a source of living for all the population."[13] And "obviously," no planning unit could disregard social and economic planning as a primary activity in the fulfillment of its duties to plan comprehensively for the community. Had not political scientist Robert A. Walker said that to do otherwise would be "to plan the super structure without providing the foundation"? Picó hoped not only for truly broad-scale planning in urban areas but also for "regional planning, side by side with social and economic planning, carried [on] at the national level."[14]

Was this distinguished man suggesting that planners think of themselves as supermen? Was he inviting them to clash with other experts who considered economic or fiscal or social planning their special preserve? Or did he simply believe in close coordination of the several kinds of planning? As in the 1930s and early 1940s, when the National Resources Planning Board ventured into various types of planning and raised deeply disturbing questions for city planners, the Picós and Walkers and others who thought like them seemed to urge the impossible, the dangerous, the philosophically untenable. Surely, no man could encompass every form of planning, nor should anyone even try. But what was the scope of city planning? Where were its territorial boundaries, so to speak? No one had ever been able to say precisely, and all that anyone knew for certain was that in recent years they had been extended — greatly extended. The trend, moreover, was toward further extension, notwithstanding strains and tensions within the planning profession, sharp debates, and occasional cries of alarm and warnings of disaster.

John T. Howard, perhaps speaking for the majority of city planners, held fast to a conception of city planning based on an image of the city as "a good or bad pattern of land uses and population densities, knitted into better or worse workability by systems of streets, utilities and public service facilities."[15] In this context, city planning had social and economic objectives and operated through political machinery, but its product was a plan, or plans, for physical change and development. "We are not talking about planning city governments, nor social structures, nor economic activity," he maintained, "though we are vitally concerned with them as they set goals for us or establish limitations."[16] If Rexford G. Tugwell and E. C. Banfield, in their review of the new edition of Walker's book, offered "developmental planning" as what city planning agencies ought to be doing, that, according to their own definition, was what Howard saw planners in Cleveland, Providence, San Francisco, and a number of other cities actually doing—exerting a daily impact upon the gradual growth of the city, guiding and shaping its elements toward the realization of the goals expressed in the general plan.

For Henry S. Churchill, too, planning was "physical planning, with consideration for economic necessity and social implications."[17] But such definitions had little meaning for some members of the American Institute of Planners, as articles in the Institute's own journal had indicated from time to time. Unanswered was the question whether anyone could draw a fine line between physical planning and, say, economic planning, especially as the planning perspective widened to include interstate and national planning. "Just as some of the leaders of thought in our cities have recognized the 'essential oneness of the community,' so we in the cities must recognize how inextricably urban development and redevelopment are entwined with the soundness and good planning of the regions of which they are a part," Eric Carlson had written in an editorial commenting on a spate of books about conservation. "We urge again the mobilization of support for the development of a national planning policy, program, and organization."[18] Even such fragmentary national planning as the United States presently knew and had known was, however, in reality a compound of economic, social, and fiscal programs, some of the elements of which were physical improvements. And Patrick Hetherton, executive officer of the Pacific Northwest Field Committee of the U.S. Department of the Interior and former executive officer of the Washington State Planning Council, could not overlook this fact when writing an article inspired by Carlson's editorial. In the larger geographic areas of the nation, economic planning and the management and development of resources were so closely related that they were well-nigh inseparable. But Hetherton wondered whether most planners were any longer concerned about "the conservation of resources and the influence of resource management on the economic base of cities, counties, metropolitan areas and regions."[19] At an important planning conference in California it seemed as if such subjects were avoided, particularly when someone suggested that there was a relationship between fast population expansion and water supply. In general, interest among city planners in resource and economic planning appeared to be at a low ebb, and Hetherton thought that some planning commissions were dangerously ignoring the depletion of resources on which the welfare of their fellow citizens depended.

These indications of dissatisfaction with definitions of planning that tended to narrow its focus to the physical environment of urban areas foreboded an eventual revolt against what some members considered the traditional conservatism of the planning profession. Meanwhile, the rejection of broader conceptions of planning was obscured by widespread efforts to make physical planning more responsive to economic and social trends and to develop effective means of carrying out general plans.

New Regulations to Meet New Conditions

City after city revised its zoning regulations to reflect recent economic research and careful land use surveys; many smaller cities adopted zoning ordinances for the first time. Most of the new measures required off-street parking and loading zones; many permitted diversified uses in "planned unit developments" of a certain minimum size; and in the larger cities the revised regulations differentiated among various types of commercial use and protected industrial districts from misplaced residential and commerical uses.

Special interest attached to a plan for rezoning the city of New York, not only because the metropolis had been the first to adopt comprehensive zoning but also because some of the new kinds of flexibility recommended by leading city planners were particularly well exemplified in the proposed scheme. The original zoning resolution of the city, amended more than fourteen hundred times since its enactment in 1916, had become so unsatisfactory that Mayor William O'Dwyer hailed the new plan formulated by the consultant firm of Harrison, Ballard and Allen as perhaps the most constructive undertaking of his administration, but other cities proved more enthusiastic about the firm's recommendations than New York itself. From coast to coast, cities availed themselves of innovations proposed in the rezoning plan, while financial, real estate, and other interests in New York City year after year opposed its adoption. Especially attractive to other cities were suggestions for controlling the total permitted floor area of a building as a multiple of the area of the lot, or what is known as the floor area ratio—a concept actually suggested by architect-planners in the early days of city planning but overlooked for decades. By means of this ratio, which establishes standards of lot coverage in relation to height of structure, and the use of new methods of providing for access to light and air, the plan contemplated the encouragement of greater freedom of architectural design—a matter of interest to architects throughout the nation, as well as to city planners concerned with urban design. Also appealing to other cities were new types of zones devised by the consultant firm with the assistance of ten advisory committees of distinguished specialists. One, for instance, was a special district to facilitate the establishment of offices, laboratories, and light manufacturing companies in the outer parts of the city. Another was a heavy commercial district to provide for automotive and other repair services, building-material yards, coal yards, and similar uses and to keep them out of retail areas. In all, the rezoning plan proposed eighteen groups of uses, in response to new linkages among establishments and the necessity of regulating activities on a much more refined basis.

In the intensive, nationwide effort to revise zoning regulations to accord with the changes in urban life, no group made more significant contributions than the National Industrial Zoning Committee (originally the Joint Committee on Industrial Zoning). Familiar with technological advances in industry and determined to make the method of operating, rather than the type of product, the basis for establishing zoning regulations for industry, the committee first drew up twelve principles that a community should observe in reserving space for manufacturing plants and related establishments. But it was no easy task for the diverse members of the committee to agree on the wording of the principles or the accompanying explanations. "We have done some scrapping," said Harold Miller, executive director of the Tennessee State Planning Commission, who essayed to draft a statement of principles that would meet the approval of "folks . . . ranging from the most idealistic planners to those most hot in pursuit of a commission on a piece of real estate"[20] — the representatives of six national organizations: American Industrial Development Council, American Institute of Planners, American Railway Development Association, American Society of Civil Engineers, Association of State Planning and Development Agencies, and the Society of Industrial Realtors. In August, 1951, however, the committee brought out the consensus of its deliberations in pamphlet form, and before the year was over it was distributing a third printing, so favorably received were its guidelines for allocating land for industry.

In the days since zoning was used chiefly to ban industry from the more desirable districts or to exclude it altogether from a city, public opinion had come to recognize that most communities require a certain amount of industrial development to produce a sound economy. Yet many municipalities still afforded industry little or no protection against encroachment, failed to designate areas served by rail lines and highways for industrial use, and installed streets that cut appropriately situated acreage into sites too small for proper use by large plants. The industrial park, convenient to necessary transportation and especially designed to accommodate modern plants, increasingly offered manufacturers the setting the community itself neglected to provide. But the National Industrial Zoning Committee, although interested in industrial parks, sought a more general solution to the problems of industry. Adequate land use planning, implemented by effective zoning, could assure industry the consideration it deserved. The principles formulated by the committee sought a reclassification of industry based on modern manufacturing processes and an end to negative zoning that stated what might not be done rather than what would be permitted. "It is manifestly impossible to anticipate all technological developments, new products and processes and to include or exclude such unborn industries from special industrial zones," the pamphlet on principles pointed out. "More recent practice has been to permit in the respective industrial districts certain classes of industrial uses which meet stated standards, others being excluded automatically."[21] The committee looked forward to the time when "performance standards," describing the operating conditions an industry would be expected to meet, would be substituted for lists of prohibited industrial uses and unsatisfactory attempts to classify industries as light or heavy and offensive or inoffensive.

The next endeavor of the National Industrial Zoning Committee appropriately was an attempt to find out what kind of performance standards modern industry had established for itself. The committee drew up a questionnaire on every aspect of production and distributed it to some thousands of concerns occupying plants constructed since 1945. But before the forms could be analyzed, Dennis O'Harrow, then director of the Youngstown Comprehensive Plan, rather stole the thunder of the committee by preparing a paper discussing the kinds of industrial nuisances to be regulated and the technology available to measure and control them. This paper, presented at the annual meeting of the American Society of Planning Officials in the fall of 1951, was immediately termed a brilliant contribution to the improvement of industrial zoning.

"The expression 'performance standard' is taken from building code terminology," O'Harrow explained.[22] Older *specification* codes stated what materials must be used and how buildings must be constructed, whereas the newer *performance* codes established what materials and methods of construction must *do,* or how they must perform under stated conditions. A wall, for example, might be built of brick, concrete, or steel so long as it could retain its strength and resist high temperatures in a fire. Most zoning ordinances, O'Harrow declared, were similar to the more primitive specification codes, but the possibility of setting up quantitative performance standards to control noise, smoke, odor, dust and dirt, noxious gases, glare and heat, fire hazards, industrial wastes, and the combination of nuisances associated with traffic and transportation appeared hopeful though difficult. One approach to the regulation of odors, for instance, was through measurements showing the minimum concentration that would give the first sensation of odor. For hydrogen sulfide, the familiar "rotten egg" gas, the minimum would be .0011 ounces in a thousand cubic feet of air. "The odor from our old friends the glue factory, the slaughterhouse, and the fish cannery can be completely eliminated—at least as far as escape into the atmosphere is concerned," O'Harrow assured his fellow planners. "On the other hand, there seems to be no prospect, present or future, for the elimination of the odor nuisance from a stockyard."[23] Even though this use and a few others might have to be prohibited by name from certain districts, the ideal zoning ordinance of the future would probably merely set up standards for most zones. Any industry able to meet the standards for a particular zone would be permitted to operate therein.

O'Harrow recommended that the National Industrial Zoning Committee pursue further its study of performance standards, indicating the need for additional research wherever knowledge was inadequate. He himself foresaw changes that would revolutionize zoning procedures. Many of his fellow planners pondered the problem of administering zoning ordinances containing highly technical performance standards.

Redevelopment: Projectitis and Creeping Blight

Although a rapidly changing technology continued to test the resourcefulness of the planning profession and to compel it to revamp concepts as well as administrative devices, the struggle against blight contributed perhaps more than anything else to the determined quest for reliable ways to translate plans into action. Had the Housing Act of 1949 proved to be the potent weapon against the forces of decay and neglect that its proponents originally thought it was, the search for surer methods of converting policies and plans into tangible accomplishments might have been less diligent, but the act had shortcomings that were soon apparent, and was itself a stimulus to the perennial hunt for mechanisms and stratagems that would enable city planners to influence urban development more directly and more certainly.

From the beginning, the urban redevelopment program authorized by the act was discouragingly slow and disappointing. Even the initial steps, taken amid the continuing housing shortage that resulted from postwar prosperity and the formation of millions of new families, aroused the resistance of families who would be displaced. Most cities, however, faced a long period of survey-making and planning before they could acquire land, relocate families in project areas, demolish structures, and prepare sites for rebuilding by private enterprise. Besides being new and a good deal more complicated than the earlier federally aided public housing program, the redevelopment program was as latent with controversial issues as its forerunner. Members of citizens' housing and planning associations argued about densities and dwelling types in proposed projects. The proponents of moderate-rental housing were disenchanted when economic studies showed that in most blighted areas only housing for families in the upper middle-income brackets would be "prac-

NUMBERS INDICATE RECOMMENDED ORDER OF PROGRAMMING

PROPOSED NEW DWELLINGS

PROPOSED NEW COMMERCIAL DEVELOPMENT

AREAS PROPOSED FOR REHABILITATION

READING RAILROAD PROPERTY

PROPOSED RECREATION AREAS PARKS AND OPEN SPACES

AREAS IN WHICH EXISTING STRUCTURES ARE NOT AFFECTED BY PRESENT DETAILED RECOMMENDATIONS

RESIDENCE   COMMERCE   INDUSTRY

MAJOR INSTITUTIONS

SOURCE SANBORN MAP, VOLUME 8 BASE PREPARED FROM CITY PLAN #119

1   HARRISON PUBLIC SCHOOL
2   PROPOSED JUNIOR HIGH SCHOOL
3   POST OFFICE
4   PUBLIC BATH HOUSE
5   ST. JOHN'S SETTLEMENT HOUSE

6   BRIGHT HOPE BAPTIST CHURCH
7   MT. OLIVE HOLY TEMPLE
8   MT. ZION METHODIST CHURCH
9   PHILADELPHIA GOSPEL TABERNACLE
10 ST. MALACHY'S ROMAN CATHOLIC CHURCH, CONVENT AND SCHOOL
11 WALTERS MEMORIAL A.M.E. ZION CHURCH
12 PLAYGROUND SHELTERS

REDEVELOPMENT AREA **PLAN**

SCALE IN FEET   200 100 0   200   400   600

DECEMBER 1949

PHILADELPHIA CITY PLANNING COMMISSION

SOUTHWEST TEMPLE AREA

92. Proposed order of programming the redevelopment of the Southwest Temple area, one of several blighted areas for which the Philadelphia City Planning Commission made redevelopment studies in the early 1950s

93. (upper) The Point, Pittsburgh, Pennsylvania, before redevelopment, 1947; (lower) the area in 1965 *(Jay Bee Studios and Allegheny Conference on Community Development)*

tical." And to the dismay of many, the war that had broken out in Korea in June posed the threat of restrictions on certain building materials and the deferral of projects even after plans had been prepared.

Seated at her typewriter in September, 1951, more than two years after passage of the Housing Act of 1949, Catherine Bauer lamented that "to many of those concerned the [redevelopment] program has become a kind of combination obstacle race and maze, a tortuous process of finding some feasible route in a vast dim wilderness full of uncharted hobgoblins, stumbling blocks, and divergent paths. . . ."[24] The next impediment would perhaps be the deathblow.

Miss Bauer and her fellow participants in the Urban Redevelopment Study—directed by Coleman Woodbury under the general supervision of an administrative committee composed of executives of the Public Administration Clearing House, American Society of Planning Officials, and the National Association of Housing Officials—found few on-site undertakings to write about. In Philadelphia only one redevelopment project was under way. In Pittsburgh the urban redevelopment authority had cleared ninety old buildings from a commercial slum at the confluence of the Monongahela and Allegheny rivers, and the Equitable Life Assurance Society was beginning construction of three office buildings; but this effort to rejuvenate the historic Point area—once occupied by Fort Duquesne, the frontier French outpost, and later by the British Fort Pitt—had been brought off without any federal aid and testified to the vision and persistence of the Pittsburgh Regional Planning Association and a committee of the Allegheny Conference rather than to the efficacy of federal inducements. In Chicago the Land Clearance Commission was just acquiring a 100-acre site for the Lake Meadows residential project to be built by the New York Life Insurance Company; and in Detroit the redevelopment program had progressed no further than submission of a councilmanic request to the federal government to designate a 131-acre blighted area near the central business district as an official Title I redevelopment project. It would be several years before most cities even received federal funds for the acquisition of properties, and still longer before any dilapidated structures were demolished.

Miss Bauer suspected that groups supporting redevelopment might be trying to do the right thing at the wrong time. The low-rent public housing program was not moving rapidly enough to provide for the relocation of low-income families living in redevelopment areas, partly because some of its long-time enemies had adopted the diabolical tactic of opposing the use of vacant sites for new projects and insisting on the demolition of slums, knowing full well that in a period of housing shortage any housing authority which attempted to evict families would immediately be in hot water. The shortage had made slums more profitable and therefore more costly for redevelopment agencies and public housing authorities to acquire, and the Korean war had caused such increases in the prices of building materials that private firms were becoming wary of undertaking redevelopment at all. Meantime, the suburbs were growing rapidly, with all too little planning, while professional planners kept their gaze on the inner cities and became more and more frustrated by the delays and difficulties of redevelopment.

Some of the delays were inevitable. The constitutionality of state laws granting redevelopment agencies the power to acquire blighted properties by condemnation, clear them, and resell them to private enterprise had to be tested in the courts, nor was there any lack of irate litigants contending that the procedure was plainly and simply a taking of the holdings of one group of owners for the benefit of another. Most of the state supreme courts held otherwise, viewing redevelopment as serving the public purpose of ridding the community of slums and therefore contributing to the general welfare. Occasionally, however, conservative justices scrutinized the kind of redevelopment contemplated and disapproved the reuse of blighted areas for commercial and industrial enterprises, indicating that in their opinion the only proper reuse would be for housing that would accommodate low-income families. Thus the supreme courts of Florida and Georgia struck down the redevelopment laws of their states. "It is inconceivable," said the Florida court, "that anyone would seriously contend that the acquisition of real estate for the declared purpose set forth in the proposed redevelopment plan is for a public use or purpose. . . . If the municipality can be vested with any such power or authority, they can take over the entire field of private enterprise without limit so long as they can find a blighted area containing sufficient real estate."[25] The supreme court of Oregon, on the other hand, took an extremely liberal view of the redevelopment statute of that state, not only upholding it but also declining to judge the wisdom of the enactment as that was "a legislative and not a judicial question." "The legislature has the right to experiment with new modes of dealing with old evils," the court stated in an opinion which further held that even though a few of the structures in a redevelopment area might be standard, that fact would not indicate that the entire section was not a blighted one within the purview of the law.[26]

In 1953 the high tribunal of Illinois reversed its earlier decision that an amendment to the state redevelopment law authorizing the taking of blighted vacant land was unconstitutional and became the first supreme court in the nation to validate the condemnation of predominantly open land that was unmarketable because of obsolete platting, diversity of ownership, deterioration of site improvements, or delinquent taxes and special assessments exceeding the fair value of the land. "In our opinion," the court said, "the interrelationships between slum clearance, the revitalization of 'dead' areas like that here involved, and the construction of additional housing which have thus been recognized by the Congress, the General Assembly, and this court, amply justify the legislature in regarding the matters involved in the present statute as germane to a single subject—the elimination of slums."[27] The justices held that the acquisition of blighted open land was for a public use or a public purpose since the taking tended to alleviate a housing shortage and could be viewed as an essential aid and adjunct to slum clearance. The decision paved the way for similar judicial opinions in Pennsylvania, California, Ohio, and other states in which redevelopment agencies awaited the opportunity to plan open-land projects that would permit resettlement of some families from densely populated slum areas or would generally increase the supply of standard housing and thus facilitate the relocation of disadvantaged groups living in blighted areas. The redevelopment agency in San Francisco, for instance, jubilantly hailed a decision of the California Supreme Court permitting acquisition and replanning of the predominantly vacant Diamond Heights area of 320 acres in the geographical center of the city—a hilly area inappropriately platted with a gridiron pattern in 1869.

All doubts about the constitutionality of redevelopment finally were ended in the fall of 1954 when the United States Supreme Court, in a milestone opinion written by Justice William O. Douglas, upheld the District of Columbia Redevelopment Act of 1945 in a case (Berman v. Parker) in which the owner of a department store in a blighted area in southwest Washington challenged the right of the local redevelopment land agency to acquire his property. Pointing out that Congress exercises over the District of Columbia "all the legislative powers which a state may exercise over its affairs," Justice Douglas indicated the nationwide applicability of the high court's decision.[28] In an important respect his reasoning was similar to that of the supreme court of Oregon. Subject to specific constitutional limitations, the legislature, not the judiciary, "is the main guardian of the public needs to be served by social legislation" enacted in the exercise of the police power, and this principle admits of no exception merely because the power of eminent domain is involved.[29] In language widely interpreted as sanctioning the use of the police power to achieve aesthetic ends as well as validating the taking of properties in blighted areas that will be rebuilt in accordance with project plans conforming to a long-range, general plan, the Justice observed,

In the present case, the Congress and its authorized agencies [the National Capital Planning Commission and the District of Columbia Redevelopment Land Agency] have made determinations that take into account a wide variety of values. It is not for us to reappraise them. If those who govern the District of Columbia decide that the Nation's Capital should be beautiful as well as sanitary, there is nothing in the Fifth Amendment [providing, among other things, for due process of law and just compensation for private property taken for public use] that stands in the way. [new paragraph] Once the object is within the authority of Congress, the right to realize it through the exercise of the power of eminent domain is clear.[30]

Though some find fault with the reasoning of the high court's decision, contending that the issue is not whether eminent domain is being used for a public purpose but rather whether the use of the land seized will be public or private,[31] the judgment in Berman v. Parker remains an outstanding affirmation of the principle of "legislative determination" of social goals and the means of attaining them, within the limitations of constitutional safeguards of individual rights.

The legal hurdles which redevelopment agencies were obliged to surmount were perhaps less troublesome, once the courts had spoken decisively, than matters of planning, relocation, disposition of sites, public relations, and liaison with other public agencies. At the beginning of the federal program only a handful of cities had general plans indicating how proposed redevelopment activities would contribute to the reshaping and long-term development of the community. Among these cities were Chicago, Detroit, Cincinnati, and Cleveland, which in 1950 published a general plan including a "neighborhood improvement" section designating redevelopment areas for residential use, others for nonresidential use, conservation areas requiring corrective action, and areas needing mainly protective measures. The Philadelphia City Planning Commission, though without a published general plan until 1960, in 1948 had certified nine areas, totaling almost six square miles, as blighted. In San Francisco and in Providence, Rhode Island, the planning commissions had also defined the areas needing reconstruction, but in many other cities there were no broad plans, merely schemes for reclaiming one or two particular areas without any studies showing how the proposed redevelopment might relate to city-wide improvement and development.

The relatively primitive state of the planning program in dozens of cities, the lack of any conception among councilmen and executives of city planning as a process carried on systematically with the cooperation of all departments, the absence of firm municipal policies concerning housing, planning, and community development—all these conditions foredoomed the larger redevelopment effort throughout the nation to a limping pace. Even in some of the cities whose planning departments envisaged slum clearance and rebuilding in the context of a sustained administrative endeavor to upgrade and conserve all neighborhoods, the machinery for enforcing housing and sanitation codes, administering zoning and subdivision regulations, and providing needed public facilities and services was underdeveloped and inadequate, nor were housing codes and other regulations always up-to-date and designed to expedite a continuing program of improvement.

Under these circumstances the Housing Act of 1949 presented the Division of Slum Clearance and Urban Redevelopment of the Housing and Home Finance Agency with responsibilities more puzzling than gratifying. The division was to approve financial aid only for redevelopment plans conforming to "a general plan for the development of the locality as a whole."[32] It was to "encourage the operations of such local agencies as are established on a State, or regional (within a State), or unified metropolitan basis," or on some other basis permitting agencies "to contribute effectively toward the solution of community development and redevelopment problems on a . . . unified metropolitan basis."[33] And it was to protect the federal investment in redevelopment by giving "consideration" to the extent to which appropriate local public bodies had undertaken "positive programs . . . for preventing the spread or recurrence . . . of slums and blighted areas through the adoption, improvement, and modernization of local codes and regulations relating to land use and adequate standards of health, sanitation, and safety for dwelling accommodations."[34] At the outset the officials of the division wondered how far they could go in applying the requirements of the act. Did all cities understand what was meant by a general plan? And how many actually had such a plan? Did the plans reflect awareness of the changes taking place in the whole urban area? Examination of the first group of applications for reservation of funds was disquieting. Of 205 localities submitting requests, only 128 had official planning agencies, and only 56 of these had full-time staffs. It was hardly to be expected that the cities lacking planning agencies or adequate staffs had plans prepared by planning consultants or that if they had such plans, the plans were all current and useful.

Appearing at the annual national conference of the American Society of Planning Officials in 1950, Carl Feiss, then chief of the Community Planning and Development Branch of the Division of Slum Clearance and Urban Redevelopment, revealed the quandaries he and his fellow federal officials faced. "The submittals which have come in to us to date indicate a wide difference of opinion or a wide difference in understanding of what the contents of a general plan may be," he said.[35] His audience would be "surprised at the number of local planning engineers who be-

lieve that the street or traffic pattern is the sole framework on which
to hang the plan, not realizing that all public works must hang on a
population plan with its attendant economic base."[36] Some cities even
presented "data of an isolated nature and evidence of data as an excuse
for plans."[37] Assuming that a locality should formulate its planning
goals and express them in a land use plan for the future development
of the community, Feiss asked whether his professional brethren would
agree that the manual of operations being prepared by his division
should require that a market analysis should support the new uses and
reuses of land proposed in the land use plan presented as part of a general plan. Would planners accept the proposition that redevelopment
areas should be designated in relation to "the logical and desirable
neighborhood and community areas which should make up the urban
locality?"[38] Would they support the Division of Slum Clearance and
Urban Redevelopment in insisting that a general plan must include, as
one element, a scheme of public facilities, utilities, and services and
that the municipality must have a program of capital expenditures for
carrying it out? "Will you go along with us," Feiss inquired, "on the
concept that the locality as a whole means the entire urban area, including more than a single political jurisdiction, so as to take into account the probable, possible, and desirable future urban development
in any given locality? Would you be willing to broaden the scope of your
local cooperation to work toward [metropolitan] planning legislation
similar to Atlanta's?"[39]

However much Feiss and others wished to carry out the mandates of
the Housing Act of 1949, they could not in all respects do so and get a
nationwide redevelopment program under way. The language of the act
expressed desires rather than the realities of the current situation; it
sought to establish a basis for raising the quality of urban planning, and
in that it somewhat succeeded from the beginning, but it assumed a
prevalence of good planning and municipal administration that did not
exist. The *Local Public Agency Manual* issued by the Division of Slum
Clearance established the essential elements of a general plan as land
use, circulation, public utilities, and community facilities, and even outlined the kinds of details that should be included in each element, but the
division had to accept the initiation of general planning programs in
many cities, rather than the presentation of integrated plans, as compliance with the requirements for reserving federal grants. It sometimes had to accept the assurances of mayors that local codes would be
modernized and enforced rather than evidence that there were adequate
codes and enforcement programs. It occasionally had to rely on the word
of local officials that families displaced by clearance activities would be
decently rehoused, even though civic groups in the community questioned

the accuracy of the official statistics showing that there was a sufficient number of standard accommodations available at reasonable rents. Not surprisingly, at times the division incurred the wrath of those who had been its friends, as when Ira S. Robbins, executive vice-president of the Citizens Housing and Planning Council of New York, declared in his anger over the handling of relocation in the nation's largest metropolis, "There is the very serious question of just how much support those of us who have fought for urban redevelopment and believed in it should give to a federal agency that takes its own rules, regulations, and standards and scraps them, and leaves it up to a local body or two which ignores the facts also."[40]

Many cities required from a year and a half to two and a half years to bring their general planning work to a stage acceptable to the federal agency. Some local redevelopment agencies, moreover, were unable to proceed expeditiously because the city planning commission was without an adequate budget and staff to provide the broad, general scheme needed as a guide for project planning, and a city could not be certain of finding experienced planners even though it responded to the inducement of federal monies for slum clearance and reconstruction and appropriated funds to inaugurate a local planning program. Planners were more than ever in short supply. But not all difficulties stemmed from lack of money or lack of planners. Planning agencies did not always cooperate with the local agency entrusted by state law with formulating project proposals. In the newsletter of the American Society of Planning Officials for July, 1952, Walter Blucher pleaded with planning agencies not to shirk their share of responsibility for the local redevelopment program or to feel aggrieved when the federal Division of Slum clearance and Urban Redevelopment negotiated directly with local redevelopment officials, as the law required it to do. "Almost universally state redevelopment legislation requires approval of the local planning commission of redevelopment project plans," Blucher noted. "Obviously, this cannot be done adequately by a planning commission unless such redevelopment project plans are related to a general plan for the locality as a whole."[41]

Notwithstanding the provisions of state laws and the stipulations in the manual of operations issued by the Housing and Home Finance Agency to local public agencies concerned with redevelopment, many proposals for the reconstruction of specific areas evidenced little relation to long-range, general plans and reflected no consideration of future areawide development. As the federal-local program proceeded, critical observers saw more and more clearly that most cities were intent on piecemeal projects and were doing little to prevent the spread of blight.

Some of the larger centers, however, were exceptions. Since their planners had outlined comprehensive programs for renewing the entire city, concerned citizens and officials launched movements for the rehabilitation of partially blighted areas and the prevention of deterioration in the better neighborhoods. In 1953 the Illinois legislature, at the urging of the Metropolitan Housing and Planning Council of Chicago, adopted an Urban Community Conservation Act designed to prevent the creation of slums. The measure authorized the appointment of municipal community conservation boards and empowered them to designate particular localities as conservation areas. Boards then had the duty of assisting in formulating plans for these areas. A conservation plan, which was required to conform to the general plan, could include proposals for the use of land, needed alterations and improvements in the street system, suggestions for additional public areas and public buildings, recommended demolition of specified structures and the rehabilitation and conversion of others, desirable zoning or rezoning, proposed building restrictions, and other matters. If the governing body of the municipality adopted the plan, the conservation board was authorized to acquire, by purchase, condemnation, or other means, any property necessary to carry out the plan, and to make repairs to privately owned structures in order to bring them up to the minimum standards of the municipality. The cost of repairs became a lien upon the property, subordinate to prior liens. Like the earlier redevelopment laws, this statute encountered legal opposition, but the Illinois Supreme Court upheld it, saying that the court was aware of no constitutional principle that would prevent a government from taking action against an evil until it had reached its maximum development.

Baltimore for some years had attracted national attention by a program of strict enforcement of building and sanitation regulations in areas which could not be cleared and rebuilt by either public or private funds. The program was a rather simple one, characterized by coordinated inspection by health officials and police sanitarians on a block-by-block basis, with violators, whether tenants or landlords, being brought to trial before a Housing Court. Salutary and educational as this "Baltimore Plan" was in holding the line against the worst forces of decay, it of course fell far short of the scope of undertakings possible under the Urban Community Conservation Act of Illinois, which set a precedent for the general neighborhood renewal plans of a later date.

Particularly noteworthy was the appointment by the mayor of Detroit of a thirty-four-member Advisory Committee for Neighborhood Conservation and Improved Housing, headed by Dr. Joseph G. Molner, commissioner of the Department of Health, with Charles A. Blessing, director of city planning, as vice-chairman. The mayor's charge to the group was to determine what could be done to halt the decline of areas that did not require complete rebuilding—the sixty-three square miles of middle-aged neighborhoods that grew up with the automobile industry during and after the First World War and before the great depression of the 1930s. Though these areas had developed with the protection of a building code adopted in 1911 and contained essentially sound structures, they evidenced the ill effects resulting from the fact that Detroit was without adequate subdivision regulations until 1918, without a zoning ordinance until 1940, and without a general plan until 1947. In many neighborhoods houses stood back to back on constricted lots; stores, factories, and houses were haphazardly intermingled; both illegal and undesirable legal conversions of residential buildings abounded; streets were crowded, partly because there was a lack of off-street parking; and playgrounds and recreation centers were generally lacking. These middle-aged areas, consequently, had been growing shabbier and losing population at an accelerating rate. Upon appointment of the advisory committee, the common council of the city requested the planning department to draft a statement outlining a general approach to the problem of arresting decay and increasing the livability of what amounted to a third of the city. Blessing and his staff suggested treatment of the problem on a community-wide basis with the cooperation of property owners, tenants, neighborhood associations, and public agencies, starting with a detailed study of housing and environmental conditions and progressing to a "pilot" project in which conservation techniques could be tested and perfected. From this beginning was to develop a ten-year conservation program proposing the scheduling of improvements in fifty-five neighborhoods in three major stages, but such a program depended upon federal legislation exceeding in scope what was available when the advisory committee and the city government began their fruitful collaboration.

The Housing Act of 1954

As dissatisfaction with the limitations of the urban redevelopment program increased, cries for broader federal legislation arose. Besides being exasperatingly slow and poorly coordinated with related federal housing activities, the program failed to strike at the roots of urban decay. It treated symptoms rather than causes. Miles Colean spurred the agitation for a more effective attack on the urban malaise with his book *Renewing Our Cities*, published by the Twentieth Century Fund. Scoring intermittent surgery to remove sick cells, he called for a continuous and coordinated process of growth, maintenance, and replacement of the parts of the urban structure.

In September, 1953, President Dwight D. Eisenhower, under pressure from Senator Robert Taft and Secretary of the Treasury George M.

Humphrey, responded to widespread demands for expansion of the federal-aid program by appointing an Advisory Committee on Government Housing Policies and Programs to investigate all aspects of federal housing activities and report its recommendations to him before the end of the year. Colean was named as one of the members, together with a large number of financiers, two labor leaders, two architects, mortgage banker James W. Rouse of Baltimore, and the redoubtable Ernest J. Bohn, director of the Cleveland Metropolitan Housing Authority and long-time chairman of the Cleveland City Planning Commission. The preponderance of bankers and executives of title companies, savings and loan associations, and life insurance companies in the group caused anxious housers and some city planners to fear that the committee had been "stacked" to emasculate the public housing program, which they regarded as an essential complement of the redevelopment program; but they were to be agreeably surprised by the committee's findings and recommendations.

A subcommittee on urban redevelopment, headed by Rouse, discovered that slum clearance projects already approved and in process would remove approximately 70,000 dwelling units in eighty-six cities. These structures occupied some 5,000 acres of land—only eight square miles out of the hundreds of square miles of blighted areas in American cities. At an average cost to the federal government of $2,500 per dwelling unit cleared, the financial authorizations already made by the Congress would provide for the demolition of perhaps 130,000 additional units in the next three or four years. Thus the nation could expect, at most, only 200,000 unfit units to be cleared under the redevelopment program that had aroused great hopes a few years earlier, whereas the subcommittee estimated that the total number of units probably requiring removal was 5,000,000. If the cost to the federal government and the localities could be reduced from $3,750 per dwelling unit ($2,500 federal and $1,250 local) to $3,000 per unit, the total cost of ridding the country of its most disgraceful urban dwellings would be $15,000,000,000.

How much conservation and rehabilitation would cost, the subcommittee could not be certain because the whole concept of conservation was relatively new. There were probably 15,000,000 dwelling units in neighborhoods threatened with blight, and if the cost of necessary spot clearance, street closings and widenings, parks, recreation areas, and other public improvements averaged $600 per unit, the total public cost of this type of program would be $9,000,000,000. The cost to property owners of rehabilitating structures and improving the immediate surroundings would undoubtedly exceed the public expenditures.

Omitting calculations of the cost of conservation and rehabilitation, the subcommittee observed that its own figures indicated the need for a budget of $1,500,000,000 annually for slum clearance alone if the job were to be done in ten years. Stepping up expenditures to five times the rate then prevailing, or to approximately $300,000,000 a year, would extend slum clearance operations over a fifty-year period; and continuing demolition and rebuilding at the rate of the moment would prolong the program for two centuries. Meanwhile, slums would accumulate faster than cities could demolish them. The subcommittee concluded,

> An examination of the cost of the problem reinforces the necessity for developing a much broader approach to slum elimination. If the nature of the problem itself did not require it, budget considerations alone would be sufficient to impel anyone who was sincerely trying to eliminate slums to find ways of preventing the spread of blight in its earliest stages; of rehabilitating dwellings worth saving and of creating sound, healthy neighborhoods out of the existing housing inventory. It is obvious that we must check the cycle of decay before slums are born.[42]

In a special report to the subcommittee, consultant Robert B. Mitchell, professor of city planning at the University of Pennsylvania, gave some perspective to the group's studies and deliberations. "We have never really faced up to the problems of our cities and determined as a Nation to solve them," Mitchell wrote. "We have talked and written for two decades about the menace of urban blight and slums. A few blighted and slum areas have been cleared through a partnership of local and Federal Government, but we have to look for these spots carefully to find them. Meanwhile the forces of obsolescence, neglect, and exploitation have been allowed to compound the problem."[43]

The failure of most Americans to recognize that "the real cities are entire metropolitan areas" contributed enormously to the difficulty of finding solutions. "We must awaken among the people of these regions an awareness that central cities and suburbs are interdependent and cannot survive in the present governmental and physical chaos," Mitchell advised the subcommittee.[44] Air pollution, heavy through traffic, inadequate public services, overcrowded land and buildings, and other influences made the central cities undesirable in competition with newer, outlying districts. The upper- and middle-income population fled, lower-income migrants moved in, trade and industry of high taxpaying ability gravitated to the suburbs, and the revenue base of the "hub" decreased while the demand for expensive services rose. Yet the suburbs, mainly developed by the "spatterdash method" and often poorly laid out, constructed, and serviced, would eventually show the symptoms of blight found in the older cities. Neither suburbs nor central cities escaped "the disorganized and conflicting problems of government finance and taxation" or the consequences of the lack of efficient areawide systems of transportation, utilities, and well-distributed parks and recreation areas. "We need some regional agencies to analyze, invent, and suggest acceptable solutions to these problems," Mitchell urged. Bold regional planning was required "to guide the regeneration of these amorphous urban areas as efficient, functionally sound, and organic physical structures." And there should be "a reshaped governmental structure" which would leave as much local determination as possible to smaller communities within the region, and yet provide on a regional basis those services which could be most effectively and efficiently provided in that way.

The task of solving metropolitan problems was not that of the federal government, Mitchell assured the subcommittee. Rather, it must be "tackled within each region, with State encouragement and assistance." But the national government could make sure that aids to programs of urban renewal or urban highway improvement or to other physical development projects in urban areas were conditioned upon a continuing effort of each region to devise programs of regional integration and development. The states might provide technical assistance for regional planning and establish special commissions to further regional integration, while the federal government might offer grants to the states on a matching basis for these purposes.

Mitchell's suggestions, foreshadowing the motivation of future federal programs of financial aid to state and local governments, appeared in the subcommittee's report as recommendation number sixteen: "That grants be made on a matching basis to State or metropolitan area governmental planning agencies to cover the cost of technical assistance for small cities and towns and for metropolitan regions within States."[45] The proposal that metropolitan planning be made a condition for receiving federal aid had already been applied, insofar as redevelopment was concerned, in the vague requirement of the Housing Act of 1949 that redevelopment plans must conform to "a general plan for the development of the locality as a whole." The subcommittee failed to recommend a broad extension of this principle to all forms of development related to renewal, but its recognition of the desirability of financial assistance for metropolitan planning provided a basis for making such planning a prerequisite for federal aid for a wide variety of urban improvements in later years.

The general report of the President's advisory committee, embodying the reports of its five subcommittees, was an astonishly bold document. The committee as much as demanded that the chief executive and the Congress accept *all* its recommendations. The member had made a thorough investigation of housing problems and had concluded that "a series of related actions" was necessary to achieve sound community development.[46] They emphasized that "no one nor even an exclusive grouping of these recommendations can serve to accomplish the aims of the Committee."[47] Coming from a group of known reformers and liberals, a demand so uncompromising would almost surely have raised hackles, but Eisenhower had appointed mostly captains of finance—and he had also appointed Rouse and Bohn. Neither the President himself nor the Congress was inclined to question the wisdom of the committee's "comprehensive program." With only minor changes the recommendations were translated into provisions of the Housing Act of 1954, including the recommendation for "a continuation of the public housing program as contained in the Housing Act of 1949," though with some amendments concerning finances, the design of projects, and preferential treatment for families displaced by various kinds of public improvements.[48]

The new legislation stressed the prevention of slums and blight. Its Title III pertained to "slum clearance and urban renewal" rather than to slum clearance and redevelopment, but since several other titles of of the act were related to this central program, the measure was, in effect, an urban renewal statute. As a condition for receiving federal assistance not only for the removal of slums but also for low-rent public housing and new FHA insurance programs designed to facilitate clearance and rebuilding, the legislation required localities to put into operation a "workable program" utilizing all means available to eliminate slums, rehabilitate still useful housing, and prevent the decline of areas as yet unaffected by blight. As indicated in the act and as specified in more detail by the administrator of the Housing and Home Finance Agency, the requirements included a long-range, general plan and such means of carrying it out as a program of public improvements, a zoning ordinance, and subdivision regulations; neighborhood analyses identifying the extent and intensity of blight and delineating residential neighborhoods conforming to the general plan; codes and ordinances assuring adequate minimum standards of health, sanitation, and safety, together with administrative agencies and personnel for enforcing them; a plan for financing the city's share of renewal projects (one-third of the total net project cost of all projects undertaken with federal assistance) as well as municipal capital improvements and planning and enforcement programs; arrangements for rehousing dislocated families; and effective participation in the whole renewal effort by community-wide organizations and neighborhood groups.

In accordance with the recommendations of the President's advisory committee and various other groups consulted before passage of the Housing Act of 1954, the administrator of the Housing and Home Finance Agency created an Urban Renewal Administration comparable in importance to the Federal Housing Administration and the Public Housing Administration, and within this new unit established an Urban Renewal

Service (also proposed by the President's committee) to assist communities in preparing the workable program and to provide professional assistance for planning and developing local urban renewal programs.

For cities with populations of less than 25,000 and for official metropolitan planning agencies the new act also authorized $5,000,000 in grants for general planning, with the requirement that grants not exceed 50 per cent of the estimated cost of the work to be done. Known as the "701 program" because it was incorporated under Section 701 of the act, this program proposed by Mitchell and endorsed by the President's committee was to prove a powerful stimulus to planning throughout the nation, and within the decade was to be enhanced by larger authorizations of funds. Further, it was to be extended to small cities struck by disaster and to counties having populations of less than 25,000 (Housing Act of 1956), to areas threatened with rapid urbanization as a result of the establishment or expansion of a federal installation (Housing Act of 1957), and to cities, counties, or groups of adjacent communities with populations of less than 50,000, as well as to state planning agencies carrying on statewide or interstate comprehensive planning (Housing Act of 1959).

The broader scope of the act of 1954 was shown by its references to "urban renewal areas," which could be slum areas requiring complete redevelopment, deteriorating areas to be restored by a program of voluntary repair and rehabilitation, or rundown areas in which a combination of demolition and rehabilitation would be appropriate. For all these types of areas it prescribed an urban renewal plan conforming to the workable program as well as to the general plan of the locality as a whole.

In every provision the new enactment linked planning to action. To encourage public agencies to experiment with new methods and techniques of preventing and eliminating slums and urban blight, it authorized the allocation of $5,000,000 in grants for speical pilot projects expected to contribute significantly to renewal techniques and to serve as guides for other communities. Grants could amount to as much as two-thirds of the estimated cost of the proposed demonstrations and tests of techniques. Under this program, within three years the commissioner of Urban Renewal Administration made twenty-three grants to cities, state agencies, universities, and redevelopment agencies for projects concerned with relocation, rehabilitation, the organization of workable programs, long-range planning for urban renewal, coordination of renewal with public roads programs, community organization and participation in understanding and developing urban renewal programs, nieghborhood conservation, and the financing, administration, and programming of renewal.

The legislation, furthermore, made the Federal Housing Administration more directly a partner in renewal efforts, though the agency's support of new building in suburban areas on a still more extensive basis may have further weakened central cities. A new section of the original law under which FHA operated authorized mortgage insurance for the rehabilitation of dwellings in deteriorating neighborhoods officially designated as renewal areas, as well as for the construction of new dwellings in clearance areas, whereas formerly the agency would not provide mortgage insurance in areas obviously in decline. Another new section of the law provided FHA insurance for low-cost housing for displaced families in communities carrying out redevelopment projects under the Housing Act of 1949.

Although the President's advisory committee had recommended continuation of the low-rent public housing program "as an essential part of the overall housing program of the Federal Government," and particularly "to provide relocation housing for families displaced through urban redevelopment, rehabilitation, and law enforcement programs,"[49] the Housing Act of 1954 authorized not more than 35,000 additional units in 1955 — 100,000 fewer than had been authorized annually for a six-year period under the Housing Act of 1949. The Congress was still generally hostile to this subsidized program and had reduced it to 75,000 units in 1950, after the outbreak of the Korean war, to 50,000 units in 1951, to 35,000 in 1952, and to as few as 20,000 in 1953. The new authorization therefore represented a slight increase but was nevertheless disappointing to agencies struggling with the problem of relocation.

The only alternative to public housing presented to the President's committee had been a "rent certificate" plan, which the committee had rejected because it could not foresee "any expansion of the supply of decent housing on a tenuous expectation that a rent subsidy will be forthcoming and continued from year to year until the investment is amortized."[50]

In addition to its various recommendations concerning federal housing programs, the President's advisory committee had proposed that "a broadly representative private organization should be formed outside the Federal Government with congressional and/or Presidential sponsorship to mobilize public opinion in support of vigorous action by the communities in slum prevention, neighborhood conservation and other urban renewal activities."[51] Three and a half months after the Housing Act of 1954 became law, President Eisenhower himself addressed a luncheon in the national capital at which the type of organization contemplated by the committee was given its public "presentation." Known as ACTION or the American Council to Improve Our Neighborhoods, it was composed of "top leaders in business and labor, trade, civic and religious organizations,"[52] as the advisory committee had suggested; and serving on its board of directors were, among others, Ernest Bohn, Robert Mitchell, Ferd Kramer, president of the Metropolitan Housing and Planning Council of Chicago, Herbert Emmerich, director of the Public Administration Clearing House, and associates who were already old hands at stimulating citizen interest in community improvement. With substantial financial support from the Ford Foundation and some funds from its own board of directors, the council carried on a well-organized program of research, public information, and assistance to local groups furthering the attainment of "the best possible environment in which to live and earn an ample livelihood."[53] In its first five years its executive vice-president, James E. Lash, former director of the redevelopment agency of San Francisco, arranged dozens of group discussions, clinics, and conferences of civic leaders throughout the nation.

The Planning Boom in Suburbia

The financial inducements and mandates of the augmented federal program, the promotional endeavors of ACTION, and worry about what Carl Feiss called "land pollution" and Lewis Mumford referred to as "the suburban fall-out from the metropolitan explosion" all combined to stimulate more urban planning in the United States in the latter half of the 1950s than at any previous time in history. Some of it was not good planning because planning activities expanded so rapidly that many unseasoned planners were thrust into positions of authority and some members of allied professions who had an inadequate understanding of planning were tempted to undertake assignments which were beyond their competence; but generally the new urban planning assistance program authorized in the Housing Act of 1954 and the broader approach to renewal provided for in the measure led to experimentation, pilot studies, and research which had far-reaching effects on the scope and impact of planning processes. Planning programs in several cities contributed to new legislation. Some metropolitan planning programs furthered intergovernmental cooperation.

The urban planning assistance program, which was independent of urban renewal or other federal aids, was intended mainly to help suburban communities and metropolitan areas that were undergoing explosive growth. As it called for matching state and local funds and for the disbursement of federal funds by state agencies, it encouraged states to pay more attention to local planning and to increase their support of local planning and development agencies. In Arkansas, Georgia, Indiana, Louisiana, Maine, Massachusetts, Montana, and Washington the state legislatures approved bills permitting or requiring the establishment of planning agencies for entire urbanized areas, usually specifically empowering such agencies to receive or apply for federal grants. Among the statutes passed were special acts creating metropolitan planning commissions in Indianapolis and Marion County (1955), the twin cities of Minneapolis and St. Paul, and the six counties in the Chicago region (the latter two in 1957). Under general laws such small centers as Portland, Maine; Hartford, Connecticut; and Lowell-Lawrence-Haverhill, Massachusetts, formed new regional planning commissions.

Officials in Washington, D.C., soon saw how widespread was the lure of federal financial aid for planning. In the first year after passage of the

94. A new freeway — and land ripe for urbanization, in southern Alameda County, California *(California Division of Highways)*

act 76 small communities, 6 metropolitan areas (Atlanta; Baton Rouge; Cleveland; Detroit; Little Rock, Arkansas; and Springfield, Ohio), and 3 urban regions benefitted by the assistance program. At the end of 1956, 242 small communities and 23 large and populous areas were receiving aid. Each year thereafter the program expanded until at the end of 1959 more than 1000 towns and small cities and 94 metropolitan areas and urban regions were participating in it and the total amount of federal monies that had been disbursed for planning assistance exceeded $8,600,000.

The growth of the program came at a time when American magazines and newspapers were running articles discussing every aspect of suburban expansion—articles entitled "Crisis in the Suburbs," "Suburban Growing Pains," "New York, the Runaway City," "Sacramento . . . A Crisis of Growth," and "The Rush to the Suburbs: It's Changing City

95. Industrial plants and new subdivisions, San Leandro–Hayward area, California, 1950s *(California Division of Highways)*

Life Everywhere." The 1950 census had revealed that 80 per cent of the national gain of 19,000,000 people in the 1940s had accrued to the 168 "standard metropolitan areas" and that half of this increase had gone to the suburban and rural areas, or rings, outside the central cities. In the latter 1950s, as the suburbs joined the central cities in a scramble for city planners, the Bureau of the Census estimated that in the six years from 1950 to 1956 the rings surrounding the central cities had increased by 9,600,000 or almost 28 per cent, while the core cities themselves had increased by only 2,000,000 or 4 per cent. And in territories just outside the standard metropolitan areas—the next places in which suburban growth could be expected—the nonfarm population had risen by 3,000,000, or 11 per cent. City planners were confronted not merely with all kinds of land use and circulation problems but with a full-scale social revolution led by the rapidly expanding middle class and abetted by American industry, the federal and state governments, financial institutions, and even the farmers who sold their pastures and orchards to developers at irresistibly high prices. Certainly, no one escaped the effects of this enormous restructuring of cities and society, whether renter in the central city or homeowner in "subtopia," whether pastor of a declining church on the periphery of a struggling downtown or minister of a brand-new suburban church encumbered by a huge mortgage, whether city councilman representing an increasingly nonwhite constituency in an old, rat-infested area or county supervisor besieged by the new residents of an unincorporated territory lacking adequate police and fire protection.

Many small suburban communities which had never had a planning program chose to contract with planning consultants for a "package deal"—a land use survey, a population forecast, a master or general plan, and a new or revised zoning ordinance. The state agencies disbursing federal urban planning assistance funds approved the contracts, provided the state funds needed to match the local contributions, and sent the proper forms to Washington. Some of the small municipalities later retained their consultants to guide them in using the plans and ordinances delivered under the original contract and to provide additional plans and services as time went on. Some received such a good initiation into the planning process under the tutelage of the consultant that they decided to employ their own planner and gradually build up a staff. But critical observers of the federal aid program saw that it was hardly a success in some places, either because the city administration failed to make adequate use of good plans or because planning consultants produced plans not really meeting local needs or performed various services indifferently. Perhaps the worst drawback of the "package-contract" method popular in the early days of the urban planning assistance program was that it fostered "the delusion," as John Howard expressed it, "that once a locality has bought a plan, it has planning."[54] The same distorted notion of planning had flourished in the City Beautiful days and in the 1920s. Its inadvertent revival under a federal-aid program in a period when the ablest city planners were striving to make planning "programmatic" or to devise procedures for carrying out each element of a broad scheme in stages with varied administrative and financial means was, to say the least, embarrassing to the leaders of the planning profession.

The suburban boom sometimes presented unexpected situations and problems of control which neither local officials nor their consultant firm had anticipated and which could not readily be dealt with under contracts for predetermined services. An out-of-town syndicate might suddenly apply for rezoning of an area for a large new shopping center, or a particularly aggressive developer might announce plans for a big residential tract that could "swamp" the local school system and call for an unforeseen expansion of the municipal sewage treatment plant and water supply. Regulating the tempo and geographical sequence of development in a period in which growth was diffuse, sporadic, and unpredictable called for exceptional planning talents and innovative legal measures. Those communities which retained able consultants on a long-term basis and assured themselves of close scrutiny of every change were perhaps in a better position to give some semblance of order to their growth than those obliged to employ relatively inexperienced planners or large planning firms spread thin by many contracts.

Most planners could cite but one community which had acquired almost all the developable land within its boundaries and which was able to regulate the tempo of its growth by marketing only a limited number of lots annually. This was the wealthy borough of Mountain Lakes, New Jersey. Few other communities had the financial resources to follow its example even if their state legislatures had given them the legal authority, and there was as yet little indication that American lawmakers were persuaded that local governments should emulate the various European municipalities which had long managed their expansion in the manner of the New Jersey borough. Police power regulations, tax measures, and administrative policies concerning the extension of utilities appeared to be the chief means available to other American communities to regulate the timing and location of development. None of these means was altogether adequate, but under the stress of circumstances some planners found ways to make old devices more effective, both as instrumentalities for directing growth and as tools for carrying out the general plan.

In Rockland County, New York, for example, planning director Richard May, Jr., aided by consultant Norman Williams, thought out new zoning procedures to slow down a wave of building set off by the construction of the New York Thruway and the Palisades Interstate Parkway. At their suggestion the community of Clarkstown adopted a zoning ordinance placing its development areas in two types of special districts, one intended for early use for regular suburban residential development, the other requiring an acre for each dwelling but permitting smaller-lot development if the planning board determined that adequate schools were available and that there would not be a strain on other community facilities. Such an ordinance, of course, served two purposes. It encouraged growth adjacent to existing settlements before more remote areas were opened to intensive use; and it adjusted the absorption of additional population to existing or planned services.

For Orangetown, in the same county, May and Williams proposed placing a schedule on all new developments, specifically limiting the number of homes to be completed each year to a number the schools in the area could reasonably prepare for. By bringing the two local school

96. Roosevelt Field Shopping Center, Long Island; office building and industrial park in foreground *(Louis B. Schlivek, photographer, and Regional Plan Association of New York)*

boards "into the town planning arena," the planners gave board members "an opportunity to make advantageous deals with the developers — for school sites where needed, or perhaps even financial aid." In the past, May said, the school boards had been "on the outside, grumbling about how the planning boards or the town boards were giving them all the headaches."[55]

As May saw it, suburban communities expected far greater integration of zoning and planning than planners had been giving them. "The classic master plan," he remarked, "generally has too loose a relationship to zoning; and where there is a relationship it frequently can only be found in the mind of the planner or by the planning board. This gap between the zoning ordinance and the master plan needs more specific legal treatment, and development timing may be a step in this direction."[56]

Henry Fagin, Planning director of the Regional Plan Association in the New York area, suggested still another way to use zoning to regulate the timing of development. In an article in *Law and Contemporary Problems,* published by Duke University, he explained a method of assigning varying priority ratings to zoning districts and limiting the issuance of building permits according to the ratings. In Fagin's view, development timing not only was permissible in the legal sense but also had become "an urgent responsibility of municipal government needed to protect the very health, safety and welfare of our rapidly growing suburban communities."[57]

The new efforts to make time a fourth dimension in planning raised problems of assessment and taxation that most planners had only briefly investigated. Land assessments for realty tax purposes had rarely been well related to the long-range land use plan or the zoning scheme supposedly designed to bring it into being by a process of progressive amendment. Priority ratings, districts in which the intensity of development could be changed under certain circumstances, and limitations on the number of houses permitted annually all indicated the need for reexamining assessment practices, lest there be opposition to some of the new regulations on grounds of financial discrimination.

Philip P. Green, Jr., assistant director of the Institute of Government at the University of North Carolina, pointed out the possibility of using taxation as a planning tool in the struggle to retard development in some areas and to encourage it in others. "If there is a great enough differential in the tax values placed upon land zoned for intensive, urban type uses as compared with agricultural uses, there will be less pressure to rezone low-value agricultural land and begin sporadic development in advance of actual real estate market demand," he observed. "Conversely, land deemed ready for immediate development can be taxed at such a level as to prod its owner into beginning development."[58]

Lack of coordination between the planning program and assessment practices, on the other hand, could have the opposite effect of forcing the premature conversion of good farmland to residential or industrial use and producing a fragmented urban pattern, as the planners of Santa Clara County, California, discovered. In that garden spot a subdivision no sooner took shape amid the prune and apricot orchards than the county assessor raised the assessments on all the surrounding acreage, on the theory that the land was ripe for urban development and should be taxed at its market potential. Unable to continue operating at a profit, many farmers capitulated to the developers, the agricultural economy of the county began to suffer, and political tensions destroyed the once harmonious atmosphere of the valley.

Seeking to counteract the undesirable effects of the assessment system, county planning director Karl J. Belser proposed that upon the request of the landowners in an area, the county establish exclusive agricultural zones from which all subdivisions and industrial and commerical uses would be barred. His thought was that such "greenbelting," as it was called in Santa Clara County, not only would reduce urban sprawl but perhaps also entitle farmers to preferential tax treatment.

The county board of supervisors adopted exclusive agricultural, or "A," zoning in the fall of 1953, and in the next three years placed some 20,000 acres under such zoning upon petition of groups of landowners. The new classification afforded farmers some protection against increased taxes for schools and other urban services required in areas dotted with subdivisions, but it did not, as was hoped, offer them any relief from assessments based on the rising market value of their land. The county assessor pointed out that the constitution of California required assessment at full cash value and that the courts had defined market value as the value for the highest and best economic use, holding that "the question is not what its value is for a particular purpose, but its value in view of all the purposes to which it is naturally adapted."[59]

The county government appealed to the state legislature to intercede on behalf of the agriculturists, with the result that the lawmakers in 1957 amended the California Revenue and Taxation Code to state that "In assessing property that is zoned and used exlusively for agricultural or recreation purposes and as to which there is no reasonable probability of the removal or modification of the zoning restrictions within the near future, the assessor shall consider no other factors than those relative to such use."[60] But the amendment proved worthless. The state attorney general, Edmund G. Brown (later governor), held that under zoning there *is* a reasonable probability that zoning will change. His point, moreover, was reinforced by amendments made in 1957 to a law passed in 1955 to protect exclusive agricultural zones from annexation to nearby cities without the consent of the owners. The weakening amendments of 1957 allowed annexation even against the wishes of agriculturists, permitted municipalities to extend shoestring strips through greenbelts in order to annex larger areas desiring to become part of the city, and allowed cities to annex land all around "A" zones, making them islands of county-governed territory within city boundaries and discouraging farmers from further pursuit of their way of life. (Residents of surrounding areas sometimes stole fruit, complained of the dust from plowing, and objected to the spraying of insecticides.)

As in many other states, the main hope of achieving the twin objectives of preventing urbanization and offering owners of farm lands, golf courses, and other open areas preferential taxation was a constitutional amendment specifically stating that certain lands must be assessed at a low rate while in open use but that owners must pay a sizable yield tax when the land is sold for building development. Such a consitutional amendment finally came before California voters in 1962 and was defeated. Revised and submitted again in 1966, the measure won approval.

Law professor Jacob H. Beuscher expressed the thought of many city planners when he said in 1958, "Probably, however, the solution of the open space problem lies in purchase of development rights by public agencies."[61] He believed that it might be well to buy the full fee simple interest in the land and then sell the land back for private use, subject to covenants barring building. Others suggested the possibility of purchase and leaseback, but either method requires financial resources exceeding those of most city and county governments.

Although the struggles of Santa Clara County to bring zoning, assessment practices, and long-term planning into harmony were only par-

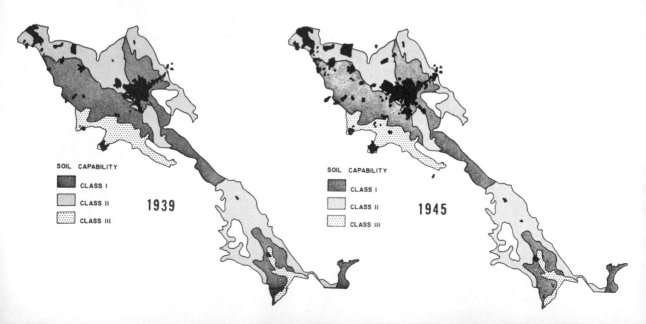

SOIL CAPABILITY

■ CLASS I
▨ CLASS II
▧ CLASS III

1939

SOIL CAPABILITY

■ CLASS I
▨ CLASS II
▧ CLASS III

1945

tially successful (a few remaining greenbelts might eventually become the urban parks in a vast area now being blanketed with subdivisions), they dramatized the necessity of relating planning to effective means of implementation, as did the attempts of other local governments to use new zoning and subdivision control devices to influence the timing and sequence of development.

A New Means of Implementing Regional Planning

While planners in individual cities and counties attempted to cope with the rush of suburban development, various metropolitan planning agencies, established both before and after the authorization of federal assistance for urban planning, struggled with some of the same problems under the serious handicap of being unable to influence the actions of municipal and county governments directly. Something of an exception was the metropolitan planning commission created in the Tulsa area in 1953 because of problems of urban overspill. It operated under a statute requiring city and county governments to refer all proposed public improvement projects and all new subdivision plans to it for review and recommendations, but most areawide or regional planning agencies had no such opportunity to try to put their general plans into effect. The decade was one in which metropolitan planning commissions exercised their ingenuity to overcome the frustration of being "orphans" with no metropolitan governing group to finance or carry out the proposals embodied in their long-range plans. The Detroit Metropolitan Area Regional Planning Commission created soon after the Second World War was perhaps the most successful in finding a way to work closely with the governments in its area and affect regional development.

When T. Ledyard Blakeman, executive director of the Detroit Metropolitan Area Regional Planning Commission, began his labors, the Detroit area included 125 cities, villages, and townships in four counties,

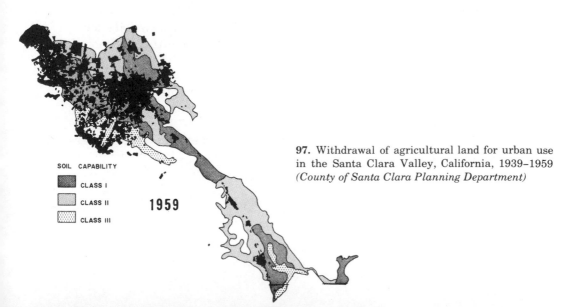

SOIL CAPABILITY

■ CLASS I

☐ CLASS II

▨ CLASS III

1959

97. Withdrawal of agricultural land for urban use in the Santa Clara Valley, California, 1939–1959 *(County of Santa Clara Planning Department)*

or a total of 129 local governments, from all of which the commission needed support in order to pursue a vigorous regional planning program. In spite of having to utilize considerable staff time in "local stimulation and aid, or other vote-getting projects,"[62] Blakeman managed to place the main emphasis on preparing a regional land use plan based on extensive research on population, industrial trends, present uses of land, zoning regulations, and local plans for public improvements. In the course of the essential fact-gathering and analysis, Blakeman's staff found that it could be extremely helpful to local officials and private interests by providing information about the region—a circumstance which helped in getting adequate appropriations from the four counties in the area while rather unglamorous preliminary work was under way. But perhaps the most significant aspect of this planner's program was his use of municipal department heads, university professors, and specialists in private industry on technical committees concerned with such regional problems as drainage and pollution abatement, sewage disposal, water supply, transportation, recreation, and industrial development. In 1953 Blakeman estimated that these experts had contributed $200,000 worth of field work to the commission, yet their most valuable aid was simply their genuine interest and active participation, particularly since some members of the forty-six-man regional commission served on each committee and subcommittee and became directly involved in discussions with these knowledgeable men. Somewhat less successful in bringing important citizens and officials into the planning program were advisory councils for several "development areas" into which Blakeman and his staff divided the 2,100-square-mile metropolitan area. Of six initially set up in the urban area contiguous to Detroit, all were not equally active and one fell by the wayside. Those which met regularly afforded communication between planners and local representatives that was valuable in developing the regional land use plan.

In April, 1953, the cooperative approach characteristic of the regional commission's whole program pervaded a conference at which two hundred officials of Detroit and the suburban municipalities discussed the future of the metropolitan area. The mayor of Detroit and two city councilmen assured the smaller communities that the metropolis had no desire to dictate policies and wished merely to work with them in solving shared problems. Dr. Thomas H. Reed, long the advocate of some form of metropolitan government, addressed the participants, telling them that financial ruin faced both the core city and the suburbs unless they agreed to merge their interests in "the family good," but he refrained from offering a prescription for areawide government, and his hearers talked of joint efforts through cooperative agencies. Blakeman himself was loudly cheered when he said, "Together we can show the other great cities not only how to produce but, more important, how to live."[63]

Meanwhile, in neighboring Canada the provincial government of Ontario, after almost three years of discussions, hearings, and studies by the Ontario Municipal Board, was concluding that "the family good" of the municipalities in the Toronto area required the kind of governmental solution that Dr. Reed avoided recommending to the elected officials of the Detroit area. Planners attending the annual meeting of the American Society of Planning Officials in the fall of the year had an opportunity to hear a municipal statesman named Frederick G. Gardiner describe a new federated metropolitan government, the first in North America, which would go into effect on January 1, 1954, as the Municipality of Metropolitan Toronto. As head of this metropolitan corporation, which not only would carry on areawide planning but also would have the authority to construct important public works conceived as elements of a general plan of development, Gardiner ignited hopes for similar unions of metropolitan planning with metropolitan decision-making in the United States.

"The Metropolitan Toronto answer to metropolitan problems," the Canadian said, "is a system whereby the thirteen municipalities [in the Toronto area] may preserve their identity and continue to administer those services which are local in nature and at the same time combine together for the provision of those services which are metropolitan in nature and essential to the whole area."[64] The metropolitan services were to be water supply, sewage disposal, arterial highways, metropolitan parks, housing and redevelopment, regional planning, certain health and welfare services, and equalization of the cost of education to permit each of the local municipalities to provide a reasonable standard of education for its children. A Metropolitan School Board, however, would designate the location of new schools and coordinate the activities of the local school boards in the thirteen municipalities of the metropolitan federation. Public transportation would also be provided by a separate authority, the thirty-year-old Toronto Transportation Commission, renamed the Toronto Transit Commission. The $60,000,000 subway of the city of Toronto, then nearing completion, and all the independent bus lines operating in the suburbs, would become the property of the transit commission on July 31, 1954. Gardiner explained that the cost of operating the metropolitan corporation and all its undertakings would be charged "equitably and evenly over the thirteen municipalities in the ratio of their aggregate assessment" as determined by the Greater Toronto Assessment Board established by the provincial government two years earlier. That same government, however, would make a capital grant of $5,000,000 to the new metropolitan corporation in 1954 and in each year thereafter a similar grant of $4 per capita, to eliminate the necessity of substantially increased municipal taxation.

American planners listening to the chairman-designate of the Municipality of Metropolitan Toronto could envy their Canadian professional brothers whose regional planning jurisdiction would be not only the 250 square miles of the Toronto metropolitan area but also the adjoining townships on its borders; they could understand the health, circulation, and suburban fiscal problems that finally impelled the Province of Ontario to impose a federated metropolitan government on Toronto and its neighboring municipalities; but they were obliged to doubt whether their own countrymen would accept similar forms of government by determination of their state legislatures. Having fought long and strenuously for freedom from the interference of state lawmakers in municipal affairs, American city dwellers, it sometimes seemed, feared encroachment on home rule even more than they dreaded impending water shortages, pollution of the streams and lakes in which they swam, or acrimonious disputes among local governments over highway routes and intercity transit services. There was, nevertheless, the possibility, as urban skies became dirtier, commuting more difficult, and regional recreation space more inaccessible, as local property taxes rose and areawide problems got worse, that state governments would be compelled to take action. And no one appreciated the threat of state intervention more keenly than some of the politicians in city halls and county courthouses. Toronto to these elected officials was more portent than promise, more the catastrophe to be avoided than the consummation devoutly to be wished.

Among those who wanted no form of government even remotely resembling the Municipality of Metropolitan Toronto were county supervisors and city councilmen in the Detroit metropolitan area. But Blakeman and energetic Councilman Edward Connor of Detroit, who was also president of the Wayne County Board of Supervisors, had in mind some collaborative endeavor which might lead to the implementation of regional planning. As executive of the Citizens Housing and Planning Council before becoming a councilman and a supervisor, Connor had been a member of the Detroit Metropolitan Area Regional Planning Commission and had been impressed by the committee technique Blakeman used. The two friends worked on the presidents of the boards of supervisors of neighboring counties (Macomb, Monroe, Oakland, and Washtenaw) until each county board agreed to appoint some of its members to a Supervisors Inter-County Committee. This organization then appointed five committees on important regional problems, and Blakeman and his staff fed information to the groups "in doses they could take" without getting mental indigestion. Gradually, under Connor's expert leadership and prodding, the aroused officials began to "move on their own steam."[65]

A sixth county, St. Clair, joined the informal "arena for the free exchange of information" in 1955, further strengthening an alliance that was explicit in its underlying repugnance to "supergovernment." Report after report of the committee included this statement: "There is no desire to superimpose another governmental layer on top of existing governments."[66] Instead, the organization proposed to "develop recommendations for ratification by the several boards of supervisors."[67]

This new intercounty group, first of the many councils of governments now functioning in American metropolitan regions, was, as Blakeman said, "about the only form of effectuation that could possibly work under the circumstances."[68] It brought together forty-two public officials, seven from each of the six counties, including the chairman of each county board of supervisors. Municipalities had no official representation although boards of supervisors selected some city councilmen to serve on each county group; nor were special districts in the Detroit area accorded direct representation—a fact noted by impartial observers many years later as contributing to some lack of harmony between the committee and these autonomous political units. But, on the whole, the committee provided a reasonably satisfactory means of focusing regional attention on some of the important problems with which Blakeman and his staff and well-known experts in the metropolitan region had been struggling. One of the publications of the committee made clear that the members thought of the Detroit Metropolitan Area Regional Planning Commission almost as the planning arm of the organization: "In formulating its resolutions the Inter-County Committee utilizes the expert knowledge of groups like the Regional Planning Commission, its planners and technicians. An invaluable characteristic of the Inter-County Committee is its ability to draw on resources like this to guide its work." Summing up the relationships, the publication stated,". . . the Regional Planning Commission, as the name suggests, is a *planning* group. The Supervisors Inter-County Committee is an *action* group. Through it plans become reality."[69]

The route of a proposal from the plan stage to actuality is by way of one of several standing committees—orginally a quintet on port, recreation, roads, sewage and waste disposal, and water—to the entire membership of the multicounty organization, meeting as a Committee of the Whole. By majority vote, standing committee reports then become recommendations to each county board of supervisors, and "as each county takes affirmative action, it carries out its segment of the complete plan— an economical practical approach to areawide problems."[70]

Like the Toronto area, the Detroit area in the mid-fifties was particularly troubled by problems of water supply, sewage and waste disposal, and regional circulation. Of the five standing committees originally appointed, the most active were the water and sewage committees, which soon discovered that Blakeman and his staff had been giving a great amount of time to an impending water crisis and to flood control and pollution problems, though without being able to make the kinds of comprehensive studies that could be undertaken only by specialized groups. The Regional Planning Commission, moreover, had been set up to serve but a little more than half of the 3,983 square miles in the six counties and lacked information on some of the areas farthest from Detroit. On recommendation of its water committee, the Supervisors Inter-County Committee engaged the National Sanitation Foundation to conduct a $100,000 study (financed by private sources), which led to the extension of the Detroit water system into three of the member counties and the avoidance of the creation of a second big system. To provide regionally integrated information concerning sewage and drainage needs, the multi-county committee established a Sanitation Council of Southeastern Michigan consisting of more than fifty members from government and industry. The Water Pollution Division of the United States Public Health Service later made its first demonstration grant, in the amount of $100,000, to this council as the federal contribution toward solving waste-disposal and drainage problems.

Having pressed for enabling legislation in 1955 that would permit two or more counties to join together under contract to create a system of expressways, superhighways, and intercounty roads with sufficient setbacks to provide for adequate future rights-of-way, the roads committee furthered the formation of an Inter-County Highway Commission. Representatives of the Regional Planning Commission, county road commissions and boards of supervisors, and the state highway department served on this six-county agency, which set to work to prepare a master plan of future highways. In this endeavor the agency was heir to a highly significant pioneering effort to develop a highway plan by deriving patterns of travel from data on the traffic-generating capacities of various uses of land—the Detroit Metropolitan Area Traffic Study completed in 1956 though begun in the fall of 1953, some months before the appearance of Robert B. Mitchell's and Chester Rapkin's book, *Urban Traffic: A Function of Land Use*.

Building on the study directed by Dr. J. Douglas Carroll, Jr., in Detroit and areas within a radius of twenty or twenty-five miles, the Inter-County Highway Commission attempted to relate a long-range highway system to a land use plan worked out by the Regional Planning Commission for the larger region. This plan suggested a modified corridor pattern of development. The proposed highway system, projecting traffic needs to 1970 or thereabouts, combined radial routes and circumferential belts, and although the counties in the region took steps to protect the required rights-of-way by adopting and enforcing setback ordinances, amendments to zoning ordinances, and use of the state's Mapped Improvement Act, the passage of years inevitably revealed shortcomings in the plan, as they did in the earlier Detroit study. In a period of eight or nine years various agencies spent almost $1,000,000 to keep Dr. Carroll's study up to date by adjusting the data to reflect current conditions and by refining and improving methods of traffic projection and assignment, yet by 1965 the Detroit Metropolitan Area Regional Planning Commission was calling the attention of public officials and citizens of the six-county region to the need for a new study of transportation and land use. The important thing, however, is not the obsolescence of the Detroit study and the regional highway plan but the continuity of planning by the Regional Planning Commission, the City of Detroit, the Inter-County Highway Commission, the Supervisors Inter-County Committee, the Michigan Highway Department, and other agencies.

In 1957 the Supervisors Inter-County Committee became a potent force in sustaining regional planning when the Michigan state legislature gave legal status ex post facto to the voluntary agreement of the six counties, formally empowering the Committee to receive and administer funds from the counties, other governmental units, and private agencies, as well as to utilize such standing committees and special groups as might be needed to study and analyze intergovernmental problems. Operating initially, and as it still does, with only a small staff, the supervisors' committee not only demonstrated that it could be effective in resolving crucial problems and steadily making progress on others less urgent, but also that it could inspire governments in other metropolitan regions to cooperate in planning for regional development. It has the distinction of being, in a sense, the parent of the 100 or more councils of governments presently active in the United States.

Before the end of the 1950s, there were three other efforts to establish similar councils, and in the early 1960s several additional voluntary associations came into being. In 1956 Mayor Robert F. Wagner of New York City invited the officials of neighboring jurisdictions to join him in forming a Metropolitan Regional Council for the New York region, but this council experienced difficulties, according to one assessment, mainly "because New York City tended to dominate it and tried to provide all staff services."[71] At the invitation of Robert E. McLaughlin, President of the Board of Commissioners of the District of Columbia, representatives of the local and state governments in the national capital region came together in 1957 to set up the Washington Metropolitan Regional

Conference, later renamed the Metropolitan Washington Council of Governments. Not until 1960 did this voluntary association employ a staff, but by that time it had created the Washington Metropolitan Regional Sanitary Board (1959) as its own technical committee rather than as an autonomous special-purpose agency, and was on the way to becoming a regional planning agency, all as a result of having responded responsibly to the recommendation of the Congressional Joint Committee on Washington Metropolitan Problems that a special board be established to prepare a comprehensive regional sewage-disposal plan. The third intergovernmental council organized in the fifties was the Mid-Willamette Valley Council of Governments in the Salem, Oregon, area, an informal alliance for eighteen months after its formation in June, 1958, and then a legal entity under a compact eventually ratified by the state legislature. Participants are the State of Oregon, the City of Salem, Marion and Polk counties, and School District 24 CJ.

In the early 1960s appeared the Association of Bay Area Governments in the San Francisco region, the Puget Sound Governmental Conference in the Seattle-Tacoma area, the Metropolitan Atlanta Council of Local Governments, the Regional Conference of Elected Officials in the Philadelphia area, and the Southern California Association of Governments. Each has been much concerned with regional planning, and some have assumed the function, as the concluding chapter will relate.

Renewal, Middle-Range Planning, and Development Coordinators

Though not eligible for urban planning assistance grants, medium-size and large cities stepped up their planning programs in order to qualify for urban renewal loans and grants, placing particular stress on the preparation of a general plan as one of the essential requirements of the workable program for preventing as well as eliminating blight and slums. A little more than a year after passage of the Housing Act of 1954 the administrator of the Housing and Home Finance Agency reported that he had approved the workable programs of eighty cities. In 1956 he certified 68 additional programs, in the following year 249, and in 1958, 338. On September 29, 1959, federal officials and citizens of Plymouth, Massachusetts, gathered at Plymouth Rock to celebrate the fact that their historic community had become the thousandth to receive certification of its workable program. From one speaker they heard that 54 per cent of the urban population of the United States then lived in communities having such programs and that all of the eighteen cities with populations of more than 500,000 were engaged in the full complement of renewal operations.

But the record of workable programs certified, grants allocated, and planning agencies organized or stirred to greater activity was more impressive than the actual results achieved in slum clearance and rehabilitation. Ten years after the passage of the Housing Act of 1949 and five years after the adoption of the measure introducing the broader concept of urban renewal, a little less than ten square miles of slums had been acquired by local public agencies and fewer than a hundred thousand substandard dwelling units had been demolished. Only 1,972 acres of cleared land had been sold for redevelopment, although 429 projects for which the paper work was well along included a total area of 22,400 acres, or thirty-five square miles—equivalent to about five-sixths of the area of San Francisco, one of the most compact cities in the nation. Forty-five thousand dwelling units were marked for rehabilitation in federally assisted projects, but reconditioning had been completed or was in process in fewer than 8,000. Of a somewhat larger number of units requiring rehabilitation in nine projects not assisted by the federal government, approximately 2,500 had been repaired and modernized.

Had the whole renewal program demanded a disproportionate amount of time and effort on the part of planning agencies, considering the limited accomplishments and the urgency of other urban problems? Or were there some long-term gains, as yet difficult to assess but certain to appear substantial at a later time?

Probably the discouragements of the moment prevented many planners from realizing that in some cities, if not their own, the planning activities associated with renewal had strengthened relations between planners, administrators, and elected officials, had made planners themselves more aware of the necessity of integrating environmental planning with planning for human welfare, and had helped to evolve new legislative and administrative tools for reducing the physical deterioration and human misery in urban centers. Generally, efforts to stem the spread of blight were retarded by conditions beyond the control of local authorities. Many legislators in Congress opposed the voting of larger appropriations for renewal, and the Eisenhower Administration itself adopted a cautious attitude about expenditures for housing and renewal, especially after the recession of 1957–1958. Public alarm over various international crises, the civil rights struggle, and the Soviet triumph in orbiting Sputnik I before the United States could launch an artificial satellite deflected attention from the worsening plight of the cities.

Public agencies in Philadelphia, Detroit, Chicago, Baltimore, St. Louis, and a few other cities nevertheless made some progress in developing overall strategies for renewal. The first two of these cities, particularly, contributed to the emergence of a new tool for making planning effective—the community renewal program, which was briefly outlined in the Housing Act of 1959 but not much discussed or used until 1961. In both Philadelphia and Detroit some of the activities leading to the formulation of this new means of translating the general plan into reality antedated the enactment of the Housing Act of 1954 and suggested the need for the workable program.

Mayor Joseph Clark of Philadelphia (later United States senator) gave impetus to a more systematic attack on blight and slums in his city when he appointed three new members to the board of the redevelopment authority in 1952: former United States Senator Francis J. Meyers; Mrs. Dorothy Montgomery, managing director of the Philadelphia Housing Association; and a prominent banker, William F. Kurtz, Jr. The reconstituted board realized that although the authority had an innovative and experimental program, it was making mistakes, undertaking projects "conceived out of context of any economic or real estate analysis," as a member of its planning staff said, and not materially aiding in checking the spread of blight.[72] To help it in shaping a long-range program, the board formed an advisory Development Committee composed of Mrs. Montgomery; Aaron Levine, executive director of the Citizens' Council on City Planning; and three professors of the University of Pennsylvania — Martin Meyerson, Robert B. Mitchell, and G. Holmes Perkins. In an interim report in December, 1952, the committee recommended "the establishment of a system for reviewing priorities as among the various redevelopment areas, together with an overall program for the prevention, control and elimination of blight throughout the City."[73]

Ideally, the kind of city-wide program the committee had in mind would be based on a comprehensive or general plan of development, but in the absence of such a plan, the redevelopment authority and its advisory committee were obliged to limit their long-range programming to the inner city. The Philadelphia Home Rule Charter adopted in 1951 charged the city planning commission with the preparation of a comprehensive plan, and pressures were rapidly building up to force the city council to appropriate sufficient funds to enable planning director Edmund Bacon and his staff to start work on one. In the meantime, the redevelopment authority and its advisors decided that the planning commission would probably be able to provide certain elements of the comprehensive plan-to-be for a study of the central urban renewal area, as the inner city was designated. A diagrammatic plan of land uses and circulation, proposed densities, and standards of public facilities were especially needed. The planning staff of the redevelopment authority would analyze the scope of the total renewal program in the inner city, measuring housing and environmental deficiencies, establishing goals and precepts to guide action, and developing possible programs to fit both short- and long-range renewal strategies and proposed policies.

In the spring of 1956 the redevelopment authority and the planning commission brought out companion studies usually referred to as the

CURA Report. The study of the redevelopment authority was of more than local significance because it suggested new approaches to renewal in other cities that had made the same mistakes in their early slum clearance programs that Philadelphia had made. On the theory that "spores" of good new housing would act as a stimulus to the revitalization and rehabilitation of nearby private property, the authority had developed its first projects in the very heart of the worst slums, most of which were occupied by Negroes. The families displaced had moved to areas immediately adjacent, further overcrowding the houses there and turning what were only somewhat deteriorated into wholly rundown sections. People living in substandard homes in other parts of the city had not moved into the good, new, middle-income accommodations because they did not wish to live in the midst of slums. The *CURA Report* did not recommend abandonment of programs already under way, but it sought to relate them to a wide range of activities designed to halt further decline in the inner city. It suggested no further slum clearance in Negro-occupied areas until the housing opportunities for Negroes could be substantially increased. It proposed a concentration of renewal efforts in the areas immediately surrounding the central business district, so that the city center would serve as the keystone of eventual renewal in the "gray areas" just beyond. In areas where chances of conservation were good—generally the areas surrounding blighted sections—the report called for a combination of public and private actions to prevent deterioration. To strengthen the economy of the city and provide new jobs, the report urged special emphasis on clearance for industry.

The Philadelphia report would have been a milestone had it gone no further in its recommendations, but it anticipated present-day model-city programs by recommending programs of adult education to aid the disadvantaged, general improvement of all city services in areas not designated for clearance, new and improved public and private programs to treat problems of family disorganization, delinquency, crime, and poverty, and legislation to induce open-occupancy housing in the suburbs and lessen the pressures that were forcing the expansion of the "black belt."

The most important feature of the report was a section presenting four different renewal policies, a program to carry out each policy, and estimated costs of each program. The planning division of the redevelopment authority, headed by David A. Wallace, did not suggest the selection of any one of these possibilities but proposed rather a combination program with two principal aims: renewal from the center out, with all kinds of public and private actions, and improvement of the economic base of the city. Such a composite of policies and programs would be realistically related to the limited financial resources—federal, state, and local—available to the city for its renewal activities and would be flexible, permitting adjustments from time to time in the light of further knowledge and experience with the program.

The proposed program represented the kind of bridge between the general plan and housing and redevelopment activities that cities had long needed. It related Philadelphia's excellent capital improvement program to a schedule of renewal actions in a six-year period and envisaged the coordination of planning, public housing, slum clearance, code enforcement, and public and private social programs to attain the ends of urban development and revitalization. Even though the overall strategy suggested in the *CURA Report* was never fully adopted, because of further controversy over whether a concentrated approach was better than the "scatter" tactics of the early days of the planning and redevelopment programs in Philadelphia, the report markedly shaped the course of development in Philadelphia and had widespread influence on planning in other cities.

The city planning commission in Detroit meanwhile was also deeply concerned with analyzing the extent and characteristics of blight, establishing priorities for action, and developing methods of conserving older neighborhoods. In 1953 the Detroit Common Council, at the urging of the mayor's Committee for Neighborhood Conservation and Improved Housing, had appropriated money to set up a separate conservation division in the city planning department. A few months before the Congress approved the Housing Act of 1954, this division completed a comprehensive survey of housing and environmental conditions that revealed the magnitude of the task of ridding the city of poor housing and neighborhood defects. Detroit had 8,000 acres of severe residential blight, mostly in the heart of the city, but surrounding this dilapidated core was a three-mile band of middle-aged areas in which most of the dwellings were worth rehabilitating. The area comprised twenty square miles in all and was home to 500,000 citizens. Convinced that a start had to be made somewhere to reverse the process of decline, the conservation division recommended an area of thirty-eight blocks on the east side of the city for detailed study.

The pilot neighborhood, known as the Mack-Concord area, was in the early stages of physical decay. Thirty per cent of its population was Negro, but this minority was increasing as white families moved out. Only 35 per cent of the homes were owner-occupied. An attitude survey conducted by a sociologist of the conservation division and a sociology professor and his students revealed that most of the people interviewed found little or nothing the matter with their houses although they were dissatisfied with traffic on residential streets, the scarcity of parking space, the lack of parks and playgrounds, noise and dirt, the inadequacy of municipal services, and "the type of new neighbors moving in"—a complaint indicating racial tensions. Particularly discouraging, or challenging, to planners was the finding that most residents, especially whites, were uninterested in participating in the neighborhood conservation program, or at least uninterested in joining a neighborhood group formed to coordinate and carry out improvements. Thus the problems of the area were clearly social as well as physical.

While the city planners of the conservation division set to work analyzing changes and improvements that could be made in the project area, the community organizer of the division met with the citizens' participation subcommittee of the Detroit Committee for Neighborhood Conservation and Improved Housing to discuss ways of achieving "grass roots" citizen participation and decision-making in the area. Since there was no neighborhood organization through which to communicate with the people, the one community organizer of the conservation division needed assistance. Several professional social workers and leaders in civic and church agencies volunteered to help organize block meetings at which the contemplated conservation program would be explained. Suspicion and distrust among residents gave way to cautious interest when the department of parks and recreation carried out a street-tree-pruning program and other municipal departments assisted a few block groups in cleaning up alleys, removing illegal waste receptacles, and controlling rodents. Six months after the first steps in the organization procedure had been undertaken, the goal of a neighborhood council was attained, and by that time the planners were ready to present tentative plans for improving the area. These were put forth merely as suggestions, in order to elicit comments and reactions. After many block discussions and general public meetings, "during which the citizens participated helpfully in decision-making with understanding of their role in the planning process," the delegates of the thirty-eight blocks voted 4 to 1 in favor of a proposed improvement plan modified in accordance with the residents' suggestions.[74]

The organizing effort, however, had been poorly timed. Two or more years passed before federal funds could be obtained for carrying out proposed improvements. In the meantime, some block leaders had become disillusioned and the majority of residents, never more than mildly interested, had lapsed into apathy. But the planning department at least had learned the difficulties of "planning for and with people," had come to understand that some of the conditions leading to urban blight are social in their origin, and had begun to realize that unless the social attitudes, values, and property-keeping habits of residents could be changed, conservation would be merely another costly means of providing physical improvements that would not fundamentally better neighborhoods and cities. Sociologist Mel Jerome Ravitz, who participated in the organization endeavors, listed five main threats to the success of urban conservation: the lack of civic interest of many residents, resistance to higher standards, inability of many families to finance home improvements, fear of increased tax assessments after renovation, and the deep-seated prejudice of whites against Negroes. He concluded that headway could be made against these interrelated problems, all woven deep into the American culture, "only if we recognize them as problems and work reasonably and determinedly on many fronts to resolve them." But so broad a revision of American thought seemed necessary that he expressed "real doubt that it will occur."[75]

Notwithstanding the discouragements experienced in the pilot project area, the city planning commission decided to proceed with a long-range, comprehensive conservation program that contemplated further employment of community organizers and volunteer social workers and the

98. Proposed improvement of alleys with parking bays and playlots, Mack-Concord conservation project, Detroit, 1958 *(Detroit City Plan Commission)*

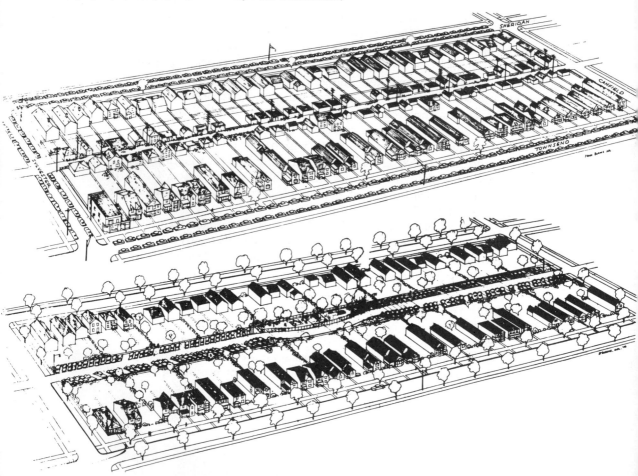

application of the kinds of corrective measures developed in the experimental neighborhood. The planning staff outlined a coordinated ten-year program based on a careful reexamination of the budget requirements of half a dozen city departments which would carry out projects in the neighborhoods. This program was related to the city's six-year and reserve capital-improvement program and took into account probable federal subventions. The planning staff suggested that fifteen neighborhoods should be improved in the first three years, twenty in the next three years, and the remaining twenty in the last four years.

In 1956 a new section entitled "Neighborhood Conservation Areas" was added to the Detroit Master Plan, and the city council officially adopted the ten-year scheme for improving the fifty-five middle-aged areas. Two years later the planning commission, with the aid of a demonstration grant from the Housing and Home Finance Agency, published a detailed report by Maurice Frank Parkins, principal planner of the conservation division, on the pilot study of the Mack-Concord area and its significance in the city's larger plans for arresting the downward trend in obsolescent neighborhoods. This study was widely distributed by the federal agency as an example of the kind of city-wide planning and detailed programming other cities might emulate. Like the *CURA Report* in Philadelphia, it suggested to Richard Steiner, commissioner of the Urban Renewal Administration, that federal housing legislation should be amended to encourage communities to plan and program urban renewal activities on a city-wide basis, utilizing all available resources, financial and otherwise, and conceiving of the whole endeavor as a more effective means of moving the general plan from vision to reality. But Steiner was to be no more successful in pressing for congressional approval of this proposal in 1958 than Detroit was to be in obtaining adequate federal funds for its ambitious renewal plans. Another year would pass before the national legislature adopted a housing act providing grants for the preparation of community renewal programs.

The cautiousness with which Capitol Hill accepted new ideas was in strong contrast to the eagerness with which many planners welcomed the new strategies suggested by the *CURA Report* and Parkins's neighborhood conservation study, once one of their leaders made them fully aware of a promising middle ground between short-range project planning and long-range comprehensive planning. This leader was Martin Meyerson, who as a member of the advisory Development Committee in Philadelphia had helped to outline the redevelopment authority's study of the inner city. His participation in that enterprise and his activities as vice-president of the American Council to Improve Our Neighborhoods were reflected in a formulation of five interrelated functions which planning agencies should undertake to make planning more useful to policy makers and developers. Described to members of the American Institute of Planners at their annual meeting in 1956, this complex of middle-ground functions appealed to a considerable number of planners as the sort of mechanism they had been seeking for some time, though in no very systematic fashion.

As Meyerson saw it, neither project planning nor general planning provided the kind of guidance that mayors, city managers, head of operating departments, home-builders, merchants, industrialists, and civic leaders needed to make rational decisions. The long-range plan, for instance, did not indicate to a home-builder how many units he should, as well as could, build next year; nor did it enable the government official to decide whether the signs of unemployment in the locality required special public action. It did not fully enlighten the industrialist who wished to know what specific land use changes probably would be made in an area in the next few years before he committed the resources of his corporation to expansion. Nor could the director of a redevelopment agency learn from the long-range plan what the effects of previous slum-clearance projects had been and what mistakes should be avoided in the future. To help all these people make decisions beneficial to the community as well as to themselves and their organizations, the planning agency, it seemed to Meyerson, should perform an intermediate set of planning functions on a sustained basis. In varying degrees most or all of them were already being performed by city planning agencies, but sporadically and not in a manner adequate to bring planning and policy closer together.

One would be a market analysis function making available special reports on the market for new homes, investment in plant, income and spending of consumers, and on land and building costs, to enable both producers and consumers to make more intelligent choices about location, investment, building, and the utilization of land for various purposes.

A second would be a pulse-taking function similar to that undertaken by the President's Council of Economic Advisers to encourage equilibrium in the national economy and new growth in employment and investment. Carried on locally, this type of activity would alert the community, by means of periodic checks, to incipient blight, potentially dangerous economic changes, and harmful shifts in population.

Closely related to this function would be a third concerned with the analysis and presentation of alternative policies that might be adopted to halt undesirable changes and achieve desired goals. In performing this function, the planning agency would determine the benefits and costs of different specific policies, on the assumption that clarification of the consequences of any particular policy would aid the political process of choosing courses of action.

A fourth function, stemming logically from the third, would be somewhat an extension of capital improvement programming. Meyerson suggested that the planning agency prepare a short-range comprehensive plan specifying the detailed course of action necessary to carry out the development policies selected in the political arena. This plan would indicate the specific changes in land use programmed each year for a period of five to ten years, the rate of new growth, the public facilities to be built, the structures to be removed, the private investment required, the extent and sources of public funds to be raised, and the tax and other local incentives to encourage private behavior requisite to the plan. "Revised yearly, it [the plan] would become the central guide to land use control, to public budgeting, and to appropriate private actions to achieve directed community improvement," Meyerson explained.[76]

His fifth proposed function was described as a review or analysis of the effect of planning measures or programs of action—something lacking in most communities. Rarely did a city government know, for example, whether public housing and redevelopment projects achieved the objectives originally established, how the construction of highways and freeways affected the demand for parking space, or precisely how zoning, as a form of public interference in the operations of the land market, affected the costs of land or encouraged or discouraged certain types of development. Consequently, in most cities there was no systematic adjustment of planning and the programming of public improvements to reflect actual experience with various kinds of public regulation and public investment. Meyerson said,

> Assuming these functions have merit, I am convinced that the planning agency should be the appropriate niche for them. This is for us in the A.I.P. to decide, or it may be decided for us. We will not have a great deal of time in which to decide. Two cities, a large one and a moderate-sized one, both known in recent years for their good government, are establishing posts called "development coordinator." Should this responsibility not have been delegated to or assumed by city planning? It is not too early, however, to say that planners have the opportunity to take on the development coordination function, to extend their range from the generalized plan on the one hand and the day-to-day demands on the other to the intermediate type of sustained, ongoing activities I have suggested.[77]

The implications of his proposals were, of course, apparent to Meyerson. Planning agencies would require more specialists than ever before—people who were generalists in planning and specialists in design or law or engineering or transportation. And these well-trained experts would require higher salaries than most planning agencies were then able to pay. In fact, the budgets of planning agencies would have to be substantially increased to permit them to perform the range of functions Meyerson thought necessary. Local communities in the United States were spending between $7,500,000 and $10,000,000 annually for planning, whereas a single public building or a mile of urban freeway frequently cost as much or more. If cities, counties, and metropolitan districts raised their planning budgets and encouraged their planning agencies to undertake the middle-ground activities, it was possible that "some of the efficiencies . . . derived from city planning in a single city could pay for the entire cost of city planning in the country."[78]

Meyerson's challenge to the planning profession was as controversial as it was stimulating. To some it seemed that he urged planning agencies to become, in part, operating agencies. Development coordination, if extended to many activities, could shift a planning agency from its advisory role to a quasi-administrative position. Indeed, the more effective planning became, the more it shaded into administration, to the philosophical dismay of some planners and the pragmatic satisfaction of others. If Meyerson was right and the drift was toward activism, then the strong planner might tend to become a superexecutive—unless, of course, a strong mayor foreclosed the opportunity by himself appointing a development coordinator, as Mayor Clark did in Philadelphia and as Mayor Richard Lee did in New Haven, Connecticut—the two cities to which Meyerson referred.

William Rafsky, who had been named housing coordinator in Philadelphia in 1954, became development coordinator in 1956. Edward Logue held the same title in New Haven, but whereas Logue rather dominated the situation in the Connecticut city, Rafsky did not overshadow planning director Edmund Bacon and his staff in Philadelphia or wholly succeed in carrying out the strategy suggested by the *CURA Report*. He proceeded with general agreement among Philadelphians that there should be concerted effort to safeguard the city center and to encourage industrial development. But he was not wholeheartedly supported in his attempts to stop the spread of blight by improving housing and neighborhood conditions in the outlying areas and then gradually working inward through increasingly serious blight to the central core of slums. Rafsky nevertheless epitomized a certain community insistence that planning in Philadelphia become more deeply concerned with economic and social issues, more encompassing and less project-oriented, and more closely coordinated with administrative policy. He shared with Logue the distinction of being the first of a new order of municipal officials conspicuously charged with producing teamwork among the agencies concerned with city building and renewal, including special districts, quasi-public agencies, and even private corporations. His and Logue's performances as development co-ordinators inspired other mayors to consider similar appointments and stimulated the reorganization of planning and development functions in several cities.

The first extensive reorganization took place in Baltimore as a result of a study made in 1956 by a special board appointed by Mayor Thomas D'Alesandro, Jr., and headed by William L. C. Wheaton, then director of the Institute of Urban Studies at the University of Pennsylvania. The board recommended vesting all project planning, clearance, code enforcement, public housing, relocation, rehabilitation, and conservation activities in a new renewal and housing agency. Further, it proposed putting an assistant to the mayor in charge of programming and supervising all public works planning and development, the capital budget, city planning, renewal, industrial and commercial development, and similar activities. The city planning commission and department, the board suggested, should be reorganized "to make them an integral part of the Mayor's coordinating machinery."[79] Richard L. Steiner later became director of the reorganized renewal and housing agency.

A Comprehensive Plan for a Central City

The new emphasis on development as a direct outgrowth of planning and on intermediate functions as bridges between forethought and accomplishment in the planning process necessarily affected the scope and nature of general plans, as the Philadelphia comprehensive plan that was prepared in the late fifties disclosed. Here was a plan which viewed Penn's city as a metropolis in intense competition with other great cities in the nation and presented needed improvements as capital requirements which would enable the city to maintain its economic position nationally and regionally. Environmental and cultural goals were not slighted or subordinated to economic objectives, but the thrust of the plan was toward its realization by orderly fiscal procedures and a definite strategy of development stressing economic aims.

When official and public pressures for crystallization of a long-range plan came to a head, the staff of the city planning commission was reorganized and a comprehensive planning division was added. Arthur Row, assistant director of the Detroit Metropolitan Traffic Study, came to Philadelphia as assistant executive director in charge of the new division. He found that although there was little agreement about what was meant by a comprehensive plan, there was general agreement on certain ends. Row later observed that "A wanted a process, B a strategy, C a credo, D a numerical accounting, E a sketch."[80] The plan prepared under his direction in some measure satisfied all desires. In a sense, the whole plan was a credo, as well as a guidepost in a continuing planning process.

The plan included a strategy of development, presented the costs to be borne, and generally depicted the physical changes that would take place if all proposals were followed.

As a credo the plan was peculiarly an expression of the civic renaissance Philadelphia experienced in the 1950s under the administrations of Joseph Clark and his successor, Richardson Dilworth. That period of governmental reorganization, physical rejuvenation of historic parts of the city, and aggressive industrial promotion had its gestation in the 1940s when Clark, Edmund Bacon, and many other activists were Young Turks championing city planning as a noncontroversial means of getting certain things they wanted and preparing the way for a housecleaning in city hall. Capitalizing on strong local patriotism, they enlisted the aid of high priests of the business community, persuaded the superintendent of schools to permit school children to participate in developing the famous Better Philadelphia Exhibition of 1947, and eventually convinced leading financiers to support political reform. By the time Clark took office in 1952 the city was ready for one of those rare flowerings that result from a fortuitous conjunction of personalities, trends, propitious developments, and recognized needs. Such eras of heady accomplishment can seldom be sustained for more than a decade, and Philadelphia's celebrated renaissance was no exception, but while it lasted it gave the city Penn Center, Independence Mall, a transformed Society Hill, the Food Distribution Center, the Schuylkill Expressway, a new housing code, an outstanding industrial development program, an effective capital improvement program, and a planning "tradition" respected by local politicians. The comprehensive plan, incorporating proposals of many public agencies and private groups invigorated by the Clark and Dilworth administrations, emerged as a declaration of faith in the ability of the city to continue the kind of progress represented by these examples of achievement. The plan was presented as "an assurance that Philadelphia, by the time it celebrates its Bicentennial as the nation's birthplace in 1976, will be well on the way toward its rendezvous with a future even greater than the one Penn planned for it."[81]

Belief in a future surpassing anything previously known was predicated, however, on the assumption that the city, by public action, could halt the commonly observed weakening of its economic position that resulted from competition of the suburbs. The plan urged a strategy of concentrating investments in public improvements designed to increase the vitality of the city economy in general and to strengthen the tax base in particular, though not at the expense of deterioration of the residential environment. Of necessity the strategy called for improvements in living areas which would prevent further flight of families in the higher income groups to the suburbs. Successful pursuit of this overall strategy of course demanded careful selection and scheduling of projects to spur growth where and when desired — for example, coordinating expressway construction with redevelopment to provide access to newly cleared industrial sites at the time they would become available for use.

A curious omission in a plan suggesting such an overall strategy was a scheme for the central business district of the city, since the one thing on which all officials and citizens saw eye to eye was the need for a plan that would preserve the central area, especially the rectangle embraced in William Penn's original plan, as a hub of economic activity, with particular emphasis on new office space, revitalized retail space, enhanced and expanded cultural activities, and unique housing. The city planning department later prepared a plan for the business core but even then failed to outline any significant treatment of the area. A still later plan for Market Street East indicated, however, that the department had in mind a strategy of project planning consistent with the overall plan.

The comprehensive plan made clear that the goal of a stronger center required the achievement of a related goal: a transportation system linking the center easily and quickly with its metropolitan market and the labor force and, equally important, with the smaller outlying regional centers to which it could provide the professional and financial services that these subcenters could not effectively provide themselves. But the system also had to be designed to assure the economic health of the entire region if the main center was to flourish. The port, two airports, the two major universities, the regional subcenters, the major industrial areas, and the growing residential areas of the suburbs needed to be readily accessible to one another. The specific policies required to achieve the kind of system outlined appeared, however, not in the general plan but in a report of a separate transportation board.

Still another objective was to meet the demands of industry for more space in Philadelphia. The plan included proposals for stimulating industrial development, providing more jobs in the city, and reducing the disparities in average family income among various areas of the city. It allotted vacant land in outlying areas for the future use of industry, and it also proposed the clearing of more than twelve hundred acres of land used for residential and commercial purposes in industrial areas and making them available for new or expanded plants.

Essential to the strategy of stemming the flight to the suburbs was a plan that treated the residential environment with considerable depth and sophistication. The plan for residence was not innovative in proposing to divide the undifferentiated mass of residential area into "imageable and functional" units of three types: districts, communities, and neighborhoods, each distinguished not so much by changes at the boundaries as by distinct centers including appropriate combinations of public facilities and service establishments. Nor was the plan exceptional in setting forth density standards indicating how many people would live in various areas when they had been developed or redeveloped. But it was unusually thorough in applying standards of housing quality to all areas, indicating the kinds of renewal or conservation treatment needed, forecasting changes in land use resulting from the removal of substandard dwellings and the provision of public facilities, and calculating prospective losses and additions to the housing stock. Such thoroughness was, indeed, to be expected in a city which had produced the *CURA Report.*

The completion of the comprehensive plan was to be accomplished by skillful capital improvement programming and budgeting, as in other cities. But the Philadelphia planners were more explicit about costs and sources of funds for recommended facilities than perhaps any other planning group, and they developed new devices to measure progress toward achievement of the plan. They estimated that all the proposals outlined in the plan would require capital investments totaling almost $3,500,000,000, but since federal, state, and board of education funds would be available for many purposes, and some projects would be self-sustaining, the "hard-cash" costs to the city would be approximately $921,000,000. Expenditures at the then current rate of $25,000,000 annually would make possible the completion in thirty-seven years of the tax-supported projects implied by the plan. If, however, the rate increased as fast as Philadelphia's total personal income was expected to increase, then all tax-supported projects could be carried out in twenty-eight years; and if a greater proportion of gross city income were used for city government, the capital improvement program could be speeded up even more. Assuming, for purposes of illustration, that the city would spend no more than $150,000,000 for its first six-year capital program, the planners indicated how funds needed to complete the comprehensive plan could be allocated so that eighteen sets of facilities would approach completion at the same rate. In actual practice, of course, some things of paramount importance would be done before others, but the even-rate capital budget device was a valuable tool enabling officials and citizens to discern how acceleration in one category must be offset by the slowing down of progress in other categories in order to hold the budget constant.

The makers of the plan hoped that the city would *not* hold the capital budget constant but would increase it to make possible the completion of the plan within the twenty-year span for which population forecasts were presented. But this the city failed to do for political as well as economic reasons. The economic growth of the city was slower than expected, especially in science-based industries, while industrial expansion outside the city was relatively great.

Unfortunately for the planners, these developments revealed the weakness of the basic assumptions underlying the comprehensive plan. In addition to the primary assumption that Philadelphia would remain the dominant regional center, there was an especially risky second assumption postulating that economic growth would proceed with sufficient rapidity to enable the city to invest in the public facilities called for. Least tenable of all was the third assumption that the city would maintain "a balanced population, including middle and high, as well as low income families."[82] In the next five or six years the city lost 150,000 or more of its long-time residents, saw its low-income population increase (mostly by in-migration of poor Negroes from the South), and watched the number of unemployed rise above 100,000. Even at the time the plan appeared, Dean Jefferson B. Fordham of the Law School of the University of Pennsylvania noted that a central city is "almost of necessity, pressed toward a line of policy which pays primary store by the potential and the future of the central city." Though he himself appreciated the historical fact that man had achieved his greatest intellectual and cultural development in urban centers, candor compelled him to say, "Viewed objectively, there is a question whether the 'save-the-center-city-area movement' is well conceived."[83]

Many Philadelphians, citizens as well as planners, understood the difficulties of attempting to formulate a plan for a central city outside the context of a regional planning and development program. Philadelphia is part of an eleven-county region embracing more than forty-five hundred square miles in Pennsylvania, New Jersey, and Delaware. Within this region, which to the north is separated from the New York region by a transition band of low-intensity development and to the south from the Baltimore-Washington region by open countryside, are 677 units of local government. Besides the counties, there are 20 cities and towns, 218 townships, 138 boroughs, 241 school districts, and 49 other special service districts. From the start, it was more an act of bravery to try to prepare a plan for Philadelphia alone than a step taken with real assurance of success. Without the cooperation of other governments in the region, Philadelphia could neither plan adequately nor hope to carry out many of the projects it conceived for its own betterment and that of the region. It had the help of some governments in transportation planning, but at the time general planning was undertaken there was no vehicle for regional consideration of common problems, although efforts were under way to create such a vehicle. (The story of that enterprise appears later.) The comprehensive plan nevertheless was needed and was not without value to the city. It contributed to advances in the art and science of city planning and was particularly imaginative in its attempts to link employment targets and industrial development with renewal and improvements in the residential environment. And it gave added impetus to the already pronounced trend toward recasting general plans as more effective instruments in a long-term developmental process.

Interstate Highways and New Crises

While Philadelphia was courageously preparing its comprehensive plan without the support of the kind of metropolitan regional planning and decision-making that might have enabled it to face its future more realistically, some other large cities and their smaller neighbors were initiating areawide planning with surprising alacrity. The motivation for their actions was the threat of outside intervention. In 1956 the Congress passed a new Federal-Aid Highway Act authorizing a multibillion-dollar highway construction program under which state highway departments would greatly expand and accelerate their activities. As one urban area after another faced the prospect of having freeways and highways imposed upon it by a state bureaucracy working in close cooperation with the federal Bureau of Public Roads, its local governments soon discovered advantages in metropolitan planning which they had previously failed to appreciate. Advocates of metropolitan planning for the Minneapolis-St. Paul area, for instance, said that but for the threat of highways where they were not wanted, some of the suburban governments in the area might never have joined with the two central cities in appealing for the enactment of legislation establishing a metropolitan planning commission. Many of these governments lacked planning commissions, had no long-range studies and plans, and realized that they had no reasonable basis for making counterproposals if they did not like the routes planned by the state highway department. A metropolitan planning agency, even though new and hard pressed to formulate an areawide plan that could serve as a guide for establishing the locations of routes, promised the smaller localities the protective intercession of a large staff of qualified planners—a boon in negotiations with a powerful state agency with millions of federal and state dollars at its disposal.

The Federal-Aid Highway Act in itself created a crisis for the city planning profession as well as for entire urban areas. No other federal-state-local program in history had ever provided so much money—an estimated $100,000,000,000 over a thirteen-year period—for a network of roads; nor had any other program aroused so much speculation, fearful as well as hopeful, about the effect it would have on the whole country, particularly the urban areas. Planners had only to consider the main feature of the program, a 41,000-mile national system of interstate and defense highways costing approximately $27,500,000,000, to know that cities would be profoundly altered by it. Funds for federal aid in urban areas had first been authorized in 1944, when the interstate system was projected as a network of 40,000 miles, but the 1956 act tremendously increased the amounts available, accelerated the whole program to meet the traffic expected in 1975, and raised the standards of design. As revised, the interstate system was to link most of the state capitals and 90 percent of the cities with populations of 50,000 or more and was to include 6,700 miles of four- to eight-lane, limited-access routes through urban areas. Though it was an undertaking equivalent to the building of sixty Panama Canals, this vast system, when finished, would constitute but one per cent of the highway and street mileage of the United States. A second part of the 1956 act authorized $2,550,000,000 in federal aid for primary, secondary, and lesser roads within the states for the period 1957–1959, with additional appropriations to be approved in the years thereafter. The exact total of federal expenditures was therefore not definite, nor could state and local outlays in this partnership effort be estimated precisely, but it was expected that the grand total spent on highways in thirteen to fifteen years would be almost as much as the estimated savings of the American people at the time the program was launched.

Leaders in the planning profession foresaw that such a deluge of expenditures would do more to change the character and structure of metropolitan areas than all the areawide planning done by city planners since the Second World War. Some of these leaders had written letters to Washington from time to time urging a higher ratio of federal to local money for highway construction, but now that Congress had voted to provide nine dollars of federal funds for every dollar the states contributed to the interstate system, they were filled with somber second thoughts and gloomy forebodings. John T. Howard said,

Most, if not all, of our metropolitan areas have not set down on paper and agreed upon any version of the development form and the development standards for future growth that could be promoted — or thwarted — by highway construction. We are ill prepared, now that the highways are upon us, to say where they should be built from the point of view of the best interests of the metropolitan areas. We cannot say we had no warnings: the interstate system was established in the middle 1940's, and we have known for that long what areas would be affected. In fact, I would guess that many of the central city planning agencies are pretty well prepared. It is in the metropolitan fringe, where the new highways will have the most influence on development and also where there is the most flexibility in route locations and the readiest opportunity for choice, that planning is generally lacking.[84]

As on many occasions in the past, there were not enough planners to meet the new emergency, and perhaps a high proportion of those available lacked the knowledge, the experience, and the wisdom to cope fully and confidently with the "monstrous dragon let loose on the American landscape," as the journalist Grady Clay described the huge federal highway program.[85] In countless areas the highway engineers would therefore decide the locations of routes, though not always blithely, because the best engineers realized that they were not experts in land use planning, industrial development, and land economics, and that they could make terrible mistakes.

But both planners and engineers were handicapped in this multi-billion-dollar enterprise. The federal government had no national planning agency to offer guidance, no national policy respecting a more desirable distribution of economic activities and a more rational pattern of urbanization, and, indeed, no way of arriving at a policy. Even though transportation had been the most powerful force throughout American history in shaping the development of cities and concentrating greater and greater proportions of the population in urban areas, vast sums of money were now going to be spent on a highway program related neither to a national urban policy nor a comprehensive transportation program such as the oft-remembered National Resources Planning Board had advocated in the early 1940s. In the name of defense a system of highways was going to be created which almost all urbanists predicted would further concentrate people and industries in megalopolitan complexes that invited attack. Equally serious was the failure of the authors of the Federal-Aid Highway Act to consider the possibility of integrating the highway program with plans for improving rail, water, and air transportation. Lewis Mumford thought that the program would "probably strike a mortal blow against our railroad system by giving the transcontinental trucker freeways and subsidies that he could never fully enjoy before."[86] If the fear was exaggerated, it nonetheless illuminated the single-minded narrowness of vision characteristic of the entire program.

To Mumford, historian John Burchard, and many planners the potentialities of the new highways for diffusing and weakening urban life were as perturbing as the likelihood that they would promote megalopolitan growth and injure other forms of transportation. Inevitably, the new routes would further extend the suburban fringe, increase the difficulty of renewing the semiblighted areas and festering slums, and would exacerbate the political and racial tensions between the inner city and surrounding municipalities. Though federal housing and redevelopment programs were themselves hardly coordinated, the Federal-Aid Highway Act made no provision whatever for linking housing construction with something as important to urban areas as rapid mass transit. The statute disregarded the problem of transit except as freeways and arterials might be used by express buses, and rather than contributing to a reduction in the number of trips made for various purposes, it envisaged a program that would increase automobile travel generally and lengthen journeys to work. The proponents of the highway program spoke of savings in time, the rise in the values per acre of undeveloped land along the expressways, and the expected decrease in accidents and deaths, but they discounted the expense to municipalities of extending services to new fringe areas, the accelerated slump in inner-city property values and tax revenues, and the strain of maintaining central cultural and educational institutions as the more affluent and better-educated families moved to more distant outlying areas.

Was the highway program a triumph for the federal and state highway engineers, the automobile manufacturers, the oil companies, and the speculators who hoped to make "killings" by subdividing fringe areas? Was it a defeat for city planning, advocates of metropolitan government, and humanists who believed in compact centers as expressions of the civilization that man had taken thousands of years to develop? The planners for the most part thought of it as a revelation of their own inadequacies as exponents of the idea of foresighted consideration of alternatives and rational choice of means to ends. "If a highway is so designed and built," said John Howard, "that it produces a pattern of land development and population distribution that worsens the livability and efficiency of a metropolitan area rather than bettering it, that highway is a disservice to the community — even if it carries traffic to capacity and all the traffic seems to want to go where it is carried."[87] Yet the highway act fostered such highways because it included no requirement that the location and design of routes be referred to city or metropolitan planning agencies for review regarding compliance with a comprehensive local plan, and this lack was at variance with other federal grant-in-aid programs, such as renewal and the advance planning of public works. This deficiency in the act was bound to cause trouble, but it was no consolation to city planners to anticipate outcries over the selection of routes and to foresee eventual revision of the federal legislation. In the largest construction program in American history the planning profession and the city planning function had been overlooked.

The criticism of the highway program and of state highway engineers as the group having prime legal responsibility for carrying it out became so intense that the American Association of State Highway Officials joined with the Urban Research Committee of the Highway Research Board, the American Municipal Association, the American Institute of Planners, and Syracuse University in sponsoring a week-long conference in October, 1958, at the Sagamore Conference Center in the Adirondack Mountains, to clear the atmosphere and arrive at some meeting of minds. The participants, sixty in number, included outstanding highway officials, city administrators, business and civic leaders, and a group of city planners, among whom were John Howard, Alan M. Voorhees, Hayden B. Johnson, and W. C. Dutton, Jr., executive director of the American Institute of Planners. Voorhees, a pioneer in the development of traffic models, particularly enjoyed the respect of highway engineers because he had been the recipient in 1955 of the Past Presidents Award of the Institute of Traffic Engineers for his ground-breaking paper, "A General Theory of Traffic Movement." From the face-to-face sessions, in which the representatives of city governments and city interests had an opportunity to present all their apprehensions, grievances, and proposals for improving relations with highway officials, emerged a series of recommendations revealing that the highway engineers had been conciliatory and that the urban spokesmen had pressed their points.

To highway departments throughout the nation the participants suggested that staffs be organized "to work cooperatively and efficiently with local authorities" in planning, designing, constructing, and operating streets, highways, and expressways in urban areas, that consultation with local officials be "on a continuing basis," and that programs be developed in cooperation with local governments for a period of at least five years in advance. In the event that a local government did not achieve community planning, the conference proposed that "the State should take the responsibility for initiating planning." Local governments, however, "should fulfill their primary responsibility for community planning needed to insure the maximum benefits to the local area from the highway program." Specifically, they should have "continuing, competent planning service" and should prepare a comprehensive plan for physical development consisting of a land use plan, a transportation plan including public transit, and a program of land use controls. But the participants, acknowledging the limitations of local planning, strongly recommended the initiation of regional planning in every metropolitan area. If enabling legislation authorizing such planning was lacking, the state government should join local governments in seeking its enactment. In fact, concluded the sixty leaders, "all levels of government should strengthen their support of city and regional planning," and, in particular, all federal agencies concerned with urban development "should continuously review their policies to achieve coordination with state and local objectives in urban development and transportation."[88]

After any peacemaking conclave attended by a select group, doubts always arise whether the resolutions and recommendations will be remembered and put into effect—whether the spirit prevailing around the conference table in the final sessions, when everyone is Bill or Hank or Steve, will actually be carried back to distant offices and transmitted to the lower echelons in the bureaucratic hierarchies. A year after the Sagamore Conference the newsletter of the American Institute of Planners reported: "A prominent official of the Bureau of Public Roads has told AIP that there is more cooperation between local planners and state highway departments than before, with the Sagamore Conference bringing about a 'marked difference.' "[89] A. E. Johnson, executive secretary of the American Association of State Highway Officials, noted that several highway departments had recently engaged city planners to assist in developing their programs and coordinating efforts with local planning agencies. The Sagamore Conference, in his opinion, represented "a beginning place for cooperation in urban development that has never existed before."[90]

Helpful as the meeting in Syracuse had been in establishing better understanding between highway departments and local officials, especially planners, it had only aggravated a permanent problem of the planning profession—the chronic shortage of trained planners. It was one thing to demand that federal and state officials respect local planning or lend support to the establishment of local and regional planning agencies, but it was something more perplexing to know how any substantial increase in the number of planning agencies could be accommodated by a profession whose membership at the time of the Sagamore Conference was only a little more than 2,100 and whose leaders spoke with embarrassment about more than 250 planning jobs which could not be filled. Always the profession came full circle to the question of increasing the supply of qualified practitioners and then to more controversial questions about the kind of education students of planning should receive.

The Discomforts of Professional Sophistication

In the academic year 1958–1959 twenty-nine universities in the United States and Canada offered programs leading to advanced degrees in city planning, but those in the United States expected to graduate only approximately two hundred students in 1959. Since the mid-years of the fifties the University of Southern California, the University of Kansas City, Ohio State University, the University of Washington, Pratt Institute, the Virginia Polytechnic Institute, and New York University had instituted graduate programs, and the University of Notre Dame had started an undergraduate program in its department of architecture. The University of Chicago, however, had discontinued its nine-year-old planning program in 1956 because of financial retrenchment. In September, 1958, the Massachusetts Institute of Technology accepted a small number of students for study leading to the degree of doctor of philosophy in city and regional planning, but these were students preparing for research and teaching careers. Eventually some of them would join the increasing number of planners being attracted to professorships of planning and would play their part in equipping an ever growing number of students for positions in planning agencies. In the meantime, though, the gap between the output of young men and women with master's degrees in planning and the total of vacancies in planning offices promised to become more and more alarming, even though additional graduate programs could be expected (such as the new program at the University of Mississippi in the fall of 1959 and a novel master's degree program in urban renewal and redevelopment at the University of Pittsburgh that same year).

Because of the intensity of their programs, most graduate schools of planning insisted upon at least two years in residence. Columbia University and the University of Kansas City were the only institutions in which it was possible to get a degree by attending classes in the evening. Persons desirous of learning some of the general principles and basic methodology of planning, and perhaps making the leap from an allied field such as architecture or engineering to a city planning office, could nevertheless enroll in evening courses in five or more planning schools in the East—the American University in Washington, Pratt Institute, Columbia University, New York University, and the University of Pennsylvania—and in several in the Middle West and West, including the Illinois Institute of Technology and Roosevelt University in Chicago, Michigan State College (now Michigan State University), Wayne University in Detroit, and the University of California, Berkeley.

In their desperate need for personnel, many planning agencies continued to open their doors to persons with bachelor's degrees in political science, economics, geography, sociology, architecture, landscape architecture, engineering, and other fields, gradually converting the new recruits into planners by giving them opportunities to work with graduates of planning schools or with older men respected for their years of practical experience. In some parts of the country where there were no planning schools, members of the American Institute of Planners took matters into their own hands and presented technical workshops for subprofessional members of planning staffs and other interested persons. The Baltimore chapter of the Institute, for instance, developed a course in 1956 that it presented once a week for three hours for a period of twelve weeks. To its surprise, sixty-one persons applied for admission, whereas it had expected perhaps fifteen. The chapter's committee on training of planners quickly quadrupled the teaching staff and accepted all applicants. In the fall of 1959 the Department of City and Regional Planning at the University of California, Berkeley, met the need for instruction in planning for members of city and county planning staffs who had had no graduate study of city planning by inaugurating a special two-year certificate program under the auspices of University Extension. Classes were held in planning offices in the afternoon or evening and were taught by practicing planners, many of whom had received their master's degrees on the Berkeley campus. This program, consisting of some electives and four courses presenting a much abbreviated version of the Berkeley curriculum, upgraded approximately eighty subprofessional staff members in the several years that it was offered.

The demand for qualified planners grew not only because of an increase in public planning agencies but also because other types of organizations discovered a need for the services of planners—the church-building departments of religious denominations; universities engaged in developing new campuses or expanding old ones; chain stores seeking sites for wholesale distribution centers and suburban branches; developers and real estate syndicates interested in creating new towns, industrial parks, and shopping centers; the Army and Navy; large architectural and engineering firms; a few of the larger school systems; research institutes serving private interests with large land holdings; and, as already mentioned, state highway departments. As yet, however, only a relatively small percentage of members of the American Institute of Planners was employed outside city, county, and metropolitan planning agencies, state planning departments, urban renewal and redevelopment agencies, and planning consultant firms. But the shifts in population from central areas to the suburbs, which caused problems for religious groups, wholesale and retail firms, and boards of education, affected other organizations as well. Planners were soon to be affiliated with hospital planning groups, councils of social agencies, banks with numerous branches, and with many federal agencies concerned in one way or another with urban areas. It was significant, for instance, that the Sears-Roebuck Foundation, established by one of the nation's largest merchandising firms, began providing scholarships for graduate students of city planning in 1957, just as it was noteworthy that in 1954 the United States Civil Service Commission recognized city planning as a profession for the first time and announced examinations for departmental and field positions in the federal government. Although many academes questioned whether there was a distinct discipline of city planning and although professors of city planning themselves acknowledged that they had not succeeded in developing much theory to support planning efforts, the nation at large increasingly turned to planners for guidance in making decisions about everything from the location of new savings-and-loan company offices to the layout of Army bases and new towns for the Navahos.

As a field that was still focused mainly on the physical environment but was more and more aware of the impact of social and economic changes on urban structure, city planning borrowed liberally from many disciplines and achieved a synthesis, however imperfect, of knowledge and techniques which many segments of American society and almost all governments found valuable if not indispensable. It was perhaps a sign of sophistication and approaching maturity that throughout the 1950s the members of the profession, far from being seduced by their acceptance as practitioners of an art and science unique in its usefulness, carried on a critical examination of their beliefs, their role in society, their methodology, their academic preparation for their work, and their relations with other professions. Sometimes crying "Mea culpa," they forswore notions and concepts that in application may have done more harm than good, and in all humility adopted new ideas or discovered timeliness and relevance in approaches and emphases earlier abandoned without good cause. Reawakened to the importance of aesthetics and again concerned with urban design, they found virtues in the old City Beautiful movement, for instance, that they would not have conceded in the 1920s or the 1930s; but their pretensions to comprehensiveness suffered serious erosion as they sought to define "planning" as a generic term and realized that their kind of planning was only a form of partial planning. Acquaintance with the new field of operations research, which like their own emphasized rationality as the best method of arriving at a solution but employed a range of mathematical and statistical tools as yet little used in city planning offices, deepened their sense of limitation—and their desire to find new horizons. Some winced when one of their own brethren who was also a member of the Operations Research Society of America drew a comparison between city planners and operations researchers that may have been oversimplified but which nevertheless revealed some of the professional deficiencies militating against the broader effectiveness of city planning. Melville C. Branch, Jr., wrote in 1957,

There are important differences as well as similarities between planners and operations researchers. Professionally, the memberships of the two groups represent different backgrounds and orientation. For the most part, physical planners are analysts and designers of space in either a narrow or the broadest sense of the terms. Because of their professional education, they tend to be visually oriented. They are more practical than theoretical, with relatively little interest at the present time in the possible development of comprehensive planning as a distinctive intellectual discipline. They are not mathematically minded, nor do they restrict their activities or judgments to those matters which are subject to reliable quantitative analysis. They are keenly aware of the socio-economic and political significance of their task. Although they work and cooperate with many different specialists, they operate as individuals in a staff, research, or consultative capacity within an organizational structure. The team approach, in the operations research sense, is rarely employed. They are advisors rather than decision makers. Their duties usually involve a coordinative function, broad or relatively narrow as the case may be. Occasionally, they occupy a line position in which they are directing action as well as research programs. Psychologically, they are probably more extravertive than intravertive; they are motivated more than most persons toward a self-realization attained by contributing to the social or public welfare.[91]

In the late fifties most discussions of city planning as a profession alluded to or stemmed from a provocative volume by Harvey S. Perloff, who had headed the University of Chicago school of planning. Entitled *The Education of City Planners,* Perloff's book thoughtfully traced the increasing concern of planners with the social and economic aspects of the urban scene and then wrestled with the problem of the kind of curriculum best suited to fit young men and women for the planning profession. Recognizing the rapidity with which rule-of-thumb procedures and routine skills become obsolete, Perloff defined the major task of professional education as that of "developing and advancing the basic principles to be used in the profession and providing an integrated set of learning experiences which would permit the student, in essence, to rediscover these principles himself and learn to apply them in a problem-solving setting."[92]

To begin with, the entering student should already have had "a sound general education," including the biological, physical, and social sciences, the humanities, and such tools of communication and thought as English, foreign languages, and mathematics. Such an education, of course, was difficult to obtain, especially in the larger universities, because of the academic pressures on the student to specialize, if not throughout his undergraduate program, at least in his junior and senior years. Assuming that the student somehow could manage to resist the pressures and to construct a broad foundation for training in city planning, Perloff conceived the assignment of the graduate school to be that of producing the generalist-with-a-specialty. This would be a practitioner who understood fundamental principles "in a broad social and intellectual context as well as in a problem-solving context." He would have a particular expertise because, said Perloff, "As a profession expands its knowledge and skills, it finds that it must develop specialists of all types if the profession is to make optimum use of the expanding know-how and if it is to speed the development of additional knowledge and skill."[93]

The main interest in Perloff's book, the first part of which had appeared as an article in the *Journal of the American Institute of Planners,* centered on his suggestion that "the planning schools of the country should make a major effort to develop a sound *planning core* in their training programs." The content of this core curriculum would "develop out of the requirement that the planner must learn to deal effectively with complex, relatively aggregate elements and interrelationships in a highly dynamic content (the evolving urban community)." No potpourri of survey and cram courses from other fields of study would suffice to equip him to see things whole, though Perloff believed that the student should take courses in other departments and schools, provided they were "directly *integrated* into his basic training or specialized training." The educator himself thought of the core as providing the student with "intellectual building-blocks" to work with—"basic substantive materials, propositions, and techniques that others have worked out and which the student can build upon."[94] Drawing on his own experience at the University of Chicago, Perloff suggested an emphasis on hypotheses, theories, and principles in the study of four main categories of essential knowledge: the planning process and decision-making; urbanism and urbanization as a dynamic process related to developments in the economy, in technology, and in social organization; the three-dimensional or physical city and its principal elements; the socioeconomic elements of planning. Analytical and design methods and tools would form a second part of the core curriculum, and problem-solving experiences—case studies, individual problems, group workshops—would constitute a third part.

Perloff thought it neither desirable nor to be expected that a uniform system of core courses would be established at all planning schools. His own outline of a core was illustrative and for the purpose of stimulating discussion, now that the planning profession was in a ferment and its leaders were "aware of a changing of directions, of exciting new opportunities just on the horizon, of glaring limitations in the profession which hinder progress."[95] He believed that the time had come for a great step forward, such as had been taken in 1928 when planners and educators had called the conference in New York City which resulted in the founding of the first planning school in the United States at Harvard University.

Generally, the planning schools agreed that a core curriculum might overcome the lamentable tendency of the profession "to ride off in all directions," as Robert Mitchell expressed it,[96] though it was still difficult for a profession concerned with a multiplicity of interrelationships to reach consensus on a common area of knowledge and to undergird it with a satisfactory theoretical base. "Above all," said Quigg Newton, president of the University of Colorado and former mayor of Denver, "your professionalism needs to be exemplified in terms of principle and of tested norms and standards which justify the practitioner in calling himself a professional, and the employer in depending upon his performance at the professional level." Newton was impressed with the wide variety of assignments undertaken by planners, but he observed that "many other professions and non-professional interests more deeply rooted than yours are involved in them too." And so, not unreasonably, he asked, "Is it altogether clear to you and to them what your contribution should be? What its essential nature is, and how it will fit in with work the others are doing?"[97]

Truly, not much more was clear than that the best city planners had developed an ability to take a broad view of community development, to think principally of goals, and to call upon a wide spectrum of knowledge in formulating solutions to particular problems and interrelated sets of problems. But recent research in the universities, private institutes and foundations, and in some planning agencies had revealed sad mistakes in planning performance in urban renewal, housing policy, transportation, zoning, and industrial development. At the annual conference of the American Society of Planning Officials in 1958 Lloyd Rodwin, director of the Center for Urban and Regional Studies of the Massachusetts Institute of Technology, presented an embarrassing list of questions for which there were no answers because of a lack of research. Assumptions, intuition, or partial knowledge had flawed many of the plans and proposals developed by members of the planning profession. Yet the future of the profession was not hopelessly clouded by its deficiencies of knowledge, its lack of theoretical structure, and its uncertainty concerning its role.

Research, now coming into its own as an adjunct of city planning, promised some alleviation of the discomforts of the profession rather than any startling "breakthroughs" that would make possible Perloff's hoped-for great step foreward. Rodwin realistically said that "given the egregious gaps in our knowledge, it is likely to take generations before we have a really reliable basis for action." Much of the research done would be done badly, he thought; and even the first-rate performances might be seriously misinterpreted. Everyone expected too much of research too soon, tended to want applied rather than basic research, and wanted to tell researchers what projects to pursue, whereas the "stubborn reality" was that inquiring minds would address themselves to what they considered important, not to what others regarded as useful. Until basic research was done, applied research would be as limited in range and depth as Edison would have been if Faraday and Maxwell had never developed their theories. "The basic studies must build up a solid hard core residue over a long period like a coral reef," Rodwin maintained. "There is no short cut."[98]

In the immediate future, however, applied research apparently could keep the profession moving forward and enable it to avoid some of the pitfalls in its line of march. Chester Rapkin, of the Institute of Urban Studies at the University of Pennsylvania, objected to the tendency among planners to exaggerate what they did not know and to overlook the considerable volume and variety of research studies already accumulated. These indicated that research could reduce the unanticipated consequences of action, could test and evaluate the feasibility of a given objective, could illuminate the consequences of policy and help in reconciling desirable but sometimes conflicting community goals. Take, for example, the problem of the central business district. If in the beginning of the redevelopment movement city planners had known as much about the processes of urban growth and economic development as they presently knew, they might not have eliminated small businesses and institutions in blighted areas "with dedicated abandon and with little consciousness of the roles and functions they served in urban life." Later research had shown that low-rent commercial floor space in such areas plays an important part in incubating new economic enterprise, but planners, in their "unsullied ignorance" of one of the important seedbeds of economic growth in large cities had tended to destroy a favorable economic environment and to disrupt complex relationships that could never be restored. Future research, providing both foresight and hindsight, could at least increase sensitivity to "the interaction of subtle forces" and make possible more intelligent public policies and decisions.[99]

The universities, then, with their graduate schools and their research institutes together seeking a theoretical as well as a practical basis for city planning, loomed large in the intellectual development of the profession. They offered little hope, however, that the troublesome shortage of qualified planners could be reduced. Indeed, it appeared likely to increase, even though the profession grew in importance and in numbers, attracting new members from other fields and gradually elevating the abler subprofessionals in planning agencies and related offices to professional status. Added to other signs that the nation was becoming intensely aware of its urban problems and would be calling for more and more persons to staff planning and renewal agencies was a movement for the establishment of a department in the federal government concerned with urban affairs. Even if such a department were not created for several years, there would surely be political pressures in the meantime for additional federal aids to cities; and the record showed that each new form of aid tended to encourage not only more planning but also a higher quality of planning.

Proposals for a Department Representing Urban Interests

In the Eighty-fourth Congress, the Eighty-fifth, and again in the Eighty-sixth, groups of senators and individual senators and representatives had introduced bills proposing an executive department that would represent the interests of urban and metropolitan areas. Each of these bills echoed in some form the earlier proposals of Senator Francis Newlands, Philip Kates, Harlean James, Charles E. Merriam, and others. Of the three bills introduced in 1955 in the Eighty-fourth Congress, that of Representative J. Arthur Younger of San Mateo County, California, attracted the most attention because he himself gave it wide publicity in an article appearing in Sunday supplements throughout the nation and because he suggested an odd name for the new department—the Department of Urbiculture. Just as Newlands and Kates had contemplated a department that would serve cities as effectively as the Department of Agriculture served rural areas, so Younger paid tribute to "the invaluable contribution made by the Department of Agriculture in promoting increasingly efficient use of farmlands" and prefaced his bill with the statement that "the Congress enacts this Act in order to provide a corresponding executive department to develop methods of dealing with pressing social, economic, and civic problems growing out of inadequate knowledge of the principles of using and developing urban lands. . . ."[100] Younger's bill gained a hearing before the House Committee on Government Operations, whereas the bill of a fellow representative and the one sponsored by such influential senators, among others, as Herbert Lehman, Hubert Humphrey, Paul Douglas, Wayne Morse, Warren Magnuson, and James E. Murray were smothered in silence. But the lawmakers failed to take any action on the Younger bill and it died with the others at the end of the Eighty-fourth Congress.

In 1957 the Californian reintroduced his bill, and a Michigan representative offered another. Senator Joseph Clark of Pennsylvania, former mayor of Philadelphia, led the group sponsoring the Senate version. None of these bills even received a hearing, and all three died at the end of the session because there was as yet insufficient demand for an executive department providing strong leadership for urban interests in national policy making. President Eisenhower and his chief advisers were, if anything, tacitly opposed to such a department. After favoring a federal Cabinet post for urban affairs in 1956, the influential American Municipal Association had cooled off and adopted a policy statement in 1957 calling merely for the President and the Congress to create a Council of Urban Advisors. The United States Conference of Mayors, though increasingly interested in metropolitan problems, was still more concerned with the needs of big cities than with urban matters generally. The National Association of County Officials feared that a federal Department of Urban Affairs would further weaken state governments and actively opposed the proposal. What support there was for such a department came mainly from the National Housing Conference and the National Association of Housing and Redevelopment Officials, but this support was indicative of the form a department of Cabinet rank was to take when finally created.

Appearing before the House Committee on Government Operations in 1955 as a spokesman for the National Housing Conference, Professor

William L.C. Wheaton of the University of Pennsylvania had argued for giving the Housing and Home Finance Agency departmental status rather than establishing an entirely new department concerned with a multiplicity of urban problems. The total financial commitments of HHFA, he had pointed out, "probably exceeded [those of] all of the other departments saving only the Treasury and the Department of Health, Education and Welfare."[101] Three years later when Wheaton spoke at the annual conference of the American Society of Planning Officials, he still favored "the creation of a federal department of housing and urban development [the name of the present department], which would confine its attention to those phases of the country's development that actively shape the working and living environment of three-quarters of its people." The operations of HHFA were already concerned with both public and private housing, urban renewal, financial aid to depressed areas, financial aids for community facilities, and some aids for local and metropolitan planning. With the addition of a few more functions and programs, the agency could become, Wheaton believed, a department that would satisfactorily represent cities and urban areas before Congress and in the confines of the White House and would provide cities "with equal strength at the bargaining table at the White House where our resource allocations are decided."[102]

In 1959 the Congress again failed to act on bills proposing a department of urban affairs, but a majority of members clearly indicated that they favored strengthening the agency which Wheaton and others wished to have transformed into such a department. At the beginning of the year funds for such important programs as urban renewal, veterans' housing, cooperative housing, and the moderate-cost housing program authorized in 1958 were almost exhausted, while construction under the much buffeted low-rent public housing program had all but ceased. Importuned by labor, the construction industry, and by mayors and other representatives of cities to authorize additional appropriations for these programs, the lawmakers twice approved omnibus housing bills, only to have them vetoed by President Eisenhower, whose advisers wished to eliminate the public housing program altogether and feared inflation if other programs were expanded. Finally, a third bill, watered down to suit the conservatives in the executive branch, was passed and signed by the President. And although it extended the established housing programs and authorized new federal programs of housing for the elderly and of privately owned nursing homes, the difficulties encountered in enacting it proved a point that Wheaton had made in testifying before the Senate Committee on Banking and Currency—that "we need a Department of Housing and Urban Development, something that will put responsibility for housing in the cabinet of the President where it is abundantly obvious the decisions are being made or not being made today."[103]

To members of the American Institute of Planners who had supported the bills vetoed by the President, the weakened Housing Act of 1959 presented an agenda for the future, not so much because of the few new programs it launched as because of several it failed to authorize. As planners had hoped, the act provided one 'thing they particularly wanted: grants for the development of community renewal programs like the one that Charles Blessing, George Vilican, and Maurice Parkins had formulated in Detroit. The Housing Administrator could now provide up to two-thirds of the cost of preparing a program that would identify all the slum or blighted areas in a city, determine the resources needed and available to renew such areas, designate potential project areas and types of action contemplated, and schedule renewal activities. In years to come, community renewal programs would be especially significant because they would introduce new techniques of urban analysis, suggest innovative ways to achieve renewal, and generate changes in the decision-making processes of local governments. The measure which encouraged this kind of planning retarded the whole renewal effort, however, by authorizing only half as much federal money for renewal as the cities required. Applications for capital grant reservations in 1958 alone had totaled $680,000,000, and many Congressmen had been willing to authorize $600,000,000 annually for a period of ten years, but under pressure from the Eisenhower Administration the lawmakers were obliged to reduce the authorization for 1959 to $350,000,000 and for the following fiscal year to $300,000,000. The renewal program was further handicapped by a meager extension of the public housing program—only 37,000 additional units—just when problems of relocating families were being increased by demolitions for the huge federal highway program.

A still further brake on the nationwide endeavor to salvage and reconstruct cities was the deletion from the federal legislation, at the insistence of the administration, of a provision authorizing an appropriation of $300,000 for a three-year period for scholarships and fellowships for the graduate training of city planners and housing specialists. The critical shortage of qualified planners, which Wheaton in his testimony before the Senate committee had estimated to be as high as 500 to 700 per year, therefore could only grow more severe. Ironical, indeed, was the section in the Housing Act of 1959 providing an additional $10,000,000 for matching grants to assist state and urban planning. Inevitably, much of this money would be spent to employ persons lacking previous planning experience or master's degrees in city planning.

A decade after the Housing Act of 1949 had raised great expectations that the United States would move expeditiously to eliminate poor housing and rebuild blighted urban areas, the National Housing Conference estimated that the country still had 13,000,000 substandard dwellings, of which at least 10,000,000 were in cities. In the years since passage of that act the nation had made spectacular technological progress. Television sets had become standard household equipment. Automation had increased production in hundreds of industries. The Navy had launched its first atomic submarine, the *Nautilus,* in 1954. Electronic computers had come into use for a variety of purposes, and city planners were fascinated by the possibility of processing volumes of statistical data previously undreamed of. The first jet planes had made transatlantic flights, foreshadowing the replacement of propeller planes on all except short intercity hops. Yet the living conditions of millions of Americans were, if anything, worse than ever, and the nation was actually losing ground in its fight against deterioration of the urban environment. Air and water pollution were more serious, many large cities feared water shortages such as New York had experienced in 1955, and accessible open space that city dwellers needed for recreation and quiet retreat from the hecticness of daily life was vanishing as the suburbs spread in all directions. There was no coordinated national planning to protect the natural resources upon which the welfare of large urban populations depended, though there were, to be sure, various departmental and divisional programs, related loosely if at all. Outside the Tennessee Valley and the Columbia River Basin there was precious little integrated state and regional planning. Grants of the Housing and Home Finance Agency to the states for state planning and local planning assistance were beginning to revive interest in the safeguarding of natural resources, but generally the states had retrogressed throughout most of the fifties in their concern for the wise use and conservation of their soils, streams, forests, and wildlife. In sum, the end of the decade found the nation with its problems compounded, its technical means of solving them vastly increased, and most of its representatives in Congress willing to liberalize and broaden programs of improvement — but not the Chief Executive and his associates.

Conscious of all the unmet needs and the beckoning opportunities, the American Institute of Planners adopted a policy report emphasizing "the urgent need for a national resources planning activity which can assist the President in formulating a comprehensive national resources development program."[104] And by "national resources" the Institute meant not only land, water, minerals, wildlife, and scenery, but also man-made, institutional, and human resources. The report, furthermore, called for state planning by an agency established as "an integral and permanent part of the administrative structure of state government," serving the governor in an advisory capacity and "acting at his direction in its relationship with the legislature and the individual operating departments."[105] It was to be expected that the Institute would reaffirm the need for metropolitan as well as city and county planning, but no one could have predicted with certainty even a few years earlier that in 1959 its members would agree that "the territorial extent and the complexity of interurban problems suggest the need for a governmental instrumentality somewhat different from the traditional forms of local government"—a federation, a multipurpose "authority," or "some new form of governmental organization." The Institute stated that, regardless of the form of the metropolitan regional government, "the planning function should be an integral part of such an instrumentality and should seek to obtain not only a wise use of resources but also a unified and sound form of urban development in the entire region."[106] The policy report could not have supported more trenchantly the view expressed ten years earlier by Luther Gulick: "By 1960 the vital, ungovernable, sprawling conurbations which will be our cities will cry out for governmental reconstruction."

But would the 1960s bring the hope-for reforms and innovations? In popular parlance, it was anybody's guess.

CHAPTER 8

THE SEARCH FOR A NEW COMPREHENSIVENESS

The Urban Vista in 1960

The shape of things to come in the decade of the sixties was perhaps discernible in the latter years of the 1950s and was reasonably clear in the election year 1960 to perceptive city planners and others who recognized the significant historical thrusts operating behind the movement of daily events. Whether a Republican or a Democrat was elected to the presidency in November, it was almost a certainty that the long-term federal

554

participation in urban affairs that had begun in the early days of the Depression would increase, but there was now a counterthrust sending the first shock waves through state governments. President Eisenhower, a conservative who failed even to mention such urban problems as housing and mass transportation in his annual message to the Congress in January, 1960, had signed an act in 1959 establishing a new national group that was intended, among other things, to spur the states to do their share in solving what some people called "the general metropolitan problem." Suggested by the first Hoover Commission during the Truman Administration and recommended by the Kestbaum Commission appointed by President Eisenhower in 1953, the Advisory Commission on Intergovernmental Relations was evidence that prominent members of Congress and many citizens throughout the nation deplored the drift toward greater reliance of the cities upon the federal government than upon their own state governments and feared a breakdown in the constitutional pattern that had worked reasonably well until recent times. Observers with some perspective nevertheless expected that mayors and city councilmen, having already found a path to Washington, would continue to appeal to the lawmakers on Capitol Hill and to future presidents to provide a larger and larger part of the financing required to develop and renew the urban plant. Nor was there much doubt that the federal government, either readily or reluctantly, would reinforce its commitment to the cities while prodding the states to assume greater responsibility for the welfare of their residents.

The dissatisfaction with the response of most state governments to the manifold problems of cities manifested itself in another way which foretold momentous changes in many state legislatures and in the nature and scope of state programs. In the fall of 1960 the National Institute of Municipal Law Officers, composed of the chief attorneys of more than twelve hundred municipalities, filed a brief *amici curiae* strongly urging the United States Supreme Court to accept jurisdiction in a case attacking the apportionment of seats in the Tennessee state legislature — a case which might decide "the great national issue" of the control of more than thirty state legislatures by predominantly rural legislators at a time when almost two-thirds of the entire population of the United States lived in metropolitan areas.[1]

To convince the high tribunal of the urgency of assuring city dwellers an equal vote in state elections, the municipal attorneys cited glaring examples of malapportionment: one state senator for the 14,000 residents of Inyo, Mono, and Alpine counties in California and the same representation for more than 4,000,000 people in Los Angeles County; 118 representatives for the 7,000,000 upstaters in New York and only 90 for the 8,000,000 residents of New York City. Yet even more pertinent were the financial injustices to cities resulting from such inequities in representation. The state legislature of Colorado doled out to the city of Denver only $2,300,000 a year in school aid to provide facilities and services for 90,000 children, whereas semirural Jefferson County, with but 18,000 pupils, received $2,400,000. Philadelphia spent $26,000,000 a year on its city highways, yet received only a $2,000,000 apportionment from state taxes, of which it contributed more than $20,000,000. A Supreme Court which had already outlawed racial discrimination in the schools could hardly ignore pleas to end discrimination against the urban areas by legislatures which, in violation of the express provisions of state constitutions, had not been reapportioned since the first decade of the century.

In the train of a decision that would force state lawmakers to redistrict "rotten boroughs," city planners could foresee an eventual end to the shortchanging of urban areas and the gradual unfolding of a new era in which municipalities and highly urbanized counties would receive more state funds to carry out certain types of public improvements and maintain state-aided services. Planners could hope, too, for the enactment of constructive legislation long overdue and for an expansion of state planning activities to provide more guidance to metropolitan areas and the smaller cities.

Not that even the most lopsidedly apportioned legislatures were wholly indifferent to the plight of the cities. The Advisory Commission on Intergovernmental Relations was at work in 1960 on a report pointing out that the growth of small urban constituencies in previously rural areas was tending to place such urban-type problems as zoning, planning, building regulations, water supply, and sewage disposal on the doorsteps of "rural" legislators. Furthermore, the migration of manpower from farming into other pursuits, the spread of industrial activity into the hinterlands, and the springing up of small business establishments in some previously agricultural areas was decreasing the number of strictly rural constituencies. And the increasing threat of judicial intervention was having the salutary effect of causing some state legislators to think that it might be wiser to make concessions voluntarily on the apportionment issue than to risk greater political losses through action of state or federal courts.

Some of the most underrepresented areas in a good many states were suburbs which had grown rapidly during the 1950s. As a result of the shift of population to outlying territories, several central cities actually enjoyed relatively good representation in generally badly apportioned state legislatures. The situation tended, however, to ally the suburban population with that of the metropolitan center in demanding an end to inequities and the reform of state policies. Suburban political leaders realized that there would be insufficient attention to urban problems until all urban areas were properly represented; and many suburbs now had such diversified economic and social activities that their problems were, with some exceptions, similar to those of central cities. In such matters as air and water pollution, water supply, waste disposal, transportation, and regional recreation the suburbs and the central cities increasingly were drawn together to find solutions to common problems.

Governors of the states were usually more sympathetic and responsive to the problems of the urban areas than legislators, if for no other reason than that the chief executives of the states had to appeal to concentrations of voters to get elected. Of the various state commissions and committees surveying metropolitan problems in 1960, many owed their creation to the initiative of governors. The Conference on Metropolitan Area Problems reported in December of that year that there were studies under way or recently completed in seventeen states.

Perhaps representative of the state groups designated to investigate the problems and needs of complex urban areas was the Governor's Commission on Metropolitan Area Problems appointed by Governor Edmund G. Brown of California in the spring of 1959. Accepting his challenge to "seek new answers, think creatively and not be bound by stereotypes in local governments and activities," this group concluded in December, 1960, that it should recommend not only improvements in laws concerning incorporation, annexation, and special districts but also some rather startling measures for bringing about metropolitan government.[2] It suggested the enactment of legislation permitting a majority of voters in a defined metropolitan area to establish a multipurpose district which *must* carry on comprehensive metropolitan planning and one or more other areawide functions. To spur action by metropolitan areas which had not taken advantage of such legislation by January, 1964, the commission proposed that a State Metropolitan Areas Commission (to be established by statute) be authorized, among other things, to put a proposal for a federated form of metropolitan government before any metropolitan electorate. If the voters turned down the proposal, the state agency would have the power to resubmit it to them every five years until they acted favorably upon it.

Although the chief executive of California shied away from the recommendations concerning metropolitan government and supported the less controversial proposals for improving incorporation and annexation laws, the commission's report was symptomatic of emerging belief in the necessity of well-financed metropolitan planning, multifunction metropolitan governmental units, and state agencies providing various types of assistance to metropolitan areas. In 1957 the Council of State Governments, for instance, had proposed the creation of an office of local affairs in state governments, to be charged with particular responsibility for assisting metropolitan areas. The congressionally supported Advisory Commission on Intergovernmental Relations early in 1961 similarly recommended state units of government for metropolitan affairs, as well as interlocal joint enterprises where appropriate, metropolitan authorities, or metropolitan service corporations empowered to carry on one or more of several areawide functions under metropolitan councils composed of representatives from the boards of county commissioners and from the mayors and councils of the component cities.

Dispassionate observers nevertheless expected no swift development of metropolitan governments but rather a continuation of *ad hoc* official commissions and councils, voluntary associations of nongovernmental leaders such as the Regional Plan Association in the New York area and the Allegheny Conference on Community Development, and consortiums of governmental leaders such as the Supervisors Inter-County Committee in the Detroit area. Donald C. Stone, dean of the Graduate School of Public and International Affairs of the University of Pittsburgh, believed, however, that by 1970 "the accumulation of past mistakes, citizen education, political necessity, business concern, and sheer desperation" would provide "the ingredients for intelligent political action on a wide scale."[3]

In the absence of broad interlocal contracts, joint governmental enterprises, metropolitan authorities, or multipurpose districts, some persons in city planning circles and some officials in state and federal agencies concerned with urban development shared a growing conviction that metropolitan planning agencies should be strengthened. The Advisory Commission on Intergovernmental Relations expressed this conviction in the form of a recommendation that Congress enact legislation requiring such agencies to review all applications of local governments in the larger urban areas for federal grants-in-aid for airport construction, waste-treatment works, urban renewal, public housing, hospital construction, urban highways, and any additional public facilities that might later qualify for federal aid. The review process would at least bring about a desirable exchange of information among local governmental officials and assure a considerable degree of coordination, as well as some development in accordance with comprehensive metropolitan planning. The precedent for this proposed requirement was, of course, the Housing Act of 1954, which stipulated that urban renewal and public housing projects must be in the context of a workable program including a comprehensive community plan.

As Dennis O'Harrow had observed in January, 1960, the outlook for metropolitan planning in the largest areas was not good, but it was promising in those areas in which a single county embraced all, or almost all, of the metropolitan sprawl. Of some hundred planning agencies in the United States serving more than a single city, almost two-thirds were county planning agencies. There were, in addition, at least eight county-city agencies. Gradually some of these agencies had been assuming increasing responsibility for guiding county-wide highway programs and inducing cities to relate their plans to general areawide schemes. Multi-county agencies numbered perhaps thirty at the most. In varying degrees they suffered from the usual handicap of having to depend upon voluntary cooperation of local governments to carry out proposed development. The appearance of a few metropolitan councils of governments that were interested in the planning function provided some augury of increased attention to the activities of these agencies. The general weakness of regional and county planning agencies was indicated, however, by the fact that all of them together spent approximately $10,000,000 a year, and of this sum the greater part was expended by a relatively small number of agencies.

One of the reasons for wishing to strengthen metropolitan planning programs was to reduce the somewhat chaotic impact of federal programs on urban areas. Since municipalities and counties bypassed their state governments and often did not consult one another before negotiating directly with federal agencies for grants and loans, developments in particular urban regions at times led to friction or even serious conflicts. Mayor Richardson Dilworth of Philadelphia pointed out that some of the more appalling examples of lack of coordination and long-range planning were federally aided highways that were pushed through newly renewed areas. An agreement negotiated between the Housing and Home Finance Agency and the Department of Commerce in November, 1960, to make a small percentage of highway funds and a larger amount of urban planning assistance funds available for joint use in comprehensive urban and metropolitan planning was designed to eliminate difficulties caused by the huge highway construction program of the Bureau of Public Roads. But ten or more important federal agencies whose programs impinged upon the physical environment had no arrangements among themselves to review their activities in particular metropolitan regions or populous counties. Proposals for a federal department of urban affairs mainly contemplated raising the Housing and Home Finance Agency to Cabinet status and therefore seemed to offer little hope that the welter of federal programs, social as well as developmental, could be effectively harmonized to contribute to the most desirable metropolitan advancement.

The situation indicated that throughout the 1960s and perhaps in the 1970s the federal government would be struggling to find some way to integrate the various kinds of aid provided to individual metropolitan areas. The suggestion of a review of all federally aided construction projects by a metropolitan planning agency apparently overlooked the equally important effect of federal health, education, and welfare programs on metropolitan areas.

Unknown outside a small inner circle was a confidential proposal by some members of the staff of the Bureau of the Budget for a single comprehensive annual grant to cities for community development. The conditions for federal assistance would be a broadened and strengthened requirement for a workable program of community improvement, a technically adequate and comprehensive plan of development, and an approved community renewal program. Cities meeting these requirements would be given broad discretion to use the annual grant for a variety of purposes. The proponents of this proposal recognized the ultimate desirability of providing the single annual grant to a metropolitan government but foresaw no prospect of such governments in the immediate or middle-range future. They hoped, though, that the scope of the workable program might be expanded to require intergovernmental coordination of planning as one means of assuring some consideration of the metropolitan aspects of development. Notwithstanding any merits this proposal may have had, it was well ahead of its time and did not emerge from the inner sanctums. It was nevertheless a sign that there were some minds grappling with the problem of simplifying federal relations with metropolitan areas.

In all these proposals for fortifying metropolitan planning, establishing permanent multijurisdictional units of government in the larger urban areas, and tying together federal programs, one thing was clear: planning had been accepted as a continuing process. Federal acts and regulations referred to comprehensive plans, but many city planners and government officials no longer viewed the plan itself as the chief product of planning. Since the mid-1940s planners had striven to relate planning more closely to decision-making in municipal and county government; now they hoped to find ways to make planning influence decisions affecting metropolitan development. Few had as yet abandoned the concept of the general plan, but many now regarded the plan more as an expression of goals and policies than as a graphic portrayal of land uses and circulation patterns to be achieved by some target date twenty or twenty-five years in the future. Many had emphasized flexibility as a characteristic related to the generality of the plan and had spoken of the necessity of revising the plan from time to time in the light of changing circumstances, yet in the 1950s few indeed were the planning offices which made revisions based on careful studies of the effects of particular public improvements on economic and social conditions in the community or altered the land use element of the general plan because some of the zoning designed to carry it out adversely affected overall development or bent before economic forces that were stronger than the planners realized. Now, however, planners stressed a process in which the plan was continually put into effect, adjusted, and improved as its impact on the community was studied in breadth and depth, thanks to an array of new analytical techniques, to a range of statistical data previously unavailable, and to electronic computers and data banks.

Varied performances resulted from the vast improvement in the technical resources of planners and the prospect of developing ever more sophisticated means of studying the economic and social functions of urban areas and testing hypotheses regarding how and why cities change. Some planning departments tended to believe that a greater and greater accumulation of data and more intensive analysis of economic trends would provide clues to the direction urban development would take. In such offices planning became a process of trying to outguess the market and move ahead of the tide—and of laboring to enhance the seemingly inevitable. In other offices agile minds seized upon more scientific methods of sampling public opinion and analyzing the complexities of urban areas as tools for making planning more effective politically. In these offices the focus was on the crucial decisions that planners could influence because of superior knowledge of the community; and matters of governmental structure, the strategic position of the planning department, fiscal mechanisms, and political alliances were of paramount importance. The head planner and his chief aids enjoyed exercising judgment and political skill rather than priding themselves on the refinements of their technical operations, though they sometimes were far ahead of less courageous and imaginative planners in devising new methodologies and administrative procedures. Clearly perceptible in still other agencies was a growing disenchantment with the idea of developing an overall plan and a determination to rely heavily upon systematic collection and analysis of data while substituting general principles, standards, goals, policies, and programming and budgeting procedures for the familiar report that presented the long-term plan graphically and verbally.

The disagreements among planners that had become pronounced in the 1950s were to become even greater in the 1960s as planning agencies experimented with a variety of approaches and as professors in university schools of planning divided into groups with disparate interests and opposing philosophies. The solidarity that the planning profession had had in earlier days would be all but gone by the latter years of the 1960s, not only because of a multiplicity of responses to the general acceptance of planning as a process but also because the technical advances of the profession revealed new relationships between the physical and social environments, suggesting the need for new conceptions of planning.

Most of all, though, planners allied themselves in various camps because they reacted differently to a rapidly changing social structure, an expanding economy, and a technology that was racing ahead of the ability of human beings to adjust to new conditions brought about by its proliferating wonders.

The Challenges of Population Growth

Even before the census of 1960 was taken, astute planners were familiar with many of the alterations in American society that had taken place in the 1950s. The tabulations merely revealed the magnitude of changes and underscored the reasons for tensions in the social fabric. Except for men and women in the late forties, every group between the ages of thirty and sixty increased at a rate below the national average, while the population under twenty increased enormously and the number of persons sixty-five or over rose from 12,300,000 to 16,600,000. Those generally considered dependents thus constituted no less than 48 per cent of the total population, compared with 42 per cent in 1950. Not only did the huge increase in their numbers place relatively greater burdens on those in the working years of life; it also foretold a rising demand for all the public services required by the younger and older age groups — education, medical care, special housing. Pointing to other social problems was a significant rise in the professions and in skilled jobs and a potentially serious decline in jobs for unskilled people, because of automation in many fields. Some of the newest migrants to cities, more than 1,450,000 Negroes from the South, already felt the pinch of unemployment or were destined soon to lack work.

Only 56 per cent of the nonwhite population of the nation remained in the South, whereas 66 per cent had lived there in 1950. Every large city on the Atlantic seaboard, in the Midwest, and in the West had attracted additional numbers of Negroes — New York, 365,000; Chicago, 328,000; Los Angeles 205,000; Detroit, 183,000; Philadelphia, 156,000; Baltimore, Cleveland, and Washington, D.C., each more than 100,000. The national capital, in fact, had become the first large city in the continental United States in which nonwhites predominated, constituting 54.8 per cent of the population. But more than a fourth of the population of Detroit, Cleveland, St. Louis, and Philadelphia was now nonwhite, and more than a fifth of the population of Chicago, Houston, and Cincinnati. In San Francisco and Dallas almost a fifth of the residents were nonwhite.

Even the bare statistics evoked visions of overcrowded slums, expanding areas of Negro occupancy, the flight of white families, *de facto* segregation in the schools, competition between low-income whites and nonwhites for unskilled jobs, mounting resentment among the Negro masses, and desperate attempts of civil rights groups and social agencies to ease the threat of conflict.

If nothing else, the census reports foreshadowed the increasing concern of city planners with the social and economic problems of urban populations, and even the growth of a conviction among many planners that the human problems required as much or more study than those associated with the physical environment. Indeed, the socioeconomic and the environmental problems would soon be judged inseparable, and new programs would be formulated to encompass the whole range of needs in rundown urban neighborhoods — more effective education, job training, job placement, better health services, coordinated welfare services, new and rehabilitated housing, additional community facilities, and improved public transportation.

Besides illuminating the social maladjustments that demanded greater national, state, and local attention, the census of 1960 brought into perspective a type of urban growth presenting still further challenges to the planning profession — the extended urban region composed of several metropolitan areas which appeared to be expanding to form a single great agglomeration. The development of the largest of these new forms, the chain of cities stretching from Boston to Washington, D.C., had been noted as early as the 1920s. Christopher Tunnard and his graduate students in city planning at Yale University had made this superregion the object of a special study in 1953 and four years later had brought out a publication in which they termed it the Atlantic Urban Region. Jean Gottman, the French geographer who was conducting a more detailed study of it under the auspices of the Twentieth Century Fund, called it Megalopolis, adopting the name of an ancient Greek city in the Peloponnesus which had acquired, in the popular mind, a sinister connotation of doomed gigantism. Though Gottman himself did not think of the name as suggesting impending malfunction and death, uneasiness pervaded the nation as it contemplated this and other conspicuous manifestations of another frightening phenomenon — the population explosion.

According to Dr. Charlton F. Chute, associate director of the Institute of Public Administration, there were, in all, nineteen of these urban regions in the United States, but in the article, published in 1956, in which he first identified them, he divided the Atlantic Urban Region into two regions, one extending from Lawrence through Boston to Providence, Rhode Island, the other from Springfield, Massachusetts, to the national capital. Chute foresaw, however, that these two groupings of metropolitan areas would grow in the future to form a single immense urban complex. Of the other urban regions, most were in the upper midwestern and northeastern parts of the country. Among the largest of these was the region dominated by Chicago and stretching from South Bend and Gary in

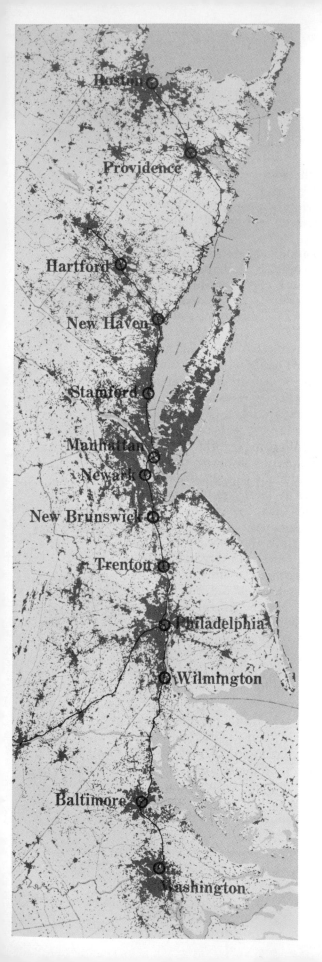

Indiana to Milwaukee in Wisconsin.
Its population of 7,600,000 exceeded
by more than a million that of
another great region including
the industrial cities of Pittsburgh,
Youngstown, Akron, and Cleveland.

On the West Coast were emerging
three urban regions, one in southern
California bordering on the Pacific
Ocean from Santa Barbara to San
Diego, another around San Francisco
Bay and the inland centers of Sacra-
mento and Stockton, and a third in
the Puget Sound area—the Seattle-
Tacoma grouping. In the South, Dr.
Chute identified five urban regions,
of which the Dallas-Fort Worth and
the Houston-Galveston regions in
Texas were the most populous.

Of the 179,000,000 people in the
United States in 1960, more than
71,500,000, or two-fifths, lived in
these burgeoning clusters of metropolitan areas. The urban region
along the Atlantic seaboard (Boston
to Washington) alone included more
than 29,000,000. But in a country in
which seven out of ten persons lived
in urban areas, there were many
large centers not related to extensive
urban regions: St. Louis, Minneapolis and St. Paul, New Orleans,
Atlanta, Denver, and Portland, Oregon, to name only a few. In these
relatively isolated metropolitan
areas the problems were, however,
little different from those in individual metropolitan communities in the
great urban regions.

99. Atlantic Urban Region *(Regional Plan
Association of New York)*

The superregion posed new kinds of problems, such as the distribution of limited water supplies among its component metropolitan areas, the provision of fast surface transportation throughout its length, the establishment of mountain or seashore recreation areas serving many metropolitan populations, the development of huge intermetropolitan airports, and the control of air and water pollution in airsheds and watersheds embracing all or parts of several metropolitan areas. Even more than in individual metropolitan areas, the resources of the federal government were needed in the extended urban regions, and the willingness of Congress to sanction interstate compacts was essential. For regional scientists among the faculties of planning schools, planners in some state and federal agencies, and planners on the staffs of private associations and research institutions the multimetropolitan region offered opportunities to revive a kind of broad-scale planning hardly attempted since the heyday of the National Resources Planning Board.

The Housing Act of 1961

Until after the elections in the fall of 1960 no one could prophesy with any certainty how much or how little the federal government's role in urban development would be expanded. Congress enacted no important housing legislation in President Eisenhower's last year in office. But upon the victory of John F. Kennedy and the election of Democratic majorities in the Senate and House, the mayors of big cities, housing commissioners, city planners, and civic groups concerned with housing and planning renewed hope for the passage of a housing act broader in scope than any previously adopted.

Three months after the young President presented his first State of the Union message, with its foreboding references to "the relentless pressures of the Chinese Communists" and solemn warnings which seemed later to have forecast years of anguish for the United States, a subcommittee of the Senate Committee on Banking and Currency began holding hearings on a dozen bills to amend the federal housing laws. As always when the economy was ailing, the course of housing construction was downward, and as usual under such circumstances, many legislators were eager to authorize further financial aids for private and public housing. But much more than housing was under consideration in the hearings. "An equal challenge is the tremendous urban growth that lies ahead," the President had pointed out in a special message on housing. "Within 15 years our population will rise to 235 million and by the year 2000 to 300 million people. Most of this increase will occur in an around urban areas. We must begin now to lay the foundations for livable, efficient, and attractive communities of the future."[4] Accordingly, the Chief Executive had called not only for a range of housing programs and more effective measures to renew blighted areas but also for loans to enable cities to build community facilities, grants to help public agencies acquire land as permanent urban open space and as reserves for future development, technical assistance to the larger urban areas for planning mass transit, financial assistance for research into housing and urban problems, and additional millions for urban and metropolitan planning. And the President had mentioned, as everyone expected, that he would soon offer a proposal for a "Cabinet-rank Department of Housing and Urban Affairs."

Testimony in the hearings indicated that there was at last a desire among city officials and business groups to treat the problems of urban areas in relation to one another rather than separately. Mayor Richardson Dilworth of Philadelphia, for instance, revealed that downtown interests in his city understood the importance not only of slum clearance and decent housing but also of adequate mass transit. They had told him, he said, that they would be willing to invest half a billion dollars in Philadelphia in the next ten years if only they could be assured of the continuity of the renewal program and of some real help for mass transportation. Mayor Richard J. Daley of Chicago, who could boast of a building boom in the central business district of his city and of "one of the most progressive, far-flung conservation programs in the nation," joined Dilworth in pleading for federal aid for mass transit, saying that he thought good transit was "as important as housing or as proper police administration."[5]

But the chief interest of the cities was still in obtaining funds to eliminate deteriorated structures, whether commercial and industrial or residential, and to undertake the public improvements that would stimulate private redevelopment and rehabilitation. Mayors and development coordinators emphasized that without additional federal funds their renewal programs could not continue. Now, however, they wanted the whole federal effort broadened, specifically by further authorizations of public housing and by major changes in what Mayor Daley called "the general policy of the FHA." The Federal Housing Administration, it seemed, was both the despair and the bright hope of the central cities. The Chicago mayor charged that it "encouraged people to move from the cities by failing to give opportunity for home ownership and general improvement of housing conditions in the cities where the majority of our people live."[6] Edward Logue, who had gained fame in New Haven, Connecticut, as a development coordinator and was now struggling with the problems of Boston, harshly seconded the criticisms of the Chicago mayor, asserting that FHA had done "as much to cause the suburban sprawl, the unplanned suburban growth and at the same time the deterioration of the middle-aged neighborhoods of the city as any other single force. . . ."[7] The problem was not that the officials of the Federal Housing Administration had "improper motives" but that the agency had "never been on the urban renewal team in the past." The Kennedy Administration's own housing bill promised to make FHA "for the first time a full partner in the urban renewal program" by authorizing mortgage amounts more nearly adequate to finance the rehabilitation of homes and by modifying the mortgage insurance program for persons displaced by urban renewal and other governmental activities so that it would serve a broad range of moderate-income families.[8]

To help curb the urban sprawl that the FHA was accused of furthering, Senator Harrison A. Williams of New Jersey had introduced a bill providing for grants to public agencies to acquire open-space land for scenic and recreational purposes, but at the request of the President the senator had substituted a new bill providing additionally for loans to assist public bodies in acquiring land for future private or public development. Among

100. Suburban sprawl in New Jersey *(Louis B. Schlivek, photographer, and Regional Plan Association of New York)*

other things, the senator's bill sought to foster better residential environments by offering grants to municipalities to promote cluster developments in which open space would be dedicated to the community without cost — a provision later deleted.

The Williams bill reflected a great wave of enthusiam for saving open land from the bulldozer and for shaping suburban development. For the past four or five years William H. Whyte, Jr., a former editor of *Fortune* magazine and author of *The Organization Man,* had made an outstanding contribution to this movement by publicizing various devices for preserving open space, particularly the use of conservation easements in California and a constitutional amendment in Maryland giving tax relief to farmers for maintaining agricultural land. Appearing at a subcommittee hearing, Whyte assured interested senators that the people of the country now realized that if they wanted the benefit of open space, they would have to pay for it. Spokesmen for ten national organizations supported the financial aids proposed in the Williams bill. But E. J. Burke, Jr., president of the National Association of Home Builders, sent a statement to the subcommittee objecting to federal loans for the acquisition of open land for future public or private development. The idea was "wholly at variance with the traditional American system of property rights," he contended. Any community empowered to compete in the private land market "would be adding more fuel to the speculative fire."[9] As Burke's statement indicated that there were other organizations opposed to the use of federal funds to enable municipalities to buy and hold land for planned expansion, political wisdom counseled sacrificing the proposal added at the urging of the President.

The various housing, mass transportation, and open-space land bills considered by the committees were eventually combined in a single bill which won approval as the Housing Act of 1961. Though the measure did not contain some of the features the American Institute of Planners and other professional organizations and governmental associations had wanted (for example, it provided no money for scholarships to study planning), it was striking proof of the vigor of the historical movement seeking greater participation of the federal government in urban development.

To the relief of anxious mayors and redevelopment officials, the act increased the urban renewal grant authorization from $2,000,000,000 to $4,000,000,000 and placed no time limit on the use of the funds. It also authorized an additional 100,000 units of public housing and liberalized the terms of financial assistance under FHA programs affecting lower-middle-income families, displaced families, and the elderly. In hearings on the legislation, however, Leon H. Keyserling, who had been the principal draftsman of the Housing Act of 1949 and had had a large part in drafting the legislation originating and improving the FHA, had warned lawmakers that the cost of housing under their proposal for lower-middle-income families would, "for the most part, be far above the income reach" of such families and that, indeed, all the housing programs they were contemplating "would not average in excess of 1.4 million units a year and probably less," or only about 70 per cent of the needed volume of nonfarm housing construction.[10] And time was to show that the distinguished economist was generally correct in his analysis of the probable effects of the housing provisions.

To city planners the breakthroughs in the legislation were the authorizations of grants for the acquisition of open-space land and the improvement of mass transportation. The act made $50,000,000 available for the new open-space land program—only half as much as Senator Williams had proposed, but sufficient to stimulate several times as much state and local spending for conservation. Localities could qualify for grants not exceeding 20 per cent of the cost of acquiring title to or interest in land of scenic or recreational value if they were carrying on a comprehensive planning program and needed land for permanent open space in order to execute an overall plan, but this limitation was increased to 30 per cent for public bodies serving all or substantial parts of metropolitan areas. Of the billions authorized for urban renewal, $25,000,000 was expressly designated for grants to local public agencies for demonstration projects designed to contribute to the improvement of mass transportation or the reduction of mass transportation needs. In addition, the housing act authorized $50,000,000 in loans to public bodies to provide for the financing of the acquisition, construction, and improvement of transportation facilities and equipment. Further, comprehensive planning for mass transportation was made eligible under the urban planning assistance program, the authorization for which was increased from $20,000,000 to $75,000,000, with the federal contribution raised from one-half to two-thirds of the planning cost.

"The new legislation provides opportunities never before possible for coordinated planning of community development," the newsletter of the American Society of Planning Officials commented.[11] There were new incentives for metropolitan planning, authorizations for the Housing Administrator to provide technical assistance to state and local governments undertaking comprehensive planning, and a provision giving the consent of Congress to interstate compacts for cooperative efforts and mutual aid in the comprehensive planning of interstate, metropolitan, or other urban areas, and to the establishment of agencies for making effective such compacts. An additional $10,000,000 was authorized for the planning of nonfederal public works, including projects to be constructed over a long period of time. The amount of renewal funds available for nonresidential projects was increased from 20 to 30 per cent in response to the desire of cities to rid themselves more rapidly of commercial and industrial as well as residential blight; and in recognition of growing concern about the "wrecker's ball" approach to urban renewal, local public agencies were authorized to carry out small rehabilitation demonstrations which in time might show the wisdom of preserving more of the existing urban texture. Though they would prove to be less effective than was desired, the middle-income housing provisions, particularly, evidenced a serious effort to assure greater flexibility in local renewal programs and make them more adaptable to social needs.

Departments of Planning and Development

By making available a greater array of tools for guiding urban development, the Housing Act of 1961 brought planning and operations closer together. The long-term shift of emphasis from plan-making to planning as a process in which proposals are systematically maneuvered through decision-making, programming, and budgeting procedures to the execution stage had already caused many planning directors to think of their departments not merely as planning organizations but as departments of planning *and* development. All the more active and effective departments were, indeed, adjuncts to a city development program embracing not only municipal departments and such semiautonomous agencies as public housing authorities and redevelopment agencies but also private syndicates and financial institutions engaged in rebuilding or rehabilitating older areas. There was a tendency, however, to relate city planning perhaps too narrowly to urban renewal and to forget that development takes place throughout a city in many fields. In Cincinnati, for instance, a proposal had been made in February, 1960, for including the functions of city planning, urban renewal, and building regulation in a single department to be called the Department of Urban Development. This proposal had been rejected and, instead, the Department of Urban Renewal had been renamed the Department of Urban Development. In Boston, on the other hand, Mayor John F. Collins soon after his election in 1960 had initiated a program calling for the integration of planning and development. The city planning board was abolished and its staff and functions were amalgamated with those of the Boston Redevelopment Authority. Edward J. Logue, lured from New Haven, had become head of the staff of the authority as well as development administrator in the mayor's Office of Development.

At the time the Housing Act of 1961 went into effect the city of Milwaukee created a Department of City Development somewhat after the model rejected in Cincinnati. The proposal had been debated for months. The staffs of the housing authority, development authority, and the city

101. (upper) Cincinnati riverfront and Fort Washington Way, cleared area being developed with a park and stadium; (lower) central riverfront before redevelopment *(Cincinnati City Planning Commission and City Engineer)*

planning commission were all assigned to the new department, although the two authorities retained their identities as independent ad hoc public bodies and the city planning commission remained essentially an advisory agency to the mayor and the city council. Heading the new department was an executive director appointed by the mayor, confirmed by the council, and approved by the constituent agencies. There were five divisions of the department: administration, management, technical and maintenance, real estate, and planning and programming. The last-named division carried on the usual range of planning activities: research, preparation of the long-range plan, housing and renewal project planning and programming, zoning administration, subdivision review, preparation of the six-year capital improvement program, and coordination of the planning activities of other city and county agencies, such as the county planning commission, the school board, and the county expressway commission.

A year later the director of this division, Vincent L. Lung, commented on the difficulties of avoiding conflicts of policies among three separate boards with widely divergent points of view and spoke of the possibility of ultimate integration of these groups. He mentioned, though, that working relationships between the Department of City Development and other city departments were good. "From the standpoint of other city departments, it is apparently easier to deal with the head of a recognizable department than it is to deal with the head of an agency whose relationship to the over-all municipal administrative structure is less clearly understood."[12]

The consolidation of planning with housing and renewal functions was apt to be considered mainly in the larger central cities in which the proliferation of agencies threatened to impede action. Mergers such as those which took place in Boston and Milwaukee were, however, relatively few, mainly because the laws of most states prevented unification of municipal departments with agencies that were legally subdivisions of state government, as public housing authorities and redevelopment commissions were in most states. Many cities took the lesser step of combining the housing inspection services of various departments in a single municipal department of urban renewal concerned principally with improving housing in areas requiring rehabilitation but not clearance. The work of such departments could readily be coordinated with that of the city planning department. In cities with strong mayors, such as Chicago, St. Louis, and San Francisco, the development coordinator, in the capacity of deputy to the mayor or head of a superdepartment, appeared on the municipal scene to assemble the professional and technical talent, the legal and intellectual skills, the public and private financing, and the civic support necessary to transform decaying areas into new residential, commercial, or industrial complexes. He was often as much concerned with economic development and race relations as with city planning and renewal. Usually he was not by profession a city planner, though under one mayor of San Francisco a former director of city planning, T. J. Kent, Jr., served as the coordinator of housing, planning, and development.

The diversity of the activities of the development coordinators seemed to belie the earlier contention of many city planners that no one man could master several types of planning. The development coordinators ranged from physical to economic and social planning without being troubled by nice distinctions, indicating by all their actions that urban development is and must be an integration of several kinds of planning.

A Policies Plan for the National Capital Region

In the urban expanse encompassing the central cities the problem of relating metropolitan planning to development seemed to defy satisfactory solution. These areas were both politically and functionally balkanized. In fact, the functional balkanization which manifested itself in independent, areawide special districts and authorities resulted almost entirely from the political fragmentation and was an attempt to overcome it. As suburbanization and the dispersion of economic activities accelerated, and as public transit became more and more inadequate and traffic on freeways reached the saturation point, the metropolitan planning in these spread-out accretions increasingly focused on the issues of transportation and the distribution of population and places of employment. Even before the Housing Act of 1961 made federal funds available for areawide transportation planning, studies were under way or contemplated in some of the more populous urban regions which indicated widespread hope that transportation systems carefully related to land use plans might be a means of achieving more orderly and satisfying development. As in earlier periods, there was a great deal of faith in the potency of mass transit as a guiding force in shaping urban areas, and there was also a fresh realization that the timing and location of new building and renewal would depend upon intergovernmental cooperation or the formation of multipurpose regional governments. Unfortunately, the uncertainty of positive action in the political sphere cast a pall over all the general metropolitan planning that was undertaken and vitiated much of the comprehensive transportation planning.

Among the more significant metropolitan plans emphasizing the importance of mass transportation was *A Policies Plan for the Year 2000*, issued by the National Capital Planning Commission and the National Capital Regional Planning Council in 1961 and later endorsed by President Kennedy himself. It had been preceded in 1959 by a comprehensive mass transportation survey of the Washington region which included a general development plan prepared by the staff of the Regional Planning

Council. That plan was a rather unusual two-part scheme that accepted the probability of "a formless sprawl" until 1965 but presented an attempt to modify the trend thereafter by a long-range proposal for planned growth that would follow main corridors of radial travel. Wedges of open space were to be retained in rural or recreational use between the sectors of concentrated urban development. The *Plan for the Year 2000* used the earlier general plan as a starting point but departed from custom by describing seven different patterns of growth graphically and in writing with the expressed hope that "there will be widespread, thorough and constructive public discussion of the issues raised in this report and the recommendations offered herein." In no sense a detailed plan for the physical development of the region, the planning report was put forth as "a set of policies to guide governmental decision-making and the preparation of physical plans."[13] Among the seven patterns was one corresponding to the long-range plan (for the year 1980) prepared by the Regional Planning Council.

For a decade or more Catherine Bauer had hoped that some planning agency would trigger lively argument about the best type of physical organization for populous urban areas by thus "dramatizing the issues." Americans, she lamented, never talked to strangers on buses and in subways about sprawl and greenbelts and new towns as the British did, mainly because planners in the United States had failed to pose the various choices so that the public could understand them. But William E. Finley, director of the staff of the National Capital Planning Commission, and his cohorts tended to foreclose debate about the seven alternatives in their report by selecting one and rejecting the others.

Written off by these planners as neither feasible nor desirable was a scheme for restricting the growth of the Washington region to a highly compact form penetrated by open space only along the rivers. Also rejected was a "planned sprawl" that would be made tolerable by minimum regulation. Far more preferable, the policies plan suggested, might be various plans to limit the size of Washington and its immediate environs by directing new growth to entirely independent cities. These might be new metropolitan centers at least seventy miles from the federal city, each spacious in conception and designed to accommodate from 300,000 to 500,000 people in the next forty years. Or the new cities might be suburban communities ten or more miles from the outer limits of the central urbanized area and at some distance from one another. Each would offer a substantial amount of employment of various kinds and would perhaps eventually have a population of 100,000 but would not, of course, compete with the central city in the range of job opportunities available. Or another possibility would be a ring of new towns at a distance of some thirty miles from central Washington. Because of their remoteness, there would be little likelihood of an eventual filling-in between these towns and the central urbanized area, but the proximity of the towns to one another would make ample employment, social, and cultural opportunities readily accessible and would compensate for the distance from Washington. Still a fourth variation on the theme of dispersed cities would be new communities at the very edge of the urbanized area, comparable in size to the towns in the urban ring or the more widely separated suburban communities built around sizeable business districts. This pattern, however, would push the open countryside farther and farther from the homes of the people and would necessitate an elaborate network of freeways, including many circumferential and diagonal routes passing through densely built-up areas.

Were any of these schemes practicable? Finley and his staff were not inclined to think so. The creation of new metropolitan centers of as many as half a million residents "would require construction efforts of unprecedented magnitude, as well as entirely new forms of political organization, legal procedures, and administrative and financial arrangements."[14] Moreover, some kind of national policy respecting the distribution of population would be essential, and the Congress and the American people had never shown serious interest in developing such policy, even when faced with the prospect of thermonuclear extinction. The other forms of dispersal were also probably no less difficult to achieve because their realization "would necessitate strong measures, such as rigorous controls over land use and public acquisition of large tracts, to assure the development of the new cities as planned, to prevent their ultimate merger with one another, and to prevent them all from being submerged in time by outward growth of the central urbanized area."[15]

The planners nevertheless foresaw the possibility of saving the open countryside near Washington as a recreational and scenic resource, of channeling future growth into well-planned new towns, and of providing everyone in the region with easy access to the central area and its offices, stores, and educational and cultural institutions. The keys to a happy solution of the problem of growth were a rapid transit system such as the one which the National Capital Transportation Agency had been created to develop and new centers of government employment, many of which would be needed as federal, state, and local government jobs in the region increased an estimated 360,000 in the next four decades. If the transit system were built with six radial routes thrusting outward from downtown Washington like the spokes of a wheel, and if the outlying stations were spaced from four to six miles apart as nodes around which to develop new towns, then the federal government, the largest employer in the region, could set the pattern of regional development by consistently dispersing additional federal activities to new locations. Clusters of federal office buildings and other facilities within walking distance of the station stops could well-nigh establish the basic form of each new town; and by careful timing of construction, cooperating governments could promote the growth of a suburban business district to serve each new community of government employees. Federal mortgage insurance and other financial aids might be used as further "leverage" to shape the desired new towns. In any event, governmental policy would be all-important in carrying out "the radial corridor plan," as Finley and his associates called their version of a well-known urban form.

In the late nineteenth century many European and American cities

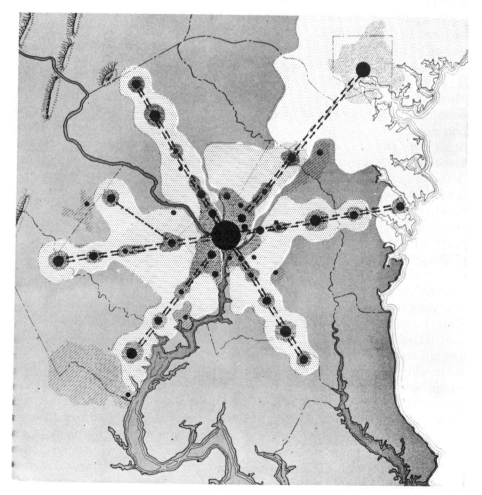

102. Radial corridor plan proposed by the National Capital Planning Commission, 1961

exhibited a pattern rather like the one these twentieth century planners proposed. Compact accretions and new suburbs along the radial commuter lines converging on the hub produced a starlike configuration set off by the wedges of open space between the urban extensions. The whole was almost a natural growth, or at least one determined by the uncoordinated decisions of thousands of individual families and businesses. Moreover, it appeared so altogether logical in the age of steam and so saving of green space in close proximity to the dwellings of men that Patrick Geddes considered the general arrangement ideal. In recent years Danish planners had found it suitable for Copenhagen, as their famous "finger plan" showed. The staff of the National Capital Planning Commission enthusiastically commended the scheme as offering "the highest promise as a guide to the growth of the National Capital region during the decades ahead."[16]

To help government officials and the public visualize the new towns that could be developed around the outlying stations of the proposed transit system, the policies plan included a sketch of the heart of a typical new suburban community. The train stop opened onto a sunken courtyard faced with small shops and restaurants at the base of office towers. Nearby high-rise apartment buildings loomed behind these tall structures. And from the sunken courtyard an escalator provided access to a larger pedestrian plaza serving as a gathering place for employees or shoppers in the suburban business district. Around some of the trees in the sunken courtyard stood large flower planters such as one sees in the public squares of Stockholm; and waiters were serving patrons seated at little tables in the open air. It was all very urbane, somewhat Scandinavian, and glamorous.

The planners obviously assumed that a goodly proportion of town dwellers would like living in high-rise and garden apartments, and the generalized town plans presented in color on another page showed schemes in which the core of each town was surrounded by areas containing from fifteen to thirty dwelling units per acre and some having eighty to a hundred units per acre. To be sure, there were substantial areas with only two to four houses per acre, and some with only one or two, yet one suspected that people in these towns would serve the transit system as much as it might serve them. Plans also showed freeways in the transportation corridors and circumferential freeways in the highly developed central sections of the metropolitan region. Still, there seemed to be a dominant assumption that people would prefer transit to the private automobile for most journeys.

In its promotion of the radial corridor plan the National Capital Planning Commission had an ally—the Maryland-National Capital Park and Planning Commission, whose jurisdiction included suburban Montgomery and Prince Georges counties. Four of the six corridors shown in the schematic plan extended into these counties, one northwest toward Rockville, a second toward Baltimore, a third toward Annapolis, and the fourth southeast into Prince Georges County. After considering this development pattern and three other possibilities — unlimited sprawl, controlled sprawl, and an arrangement of dispersed satellite cities — the Maryland commission recommended the corridor plan as the most likely to achieve the goals of pleasant living and economical public services. As an agency with direct responsibility for providing parks and recreation centers, the commission understandably had a strong interest in retaining large open spaces for the benefit of present and future generations.

On Wedges and Corridors, the report in which the commission presented its recommendations, attempted to carry policies planning some steps farther than the year-2000 plan of the National Capital Planning Commission. The concluding section of the latter plan had suggested that federal departments, the National Capital Transportation Agency (created in 1960), state highway departments, and the local governments in the capital region could all play important parts in making the corridor pattern a reality. The purchase of sites for buildings and rights-of-way for transit lines and freeways well in advance of need would be one means of establishing the skeleton of the proposed metropolitan form. To preserve the wedges of open space, city and county governments in the region could utilize "the full range of public powers, including zoning, acquisition of land for development rights, and tax concessions." And the National Capital Planning Commission did not overlook the possibility that somehow a new division of local governments, perhaps an urban development agency similar to the public corporations created to build new towns in Great Britain, might be established in each outlying jurisdiction in which a town was to be constructed. But these were the merest suggestions compared with the rather detailed recommendations of the Maryland-National Capital Park and Planning Commission for "making the urban pattern work."[18]

The Maryland commission listed twelve tools needed to achieve successful development of the corridor scheme in accordance with its general plan. Among them were local master plans conforming with its overall plan; new zoning designed to carry out the local plans; improved procedures for granting special exceptions to zoning ordinances; strict review of applications for all rezonings, subdivisions of land, and building permits; new tax policies relating land assessments to zoning; review of all federal, state, local, and utility capital improvements projects "to help assure conformance with adopted master plans," and improved procedures for preparing and reviewing long-range capital improvement budgets. The commission also advocated acquiring additional parks, establishing urban renewal programs, improving intergovernmental cooperation and coordination, and appointing "a Community Appearance Advisory Committee to act as a community conscience for the Regional District, spurring good public and private design."[19]

The catalogue of laws to be enacted, programs to be developed and vigorously pursued, and civic good works to be accomplished indicated such a wide gulf between the commission's hopes and the regional district's current legal, financial, and administrative resources for implementing planning policies that only the most incurable optimist would expect much progress in carrying out the corridor scheme.

The National Capital Transportation Agency, charged with preparing a preliminary plan for a rapid transit system, submitted a report to President Kennedy in 1962 which Warren Jay Vinton, mayor of suburban Somerset, Maryland, thought would "afford a potent and essential support for the policies set forth in the two plans for the year 2000."[20] But how, he asked, could people be assured that the proposed corridors would "develop according to the neat designs of the two plans or even develop at all?"[21] Most suburban governments, he observed, were so dominated by speculative land owners, developers, and builders whose "generous campaign contributions guarantee them an overwhelming voice in county affairs" that any attempt to keep areas open by means of zoning or to follow British or New Deal precedents in establishing special governmental units to build new towns would meet violent opposition.[22]

In 1963 the President recommended construction of a $792,000,000 rail rapid transit system for the District of Columbia and the suburban areas in Maryland and Virginia, but the opposition of highway interests resulted in a congressional decision in 1965 to approve only an initial 25-mile system lying almost entirely within the District of Columbia. In 1966, however, a movement developed to replace the interim National Capital Transportation Agency with a new regional entity of the type recommended by the National Capital Planning Commission and an advisory committee of experts in 1960. With the consent of Congress, Maryland and Virginia and the District of Columbia entered into an interstate compact creating the Washington Metropolitan Area Transit Authority, an agency responsible to the electorate of the political units of the metropolitan area. The new agency took over the functions of its predecessor in 1967 and boldly proposed a 95.3-mile regional network composed basically of three through routes which traverse the District of Columbia and then enter Maryland and Virginia. In referendums held in November, 1968, the voters in five suburban sections of the metropolitan area overwhelmingly approved bond issues to finance their portions of the projected $2,500,000,000 rapid transit system. Since the Maryland legislature had previously authorized funds for the system, the transit authority needed only the approval of additional funds by Congress to begin construction of a revised 97.9-mile system.

In the years immediately following 1962, though, Mayor Vinton's observations about the influence of speculators proved to be only too realistic. Developers gained control of the Montgomery County Council and for four years had their way in many parts of the county, by their activities precluding the full realization of the urban pattern suggested in the two policies plans for the year 2000. The fate of the corridor schemes illustrated with particular force the limited usefulness of areawide planning in an urban region lacking a certain degree of political cohesion.

In the early years of the 1960s the capital region was only beginning to develop an instrument for regional decision-making tied to the political process. The Metropolitan Washington Council of Governments, composed of representatives of the counties and cities in the region, was for many years little more than a "metropolitan marching and chowder society," in the opinion of one observer, and did not attain legal status, by incorporating as a nonprofit corporation, until 1965. In the meantime it cooperated with the National Capital Planning Commission and the Regional Planning Council in supporting a Joint Open Space Project to preserve areas of open countryside for scenic and recreational use, thus in some measure attempting to carry out policies proposed in the plans for the year 2000. This and other ventures in meeting regional needs determined its leaders to assume a regional planning function. By order of President Johnson the less potent Regional Planning Council was abolished in 1966 under an executive reorganization; the Council of Governments became the recognized regional planning agency for the capital region, took over the review of open-space land projects, and began to develop a new comprehensive areawide plan to use as a basis for resolving regional conflicts. But the slow emergence of this vehicle for achieving consensus on regional development illuminated the fact that most planning previously undertaken in the region, including the *Plan for the Year 2000*, had been unrelated to any areawide political mechanism for providing widespread local governmental approval and co-operative execution.

Attempts to Relate Planning to Regional Decision-Making

In an article on planning and development in metropolitan affairs published some months after the release of the policies plan for the capital region, Harvey S. Perloff and Lowdon Wingo, Jr., urged city planners to create "the urgently needed institutions" to prevent the political and functional balkanization of metropolitan regions from restricting their role in "formulating the strategy of development."[23] But most professional planners were by temperament or training incapable of fashioning or helping to fashion the regional political forums or legal entities needed to lift regional planning above the level of an academic exercise. T. Ledyard Blakeman, who had taken a hand in creating the Supervisors Inter-County Committee in the Detroit area in the 1950s, was an exception. In the early 1960s Henry Fagin, then working in the Philadelphia region, proved to be another, though Fagin had somewhat less success than Blakeman in hitching planning to regional decision-making. Fagin attempted, however, to effect a much more intimate relationship between planning and political action than his fellow planner had essayed. The very shortcomings of political processes in the Philadelphia region indicate the necessity of having strong political leadership to make planning effective.

In 1959 Fagin, formerly of the Regional Plan Association in New York, became head of the staff of the Penn-Jersey Transportation Study in the Philadelphia region. This planning program was an outgrowth of the activities of the Urban Traffic and Transportation Board created in Philadelphia in 1954 and was jointly sponsored by twelve governments, including the central city, several counties, the states of Pennsylvania and New Jersey, and the federal government. The study was to determine what general type of transportation program would best serve the needs of the Philadelphia and Trenton metropolitan areas. Unfortunately, the Wilmington metropolitan area, encompassing Salem County, New Jersey, and New Castle County in Delaware, was not willing to be included although it is economically part of Greater Philadelphia. The study was also limited functionally by the exclusion of programs to develop air and water transportation. The planners therefore worked under certain handicaps and restraints but sought to transcend them by developing new techniques and procedures designed to yield a more realistic view of probable regional changes and future transportation needs than any previous studies of metropolitan regions.

Instead of attempting to forecast probable land use at some future date and then fashioning a transportation system to serve the projected spatial arrangement, as was done in the monumental Chicago Area Transportation Study (1960–1962), or to prepare a single "desirable" land use plan and similarly devise a transportation system to fit it, as planners in the Detroit and San Francisco Bay areas had done in 1954, the Penn-Jersey group attempted to study the region as it might grow and develop through future time under various assumed market conditions, governmental policies, hypothetical transportation systems, and individual and corporate responses to new social and economic opportunities. In the "growth models" formulated to show sequential changes under alternative sets of circumstances, transportation was treated both as a cause and as a result of other developments. Notwithstanding the sophistication of this approach and the great amount of economic and social theory utilized in attempting to simulate the processes and the spatial patterns of growth, the Penn-Jersey planners eventually realized that the lack of strong political support for this difficult task for a reasonable period of time would preclude fully usable results. Moreover, built into the method was the requirement that certain political decisions be made during, as well as at terminal points in, the research. Fagin therefore joined forces with the regional civic group known as Penjerdel (an abbreviation for the Pennsylvania-New Jersey-Delaware Metropolitan Project, Inc.) to stimulate the formation of a mechanism for focusing attention on interrelated regional problems which could be solved only through intergovernmental cooperation.

The organization that was brought into being in 1961, the Regional Conference of Elected Officials, is a voluntary association similar to the Metropolitan Washington Council of Governments. The guiding spirit of Penjerdel, its president and executive director, John W. Bodine, drafted the bylaws of the Regional Conference, extended staff assistance to it for the first year, and served as its official adviser. Its purpose, as stated in the bylaws, was "to promote the continuous gathering, analysis, and communication of facts about the Region useful to the governments in it; to study and discuss governmental matters of concern to the Region; to identify areas of agreement on regional matters for voluntary cooperative action; and to make recommendations, to other governments and to nongovernmental bodies, on matters of concern to the Region."[24]

With support from a vigorous civic organization, the Regional Conference might have become the sort of organization Fagin hoped for. But, unfortunately, Penjerdel was not dynamic. It foundered in 1964 after it had been unsuccessful in raising local money to match further grants from the Ford Foundation. Formed in 1957, Penjerdel had had great difficulty in proving to the satisfaction of the Internal Revenue Service that it should be given tax-exempt status as an educational organization and had been delayed in getting under way until the fall of 1959. The attitude of the federal agency caused the board of directors to favor nonaction programs; and so did the traditional hostilities between Philadelphia and its suburbs. "As a result," concluded civic leader Walter M. Phillips in a study seeking to ascertain whether there might be some new role for Penjerdel to play, "Penjerdel's program lacked from the start the specific focus which ordinarily attracts philanthropic money."[25] Much of the research sponsored by the organization was, though fundamental, "too academic for a civic agency," and the understandable caution of the directors about offering recommendations or a program of action to solve immediate problems denied Penjerdel a dynamic image. "But perhaps, in the end," wrote Phillips, "the effort to finance Penjerdel failed mostly because the absence of a sense of region made it difficult to persuade potential donors of the importance of developing public support for regional approaches to regional problems. This is a dilemma of the first order."[26]

The "sense of region" was not yet strong in the Regional Conference, either. When an areawide governmental organization exercising the power of decision over major regional developments failed to materialize for lack of forceful political leadership, effective transportation planning became extremely difficult if not impossible. Certainly, transportation planning could not be isolated from other kinds of planning. In an infinitely complex metropolitan region subject to the political decisions of hundreds of local governments but not to those of any higher authority concerned with matters affecting the entire region, assumption and prediction tended to become merely intellectual exercises, even when facilitated by computers capable of handling large numbers of variables. Each regional extrapolation tested in the growth model of the Penn-Jersey Transportation Study was no better than the sum of staff judgments entering into the design of the various inputs. "With no serious political inputs, the outputs were politically irrelevant," the first executive director concluded.[27]

In 1965, when the money and authority of the Penn-Jersey Transportation Study were about to run out, Pennsylvania and New Jersey began taking steps to continue transportation planning while they worked out measures to create an interstate planning agency. Finally, in 1967, the two states set up the Delaware Valley Regional Planning Commission, which was later recognized by the federal Department of Housing and Urban Development as the areawide agency whose review is necessary as a condition for receiving federal grants for many kinds of projects. But since this agency is not directly related to the Regional Conference, the links between planning and regional decision-making are still somewhat weak. Since 1968, however, the Greater Philadelphia Movement, an organization of business and industrial leaders, has attempted to strengthen cooperation in the lower Delaware Valley by establishing a Committee on Regional Development. The committee sponsors an annual regional leadership conference at Swarthmore College and has initiated arrangements for a broad-based regional citizens' organization which can give community-wide attention to three important matters: transportation, environmental quality, and human resources (embracing the three general subjects of housing, training, and employment).

Experience in the Washington and Philadelphia regions indicates that if areawide planning is to have substantial influence on development, the planning process itself must become part of a regional decision-making process, especially since present-day planning methodology requires, as Fagin and the staff of the Penn-Jersey Transportation Study realized, decisions on matters of regional policy at various steps in planning studies and, even more than that, commitments to certain actions to be taken sequentially toward the attainment of definite regional goals. The councils of governments thus far formed in metropolitan areas are, of course, no substitute for genuine limited-function, areawide government, but perhaps they serve the purpose of showing the need for such government. These loose associations of local governments, as yet plagued by a considerable amount of parochialism, probably will not move toward the creation of permanent metropolitan government until prodded by federations of civic groups, though the history of civic endeavor in metropolitan areas points up the difficulties of organizing and sustaining regional activities among well-meaning volunteers. Governors and state legislatures should at least promote discussion of the desirability of areawide government in the chief metropolitan communities of their states, particularly since temporary commissions submitted reports on the subject in many states in the late 1950s and early 1960s.

Developments leading toward regional planning under the auspices of a limited-function metropolitan government have probably gone further in the Minneapolis–St. Paul and San Francisco Bay areas than in any other large urban areas in the United States. The Metropolitan Council established by the Minnesota state legislature for the seven-county region encompassing the twin cities is an appointed body exercising the regional planning function and having authority to review proposals and projects of almost a score of independent agencies whose plans have a multicommunity effect. In addition, it is empowered to appoint non-voting members of metropolitan commissions and boards, to review all comprehensive municipal plans, to carry on research on areawide problems and needs, and to make recommendations to the legislature regarding the kind of governmental organization or agency best suited to discharge the functions proposed. The council might, however, someday become a directly elected metropolitan government with operating responsibility, since the original legislative proposal was for such an entity and since there is still considerable support for that type of organization rather than the present appointed, coordinating agency.

In the same year in which Penjerdel served as midwife at the birth of the Regional Conference of Elected Officials in the Philadelphia region, local public officials in the San Francisco Bay Area formed the Association of Bay Area Governments, to provide a forum for the consideration of regional needs. After some years the association assumed the regional planning function and appointed a Committee on Goals and Organization to investigate regional problems, particularly those not being handled by any existing agency. On the recommendation of this committee, in

1966 the association sponsored a bill proposing the creation of a limited-function governing agency to assume full responsibility over regional planning, disposal of refuse, open space and parks, and airports. Other organizations proposed an even broader agency that would absorb some of the areawide special districts in the Bay Area.

In 1967 and 1968 a joint legislative committee on Bay Area regional organization held hearings throughout the region to determine what sort of areawide government would be acceptable to the populations of all nine Bay Area counties. On the basis of these hearings, it proposed in March, 1969, a limited-purpose regional government with jurisdiction restricted to the "natural watershed and physical boundaries" in the region, or to an area coinciding with lines of the existing Bay Area water quality control board. The proposed government would control pollution and regulate land development on the shores of San Francisco Bay and would plan coordinated transportation, land management, and utility facilities throughout its area of jurisdiction, without, the chairman of the joint committee pointed out, taking over powers of the nine counties and ninety-one cities in the region.[28] Some proponents of regional government immediately foresaw that there would be difficulty obtaining a favorable vote on this proposal in a referendum and were inclined to view the development of additional special districts as a practical, indirect approach to the ultimate goal of a single policy-making and administrative unit consolidating all multicommunity functions.

Pressures for Metropolitan Planning

Throughout the Kennedy and Johnson administrations much of the pressure upon state and local governments to cooperate in metropolitan planning and to experiment with new metropolitan political mechanisms came from the federal establishment—directly from the Congress and the executive branch and indirectly from the Supreme Court and lower federal courts. For example, the Congress included in the Federal-Aid Highway Act of 1962 a provision that after July 1, 1965, the Secretary of Commerce must not approve aid to highway programs in any urban area of more than 50,000 population unless projects were based on a continuing comprehensive transportation process carried on cooperatively by state and local governments. The effect of this requirement was to precipitate a headlong rush into areawide transportation and land use planning, either under the auspices of agencies with statewide planning authority or new metropolitan or county planning agencies. The earlier policy of the Secretary of Commerce and the Housing Administrator for joint financing of cooperative planning projects facilitated the new transportation planning efforts, and the availability of funds under the Housing Act of 1961 for transit planning and demonstration grants designed to improve transit services tended to broaden the studies to include consideration of the whole range of transportation needs.

Some urban areas, such as Seattle, Boston, and New York, already had large-scale transportation studies under way before the Highway Act of 1962 was adopted. So far as the Seattle area was concerned, the emphasis in this act on the continuing and comprehensive nature of the planning required was not needed to assure long-term intergovernmental cooperation. The four counties and larger cities in the area had previously formed the Puget Sound Governmental Conference, a voluntary association organized under state enabling legislation, had already set up the advisory Puget Sound Regional Planning Council and a Planning Directors Committee, and were fully collaborating with state and federal agencies in formulating a transportation plan as part of a general development plan for the region. In the Boston area, however, the congressional mandate for ongoing planning affecting the entire metropolitan community gave impetus to the formation of a new Boston Metropolitan Area Planning Council in which state interest was perhaps as great as that of local governments. Twenty-one gubernatorial appointees and the heads of nine state agencies served with representatives of fifty towns and cities in the area. This new council provided further support for the regional planning and transportation studies lodged administratively in a statewide agency, the Mass Transportation Commission. Even in the New York metropolitan region, where transit problems received special attention, the planning requirement of the highway act aided efforts to form a tristate transportation commission that would be, in effect, a regional planning agency.

The Baltimore area was another in which a regional planning council emerged after enactment of the Highway Act of 1962 and the initiation of an areawide transportation study. This council, like the one in the Boston area, included statutory representation of state planning and transportation agencies and several appointees of the governor.

Commenting on the increasing tendency of federal officials and agencies to regard metropolitan planning as a means of assisting them in coordinating their programs, Frederick Hayes, assistant commissioner of the Urban Renewal Administration, told members of the American Institute of Planners at a conference in 1963 that "we are and have been working with nearly every other federal agency with any programs of development or developmental assistance in our metropolitan areas." As joint projects assumed more permanent form, he believed that they would increasingly represent "the mixing bowl of the American federal system," harmonizing federal, state, and local activities.[29]

Hayes indicated, though, that the potentialities of metropolitan planning could not be realized until more attention was given to such nontransportation issues of metropolitan development as areawide sewer and water systems, and water and air pollution-abatement problems. The popularity of open-space planning and its inclusion in an ever larger number of metropolitan programs was interesting more citizens in regional issues, but as yet the process of communication with the public was weak, and until it was strengthened, the political force for implementing plans would not be generated.

Even more profoundly affecting the development of urban areas than the Housing Act of 1962 and other federal legislation requiring or encouraging intergovernmental cooperation in metropolitan planning was the United States Supreme Court decision in *Baker v. Carr*, the case involving an attack on the apportionment of seats in the Tennessee legislature. The court's ruling on March 26, 1962, that the federal courts have the right to review the distribution of seats in a state legislature and to decide whether the state's voting districts are unreasonably disproportionate marked a turning point in American history. Peter H. Nash and Richard L. Strecker, writing in the *Journal of the American Institute of Planners,* asserted that without doubt the decision ranked with four others in its impact on urban affairs: *Euclid v. Ambler Realty,* upholding the validity of zoning (1926); *Shelley v. Kramer,* denying enforcement to racial restrictive covenants (1948); *Brown v. Board of Education,* prohibiting public school segregation (1954); and *Berman v. Parker,* validating urban renewal (1954). Whereas these four cases primarily influenced process and goals, *Baker v. Carr,* by setting in motion a shift of power from predominantly rural to predominantly urban representatives in most state legislatures, inevitably changed the types of issues acted upon. Nash and Strecker at once foresaw that slum housing, mass transportation, civil rights, care for the aged, and other matters of great concern to urban populations would receive priority on legislative agendas in the future.

The two professors added an interesting footnote to history by revealing that professional planners had played an important role in the historic case. At the request of Mayor Ben West of Nashville several members of the staff of the Nashville City and Davidson County Planning Commission's Advance Planning Division had worked intensively from time to time for a period of two years preparing data and doing research documenting the constitutional and fiscal inequities resulting from the illogical apportionment of the Tennessee legislature. Their reports and visual exhibits, without which the case might have been severely handicapped, were used effectively in the arguments before the highest court.

The court's decision in *Baker v. Carr* convinced many persons that a federal Department of Urban Affairs would be needed more than ever. Although the states could be expected to take renewed interest in urban problems, cities would nevertheless continue to make direct appeals for federal assistance because the cost of urban development was so great that only the federal government, with its enormous revenue-producing power, could provide financial help to the extent required. Nash and Strecker prophesied an acceleration of federal activities on behalf of urban areas because state legislators elected in the future would be more responsive to urban needs and would be willing to delegate to a federal department the problems they considered too complex or too costly for the states to solve unaided. The initiation of additional urban programs would, of course, pose a problem of coordination, which might well be entrusted to the proposed department, the two professors believed.

The Congress, however, was in no hurry to accede to President Kennedy's repeated requests for a Department of Urban Affairs. He failed in 1962 and 1963, as in 1961, to obtain favorable action on bills authorizing such a department, and his successor, Lyndon B. Johnson, had no better fortune in 1964 when he, too, urged passage of the necessary legislation.

In the meantime, citizens in states throughout the land hastened the process of change by bringing suit to force reapportionment. Within nine months of the Supreme Court's decision in *Baker v. Carr,* litigation challenging the constitutionality of state legislative apportionment schemes had been instituted in at least thirty-four states. On June 15, 1964, the high tribunal pronounced judgment in a case (*Reynolds v. Sims*) involving the existing and two legislatively proposed plans for the apportionment of seats in the two houses of the Alabama legislature, and this time the justices spelled out the requirements for apportionment: "We hold, as a basic constitutional standard, the Equal Protection Clause [of the United States Constitution] requires that the seats in both houses of a bicameral state legislature must be apportioned on a population basis."[30] In thus establishing the principle of "one person, one vote," the court noted that "citizens, not history or economic interests, cast votes," that "people, not land or trees or pastures, vote."[31] Modern developments and improvements in transportation and communications made rather hollow, in the mid-1960s, most claims that deviations from population-based representation could validly be based solely on geographical considerations, the court stated. Arguments for allowing such deviation in order to insure effective representation for sparsely settled areas, and to prevent legislative districts from becoming so large that the availability of access of citizens to their representatives would be impaired, were nowadays, for the most part, "unconvincing."

The reasoning of a majority of the justices foreshadowed still another decision on April 1, 1968, extending the "one person, one vote" doctrine to elected local governments. But state supreme courts in California,

New York, Wisconsin, Missouri, Minnesota, Maryland, and South Dakota had already applied the precept of substantial equality in population among voting districts to local governments before the highest court rendered its decision in a test case arising in Midland County, Texas.

The repercussions of the "reapportionment revolution" were significant even before the states themselves began compelling local governments to follow the "one person, one vote" principle. As a result of the redistricting struggle, Connecticut adopted a new state constitution. In Vermont, a predominantly rural state, the percentage of state legislators living in towns of more than 10,000 population rose from 2.4 to 27.3; and political scientists observed that the new system of representation "produced a mass of progressive legislation." The House, for instance, in 1966 passed a fair housing bill, established a human rights commission, conducted reform in the state judiciary system, regulated outdoor advertising, attacked water pollution, and considered child day-care facilities, educational television, and penal reform. In Ohio a change from election at large to election by single-member districts resulted in a breakthrough for minority groups. Three Negroes were elected to the legislature from Hamilton County (Cincinnati), one to the Senate and two to the House. None had previously been elected to the Senate from the Cincinnati area although the city includes 100,000 or more Negroes. Changes such as these indicated to city planners that the kinds of programs with which they were concerned would receive closer attention than in the past and that planning programs themselves probably would reflect an emphasis on human rights and social problems.

A New Professional Concern with Human Problems

The "reapportionment revolution" was essentially part of a much larger urban revolution whose magnitude and complexity city planners had been trying to understand ever since they first perceived it—at about the time they formed a professional institute. Perhaps their first important assessment of it was made in the late 1930s when the National Resources Committee published *Our Cities: Their Role in the National Economy.* Throughout the 1940s there had been various other valuable appraisals as interest centered on the problem of blight and on the postwar accompaniment of central decay, the peripheral "explosion." Intellectual castigation of suburbia marked most of the 1950s, while efforts to view both the outward push and internal deterioration in a broader metropolitan context occupied the more thoughtful analysts. By the 1960s the focus was on an aspect of urban change that had been in process ever since the 1920s, when some sociologists had first noted substantial Negro migration to cities of the North.

City planners, as well as persons in many other fields, began to be painfully aware that urbanization had placed on the political doorstep problems of race and poverty unlike any that had previously been brought to the attention of earnest social workers, elected officials, and the general public. The immigrant poor of earlier days had gradually been assimilated into the mainstream of American life, but now there were in the cities the native white poor of Appalachia and other depressed areas, illiterate and unskilled Negroes from the rural South, Indians from overpopulated reservations, and equally impoverished, desperate, and yet somehow expectant Puerto Ricans, Spanish Americans, and Mexicans by the thousands—subcultures enervated by a sense of rejection and inadequacy and characterized by a sullen solidarity which defied the inept advances of officialdom and the well-meaning proffers of assistance of voluntary institutions. By force of circumstance these alienated groups inhabited the meanest sections of the older cities and increased alarmingly. Their very presence belied the boasted affluence of American society and constituted an indictment of both the economic system and the political order.

In their attempts to rid cities of slums and the economic problems associated with them, city planners tended at first to overlook the web of relationships binding together these disadvantaged elements in their various communities. The law required that displaced families be relocated, and relocated they were if they would accept aid, although in some cities as many as half of the uprooted families refused help and found new quarters on their own initiative. For the most part they obtained housing only slightly better than that which they had occupied previously, but usually at higher rents and not always in as desirable locations. Lost in the moves, however, were neighbors of many years, the reassuring and protective physical and social environment, the parish churches, and the corner groceries that would give a family credit in hard times, and in all too many cases the means of livelihood. So many of the families relocated were nonwhite that it became a common saying that "slum removal is Negro removal." And as the pace of demolition and clearance accelerated, politicians grew attentive to the outcries, and journalists exploited examples of extreme hardship.

Peter Marris, a British sociologist who essayed to evaluate urban renewal in eleven American cities in the summer of 1961, concluded that relocation had achieved little overall improvement in the circumstances of the people displaced and had merely hastened the decay of other areas. Social welfare programs, he maintained, could not succeed in integrating slum communities with the wider society because the members of subcultures could not endure the humiliation of admitting weaknesses in order to be helped. It would be wiser, Marris suggested, to rebuild

103. (upper) Constitution Plaza, Hartford, Connecticut, 1965; (lower) the Hartford riverfront before redevelopment, 1953 *(The Travelers Insurance Companies)*

or rehabilitate slum areas as homes for the slum dwellers themselves, "not to a perfunctory minimum standard, but as places in which people can live with pride, and which will enhance the appearance of the city." Such a policy would not preclude the clearance of sites for other uses, but those displaced should be rehoused together in "a comprehensively developed community near their place of work."[32]

If Marris's prescription for solving the social problems of slum dwellers was controversial, it was at least based on long study of cities and careful observation of the efforts of all classes to carve out social space they could master. Having a scholarly appreciation of the value of diversity within the urban superstructure, the sociologist advocated an approach to the problems of minority groups somewhat resembling the "model cities" program initiated later. But no such disciplined analysis supported the opinions of a writer who suddenly raised the wails about urban renewal into a popular howl. In *The Death and Life of Great American Cities,* Jane Jacobs, an associate editor of *Architectural Forum,* not only excoriated the havoc wrought upon the families dislocated by renewal but also contributed to the growing recognition of the subtle relations between people and place. Denouncing overstandardized, overspecialized public housing and redevelopment projects, the destruction of the "close-grained" diversity of older low-income neighborhoods, and the evisceration of cities by expressways, Mrs. Jacobs appealed to tens of thousands of readers who had grave doubts about many of the things they saw being done in the name of progress. Her pages were brilliant and emotional, much of her criticism valid and effective, but her desire for cities composed almost exclusively of neighborhoods like her own beloved Greenwich Village or Boston's North End entirely ignored the fact that the overwhelming majority of Americans did not like high-density development, high land coverage, and mixed land uses.

Readers who shared her apprehensions about muggings on city streets and robbery and rape in city parks or who also deplored the brutal appearance of high-rise structures in renewal areas were apt, however, to overlook her personal biases because she identified the villains responsible for the inhumane treatment of slum dwellers and the ruin of the city. They were the city planners, who branded whole areas substandard, zoned cities into dull, single-use districts, delighted in divisive freeways, and created dangerous open spaces in which hoodlums lurked and attacked. Exempting none from her blanket indictment and not once indicating that private entrepreneurs, architects, redevelopment officials, highway engineers, and assorted state and federal bureaucrats participated in fashioning the developments she found wanting, Mrs. Jacobs flayed her scapegoats without acknowledging that many of them were already engaged in salutary reexamination of the formulas and clichés that led to some of the horrible examples she cited. She herself, it seemed to most planners, did not believe in planning at all. Yet they conceded that she had done them a service by challenging their ideas and their performance. And with the passage of years it now appears that she helped to point the way to renewal in which the human considerations are as important as the physical.

For time to time professional journals of many sorts, as well as widely read magazines and newspapers, had been scoring the very weaknesses of public housing and urban renewal that Mrs. Jacobs singled out for attack. No one any longer defended institutional-looking public housing projects which isolated low-income families from other elements of the population; and almost everyone agreed that there was something socially reprehensible about forcing the underprivileged inhabitants of blighted areas to pack up and get out so that insurance companies and realty syndicates could build expensive apartments for account executives and the professional elite. Many planning, housing, and renewal officials favored distributing public housing units in small groups throughout cities and rehabilitating older dwellings that were still structurally sound and in reasonably satisfactory neighborhoods, and even leasing private units for the use of low-income families qualifying for public housing. Hundreds of planners thought that far more attention should be given to maintaining the visual and historical continuity of the city by saving and reconditioning older structures worthy of further economic investment.

The disenchantment with much that had been done presumably in the public interest was now matched with a realization that a great deal of the previous faith in the efficacy of sanitary housing and showy renewal was naïve. Hygienic dwellings did not automatically reform slovenly or disorganized households; nor did huge public and private expenditures for slum clearance and rebuilding necessarily revitalize declining central business districts. "Projects" had no magic to solve either the social or the economic problems of people and cities. If the word "comprehensive" meant anything, it meant that planned change should be examined for the effects it would have on the social and economic relations of human beings as well as on their bodily comfort and health. William L. Slayton, Urban Renewal Commissioner, expressed the new concern with the human aspects of renewal when he said that "it must not only rehouse families in equal or better quarters, it must also highlight some of the other problems of these families—poverty, unemployment, and inadequate education—and lead communities to develop better techniques for dealing with these problems."[33] He mentioned to the participants in the annual conference of the American Society of Planning Officials in 1963 that both the Department of Health, Educa-

tion and Welfare and the President's Committee on Juvenile Delinquency were working on this social goal of urban renewal. And Robert
C. Weaver that same year told a conference at the University of California, Berkeley, that the federal government should "recognize that
human renewal is a part and a legitimate cost of urban renewal."[34]
Years of experience with renewal plus the chorus of criticism of the
results achieved had thus prepared the way for broader legislation and an
expansion of the scope of programs.

Some of the shortcomings of renewal in particular and of a great deal
of other urban development doubtless stemmed from artificial distinctions between physical planning and other types of planning. City planners with a knowledge of the history of their profession had long regarded
the early split between the planners and housing reformers, soon after
the first national conference on city planning, as one of the great mis-
fortunes of American professional life. That meeting had brought together architects and landscape architects of the City Beautiful movement, settlement-house workers, public health officials, philanthropists,
enlightened financiers, attorneys, transportation engineers, and many
others. It had raised the hope of close, fruitful collaboration among all
the professions interested in the welfare of the city. But that hope had
not materialized, and for more than fifty years each confraternity, including the city planning profession, had been separated from the main
stream of concern with urban affairs. Indeed, there had hardly been a
main stream until the 1950s, when at last persons in many endeavors
had begun to glimpse the sweeping currents of a national involvement
in urban problems. To this broad flow, with its eddies of anxiety and its
flotsam of capsized reforms, the social scientist had contributed their
studies of the pathology and the ecology of the city, their investigations
of political structure and power, their analyses of urban and regional
economies, and their histories of the rise of individual cities and constel-
lations of cities. Their findings often derived from the records amassed by
welfare agencies, police departments, public health offices, housing and
redevelopment authorities, school systems, churches, and hospitals; and
in time the insights afforded by these accumulations of data influenced
the professional practice of social workers, criminologists, health officers,
housing managers, teachers and school administrators, clergymen, and
city planners. All these perceived, more and more clearly, how their
activities and those of others were tributary to the great tide bearing the
nation toward understanding of its urban needs. To the deepening drift
the biological and physical sciences, mathematics and engineering, and a
new technology added their special contributions, providing not only
essential knowledge but also electronic devices capable of processing
vast amounts of urban data.

Perhaps no one in the city planning profession stated more cogently than Melvin M. Webber, professor and former editor of the *Journal of the American Institute of Planners,* the new commonality of interests among the professions as the nation discovered that many of its most pressing problems were urban problems. City planners not only were gaining a new appreciation of the value of their historic responsibility for guiding land use patterns and appraising the relative effectiveness of various proposed public services and facilities but also were coming to understand that they must seek, with their colleagues in public health, education, law enforcement, engineering, and public administration, a systematic integration of programs for improving urban communities. "We are coming to comprehend the city as an extremely complex social system, only some aspects of which are expressed as physical buildings or as locational arrangements," Webber noted. "As the parallel, we are coming to understand that each aspect lies in a reciprocal causal relation to all others, such that each is defined by, and has meaning only with respect to, its *relations* to all others."[35]

As one result of this broadened conception of the city system, planners no longer could speak of the physical city as distinct from the social city or the economic city or the political city or the intellectual city; nor could they any longer dissociate a building from the social meanings that it carries for its users and viewers or from the social and economic functions of the activities conducted within it. If distinguishable at all, the distinction was that of constituent components, as with metals composing an alloy. Nor could planners continue to think of capital exclusively as material things. The skills and capacities of urban populations, the accumulated knowledge and wisdom of the culture, and the ways in which people organized themselves for the joint conduct of their affairs, all contributed to human productive capacities and wealth in ways that were inseparable from those of the physical equipment and natural resources used.

In this encompassing view of the city the glaring failures of American society stood revealed: the poverty and cultural deprivation of a large proportion of the population; the insufficiency of federal and state assistance to urban areas and the lack of coordination between local activities and federal and state activities; the uncontrolled expansion and political disunity of metropolitan areas. Metropolitan growth had shifted the middle class and many opportunities for employment to the outlying areas, leaving behind in the central cities the unskilled and undereducated. The inadequacy or high cost of public transit, together with the lack of skills, made inaccessible many of the jobs needed by these groups. To make matters worse, redevelopment in central cities had often eliminated enterprises providing employment for low-income workers. Neither single-function programs nor efforts in individual municipalities could extricate the racial minorities and other poor from the conditions entrapping them. An areawide and integrated approach, in which city planners joined forces with social service, health, and educational groups, alone would eliminate poverty and discrimination and the most urgent social issues confronting municipal governments and the nation. And if many of the activities required to achieve this end did not fall within the city planner's areas of special competence, he was nonetheless "a key agent in setting minicipal-investment priorities" and was thus "in a position to guide municipal policies toward the issues that really matter."[36]

"Our purpose is to find those wealth-increasing approaches that will benefit *all* members of the society," Webber asserted. "Where such consummate returns are not possible, we seek to design those minimum controls that will avoid abuses by forestalling probabilities of individuals or groups harming others. Where income-redistribution effects are either unavoidable or publicly intended, we would have the gains go to those most in need of help. And when sacrifices must be made, especially when they must be made by those least able to sustain them, we would have them accompanied by commensurate payments."[37]

Webber's new interpretation of the social responsibility of planners, indicating that the profession was redirecting its attention from the form of the city to "the processes that relate the interdependent aspects of the city one to another," was but another sign that the American people were caught up in a movement for recognition of urban areas as the foci of national growth and development. This movement, of course, had its origins in the redistributions of population and productive activity that had been accelerating since the First World War, chiefly as the result of rapid technological advances. Since the imbalances of our society necessarily became most conspicuous in the areas of greatest population concentration, it was perhaps inevitable that the vanguard of a profession which had long regarded itself as the custodian of a utopian tradition in urban development and a holistic view of communities should become alarmed at the stultifying effects of bureaucratization and should seek to restate its dedication to human purposes in broader terms.

The Many Ramifications of the Community Renewal Program

Ironically, a program which at first appeared to be more concerned with buildings than with people contributed significantly to the enlargement of the social vision of planners, though even the brief statutory description of it in the Housing Act of 1959 indicated that it included elements ramifying into the fields of social welfare, finance, and economic development. The community renewal program ostensibly invited planning agencies to measure varying degrees of blight throughout an entire city and to determine appropriate actions for removing slums, renewing deteriorating areas, and preserving relatively stable areas. The "blighting factors" to be studied were obviously economic and social as well as physical; the resources needed and available to renew rundown areas were surely more than financial and administrative; and the relocation of families whose dwellings were to be demolished or renovated certainly required the cooperation of social agencies, yet on the whole the community renewal program initially seemed to be chiefly a comprehensive way of approaching the physical problem of obsolescence and decay. To professional men fascinated by new techniques of analysis and the potentialities of the computer, it also offered opportunities to advance the "science" of planning and to test theories of urban growth and development. Fortunately, too, the program held new and exciting possibilities of relating city planning to governmental policy and the processes by which crucial decisions and courses of action are determined — of continually presenting the reasonable alternatives to elected officials and administrators and enabling them to make rational, circumspect choices about the investment of public funds in the ever renewable urban plant. In all these respects the community renewal program promised to fulfill some of the more recent as well as some of the long-term dreams of city planners. That it would do much more and would open the way to close collaboration with specialists in many fields, particularly health, education, and welfare, and would raise hopes of initiating a community development program embracing all forms of planning, was far from the thoughts of most planners as they began devising programs designed mainly to replace, rehabilitate, or maintain structures and to improve neighborhoods.

Relatively few cities were interested in the community renewal program in the early 1960s. Some officials mistakenly thought that it altered the nature of federal assistance for projects, and others believed that it somehow duplicated the general plan or overlapped the workable program for community improvement established as a prerequisite to various federal housing and urban renewal aids. In mid-1961 only a score or more of cities had applied for and received grants for the preparation of this new type of city-wide program, though among them were some of the largest: New York, Chicago, Houston, Pittsburgh, and Denver. On the other hand, the number of cities engaged in various forms of urban renewal was approximately five hundred, and together they had received approval of some nine hundred renewal projects. But the whole purpose of the community renewal program was to substitute systematic, sustained prevention and eradication of blight for the often opportunistic, spotty re-creation of residential, commercial, or industrial slums; and as an increasing number of localities realized the desirability of thoroughly analyzing all areas and formulating short-term as well as middle-range and long-range measures for improving conditions and arresting the spread of blight, a greater and greater number of applications for grants flowed into the Urban Renewal Administration in Washington. At the end of 1963 more than a hundred cities were undertaking community renewal programs, including one in every three cities with populations between 250,000 and a million.

By that time city planners throughout the nation had begun to have strangely mixed feelings about this innovative program. It had inspired some remarkable technical achievements. Planners were fascinated, for instance, by the development, in the Pittsburgh program, of a mathematical simulation model intended to make possible rapid and comprehensive analysis of the implications of alternative urban renewal decisions. They learned with pleasure of the creation in San Francisco of a model showing how the supply of housing and nonresidential structures would be affected by the pattern of investment flows and decision-making in the city and metropolitan area. They heard that Spokane, Washington, boasted a new technique of graphic analysis through the use of computers, and that New York City had led the way in developing a computer program designed to print out great quantities of otherwise unavailable data on a tract basis from original census tapes. They noted with interest that in Pittsburgh, Philadelphia, and Detroit the techniques of program evaluation and review developed by the Defense Department and the National Aeronautics and Space Agency were being utilized in scheduling the community renewal program itself. Such pioneering ventures foretold still more technical progress in the years ahead. But the social problems uncovered by the community renewal program caused uneasiness among men traditionally concerned with land use, circulation, and other aspects of the spatial city.

These problems suggested that social action should accompany the clearance or rehabilitation of buildings and the provision of public improvements; yet most planners, even the most sensitive and liberal, had given all too little thought to the relation between social planning and their kind of planning, had only a superficial knowledge of the welfare resources of their communities, and had made no detailed study of the needs and desires of minority groups and the victims of poverty found in large numbers in deteriorating sections. In the usual course of their endeavors, most planners had neither worked closely with social agencies and associations concerned with economic development nor familiarized themselves with the objectives and programs of such organizations. Studies of blight commonly presented a wealth of data on incomes, dependency, unemployment, marginal businesses, communicable disease, mortality, crime, and delinquency, but mainly as supporting evidence

and not for the purpose of indicating needed public and private programs
to aid the residents of deteriorating areas as well as facilitate the reconstruction and improvement of the city. Planners were therefore at a disadvantage to know how to integrate social action with plans for the inspection of housing, rehabilitation efforts, or the clearance of slums and
the relocation of the occupants. Professional journals and speakers at
conferences had said, again and again, that planning was for people,
but city planners knew more about the three-dimensional city than about
the human beings in it, and now, at last, the fact profoundly troubled
them—and opened their eyes to the necessity of broadening their knowledge and redefining their professional role.

The events of the times hastened their quest for more inclusive approaches. The nation was in the grip of a struggle to end segregation or
discrimination in education, housing, jobs, public accommodations, and
voting; and in the course of this struggle came forth executive orders,
rules and regulations, laws, court decisions, and reports which affected
the community renewal program in particular and city planning generally. President Kennedy, for example, on November 20, 1962, signed
an Executive Order on Equal Opportunity in Housing which prohibited
discrimination because of color, creed, national origin, or race in the
sale or rental of housing financed in whole or in part with federal aid.
On June 20, 1963, only two months before 200,000 freedom marchers
assembled in Washington to support a civil rights bill, Urban Renewal
Commissioner Slayton announced that his agency would assist in meeting the objectives of the executive order by requiring that all future community renewal programs consider the special housing problems faced
by minority groups. Programs were to include an analysis of the current
pattern of housing occupied by Negroes and other minorities and the
extent to which this pattern resulted from discrimination; they were to
project the housing needs of minority families, including those of newcomers as well as those displaced by urban renewal and other public
action; and they were to outline "an affirmative program to increase the
quantity, improve the quality, and eliminate barriers to housing for
Negro and other minority families."[38] Furthermore, the new requirement was coupled with another which was also certain to plunge city
planners deeper into problems of community organization and social
action. In addition to determining the financial and relocation resources
needed and available for urban renewal, they were to investigate the
social resources, including means of mobilizing citizen participation in
the renewal process. If they had neglected to learn the details of public
and private welfare and assistance programs and to evaluate the community facilities which could be utilized by cooperating groups, they
were now confronted with the necessity of surveying and analyzing the

work of United Fund agencies, welfare planning councils, and religious institutions. The imperative to enlist such organizations in the city-wide renewal effort foreshadowed no early integration of city planning and social action, but it brought nearer that long-sought goal.

City planners soon discovered, if they had not already known, that social planning in their communities was in a somewhat primitive state of development. In their own field there was a diffusion of developmental policy and decision-making among various tiers of government and innumerable private enterprises; but at least the typical city planning department represented a certain formal focusing of planning activities, because it maintained some kind of general development scheme, performed a coordinating function, and used its accumulated knowledge and its general plan in advising the city fathers, the city executive, department heads, and private citizens. In the field of social welfare, however, there was no one well-recognized center of planning. The most important programs — social security, temporary relief, and federally aided public assistance — were governmental and were administered by federal, state, and county agencies. The more experimental, peripheral programs in the fields of family counseling, youth services, and special health problems were in the hands of voluntary agencies, which might or might not be associated in a local or metropolitan welfare planning council including some representatives of governmental agencies. Usually chambers of commerce and economic development groups concerned with jobs and income were not even represented in such councils though their contributions might be essential in any concerted attack on problems of unemployment, underemployment, poverty, and economic discrimination. City planners attempting to achieve some working relationship between the public agencies directly engaged in urban renewal and the social agencies providing a wide range of health and welfare services were therefore often discouraged by the organizational difficulties of combining social planning with so-called physical planning.

These difficulties were compounded by others: the long lack of communication between planning and welfare groups, the traditional emphasis of social agencies on immediate problems and individual case work, and the unfamiliarity of most social workers and lay boards with the long-range planning process in city government, the main features of the general plan, and generally accepted planning policies. Wherever a welfare planning council had been formed, it provided a means of widening social planning to embrace the activities of governmental agencies and private organizations promoting economic development, not to mention civic associations furthering such things as areawide open-space land planning and the elimination of air pollution. Almost invariably, though, such councils had insufficient budgets, owing mainly to the relative newness of cooperative planning. Their studies were apt to be limited to filling some of the more obvious gaps in services or effecting closer collaboration among agencies with similar programs. To suggest that a council undertake additional studies was sometimes unrealistic or posed the problem of raising much larger sums for social planning. City planners seeking help in making community renewal programs more effective consequently found themselves hampered not only by their own sketchy knowledge of the welfare field but also by the fact that social planning was almost everywhere in its infancy and would require time to evolve.

Time, however, was in short supply in an America shaken by the murder of civil rights workers, riots in northern cities, and mounting evidence of failures in both the political and economic systems. There was the same urgency for speedier development of welfare planning as there was for the broadening of city planning. In every field of endeavor the times cried out for faster action, and yet in the Congress there was fateful procrastination about important legislation, especially a new civil rights act proposed by President Kennedy in June, 1963. While tensions of all kinds increased, an assassin cut short the life of the Chief Executive who had bade his fellow citizens, "Ask not what your country can do for you but what you can do for your country." Again the nation experienced a purgation of tears and for a time reflected on its shortcomings and on the great hopes and dreams that had carried it forward. The vision of the New Frontier became transformed into a vision of the Great Society as another President took up the burdens of office and attempted to express anew the heritage of idealism that has given meaning to action and continuity to sporadic achievement throughout American history.

In a speech at the University of Michigan on May 22, 1964, Lyndon B. Johnson made it clear that the Great Society is an urban society. He quoted Aristotle: " 'Men come together in cities in order to live, but they remain in order to live the good life.' " It was more and more difficult to live the good life in American cities, the thirty-sixth President told his youthful audience. The catalogue of ills was long. Worst of all, expansion of urban areas was eroding "the precious and time-honored values of community with neighbors and communion with nature." The loss of these values bred loneliness and boredom and indifference. "Our society will never be great until our cities are great," the President declared. "Today the frontier of imagination and innovation is inside those cities, and not beyond their borders. New experiments are already going on. It will be the task of your generation to make the American city a place where future generations will come, not only to live but to live the good life."[39]

The new president was distressed that the good life was little more than a mirage for millions of his countrymen. Only a few months before he addressed the students at Ann Arbor, he had transmitted the annual report of the Council of Economic Advisers to the Congress—a report stating that notwithstanding all the economic gains since the Second World War, almost a fifth of the nation, from 33,000,000 to 35,000,000 Americans, still lived in poverty:

> The poor inhabit a world scarcely recognizable and rarely recognized, by the majority of their fellow Americans. It is a world apart, whose inhabitants are isolated from the mainstream of American life and alienated from its values. It is a world where Americans are literally concerned with day-to-day survival—a roof over their heads, where the next meal is coming from. It is a world where a minor illness is a major tragedy, where pride and privacy must be sacrificed to get help, where honesty can become a luxury and ambition a myth. Worst of all, the poverty of the fathers is visited upon the children.[40]

To wage a "war on poverty," the President needed legislative weapons that would be as helpful to social workers and city planners as to federal officials. To make the cities places where men could live the good life, he needed legal instruments that would be as useful to transportation engineers, conservationists, development coordinators, and businessmen as to planning directors and heads of welfare agencies. In his first year in office he obtained four measures which were interrelated in their effect on cities and on conditions of poverty. The Civil Rights Act of 1964, won only after a three-month filibuster, the Economic Opportunity Act (popularly referred to as the Anti-Poverty Act), the Housing Act of 1964, and the Urban Mass Transportation Act of 1964 all contained provisions which aided urban strategists who were beginning to conceive of a multi-pronged attack on the ills of the city. The sections of the Civil Rights Act forbidding racial discrimination by either employers or labor unions and permitting the withholding of federal funds from projects in which racial discrimination persisted were as important in strengthening the city as sections of the housing act authorizing an additional $750,000,000 for urban renewal. The authorization of $375,000,000 to aid urban mass transportation systems for a three-year period was in many ways as much a measure to help the urban poor as the community action programs, youth programs, and work-experience programs provided for in the Economic Opportunity Act. Studies carried out later would show, for instance, that inadequate transit deprived Negroes living in central Chicago of as many as 35,000 jobs in outlying areas and Negroes in Detroit of 9,000 suburban jobs.

Of these statutes, the two of greatest interest to city planners were, of course, the housing and transportation acts. Although the former provided funds for further slum clearance, it represented a shift in emphasis from large-scale reconstruction of badly blighted areas to greater concentration on rehabilitation of the existing housing supply and less disruption of the social fabric of the city. The measure thus reflected popular dissatisfaction with the overall renewal program as well as partisan efforts to make capital of the mistakes of the party in power. But the renewal program was neither Democratic nor Republican and had developed under both political parties. Its weaknesses could be attributed as much to hundreds of local administrations and civic leaderships as to the federal bureaucracy. If not enough had been done to prevent the spread of blight, to rehouse displaced families in better neighborhoods as well as better quarters, and to conserve rather than demolish still useful older structures, it was because the whole program, even after fifteen years, was still somewhat experimental and the laws authorizing it were evolving in the light of experience. The 1964 act nevertheless was a response to demands for closer attention to the human problems of renewal, and it obliged city planners to study more circumspectly the social issues associated with older areas.

The act permitted the use of urban renewal funds to enforce health, sanitation, and occupancy codes in renewal areas, provided localities increased their own expenditures for enforcement. It served notice on cities that had failed to put into practice a satisfactory minimum-standard housing code as part of a workable program for community improvement that after 1967 they could not qualify for federal assistance if they had not had an adequate code in effect for at least six months. To lighten the impact of code enforcement on property owners who could not afford to bring structures up to standard, the law authorized a new program of twenty-year, low-interest loans to finance repairs and modernization, but it did not take into account property owners who were so poor that they would need outright subsidies to comply with code requirements. As a condition of support for the legislation, conservatives had also inserted in it a stipulation that no demolition project should be started unless the Housing Administrator determined that renewal could not be achieved by rehabilitation. And although relocation activities had always been hampered by an insufficiency of low-rent public housing, the Congress provided for only 37,500 additional units instead of the 50,000 annually for four years that the President had requested. The act, in sum, was a timid measure further underscoring the fact that Congress at no time had been willing to underwrite a construction program that would produce as many new dwellings each year as the country needed, including an adequate increase in housing for low-income families. In this respect, it aggravated the housing problem while somewhat "humanizing" the renewal program.

President Johnson had suggested a program of new towns "with all public services, all the industry and commerce needed to provide jobs, and sufficient housing and cultural and recreation facilities for moderate- and low-income families as well as for the well-to-do" as one means of improving the lot of minorities bottled up in urban ghettos,[41] but even cities struggling with the explosive issues of race and unemployment feared the competition of new communities and further loss of their middle-class residents. The lawmakers therefore took no action on proposed programs to enable states and local governments to collaborate with private industry in planning and building exemplary new towns.

The Urban Mass Transportation Act, a logical sequel to the modest program of federal aids for urban transportation initiated in the Housing Act of 1961, authorized the substantial developmental capital needed to carry out some of the improvements in transit systems devised with urban planning assistance grants or tried out with the help of demonstration grants. Under that earlier act the Mass Transportation Commission of Massachusetts, for example, had received several grants for transportation planning in the Boston metropolitan region, the first for a regional survey, the second for a large-scale planning program, and a third for a study to determine the effects of various service improvements and fare adjustments on the use of commuter railroad, rapid transit, and bus lines. As a result of tests conducted under agreements with commuter railroads and several local bus companies, the commission obtained data which were used in formulating comprehensive legislation establishing the Massachusetts Bay Transportation Authority, a regional agency with power to engage in transportation planning, to construct facilities and purchase equipment, and to contract for service with private companies. Under the federal act of 1964 this new agency received the largest of five initial grants made by the Housing and Home Finance Agency — $4,558,000 of a projected expenditure of some $9,000,000 for the modernization of approximately forty stations on various subway lines and the improvement of surface-line shelters and parking facilities, but the federal government had already contributed even more millions in planning and demonstration grants as well as some funds of the U.S. Bureau of Public Roads, and these federal monies had been matched by several millions in state funds.

The Minneapolis-St. Paul and Memphis areas were other early beneficiaries under the Urban Mass Transportation Act, which authorized two programs of matching grants as well as loans for projects in an urban transit system conceived as part of an areawide development scheme, but only if no capital-grant assistance was required. Under one of the grant programs, if an urban area had a program for developing a unified or coordinated transportation system as part of a comprehensively planned development, a public agency wishing to purchase buses (as in Memphis), extend a rapid transit system, or modernize terminals and stations (as in Boston) could apply for a grant covering as much as two-thirds of that portion of the project cost which could not reasonably be financed from fares. Under the other program of grants, the Housing Administrator received further authority to undertake or contract for projects to study, develop, test, and demonstrate new or improved mass transportation facilities, equipment, services, or techniques. The loans available for proj-

104. Model of the South Hayward station of the San Francisco Bay Area Rapid Transit District, a special district which has received some federal aid under the Urban Mass Transportation Act of 1964; designed by architects Kitchen and Hunt *(San Francisco Bay Area Rapid Transit District)*

ects not requiring grants were limited to the balance of the $50,000,000 authorization for mass transportation loans in the Housing Act of 1961.

The satisfaction which federal officials and city planners obtained from seeing transportation plans actually being carried out by means of large federal grants for transit as well as highways was tempered by the realization that some of the planning contributed neither to the creation of great cities and the Great Society nor to the solution of problems of poverty. For several years state highway departments had controlled the only adequate developmental capital in sight. In many areas transportation planning had therefore tended to be mainly highway planning. The comprehensive planning of which it was supposed to be an element was secondary, merely supporting the schemes of highway engineers with data based on the past and current behavior of land users, motorists, and patrons of public carriers. Large issues of increasing the economic productivity of urban areas and enhancing employment and social opportunities for every segment of the population tended to be overlooked as specialists sought just to relieve traffic congestion or to reduce total transportation costs.

Victor A. Fischer, the Housing and Home Finance Agency's assistant administrator for metropolitan planning, was particularly critical of the philosophy, the approach, and the techniques employed in most of the transportation studies he had observed. They were "conservative by nature," trend-oriented rather than policy-oriented.[42] They did not consider what ideally should be sought, what changes could be induced, or how preferences might be shifted toward more desirable public objectives. Nor was Fischer alone in suggesting that in a society conducting a war on poverty a metropolitan community might be justified in regarding an areawide mass transit system as a basic utility providing low-fare transportation to the poor and carless, the aged, the young, and the handicapped as well as meeting the usual rush-hour needs. Judgments entering into the design of such a system could not, of course, be predicated solely on "scientific" studies of trends and projections of trends.

The social orientation of Fischer and many other federal officials, the general atmosphere of concern about the problems of the poor and minority groups, and the increasing social emphasis in the community renewal program and transit planning all combined to shift the city planning profession farther and farther from its once almost exclusive interest in land use planning and control. But as yet there was tension and conflict between those interested in physical planning and development and those concerned with human-resources programs, as Harvey Perloff pointed out in a Pomeroy Memorial Lecture entitled "Common Goals and the Linking of Physical and Social Planning," delivered at the annual conference of the American Society of Planning Officials in the spring of 1965. In the minds of many social workers city planning was associated with the dislocation of minority families and small merchants by slum clearance, large-lot suburban zoning directed specifically at keeping lower-income families out, and freeways which disrupted stable and cohesive neighborhoods. It was a "plaything of the neatness-minded middle classes" rather than the boon city planners said it was.[43] The planning fraternity, on the other hand, tended to find welfare workers unduly concerned with problem families and the social pathology of the city.

To close the gap between social planners and physical planners, Perloff suggested a search for "integrating concepts and goals" around which approaches to the solution of urban problems might be brought together.[44] Such common goals would be a "decent home and suitable environment" for every family, as stated in the Housing Act of 1949; jobs for all and a minimum family income; and adequacy and equality in public services and facilities. Presumably city planners had long accepted the first and third of these goals, though not with the breadth of vision, imagination, and political astuteness required to break through obstacles to racial integration in suburban areas and to achieve new towns designed for open occupancy or really low-cost housing near factories in outlying areas.

The community renewal program, in Perloff's opinion, was perhaps the one type of urban planning that offered significant opportunities for joint effort by social and physical planners. It suggested the "possibility of a co-ordinated attack on urban problems through long-term improvement programs for individual neighborhoods, particularly in neighborhoods where community action and human resources projects loom large."[45] Indeed, several cities had already made a beginning on such improvement programs — the forerunners of the "model cities" programs of today. And as Perloff outlined five-year development programs that might be prepared for neighborhoods in which physical structures were not beyond redemption, he came close to describing the kind of social-physical planning many cities are presently undertaking: "Such development programs would have to be evolved from community efforts broadly involving the residents of the neighborhood, but bringing to bear as well the know-how and strength of the city-wide planning and action agencies. Such programs could be prepared by technicians from the city planning agency, in co-operation with technicians from the human resources agencies, seeking ways in which the problems of the neighborhood could be overcome and the realistic aspirations of the residents achieved." The programs would include many elements, "ranging from spot redevelopment and rehabilitation of existing housing to the improvement of traffic flows for safety, the improvement of the public facilities, and the strengthening of various human resources programs such as education, health, welfare, and recreation."[46]

Ira M. Robinson, who was project director of the San Francisco community renewal program study, was so impressed by the technical, administrative, and social gains from the various community renewal programs carried on throughout the United States that he believed the city planning profession, after several generations of search, might now be "equipped to undertake comprehensive planning." As members of the staffs of these programs, city planners had come to recognize the importance of adequate, quantified information as an aid in monitoring conditions, changes, and trends; in detecting trouble and danger signs before they became too serious; in assessing the costs and benefits of alternative policies; and in evaluating the impacts and consequences, intended and unintended, of public and private programs. They had also realized the need to establish planning-and-programming as a continuing process of city government, related to and integrated with the everyday operations of city departments and agencies. And they had found themselves performing as policy formulators in the once-foreign fields of finance, monetary policy, social welfare, economic development, and more. If planners could now take the creative and unifying ideas from the federal community renewal program concept, draw upon the innovative approaches and methods developed in practice, and then extend these ideas in scope, content, and function, they might soon be establishing "truly comprehensive Community Development Programming processes in city governments."[47]

Community development programming, Robinson explained, would differ from the community renewal program in three significant respects. It would be directly concerned with "all aspects of the city system relevant to specific social, economic, and physical programs."[48] It would be concerned with *all* programs and activities of local government that directly or indirectly affected economic, social, and physical renewal and development. And it would formally and explicitly recognize the importance of establishing community-wide programming as an ongoing process of city government.

Among the principal activities of the central planning and programming agency would be the assembly and recommendation of an annual budget for development and renewal, the formulation of policy guides, and the preparation of a six-year schedule of the elements of the program, as in the capital improvement program familiar to most city administrations. Each year the six-year program would be reviewed and revised in the light of information fed back to the programmers regarding the success of public actions taken the previous year. The policy guide and program officially adopted by the city fathers would include "a time-phased and costed" set of public programs to be carried out by various departments and agencies in the future six-year period, together with a statement of the objectives of each program, the agency responsible for its execution, the foreseeable performance targets of each program, the method of evaluating performance, and the costs of the program year by year. The city council would adopt a budget and "action plan" for the first year of the six-year program.

Robinson himself wondered whether he was too optimistic about the prospects for community development programming. "Will it become standard operating procedure in all large central cities," he asked, "or remain just another good idea which nobody implements?"[49] Although he obviously could not answer his question, he noted that in a good many cities the community renewal program had already brought about the appointment of a renewal coordinator or development director serving directly under the chief executive and participating in a policy-making committee composed of the heads of the principal planning, renewal, and development agencies. "The next logical step," Robinson asserted, "is to subsume under his responsibility all developmental functions as well." Robinson thought community development programming would appeal to city managers and controllers who had pioneered in the use of such new tools of public management as performance budgeting and the program budget, and he believed that citizens exhibiting "uneasy impatience and skepticism" about traditional planning approaches would also welcome the more inclusive programming because its focus would be on "people rather than buildings." His own enthusiasm for the concept sprang mainly from the belief that it would "reunite the various professional interest groups and disciplines traditionally concerned with urban problems: the city planners, the housing and urban renewal specialists, the social scientists concerned with such urban problems as crime, delinquency, mental health, and poverty."[50] Robinson wrote,

> This union between planning, renewal, and housing is taking place not because of exhortation or because it is "right" and "logical," but primarily because of the developing theories and the technical advances in urban model-building, which explicitly illuminate the interrelations among long-range planning goals and policies, renewal activities, and the housing market. Without these developments no amount of hortatory advice would bring these groups out of their separate compartments. Similarly, as new theories and models of human behavior are built, especially those relating social behavior, human development, and physical environment, we will find closer ties among the social scientists and those traditionally associated with city planning, renewal and housing. Inevitably, these technological developments will be reflected in administrative and governmental rearrangements.[51]

In his eagerness to point out the potentialities of community development programming, Robinson tended to overlook some of the political realities which might prevent the process from operating effectively. They were the very conditions that David A. Grossman, director of the Community Development Branch of the Urban Renewal Administration, had cited earlier when discussing the community renewal program. Even though the community development program of a central city, for instance, might attempt to provide a metropolitan context for local decisions, it might not wholly resolve the problem of coordination with neighboring municipalities. As for a truly metropolitan development program, how could it be conceivable without an areawide government to make policy decisions and its own operating agencies to carry them out? Robinson also probably underestimated the willingness of elected officials to make advance commitments, especially in times of social ferment and economic uncertainty. Further, he may have miscalculated the ability of many city managers and chief executives to understand and fully utilize highly rational planning and programming processes employing electronic data-processing, simulation models, and other advanced techniques.

A Message on Cities, and Far-Reaching Legislation

Broad programs such as Perloff, Robinson, and other city planners envisaged demanded not only better-educated and more competent professional men in ever increasing numbers but also legislation of expanded scope, as well as much larger appropriations of developmental capital than the federal and state governments had ever contemplated. Of these needs President Johnson was perhaps more acutely aware than any previous Chief Executive. In a message sent to the Congress only four months after his landslide victory over Senator Barry Goldwater in November, 1964, the President asked for the most far-reaching housing and urban development legislation since the Housing Act of 1949. His message, moreover, was the first of its kind, a document "Relative to the Problems and Future of the Central City and Its Suburbs." City planners appreciated it not alone because throughout the text the President used the word "city" to mean the entire urban area but because he was unmistakably clear about the core of the urban problem. "The problem is people and the quality of the lives they lead," he stated. "We want to build not just housing units, but neighborhoods; not just to construct schools, but to educate children; not just to raise income, but to create beauty and end the poisoning of our environment."[52] The emphasis on goals rather than means could not have been more in accord with the views of planners who were themselves striving to reassert the primacy of human considerations and the overriding importance of "enriching the quality of American civilization."[53]

The enormous plurality of the Democratic triumph at the polls as well as the gravity of urban problems at last assured the enactment into law of many proposals foreshadowed in earlier legislation and presidential messages. The Congress transformed the Housing and Home Finance Agency into a new Cabinet-rank Department of Housing and Urban Development and adopted an omnibus housing and urban development act giving the new department supervision over a much wider range of programs than the predecessor agency had administered. The authorizations for new or relatively new programs for improving urban areas were particularly impressive: $200,000,000 annually for four years for grants to finance basic public water and sewer facilities; $25,000,000 annually for the same period of time for grants to assist public bodies in acquiring sites for future construction of public works; $50,000,000 annually for grants to finance community or youth centers, health stations, and similar public buildings in disadvantaged areas; and $310,-000,000 for open-space land grants, of which $64,000,000 could be used to provide parks and playgrounds in built-up areas and $36,000,000 could be expended for urban beautification; and, in addition, $5,000,000 for demonstration grants to encourage experimentation and innovation in programs of beautification and improvement of public lands.

City planners noted that grants for water and sewer facilities, advance acquisition of land for public works, and the acquisition and development of open-space land were all conditioned upon conformity of projects to an areawide or comprehensive plan. Not, as the President said in his message, that metropolitan planning was "a cure-all or a panacea." Sometimes it could be "a slender reed," and sometimes communities could not wait for completed plans, but such planning would "teach us to think on a scale as large as the problem itself, and act to prepare for the future as well as to repair the past."[54]

Even more significant than the requirement of metropolitan planning was an amendment to Section 701 of the Housing Act of 1954 authorizing grants to areawide councils of elected government officials such as the Association of Bay Area Governments and the Metropolitan Washington Council of Governments. The purpose of the grants, which might cover up to two-thirds of the cost of a broad range of planning and study activities (including general administrative support), was to stimulate the formation of additional metropolitan councils or conferences of local government officials, since federal agencies found such councils effective forums for resolving issues raised by metropolitan problems and for preparing comprehensive plans and developing programs for carrying them out. Urban Renewal Commissioner Slayton, for instance, lost no time issuing a directive stating that any metropolitan planning agency supported by "701" funds and operating in an area having a council of governments must coordinate its activities with those of the council.

The most controversial feature of the new act was one designed to provide a metropolitan solution to a problem which not even councils of governments acknowledged as their affair. This was the rent supplement program, authorized only by narrow votes in both houses of Congress. Originally the Johnson Administration had intended the program to help families with incomes too high for public housing yet not sufficient to enable them to obtain good private housing, but as it emerged in the act of 1965 it had all the appearances of a stratagem for breaking the "white noose" around central cities and permitting low-income families, including Negroes, to live in the suburbs. The rent supplement, bridging the gap between 25 per cent of a poor family's income and a fair market rental, was a device to induce nonprofit, cooperative, and limited-dividend organizations to build housing developments under FHA's moderate-income housing program at regular market interest rates in any part of a metropolitan area and rent them to low-income families. The program was expected to generate approximately 375,000 units by 1969 that would be occupied by some of the families on public housing waiting lists and some of the 6,000,000 families with incomes below $4,000 living in sub-standard housing. Presumably it would avoid the issues and emotions aroused by the construction of public housing projects, and it would be one way to introduce low-income families into suburban areas that had consistently opposed the establishment of public housing authorities. But the representatives of suburban communities soon detected the "plot" to crack the white, middle-class ring around the central cities, and though they were unsuccessful in blocking approval of the rent supplement program, they and their allies managed to delay an initial appropriation for it until 1966 and to keep all funding thereafter well below the amounts authorized in the housing act of 1965. The uncertainty about the program also made it for some time unattractive to insurance companies and other large interests.

The struggle between central cities and suburbs left other marks on the housing legislation of 1965. The mayors and councilmen of central cities again made common cause with insurance companies and private developers to defeat the President's attempts to obtain financial assistance for the planning and development of new towns. Though he still wanted to relieve some of the tensions in central cities by opening brand-new communities to racial minorities, the mayors of big cities feared risking the loss of more middle- and upper-class residents. All that the Congress would grant the Administration was an authorization for the Federal Housing Administration to insure mortgages for private developers wishing to acquire land for residential subdivisions and install site improvements. The lawmakers stipulated, however, that the new areas must be consistent with a comprehensive plan for the locality.

The central cities won further authorizations for urban renewal, but these were in the conservative range of $675,000,000 on enactment to $750,000,000 in 1967 and 1968, whereas some voices insisted that the nation should be spending as much as $2,000,000,000 a year for reconstruction and rehabilitation. Again the law stressed intensive code enforcement in deteriorating areas. The measure provided for grants to localities of up to two-thirds of the cost of enforcement programs (three-fourths for towns of 50,000 or less), as well as for grants covering two-thirds of the cost of demolishing unsound structures in urban renewal areas. But to complement enforcement activities, the act increased the authorizations for low-interest rehabilitation loans, and it made grants available to homeowners with incomes of $3,000 or less to enable them to modernize their homes when required, so that they would not be compelled to move. In recognition of the manifold financial problems of central cities and their desire to promote the economic improvement of older areas, the Congress also increased the proportion of the capital-grant authority which could be used for nonresidential renewal from 30 to 35 per cent.

Modifications in a few of the FHA mortgage insurance programs and the public housing program met some of the frequent criticisms leveled against federal housing policies and made these programs more adaptable to overall efforts at community renewal. The FHA program of moderate-income housing authorized in the Housing Act of 1961, and the program of direct loans for nonprofit housing for the elderly and handicapped, for example, were extended to larger numbers of persons by reducing the maximum interest rate to 3 per cent. Legislators countered the criticism that public housing was institutional-looking and isolated from its surroundings by approving provisions permitting public housing authorities to purchase and rehabilitate as many as 15,000 existing units out of a total of 60,000 units authorized annually for a period of four years. Other provisions allowed 10,000 units annually to be leased from private owners and used for low-income families; and tenants living in detached or semidetached dwellings could enter into a contract to buy the dwelling if an increase in income threatened to make them ineligible for public housing.

All in all, the President obtained much that he asked for in his message on cities, but after signing the Housing and Urban Development Act of 1965, he still had two matters included in the message to act upon. One was to appoint a commission to study housing for low-income families, zoning and land use, building codes and technology, housing codes, and local, state, and federal taxation affecting housing and urban growth. The other was to establish an Institute of Urban Development to support the training of local officials in a wide range of administrative and program skills and to administer grants to states and cities "for studies and the other basic work which are the foundation of long-term programs."[55]

As Congress did not appropriate funds for the commission until the fall of 1966, the President did not appoint the members until early 1967. Called the National Commission on Urban Problems, the group was chaired by former Senator Paul H. Douglas. It issued its findings and recommendations in five volumes in 1968 after holding hearings in eighteen cities throughout the country. Though the massive testimony of officials and citizens presented little that was not already known about urban problems, it at least clarified the issues.

The Urban Institute, which the President at first had thought might be created as a part of the new Department of Housing and Urban Development, was established in April, 1968, as a private, nonprofit organization, with Arjay Miller, vice-chairman of the Ford Motor Company, as its chairman. A few weeks later the federal department awarded a $3,000,000 contract to the new institute to carry out "research related to the Department's mission and program."[56] Other federal departments having important urban-related responsibilities later contracted with the institute to develop new knowledge and obtain information needed in their programs.

A Broader Statement of Purpose in the AIP Constitution

When members of the American Institute of Planners met at St. Louis in October, 1965, for their annual conference, they said little about the recent "escalation" of the war in Vietnam but much about the changes taking place on the domestic scene and their professional response to a transitional era. The passage of legislation establishing a federal Department of Housing and Urban Development clearly signified that planning had come of age and was recognized as a necessary function of government in nation, state, and municipality. Yet, paradoxically, in the very hour of success the city planning profession was engaged in an agonizing reappraisal of its purposes and a search for its identity. Its membership had grown by 50 per cent in the past five years and now numbered more than 3,800, but growth had resulted in the enrollment of men and women of heterogeneous background and outlook, and there was no longer agreement regarding the problems with which the profession should be concerned. Particularly troubled and almost defensive were some of the older planners who believed that the spatial arrangement of cities was still of paramount importance. On all sides their views were challenged, and the challenges came as much from the new conditions of American society as from some of their fellow members with prior allegiances to sociology, economics, political science, and law.

Aroused by such writers as Michael Harrington, Rachel Carson, and the scholarly James Bryant Conant, the public conscience was on fire with demands to help the poor, to preserve the natural environment, and to reform education. Though the typical planner of land use and circulation labored on behalf of people, he had already learned through the community renewal program that the poor and illiterate or undereducated had problems beyond his sphere of competence; and some of the proposals for dealing with them confronted him with the necessity of reexamining long-cherished concepts. For example, some liberal educators and minority leaders urged sending all children to school parks serving a whole city or a large part of a city. The very idea undermined the notion of the elementary school as the nucleus of the neighborhood and made questionable the value of general plans based on the neighborhood unit. The appeal to save the environment struck a responsive chord in the land use planner, but he had to admit that he knew little about ecological systems, the food chain in lakes, rivers, and saltwater estuaries, and the new proposals for waste disposal. Even in the field of transportation, which had occupied a great deal of his attention in recent years, there were technological developments in the offing that might upset plans for rail rapid transit systems and connecting bus lines. The "spin off" from the efforts of scientists working to put men on the moon and to develop habitable platforms that would orbit the globe might be systems of economical public transportation capable of neighborhood circulation as well as high-speed, automated trunk-line service. It was as difficult to foresee the effects of technological breakthroughs as it was to embrace new social theories and adjust to new political relationships.

So many people in other fields now called themselves planners that a land use planner might be considered presumptuous for assuming that he had a prior claim to the title. In forward-looking activities of hospital and health associations, welfare groups, the military, financial institutions, and even grocery chains, men who held graduate degrees in economics, urban geography, public health, or architecture not only understood and carried on the planning process but also utilized all the new computer techniques of which the land use planner had become enamored. If city planning had borrowed heavily from other professions and disciplines, they had more than repaid the compliment and had perhaps deprived it of a supposed guardianship of a special core of knowledge and the generalist approach.

Before the city planners at St. Louis was a proposed amendment to the constitution of their professional organization intended to acknowledge the greater breadth that planning had acquired in the past decade or more. Since 1938 the statement of purposes in Article II had described the professional sphere of activity as "the planning of the unified development of urban communities and their environs and of states, regions, and the nation, as expressed through determination of the comprehensive arrangement of land uses and land occupancy and the regulation thereof." A committee headed by Professor Louis Wetmore of the University of Illinois suggested deleting from this statement the entire last phrase referring to land uses. The emphasis would then be on the planning of the "unified development" of delimited geographical areas, and such planning might be interpreted to include social and economic plans and programs as well as proposals for land use and appropriate actions to carry them out. Wetmore's committee failed, however, to make the case for eliminating the familiar phrase about land use and gave some planners the impression that the profession contemplated downgrading its historic concern with spatial relationships, whereas the committee meant instead to indicate that comprehensive planning for development should encompass all relevant social and economic considerations.

The lack of clarity of the committee report touched off searching discussions of the proper role of the planner, or as Henry Fagin said, the proper roles of the planners, in a predominantly urban society. Fagin was one of four panelists chosen to confront the challenges to the profession in one of the sessions at the St. Louis conference. "Isn't planning for the physical environment enough of a job?" he asked. "Why don't we wait until we do this well before we think of enlarging the scope of the Institute?" But he saw no reason to exclude other planners who were coping directly with poverty, employment, economic development, segregation, renewal, and new cultural, educational, and health opportunities if they, too, had the knowledge and understanding required "to analyze what is relevant, to prepare plans and to manage the effectuation essential to the realization of plans." Their presence in the Institute might even protect its present members from "unknowingly undertaking responsibility in aspects of planning in which other planners are more specifically competent."[57]

Fellow member Patrick J. Cusick, Jr., similarly believed that rather than enlarge the professional sphere of interest, planners should first "achieve mastery" over the physical environment and welcome into their ranks, to aid them in the task, "all professional specialists involved in any phase of the comprehensive physical planning process who are able to demonstrate a minimum basic competence in this form of planning."[58]

With these views the greater proportion of Institute members agreed. The panelist who startled the assembled planners was Professor T. J. Kent of the University of California. "I don't think we're a profession today," he observed. Since World War II the Institute had "opened the gates" to persons interested in cities but concerned less with the physical environment than with social and economic improvement. As a result, the so-called city planning profession had become "a free association of people with common interest in cities and people," but with various groupings within this free association.[59]

Kent saw new planning professions emerging, one concerned with "the whole range of welfare and social objectives and programs," another with "the kinds of economic activities most needed to increase productivity and to broaden the distribution of wealth within our great metropolitan communities," and perhaps a third concerned with "a whole range of public health activities." The first of these professions would be "far more influential in terms of dollars than the physical planner can ever hope to be or ever should want to be." Kent himself had long been identified with the land use planners and still wished to be affiliated with a group concerned principally with physical development, but on the other hand he "would like very much to have an association of professional societies which share a common concern for life in cities, primarily cities in great metropolitan regions." In the next twenty to fifty years, however, he foresaw "professional longings for more completeness and relatedness" being disappointed as new political leaderships emerged in cities and the larger urban regions. These new combinations, far more aggressive and sophisticated than present leadership groups, would reassert civilian control over the professional leadership not only in municipal government but also in the new metropolitan governments that would eventually come "at a time unanticipated." In the meantime, city planners might succeed in influencing "top-level decisions in governing and building because they have an impulse to do this," but inevitably they would be obliged to share the advisory role with other professions.[60]

As Kent analyzed the problem of the American Institute of Planners, it was to enable those interested in planning urban and metropolitan physical development to improve the quality of their work by carrying on a lively exchange among themselves yet somehow not exclude from their confrontation of the urban challenges many others who were interested mainly in economic planning and social planning. How this could be done without assimilating them and thereby inhibiting or precluding the development of the much-needed new professions he envisaged, he really did not know.

After further debate and clarification of views, in 1967 the membership of the Institute accepted the amendment proposed by the Wetmore committee with the understanding that it broadened the scope of professional concern by removing the apparent limitation on planning practice implied in the direct references to land use. The aspiration of members was for a comprehensive planning approach in which social development and economic development were integral with, but not independent of, physical development. As a committee of the California chapter of the organization observed, the problems of a society struggling to secure full rights for all citizens, eliminate poverty, and allocate resources in a socially responsible manner demand planning that is not unduly circumscribed. Persons trained in disciplines other than city and regional planning belonged in the Institute if they met the qualifications of devotion to the public interest and mastery of the principles and techniques employed in the comprehensive planning process.

In a sense, the decision to modify the constitutional statement of purpose sanctified the enlistment of persons from other fields and other disciplines that had been going on for some years. The profession also formally acknowledged that in practice it had long ago accepted a teamwork approach to planning, the chief requisite of which was that all participants demonstrate an understanding of comprehensive planning. Sometimes planners with a background in economics led the team; upon other occasions the problem called for a team captain whose specialty was public administration or sociology. The adoption of a broader statement of purpose and of a policy of welcoming members from a wider spectrum of interests assured a still greater flexibility in the interdisciplinary approach to planning problems, though the danger of arousing the hostility of other professions was perhaps as great as the possibility of entering into closer collaboration with some of them, such as the professions of medicine, social work, engineering, architecture, and law. Growth through the inclusion of persons concerned with social planning and economic planning necessarily increased the tendency for subgroups to form and to rob the Institute of some of the cohesiveness it enjoyed as a smaller organization of like-minded members. Yet its latter-day heterogeneity was appropriate, if not inevitable, in a society characterized by complexity, pluralism, and interdependence. Political parties, religious denominations, labor unions, and other professions all exhibited the same tendency to embrace and accommodate a multiplicity of views.

The Great Shift in Federal Aid to Cities

A few weeks after the St. Louis meeting of the American Institute of Planners, President Johnson made known the members of an eight-man Task Force on Urban Problems that he had selected a year earlier. Their assignment was to propose an organization for the new Cabinet-rank Department of Housing and Urban Development and make recommendations for reorganizing federal assistance to cities.

The very names of the members indicated that the President invited bold and innovative ideas and that the group would give him what he expected. Every member was known for fresh approaches to old problems, for a willingness to entertain new ideas, and for an exploratory cast of mind. Heading the group was Professor Robert C. Wood of the political science department of the Massachusetts Institute of Technology, who had been consultant to the Bureau of the Budget and was widely known as the author of *Metropolis Against Itself* and *Suburbia: Its People and Their Politics*. Mayors, city managers, and county officials identified him with a proposal, first made in 1962, for establishing a network of "urban observatories" throughout the nation to study local governmental efforts to solve urban problems and to carry on research with the cooperation of urban universities. Serving with Wood were Kermit Gordon, former director of the Bureau of the Budget; Professor Charles M. Haar of the Harvard Law School, who was known to city planners as an authority on land planning and zoning law; William L. Rafsky, economist and former urban development coordinator in Philadelphia; Walter P. Reuther, president of the United Auto Workers; industrialist Edgar F. Kaiser; Whitney M. Young, Jr., executive director of the National Urban League; and Ben W. Heineman, chairman of the Chicago and North-Western Railway, which was one of the few profitable commuter services in the country.

To coordinate the work of the group, the President appointed Senator Abraham A. Ribicoff, chairman of the Senate Subcommittee on Governmental Reorganization and one of the most progressive legislators in the nation. On the staff of the task force was Chester Rapkin, land economist and author, with Robert Mitchell, of *Urban Traffic, A Function of Land Use*.

Wood and his colleagues proposed a federal effort to help cities that would be "larger in scope, more comprehensive, more concentrated" than any that had gone before, as the President revealed in a message to the Congress on January 26, 1966.[61] Indeed, his task force by the strength of its collective vision created a receptivity to new ideas that was to continue throughout the President's term of office, unleashing a flood of unusual suggestions for meeting housing and urban development problems and resulting in the passage of not one but two more major housing acts as significant as those of 1961, 1964, and 1965 – the Demonstration Cities and Metropolitan Development Act of 1966 and the Housing and Urban Development Act of 1968. The latter omnibus statute was in many ways the product of the seminal thought of the task force, because federal housing legislation is cumulative; the effective provisions of one act appear in the next and the next, broadened, strengthened, bolstered by usage and popular acceptance. Moreover, the inventiveness of one group inspires ingenuity in others, witness the eagerness with which forward-looking legislators, Republican and Democratic, expanded the act of 1966 into the still more flexible and wide-ranging act of 1968. But had not the ghettos of big cities ignited with hatred and violence, there might have been no congressional "market" for such audacious pragmatism as these two measures exhibited. Only the appalling destruction in a series of long, hot summers and the frightening implications of black revolt could have moved most senators and representatives to approve some of the novel alliances of public and private enterprise authorized in these enactments.

President Johnson, however, presented the proposals of his Task Force on Urban Problems not as measures to meet a crisis but as considered responses to persistently difficult problems. From the experience of three decades, it had become clear, he said, that every forward step taken to assist cities had had its severe limitations. Urban redevelopment had been attended by the hardships of relocation; the relief of traffic congestion had widened the gulf between the affluence of suburbia and the poverty of the city; and the struggle to preserve the autonomy of local agencies had crippled attempts to attack regional problems on a regional basis. Such dilemmas could not be resolved by any single program, but there could be new, multipurpose endeavors that would "concentrate our available resources—in planning tools, in housing construction, in job training, in health facilities, in recreation, in welfare programs, in education—to improve the conditions of life in urban areas." The President called for "experiment with a dozen approaches, or a hundred" under a "demonstration cities" program, later to be known as the "model cities" program. Wherever this kind of program was organized it should be of sufficient magnitude, both in its physical and social dimensions, to arrest blight and decay in entire neighborhoods and make "a substantial impact" on the development of the whole urban area within a few years.[62]

Such a program Mayor Richard C. Lee of New Haven, Connecticut, no doubt had had in mind when he proposed in 1962 that the federal government assist "a few pilot cities" to carry on "a total program for both physical and human renewal."[63] Since that time, of course, Harvey Perloff and several other planners had also urged combining physical rebuilding and rehabilitation with effective social programs.

The complement of an inner-city demonstration should be a far more vigorous metropolitan planning undertaking, the President stated. "What happens in the central city, or the suburb, is certain to affect the quality of life in the other."[64] Recognizing this fact, the Congress for the past five years had brought more and more grant-in-aid programs under the requirement that projects be consistent with comprehensive planning for an entire urban or metropolitan area. But the President and his task force believed that more should be done to stimulate cooperation and joint planning among neighboring jurisdictions. He recommended a new incentive "to help assure that metropolitan plans achieve their potential": the federal government should bear a larger share of the total cost of related federal-aid programs in areas showing willingness to be guided by their own plans in working out future development and to establish joint institutional arrangements necessary to carry out plans.[65] He proposed that a series of demonstrations in effective metropolitan planning be undertaken promptly.

While the Congress held hearings and debates on the handiwork of the President's task force, the organization of the Department of Housing and Urban Development got under way. The appointment of Robert C. Weaver as Secretary was a surprise to no one. The naming of Professor Wood as Under Secretary and of Professor Haar as Assistant Secretary for Metropolitan Development placed in the department two of the most articulate and able members of the task force, the latter to take jurisdiction over urban planning assistance, mass transit, open-space land, public works and public facilities programs. But perhaps just as much significance attached to Secretary Weaver's borrowing of Dr. Leonard Duhl, the psychiatrist, from the Department of Health, Education and Welfare, in which he was chief of the Office of Planning in the National Institute of Mental Health. As Weaver's senior consultant on social programs and resources, Duhl was expected to review all departmental programs for their social implications.

The psychiatrist soon indicated that he favored a reexamination of old premises and a reorientation of federal programs. Addressing a meeting of the Washington, D.C., chapter of the American Institute of Planners in May, he enunciated his belief in interprofessional, interorganizational effort. City planners and most other professionals were like members of craft guilds, narrowly concerned with very limited projects and jurisdic-

105. Robert C. Weaver, Secretary of Housing and Urban Development in the administration of President Lyndon B. Johnson *(U.S. Department of Housing and Urban Development)*

tions and not inclined to "link up" with other professionals even when concerns overlapped and work was duplicated.[66] But Duhl saw an interdisciplinary era dawning, and he himself hoped that interagency coordination would become the order of the day among the Department of Housing and Urban Development, the Department of Health, Education and Welfare, the Office of Economic Opportunity, the Department of Labor, and other agencies and groups having anything to do with poverty, employment, health services, and a multitude of social concerns.

The Demonstration Cities and Metropolitan Development Act signed by the President on November 3, 1966, was, in a sense, the manifesto of the cooperative, interprofessional approach proclaimed by Duhl and envisaged by the presidential task force. Months before the act was approved by the Congress and sent to the Chief Executive, Senator John Sparkman of Alabama had foreseen that it would represent "a complete shift in the form of federal housing assistance from that which was started in 1932" in the last year of Herbert Hoover's presidency. The nation had moved, the senator pointed out, from a single federal program established to help finance homes to a multilateral program designed to help finance all sorts of city improvements and environmental amenities and even direct assistance to the people themselves.

Perhaps because racial demonstrations in many cities in recent years had made the name used in the title of the act distasteful, the President preferred to term the provisions for restoring quality to older neighborhoods a "model cities" program. But the change in terminology in no way altered the intent of the legislation to give new meaning to the word "comprehensive" as applied to plans for creating several score of exemplary areas that would inspire other cities to bring all their resources to bear on revitalizing large slum and blighted areas.

Broadly interpreting the purposes stated in Title I of the act, the Department of Housing and Urban Development suggested that an adequate program for a model neighborhood should include plans to expand housing, increase job and income opportunities, reduce dependence on welfare payments, improve educational facilities and programs, combat disease and ill health, reduce the incidence of crime and delinquency, enhance recreational and cultural opportunities, establish better access between homes and jobs, and, in general, improve living conditions for the residents. No mere packaging together of existing plans and programs would suffice. The components of the program should be interrelated, so that projects and activities in one could reinforce and support those in others. To develop such integrated measures for achieving specific goals, a wide range of local public and private agencies would necessarily be required to work with a similarly wide range of federal and state agencies, but under the authority of a single local public agency "closely related to the governmental decision-making process in a way that permits the exercise of leadership by responsible elected officials in the establishment of the policies, plans and activities of the local program."[67]

The act authorized the Department of Housing and Urban Development to make grants amounting to 80 per cent of the cost of planning a "model neighborhood" program, but since the initial grants were to be distributed among carefully chosen cities of various sizes, the department announced that only those cities would be favored whose proposals reflected "an understanding of the conditions of the neighborhood area selected, how these conditions have developed, and what will be necessary to overcome them."[68] Upon submission of a satisfactory program, cities might receive four-fifths of the cost of administering the undertakings contemplated, but not the cost of administering any projects assisted by federal grant-in-aid programs.

A second main emphasis of the 1966 act was, as its title indicated, metropolitan development. In accordance with the President's recommendations in his message to the Congress, the act authorized incentive payments for development projects conforming to areawide plans, but there was so much opposition to this idea that legislators later refused to vote an appropriation for bonus grants amounting to 20 per cent of the cost of projects. The lawmakers, however, apparently genuinely favored the principle of coordinated planning in metropolitan areas as much as in model neighborhoods. Section 204 of the act provided that after June 30, 1967, all applications for loans and grants to assist in carrying out open-space land projects and for planning or constructing hospitals, airports, libraries, water supply and distribution facilities, sewerage facilities and waste treatment works, highways, transportation facilities, and water development and land conservation projects within any metropolitan area must be accompanied by the comments and recommendations of a metropolitan or regional planning agency composed of elected officials or responsible to a council of governments or an areawide government. Inclusion of this requirement of course meant that urban areas lacking associations of governments or metropolitan planning agencies functioning as arms of such associations must create them, lest cities and counties in the area be cut off from federal aid for development projects.

If the act of 1966 had included nothing more than the authorization of the model cities program and the requirement that areawide bodies must review federally aided development projects, it would have been one of the landmark statutes of the 1960s. But it included much more. It authorized FHA mortgage insurance to finance and equip facilities for the group practice of medicine, optometry, or dentistry; it made grants available for surveys of historic structures and sites and for the preservation of areas, sites, and structures of historical or architectural value; it sanctioned "a comprehensive program of research . . . to improve understanding of the environmental conditions necessary for the well-being of an urban society, and for the intelligent planning and development of viable urban centers";[69] it authorized grants to states to provide information and technical assistance to communities of less than 100,000 population; and it at last fulfilled the President's desire for mortgage insurance for the development of new communities, though the Congress limited the program to six years, restricted the maximum amount of insured loans outstanding at any one time to $250,000,000, and required governing bodies of adjoining localities, and in most instances even the governors of states, to approve the proposed new towns.

All these restrictions on the new-communities program indicated that the prospect of new outlying development still aroused as many misgivings among the officials and business leaders of central cities as among the officials and residents of suburban communities, albeit the reasons for dread were altogether different in the two camps. The suburbanites had not forgotten that the President had once advocated new towns as areas that should be open to minorities, although he had refrained from mentioning this possibility in his 1966 message on cities and metropolitan areas.

Of the new programs authorized in the act, the model cities program attracted the most attention nationally because it seemed to be the quintessence of the war on poverty. One hundred ninety-three cities throughout the country filed applications with the Department of Housing and Urban Development for planning grants to develop proposals for using various federal urban-aid programs to improve selected blighted areas, but before the department could review the applications and make grants to the cities promising especially innovative approaches, riots in the ghettos of Newark, Detroit, and several other cities again revealed that even such enlightened legislation as the Demonstration Cities and Metropolitan Development Act of 1966 came too late to heal the deep wounds inflicted by discrimination and callous indifference to the problems of black people. The riot in Newark, brought on by the determination of the city administration to remove hundreds of Negro families from a forty-six-acre site offered for a state medical school, was proof to black militants in cities across the land that the white population would not respect Negro interests or listen to legitimate protests. Mixed with the whites' cries of dismay and outrage, of course, was a heavy sense of guilt born of the knowledge that, in truth, too little had been done to lift the stigma of second-class citizenship from the Afro-American and make him a partner in the political and economic system. Liberal senators, however, had realized, even before this latest outbreak of violence, arson, and looting, that additional constructive measures were needed; they had introduced approximately three dozen pieces of urban legislation, which were before the Senate Banking and Currency Subcommittee on Housing when the riots began, whereas the Johnson Administration had been trying to consolidate the gains made in the previous Congress and was not planning to ask for any major new urban programs. The President had but one modest request to make of the Congress—that it provide $40,000,000 for the extermination of rats in city slums. Discussion of the bill embodying this proposal opened in the House a few days after the riots in Newark.

"Why not just buy some cats and turn them loose on the rats and thereby we could take care of this situation without any $25,000,000 from the Treasury of the United States," suggested Representative James A. Haley (D., Fla.) with a grin.

"Mr. Speaker," said Representative Joel T. Broyhill (R., Va.) archly, "I think the 'rat smart thing' for us to do is to vote down this rat bill 'rat now.' "

As laughter swept the chamber and Representative H. R. Gross (R., Iowa) asked whether there was going to be a high commissioner or administrator of the rat corps, Representative Martha W. Griffiths (D., Mich.) attempted to face a serious issue seriously. "Rats are a living cargo of death," she reminded her fellow legislators. "Their tails swish through sewers and over that food we eat. Their stomachs are filled with tularemia, amoebic dysentery. They carry the most deadly diseases, and some think it funny. . . ."[70] But the mood of hilarity was not to be dismissed, and by a vote of 207 to 176 the House refused to permit formal debate and action on the bill.

The performance of the majority was one of the most disgraceful ever witnessed on Capitol Hill. It provoked editorial condemnation from coast to coast. Offending congressmen smarted with shame. Yet unwittingly they had set the stage for consideration of broader urban legislation in the next session of Congress; and they had given the proponents of such legislation the moral upper hand in the deliberations.

From the committee hearings, the debates in chambers, and the conference sessions emerged a housing and urban development act beside which all previous attempts to dignify family life and improve cities seemed almost halfhearted. The measure signed into law on August 1, 1968, created twelve new programs and expanded seven others, including low-rent public housing and urban renewal, model cities, and rent supplements. Still, it was not the variety of programs provided for but the focus of all programs on a ten-year timetable for achieving the goal of a good home and a suitable living environment for every American family that made this act different from others. Not since the general goal was stated in the Housing Act of 1949 had any administration sought to have the Congress say how soon America should replace the 6,000,000 housing units beneath the lowest standards of decency, rehabilitate millions of others, and enlarge the supply of middle-income housing—26,000,000 units in all. The authorizations in the act were, however, for only the first three years of the ten-year effort and for but 1,470,000 of the 6,000,000 dwellings needed by low- and moderate-income families. Yet to be presented was a plan for reaching the goal in the remaining years of the decade, and clouded with uncertainty were the actions that future administrations and Congresses would take to finance the programs authorized.

The best augury for the long-term usefulness of this most voluminous of all housing acts was the considerable bipartisan support given several revolutionary new programs recognizing the aspirations of the poor, particularly Negroes and other minorities. For families with incomes between $3,000 and $7,000 or thereabouts the act established an unprecedented program of home ownership under which the federal government pays part of the interest cost of a purchaser's mortgage. There was also a rental assistance program to aid low-income families indirectly by federal subsidies on the mortgage interest costs of apartment projects sponsored by nonprofit organizations. Residents of ghettos and other blighted areas benefit by a provision relaxing FHA mortgage insurance requirements in older neighborhoods and by still another provision offering credit assistance and debt management on an experimental basis to low- and moderate-income families with poor credit and irregular employment patterns who are unable to meet required credit standards for purchasing homes under FHA mortgage insurance programs. To protect homeowners and businessmen in areas of racial tension and to assure them that insurance coverage will be continuously available, the act created a program providing the private insurance industry with federal reinsurance against losses resulting from riots or civil disorders.

Yet another feature of the act specifically signifying a desire to meet the needs of the underprivileged was a directive to the Secretary of Housing and Urban Development to require that housing programs for low-income families provide jobs and training for lower-income persons living in the vicinity of projects and that contracts be awarded, to the greatest extent possible, to firms situated in the immediate area or owned by persons in the area.

Significantly, the general intent of the law to broaden opportunities for families at the lower end of the economic scale specifically extended to a title of the act providing additional federal assistance for the development of new communities. Among other determinations, the Secretary of Housing and Urban Development must find that federally aided new communities will include a "substantial number" of housing units for families of low and moderate income. The Demonstration Cities and

Metropolitan Development Act of 1966 had required developers to obtain funds from private lenders, but the act of 1968 authorized the secretary to guarantee bonds and other obligations issued by developers to help finance land acquisition and land development if plans were sound and were consistent with the comprehensive planning in the area.

All these new programs directly or obliquely attacking problems of race, unemployment, and low income could not but thrust city planners in the larger urban areas more deeply into social issues. In addition, there were amendments to the Section 701 planning assistance program which insured that almost every planning agency benefitting by federal aid would develop stronger social commitments. The definition of comprehensive planning was broadened to include planning for the provision of governmental services and for the development and utilization of human and natural resources. For the first time it became mandatory for planning agencies to consider housing needs as an element of land use planning. By making assistance available through state planning agencies to district planning agencies in rural and other nonmetropolitan areas, the 1968 act gave wider currency to these enlarged conceptions of planning. Provisions enabling the Department of Housing and Urban Development to give financial aid for metropolitan planning efforts in cities without regard to population also furthered widespread acceptance of these more inclusive views of professional responsibility.

Like all the housing and urban development legislation since 1949, this crowning achievement of the Johnson Administration in equipping the nation with the legal tools to renew and develop cities gave the federal blessing to things which the most progressive — or most distressed — cities realized should be done. It set no radical new goals for the leading planning agencies, but it did provide inducements and compulsions for less enlightened agencies to catch up with them. In its totality it perhaps reflected a greater awareness of the gravity of city problems by a partnership of liberal legislators and federal officials than by Congress as a whole or the nation Congress represents. The approach of a national election no doubt influenced many conservatives to vote for the 1968 act who were lukewarm about its more advanced programs or were secretly opposed to them. Certainly, the later refusal of the majority to appropriate the amounts authorized for such programs as urban renewal, model cities, and rent supplements indicated general unwillingness to give appropriate support to the goals and policies stated in the act. The statute has thus become more a moral injunction to a troubled and confused people to address themselves to matters of the most vital concern than an instrument for doing so. Until the financial means for carrying out programs on the scale envisaged in the act are made available, the problems which it treats, or seeks to treat, can only intensify, because as yet the nation is engaged not in rebuilding its cities but in mounting various demonstrations, whether renewal projects initiated several years ago or model cities programs started in the past year or two. All these relatively small, experimental undertakings serve mainly to reveal the magnitude of the problem of reorienting city planning, reorganizing city governments, reforming state governments, and bringing federal programs closer to the cities and the citizens they are designed to help.

The Model Cities Program

In November, 1967, the Department of Housing and Urban Development announced that sixty-three cities in thirty-three states, the District of Columbia, and Puerto Rico had been chosen to proceed with detailed plans for model neighborhoods. In March, 1968, twelve additional cities received grants. Thus only seventy-five of the hundreds of American cities provide some basis for judging the strengths and weaknesses of the model cities program, but this first group of cities includes more than half of the municipalities in the country with populations over 250,000, fourteen with populations ranging from 100,000 to 250,000, and some smaller cities, among which the least populous are Pikesville, Kentucky (population 5,000), and Winoosky, Vermont (population 8,000). The group, in short, constitutes a reasonably good sample of the nation's cities.

In the neighborhoods which these communities propose to upgrade live a million families, or more than 4,000,000 persons. The social statistics on these families show that the cities have chosen areas of urban pathology, or, as Secretary Weaver preferred to put it, areas representing "the hard core both of need and opportunity in meeting our urban problems."[71] At the time the areas were selected, almost a third of the families had incomes of less than $3,000 a year, and the vast majority earned less than the median income in the locality. Unemployment was twice the national percentage. A third of the adults had less than an eighth-grade education—a fact closely related to low income and unemployment. A fourth lived in substandard housing, and many more were overcrowded in deteriorated buildings. The infant mortality rate, an indicator of the combined effects of poverty, ignorance, poor sanitation, and inadequate medical care, was double that for the nation as a whole. Although no information was provided on crime, delinquency, communicable disease, and family disorganization, doubtless the statistics on these subjects exceeded the norms.

The application of the city of Buffalo disclosed something else that could be said of most of the areas in which the larger cities are carrying on model neighborhood programs: "Many of the residents [in the area selected] are relatively new arrivals on the urban scene from the rural

South, and most are Negroes unprepared to participate in an increasingly technological society."[72]

Since the fundamental principle of the model cities effort is that citizens have a right to participate in and influence the development of plans affecting their lives, it was evident from the beginning that city planners and many other professional people would be obliged to engage in a form of face-to-face democracy for which most of them were ill prepared. It was equally clear that the preponderance of residents of the demonstration areas were even less well prepared to join in making decisions affecting their futures. At the annual national conference of the American Society of Planning Officials in the spring of 1967, Paul Davidoff, director of the department of urban planning at Hunter College in New York City, chided his professional brothers for being "as indifferent to the problem of racial injustice as . . . the rest of society." No city plan that he could think of had attacked the problem of discrimination and segregation "openly and with strength."[73] But planners were at a disadvantage in the model cities program not merely because of their seeming neglect of racial issues but also because of their lack of training for direct work with poorly educated people of different social strata. A few planners who had attempted to involve the residents of ghettos in planning had discovered that most of them had little or no experience in social or civic programs and were inarticulate, timid, suspicious, or indifferent. The Regional Plan Association in New York had attempted, for instance, to elicit the participation of people of low income and less-than-average education in its famous Goals for the Region Project, a pioneering venture in giving large numbers of citizens an opportunity to "influence the big decisions" affecting their environment, but the association had found that a special effort in a single Puerto Rican neighborhood in the Bronx failed to bring out large enough numbers of residents for an adequate sample of opinion despite intensive recruitment by neighborhood leaders.[74] It was hardly surprising, therefore, that the Department of Housing and Urban Development gave early indications of widespread inclination to avoid the difficult or inconclusive face-to-face meetings and to stress action. In January, 1968, the department issued a revised model cities program guide urging communities to put greater effort into bringing together local public and private groups and neighborhood residents to develop a deep, probing analysis of the problems in the project area and not to concentrate prematurely on developing specific program proposals. Yet it was easier to advise communities to work closely with site residents than it was for planners of model neighborhoods to master the art of communicating with those needing help.

In a review of the first ten months of the model cities program presented at a midwest regional conference in September, 1968, H. Ralph Taylor,

Assistant Secretary for Model Cities and Governmental Relations, confirmed the general impression that the necessary partnership between city government and citizens is endangered by certain professional attitudes. "We still find people in public positions—more frequently local bureaucrats than elected officials—who resent the restraints on their power implicit in citizen involvement," he noted. Did he include city planners among the local bureaucrats? He was too tactful to say, but some planners may have felt guilty as he went on to say, "They mask their resentment in the rhetoric of the importance of *action,* and the difficulty of getting citizens to agree on a plan for action. They point to the fragmentation in the neighborhoods, the conflict between groups, and the absence of an accepted spokesman as justification for their attempt to retain full control. They have the arrogance of professionals who believe that citizens, particularly poor and black citizens, lack the necessary credentials."[75] Such an attitude, Taylor pointed out, reinforces the suspicion of underprivileged citizens toward city government, and a self-fulfilling prophecy results.

Arrogance, sometimes not acknowledged by those who exhibit it, has long been a shortcoming of most professionalism. City planners, especially when associated with other professionals, would hardly be human if they did not manifest various degrees of superiority in their relations with folk separated from them by a very great intellectual gulf. The gulf alone tends to make even the most well-meaning planner appear patronizing or condescending to the already mistrustful residents of blighted areas. Perhaps for the first time in his life he is cast in a role akin to teacher or counselor, the essence of which is humility and patience. Others more experienced in working with poorly educated and disadvantaged people may help him, but he will be obliged to learn mainly by trial and error how to become not only coplanner and adviser but also cultural anthropologist, psychologist, social worker, and public relations expert. While the learning process is under way, the model cities program will reflect the mistakes of individual planners and planners collectively, just as the earlier urban redevelopment program did. But the mistakes will be shared by others because, as Taylor observed, "there has been virtually no experience in American cities with broad-scale planning that related physical planning and social and economic planning."[76] Nor has there been experience with this kind of planning as a collaborative enterprise between city government and the citizens of segregated, blighted neighborhoods.

The federal official expressed the belief that the model cities program would have a profound effect on municipal governments, increasing their responsiveness to citizen needs, their ability to measure the resources required for problem-solving, and their competence to develop institutions that "will help the individual overcome the feeling that he has no role to play in an impersonal society."[77] But Taylor saw "little evidence of enlarged state capacity or of state commitment to focus resources on the problems of the inner city."[78] In many states, bureaucracies that have been unsympathetic to, or even unaware of, what is happening in central cities have controlled the distribution of federal funds and set the pattern of technical assistance in federally aided programs; and few governors have known the full extent and nature of the flow of federal funds into their states and how the funds have been allocated to cities. The model cities effort, demanding recognition of carefully established priorities and the funding of related components of programs in an appropriate time sequence, cannot succeed unless the whole system of processing applications and grants becomes speedy and flexible. Great changes in federal-state relations and in state and federal procedures are required. As Taylor pointed out, various federal departments with urban programs are substantially strengthening regional offices, so that they can work more closely with cities, and are making other adjustments that can be accomplished without additional legislation, yet it is obvious that in the long run outmoded state government and cumbersome intergovernmental relationships must be overhauled.

City planners engaged in model neighborhood planning have the opportunity to become participants in the larger task of reshaping local and state government, not to mention the federal government. The political role may be thought of as an administrative one, since the context of activities is the municipal administration, but the planner's function is nevertheless political if he directs attention to reforms needed in the city hall, the state capital, and the national capital and works in every way that he can to effect governmental reorganization and the improvement of governmental services. The housing and urban development acts passed in this decade have permanently shifted the planner from the role of technician and adviser on physical development to the role of quasi-political strategist of social change.

Ghettos and Metropolitan Planning

When the model cities program was first instituted, cynics referred to it as a means of fashioning "gilded ghettos" and keeping black people as segregated as ever. Secretary Weaver expressed a more sanguine opinion: "I do not see the improvement of living conditions or job or education conditions in the ghetto as the creation of a gilded ghetto, *provided these improvements are coordinated with effective efforts to remove the barriers that confine people to segregated areas. Without both, there is no solution* [emphasis added]."[79]

Since then black militants have advocated separatism and have demanded complete control by blacks of the areas in which they live and carry on businesses serving their own race. Some whites, though rejecting the idea of permanent apartheid, have concluded that disadvantaged blacks must first learn to manage their own communities before they can successfully become members of the larger society. Still other whites deplore the trend toward increasing acceptance by blacks, for whatever reasons, of separatism and maintain that the only long-term solution of minority problems is gradual elimination of discrimination and eventual free association of all elements in a completely democratic system.

The hopes of those who cling to the ideal of integration seem, however, to be frustrated by the tide of events since the Supreme Court's school desegregation decision of 1954. Notwithstanding all the gains in civil rights legislation and various federal acts creating greater opportunities for blacks and other minorities, American cities today are more segregated than at any time in history. Moreover, the trend is toward still greater separation of the races even though the Housing and Urban Development Act of 1968 provides new means for low-income families, including blacks, to own or rent homes outside ghetto areas. In the fall of 1968 the House refused to appropriate money for the enforcement of the open-housing provisions of the legislation which might be regarded as the companion of the housing act — the Civil Rights Act of 1968, passed soon after the assassination of the Reverend Dr. Martin Luther King. The effectiveness of this measure — designed to topple racial barriers in 80 per cent of the nation's housing in three stages between 1968 and 1970 — may, therefore, be nullified or greatly diminished. Blacks willing to venture into the outlying neighborhoods of big cities or into suburbia may find as much difficulty as ever in purchasing or renting homes. Not to be overlooked is the Supreme Court decision in June, 1968, holding that an almost-forgotten civil rights act of 1866 totally prohibits discrimination in sales and rentals of property throughout the nation, but the enforcement provisions of the old law are weaker than those of the new one. The widespread interest of blacks in organizing and improving their own areas may even be creating a climate of opinion inhibiting Negro families from forsaking familiar territory. Thus the future movement of the black population within metropolitan areas is somewhat unpredictable.

The situation casts a shadow over the planning of model neighborhoods and raises questions about metropolitan planning generally. Ideally, ghetto neighborhoods should be re-created as coherent parts of metropolitan areas. One of the objectives of the model cities program, moreover, is to relate planning in these demonstration neighborhoods to metropolitan planning. If the view of Secretary Weaver prevails, ghettos will be replanned as stepping-stones to less-restricted living. Physical, social, and economic planning will be combined to fit the residents of blighted districts to participate more effectively in urban life and someday to live wherever they can afford the housing costs. And metropolitan planning will further this possibility and facilitate the upward social mobility of all minorities. But does areawide planning as presently carried on enhance opportunities for blacks and other underprivileged people to achieve equality in the American scheme of things?

The Department of Housing and Urban Development probably has done more, specifically, to help blacks overcome the injurious effects of segregation than metropolitan planning agencies. It has provided grants to universities for several studies of the problem of opening the metropolitan job market to Negroes. Since most of the new factory jobs, and many of the new service jobs as well, are in outlying areas served by inadequate public transportation, one of the main difficulties for blacks is the inaccessibility of employment. An investigation by Washington University, in St. Louis, of ways in which transportation could assist in alleviating unemployment in the inner city is among the studies promising some relief to economically disadvantaged blacks. But the federal department has not, of course, limited its interest in transportation to research; it has made hundreds of grants, some amounting to many millions of dollars, to improve mass transit in urban areas of all sizes.

The long-run hope of bettering the lot of the poor, more than half of whom are not members of minority groups, undoubtedly lies, however, in the development of a broader vision of the potentialities of the metropolitan aggregation. To the slow process of developing such a vision the Demonstration Cities and Metropolitan Development Act of 1966 has made a signal contribution. The requirement that after June 30, 1967, all applications for certain federally aided projects must be reviewed by an "areawide agency which is designated to perform metropolitan or regional planning" resulted in the selection of 171 agencies to exercise the review function, among which were thirty-three of the forty-seven or more councils of governments active when the Bureau of the Budget released the list of designated agencies on September 15, 1967. Only a little more than six months later the number of councils had increased to eighty-eight, of which fifty-nine were undertaking metropolitan planning. Several metropolitan planning commissions had been converted partially or entirely into councils of elected officials, and a few commissions had become the secretariats for the councils of governments.

In this trend toward greater cooperation among local units of government and the gradual alliance of areawide policy-making and decision-making with areawide planning can perhaps be seen some prospect that racial problems and all the thorny issues of class intertwined with them will be confronted and steps taken to resolve them, little by little. Officials of central cities cannot but bring various aspects of poverty and discrimination into metropolitan planning discussions, though presently most review agencies tend to restrict themselves to somewhat piecemeal consideration of projects and to avoid examining the social dimensions of such things as local comprehensive plan, public housing and renewal programs, and model cities efforts. No one aware of the long process of self-education through which the members of councils of govern-

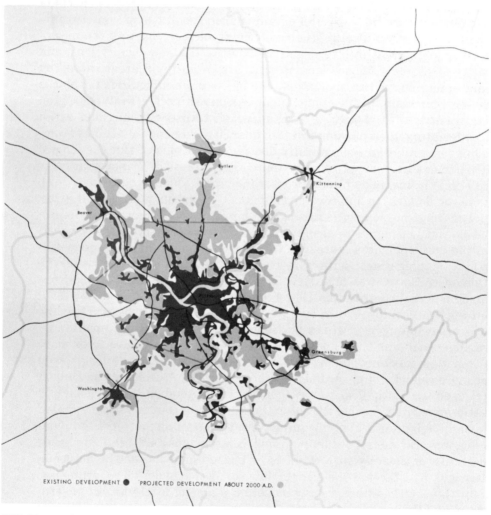

EXISTING DEVELOPMENT ●   ˙PROJECTED DEVELOPMENT ABOUT 2000 A.D. ●

106. Future development of the Pittsburgh, Pennsylvania, area as projected by the Southwest Pennsylvania Regional Planning Commission

ments will be obliged to make their way can expect rapid progress in either better planned regional development or racial integration; but there are political compulsions on the national scene forcing state governments to pay more attention to regional and local affairs, and these pressures may somewhat accelerate change in metropolitan communities.

Since the early months of 1967, when the effects of the reapportionment of state legislatures began to be felt, a score or more of states have provided financial assistance to local governments for such urban programs as housing, renewal, mass transportation, sewage disposal, and water supply. At the end of 1968 more than half of the states had established departments of urban affairs or had authorized some other administrative unit of government to provide advisory, coordinating, or technical assistance to local governments. At the urging of the National Governors' Conference, which opened a Washington office in the spring of 1967, almost all the states have designated federal-state coordinators, so that they can closely follow federal legislative developments and become better informed about federal programs requiring state cooperation. One of the first reports of this organization's Committee on State-Urban Relations offered eighty-five specific proposals for action by state governments. The list ranged from studies and reappraisals of local governmental structure to state financing of rent supplements.

Governor Nelson A. Rockefeller of New York contributed to the growing interest of the states in urban affairs when he established a privately financed State-Urban Action Center to provide technical assistance to governors and state legislative leaders seeking solutions to urgent urban problems. His initiative was matched by that of former North Carolina Governor Terry Sanford, under whose leadership, and with the financial support of the Ford and Carnegie Foundations, an institute of state planning was opened at the University of North Carolina — the first of a series of institutes serving as centers for shaping tools and techniques to improve state government. So numerous and promising, indeed, have been developments on the state scene in the past few years that many persons are hopeful that all of the states at length will assume their proper responsibilities in meeting the crisis of the cities.

The Need for "A Whole New Order of Urban Expert"

In this crisis the federal government, the states, and thousands of local governments, while taking timely action, increasingly have sought assistance from institutions traditionally committed to the long view — the universities and colleges and the private foundations engaged in financing many of the research projects carried on in special institutes established on campuses in the past ten or fifteen years. From these centers of higher education almost every agency of the federal government has plucked high administrative officers. But what is needed is not so much the immediate enlistment of gifted professors and researchers in government service as the assurance that in the future there will be a growing number of highly educated professionals entering public service annually, and in the universities themselves brilliant corps of specialists and generalists to instruct them. At no time in history have the trustees, presidents, and faculties of universities been so intensely aware of the immensely important supporting role higher education must play in a society geared to change—seemingly rapid but in many respects long-overdue change.

From the beginning of the 1960s an obvious need has been a greater number of city planners holding graduate or undergraduate degrees in planning, preferably the former. Among the institutions inaugurating new planning programs in response to the need have been the Catholic University of America, University of Tennessee, Iowa State University, Hunter College, Pennsylvania State University, University of California at Los Angeles, Florida State University, University of Arizona, and Texas A&M University. The older planning schools have enlarged their faculties and enrolled more students.

As the number of planning schools has increased, so too has the number of scholarships available to their students. In 1960 the firm of Harland Bartholomew and Associates became the first consultant organization to provide a planning fellowship—to the University of Pennsylvania. In the single year 1962 the Sears–Roebuck Foundation doubled the number of fellowships it provided to planning schools; and the Pittsburgh Plate Glass Company, the Loula D. Lasker Foundation, and the State of Kentucky began offering fellowships. Two years later the Richard King Mellon Charitable Trusts provided the largest of all the benefactions to students and their instructors: $50,000 a year—$25,000 for fellowships and $25,000 for faculty salaries—to each of more than a dozen planning schools for the five-year period 1964–1969. In May, 1968, the American Society of Planning Officials reported that thirty-seven institutions having graduate or undergraduate programs in city planning had a total of 586 students receiving scholarships and other forms of financial assistance.

Of the various scholarships, none more significantly attests to the importance of city planning than those granted by the federal Department of Housing and Urban Development. The Congress first authorized these financial aids in the Housing Act of 1964 but did not appropriate funds for them until the fiscal year 1967. In the fall of 1968 ninety-five students in forty planning schools were pursuing their studies with the benefit of federal monies.

Even though scholarships enable a larger number of students to prepare themselves for careers in planning, the output of the planning schools is still relatively small compared with that of schools of architecture, engineering, law, or medicine. Together, all the universities offering programs in planning awarded 446 undergraduate degrees and 2,050 master's degrees in the five-year period 1963–1968, but the total "crop" was insufficient to meet the need in city, county, metropolitan, federal, and private planning offices. In 1968 the Department of Housing and Urban Development estimated the shortage of urban planners at 1,500 to 1,700.

At that time Robert Weaver called not just for more city planners but for "a whole new order of urban expert." Even vastly increased programs of training for people in planning, public administration, sociology, and other fields would not be enough, he said. "We need to train a new kind of urban generalist, the man who can administer the kinds of new programs — such as Model Cities — which are going to make their appearance in the next few years. And it is the universities which must bear most of the burden of producing this new kind of modern Renaissance Man."[80]

Nor have the universities been waiting to be prodded into revising their curriculums and making the new academic arrangements necessary to educate men of broader competence. New interdisciplinary programs have appeared in many institutions. The departments of city planning and political science at the Massachusetts Institute of Technology, for example, together sponsor a program leading to the degree of doctor of philosophy in urban politics and planning, in an effort to integrate the increasing research capability of the social sciences with environmental and humanistic perspectives on the city. The University of North Carolina offers a master's degree program in health services planning through joint efforts of the schools of public health and medicine and the department of city and regional planning. Michigan State University has a Ph.D. program in urban and regional planning under the aegis of the College of Social Science.

The city and regional planning department of the University of California at Berkeley has a particularly interesting program in the new field of social policies planning, instituted in 1967 with the aid of a five-year grant from the Center for Studies of Metropolitan and Regional Mental Health Problems of the National Institute of Mental Health. This Ph.D. program, under the direction of Professor Melvin M. Webber, developed from the belated discovery by professionals in the fields of city planning, social work, public health, mental health, medicine, education, and law that their separate efforts to alleviate the deprivations of low-income groups were only partially successful and should be redirected to the larger task of cooperatively guiding social change and accelerating social mobility. As Webber pointed out in a prospectus of the unique program, it is designed to "train a new kind of interprofessional professional" capable of planning changes in the institutional organizations through which services to individuals, families, and groups are initiated and administered.[81] Some having competencies in social policies planning will find careers in the budgeting offices of government, some in agencies with specific but all too limited programs, and others in the quasi-governmental organizations that are becoming increasingly numerous in the social- and human-services fields.

Besides preparing new types of planners, the planning schools have undertaken to expand the ranks of the teaching profession through their Ph.D. programs. In these offerings they seek not only to train men and women who can develop the new knowledge and theory required in the urban planning field but also to assure themselves of the exceptional minds that can guide research undertaken on behalf of the federal government, state governments, quasi-public institutions, and important civic groups. Without an oncoming supply of innovative young professor-researchers, the schools can neither fulfill their obligations to equip students for the higher positions in planning agencies nor staff the research centers and institutes that are becoming integral parts of the academic shop.

But planners outside the groves of Academe do not always appreciate the new emphasis on Ph.D. programs. At the 1967 annual national conference of the American Society of Planning Officials applause greeted a suggestion by Robert M. Leary, assistant general manager of the National Capital Commission of Ottawa, Canada, that Ph.D. candidates in planning should be allowed to do only research and should be "kept away from other planning students, unless they have had some practical experience."[82] To Professor Leo Jakobson, chairman of the department of urban and regional planning at the University of Wisconsin, this endorsement of the idea of quarantining men interested in higher degrees, lest they infect and ruin students capable of becoming practical planners, was "sad indeed," if not alarming, because if it represented the true sentiment of the profession, the time might come when planners would be divided into two separate groups, one composed of bureaucratic technicians "whose horizon is as limited as that of the guy obsessed with the engineering fix," the other made up of planners "concerned with theory in the abstract only." Jakobson was convinced that neither group could succeed, "for the simple reason that the former will be lacking in a theoretical framework within which to operate, and the latter because of want in practical applications."[83]

An opponent of doctoral work in planning some years earlier, the professor had wholly changed his views since returning from India, where he had been engaged in a planning program in Calcutta. "The disparities between the advances in the technology of planning, on the one hand, and the conceptual poverty in planning theory, on the other, stood out more clearly than ever. . . . To apply modern planning technology to indigenous concepts, plans, and programs was impossible because an abstract, theoretical frame of reference does not, at present, exist." As long as planners failed to develop "an explicit, concise theoretical framework for planning," they would be unable to assist the so-called developing nations in "finding solutions to the impact of rapid industrialization" or to "counteract efficiently the projected further deterioration of our own development patterns." Jakobson therefore urged that "many more of our talented young people in planning schools, and in the profession, pursue advanced academic work."[84]

Surrounded by professors in other disciplines who assume that they possess theories adequately explaining the behavior of certain kinds of phenomena, professors of city planning feel particularly keenly the lack of any "theoretical framework" to give their own field not only respectability and status but also validity. If many planners are merely "urban carpenters" making repairs to cities and tacking on additions without really knowing what they are doing, what can be said of professors who are unable to offer all-embracing principles and laws to elucidate how and why cities grow and develop and how they should be planned? It is little consolation to realize that none of the social sciences and not even the physical and biological sciences have yet achieved a body of precept wholly dependable in every situation requiring clarification. Some of these fields of learning at least have theoretical foundations which suffice most of the time. But planning—which might be a process but which is impossible to define as a discipline, so imprecise and extended are its outer limits—sends one groping among all the other fields for illuminating abstractions and synthesizing principles. Is it an illusion that in the vast realm of human thought there must be theoretical constructs to guide the patterning of urban regions and even entire countries? Or can the planning profession actually look forward to the development of the theory it seeks and needs?

As Jakobson indicated, the profession has missions elsewhere in the world—in Asia, Africa, Latin America, and the Caribbean, as well as in the United States and Europe. To those in quest of theory, it seems that if in the long run planners fail to develop genuine understanding of man as a creator and user of cities, then the failure will be of global magnitude. But surely this is a view as naïve as it is presumptuous. It is naïve because it assumes that man behaves in ways which can be reduced to scientific formulations—when all history shows him to be a creature at times as distressingly irrational and erratic as he is upon other occasions superbly logical and steadfast; it is presumptuous because it presupposes that planners will someday enjoy greater influence than they are ever likely to have in any society, democratic or autocratic. The yearning for all-encompassing theory is an overreaching characteristic of an age dominated by science, if not by the wise use of science. Just as science can never explain the combining of genes which results in genius, so it probably can never fully explain the complex interactions of human beings as members of society. Frustration will be the lot of those who forget the art in the "art and science of city planning." Cities are such amalgams of memory and hope, clutter and space, drabness and glitter, the tangible and the intangible that it is inconceivable they could ever be mastered by analysts and systematizers of knowledge. Not that professors and researchers should abandon the search for theory, but that they should expect to be disappointed and come at length to acknowledge that emotion and judgment and intuition have as much to contribute to the development of cities and society as generalizations from empirical data and postulates derived from statistical calculations.

American city planning has arrived at that stage of sophistication in which it is overly self-critical, sometimes almost to the point of flagellation. A more balanced appraisal suggests that even now the field commands more knowledge, methodological capability, and philosophical insight than society is willing or able to utilize. In the United States and Canada the persistent disposition to favor private gain rather than the enlargement of opportunity for the general public dooms many plans and blights many planning recommendations. Until attitudes change appreciably—and they are changing, though very slowly—the quality of planning presently attainable may be somewhat better than the society expects or deserves. The lack of satisfactory theory and of certain kinds of knowledge therefore may not be so lamentable as some imagine. By the time there is a greater desire for sound planning, there may be a firmer theoretical basis for planning, and planners may have learned more about how to unite theory and art in actual practice.

The Commitment to the American Dream

In a commemorative volume such as this one, it is well to consider briefly the kind of society in which planners will be serving in the future. Though prophecy is hazardous, perhaps there is no better way to prefigure the social milieu of coming decades than to note the main currents flowing from the past and to examine them for hints about tomorrow. The city planning movement at the beginning of the century was part of a reform movement affecting almost every aspect of American life—business and industry, government and politics, the arts, and the growth and development of cities. Without the Progressive impulse that animated local as well as national politics, there might have been no McMillan Commission to prepare a plan of Washington, no civic associations and business groups eager to employ Robinson, Olmsted, Burnham, and Nolen, and no large number of citizens willing to vote huge bond issues to carry out some of the principal features of the Burnham plan of Chicago.

In the cynical, materialistic, business-dominated twenties almost everyone pronounced the reform movement dead; and indeed in that time of technological change and popular obsession with such wonders as the long-distance transmission line, the radio, and the mass-produced automobile, it was difficult to find much evidence of social concern. Yet in that period of speculation and excess, Henry Wright prepared his prophetic, though neglected, plan of the state of New York, Thomas Adams and his cohorts envisaged a less congested and more livable environment for the people of the nation's largest metropolis, and Wright and Clarence Stein planned Radburn as a safe and neighborly city for the motor age. Planning consultants, among whom Harland Bartholomew was the most active, were called upon mainly to prevent gross disorder by drafting zoning ordinances and devising street and highway plans, but almost to a man they upheld the ideal of a more inclusive plan and at times persuaded city councils to respect and follow the broad outlines of a plan embodying several closely related elements.

When the economy faltered in the early thirties and Americans realized how hollow their vaunted prosperity had been, reform again swept through the whole institutional structure of the nation. Millions were unemployed, millions were ill-fed, ill-housed, and ill-clothed. Millions, moreover, had always been deprived. The focus was now on fundamental human needs. President Franklin D. Roosevelt's New Deal created emergency agencies to put men to work, initiated a long-needed social security system, and embraced housing and planning proposals previously considered visionary if not radical. For the first time there was a national planning agency to encourage states, counties, and municipalities to plan, to foster the planning of entire river basins, and to study and propose improvements in such varied matters as the economy, welfare, housing, and transportation. Abolished after a decade of activity, it left as its legacy a conception of planning that was so encompassing that many planners have not accepted it to this day.

The National Resources Planning Board was not, however, the only governmental agency of the thirties and early forties that contributed to the development of a more comprehensive type of planning. The Tennessee Valley Authority, the Resettlement Administration, the United States Housing Authority, and various other agencies created in response to temporary or long-term needs also helped to enlarge the scope of planning, whether urban or state planning or planning within the federal establishment. The planning profession emerged from the Roosevelt era with new alliances, new responsibilities, and a deeper concern for the social and economic needs of people. Always dedicated to serving the public interest, its members had gained knowledge and experience that enabled them to champion the public interest more effectively. In some of the large cities, at least, they were at work in departments authorized by law to exercise strong influence in the determination of development policy.

In the postwar years the evolutionary expansion of the functions of American government continued under the impelling force of the American dream of equality of opportunity and a more ample life for everyone. Congress enacted an omnibus housing measure in 1949 setting forth the national goal of a decent home and a suitable environment for every American family. The statute was but the first of a series of multiprogram housing and urban development acts recognizing the interrelated needs of cities and the importance of cities in the life of the nation. Each act in varying degrees incorporated the ideas of leading city planners and represented professional response to old problems that were becoming more critical and to new ones that were arising as urban areas increased in population and spread into surrounding territories.

Alarmed by the gathering momentum of change, planners in public agencies as well as in schools of planning and special research institutes plunged into intensive study of the nature of cities, the historic forces shaping cities, and specific problems demanding amelioration if not solution. Investigations of the deterioration of central areas, the unmet needs and desires of minority groups, the inadequacy of mass transportation, the loss of open space, air and water pollution, and the growing complexity of governmental organization in metropolitan areas revealed that planning restricted mainly to manipulation of the physical environment falls short of the mark. As some of the planners affiliated with the National Resources Board had understood, all forms of planning— economic, social, and environmental—must be linked, difficult as it may be to develop a truly encompassing planning process. The rediscovery of this basic principle sustains a new conviction: social change not only can be planned but also must be. Some of the more advanced schools of planning now offer courses in the planning of social change.

The model cities program authorized in the Demonstration Cities and Metropolitan Development Act of 1966 may be regarded as the first significant political expression of the need for a new type of planning. The program is the harbinger of still broader programs designed to relieve the United States of deprivation—the deprivation signified by dirty skies and polluted rivers as well as by children with spindly legs and distended abdomens—and to fulfill what an early Progressive, Herbert Croly, called the promise of American life. Credit for formulating the program belongs not alone to city planners but also to members of a presidential task force representing many fields of interest, yet it is heartening to note that the long liberal tradition of planning shines through in this new means of bettering human lives and the urban environment.

Planners will play more influential roles in American society in the decades ahead only if they continue to act in accordance with that optimistic and humanitarian tradition. Though riots in ghettos, fiscal crises in city halls, student rebellions on university campuses, and strikes of teachers and other public employees sometimes seem to indicate that the nation is incapable of handling its social and economic problems, the reality is that all these upheavals and protests testify to the strength of American determination to achieve a more just and beneficent society. Blacks and other minorities aspire to the material comforts and amenities they see others enjoying. Mayors of big cities are troubled by deficits partly because municipal governments have striven to provide a wider and wider range of public services. Students revolt not just because they resent authority but also because many of them wish to redirect society from the pursuit of affluence to the pursuit of some deeper meaning in life, and because they are acutely aware of the deficiencies of the corporate system and the governmental mechanisms it frequently uses for its own ends. Teachers, policemen, sanitation workers, and firemen strike to gain salaries and working conditions comparable to those already won by many industrial unions. The atmosphere of strife is a reverse tribute to the vigor of the American ideal of meeting human needs adequately; and the idea of adequacy implies spiritual and intellectual satisfactions as well as material well-being. The strident voice of protest says clearly that America can and must move forward decisively to attain the goals stated in legislation of the past several decades, in presidential addresses and special messages, and in the reports of innumerable state and federal commissions.

To those who listen carefully, this clamorous voice also speaks of apprehensions generated by the impersonality of numbers. Urban populations are large and are growing still larger. Big corporations and many public agencies count their employees by the tens of thousands. Big high schools and big universities "process" thousands of graduates annually. No one doubts that a society capable of manning almost any productive enterprise with as many workers as may be required can provide abundantly for all bodily needs. But millions fear the loss of their identity in the rising tide of numbers. Indeed, millions are saying that they have already become mere statistics and have been shorn of their natural uniqueness by the punch card and the computer; and still other millions, whose skin is pigmented, angrily cry out that white men made them anonymous long ago and must now give back the badge of individuality. In all, the sense of being deprived of essential self-esteem exacerbates dissatisfaction with the shortcomings and failures of "the system." And to what pathetic measures the belittled men resort to assert their faith in self! They move to the suburbs and live in look-alike houses, treasuring the thought that they have a piece of ground and a home of their own. Some of the young affect odd dress, as if beads and sandals and fringed jackets had any distinction at all when worn by entire colonies. In the bitterest extremity those who have an overwhelming feeling of being nobody become drug addicts or commit suicide. The malaise of facelessness strikes at all too many of our 200,000,000 citizens and threatens the health of our democracy. Men who resent being considered unimportant or subject to the control of remote, technological contrivances or the regulations of distant bureaucracies are emotional men, at times irrational men, lashing out intemperately at whomever or whatever they take to be the deniers of their worth. In their wrath they could destroy the best as well as the worst in the social order.

In various ways city planners have long affirmed the value of the individual, but they must now reaffirm it with more telling effect than heretofore, as speaker after speaker declared at meetings of the American Institute of Planners in Portland, Oregon, in 1966 and in Washington, D.C., in 1967.[85] At these sessions commemorating a half century of professional growth and setting forth the prospects for the next fifty years, planners were mindful of the enthusiasm with which, in years past, they embraced the idea of the neighborhood unit and prepared city plans in which residential districts were divided into areas that might gradually be organized or reorganized to resemble Clarence Arthur Perry's ideal construct. The theory was that a relatively small area which provided for most of man's daily needs would enable people to know their neighbors, to form enduring friendships, to take an interest in parochial and city-wide affairs, and generally to fulfill themselves as human beings and good citizens. Even though changing economic and social relationships in urban areas have suggested the desirability of reformulating ideas about social interaction and spatial arrangements, the theory and the concept still have considerable usefulness. The community renewal program and more recently the model cities program have again emphasized the importance of creating intimate urban environments in which people frequently meet one another face to face, share their joys and sorrows, and participate together in improving their surroundings.

Developers of at least two new towns—Reston, Virginia, and Columbia, Maryland—have made unusual efforts to bring into being communities that by their very design and provision of services contribute to personal development. The Rouse Company, for instance, engaged experts in public administration, family life, recreation, education, health, housing, transportation, and community structure to help plan Columbia as a city in which everyone, child, teenager, or adult, could enjoy the possibility of a happy family life and a rewarding communal experience. But for every Reston or Columbia that has been planned with concern for human values, dozens of dreary tracts and half-cities have been built, not to mention some of the poorly conceived projects that have replaced slums in central cities. Often city planners have disapproved of many features of the plans but have been unable, under the law or local political conditions, to require much improvement.

Too much is at stake in the future of the United States, however, to permit amorphous, unfocused accretions to befoul the urban scene, or to allow deteriorated areas to be rebuilt with brutal megastructures and

107. New town of Reston, Virginia *(Louis B. Schlivek, photographer, and Regional Plan Association of New York)*

monolithic high-rise apartments. The commitment of the planning profession is to a rich diversity that will satisfy many tastes, styles of living, personal aspirations, and communal needs. This commitment becomes all the more relevant in view of the crises and protests which show how severely choice has been restricted for many, how fatuous have been our pretensions that social mobility was possible for everyone, and how dangerous our neglect of individual preference and individual expression has been. In a society that can replace men with machines in the office as well as in the factory and can standardize the production of everything from houses to hot cakes, the temptation to think of masses and averages and to overlook the full range of human differences is well-nigh irresistible. But the differences must be kept in mind as we replan the old cities and fashion the new ones.

A growing concern for the quality of life has begun to act as a counterforce to the facile production of carbon-copy neighborhoods, identical supermarkets, uniform playgrounds, and cliché office buildings—all symbols of disrespect for men as individuals. Millions have more leisure in which to sharpen critical judgments; millions can now afford to travel and savor the variety of the world. The environment that is nothing more than the callous manifestation of profit-seeking will someday be wholly unacceptable to large numbers of Americans. Indeed, the rising generation, or at least a significant proportion of young people, has indicated rather definitely that it is not interested in the quantitative aspects of life, material success, and conformity. Rather, its goals are a more humane society, opportunities for service, and a man-made environment in harmony with the natural environment, not destructive of it. This generation and those that follow it may succeed in placing the accent where it belongs: on the satisfaction of the special needs of individuals and groups, on distinction of design, on preservation of the cultural heritage and natural resources, and on the search for political institutions that are more sensitive to and more readily responsive to emerging social problems.

In a time when urban areas, corporations, and governmental agencies are all growing bigger, some of the goals of the newer generations may seem particularly incompatible with long-range trends. Yet the challenge to reassert the primacy of the individual can be met, and must be met. Entire new cities can be built to accommodate some of the population increase foreseen in the decades ahead, and in these cities serious efforts can be made to utilize the planning approach employed at Columbia, Maryland. The new cities, however, should be several times larger than Columbia (which will eventually have a population of 100,000), in order to provide the variety of employment, educational, and recreational opportunities needed to assure genuine freedom of choice.

Thus far the nation has taken only the first timid steps toward the development of perhaps scores of new cities required to absorb some of the millions who will be added to the population. The "New Communities Act of 1968," Title IV of the Housing and Urban Development Act of 1968, indicates that Congress expects private developers to propose new communities that will be "economically feasible" and will also include "a proper balance of housing for families of low and moderate income." Even with some of the new federal aids for home ownership, the social hopes of our legislators may be irreconcilable with the unvarnished facts

108. Model of the downtown area of the new town of Columbia, Maryland (*The Rouse Company*)

of the market place. In any event, the revolving fund established for the purpose of financing new communities will spawn but a few, and probably none of them will be large enough. The conception and promulgation of a "new communities" program commensurate with America's need for a better urban environment remains one of the great unfinished tasks of the city planning profession and of the legislators, public officials, social scientists, and civic groups with which it has alliances. New communities "varied in their scale, location and type would offer every individual or family selecting a place to live a wider range of choices in keeping with the principles of a democratic society," an A.I.P. Task Force on New Communities points out in a paper recommending the creation of a National Urban Communities Commission through congressional action, to formulate and administer a national settlement policy and to grant sponsorship franchises to qualified corporations and agencies for the development of new communities.

Notwithstanding any number of new cities that might be developed, the bulk of the expected population increase will undoubtedly accrue to metropolitan agglomerations. In these areas the struggle to dignify the individual and to eradicate the feeling among many elements, particularly the minorities, that they are insignificant and socially ineffective will be especially intense. But the Second Regional Plan of the Regional Plan Association of New York suggests that even in the densely settled Atlantic Urban Seaboard the battle against the dehumanizing effects of numbers and the downgrading of entire groups can be won. The plan maintains that additional population can be accommodated without undue crowding at least until the year 2000 if there is a will to achieve a good environment. It also contends that there can be enough open space for visual and spiritual relief, that there can be enough recreation land to serve all needs, and that there can be a sense of community.[86] Everything depends, however, upon the all-important matter of willingness not only to plan a better environment but also to sustain long-term programs for carrying out plans.

In the Atlantic Urban Region, as well as in every other large and populous area of the United States, a more truly comprehensive planning should be instituted. This planning should extend from the metropolitan planning agency to every local planning agency and should include many public and private groups not generally thought of as planning organizations. The planning done thus far in most jurisdictions has of course been comprehensive in name only. Planning for social services, economic development, governmental reorganization, and cultural advancement has usually been conducted by separate groups independently of city or regional planning. All too few attempts have been made to develop uniform assumptions and forecasts or to exchange information,

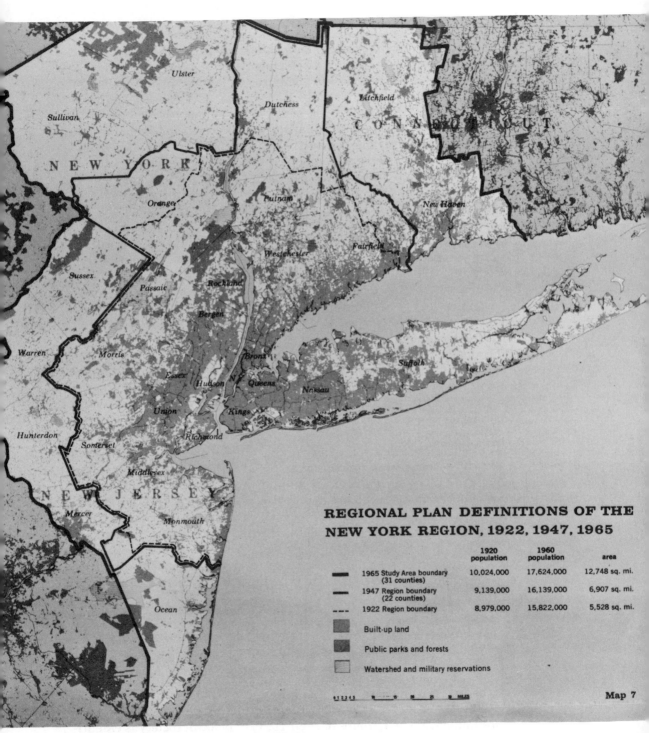

REGIONAL PLAN DEFINITIONS OF THE
NEW YORK REGION, 1922, 1947, 1965

		1920 population	1960 population	area
▬▬▬	1965 Study Area boundary (31 counties)	10,024,000	17,624,000	12,748 sq. mi.
▬▬▬	1947 Region boundary (22 counties)	9,139,000	16,139,000	6,907 sq. mi.
- - -	1922 Region boundary	8,979,000	15,822,000	5,528 sq. mi.
▨	Built-up land			
▨	Public parks and forests			
▨	Watershed and military reservations			

Map 7

109. *(Regional Plan Association of New York)*

relate goals and proposals, and plan for the same areas and periods. Now that the Housing and Urban Development Act of 1968 has broadened the definition of comprehensive planning to include planning for the provision of governmental services and for the development and utilization of human and natural resources, the way has been prepared for very broad-scale planning eliminating the old, artificial demarcations that tended to narrow the perspective of planning agencies. The definition is not yet so inclusive as would be desirable, and the planning agencies with the greatest vision will press for an even more comprehensive definition that will give them the scope they believe necessary. Ideally, the metropolitan planning agency should have the superior outlook and should establish the general framework within which local planning groups develop their plans and proposals, but it is realistic to expect that in some areas a city or county planning agency, or perhaps a civic association, will have a larger view of regional possibilities and will have to prod the metropolitan agency and other organizations to strive for a higher quality of planning.

The metropolitan agencies, however, will be operating under the scrutiny of various congressional committees, federal advisory commissions and councils, the Bureau of the Budget, and executive departments that provide grants for planning or funds for certain types of federally aided projects. There will therefore be substantial pressure on the metropolitan agencies to achieve a more integrated and effective planning process. Washington is not, of course, the seat of all wisdom, but it has become, for the planning profession as well as for many other professions, the focus of efforts to improve the laws under which a great deal of planning is done. The incentives for the widespread formation of metropolitan councils of governments and for allying metropolitan planning with these policy-forming organizations have come mainly from the national capital, though it is true that planners in particular metropolitan areas first showed how to join planning with intergovernmental cooperation and action. It is reasonable to expect that fresh ideas will continue to attract attention in Washington and that they will be embodied in laws, regulations, and reports designed to raise the quality of planning throughout the nation.

No matter how much effort metropolitan planning agencies make to elevate their own sights, though, the general tone of planning in any one multicommunity area will depend in large measure upon the kind of planning carried on in city and county planning departments. The metropolitan agency can envisage the overall systems of facilities and services and can indicate, in the main, how areas for urban expansion should be developed, but the more detailed planning which is needed to assure individuals and groups of their rightful place in society is essentially the responsibility of local agencies, especially if the principle of genuine citizen participation (rather than token participation) is to be invoked, as in the model cities program. There will be times, nevertheless, when the metropolitan agency should intercede on behalf of certain groups to protect them from parochial prejudices and infringements and to maintain desirable standards throughout the whole urban area. Metropolitan agencies have thus far been reluctant to review the comprehensive plans of local agencies and to offer the kind of guidance many state and federal officials expect, yet they must do so if areawide planning is to serve the additionally important function of stimulating discussion and illuminating issues and problems.

If it seems naïve to assume that metropolitan planning agencies, some of which are councils of governments, will actually disapprove of local plans, censure individual communities for attempting to violate generally accepted standards, and at times expose instances of discrimination, let it be remembered that in our society the chief defense against the selfishness or unfairness of persons, special interests, and intransigent political units is the large, representative body that is presumably capable of acting for the good of all. But occasionally such bodies fail to perform justly or farsightedly, and aroused citizens must then appeal to some higher authority. If the council of governments, having taken unto itself the planning function, cannot protect the larger public interest, the state or federal government may have to do so. Ultimately, redress can be sought in the courts. These, too, sometimes fail. But we could maintain no society at all if we did not make the assumption that generally the representative group will express the higher values of the majority of people. In our large urban areas we are therefore obliged to look mainly to the metropolitan planning agency and the policy-forming or decision-making council that it advises, or to the council itself, for the overall direction that will enable every part of the area to meet human needs adequately. Meanwhile, the hope abides that an even more representative type of metropolitan group, directly elected and responsible for all truly areawide functions, will emerge.

All metropolitan areas will nevertheless require certain guidelines from the federal government, in addition to those now embodied in congressional enactments, as they struggle to accommodate increases in numbers and to make sure that individual citizens enjoy the rights, amenities, and opportunities to which they are entitled. The Regional Plan Association of New York suggests that the federal government must look beyond the year 2000, when further population growth in the megalopolitan areas might result in dangerous overcrowding, by undertaking a study leading to the formulation of national policies concerning the future distribution of population. One aspect of the study should be an investigation of the effect of projected world and national population growth on living conditions in all parts of the country.

The association points out that approximately 30 billion people could live on only a tenth of the habitable land on the globe, at densities not exceeding those common in European urban areas today, "but if world population is to level off at 30 billion people, the growth rate will have to begin declining by the year 2000 at the same rate as it has been increasing in modern time."[87] The last third of the twentieth century, then, becomes a period in which the United States not only should carry on intensive public education among its own citizens to lower birth rates but should also join with other leading nations to reduce birth rates in less developed countries, especially those of Asia, Africa, and South America.

The knowledge among planners that the end of the century represents the beginning of a critical era for mankind should convince them that programs encouraging family planning bear as much relation to the comprehensive planning process as programs for providing community facilities and services. The new planning thus literally takes on global dimensions and ceases to be merely regional or national in its implications. Whatever the larger American urban regions learn about preserving the sense of community as they make room for additional hundreds of thousands or millions may have widespread application on other continents.

Truly, the opportunities for the planning profession were never greater—or its responsibilities more awesome. The world lives under the double threat of swift extinction in a nuclear holocaust or slow submergence in an uncontrolled flood of humanity. An intolerable increase in numbers could, in fact, bring on wars resulting in the cremation of mankind. Peace and birth control are therefore the indispensable requirements for the solution of human problems. The nation has an imperative need to improve its performance at the international conference table, since the lessening of tensions at various places on the globe might mean that the United States could afford to extend greater financial and technical aid to the teeming underdeveloped nations. These nations undoubtedly must achieve higher levels of economic well-being and literacy before they can be expected to make much progress in reducing their birth rates. But the ability of the United States to provide greater help to developing nations depends in some measure upon its achieving domestic peace. So long as minority groups cannot contribute fully to national productivity because their members are undereducated, unskilled, unemployed, or only partially employed, this nation will neither enjoy tranquillity at home nor be able to work effectively to reduce tensions abroad. To the extent that planners can improve living conditions in ghettos, prepare cities for the time when there will no longer be any ghettos at all, and shape urban areas to satisfy diverse human needs, they will be furthering international cooperation as well as national stability. Just as local and metropolitan planning have become immensely more challenging and difficult, so also have they gained much more than local or metropolitan significance.

To serve well in any planning capacity these days is to serve not merely the immediate community, small or large, but humanity. Planners in an earlier day were perhaps less conscious of the worldwide potentialities of their activities, but they were also less cognizant of dangers that make a new dedication to peaceful purposes essential. We do not have unlimited time to test our faith that reason and compassion will prevail in a world plagued by ignorance, mistrust, hatred, malnutrition, disease, and untimely death.

Reference Material

Chapter 1   The Spirit of Reform

1. Quoted in Flavel Shurtleff, *Carrying Out the City Plan* (New York, 1914), pp. 177–178.

2. Quoted from the act in Boston Chamber of Commerce, *Report on City Planning in Relation to the Street System in the Boston Metropolitan District* (1914), p. 3.

3. Edwards *v.* Bruorton, 184 Mass., 533.

4. Joseph W. Shirley, "The Problem of Extending the City Plan," *Proceedings of the Second National Conference on City Planning and the Problems of Congestion*, p. 165.

5. W. P. Richards, "A Street Extension Plan for the Entire District of Columbia," in U.S. Congress. Senate. 55th Cong., 3d sess., Senate Document No. 38, p. 56.

6. Quoted by Richards, *op. cit.*, p. 56.

7. Quoted from the act in Andrew W. Crawford, "How to Secure Power to Prevent Building Within the Lines of Platted Streets," *City Plan,* II (January, 1917), 9.

8. *Ibid.*, p. 9.

9. U.S. Commissioner of Labor, *The Slums of Baltimore, Chicago, New York, and Philadelphia* (Washington, 1894), pp. 12–13.

10. *Ibid.*, p. 19.

11. *Ibid.*, p. 100.

12. U.S. Commissioner of Labor, *The Housing of the Working People* (Washington, 1895), p. 419.

13. *Ibid.*, p. 439.

14. Quoted by Francis H. McLean, "South End – Boston," *Municipal Affairs,* III (March, 1899), 154.

15. Horace W. S. Cleveland, *Landscape Architecture as Applied to the Wants of the West,* ed. Roy Lubove (University of Pittsburgh Press, 1965), p. 52.

16. *Ibid.*, p. 50.

17. *Ibid.*, p. 25.

18. Advertisement quoted by William H. Wilson, *The City Beautiful Movement in Kansas City* (University of Missouri Press, 1964), p. 42.

19. Wilson, *op. cit.*, pp. 46–47.

20. Kessler's report, as quoted by Wilson, *op. cit.*, p. 48.

21. Charles Eliot, "Report of the Landscape Architect," in Massachusetts, *Report of the Board of Metropolitan Park Commissioners* (January, 1893), p. 90.

22. Quoted by Eliot C. Clarke, *Main Drainage Work of the City of Boston* (Boston, 1885), p. 14.

23. Quoted by Charles W. Eliot, *Charles Eliot, Landscape Architect* (Boston: Houghton, Mifflin, 1902), p. 353.

24. Quoted by Charles W. Eliot, *op. cit.*, pp. 354–355.

25. Acts of 1892, Chapter 342, as quoted in *Report,* p. ix.

26. *Ibid.*

27. Charles Eliot, "Report of the Landscape Architect," p. 91.

28. *Report of . . . Metropolitan Park Commissioners,* p. 12.

29. *Ibid.*, p. 12.

30. *Ibid.*, p. 71.

31. *Ibid.*, p. 75.

32. *Ibid.*, p. 79.

33. Charles Eliot, "Report of the Landscape Architect," pp. 89, 82.

34. The act as quoted in National Municipal League, *The Government of Metropolitan Areas in the United States* (New York, 1930), p. 368.

35. Report of the commission as quoted, *ibid.,* p. 369.

36. Quoted, *ibid.,* p. 370.

37. Julius F. Harder, "The City's Plan," *Municipal Affairs,* II (1898), 45.

38. *Ibid.,* p. 38.

39. *Ibid.,* p. 37.

40. *Ibid.*

41. "The City's Plan," p. 30.

42. *Ibid.*

43. *Ibid.*

44. "The City's Plan," p. 29

45. Adna F. Weber, "Growth of Cities in the United States: 1890–1900," *Municipal Affairs,* V (June, 1901), 375.

46. Quoted by Charles Mulford Robinson, "Improvement in City Life, III. Aesthetic Progress," *Atlantic Monthly,* LXXXIII (June, 1899), 772.

47. John A. Kouwenhoven, *The Columbia Historical Portrait of New York* (Garden City, N.Y., 1953), p. 394.

48. *Chicago Tribune,* June 30, 1889, p. 4.

49. *Ibid.*

50. *Chicago Tribune,* July 31, 1889, p. 4.

51. Quoted in *Chicago Tribune,* May 17, 1889, p. 6.

52. *Chicago Tribune,* June 26, 1889, p. 1.

53. Quoted in *Chicago Tribune,* September 25, 1889, p. 9.

54. *Chicago Tribune,* August 8, 1889, p. 1.

55. *Chicago Tribune,* August 4, 1889, p. 10.

56. *Chicago Tribune,* May 28, 1890, p. 4.

57. Charles C. McLaughlin, "Selected Letters of Frederick Law Olmsted" (Unpublished Ph.D. thesis, Harvard University, 1960), p. 418.

58. Louis H. Sullivan, *Autobiography of an Idea* (New York: Dover Publications, Inc., 1956), pp. 324–325.

59. Burnham Diaries, Chicago Art Institute, entry for July 27, 1896.

60. Charles Moore, *Daniel H. Burnham, Architect, Planner of Cities* (Boston and New York, 1921), II, 103.

61. *Ibid.,* p. 106.

62. *American Architect and Building News,* LV (January 9, 1897), 11.

63. *Ibid.,* p. 12.

64. *Ibid.*

65. Quoted in Herbert Croly, *The Promise of American Life* (New York, 1911), p. 19.

66. Henry Demarest Lloyd, *Wealth Against Commonwealth* (New York, 1894), p. 3.

67. *Ibid.,* p. 517.

68. Frank P. Prichard, "The Study of the Science of Municipal Government," *Annals of the American Academy of Political and Social Science,* II (July, 1891–June, 1892), 452.

69. *Ibid.,* p. 455.

70. Edward M. Hartwell, "Municipal Statistical Offices in Europe," *Municipal Affairs,* I (1897), 548.

71. League of American Cities, *The Book of American Municipalities, 1907,* p. 8.

72. *Ibid.,* p. 11.

73. Charles Moore, *Daniel H. Burnham,* II, 101.

74. Charles M. Robinson, *op. cit.* (see n. 46 above), p. 771.

75. *Municipal Affairs,* III (1899), footnote, p. 706.

76. *Ibid.,* p. 706.

77. Edwin H. Blashfield, "Municipal Art," *Municipal Affairs,* III (1899), 584.

78. George Kriehn, "The City Beautiful," *Municipal Affairs,* III (1899), 594.

79. Philip Mairet, *Pioneer in Sociology: The Life and Letters of Patrick Geddes* (London: Lund Humphries, 1957), pp. 79–81, as quoted by John Hancock, "John Nolen and the American City Planning Movement" (Unpublished Ph.D. thesis, University of Pennsylvania, 1964), p. 31.

Chapter 2   The Heyday of the City Beautiful

1. Unfortunately, careless placement of many buildings later destroyed some of L'Enfant's splendid vistas. The old Treasury blocks the view of the White House from Pennsylvania Avenue; the structure once occupied by the State Department obstructs it from New York Avenue; and the Library of Congress stands athwart the vista of the Capitol from eastern Pennsylvania Avenue.

2. Glenn Brown, *History of the United States Capitol,* 54th Cong., 1st sess., Senate Document No. 60, 2 vols. (Washington, 1900–1903), I, 3.

3. *Ibid.*

4. *Proceedings of the Thirty-fourth Annual Convention of the American Institute of Architects* (Washington, 1900), p. 15.

5. *Ibid.*

6. *Ibid.,* p. 113.

7. *Report of the Park Commission to the Senate Committee on the District of Columbia,* 57th Cong., 1st sess., Senate Report No. 166 (Washington, 1902), p. 105.

8. Quoted by H. P. Caemmerer, *Washington the National Capital,* 71st Cong., 3d sess., Senate Document No. 332 (Washington, 1932), p. 75.

9. *Ibid.*

10. *Report of the Park Commission,* p. 25.

11. *Proceedings of the Thirty-sixth Annual Convention of the American Institute of Architects* (Washington, 1903), p. 53.

12. Frederick Gutheim, "Capital Planning," review of *Monumental Washington,* by John W. Reps, in *Landscape,* XVII (Spring, 1968), 28.

13. *Report of the Park Commission,* p. 75.

14. *Ibid.,* p. 76.

15. *New York Times,* March 5, 1902, p. 8.

16. Frederick L. Olmsted, "The Town-Planning Movement in America," *Annals of the American Academy of Political and Social Science,* LI (January, 1914), 177.

17. *The Philadelphia Inquirer,* February 26, 1892, p. 1.

18. Letter of Theodore Marburg, President, Municipal Art Society of Baltimore, to Board of Park Commissioners of Baltimore, in Olmsted Brothers, *Report upon the Development of Public Grounds for Greater Baltimore* (1904), p. 8.

19. Olmsted Brothers, *Report,* p. 8.

20. *Ibid.,* p. 110.

21. John de Witt Warner, "Civic Centers," *Municipal Affairs,* VI (March, 1902), 23.

22. John Reps, *The Making of Urban America* (Princeton, 1965), p. 517.

23. Charles M. Robinson, *Modern Civic Art* (New York, 1904), p. iii.

24. J. Horace McFarland, "The Nationalization of Civic Improvement," *Charities and the Commons* [*Survey*], XVII (1906), 231, 234.

25. *Ibid.,* p. 230.

26. C. M. Robinson, *Modern Civic Art,* p. 27.

27. *Ibid.,* p. 29.

28. *Ibid.,* p. 271.

29. *Ibid.,* p. 285.

30. *Ibid.,* p. 259.

31. *Ibid.*

32. *Modern Civic Art,* p. 281.

33. *Ibid.*

34. David R. Francis, *The Universal Exposition of 1904* (St. Louis, 1913), p. 318.

35. *Ibid.,* p. 341.

36. John Nolen and F. L. Olmsted, "The Normal Requirements of American Towns and Cities in Respect to Public Open Spaces," *Charities and The Commons* [*Survey*] XVI, (June 30, 1906), 411.

37. *Ibid.,* p. 416.

38. *Ibid.,* p. 417.

39. *Ibid.,* p. 418.

40. *Ibid.*, p. 426.

41. Civic League of St. Louis, *A City Plan for St. Louis* (St. Louis, 1907), p. 37.

42. *Ibid.*, p. 53.

43. *Ibid.*

44. *A City Plan for St. Louis,* pp. 37–39.

45. *Ibid.*, p. 14.

46. *Ibid.*, p. 11.

47. "The Movement in Chicago," editorial in *Chicago Post,* quoted in *Current Literature,* XXXII (April, 1902), 421.

48. *Chicago Tribune,* December 29, 1907, as quoted by John Hancock, "John Nolen and the American City Planning Movement" (Unpublished Ph.D thesis, University of Pennsylvania, 1964), p. 117.

49. J. Horace McFarland, "The Growth of City Planning in America," *Charities,* XIX (February 1, 1908), 1528.

50. Robert W. de Forest, "The Practical Side of City Planning," *Charities,* XIX (1907–1908), 1550.

51. *Ibid.*

52. *Ibid.*

53. Frederick S. Lamb, "New York City Improvement Report," *Charities,* XIX (1908), 1536.

54. Benjamin C. Marsh, "City Planning in Justice to the Working Population," *Charities,* XIX (Feb. 1, 1908), 1514.

55. Quoted by Marsh in *An Introduction to City Planning: Democracy's Challenge to the American City* (New York, 1909), p. 107.

56. *Ibid.*

57. Simon Patten, "A Program of Social Work," a chapter of *The New Basis of Civilization, Charities,* XVIII (April 20, 1907), 97.

58. B. C. Marsh, "City Planning in Justice to the Working Population," p. 1514.

59. John Martin, "The Exhibit of Congestion Interpreted," *Charities,* XX (April 4, 1908), 27.

60. B. C. Marsh, "City Planning in Justice to the Working Population," p. 1515.

61. *Ibid.*, pp. 1515–1516.

62. *Ibid.*, p. 1516.

63. *Ibid.*, pp. 1516–1517.

64. *Ibid.*, p. 1517.

65. *Ibid.*, p. 1518.

66. *Ibid.*

67. B. C. Marsh, *Lobbyist for the People: A Record of Fifty Years* (Washington, D.C., 1953), p. 19.

68. B. C. Marsh, *An Introduction to City Planning* (New York, 1909), p. 98.

69. "Garden Cities Association of America," *Charities,* XVII (November 17, 1907), 286.

70. Quoted by C. M. Robinson, "The City Plan Exhibition," *Survey,* XXII (1909), 314.

71. *Ibid.,* p. 314.

72. *Ibid.,* p. 317.

73. *Ibid.,* p. 318.

74. *Ibid.*

75. "The Pittsburgh Survey," *Survey,* XIX (March 7, 1908), 1666.

76. Herbert Croly, *The Promise of American Life* (New York, 1911), pp. 24, 22.

77. *Ibid.,* p. 24.

78. *City Planning,* U.S. 61st Cong., 2d sess., S. Doc. 422 (1910), p. 59.

79. *Ibid.,* p. 76.

80. *Ibid.*

81. Letter of Hon. James Bryce, British Embassy, Washington, May 19, 1909, in *City Planning,* p. 58.

82. *City Planning,* p. 66.

83. *Ibid.,* p. 69.

84. *Ibid.,* p. 70.

85. *Ibid.,* p. 74.

86. *Ibid.,* p. 75.

87. *Ibid.,* p. 76.

88. *Ibid.,* p. 61.

89. *Ibid.*

90. *Ibid.*

91. *City Planning,* p. 79.

92. *Ibid.,* p. 92.

93. *Ibid.,* p. 73.

94. *Ibid.,* p. 78.

95. Daniel H. Burnham and Edward H. Bennett, *Plan of Chicago* (Chicago, 1909), pp. 36–37.

96. *Ibid.,* p. 39.

97. *Ibid.,* p. 36.

98. *Ibid.,* p. 91.

99. Walter L. Fisher, "Legal Aspects of the Plan of Chicago," *Plan of Chicago,* p. 154.

100. *Ibid.,* pp. 155–156.

101. *Plan of Chicago,* p. 8.

102. *Ibid.,* pp. 32–33.

103. *Ibid.*, p. 32.

104. George E. Hooker, "A Plan for Chicago," *Survey*, XXII (September 4, 1909), 790.

105. *Plan of Chicago*, p. 108.

106. *Ibid.*, p. 109.

107. *Ibid.*, pp. 83–84.

108. *Ibid.*, p. 778.

Chapter 3 Science and the City Functional

1. "Plan for a Boston Plan," *Survey*, XXII (June 5, 1909), 396.

2. *Ibid.*

3. *Ibid.*

4. *Ibid.*

5. *Ibid.*

6. Paul U. Kellogg, "Boston's Level Best," *Survey*, XXII (June 5, 1909), 392.

7. Mentioned by Kellogg, *loc. cit.*

8. John Nolen, "General Planning Board for Metropolitan Boston," *National Municipal Review*, I (April, 1912), 234.

9. John F. Fitzgerald, "Address of Welcome," *Proceedings of the Fourth National Conference on City Planning*, p. 2.

10. Frederick L. Olmsted, "Introductory Address on City Planning," *Proceedings of the Second National Conference on City Planning and the Problems of Congestion*, p. 15.

11. *Ibid.*, p. 16.

12. *Ibid.*

13. *Ibid.*, p. 18.

14. *Ibid.*, p. 15.

15. Cass Gilbert and F. L. Olmsted, *Report of the New Haven Civic Improvement Commission to the New Haven Civic Improvement Committee*, p. 99.

16. *Ibid.*, p. 130.

17. George B. Ford, "Recent City-Planning Reports," *National Municipal Review*, I (April, 1912), 262.

18. Cass Gilbert and F. L. Olmsted, *op. cit.*, pp. 13–14.

19. *Ibid.*, p. 14.

20. *Ibid.*, p. 13.

21. *Ibid.*, p. 16.

22. *Ibid.*, p. 15.

23. George B. Ford, "Digging Deeper in City Planning," an address before the Seventh Annual Convention of the American Civic Association, *American*

City (March, 1912), p. 558, as quoted in Norman J. Johnston, "Harland Bartholomew: His Comprehensive Plans and Science of Planning" (Unpublished Ph.D. thesis, University of Pennsylvania, 1964), p. 78.

24. Ford's address as quoted in Johnson, p. 80.

25. George B. Ford, "The City Scientific," *Proceedings of the Fifth National Conference on City Planning,* p. 31.

26. *Ibid.,* p. 32.

27. *Ibid.*

28. "The City Scientific," p. 37.

29. "Efficiency in City Planning," *American City,* VIII (February, 1913), 139.

30. *Ibid.,* pp. 142–143.

31. Charles M. Robinson, *The Improvement of Fort Wayne, Indiana* (1910), p. 52.

32. George E. Kessler, *A City Plan for Dallas,* (1910), p. 8.

33. *Ibid.*

34. Pittsburgh Civic Commission, "City Planning and the Cost of Living in Pittsburgh," in Frederick Law Olmsted, *Pittsburgh: Main Thoroughfares and the Down Town District* (Pittsburgh, 1911), p. xv.

35. Olmsted, *Pittsburgh,* p. 1.

36. *Ibid.,* p. 94.

37. *Ibid.,* p. 21.

38. F. L. Olmsted, "Introductory Address on City Planning," *Proceedings of the Second National Conference on City Planning and the Problems of Congestion,* p. 30.

39. Municipal Plans Commission, *Plan of Seattle* (Seattle, 1911), p. 45.

40. *Ibid.,* p. 131.

41. John Nolen, *Madison: A Model City* (1911), pp. 126–128.

42. *Ibid., passim.*

43. *Madison,* p. 136.

44. Quoted by Nolen in *Madison,* p. 137.

45. Arnold W. Brunner, F. L. Olmsted, and B. J. Arnold, *A City Plan for Rochester,* p. 8.

46. *Ibid.* p. 25.

47. Edward T. Hartman, "Causes of Congestion in Boston," *Proceedings of the Second National Conference on City Planning and the Problems of Congestion,* p. 63.

48. Grosvenor Atterbury, "An Introductory Outline," *Proceedings of the Second National Conference,* p. 68.

49. Lawrence Veiller, "The Safe Load of Population on Land," *Proceedings of the Second National Conference,* p. 77.

50. *Ibid.*

51. Edward E. Pratt, "Relief Through Proper Distribution of Factories," *Proceedings of the Second National Conference*, p. 111.

52. *Ibid.*

53. *Ibid.*

54. Henry C. Wright, "Rapid Transit in Relation to the Housing Problem," *Proceedings of the Second National Conference*, p. 130.

55. Frederick C. Howe, "The Municipal Real Estate Policies of German Cities," *Proceedings of the Third National Conference on City Planning*, p. 15.

56. *Ibid.*, p. 23.

57. J. Randolph Coolidge, Jr., "The Problem of the Blighted District," *Proceedings of the Fourth National Conference on City Planning*, p. 105.

58. Edith Elmer Wood, *Housing of the Unskilled Wage Earner* (New York: Macmillan, 1919), p. 7.

59. Interview with Flavel Shurtleff, Boston, June 12, 1965.

60. Interview with Shurtleff.

61. Flavel Shurtleff, *Carrying Out the City Plan* (New York, 1914), p. 3.

62. *Ibid.*, p. 148.

63. *Ibid.*, p. 158.

64. *Ibid.*, p. 202.

65. *Ibid.*, p. 206.

66. *Ibid.*, p. 207.

67. Arnold W. Brunner and John M. Carrère, *Preliminary Report for a City Plan for Grand Rapids*, p. 39.

68. John Nolen, *Replanning Small Cities* (New York: B. W. Huebsch, 1912), p. 161.

69. *Ibid.*

70. *Ibid.*, p. 162.

71. *Ibid.*

72. *Ibid.*

73. A. W. Crawford, "Certain Aspects of City Financing and City Planning," *Proceedings of the Sixth National Conference on City Planning*, p. 62.

74. George McAneny, "Remarks" at the closing dinner, *Proceedings of the Sixth National Conference on City Planning*, p. 339.

75. Quoted by Charles H. Wacker, "Gaining Public Support for a City Planning Movement," *Proceedings of the Fifth National Conference on City Planning*, p. 227.

76. F. L. Olmsted, "President's Address of Welcome," *Proceedings of the Third National Conference on City Planning*, p. 12.

77. F. L. Olmsted, "A City Planning Program," *Proceedings of the Fifth National Conference on City Planning*, p. 16.

78. *Ibid.*, pp. 2–3.

79. *Ibid.*, p. 2.

80. *Ibid.*, pp. 9–10.

81. *Ibid.*, p. 2.

82. William A. Magee, "The Organization and Functions of a City Planning Commission," *Proceedings of the Fifth National Conference on City Planning,* p. 79.

83. *Ibid.*, p. 84.

84. "Report of the Committee on Legislation," *Proceedings of the Fifth National Conference on City Planning,* pp. 248–250.

85. George B. Ford, "Report of the Conference of Delegates from National Organizations to Consider City Planning Cooperation," *Proceedings of the Seventh National Conference on City Planning,* p. 233.

86. Walter D. Moody, "How to Go About City Planning," *City Plan,* I (March, 1915), p. 16.

87. National Municipal League, *A Model City Charter and Municipal Home Rule* (Philadelphia, 1916), p. 51.

88. *Ibid.*, p. 51.

89. F. L. Olmsted, "Introduction," in *City Planning,* ed. John Nolen (New York, 1916), p. 1.

90. *Ibid.*, p. 3.

91. Nelson P. Lewis, *The Planning of the Modern City* (New York, 1916), p. iii.

92. *Ibid.*, p. 1.

93. *Ibid.*, pp. 17–18.

94. *Ibid.*

95. *Planning of the Modern City,* pp. 412–413.

96. *Ibid.*, p. 298.

97. *Ibid.*, p. 403.

98. George Hooker, "Remarks" at closing dinner, *Proceedings of the Eighth National Conference on City Planning,* p. 271.

99. *Ibid.*, p. 272.

100. Philip Kates, "Remarks" in discussion of "Certain Principles of a Uniform City Planning Code," *Proceedings of the Third National Conference on City Planning,* p. 257.

101. Philip Kates, "A National Department of Municipalities," *American City,* VI (January, 1912), 405.

102. Thomas Adams, "State, City and Town Planning," *Proceedings of the Eighth National Conference on City Planning,* pp. 141–142.

103. John Nolen, "Planning Problems of Smaller Cities in the United States," *Proceedings of the Eighth National Conference on City Planning,* p. 190.

104. Frank B. Williams, "Remarks" in discussion of Lawrence Veiller's paper entitled "Protecting Residential Districts," *Proceedings of the Sixth National Conference on City Planning,* p. 115.

105. Alfred Bettman, "Remarks" in discussion of Veiller's paper, *Proceedings of the Sixth National Conference on City Planning,* p. 190.

106. *Ibid.,* p. 113.

107. Alfred Bettman, "Brief in Euclid Village Zoning Case," *City and Regional Planning Papers* (Cambridge, Mass.: Harvard University Press, 1946), p. 162.

108. Advertisement in the *Evening Post,* New York, March 6, 1916, reproduced in American Institute of Architects, *City Planning Progress* (Washington, 1917), p. 124.

109. Edward M. Bassett, "Remarks" in discussion of paper entitled "Districting by Municipal Regulation," *Proceedings of the Eighth National Conference on City Planning,* pp. 161–162.

110. *Ibid.,* p. 161.

111. *Ibid.,* p. 160.

112. Harrison, Ballard & Allen, *Plan for Rezoning the City of New York* (New York: City Planning Commission, 1950), p. 8.

113. Frank B. Williams, Letter to the editor, *American City,* May, 1916, quoted by Harold S. Buttenheim in "Frank Backus Williams, 1864–1954," *Journal of the American Institute of Planners,* XXI (Winter 1955), 61.

114. *Ibid.*

115. George B. Ford, "Remarks" in panel discussion, *Proceedings of Eighth National Conference on City Planning,* p. 165.

116. *Ibid.,* p. 167.

117. *Ibid.,* p. 170.

118. Williams, "Letter," p. 61.

119. G. B. Ford, "Remarks," pp. 164–165.

120. Charles H. Cheney, "Districting Progress and Procedure in California," *Proceedings of the Ninth National Conference on City Planning,* p. 185.

121. American Institute of Architects, *City Planning Progress* (Washington, 1917), p. iii.

122. *Ibid.,* p. 2.

123. *Ibid.,* p. 3.

124. Lawrence Veiller, "Districting by Municipal Regulation," *Proceedings of the Eighth National Conference on City Planning,* p. 158.

125. *City Planning Progress,* p. 194.

126. A. W. Crawford, "Remarks," *Proceedings of the Eighth National Conference on City Planning,* p. 83.

127. F. L. Olmsted, "War Housing," *Proceedings of the Tenth National Conference on City Planning,* p. 90.

128. *Ibid.,* p. 99.

129. F. L. Olmsted, "Planning Residential Subdivisions," *Proceedings of the Eleventh National Conference on City Planning,* p. 6.

130. *Ibid.*

131. Quoted in editorial entitled "Why Not Make States Out of Our Largest Cities," *American City,* X (January, 1914), 1.

132. J. H. McFarland, "Shall Our Great Cities Be Made States?" Answers Pro and Con to Questions on This Subject as Propounded in the January Number, *American City,* X (February, 1914), 142.

133. Frederic C. Howe, "Shall Our Great Cities Be Made States?" *American City,* X (February, 1914), 142.

134. John H. Gundlach, "A City's Control of Outlying Districts," *American City,* IV (January–June, 1911), 224.

135. Laws of Pennsylvania, General Assembly, No. 226, of 1913, as quoted by F. Shurtleff, *Carrying Out the City Plan* (New York, 1914), p. 300.

136. Letter of Charles D. Norton to Frederic A. Delano, New York, Nov. 24, 1921, Files of the Regional Plan Association, New York, p. 7.

137. *Ibid.,* p. 3.

138. Memorandum in Norton letter, p. 7.

139. *Ibid.,* p. 8.

140. *Ibid.*

141. Letter of John B. Pine to C. D. Norton, quoted in letter of Norton to Delano, pp. 9–10.

142. Letter of Frederic B. Pratt to Norton, quoted in letter of Norton to Delano, p. 11.

143. Norton letter, p. 12.

144. *Ibid.,* p. 13.

145. Thomas Adams, "Regional and Town Planning," *Proceedings of the Eleventh National Conference on City Planning,* p. 77.

146. *Ibid.,* p. 77.

147. *Ibid.,* p. 88.

148. *Ibid.,* p. 79.

149. Morris Knowles, "Engineering Problems of Regional Planning," *Proceedings of the Eleventh National Conference on City Planning,* p. 132.

150. *Ibid.,* p. 130.

151. *Ibid.,* p. 132.

152. W. J. Donald, "Regional Planning in Motion," *Proceedings of the Eleventh National Conference on City Planning,* pp. 107, 111.

153. A. W. Crawford, "A Proposed Federal Agency to Deal With Housing, Town Planning and Other Municipal Affairs," *American City,* XX (February, 1919), 179.

154. Harlean James, "Service—The Keynote of a New Cabinet Department," *American Review of Reviews,* LVIX (February, 1919), 187–188.

155. F. L. Ackerman, "Where Goes the City-Planning Movement?" *Journal of the American Institute of Architects,* VII (December, 1919), 519–520.

156. John Nolen, "Planning Problems of Industrial Cities—Niagara Falls as an Illustration," *Proceedings of the Eleventh National Conference on City Planning,* pp. 30–31.

Chapter 4 City Planning in the Age of Business

1. William E. Harmon, "Playgrounds in New Land Subdivisions," *City Planning,* II (April, 1926), 86.
2. Frederic A. Delano, "Skyscrapers," *American City,* XXXIV (January, 1926), 1.
3. *Ibid.,* p. 3.
4. *Ibid.,* p. 8.
5. B. Antrim Haldeman, "Report on Regional Planning," *Proceedings of the Twelfth National Conference on City Planning,* p. 128.
6. *Ibid.,* p. 126.
7. Thomas Adams, "Remarks," *Proceedings of Twelfth National Conference,* p. 128.
8. *Ibid.,* p. 129.
9. Herbert Hoover, "Foreword," U.S. Department of Commerce, Advisory Committee on Zoning, *A Standard State Zoning Enabling Act* (Washington, 1924), p. iv.
10. *Ibid.*
11. Quoted by Edward M. Bassett, "Present Attitude of the Courts Toward Zoning," *Proceedings of Fifteenth National Conference on City Planning,* pp. 128–129.
12. *Standard State Zoning Enabling Act,* p. 9, n. 41.
13. *Standard State Act,* p. 6.
14. *Standard State Act,* p. 6, n. 25.
15. Walter H. Blucher, "Zoning and Quitting," *Proceedings of the First Annual Indiana State-wide Planning Conference,* p. 41.
16. *Ibid.*
17. George H. Gray, "Remarks," *Proceedings of Thirteenth National Conference on City Planning,* p. 66.
18. Robert H. Whitten, "Zoning and Living Conditions," *Proceedings of Thirteenth National Conference,* p. 28.
19. George B. Ford, "What Planning Has Done for Cities," *Proceedings of Sixteenth National Conference on City Planning,* pp. 18–19.
20. Letter of Charles D. Norton to Frederic A. Delano, Nov. 24, 1921, p. 18.
21. Memorandum of Jan. 31, 1921, quoted in letter of Norton to Delano, p. 20.
22. *Ibid.*
23. *Ibid.*

24. Memorandum, p. 21.

25. *Ibid.*

26. *Ibid.*

27. Minutes of meeting of trustees of the Russell Sage Foundation, Feb. 4, 1921, as corrected at meeting of May 17, 1921, quoted by Norton in letter to Delano, Nov. 24, 1921, p. 26.

28. Quoted by R. L. Duffus, *Mastering A Metropolis: Planning the Future of the New York Region* (New York, 1930), p. 126.

29. Quoted by Duffus, p. 127.

30. *Ibid.*

31. Regional Plan of New York and Its Environs, Miscellaneous Papers, No. 1.

32. Gordon Whitnall, "City and Regional Planning in Los Angeles," *Proceedings of the Sixteenth National Conference on City Planning,* p. 110.

33. Graham R. Taylor, "City-County Challenge West and East," editorial in *Chicago Daily News,* Feb. 4, 1922, reproduced in *Proceedings of First Regional Planning Conference of Los Angeles County, California,* p. 23.

34. Quoted in Daniel H. Burnham, Jr., and Robert Kingery, *Planning the Region of Chicago* (1956), p. 21.

35. Quoted in Burnham and Kingery, p. 23.

36. Quoted in Theodora K. Hubbard and Henry V. Hubbard, *Our Cities To-day and To-morrow. A Survey of Planning and Zoning Progress in the United States* (Cambridge, Mass., 1929), p. 50.

37. Alfred Bettman, "How to Lay Out Regions for Planning," *Planning Problems of Town, City, and Region: Papers and Discussions at the International City and Regional Planning Conference, 1925,* p. 289.

38. Quoted in Mel Scott, *The San Francisco Bay Area: A Metropolis in Perspective* (Berkeley: University of California Press, 1959), p. 191.

39. Letter of Russell Van Nest Black to the author, May 5, 1965, p. 2.

40. R. V. Black, "Theory of Planning the Region as Exemplified by the Philadelphia Tri-State Plan," *City Planning,* VI (July, 1930), 185.

41. *Ibid.,* p. 187.

42. *Ibid., passim.*

43. Letter of Black to the author, May 5, 1965, p. 2.

44. Letter of Black to the author, Nov. 4, 1966, p. 2.

45. Charles A. Beard, "Some Aspects of Regional Planning," *American Political Science Review,* XX (May, 1926), 276.

46. *Ibid.,* p. 277.

47. *Ibid.,* p. 278.

48. *Ibid.,* p. 282.

49. *Ibid.*

50. Commission of Housing and Regional Planning, *Report to Governor Alfred E. Smith,* p. 67.

51. Lewis Mumford, article in *Survey Graphic,* May 1, 1925, p. 151, as quoted in Commission of Housing and Regional Planning, *Report,* p. 66.

52. Commission of Housing and Regional Planning, *Report,* p. 64.

53. *Ibid.,* p. 72.

54. *Ibid.,* p. 73.

55. Thomas Adams, *Planning the New York Region* (New York, 1927), p. 76.

56. *Ibid.,* p. 77.

57. *Ibid.,* p. 124.

58. *Ibid.,* p. 125.

59. Interview with Flavel Shurtleff, Boston, June 12, 1965.

60. Adams, *op. cit.,* p. 124.

61. *Ibid.*

62. Adams, *op. cit.,* p. 25.

63. Thomas H. Reed, "The Government of Metropolitan Areas," *Planning Problems of Town, City, and Region: Papers and Discussions at the Seventeenth National Conference on City Planning,* p. 302.

64. *Ibid.,* p. 311.

65. *Ibid.,* p. 302.

66. *Ibid.,* pp. 306–307.

67. *Ibid.,* pp. 308–309.

68. *Ibid.,* p. 310.

69. *Ibid.,* p. 311.

70. George B. Ford and E. P. Goodrich, *The Official City Plan of Cincinnati, Ohio* (1925), p. 51.

71. G. B. Ford, "Planning the Attractive Town," *Proceedings of the Thirteenth National Conference on City Planning,* p. 198.

72. *City Plan of Cincinnati,* p. 31.

73. G. B. Ford, "The Cincinnati City Plan is Now Law," *City Planning,* II (April, 1926), 117.

74. Alfred Bettman, "The Ohio Statute," *City Planning,* II (April, 1926), 119–120.

75. Harland Bartholomew, "Public Support and Understanding," *City Planning,* II (April, 1926), 124.

76. Quoted in John L. Hancock, "John Nolen and the American City Planning Movement" (Unpublished Ph.D. thesis, University of Pennsylvania, 1964), p. 368.

77. Quoted in Urbanism Committee of National Resources Committee, *Urban Planning and Land Policies* (Washington, 1939), p. 92.

78. F. L. Olmsted, quoted in Urbanism Committee, *Urban Planning,* p. 86.

79. Quoted in John Hancock, *op. cit.,* p. 393.

80. Frank F. Jonsberg, "Address of Welcome," *Proceedings of Eighteenth National Conference on City Planning*, p. 1.

81. F. L. Olmsted, "The Planning of Pleasure Resort Communities," *Proceedings of Eighteenth National Conference*, p. 92.

82. *Ibid.*, p. 103.

83. Robert Whitten, "Combined Zoning and Planning Control of Unsubdivided Areas," *Proceedings of Eighteenth National Conference*, p. 57.

84. *Ibid.*, p. 58.

85. *Ibid.*, p. 59.

86. Urbanism Committee, *Urban Planning*, p. 119.

87. Alfred Bettman, "Village of Euclid *et al. v.* Ambler Realty Company, Brief, *Amici Curiae*. In the Supreme Court of the United States," in his *City and Regional Planning Papers* (Cambridge, Mass., 1946), p. 164.

88. *Ibid.*, p. 166.

89. Bettman, "The Decision of the Supreme Court of the United States in the Euclid Village Zoning Case," *City and Regional Planning Papers*, p. 51.

90. Bertram H. Saunders, "Zoning: What Can Be Done for It Where the Courts Are Unfavorable?" *American City*, XXXIV (March, 1926), 238.

91. Coleman Woodbury, "The Size of Retail Business Districts in the Chicago Metropolitan Region," *Journal of Land & Public Utility Economics*, IV (July, 1928), 91.

92. George H. Coffin, Jr., "To What Extent Should Business Areas Be Limited?" *Municipal and County Engineering*, LXXXI (October, 1926), 249.

93. *Ibid.*, p. 250.

94. U.S. Department of Commerce, Advisory Committee on City Planning and Zoning, *A Standard City Planning Enabling Act* (Washington, 1928), p. 16.

95. *Ibid.*, p. 16.

96. *Ibid.*, p. 17, n. 42.

97. "General Statement," *Standard Enabling Act*, p. 1.

98. *Ibid.*, p. 49.

99. *Ibid.*, p. 50.

100. *Ibid.*, p. 51.

101. *Ibid.*, p. 49, n. 135.

102. *Ibid.*, p. 44, n. 123.

103. John Nolen, "Twenty Years of City Planning Progress in the United States," *Planning Problems of Town, City, and Region: Papers and Discussions at the Nineteenth National Conference on City Planning*, p. 7.

104. *Ibid.*, p. 8.

105. *Ibid.*, pp. 18–19.

106. Lewis Mumford, "The Next Twenty Years in City Planning," *Papers . . . at Nineteenth National Conference*, p. 50.

107. *Ibid.*, p. 47.

108. *Ibid.*, p. 57.

109. *Ibid.*, pp. 57–58.

110. John Ihlder, "How City Planning Affects Real Estate Values," *Papers . . . at Nineteenth National Conference*, p. 73.

111. Thomas Adams, "Regional Highways and Parkways in Relation to Regional Parks," *Papers . . . at Nineteenth National Conference*, p. 176.

112. Quoted in C. E. Rightor, "The Preparation of a Long-term Financing Program," Publication No. 5, Municipal Administration Service, 1927, p. 10.

113. "Budgeting of Capital Expenditures," *Papers . . . at the Twentieth National Conference on City Planning*, p. 236.

114. Walter H. Blucher, "Planning a Housing Project," *City Planning*, X (July, 1934), 114.

115. Detroit City Plan Commission, *Annual Report – 1928*, p. 14.

116. *Ibid.*, p. 16.

117. Edith E. Wood, "Housing in My Time," *Shelter*, III (1938), 4.

118. Quoted in *American City*, XXXV (November, 1926), 620.

119. Edith E. Wood, "Is Government Aid Necessary in House Financing?" *Proceedings of the Tenth National Conference on Housing*, p. 59.

120. *Ibid.*, pp. 55–56.

121. *Ibid.*, p. 61.

122. Lawrence Veiller, "Slum Clearance," *Proceedings of Tenth National Conference on Housing*, p. 80.

123. Harold S. Buttenheim, "Slum Improvement by Private Effort," *Proceedings of Tenth National Conference on Housing*, p. 93.

124. *Ibid.*, p. 92.

125. *Ibid.*, p. 93.

126. Robert Whitten, "A Neighborhood Scientifically Conceived and Developed," *Proceedings of the Tenth National Conference on Housing*, p. 182.

127. Louis Brownlow, "Building for the Motor Age," *Proceedings of the Tenth National Conference on Housing*, p. 151.

128. John Nolen, "Remarks," in discussion of talk by Louis Brownlow, *Papers and Discussions at the Twenty-first National Conference on City Planning*, p. 12.

129. *Ibid.*, p. 13.

130. John M. Glenn, Lilian Brandt, and F. Emerson Andrews, *Russell Sage Foundation, 1907–1946*, II, 451.

131. Committee on the Regional Plan of New York and Its Environs, *The Graphic Regional Plan*, Vol. II of *Regional Plan of New York and Its Environs*, p. 132.

132. *Ibid.,* p. 408.

133. *Ibid.,* p. 409.

134. *Ibid.,* pp. 149–150.

135. Melvin M. Webber, "Transportation Planning for the Metropolis," *Urban Research and Policy Planning,* ed. Leo F. Schnore and Henry Fagin (Beverly Hills, Calif., Sage Publications, Inc., 1967), p. 391.

136. Thomas Adams, E. M. Bassett, and Robert Whitten, "Problems of Planning Unbuilt Areas," *Neighborhood and Community Planning,* p. 256.

137. *Ibid.,* p. 263.

138. "Report of Conference," in John M. Gaus, *The Graduate School of Design and the Education of Planners* (Cambridge, Mass., 1943), Appendix, p. 48.

139. *Ibid.,* p. 49.

140. *Ibid.,* p. 50.

141. Henry V. Hubbard, "The Profession of City Planning," *City Planning,* III (July, 1927), 203.

142. The Planning Foundation of America, *New Cities for the New Age,* p. 23.

143. *Ibid.*

144. Quoted in Arthur M. Schlesinger, Jr., *The Age of Roosevelt: The Crisis of the Old Order, 1919–1933,* p. 89.

Chapter 5   A New Perspective: The Urban Community in National Life

1. Federated Societies on Planning and Parks: Joint Committee on Bases of Sound Land Policy, *What About the Year 2000?* (Washington, 1929), p. 2.

2. *Ibid.,* p. 3.

3. *Ibid.,* pp. 13–14.

4. *Ibid.,* p. 145.

5. *Ibid.,* p. 69.

6. Committee on Recent Economic Changes, *Report,* p. xxii.

7. *Ibid.,* p. xxi.

8. Wesley C. Mitchell, "A Review," in *Recent Economic Changes in the United States* (textbook edition) (New York, 1929), p. 910.

9. *Ibid.,* p. 909.

10. President's Research Committee on Social Trends, *Recent Social Trends in the United States* (New York, 1933), p. xi.

11. Herbert Hoover, "Foreword," *Recent Social Trends in the United States,* p. v.

12. R. D. McKenzie, *The Metropolitan Community* (New York, 1933), p. 315.

13. *Ibid.,* p. 316.

14. *Ibid.,* p. 318.

15. Quoted by Edward M. Bassett in "Difficulties During the Depression," *City Planning,* VIII (April, 1932), 134.

16. John E. Surratt, "The Effect of the Depression on City Building in Texas," *City Planning*, VIII (October, 1932), 204.

17. Flavel Shurtleff, "What the Plan Commissions Are Doing," *American Civic Annual, 1932*, p. 178.

18. Edith Elmer Wood, *Recent Trends in American Housing* (New York, 1931), p. 286.

19. *Ibid.*

20. *Recent Trends . . .* , p. 287.

21. Herbert Hoover, "Address," in *Housing Objectives and Programs*, Vol. XI of *The President's Conference on Home Building and Home Ownership*, p. 4.

22. *Ibid.*, p. 1.

23. *Ibid.*, p. 3.

24. Ray Lyman Wilbur, "Foreword," *Slums, Large-Scale Housing and Decentralization*, Vol. III of *The President's Conference*, p. xii.

25. *Slums, Large-Scale Housing and Decentralization*, p. 108.

26. *Ibid.*, p. 110.

27. The Editors of *Fortune, Housing America*, p. 21.

28. *Ibid.*, p. 131.

29. Orrin C. Lester, "Financing New Housing," in *Planning Problems of Town, City and Region, 1932*, p. 42.

30. *Ibid.*, p. 45.

31. *Ibid.*, p. 42.

32. Robert D. Kohn, "What Next in Housing? The Opportunity," in *Planning Problems of Town, City and Region, 1932*, p. 27.

33. Franklin D. Roosevelt, "Growing Up By Plan," *Survey*, LXVII (Feb. 1, 1932), 483.

34. Thomas Adams, *The Building of the City*, p. 66.

35. *Ibid.*, p. 588.

36. *Ibid.*, p. 90.

37. *Ibid.*, p. 92.

38. *Ibid.*, p. 216.

39. E. E. Wood, *Recent Trends in American Housing*, p. 279.

40. Lewis Mumford, "The Plan of New York, I," *New Republic*, LXXI (June 15, 1932), 122.

41. *Ibid.*, p. 123.

42. Lewis Mumford, "The Plan of New York, II," *New Republic*, LXXI (June 22, 1932), 152.

43. *Ibid.*, p. 151.

44. Thomas Adams, "A Communication in Defense of the Regional Plan," *New Republic*, LXXI (July 6, 1932), 208.

45. Thomas Adams, *The Building of the City*, p. 202.

46. Jacob L. Crane, Jr., "State Planning in Illinois and Iowa," *City Planning,* VIII (April, 1932), 94.

47. *Ibid.,* p. 96.

48. *Ibid.,* p. 94.

49. *Ibid.,* p. 95.

50. Quoted by Joseph T. Woodruff in "Greater Pennsylvania Council," *City Planning,* VIII (April, 1932), 129.

51. Quoted in "Report on Land Utilization Conference," *Agricultural Review,* I (December, 1931), 11.

52. Quoted in Harold S. Buttenheim, "Trends in Present-day City and Regional Planning in the United States, 1932," *City Planning,* IX (April, 1933), 81.

53. Jacob L. Crane, Jr., "Whither State Planning?" in *Problems of Town, City and Region, 1932,* p. 143.

54. *Ibid.,* p. 149.

55. President's Research Committee on Social Trends, *Recent Social Trends,* p. xxxiii and p. lxxi.

56. *Ibid.,* pp. lxxiii–lxxiv.

57. *Ibid.,* p. lxxiii.

58. President Roosevelt's *Message to Congress on Muscle Shoals Development,* House Doc. 15, 73rd Cong., 1st sess., p. 1, as quoted by Charles L. Hodge, *The Tennessee Valley Authority* (Washington, 1938), pp. 33–34.

59. Harold L. Ickes, "Federal Emergency Administration of Public Works," *Planning and National Recovery* (1933), p. 22.

60. *Ibid.,* p. 25.

61. Charles W. Eliot II, "Planning by the Federal Government," *Planning and National Recovery* (1933), p. 38.

62. Ickes, *op. cit.,* p. 23.

63. *Ibid.,* p. 24.

64. *Ibid.,* pp. 24-25.

65. Letter of R. V. Black to the author, Jan. 5, 1967.

66. Philip H. Elwood, "Briefs from the Progress of State Planning Boards," in *Planning Problems of City, Region, State and Nation* (1934), p. 76.

67. Lawrence Sheridan, "Organization and Personnel of State Planning Boards," in *Planning Problems . . .* (1934), p. 75.

68. L. D. Tilton, "Briefs from the Progress of State Planning Boards," *Planning Problems . . .* (1934), p. 86.

69. Quoted in National Resources Board, *State Planning: Review of Activities and Progress* (June, 1935), p. 269.

70. Quoted by National Resources Committee, *State Planning: Programs and Accomplishments* (December, 1936), p. 97.

71. *Ibid.,* p. 98.

72. Charles W. Eliot II, "New Approaches to Urban Planning," *Planning for the Future of American Cities, 1935,* p. 111.

73. Ladislas Segoe, "City Planning and the Urbanism Study," *Planning for City, State, Region and Nation, 1936,* p. 7.

74. *Ibid.,* p. 12.

75. *Ibid.*

76. Interview with Tracy Augur, Cosmos Club, Washington, D.C., May 27, 1965.

77. Earle S. Draper, "Housing by the TVA," *American Planning and Civic Annual, 1935,* p. 90.

78. *Ibid.,* p. 91.

79. Earle S. Draper, "The New TVA Town of Norris, Tennessee," *American City,* XLVIII (December, 1933), 68.

80. Harold S. Buttenheim, "Trends in Present-day City and Regional Planning in the United States, 1933," *City Planning,* X (April, 1934), 64.

81. Quoted by Robert B. Navin, *Analysis of a Slum Area* (Washington: The Catholic University of America, 1934), p. 7.

82. Harold L. Ickes, "Slum Clearance by Private Enterprise Impossible," *City Planning,* IX (October, 1933), 180.

83. Quoted by Buttenheim, *op. cit.,* pp. 63–64.

84. "Suggestions for Legislation Setting up Housing Authorities," memorandum drafted by committee of National Conference on Slum Clearance, p. 1.

85. *Ibid.,* p. 4.

86. Horatio B. Hackett, "Problems and Policies of the Housing Division of PWA," *Housing Officials' Year Book, 1935,* p. 3.

87. Illinois Housing Commission, *Final Report,* p. 25.

88. Albert Mayer, "Let Us Demand a Housing Program," *Nation,* CXXXIX (October 10, 1934), 403.

89. Albert Mayer, Henry Wright, and Lewis Mumford, "New Homes for a New Deal," *New Republic,* LXXVIII (March 7, 1934), 91–94.

90. Harold L. Ickes, "The Federal Housing Program," *New Republic,* LXXXI, (December 19, 1934), 157.

91. Sir Raymond Unwin, "Low-cost Housing in England and America," a talk given in Cincinnati, Ohio, Sept. 28, 1934, in *Housing Officials' Year Book, 1935,* p. 54.

92. "Summary of 'A Housing Program for the United States,'" *Housing Officials' Year Book, 1935,* p. 54.

93. *Ibid.,* p. 55.

94. *Ibid.*

95. "A Housing Program for the United States," *Housing Officials' Year Book, 1935,* p. 9.

96. "Summary," p. 56.

97. *Ibid.,* p. 57.

98. *Ibid.*

99. Quoted by A. R. Clas in "Housing Achievement of the PWA," *American Planning and Civic Annual, 1935,* p. 99.

100. Hearings on S. 4424 (United States Housing Act of 1936), p. 191.

101. The United States Housing Act of 1937, as Amended, Sec. 2 (2). [Public Law No. 412, 75th Cong., 1st sess.]

102. R. V. Black, "Large-scale Housing and the City Plan," *Planning for City, State, Region, and Nation, 1936,* p. 13.

103. Coleman Woodbury, "Another Year in Housing," *Housing Officials' Year Book, 1937,* p. 149.

104. Walter Blucher, "Revive the Old Ones," *ASPO News Letter,* III (November, 1937), 89.

105. Black, *op. cit.,* p. 17 and p. 13.

106. *Ibid.,* p. 14.

107. *Ibid.,* p. 16.

108. Charles B. Bennett, J. L. Crane, and John Ihlder, "Planning a Housing Program," *American Planning and Civic Annual, 1938,* p. 194.

109. *Ibid.,* p. 191.

110. *Ibid.,* p. 192.

111. *Ibid.,* p. 191.

112. Robert B. Mitchell, "Prospects for Neighborhood Rehabilitation," *Housing Yearbook, 1938,* p. 147.

113. *Ibid.,* p. 21.

114. Jacob Crane, Jr., "Let Us Build Some Garden Cities," *American City,* L (February, 1935), 65.

115. William A. Robson, "Municipal Government a Century Hence," *American City,* L (December, 1935), 53.

116. Rexford G. Tugwell, "Housing Activities and Plans of the Resettlement Administration," *Housing Officials' Year Book, 1936,* p. 28.

117. Quoted in Arthur Schlesinger, Jr., *The Age of Roosevelt: The Coming of the New Deal* (Boston, 1958), pp. 370–371.

118. Interview with Tracy Augur, Washington, D.C., May 27, 1965.

119. Tugwell, *op. cit.,* p. 30.

120. Coleman Woodbury, "Summary of a Busy Year," *Housing Yearbook, 1938,* p. 250.

121. Justin R. Hartzog, "Planning of Suburban Resettlement Towns," *Planners Journal,* IV (March–April, 1938), 29–30.

122. Henry Churchill, "Henry Wright: 1878–1936," *Journal of the American Institute of Planners,* XXVI (November, 1960), 297.

123. John S. Lansill and Jacob Crane, "Metropolitan Land Reserves as Illustrated by Greendale, Wisconsin," *American City,* LII (July, 1937), 58.

124. Ladislas Segoe, "The Urban Community and Its Problems," *New Horizons in Planning: Proceedings of the National Planning Conference, 1937*, p. 3.
125. National Resources Committee, "Foreword," *Our Cities: Their Role in the National Economy* (Washington, 1937), p. vii.
126. *Ibid.*, p. viii.
127. *Ibid.*, p. xii.
128. *Ibid.*, p. x.
129. *Ibid.*, p. xi.
130. Segoe, *op. cit.* (n. 124 above), p. 11.
131. *Ibid.*, p. 12.
132. *Our Cities: Their Role in the National Economy*, p. 85.
133. Louis Wirth, "The Urban Mode of Life," *New Horizons in Planning, Proceedings of the National Planning Conference, 1937*, p. 24.
134. *Ibid.*, p. 29.
135. Albert Lepawsky, "Planning and Urban Government," *New Horizons in Planning*, p. 32.
136. *Ibid.*, p. 33.
137. Warren J. Vinton, "Has Physical Planning Been Over-Emphasized?" *American Planning and Civic Annual, 1937*, p. 195.
138. *Ibid.*, p. 196.
139. R. V. Black, "Is Social and Economic Planning Being Over-Emphasized in Current State Planning Programs?" *American Planning and Civic Annual, 1937*, p. 186.
140. Walter Blucher, "Zoning and Quitting," *Proceedings of the First Annual Indiana State-wide Planning Conference*, p. 44.
141. Hugh R. Pomeroy, "Marin County (California) Zoning," *ASPO News Letter*, IV (October, 1938), 82.
142. In the Superior Court of the State of California, in and for the County of Monterey: County of Monterey, Plaintiff *v.* William Thomas Bassett et al., Defendants, No. 16969. Memorandum Order Overruling Demurrer, as quoted in *ASPO News Letter*, IV (December, 1938), 97.
143. National Resources Planning Board, *Long-range Programming of Municipal Public Works* (Washington, 1941), p. 23.
144. *Ibid.*, p. 27.
145. Earle S. Draper, "New Developments in the Planning Field Bearing on Problems of Municipal Planning," *American Planning and Civic Annual, 1938*, pp. 212–213.
146. Quoted in "Los Angeles' New Mayor for Planning," *ASPO News Letter*, V (August, 1939), 66.
147. Quoted in "Philadelphia Charter Commission Urges Better Planning," *ASPO News Letter,* IV (November, 1938), 91.
148. George McAneny, "Foreword," *From Plan to Reality, Two* (New York: Regional Plan Association, 1938), p. v.

149. National Resources Committee, *The Future of State Planning,* p. 3.

150. Act No. 32, Acts of 1936, State of Pennsylvania, as quoted in *ASPO News Letter,* II, (August, 1936), 63.

151. *The Future of State Planning,* p. 10.

152. Quoted in "President Urges Regional Planning," *ASPO News Letter,* III (June, 1937), 48.

153. Quoted in President's veto message as reported in *The New York Times,* Aug. 14, 1937, and as reproduced in *ASPO News Letter,* III (September, 1937), 76.

154. *Ibid.*

155. Miller McClintock, "Of Things to Come," *New Horizons in Planning, Proceedings of the National Planning Conference, 1937,* p. 34.

156. Neighborhood Improvement Act, Sec. 3, as reproduced in "For the Replanning of Cities by Neighborhood Areas," *American City,* LIII (February, 1938), 56.

157. Harland Bartholomew, "Neighborhood Rehabilitation and the Taxpayer," *American City,* LIII (February, 1938), 57.

158. Quoted in "For Large-Scale City Rebuilding," *American City,* LIII (August, 1938), 5.

159. "Report of the Committee of the American City Planning Institute on Professional Education," Oct. 9, 1936, p. 3.

160. Carl Feiss, "Status of Planning Instruction in Institutions of Higher Education," *Proceedings of National Conference on Planning, 1938,* p. 145.

161. *Ibid.,* p. 146.

162. "Summary of Discussion [of Report of Committee on Education for Planning in the United States]," *Proceedings of National Conference on Planning, 1938,* p. 159.

163. Thomas Adams, *Outline of Town and City Planning,* (New York, 1936), p. 19.

Chapter 6   Defense, War, and the Struggle Against Blight

1. Urban Land Institute, *Decentralization: What Is It Doing to Our Cities?* (Chicago, 1940), p. 5.

2. Quoted in "Rebuilding Atlanta, A Fifteen-Year Effort in Progress," *American City,* LV (February, 1940), 79.

3. Quoted in "Our Defense Must Be from Within," *American City,* LV (June, 1940), 36.

4. Charles E. Merriam, "Planning in a Democracy," *Proceedings of the National Conference on Planning, 1940,* p. 178.

5. Rexford G. Tugwell, "San Francisco as Seen from New York," *Proceedings of the National Conference on Planning, 1940,* p. 187.

6. *Ibid.*, p. 188.

7. Tracy B. Augur, "City Planning and Housing—May They Meet Again," *Proceedings of the National Conference on Planning, 1940*, p. 163.

8. *Ibid.*, p. 164.

9. *Ibid.*

10. Quoted in Herbert Charles O'Neill, *A Short History of the Second World War* (London: Faber and Faber, 1950), p. 71.

11. Walter Blucher, "Planning Commissions Must Be Prepared," *ASPO News Letter,* VI (July, 1940), 49.

12. Glenn A. Rick, "How San Diego is Meeting Its Great Local Problems in Defense Programs," *Western City,* XVI (December, 1940), 18.

13. Quoted in "Federal Cooperation (?) with San Diego," *ASPO News Letter,* VII (October, 1941), 89.

14. National Resources Committee, Urbanism Committee, *Our Cities: Their Role in the National Economy* (Washington, 1937), pp. 63–64.

15. Ladislas Segoe *et al., Local Planning Administration* (Chicago, 1941), p. 38.

16. *Ibid.*, p. 39.

17. Federal Home Loan Bank Board, *Waverly, A Study in Neighborhood Conservation* (Washington, 1940), p. 62.

18. *Ibid.*, pp. 64–65.

19. T. T. McCrosky, "Foreword," Chicago Plan Commission, *Rebuilding Old Chicago* (1941), p. 3.

20. Guy Greer and Alvin H. Hansen, *Urban Redevelopment and Housing,* Planning Pamphlet No. 10 (Washington, D.C.: National Planning Association, 1941), p. 7.

21. *Ibid.*, p. 10.

22. Federal Housing Administration, *A Handbook on Urban Redevelopment for Cities in the United States* (Washington, 1941), p. 104.

23. Greer and Hansen, *op. cit.*, p. 14.

24. *Ibid.*, pp. 17–18.

25. *Ibid.*, p. 7.

26. National Resources Planning Board, *National Resources Development Report for 1942*, p. 107.

27. *Ibid.*, p. 105.

28. National Resources Planning Board, *After Defense—What?*, pp. 12-13.

29. Urban Land Institute, *Outline for a Legislative Program to Rebuild Our Cities* (Washington, 1942), p. 4.

30. *Ibid.*, p. 5.

31. *Ibid.*, p. 6.

32. *Ibid.*, p. 4.

33. Greer and Hansen, *Urban Redevelopment and Housing,* p. 10.

34. *Ibid.*, p. 11.

35. U.S. House. Select Committee Investigating National Defense Migration, *Hearings,* 77th Cong., 1st sess. (Washington, 1941), Part I, p. 6418.

36. Walter Blucher, "Don't Let Down All the Bars," *ASPO News Letter,* VII, (November, 1941), 93.

37. "The President's Address," New York *Times* (Dec. 10, 1941), p. 1.

38. "Zoning Experiences During Wartime Hysteria," *ASPO News Letter,* VIII (October, 1942), 82.

39. Quoted in "Relaxation of Ordinances for War Purposes," *ASPO News Letter,* IX (July, 1943), 60.

40. Walter Blucher, "Evacuation Planning," *ASPO News Letter,* VIII (March, 1942), 21.

41. Quoted in L. J. Carr and J. E. Stermer, *Willow Run: A Study of Industrialization and Cultural Inadequacy* (New York, 1952), p. 9.

42. Mayor's Advisory Committee on Planning Organization, *Report to the Hon. Frank J. Lausche, Mayor of the City of Cleveland* (Cleveland, 1942), p. 2.

43. Amendment to the Charter of the City of Cleveland Establishing a City Planning Commission, Sec. 76-2.

44. National Resources Planning Board, *Better Cities,* by C. S. Ascher, p. 1.

45. *Ibid.,* p. 21.

46. National Resources Planning Board, *The Role of the Housebuilding Industry,* by Miles Colean, p. 3.

47. National Resources Planning Board, *Post-War Planning,* p. 25.

48. National Resources Planning Board, *The Future of Transportation,* p. 36.

49. Quoted in "Planning Revitalized in Kansas City," *ASPO News Letter,* IX (May, 1943), 38.

50. Harland Bartholomew and Associates, *Your Dallas of Tomorrow: A Master Plan for a Greater Dallas* (St. Louis, 1943), p. 32.

51. Robert Moses *et al., Portland Improvement* (New York, 1943), p. 85.

52. *Ibid.,* p. 10.

53. Quoted in Christopher Tunnard, "Portland Improvement," *Task 5* (Spring, 1944), p. 21.

54. Moses, *op. cit.,* p. 10.

55. Tunnard, *op. cit.,* p. 21.

56. Reproduced in *ASPO News Letter,* IX (September, 1943), 79.

57. *Action for Cities: A Guide for Community Planning* (Chicago: Public Administration Service, 1943), p. 76.

58. Interview with Charles Eliot II, Cambridge, Mass., June 14, 1965.

59. Interview with Walter Blucher, Detroit, June 19, 1965.

60. George S. Duggar, "Experiment in Planning," *Task 5* (Spring, 1944), p. 19.

61. Norman Beckman, "Federal Long-Range Planning," *Journal of the American Institute of Planners (AIP),* XXVI (May, 1960), 93.

62. Interview with Charles Eliot II.

63. Charles W. Eliot II and Harold A. Merrill, *Guide to the Files of the National Resources Planning Board and Predecessor Agencies. Ten Years of National Planning, 1933–1943,* p. 28.

64. Charles W. Eliot II, *Final Report: Status of Work, National Resources Planning Board,* p. 17.

65. Charles E. Merriam, "The National Resources Planning Board; A Chapter in American Planning Experience," *American Political Science Review,* XXXVIII (December, 1944), 1086.

66. Quoted in Cleveland Rodgers, *American Planning: Past, Present, Future* (New York, 1947), p. 171.

67. Louis Wirth, "Illinois," one of a series of talks on "How States Are Preparing for the Post-War Period," *Planning, 1944,* p. 121.

68. *Ibid.,* p. 122.

69. *Proceedings of the National Conference on Postwar Housing* (New York, 1944), pp. 93–94.

70. *Ibid.,* p. 99.

71. *Ibid.,* p. 103.

72. *Ibid.,* p. 104.

73. *Ibid.,* p. 109.

74. *Ibid.,* p. 110.

75. *Ibid.,* p. 113.

76. U.S. Senate. Special Committee on Post-war Economic Policy and Planning. Subcommittee on Housing and Urban Redevelopment. *Hearings on Post-war Economic Policy and Planning,* Part 9. 79th Cong., 1st sess. (Washington, 1945), p. 1602.

77. *Ibid.,* p. 1603.

78. *Ibid.,* pp. 1602–1603.

79. *Ibid.,* p. 1615.

80. *Ibid.,* p. 1617.

81. *Ibid.,* p. 1617.

82. *Ibid.,* pp. 1618–1619.

83. U.S. Senate. Special Committee on Postwar Economic Policy and Planning. Subcommittee on Housing and Urban Redevelopment. *Postwar Housing.* 79th Cong., 1st sess. (Washington, 1945), p. 18.

84. *Ibid.,* p. 17.

85. U.S. Senate. Committee on Banking and Currency. *Hearings on the General Housing Act of 1945* [S. 1592], Part I. 79th Cong., 1st sess. (Washington, 1946), p. 2.

86. *Ibid.,* p. 440.

87. *Ibid.,* p. 451.

88. *Hearings,* Part II, pp. 893–894.

89. "No Holds Barred," *Architectural Forum,* LXXVIII (June, 1943), 50.

90. Quoted in Joseph B. Robison, "The Story of Stuyvesant Town," *Nation,* CLXXI (June 2, 1951), 514.

91. *Ibid.* Later the Metropolitan Life Insurance Company voluntarily instituted a nondiscriminatory policy in the selection of tenants.

92. *Hearings on the General Housing Act of 1945,* Part II, p. 889.

93. *Ibid.,* p. 888.

94. "General Housing Act of 1945," Title VI, Sec. 604 (2).

95. Tracy B. Augur, "An Analysis of the Plan of Stuyvesant Town," *Journal of the AIP,* X (Autumn, 1944), 11.

96. *Ibid.,* p. 13.

97. O'Brien Boldt, "Proposal for a Regional Council," *Organization for Metropolitan Planning: Four Proposals for Regional Councils* (Chicago: American Society of Planning Officials, 1943), p. 36.

98. C. McKim Norton and Frederick P. Clark, "Proposal for a Regional Council," *Organization for Metropolitan Planning,* p. 65.

99. *Ibid.,* p. 64.

100. Norman J. Gordon, "Proposal for a Regional Council," *Organization for Metropolitan Planning,* p. 52.

101. Quoted in Citizens Regional Planning Council, *Annual Report,* by Lyman Field (March, 1951), p. 1.

102. Carl J. Friedrich, "First Prize Program," *The Boston Contest of 1944* (Boston, 1945), p. 9.

103. Elizabeth Herlihy, remarks in session on "Intra-State and Inter-State Planning," Proceedings of a Discussion Conference on State Planning Problems, in *Planning, 1945,* Part II, p. 62.

104. T. T. McCrosky and Charles A. Blessing, "An Action Program for Metropolitan Boston," *Journal of the AIP,* XIII (Spring, 1947), 29.

105. *Ibid.,* p. 30.

106. Louis M. Lyons, "What Has Been Done in Boston: The Boston Contest, *Symposium 2—Metropolitan Planning,* Harvard University (1951), p. 29.

107. Catherine Bauer, "What Boston Can and Must Do Now," *Symposium 2,* pp. 31–32.

108. Sherwood L. Reeder, "Revamping the Master Plan," *Journal of the AIP,* XIII (Summer-Fall, 1947), 8.

109. Ladislas Segoe, "Planning Metropolitan Cincinnati, III—Basic Policies," *Planning, 1947,* p. 57.

110. *Ibid.,* p. 59.

111. *Ibid.,* p. 61.

112. *Ibid.,* p. 61.

113. Malcolm H. Dill, "The Cincinnati Metropolitan Master Plan," *Planning, 1947,* p. 71.

114. W. R. Kellogg, "Planning Metropolitan Cincinnati, I—The Administrative Viewpoint," *Planning, 1947,* p. 54.

115. Victor Jones, "Government in the Future City," *Building the Future City, Annals of the American Academy of Political and Social Science*, CCXLII (November, 1945), 86.

116. Thomas H. Reed, *The Governments of Atlanta and Fulton County, Georgia*, p. 61.

117. Quoted in Milton M. Kinsey, "The Bi-State Development Agency for the Missouri-Illinois Metropolitan District," *American Planning and Civic Annual, 1951*, p. 54.

118. Malcolm Elliott and W. Phillip Shatts, "Foreword," Harland Bartholomew and Associates, *Guide Plan, Missouri-Illinois Metropolitan Area* (St. Louis, 1948), p. 3.

119. *Guide Plan*, p. 9.

120. *Ibid.*, p. 6.

121. *Ibid.*, p. 6.

122. *Ibid.*, p. 7.

123. *Ibid.*, p. 48.

124. Paul Windels, "The Metropolitan Region at the Crossroads," *American Planning and Civic Annual, 1948*, p. 64.

125. *Ibid.*, p. 65.

126. *Ibid.*, p. 66.

127. Quoted in "Factory Dispersal for National Security and Rational Town Planning," *American City*, LXIII (September, 1948), 5.

128. *Ibid.*

129. Tracy B. Augur, "Decentralization Can't Wait," *Planning, 1948*, p. 32.

130. Hans Blumenfeld, "Alternative Solutions for Metropolitan Development," *Planning, 1948*, p. 20.

131. *Ibid.*, p. 22.

132. *Ibid.*, p. 23.

133. "Shall We Subdivide Again," *Municipal Finance News Letter*, XVII (August 16, 1944), 1.

134. *Ibid.*, p. 3.

135. Quoted in "Land Planning and Community Protection in the Emergency Housing Program," *ASPO News Letter*, XII (July, 1946), 57.

136. *Ibid.*, p. 58.

137. *Ibid.*, p. 58.

138. *Ibid.*

139. Quoted in "Planning in Los Angeles," *ASPO News Letter*, VI (February, 1940), 12.

140. Kenneth C. Welch, "Regional Shopping Centers—Some Projects in the Northeast," *Journal of the AIP*, XIV (Fall, 1948), 7.

141. U.S. Congress. Joint Committee on Housing. *Housing Study and Investigation*. Final Majority Report. 80th Cong., 2d sess., House Report No. 1564. (Washington, 1948), p. 1.

142. National Association of Housing Officials, *Legislative History of Certain Aspects of the Housing Act of 1949*, Publication No. N278, p. 5.

143. Quoted in *Legislative History*, p. 5.

144. Public Law No. 171, 81st Cong., 1st sess. "Housing Act of 1949," Sec. 2.

145. William L. C. Wheaton, "The Housing Act of 1949," *Journal of the AIP*, XV (Fall, 1949), 36.

146. G. Holmes Perkins, "Editorial," *Journal of the AIP*, XV (Fall, 1949), 2.

147. Nathaniel S. Keith, "Urban Redevelopment — A Challenge to Cities," *Planning, 1949*, p. 39.

148. Public Law No. 171, "Housing Act of 1949," Title I, Sec. 101 (b), p. 2.

149. *Ibid.*, Title I, Sec. 105 (a) (iii), p. 5.

150. In a bill introduced by Senator Elbert D. Thomas of Utah in 1943 and cited as the Federal Urban Redevelopment Act of 1943, Bettman had contributed a provision specifying the required elements of a master plan as all proposed uses of land, a complete system of circulation and transportation, and standards of population density and building intensity, together with "estimates of population growth and a general description of the amount and kind of industrial, business and other economic activities for which the planning agency deems that space should be supplied . . . all correlated with the land-use plan."

151. "Housing Act of 1949," Title I, Sec. 110 (b) (1), p. 9.

152. *Ibid.*, Title IV, Sec. 301 (c), p. 22.

153. John T. Howard *et al.*, "The Content of Professional Curricula in Planning," *Journal of the AIP*, XIV (Winter, 1948), 6.

154. *Ibid.*, pp. 6–7.

155. *Ibid.*, p. 8.

156. *Ibid.*

Chapter 7   Inquiry and Innovation: Responses to Urban Flux

1. Luther Gulick, statement in "What Next for Our American Cities," *American City*, LXIV (December, 1949), 80.

2. "Statement of Policy on Urban Development and Expansion," *Journal of the American Institute of Planners (AIP)*, XVI (Spring, 1950), 94.

3. *Ibid.*, p. 95.

4. *Ibid.*, p. 96.

5. *Ibid.*

6. Catherine Bauer, "The Increasing Social Responsibility of the City Planner," *Proceedings of a Joint Annual Meeting of the American Institute of Planners and the Canadian Institute of Professional Town Planners, Niagara Falls, Ontario, March 3–5, 1950*, pp. 11–12.

7. American Institute of Planners, "Suggestions for a Program of Research in the Urban Environment" (Cambridge, Mass., 1949), p. 24.

8. *Ibid.,* p. 2.

9. *Ibid.,* p. 4.

10. George S. Duggar, "Reporter's Summary of Meeting on Metropolitan Regional Research," *Journal of the AIP,* XVIII (Spring, 1952), 75.

11. Rafael Pico, "The Role of Planning in the 1950's," *Planning, 1951,* p. 3.

12. *Ibid.,* p. 2.

13. *Ibid.,* p. 4.

14. *Ibid.*

15. John T. Howard, "In Defense of Planning Commissions," *Journal of the AIP,* XVII (Spring, 1951), 90.

16. *Ibid.* Like many other planners, Howard now has a different conception of city planning. It is well to remember what Emerson said about consistency and little minds.

17. Henry S. Churchill, "Some Definitions," *Journal of the AIP,* XVIII (Spring, 1952), 82.

18. Eric Carlson, "Are We on the Road to Survival?" *Journal of the AIP,* XVI (Spring, 1950), 58.

19. Patrick Hetherton, "Regional Planning in the Pacific Northwest," *Journal of the AIP,* XVI (Winter, 1950), 28.

20. Harold Miller, "National Industrial Committee Survey," *Planning, 1951,* p. 56.

21. National Industrial Zoning Committee, *Principles of Industrial Zoning,* p. 12.

22. Dennis O'Harrow, "Performance Standards in Industrial Zoning," *Planing, 1951,* p. 42.

23. *Ibid.,* pp. 46–47.

24. Catherine Bauer, "Redevelopment: A Misfit in the Fities," in *The Future of Cities and Urban Redevelopment,* ed. Coleman Woodbury (Chicago, 1953), p. 8.

25. T. A. Adams, Appellant *v.* Housing Authority of the City of Daytona Beach and City of Daytona Beach, Supreme Court of Florida, 60 So. 2d 663, as quoted by Walter H. Blucher, "Planning Legal Notes," *ASPO Newsletter,* XVIII (November, 1952), 93.

26. Foeller *et ux v.* Housing Authority of Portland *et al.,* Supreme Court of Oregon, April 29, 1953, 256 P. 2d 752, as quoted by W. H. Blucher, "Planning Legal Notes," *ASPO Newsletter,* XIX (July, 1953), 55.

27. People *ex rel* John Gutknecht, State's Attorney, Appellant, *v.* The City of Chicago *et al.,* Appellees, Supreme Court of Illinois, January, 1953, unreported, as quoted by W. H. Blucher, "Planning Legal Notes," *ASPO Newsletter,* XIX (April, 1953), 31.

28. Berman *v.* Parker, 348 U.S. 26, 75 Sup. Ct. 98, 99 L. Ed. 27 (1954), p. 31.

29. *Ibid.,* p. 32.

30. *Ibid.,* p. 33.

31. See Martin Anderson, "The Sophistry That Made Urban Renewal Possible," *Law and Contemporary Problems,* XXX (Winter, 1965), 198 and 201–211.

32. Housing Act of 1949, Public Law No. 171, Sec. 105 (a).

33. *Ibid.,* Sec. 101 (b).

34. *Ibid.,* Sec. 101 (a).

35. Carl Feiss, "Urban Redevelopment and Urban Planning," *Planning, 1950,* p. 24.

36. *Ibid.,* p. 27.

37. *Ibid.,* p. 23.

38. *Ibid.,* p. 27.

39. *Ibid.,* p. 23.

40. Ira S. Robbins, remarks in "Clinic: Relocation Problems in Urban Redevelopment," *Planning, 1952,* p. 175.

41. Walter H. Blucher, "Planners Must Provide Leadership in Urban Redevelopment," *ASPO Newsletter,* XVIII (July, 1952), 49.

42. "Report of the Subcommittee on Urban Redevelopment, Rehabilitation, and Conservation," in Advisory Committee on Government Housing Policies and Programs, *Recommendations on Government Housing Policies and Programs* (1953), pp. 111–112.

43. Robert B. Mitchell, "National Objectives for Housing and Urban Renewal," in *Recommendations . . . ,* p. 130.

44. R. B. Mitchell, letter to J. W. Rouse, Nov. 24, 1953, in *Recommendations . . . ,* p. 131.

45. Appendix 2, "Report of the Subcommittee on Urban Redevelopment . . . ," in *Recommendations . . . ,* p. 125.

46. *Recommendations . . . ,* p. 1.

47. *Ibid.,* p. 3.

48. *Ibid.,* p. 15.

49. *Recommendations on Government Housing Policies and Programs,* p. 261.

50. *Ibid.,* p. 263.

51. *Ibid.,* p. 7.

52. American Council to Improve Our Neighborhoods, *This is ACTION* (New York, 1960), p. 8.

53. *Ibid.,* p. 5.

54. John T. Howard, "The Role of the Federal Government in Urban Land Use Planning," *Fordham Law Review,* XXIX (April, 1961), 663.

55. Richard May, Jr., talk in "Clinic on Development Timing," *Planning, 1955,* p. 93.

56. *Ibid.*

57. Henry Fagin, quoting his own article in *Law and Contemporary Problems* in "Clinic . . . ," *Planning, 1955,* p. 95.

58. Philip P. Green, Jr., talk in "Clinic . . . ," *Planning, 1955,* p. 85.

59. Wild Goose Country Club *v.* County of Butte, 60 Ca. App. 339, as quoted by Donald de la Peña, *Vineyards in a Regional System of Open Space . . .* , (Unpublished Master's thesis in City Planning, University of California, Berkeley, 1962), p. 83.

60. Sec. 402.5, California Revenue and Taxation Code, as quoted by De la Peña, *op. cit.,* p. 84.

61. Jacob H. Beuscher, "The Land Use Plan," *Planning, 1958,* p. 189.

62. T. Ledyard Blakeman, "Role of Regional Planning in Solving Suburban Problems," *Planning, 1951,* p. 71.

63. *Detroit News,* Feb. 27, 1953.

64. Frederick G. Gardiner, "Metropolitan Toronto: A New Answer to Metropolitan Area Problems," *Planning, 1953,* p. 43.

65. Letter of T. Ledyard Blakeman to the author, Feb. 20, 1968, p. 1.

66. Michigan, Supervisors Inter-County Committee, *Third Annual Meeting Report* (Detroit, 1960), p. 1.

67. Bylaws, Supervisors Inter-County Committee, as quoted in *This is the Supervisors Inter-County Committee* (Detroit, 1959), p. 3.

68. Blakeman letter, p. 1.

69. *This Is the Supervisors Inter-County Committee,* p. 5.

70. *Ibid.,* p. 3.

71. Confession: The author failed to note the source of this quotation.

72. David A. Wallace, "Renaissancemanship," *Journal of the AIP,* XXVI (August, 1960), 160.

73. Planning Division, Redevelopment Authority of the City of Philadelphia, *Summary Report on the Central Urban Renewal Area* (CURA), 1956, p. 7.

74. Detroit City Plan Commission in cooperation with Housing and Home Finance Agency, *Neighborhood Conservation: A Pilot Study* (1958), p. 94.

75. Mel J. Ravitz, "Urban Renewal Faces Critical Roadblocks," *Journal of the AIP,* XXI (Winter, 1955), 21.

76. Martin Meyerson, "Building the Middle-Range Bridge for Comprehensive Planning," *Journal of the AIP,* XXII (Spring, 1956), 62.

77. *Ibid.,* p. 63.

78. *Ibid.*

79. Baltimore Urban Renewal Study Board, *Report,* p. 3.

80. Arthur Row, "The Physical Development Plan," *Journal of the AIP,* XXVI (August, 1960), 182.

81. Philadelphia City Planning Commission, *Comprehensive Plan* (1960), p. 13.

82. *Ibid.,* p. 16.

83. Jefferson B. Fordham, "Planning for the Realization of Human Values," *Planning, 1960,* p. 6.

84. John T. Howard, "Metropolitan Planning and the Federal Highway Program," *Planning, 1957,* p. 37.

85. Grady Clay, "Impact of the Federal Highway Program," *Planning, 1957,* p. 49.

86. Lewis Mumford, "Address," *Symposium on "The New Highways: Challenge to the Metropolitan Region,"* p. Z1972 (4).

87. J. T. Howard, *op. cit.,* p. 39.

88. *AIP News,* October, 1958, pp. 4–5.

89. *AIP News,* August–September, 1959, p. 10.

90. *Ibid.*

91. Melville C. Branch, Jr., "Planning and Operations Research," *Journal of the AIP,* XXIII (Fall, 1957), 173.

92. Harvey S. Perloff, "Education of City Planners: Past, Present and Future," *Journal of the AIP,* XXII (Fall, 1956), 203.

93. *Ibid.,* p. 203.

94. *Ibid.,* quotations from pp. 204–205.

95. *Ibid.,* p. 212.

96. Quoted in A. Benjamin Handler, "What is Planning Theory?" *Journal of the AIP,* XXIII (Summer, 1957), 150.

97. Quigg Newton, "Planning Comes of Age," *Journal of the AIP,* XXIII (Fall, 1957), 189.

98. Lloyd Rodwin, "Research in Planning," *Planning, 1958,* pp. 232–233.

99. Chester Rapkin, "Research in Planning," *Planning, 1958,* p. 237.

100. Sec. 2, H.R. 1019, 85th Cong., 1st sess., as quoted by Robert H. Connery and Richard H. Leach in *The Federal Government and Metropolitan Areas* (Cambridge, Mass.: Harvard University Press, 1960), p. 172.

101. Quoted in *ibid.,* p. 177.

102. William L. C. Wheaton, "A Federal Department of Urban Affairs," *Planning, 1958,* p. 171.

103. U.S. Senate. Committee on Banking and Currency. *Housing Act of 1959;* Hearings on various bills to amend the federal housing laws. Statement of William L. C. Wheaton, Washington, Jan. 23, 1959, p. 255.

104. American Institute of Planners, *Proposed 1959 Position Statement,* p. 8.

105. *Ibid.,* p. 8.

106. *Ibid.,* p. 5.

Chapter 8   The Search for a New Comprehensiveness

1. Brief *Amici Curiae* of National Institute of Municipal Law Offices in *Baker v. Carr,* Supreme Court of the United States, October term, 1960 (No. 103).

2. Governor's Commission on Metropolitan Area Problems, *Meeting Metropolitan Problems* (Sacramento, Calif., 1960), p. 1.

3. Donald C. Stone, "Adjustment of Planning to the Sixties," *Planning, 1960,* p. 44.

4. "Our Nation's Housing," Message of the President of the United States, March 9, 1961, in *Hearings on Housing Legislation of 1961*, 87th Cong., 1st sess., p. 7.

5. Statement of Mayor Richard J. Daley of Chicago, *Hearings* . . . , pp. 499, 505.

6. *Ibid.*, p. 501.

7. Statement of Edward Logue, *Hearings* . . . , p. 558.

8. *Ibid.*, p. 555.

9. Statement of E. J. Burke, Jr., *Hearings* . . . , p. 1037.

10. Statement of Leon H. Keyserling, *Hearings* . . . , p. 631.

11. "Congress Provides New Aid for Urban Programs in Housing, Open Space, Transportation," *ASPO Newsletter*, XXVIII (August, 1961), 71.

12. Vincent L. Lung, "Administrative Organization for Planning – I," *Planning, 1962*, p. 28.

13. National Capital Planning Commission and National Capital Regional Planning Council, *A Policies Plan for the Year 2000* (Washington, 1961), p. v.

14. *Ibid.*, p. 36.

15. *Ibid.*, p. 42.

16. *Ibid.*, p. 46.

17. Maryland-National Capital Park and Planning Commission, *On Wedges and Corridors* (Riverdale, Maryland, 1964), p. 111.

18. *Ibid.*, p. 43.

19. *Ibid.*, p. 43.

20. Warren Jay Vinton, "The Urban Revolution: Challenge to the Next Generation," Address to the Conference on the Teacher and the Metropolis, Washington, November 29, 1962 (Washington Center for Metropolitan Studies, 1962), p. 20.

21. *Ibid.*, p. 16.

22. *Ibid.*, p. 30.

23. Harvey S. Perloff and Lowdon Wingo, Jr., "Planning and Development in Metropolitan Affairs," *Journal of the AIP*, XXVIII (May, 1962), 89.

24. Quoted by Walter M. Phillips, *A Future for Penjerdel* (Philadelphia: The Pennsylvania–New Jersey–Delaware Metropolitan Project, Inc., 1965), p. 81.

25. *Ibid.*, p. 86.

26. *Ibid.*

27. Letter of Henry Fagin to the author, February 27, 1968.

28. "Bay Government Plan Introduced," San Francisco *Chronicle*, March 4, 1969, p. 2.

29. Frederick O'R. Hayes, "Urban Planning and the Transportation Study," *Proceedings of the 1963 Annual Conference of the AIP*, p. 114.

30. Reynolds *v.* Sims, 377, U.S. 533 (1964), p. 33.

31. *Ibid.,* p. 45.

32. Peter Marris, "The Social Implications of Urban Redevelopment," *Journal of the AIP,* XXVIII (August, 1962), p. 186.

33. William L. Slayton, "Urban Renewal Philosophy," *Planning, 1963,* p. 157.

34. Robert C. Weaver, "Social Issues: The Disadvantaged and the Amenity Seekers," in *The Metropolitan Future: California and the Challenge of Growth* (Berkeley: University of California, 1965), p. 114.

35. Melvin M. Webber, "Comprehensive Planning and Social Responsibility. Toward an AIP Consensus on the Profession's Roles and Purposes," *Journal of the AIP,* XXIX (November, 1963), 235.

36. *Ibid.,* p. 241.

37. *Ibid.*

38. Quoted in David A. Grossman, "The Community Renewal Program," *Journal of the AIP,* XXIX (November, 1963), 263.

39. "President's Talk at Michigan U.," Washington *Post,* May 23, 1964, p. A6.

40. Council of Economic Advisers, *Annual Report* (Washington, 1964), p. 55.

41. *Message from the President of the United States Relative to Drafts of Bills Relating to Housing,* 88th Cong., 2nd sess., House Document No. 206 (Washington, 1964), p. 6.

42. Victor A. Fischer, "The New Dimensions of Transportation Planning," *Proceedings of the 1964 Annual Conference of the AIP,* p. 98.

43. Harvey Perloff, "Common Goals and the Linking of Physical and Social Planning," *Planning, 1965,* p. 171.

44. *Ibid.,* p. 172.

45. *Ibid.,* p. 176.

46. *Ibid.*

47. Ira M. Robinson, "Beyond the Middle-Range Planning Bridge," *Journal of the AIP,* XXXI (November, 1965), 309.

48. *Ibid.,* p. 309.

49. *Ibid.,* p. 310.

50. *Ibid.*

51. *Ibid.,* pp. 310–311.

52. President Lyndon B. Johnson, "Special Message to the Congress on the Nation's Cities," (House Document No. 99), *Congressional Record – House,* March 2, 1965, p. 3814.

53. *Ibid.*

54. *Ibid.*

55. *Ibid.*

56. U.S. Department of Housing and Urban Development (HUD), news release No. 68–1914, June 6, 1968.

57. Henry Fagin, "Expansion of AIP Presents No Real Dangers," *Proceedings of the 1965 Annual Conference of the AIP,* pp. 69–70.

58. Patrick J. Cusick, Jr., "Views at Variance with the Report," *Proceedings . . . ,* p. 68.

59. Thomas J. Kent, "Planning Done on Many Levels of City Government," *Proceedings . . . ,* p. 71.

60. *Ibid.,* pp. 72–73.

61. "Demonstration Cities Act of 1966 — Message from the President (House Document No. 368)," *Congressional Record — Senate,* January 26, 1966, p. 1102.

62. *Ibid.,* pp. 1102–1103.

63. Richard C. Lee, "Address at the Thirty-first Annual Banquet of the National Housing Conference," reprinted in *Congressional Record — Appendix,* March 20, 1962, p. A2123.

64. "Demonstration Cities Act of 1966 — Message from the President," p. 1103.

65. *Ibid.,* p. 1104.

66. "Social Program Coordinator on Loan to Secretary's Office," *AIP Newsletter,* June, 1966, p. 4.

67. U.S. Department of Housing and Urban Development, *Improving the Quality of Urban Life, A Program Guide to Model Neighborhoods in Demonstration Cities* (Washington, 1966), p. 11.

68. *Ibid.,* p. 1.

69. Demonstration Cities and Metropolitan Development Act of 1966, Sec. 1011 (a).

70. Quoted in "Deliberations," *City,* I (September, 1967), 15.

71. Robert C. Weaver, "Statement Announcing the First Model Cities Planning Grants," HUD news release, November 16, 1967, p. 7.

72. Quoted in New York *Times,* July 4, 1967, p. 20.

73. Paul Davidoff, "A Rebuilt Ghetto Does Not a Model City Make," *Planning, 1967,* p. 188.

74. Regional Plan Association of New York, *Public Participation in Regional Planning* (New York, 1967), p. 62.

75. H. Ralph Taylor, "Model Cities: Progress and Problems in the First Ten Months," speech at Model Cities Midwest Regional Conference, Dayton, Ohio, September 6, 1968; HUD release, September 6, 1968, p. 15.

76. *Ibid.,* p. 3.

77. *Ibid.,* p. 7.

78. *Ibid.,* p. 6.

79. Robert C. Weaver, "Problems of Urban Development," lecture at Great Issues Symposium, Oklahoma State University, January 11, 1968; HUD release, September 11, 1968, p. 21.

80. Robert C. Weaver, "The Urban Opportunity: Roles for the University," address at Howard University-Georgetown University, December 8, 1966; HUD release, December 8, 1966, p. 11.

81. Melvin M. Webber, "A Ph.D. Field in Social Policies Planning: A Proposal for a Pilot Graduate Training Grant, National Institute of Mental Health" (University of California, Berkeley, August 1, 1966), p. 15.

82. Robert M. Leary, "Are Planning Schools Interfering with Planning Education?" *Planning, 1967,* p. 130.

83. Leo Jakobson, "Planning Education: A Response," *Planning, 1967,* p. 146.

84. *Ibid.,* pp. 145–146.

85. See volumes edited by William R. Ewald, Jr.: *Environment for Man: The Next Fifty Years.* Based on papers commissioned for the American Institute of Planners' two-year consultation, Part I: Optimum Environment with Man as the Measure, Portland, Oregon, August 14–18, 1966 (Bloomington, Indiana: Indiana University Press, 1967); and *Environment and Policy: The Next Fifty Years,* together with *Environment and Change: The Next Fifty Years,* Part II of a consultation on the years 1967–2017, and the future environment: papers presented at a conference in Washington, D.C., October 1–6, 1967 (Bloomington, Indiana: University of Indiana Press, 1968).

86. Regional Plan Association of New York, *The Second Regional Plan: A Draft for Discussion* (New York, 1968), p. 33.

87. *Ibid.,* pp. 33–34.

SELECTED BIBLIOGRAPHY

697

Principal Sources

In preparing this work I have used as principal sources the *Journal of the American Institute of Planners* and the monthly newsletter of the institute; the proceedings of the annual meeting of the American Society of Planning Officials and the monthly newsletter of the society; the proceedings of the National Conference on City Planning, which was held annually from 1909 to 1934 and was superseded by the National Conference on Planning (1935–1942), which in turn was superseded in 1943 by the annual meeting of the American Society of Planning Officials; and the *American Planning and Civic Annual* of the American Planning and Civic Association, as well as its monthly publication, entitled *City Planning* from April, 1925, to October, 1934, and thereafter known as *Planning and Civic Comment*. So numerous are the articles and addresses quoted from these sources that I have not attempted to list them in the bibliography, but all are properly cited in the notes to each chapter.

I have also made liberal use of articles on city planning published in the *American City*. If he had not passed on, I would say "Thank you" personally to publisher Harold Buttenheim, whom I once knew briefly, for providing a forum for planners decade after decade.

I wish especially to express my appreciation of two Ph.D. theses which have been of invaluable help to me: John Loretz Hancock's "John Nolen and the American City Planning Movement: A History of Culture Change and Community Response, 1900–1940 (University of Pennsylvania, 1964); and Norman J. Johnston's "Harland Bartholomew: His Comprehensive Plans and Science of Planning" (University of Pennsylvania, 1964).

Books

ADAMS, THOMAS. *Outline of Town and City Planning. A Review of Past Efforts and Modern Aims.* Foreword by Franklin D. Roosevelt. New York: Russell Sage Foundation, 1936.

AMERICAN INSTITUTE OF ARCHITECTS. Committee on Town Planning. *City Planning Progress, 1917.* Washington D.C.: The Institute, 1917.

ARONOVICI, CAROL. *Housing and the Housing Problem.* Chicago: A. C. McClurg & Co., 1920.

ATWATER, ISAAC, ED. *History of the City of Minneapolis, Minnesota.* 2 vols. New York: Munsell & Co., 1893.

BARCK, OSCAR T., JR. *A History of the United States Since 1945.* New York: Dell Publishing Co., 1965.

BARTHOLOMEW, HARLAND. *Urban Land Uses.* Harvard City Planning Studies, No. 4. Cambridge, Mass.: Harvard University Press, 1932.

BASSETT, EDWARD M. *The Master Plan.* New York: Russell Sage Foundation, 1938.

BAUER, CATHERINE. *Modern Housing.* Boston: Houghton Mifflin Co., 1934.

BEARD, CHARLES A. *American City Government. A Survey of Newer Tendencies.* New York: The Century Co., 1912.

BETTMAN, ALFRED. *City and Regional Planning Papers,* ed. Arthur C. Comey. Cambridge, Mass.: Harvard University Press, 1946.

BLACK, RUSSELL VAN NEST. *Planning for the Small American City. An Outline of Principles and Procedure Especially Applicable to the City of Fifty Thousand or Less.* Chicago: Public Administration Service, 1944.

BOLLENS, JOHN C., and HENRY J. SCHMANDT. *The Metropolis. Its People, Politics, and Economic Life.* New York: Harper and Row, 1965.

BROWNLOW, LOUIS. *A Passion for Anonymity: The Autobiography of Louis Brownlow.* Chicago: University of Chicago Press, 1958.

BURCHARD, JOHN, and ALBERT BUSH-BROWN. *The Architecture of America. A Social and Cultural History.* Boston: Little, Brown and Company, 1961.

CARR, LOWELL JUILLIARD, and JAMES EDSON STERMER. *Willow Run: A Study of Industrialization and Cultural Inadequacy.* New York: Harper & Brothers, 1952.

CHURCHILL, WINSTON S., and THE EDITORS OF *Life. The Second World War.* Vol. 1. New York: Time Incorporated, 1959.

CLEVELAND, H. W. S. *Landscape Architecture as Applied to the Wants of the West,* ed. Roy Lubove. University of Pittsburgh Press, 1965.

CONKIN, PAUL K. *Tomorrow a New World: The New Deal Community Program.* Published for the American Historical Association. Ithaca, N.Y.: Cornell University Press, 1959.

CROLY, HERBERT. *The Promise of American Life.* New York: The Macmillan Co., 1911.

DOELL, CHARLES S., and GERALD B. FITZGERALD. *A Brief History of Parks and Recreation in the United States.* Chicago: The Athletic Institute, 1954.

DUFFUS, R. L. *Mastering a Metropolis: Planning the Future of the New York Region.* New York: Harper & Brothers, 1930.

THE EDITORS OF *Fortune. Housing America.* New York: Harcourt, Brace and Company, 1932.

EWALD, WILLIAM R., JR., ED. *Environment for Man: The Next Fifty Years.* Based on papers commissioned for the American Institute of Planners' two-year consultation, Part I: Optimum Environment with Man as the Measure, Portland, Oregon, August 14–18, 1966. Bloomington, Indiana: Indiana University Press, 1967.

————. *Environment and Policy: The Next Fifty Years* (Part II, first volume); *Environment and Change: The Next Fifty Years* (Part II, second volume). A consultation on the years 1967–2017, and the future environment: papers presented at a conference in Washington, D.C., October 1–6, 1967. 2 vols. Bloomington, Indiana: University of Indiana Press, 1968.

FITCH, LYLE C., and ASSOCIATES. *Urban Transportation and Public Policy.* San Francisco: Chandler Publishing Company, 1964.

FORD, JAMES. *Slums and Housing, with Special Reference to New York City.* 2 vols. Cambridge, Mass.: Harvard University Press, 1936.

FRANCIS, DAVID R. *The Universal Exposition of 1904.* St. Louis, Mo.: Louisiana Purchase Exposition Company, 1913.

FULMER, O. KLINE. *Greenbelt.* Introduction by Lewis Mumford. Washington: American Council on Public Affairs, 1941.

GALLION, ARTHUR B., in collaboration with SIMON EISNER. *The Urban Pattern. City Planning and Design.* New York: The D. Van Nostrand Co., 1950.

GALLOWAY, GEORGE B. *Postwar Planning in the United States.* New York: The Twentieth Century Fund, 1942.

GLENN, JOHN M., LILIAN BRANDT, and F. EMERSON ANDREWS. *Russell Sage Foundation 1907–1946.* 2 vols. New York: Russell Sage Foundation, 1947.

GOLDMAN, ERIC F. *Rendezvous with Destiny: A History of Modern American Reform.* New York: Vintage Books, 1952.

GUTHEIM, FREDERICK. *The Potomac.* In the Rivers of America Series, Hervey Allen and Carl Carmer, eds. New York: Rinehart & Company, 1949.

HAYS, FORBES. *Community Leadership.* New York: The Regional Plan Association, 1965.

HAYS, SAMUEL P. *Conservation and the Gospel of Efficiency. The Progressive Conservation Movement, 1890–1920.* Cambridge, Mass.: Harvard University Press, 1959.

————. *The Response to Industrialism.* Chicago: The University of Chicago Press, 1957.

HILLMAN, ARTHUR, and ROBERT J. CASEY. *Tomorrow's Chicago.* Chicago: The University of Chicago Press, 1953.

HODGE, CLARENCE LEWIS. *The Tennessee Valley Authority: A National Experiment in Regionalism.* Washington, D.C.: The American University Press, 1938.

HOFSTADTER, RICHARD. *The Age of Reform.* New York: Vintage Books, 1955.

HOYT, HOMER. *One Hundred Years of Land Values in Chicago.* Chicago: The University of Illinois Press, 1933.

HUBBARD, THEODORA KIMBALL, and HENRY VINCENT HUBBARD. *Our Cities To-day and To-morrow. A Survey of Planning and Zoning Progress in the United States.* Cambridge, Mass.: Harvard University Press, 1929.

HUBBARD, THEODORA KIMBALL, and KATHERINE MCNAMARA. *Planning Information Up-to-Date. A Supplement, 1923–1928, to Kimball's Manual of Information on City Planning and Zoning.* Cambridge, Mass.: Harvard University Press, 1928.

HUNT, EDWARD EYRE. *An Audit of America: A Summary of Recent Economic Changes in the United States.* New York: McGraw-Hill Book Co., 1930.

JANEWAY, ELIOT. *The Struggle for Survival. A Chronicle of Economic Mobilization in World War II.* New Haven, Conn.: Yale University Press, 1951.

KENT, T. J., JR. *The Urban General Plan.* San Francisco: Chandler Publishing Co., 1964.

KOUWENHOVEN, JOHN A. *The Columbia Historical Portrait of New York. An essay in graphic history in honor of the Tricentennial of New York City and the Bicentennial of Columbia University.* Garden City, N.Y.: Doubleday & Co., 1953.

LEWIS, HAROLD MCLEAN. *Planning the Modern City.* 2 vols. New York: John Wiley & Sons, 1949.

LEWIS, NELSON P. *The Planning of the Modern City.* New York: John Wiley & Sons, 1916.

LOHMANN, KARL B. *Principles of City Planning.* New York: McGraw-Hill Book Co., 1931.

LUBOVE, ROY. *The Progressives and the Slums: Tenement House Reform in New York City, 1890–1917.* Pittsburgh, Penna.: University of Pittsburgh Press, 1962.

MCKELVEY, BLAKE. *The Urbanization of America.* New Brunswick, N.J.: Rutgers University Press, 1963.

MCKENZIE, R. D. *The Metropolitan Community.* New York: McGraw-Hill Book Co., 1933.

MARSH, BENJAMIN CLARKE. *An Introduction to City Planning: Democracy's Challenge to the American City.* With a chapter on the Technical Phases of City Planning, by George B. Ford, Architect. New York: B. C. Marsh, 1909.

———. *Lobbyist for the People: A Record of Fifty Years.* Washington, D.C.: Public Affairs Press, 1953.

MOORE, CHARLES. *Daniel H. Burnham, Architect, Planner of Cities.* 2 vols. Boston and New York: Houghton Mifflin Co., 1921.

NOLEN, JOHN, ED. *City Planning.* New York: D. Appleton and Co., 1916.

PATTON, CLIFFORD. *The Battle for Municipal Reform.* Introduction by Arthur M. Schlesinger. Washington, D.C.: American Council on Public Affairs, 1940.

PIERCE, BESSIE LOUISE. *The Rise of a Modern City, 1871–1893.* Vol. III of *A History of Chicago.* New York: Alfred A. Knopf, 1958.

REPS, JOHN W. *The Making of Urban America.* Princeton, N.J.: Princeton University Press, 1965.

ROBINSON, CHARLES MULFORD. *The Improvement of Towns and Cities.* New York: G. P. Putnam's Sons, 1907.

———. *Modern Civic Art, or the City Made Beautiful.* 2d ed. New York: Putnam's, 1904.

RODGERS, CLEVELAND. *American Planning: Past, Present, Future.* New York: Harper & Brothers, 1947.

SCHLESINGER, ARTHUR M. *The Rise of the City, 1878–1898.* Vol. X of *A History of American Life,* eds. A. M. Schlesinger and D. R. Fox. New York: The Macmillan Co., 1933.

SCHLESINGER, ARTHUR M., JR. *The Age of Roosevelt: The Coming of the New Deal.* Boston: Houghton Mifflin Co., 1958. (Sentry Edition, 1965.)

———. *The Age of Roosevelt: The Crisis of the Old Order, 1919–1933.* Boston: Houghton Mifflin Co., 1957. (Sentry Edition, 1964).

SCOTT, STANLEY, and JOHN C. BOLLENS. *Governing a Metropolitan Region: The San Francisco Bay Area.* Berkeley: Institute of Governmental Studies, University of California, 1968.

SEGOE, LADISLAS, with the collaboration of WALTER H. BLUCHER *et al. Local Planning Administration.* Chicago: The International City Managers' Association, 1941.

SHURTLEFF, FLAVEL. *Carrying Out the City Plan.* New York: Survey Associates, 1914.

SOMERS, HERMAN MILES. *Presidential Agency: The Office of War Mobilization and Reconversion.* Cambridge, Mass.: Harvard University Press, 1950.

STOKES, ISAAC NEWTON PHELPS. *The Iconography of Manhattan Island, 1498–1909, Compiled From Original Sources and Illustrated by Photointaglio Reproductions of Important Maps, Plans, Views, and Documents in Public and Private Collections.* Vol. III. New York: R. H. Dodd, 1915–1928.

STRATEGICUS [pseud] O'NEILL, HERBERT CHARLES. *A Short History of the Second World War.* London: Faber and Faber, 1950.

TAEUBER, CONRAD, and IRENE B. TAEUBER. *The Changing Population of the United States.* A Volume in the Census Monograph Series. New York: John Wiley & Sons, 1958.

WALKER, ROBERT A. *The Planning Function in Urban Government.* Chicago: The University of Chicago Press, 1941.

WHITEHILL, WALTER MUIR. *Boston: A Topographical History.* Cambridge, Mass.: The Belknap Press of Harvard University Press, 1959.

WILSON, MARION F. *The Story of Willow Run.* Ann Arbor, Michigan: The University of Michigan Press, 1956.

WILSON, WILLIAM H. *The City Beautiful Movement in Kansas City.* University of Missouri Studies Volume XL. Columbia, Mo.: University of Missouri Press, 1964.

WOLOZIN, HAROLD, ED. *The Economics of Air Pollution.* New York: W. W. Norton & Co., 1966.

WOOD, EDITH ELMER. *Recent Trends in American Housing.* New York: The Macmillan Co., 1931.

WOODBURY, COLEMAN, ED. *The Future of Cities and Urban Redevelopment.* Chicago: The University of Chicago Press, 1953.

———, ED. *Urban Redevelopment: Problems and Practices.* Chicago: The University of Chicago Press, 1953.

Articles

ACKERMAN, FREDERICK L. "Where Goes the City-Planning Movement?" *Journal of the American Institute of Architects,* VII (December, 1919), 418–520.

ADAMS, THOMAS. "A Communication in Defense of the Regional Plan," *New Republic,* LXXI (July 6, 1932), 207–210.

———. "Regional Planning in Relation to Public Administration," *National Municipal Review,* XV (January, 1926), 35–42.

———. "The Social Objective in Regional Planning," *National Municipal Review,* XV (February, 1926), 79–87.

"American Society of Landscape Architects Minute on the Life and Services of Charles Mulford Robinson, Associate Member," *Landscape Architect,* IX (July, 1919), 180–193.

AUGUR, TRACY B. "Planning Principles Applied in Wartime. An Account of the Planning of a Town for Willow Run Workers," *Architectural Record,* XCIII (January, 1943), 72–77.

BACHA, MARY et al. "The Pittsburgh Survey of the National Publication Committee of Charities and the Commons," *Charities and The Commons* [*Survey*], XIX (March 7, 1908), 1665–1670.

BARTHOLOMEW, HARLAND. "Planning Progress in St. Louis," *City Planning*, V (July, 1929), 141–162.

BAUER, CATHERINE. "Cities in Flux," *American Scholar*, XIII (Winter, 1943–44), 70–84.

BEARD, CHARLES A. "Conflicts in City Planning," *Yale Review*, XVII (October, 1927), 65–77.

————. "Some Aspects of Regional Planning," *American Political Science Review*, XX (May, 1926), 273–283.

BLACK, RUSSELL VAN NEST. "Theory of Planning the Region as Exemplified by the Philadelphia Tri-State Plan," *City Planning*, VI (July, 1930), 184–198.

BOGUE, DONALD J. "Urbanism in the United States, 1950," *American Journal of Sociology*, LX (March, 1955), 471–486.

CARHART, ARTHUR H. "Denver Makes a Plan," *City Planning Quarterly*, VI (April, 1930), 73–85.

CHURCHILL, HENRY S. "Met Gits the Mostest," *Architectural Forum*, LXXVIII (June, 1943), 34, 128.

CHUTE, CHARLTON F. "Today's Urban Regions," *National Municipal Review*, XLV (June and July, 1956), 274–280; 334–339.

COMEY, ARTHUR C. "A State Plan for Massachusetts," *City Plan*, I (March, 1915), 5–8.

COX, JAMES L. "Federal Urban Development Policy and the Metropolitan Washington Council of Governments: A Reassessment," *Urban Affairs Quarterly*, III (September, 1967), 75–94.

CRANE, JACOB. "Let Us Build Some Garden Cities," *American City*, L (February, 1935), 65.

CRAWFORD, ANDREW WRIGHT. "City Planning and Philadelphia Parks," *Annals of the American Academy of Political and Social Science*, XXXV (February, 1910), 76.

CRAWFORD, ANDREW WRIGHT. "A Proposed Federal Agency to Deal with Housing, Town Planning and Other Municipal Affairs," *American City*, XX (February, 1919), 179.

CURRY, S. LEIGH, JR. "The Community Renewal Program," *Federal Bar Journal*, XXI (Summer, 1961), 358–371.

DELANO, FREDERIC A. "To Meet the Housing Needs of the Lower Income Groups," *American City*, LII (January, 1937), 45–48.

DRAPER, EARLE S. "The New TVA Town of Norris, Tennessee," *American City*, XLVIII (December, 1933), 67–68.

DUGGAR, GEORGE S. "Experiment in Planning," *Task 5* (Spring, 1944), 14–20.

"Factory Dispersal for National Security and Rational Town Planning," *American City*, LXIII (September, 1948), 5.

GRUNDLACH, JOHN H. "A City's Control of Outlying Districts," *American City*, IV (May, 1911), 224–226.

GUTHEIM, FREDERICK. "Capital Planning," review of *Monumental Washington,* by John W. Reps, in *Landscape,* XVII (Spring, 1968), 26–28.

HENRY, LAURIN L. "Louis Brownlow and the Governmental Arts," *Western Political Quarterly,* VIII (September, 1955), 453–464.

HOOKER, GEORGE E. "A Plan for Chicago," *Survey,* XXII (September 4, 1909), 778–790.

"Housing News: Rehousing Survey," *Architectural Record,* XCVII (March, 1945), 132, 134.

HOWARD, JOHN T. "The Role of the Federal Government in Urban Land Use Planning," *Fordham Law Review,* XXX (April, 1961), 657–672.

ICKES, HAROLD L. "The Place of Housing in National Rehabilitation," *Journal of Land and Public Utility Economics,* XI (May, 1935), 109–116.

JAMES, HARLEAN. "Service – The Keynote of a New Cabinet Department," *American Review of Reviews,* LVIX (February, 1919), 187–190.

JONES, VICTOR. "Government in the Future City." *Annals of the American Academy of Political and Social Science,* CCXLII (November, 1945), 79–87.

KATES, PHILIP. "A National Department of Municipalities," *American City,* VI (January, 1912), pp. 405–407.

KELLOGG, PAUL U. "Boston's Level Best – The '1915 Movement' and the Work of Civic Organizing for Which It Stands," *Survey,* XXII (June 5, 1909), 382–396.

———. "The 1915 Boston Exposition," *Survey,* XXIII (Dec. 4, 1909), 328–334.

LANSILL, JOHN S. and JACOB CRANE. "Metropolitan Land Reserves as Illustrated by Greendale, Wisconsin," *American City,* LII (July, 1937), 55–58.

LOVEJOY, OWEN R. "Making Boston Over," *Survey,* XXII (September 4, 1909), 764–778.

McFARLAND, J. HORACE. "The Great Civic Awakening," *Outlook,* LXXIII (April 18, 1903), 917–920.

———. "The Nationalization of Civic Improvement," *Charities and the Commons,* XVII (1906), 229–234.

McLEAN, FRANCIS H. "South End – Boston," *Municipal Affairs,* III (March, 1899), 152–154. A review of *The City Wilderness: A Settlement Study,* by Residents and Associates of the South End House. Edited by Robert A. Woods, Head of the House. Boston and New York: Houghton Mifflin Co., 1898.

"Markets in the Meadows," *Architectural Forum,* XC (March, 1949), 114–124.

MARSH, BENJAMIN C. "City Planning in Justice to the Working Population," *Charities and The Commons [Survey],* XIX (1907–1908), 1514–1518.

MARTIN, JOHN. "The Exhibit of Congestion Interpreted," *Charities and The Commons [Survey],* XX (1908), 27–39.

MAYER, ALBERT. "New Homes for a New Deal. I: Slum Clearance – But How?," *New Republic,* LXXVIII (February 14, 1934), 7–9.

———, HENRY WRIGHT, and LEWIS MUMFORD. "New Homes for a New Deal. IV: A Concrete Program," *New Republic,* LXXVIII (March 7, 1934), 91–94.

MERO, EVERETT B. "City Improvement Program for Boston," *American City,* IV (January–June, 1911), 233–234.

MERRIAM, CHARLES E. "The National Resources Planning Board; A Chapter in American Planning Experience," *American Political Science Reveiw,* XXXVIII (December, 1944), 1075–1088.

MEYERSON, MARTIN. "Post-War Plans: A Survey," *Task 5* (Spring, 1944), 8–11.

MOODY, WALTER D. "How to Go About City Planning," *City Plan,* I (March, 1915), 12–16.

MORRIS, JUDY K. "U.S.A. Population Changes: 1950–60," based on a research report by Judah Matras. *Population Bulletin,* Population Reference Bureau, Inc., XIX (March, 1963), 25–50.

MUMFORD, LEWIS. "The Fourth Migration," *Survey,* LIV (May 1, 1925), 130–133.

_____. "The Plan of New York," *New Republic,* LXXI (June 15, 1932) 121–126; (June 22, 1932), 146–154.

"National Conference on Highways Held," *American Municipal News,* October 31, 1958.

"No Holds Barred," *Architectural Forum,* LXXVIII (June, 1943), 50.

NOLEN, JOHN. "General Planning Board for Metropolitan Boston," *National Municipal Review,* I (April, 1912), 231–235.

OLMSTED, FREDERICK LAW, JR. "The Town-Planning Movement in America," *Annals of the American Academy of Political and Social Science,* LI (January, 1914), 172–181.

_____, and JOHN NOLEN. "The Normal Requirements of American Towns and Cities in respect to Public Open Spaces," *Charities and The Commons,* XVI (June 30, 1906), 411–426.

PATTEN, SIMON N. "The Decay of Local Government," *Annals of the American Academy of Political and Social Science,* I (July, 1890–June, 1891), 26–42.

PEEL, ROY V. "Political Implications of the 1950 Census of Population," *Western Political Quarterly,* III (December, 1950), 615–619.

POLLARD, W. L. "Outline of the Law of Zoning in the United States," *Annals of the American Academy of Political and Social Science,* CLV (May, 1931), 15–33.

"Redevelopment Plan for Cincinnati's Blighted Riverfront," *American City,* LXII (January, 1947), 78–79.

"Regional Councils Explore Future," *National Civic Review,* LVI (May, 1967), 281–285.

"Regional Plan Association: 1957–67," *Regional Plan News,* LXXXIV (May, 1967), 1–17.

"Report of Land Utilization Conference," *Agricultural Review,* I (December, 1931), 11–14.

RICK, GLENN A. "How San Diego is Meeting Its Great Local Problems in Defense Programs," *Western City,* XVI (December, 1940), 14–19.

ROBINSON, CHARLES M., ED. "The City Plan," a "civic broadside" in *Charities and The Commons,* XIX (February 1, 1908), 1487–1562.

_____. "The City Plan Exhibition," *Survey,* XXII (1909), 313–318.

_____. "Improvement in City Life. III. Aesthetic Progress," *Atlantic Monthly,* LXXXIII (June, 1899), 771–785.

_____. "The Street Plan of a City's Business District," *Architectural Record,* XIII (March, 1903), 235–247.

ROBISON, JOSEPH B. "The Story of Stuyvesant Town," *Nation,* CLXXI (June 2, 1951), 514–516.

ROBSON, WILLIAM A. "Municipal Government a Century Hence," *American City,* L (December, 1935), 52–53.

RODWIN, LLOYD. "Garden Cities and the Metropolis," *Journal of Land and Public Utility Economics,* XXI (August, 1945), 268–281.

ROOSEVELT, FRANKLIN D. "Growing Up by Plan," *Survey,* LXVII (February, 1, 1932), 483–485, 506–507.

"Shall Our Great Cities be Made States? Answers Pro and Con to Questions on This Subject as Propounded in the January Number of The American City," *American City,* X (February, 1914), 142–144.

"Shall We Subdivide Again?" *Municipal Finance News Letter,* XVII (August 16, 1944), 1–3.

SHATTS W. PHILLIP. "A Big-State Compact for Metropolitan St. Louis Area Development," *State Government,* XXII (April, 1949), 108–111, 122.

STEDMAN, GORDON H. "The Rise of Shopping Centers," *Journal of Retailing,* XXXI (Spring, 1955), 11–26.

"Stuyvesant Town," *Architectural Forum,* LXXIX (July, 1943), 40–41.

TUGWELL, R. G. "The Principle of Planning and the Institution of Laissez Faire," *American Economic Review,* XXII (March, 1932), Supplement. Includes discussion, 75–104.

TUNNARD, CHRISTOPHER. "Portland Improvement," *Task 5* (Spring, 1944), 21.

"U.S.A. Population Changes: 1950–60," *Population Bulletin,* XIX (March, 1963), entire issue.

WARNER, JOHN DE WITT. "Civic Centers," *Municipal Affairs,* VI (March, 1902), 1–23.

"What Next for Our American Cities? Predictions of Further Progress in the 1950's." *American City,* LXIV (December, 1949), 79–81; LXV (January, 1950), 75–78; and LXV (February, 1950), 81–83.

WHITNALL, GORDON. "History of Zoning," *Annals of the American Academy of Political and Social Science,* CLV (May, 1931), 1–14.

"Why Not Make States Out of Our Largest Cities? Editorial Comment," *American City,* X (January, 1914), 1–2.

WOOD, EDITH ELMER. "Housing in My Time," reprinted from *Shelter,* December, 1938. 4 pp.

ZACHARY, JAMES E. "When a Defense Boom Hits a Defenseless Village," *American City,* LVI (October, 1941), 47–49.

ZETTEL, RICHARD M. "Financing Highways Now and in the Future," *Traffic Quarterly,* X (October, 1956), 433–453.

Planning Reports

Action for Cities: A Guide for Community Planning. Chicago: Public Administration Service, 1943.

ADAMS, FREDERICK J. *Urban Planning Education in the United States.* Cincinnati: The Alfred Bettman Foundation, 1954.

ADAMS, THOMAS. *Planning the New York Region.* New York: Committee on Regional Plan of New York and its Environs, 1927.

AMERICAN INSTITUTE OF PLANNERS. *Proposed 1959 Position Statement,* prepared by F. Stuart Chapin, Jr., Washington, 1959.

_____. "Suggestions for a Program of Research in the Urban Environment." Cambridge, Mass.: The Institute, 1949. Mimeo.

_____. Task Force on New Communities. *New Communities: Challenge for Today.* Background Paper No. 2. Washington, 1968.

BALTIMORE. Urbal Renewal Study Board. *Report to Mayor Thomas D'Alesandro, Jr.* Baltimore, 1956.

BARTHOLOMEW, HARLAND, "City Planning in Washington, D.C., 1790–1958." September, 1958. Mimeo.

_____, and ASSOCIATES. *Guide Plan, Missouri-Illinois Metropolitan Area.* An overall analysis of the major metropolitan development problems with some tentative proposals for their solution. Prepared for the Metropolitan Plan Association, Inc. St. Louis, the Association, 1948.

_____. *A Preliminary Report upon Your City and Planning: Wichita, Kansas.* St. Louis, 1943.

_____. *Your Dallas of Tomorrow: A Master Plan for a Greater Dallas.* St. Louis, 1943.

BOSTON CHAMBER OF COMMERCE. Committee on City Planning. *Report on City Planning in Relation to the Street System in the Boston Metropolitan District.* Boston, 1914.

BRUNNER, ARNOLD W., and JOHN M. CARRERE. *Preliminary Report for a City Plan for Grand Rapids.* Grand Rapids: Common Council of Grand Rapids, Mich. [1909.]

_____, FREDERICK LAW OLMSTED, and BION J. ARNOLD. *A City Plan for Rochester.* Rochester, N.Y.: Rochester Civic Improvement Committee, 1911.

BURNHAM, DANIEL H., and EDWARD H. BENNETT. *Plan of Chicago,* ed. Charles Moore. Chicago: The Commercial Club, 1909.

_____, and EDWARD H. BENNETT. *Report on a Plan for San Francisco,* ed. Edward F. O'Day. San Francisco: Published by the City, 1905.

BURNHAM, DANIEL H., JR., and ROBERT KINGERY. *Planning the Region of Chicago.* Chicago: Chicago Regional Planning Association, 1956.

CHICAGO. Plan Commission. *Rebuilding Old Chicago—City Planning Aspects of the Neighborhood Redevelopment Corporation Law.* Chicago, 1941.

CINCINNATI. City Planning Commission. *The Official City Plan of Cincinnati, Ohio,* by George B. Ford and E. P. Goodrich. Cincinnati, 1925.

CITIZENS' COUNCIL ON CITY PLANNING and PHILADELPHIA HOUSING ASSOCIATION.

Organizations for Metropolitan Planning. Philadelphia, 1949.

THE CIVIC LEAGUE OF SAINT LOUIS. *A City Plan for Saint Louis.* St. Louis, 1907.

CLEVELAND. City Planning Commission. *Cleveland Today . . . Tomorrow. The General Plan of Cleveland.* Cleveland, 1950.

CLEVELAND. City Planning Commission. *Planning in Cleveland.* Including Summary Report for 1963. Cleveland, 1963.

CLEVELAND. Mayor's Advisory Committee on Planning Organization. *Report.* Cleveland: July 10, 1942.

COLUMBUS, OHIO. Plan Commission. *The Plan of the City of Columbus.* Columbus, 1908.

COMMITTEE ON REGIONAL PLAN OF NEW YORK AND ITS ENVIRONS. *Regional Plan of New York and Its Environs.* Regional Survey, 8 vols.; Regional Plan, 2 vols.: *The Graphic Regional Plan,* I, and *The Building of the City,* II, by Thomas Adams, assisted by Harold M. Lewis and Lawrence M. Orton. New York: Regional Plan of New York and Its Environs, 1929–1931.

CONNECTICUT. Capitol Regional Planning Authority. *First Annual Report.* East Hartford, Conn., 1959.

CONNECTICUT. Development Commission. *Progress Toward Regional Planning in Connecticut.* Hartford, Conn., 1959.

DETROIT. City Plan Commission. *Neighborhood Conservation: A Pilot Study,* by Maurice Frank Parkins. Detroit, 1958.

FIELD, LYMAN. *Guiding the Growth of the Metropolitan Area, 1950–51,* Annual Report of the General Chairman, Citizens Regional Planning Council. Kansas City, Missouri, 1951.

GAUS, JOHN MERRIMAN. *The Graduate School of Design and the Education of Planners.* Cambridge, Mass.: The Graduate School of Design, Harvard University, 1943.

GREER, GUY, and ALVIN H. HANSEN. *Urban Redevelopment and Housing.* Planning Pamphlet No. 10. Washington, D.C.: National Planning Association, 1941.

JAMISON, JUDITH N. *Regional Planning in Los Angeles. Metropolitan Los Angeles: A Study in Integration,* III. Los Angeles: The Haynes Foundation, 1952.

LOS ANGELES COUNTY. County Regional Planning Commission. *Regional Planning in Practice. First Annual Report.* Los Angeles, 1924.

MARYLAND. The Maryland-National Capital Park and Planning Commission. *On Wedges and Corridors.* Riverdale, Maryland, 1964.

MASSACHUSETTS. Board of Metropolitan Park Commissioners. *Report.* January, 1893.

MICHIGAN. Detroit Metropolitan Area Regional Planning Commission. *Annual Report.* Detroit, 1949.

MICHIGAN. Detroit Metropolitan Area Regional Planning Commission. *Study Design for a Comprehensive Transportation and Land Use Program for the Detroit Region.* Detroit, 1965.

MILLS, EARL O., *et al. Zoning and Civic Development.* Washington, D.C.: Chamber of Commerce of the United States, 1950.

MOSES, ROBERT, *et al. Portland Improvement.* New York, 1943.

NATIONAL CAPITAL PARK AND PLANNING COMMISSION. *Washington, Present and Future.* Monograph No. 1. Washington, 1950.

NATIONAL CAPITAL PLANNING COMMISSION. *1965–1985 — Proposed Physical Development Policies for Washington, D.C.* Washington, 1965.

NATIONAL CAPITAL PLANNING COMMISSION AND NATIONAL CAPITAL REGIONAL PLANNING COUNCIL. *General Development Plan for the National Capital Region. Mass Transportation Survey.* Washington, 1959.

————. *A Policies Plan for the Year 2000 — The Nation's Capital.* Washington, 1961.

NATIONAL CAPITAL REGIONAL PLANNING COUNCIL. *Annual Report.* Washington, 1964.

NATIONAL INDUSTRIAL ZONING COMMITTEE. *Principles of Industrial Zoning.* Columbus, Ohio: The Committee, 1951.

NEW YORK CITY. City Planning Commission. *Plan for Rezoning the City of New York,* by Harrison, Ballard & Allen. New York, 1950.

NEW YORK CITY. Commission on Congestion of Population. *Report.* New York, 1911.

NEW YORK [STATE] COMMISSION OF HOUSING AND REGIONAL PLANNING. *Report.* Albany, May 7, 1926.

NOLEN, JOHN. *Madison: a Model City.* Boston, 1911.

O'HARROW, DENNIS. *Performance Standards in Industrial Zoning.* Columbus, Ohio: National Industrial Zoning Committee, 1952.

OLMSTED BROTHERS. *Report upon the Development of Public Grounds for Greater Baltimore.* Baltimore: The Board of Park Commissioners of Baltimore City, 1904.

OLMSTED, FREDERICK LAW, JR. *Pittsburgh: Main Thoroughfares and the Down Town District. Improvements Necessary to Meet the City's Present and Future Needs.* Pittsburgh: Pittsburgh Civic Commission, 1911.

————. *Report of the Committee on Improving and Beautifying Utica of the Utica Chamber of Commerce.* Utica, N.Y.: The Chamber of Commerce, 1908.

————, and CHARLES MULFORD ROBINSON. *Improvement of the City of Detroit.* Detroit: Board of Commerce, 1905.

Organization for Metropolitan Planning: Four Proposals for Regional Councils. Chicago: American Society of Planning Officials, 1943.

PHILADELPHIA. City Planning Commission. *Comprehensive Plan — The Physical Development Plan for the City of Philadelphia.* Philadelphia, 1960.

PHILADELPHIA. City Planning Commission. Comprehensive Planning Division. *Summary Report on the Central Urban Renewal Area.* Philadelphia, 1956.

PHILADELPHIA. Office of the Development Coordinator. *A New Approach to Urban Renewal for Philadelphia.* Philadelphia, 1957.

PHILADELPHIA. Office of the Development Coordinator. *Partnership for Renewal. A summary of the accomplishments of Philadelphia's experiment in improving housing and neighborhood conditions through City-citizen cooperation....* Philadelphia, 1960.

PHILADELPHIA. Redevelopment Authority. Planning Division. "Summary Report on the Central Urban Renewal Area." Philadelphia, 1956. Mimeo.

REGIONAL ASSOCIATION OF CLEVELAND. *Regional Land Use Plan, Stage One. A Plan for Present Urban Areas.* Plan Bulletin No. 6. Cleveland, 1941.

REGIONAL PLAN ASSOCIATION. *Public Participation in Regional Planning,* by William B. Shore; ed. John P. Keith. New York, 1967.

_____. *The Region's Growth: A Report of the Second Regional Plan.* New York, 1967.

_____. *The Second Regional Plan: A Draft for Discussion.* New York, 1968.

_____. *Spread City—Projections of Development Trends and the Issues They Pose: The Tri-State New York Metropolitan Region, 1960–1985.* Bulletin 100. New York, 1962.

REGIONAL PLANNING FEDERATION OF THE PHILADELPHIA TRI-STATE DISTRICT. *The Regional Plan of the Philadelphia Tri-State District.* Philadelphia, 1932.

ROBINSON, CHARLES MULFORD. *The Improvement of Fort Wayne, Indiana.* Fort Wayne: Civic Improvement Association, 1910.

SEATTLE. City Planning Commission. *Comprehensive Planning in Seattle: 1911–1954,* by James A. Barnes. Seattle, 1954.

SEATTLE. Municipal Plans Commission. *Plan of Seattle. Report of the Municipal Plans Commission Submitting Report of Virgil G. Bogue, Engineer.* Seattle: Lowman & Hanford Co., 1911.

WASHINGTON METROPOLITAN AREA TRANSIT AUTHORITY. *Metro: A Rapid Rail Transit System for the National Capital Region.* Washington, 1968.

Federal Documents

Congress of the United States

HOUSE OF REPRESENTATIVES

"Housing Act of 1949," Public Law No. 171. 81st Cong., 1st sess. Washington, 1949.

Housing Act of 1959. 86th Cong., 1st sess., House Report No. 1040. [To accompany S. 2539] Washington, 1959.

Missouri–Illinois By-State Development Agency Compact. 86th Cong., 1st sess., Report No. 950. Washington, 1959.

The State of the Union. Address of the President of the United States. 86th Cong., 1st sess., Document No. 1. Washington, Jan. 9, 1959.

COMMITTEE ON BANKING AND CURRENCY. *Basic Laws and Authorities on Housing and Urban Development, revised through May 15, 1967.* 90th Cong., 1st sess. Washington, 1967.

_____. Subcommittee on Housing. *Demonstration Cities, Housing and Urban Development, and Urban Mass Transit;* Hearings on H.R. 12341, H.R. 12946, H.R. 13064, H.R. 9256, and related bills. 2 pts. 89th Cong., 2d sess. Washington, 1966.

———. *Housing Act of 1961;* Hearings on H.R. 6028, H.R. 5300, and H.R. 6423. 87th Cong., 1st sess. Washington, 1961.

JOINT COMMITTEE ON HOUSING. *Housing in America: Its Present Status and Future Implications.* 80th Cong., 2d sess., House Document No. 629. Washington, 1948.

———. *Housing Study and Investigation;* Final Majority Report. 2 pts. 80th Cong., 2d sess., House Report No. 1564. Washington, 1948.

———. *Study and Investigation of Housing;* Hearings. 80th Cong., 1st sess. 5 pts. Washington, 1948.

SELECT COMMITTEE INVESTIGATING NATIONAL DEFENSE MIGRATION. *Hearings.* 77th Cong., 1st sess. Washington, 1941.

SENATE

History of the United States Capitol; by Glenn Brown. 54th Cong., 1st sess., Senate Document No. 60. 2 vols. Washington, 1900–1903.

S. 1592, A Bill to Establish a National Housing Policy and Provide for Its Execution, cited as "General Housing Act of 1945." 79th Cong., 1st sess. Washington, 1945.

Washington, The National Capital; by H. P. Caemmerer. 71st Cong., 3d sess., Senate Document No. 332. Washington, 1932.

COMMITTEE ON BANKING AND CURRENCY. *Hearings on the General Housing Act of 1945;* Hearings on S. 1592. 2 pts. Washington, 1946.

———. *Housing Act of 1949; Report to accompany S. 1070.* 81st Cong., 1st sess., Report No. 84. Washington, 1949.

———. *Housing Act of 1959;* Hearings on various bills to amend the federal housing laws. 86th Cong., 1st sess. Washington, 1959.

———. *Housing Act of 1961; Report to accompany S. 1922.* 87th Cong., 1st sess., Report No. 281. Washington, 1961.

———. *Housing Legislation of 1961;* Hearings before a subcommittee on various bills to amend the federal housing laws. 87th Cong., 1st sess. Washington, 1961.

COMMITTEE ON THE DISTRICT OF COLUMBIA. *City Planning;* Hearing. 61st Cong., 2d sess., Senate Document No. 422. Washington, 1910.

COMMITTEE ON THE DISTRICT OF COLUMBIA AND PARK COMMISSION. *The Improvement of the Park System of the District of Columbia;* edited by Charles Moore. 57th Cong., 1st sess., Senate Report No. 166. Washington, 1902.

COMMITTEE ON EDUCATION AND LABOR. *United States Housing Act of 1936;* Hearing. 74th Cong., 2d sess. Washington, 1936.

COMMITTEE ON MANUFACTURES. *Establishment of National Economic Council;* Hearings on S. 6215. Washington, 1932.

SPECIAL COMMITTEE ON POST-WAR ECONOMIC POLICY AND PLANNING. Subcommittee on Housing and Urban Redevelopment. *Hearings on Post-war Economic Policy and Planning.* Pts. 6, 9. Washington, 1945.

———. ———. *Postwar Economic Policy and Planning.* 79th Cong., 1st sess., Report No. 539. Washington, 1945.

Special Agencies, the Executive Branch, and the Judiciary

ADVISORY COMMISSION ON INTERGOVERNMENTAL RELATIONS

Alternative Approaches to Governmental Reorganization in Metropolitan Areas. Washington, 1962.

Governmental Structure, Organization and Planning in Metropolitan Areas. Washington, 1961.

Metropolitan Councils of Governments, by Royce Hanson. Washington, 1966.

Metropolitan Social and Economic Disparities: Implications for Intergovernmental Relations in Central Cities and Suburbs. Washington, 1965.

Fifth Annual Report. Washington, 1964.

Sixth Annual Report. Washington, 1965.

Seventh Annual Report. Washington, 1966.

Eighth Annual Report. Washington, 1967.

Ninth Annual Report. Washington, 1968.

Tenth Annual Report. Washington, 1969.

BUREAU OF INDUSTRIAL HOUSING AND TRANSPORTATION

Report of the United States Housing Corporation. 2 vols. Washington, 1920.

COMMISSIONER OF LABOR

The Housing of the Working People. Eighth Special Report. Washington, 1895.

The Slums of Baltimore, Chicago, New York, and Philadelphia. Seventh Special Report. Washington, 1894.

DEPARTMENT OF COMMERCE

ADVISORY COMMITTEE ON CITY PLANNING AND ZONING. *A Standard City Planning Enabling Act.* Washington, 1928.

ADVISORY COMMITTEE ON ZONING. *A Standard State Zoning Enabling Act.* Washington, 1924.

DEPARTMENT OF HEALTH, EDUCATION, AND WELFARE

PUBLIC HEALTH SERVICE. *Air Pollution . . . A National Problem.* Washington, 1962.

DEPARTMENT OF HOUSING AND URBAN DEVELOPMENT

Annual Report, 1965. Washington, 1966.

"Better Communities: Designs and Plans," by Secretary Robert C. Weaver, National Conference of American Institute of Planners, Hilton Hotel, Pittsburgh, Pennsylvania, Oct. 14, 1968. News release, Oct. 14, 1968.

General Summary, Housing and Urban Development Act of 1968. Public Law 90–448. Washington, 1968.

Improving the Quality of Urban Life: A Program Guide to Model Neighborhoods in Demonstration Cities. Washington, 1966.

"Model Cities: Progress and Problems in the First Ten Months," by Assistant Secretary H. Ralph Taylor, Model Cities Midwest Regional Conference, Statler-Hilton Hotel, Dayton, Ohio, Sept. 6, 1968. News release, Sept. 6, 1968.

"The Rediscovery of the American City," by Under Secretary Robert C. Wood, MIT Alumni Seminar, Cambridge, Mass., Sept. 8, 1967. News release, Sept. 8, 1967.

"The Urban Opportunity: Roles for the University," by Robert C. Weaver, Howard University-Georgetown University, International Inn, Washington, D.C., Dec. 8, 1966. News release, Dec. 8, 1966.

EXECUTIVE OFFICE OF THE PRESIDENT

NATIONAL RESOURCES PLANNING BOARD. *Final Report: Status of Work, National Resources Planning Board;* by Charles W. Eliot II. Washington, Dec. 31, 1943.

_____. *Guide to the Files of the National Resources Planning Board. Ten Years of National Planning, 1933–1943;* by Charles W. Eliot II, assisted by Harold A. Merrill. Washington, 1943.

_____. *Long-range Programming of Municipal Public Works.* Washington, 1941.

_____. *National Resources Development Report for 1942.* Washington, 1942.

FEDERAL EMERGENCY ADMINISTRATION OF PUBLIC WORKS

NATIONAL PLANNING BOARD. *State Planning Progress;* Thirteenth Circular Letter. Washington, May 31, 1934 (mimeo).

_____. *Status of City and Regional Planning in the United States;* Eleventh Circular Letter. Washington, May 15, 1934 (mimeo).

FEDERAL HOME LOAN BANK BOARD

Waverly, A Study in Neighborhood Conservation. Washington, 1940.

FEDERAL HOUSING ADMINISTRATION

A Handbook on Urban Redevelopment for Cities in the United States. Washington, 1941.

HOUSING AND HOME FINANCE AGENCY

Thirteenth Annual Report, 1959. Washington, 1960.

Eighteenth Annual Report, 1964. Washington, 1965.

DIVISION OF HOUSING RESEARCH. *The Housing Situation, 1950: An Analysis of Preliminary Results of the 1950 Housing Census.* Washington, 1951.

_____. *Population Growth in Standard Metropolitan Areas 1900–1950, with an Explanatory Analysis of Urbanized Areas;* by Donald J. Bogue. Washington, 1953.

OFFICE OF THE ADMINISTRATOR. *A Summary of the Evolution of Housing Activities in the Federal Government.* Washington, 1950.

OFFICE OF THE GENERAL COUNSEL. *Chronology of Major Federal Actions Affecting Housing and Community Development, July, 1892, through 1963.* Washington, 1964.

NATIONAL HOUSING AGENCY

OFFICE OF THE ADMINISTRATOR. Urban Development Division. *A Summary of Studies and Proposals in the U.S.A. on Assembly of Land for Urban Development and Redevelopment.* Bulletin No. 14. Washington, 1944.

OFFICE OF THE GENERAL COUNSEL. *Comparative Digest of the Principal Provisions of State Urban Redevelopment Legislation.* Washington, 1947.

NATIONAL RESOURCES BOARD

Report on Land Use Problems and Conditions in Florida; by Colin D. Gunn and John Wallace. Washington, 1935.

Report on National Planning and Public Works in Relation to Natural Resources and Including Land Use and Water Resources, with Findings and Recommendations. Washington, 1934.

State Planning: A Review of Activities and Progress. Washington, 1935.

NATIONAL RESOURCES COMMITTEE

The Future of State Planning. Washington, 1938.

State Planning: Programs and Accomplishments (Supplementing State Planning Report of 1935). Washington, 1937.

URBANISM COMMITTEE. *Our Cities, Their Role in the National Economy.* Washington, 1937.

―――. *Urban Planning and Land Policies.* Washington, 1939.

OFFICE OF WAR INFORMATION

Victory; Official Weekly Bulletin of the Office of War Information. Vol. 3, Nos. 1 to 4, Jan. 6, 13, 20, and 27, 1942.

PRESIDENT OF THE UNITED STATES

Economic Report of the President, Together with the Annual Report of the Council of Economic Advisers. Washington, 1964.

Public Papers of the Presidents of the United States, Lyndon B. Johnson, 1965, Book 1. Washington, 1966.

ADVISORY COMMITTEE ON GOVERNMENT HOUSING POLICIES AND PROGRAMS. *Recommendations on Government Housing Policies and Programs.* Washington, 1953.

COMMISSION ON NATIONAL GOALS. *Goals for Americans, Comprising the Report of the President's Commission on National Goals and Chapters Submitted for the Consideration of the Commission.* Englewood Cliffs, N.J.: Prentice-Hall, Inc., 1960.

COMMITTEE ON RECENT ECONOMIC CHANGES. *Recent Economic Changes in the United States.* New York: McGraw-Hill Book Co., 1929.

CONFERENCE ON HOME BUILDING AND HOME OWNERSHIP. *Housing Objectives and Programs; Slums, Large-scale Housing and Decentralization;* edited by John M. Gries and James Ford. Washington, 1932.

RESEARCH COMMITTEE ON SOCIAL TRENDS. *Recent Social Trends in the United States.* 2 vols. New York: McGraw-Hill Book Co., 1933.

RESETTLEMENT ADMINISTRATION

Greenbelt Towns. Washington, 1936.

SUPREME COURT

BAKER v. CARR; Brief *Amici Curiae* of the National Institute of Municipal Law Officers. (October Term, 1960, No. 103) [1960].

UNITED STATES HOUSING AUTHORITY

The United States Housing Act of 1937 as Amended, and Provisions of Other Laws and of Executive Orders Pertaining to the United States Housing Act of 1937, as Amended. Washington, 1938.

Miscellaneous Public and Semipublic Documents

AMERICAN COUNCIL TO IMPROVE OUR NEIGHBORHOODS. *This Is ACTION.* New York, 1960.

BAUER, CATHERINE. *Housing in the United States.* Reprinted from the *International Labour Review,* LII (July, 1945). Montreal: International Labour Office, 1945.

The Boston Contest of 1944. Boston: The Boston University Press, 1945.

CALIFORNIA HOUSING AND PLANNING ASSOCIATION. Committee on Urban Redevelopment. *A Chart for Changing Cities.* San Francisco, 1944.

CLARKE, ELIOT C. *Main Drainage Work of the City of Boston.* Boston: Rockwell and Churchill, City Printers, 1885.

CLEVELAND. "Amendment to the charter of the City of Cleveland Establishing a City Planning Commission." Adopted Nov. 3, 1942. Mimeo.

CONNECTICUT. Capitol Region Planning Agency. *Governmental Organization for the Capitol Region.* Part 1: *Regional Organizations in Other Metropolitan Areas. Inventory and Analysis.* Prepared by the Regional Affairs Center, University of Hartford. Hartford, Conn., 1966.

FEDERATED SOCIETIES ON PLANNING AND PARKS. Joint Committee on Bases of Sound Land Policy. *What About the Year 2000?* Washington, 1929.

GREATER PHILADELPHIA MOVEMENT. Committee on Regional Development. *Profile: The Pennsylvania–New Jersey–Delaware Region.* Philadelphia, 1968.

HANSON, ROYCE. *The Politics of Metropolitan Cooperation: Metropolitan Washington Council of Governments.* Washington: Washington Center for Metropolitan Studies, 1964.

HARTFORD, CONN. Charter and Ordinances. *The Compiled Charter and Revised Ordinances of the City of Hartford, Including All Amendments to the Charter and All Ordinances in Force October 1, 1907, with an Appendix Containing All Ordinances Enacted from October 1, 1907, to May 1, 1908.* Hartford, 1908.

HARVARD UNIVERSITY. Graduate School of Design. The Council for Planning Action. *Symposium 2 — Metropolitan Planning.* Cambridge, Mass., 1951.

ILLINOIS. Legislative Council. *Air Pollution Legislation.* Publication 101. Springfield, Ill., 1950.

METROPOLITAN WASHINGTON COUNCIL OF GOVERNMENTS. *Metropolitan Councils of Governments in the United States.* Washington, 1967.

MICHIGAN. Supervisors Inter-County Committee. *Supervisors Inter-County Committee: What it is; How it works; Its Accomplishments.* Detroit, 1963.

MICHIGAN. Supervisors Inter-County Committee. *Third Annual Meeting Report.* Detroit, 1960.

MICHIGAN. Supervisors Inter-County Committee. *This Is the Supervisors Inter-County Committee.* Detroit: Area Development Division, The Detroit Edison Company, 1959.

NATIONAL ASSOCIATION OF HOUSING OFFICIALS. *Housing Officials' Yearbook, 1935.* Chicago, 1935.

NATIONAL ASSOCIATION OF HOUSING OFFICIALS. *Legislative History of Certain Aspects of the Housing Act of 1949.* Publication No. N278. Chicago, 1949.

NATIONAL ASSOCIATION OF HOUSING OFFICIALS. Committee on Postwar Housing. *Housing for the United States After the War.* Publication No. N193. Chicago, 1944.

NATIONAL ASSOCIATION OF HOUSING OFFICIALS. Joint Committee on Housing and Welfare. *The Rent Certificate Plan.* Publication No. N204. Chicago, 1944.

NATIONAL MUNICIPAL LEAGUE. Committee on Metropolitan Government. *The Government of Metropolitan Areas in the United States.* New York, 1930.

NATIONAL MUNICIPAL LEAGUE. Committee on Municipal Program. *A Model City Charter and Municipal Home Rule.* Philadelphia, 1916.

OGBURN, WILLIAM F. *War, Babies, and the Future.* Public Affairs Pamphlet No. 83. New York: Public Affairs Committee, 1943.

PHILADELPHIA. Charter Commission. *Philadelphia Home Rule Charter, Annotated.* Philadelphia, 1951.

PHILLIPS, WALTER M. *A Future for Penjerdel. A Report on Penjerdel, The Organization and the Region, with Recommendations for New Directions.* Philadelphia: The Pennsylvania-New Jersey-Delaware Metropolitan Project, Inc., 1965.

Puget Sound Governmental Conference. Seattle: The Conference, 1966.

REED, THOMAS H. *The Governments of Atlanta and Fulton County, Georgia.* New York: The National Municipal League, 1939.

REID, PAUL M. "Planning for Urban and Regional Development." Address to the 79th Annual Convention, Michigan Engineering Society, Ann Arbor, April 4, 1959. Mimeo.

RIGHTOR, C. E. *The Preparation of a Long-Term Financial Program.* Publication No. 5. New York: Municipal Administration Service, 1927.

SWEENEY, STEPHEN B., and JAMES C. CHARLESWORTH, EDS. *Governing Urban Society: New Scientific Approaches.* Monograph 7 in a series sponsored by The American Academy of Political and Social Science. Philadelphia: The Academy, 1967.

URBAN LAND INSTITUTE. *Decentralization: What Is It Doing To Our Cities?* Chicago, 1940.

URBAN LAND INSTITUTE, *Outline for a Legislative Program to Rebuild Our Cities.* Washington, 1942.

Miscellaneous Conference Proceedings and Addresses

AMERICAN INSTITUTE OF ARCHITECTS. *Proceedings of the Thirty-fourth Annual Convention, American Institute of Architects, Washington, D.C., December 12, 13, 14, and 15, 1900.* Washington, 1900.

A.I.A. *Proceedings of the Thirty-sixth Annual Convention, American Institute of Architects, Washington, D.C., December 11, 12, and 13, 1902.* Washington, 1903.

BLANFORD, JOHN B., JR. "The Cincinnati Plan for Programming Public Improvements," *Proceedings of the Thirty-third Annual Convention.* St. Louis: American Society for Municipal Improvements, 1928.

BLUCHER, WALTER H. "Zoning and Quitting," *Proceedings of First Annual Indiana State-wide Planning Conference.* State Planning Board of Indiana, 1938.

CALIFORNIA. Los Angeles County. *Proceedings of the First Regional Planning Conference of Los Angeles County, California, at Pasadena, Jan. 21, 1922.*

Community Renewal Program Roundtable. Proceedings of a roundtable sponsored by the American Institute of Planners and the National Association of Housing and Redevelopment Officials, Washington, D.C., May 8 and 9, 1961. Washington: American Institute of Planners, 1961.

CONNECTICUT. Governor's Regional Planning Conference. *Let's Plan for Tomorrow Together Through Regional Planning for the Capital Area.* Hartford, Conn.: Regional Planning Committee, Hartford Chamber of Commerce, 1957.

NATIONAL COMMITTEE ON HOUSING, INC. *Proceedings of the National Conference on Postwar Housing, Chicago, March 8, 9, 10, 1944.* New York, 1944.

The New Highways: Challenge to the Metropolitan Region, A Symposium Sponsored by the Connecticut General Life Insurance Company. Hartford, Conn.: Connecticut General Life Insurance Company, 1957.

ORGANIZATION OF CORNELL PLANNERS. *Training the Urban Renewal Team, a Summary of the Proceedings of the First Annual Spring Conference Sponsored by the Organization of Cornell Planners.* Ithaca, N.Y.: Department of City and Regional Planning, Cornell University, 1958.

The Problem of the Cities and Towns, Report of the Conference on Urbanism, Harvard University, March 5–6, 1942. Edited by Guy Greer. Cambridge, Mass.: Harvard University Press, 1942.

VINTON, WARREN JAY. "The Urban Revolution: Challenge to the Next Generation." Address to the Conference on the Teacher and the Metropolis, of the Washington Center for Metropolitan Studies, Thursday, November 29, 1962. Mimeo.

WOOD, EDITH ELMER. "Is Government Aid Necessary in House Financing?" in *Housing Problems in America. Proceedings of the Tenth National Conference on Housing, Philadelphia, January 28, 29, 30, 1929.* New York: National Housing Association, 1929.

Manuscripts

HALL, BRYANT. "The History of City Planning in California," a paper prepared for the meeting of the Association of City Planners of Los Angeles County at Avalon, June 8, 1929. MS in author's possession.

GREATER PHILADELPHIA MOVEMENT. Committee on Regional Development. "First Annual Report on Regional Affairs." Philadelphia, 1969. Typewritten.

JOHNSTON, NORMAN J. "Harland Bartholomew: His Comprehensive Plans and Science of Planning." Ph.D. dissertation, University of Pennsylvania, 1964. Mimeo.

LA PEÑA, DONALD J. DE. "Vineyards in a Regional System of Open Space in the San Francisco Bay Area: Methods of Preserving Selected Areas. Master's thesis in City Planning, University of California, Berkeley, 1962. Mimeo.

McLAUGHLIN, CHARLES CAPEN. "Selected Letters of Frederick Law Olmsted." Unpublished Ph.D. thesis, Harvard University, 1960.

NORTON, CHARLES DYER. Letter to Frederic A. Delano, New York, Nov. 24, 1921. Files of the Regional Plan Association, New York.

SIMPSON, MICHAEL A. "People and Planning: A History of the Ohio Planning Conference, 1919–1965." First draft of a book written by Mr. Simpson while he was a graduate student of urban history at the Ohio State University; lent to the author by Professor Israel Stollman, chairman of the Division of City and Regional Planning.

In addition to the foregoing manuscripts, letters from the following persons to the author have been used in the preparation of this book:

HARLAND BARTHOLOMEW, Nov. 4, 1966; July 16, 1968.

RUSSELL VAN NEST BLACK, Nov. 4, 1966; Nov. 14, 1966; Dec. 8, 1966.

T. LEDYARD BLAKEMAN, Feb. 20, 1968.

EARLE S. DRAPER, May 5, 1965; Dec. 5, 1966.

HENRY FAGIN, Feb. 27, 1968.

WALTER M. PHILLIPS, Feb. 22, 1968; Mar. 5. 1968.

GORDON WHITNALL, Nov. 17, 1966.

The following abbreviations have been used throughout this index:

ACPI	American City Planning Institute	NAHO	National Association of Housing Officials [now National Association of Housing and Redevelopment Officials]
ACTION	American Council to Improve Our Neighborhoods		
AIA	American Institute of Architects	NCCP	National Conference on City Planning
AIP	American Institute of Planners		
ASPO	American Society of Planning Officials	NRPB	National Resources Planning Board
CRPNY	Committee on the Regional Plan of New York and Its Environs	PWA	Public Works Administration
FHA	Federal Housing Administration	RPAA	Regional Planning Association of America
FSPP	Federated Societies on Planning and Parks	RPNY	Regional Plan of New York and Its Environs
HHFA	Housing and Home Finance Agency	SCPA	Standard City Planning Enabling Act
HUD	Department of Housing and Urban Development	TVA	Tennessee Valley Authority

722   INDEX

Adams, Thomas (continued)
gional plan carried out, 447; mentioned, 28, 211, 265, 641
Addams, Jane, 10, 72
Adler, Dankmar, 36
Advisory Commission on Intergovernmental Relations: establishment of, 555; report on problems in previously rural areas, 556; recommended state departments of metropolitan affairs, 558; recommended legislation requiring review of applications for federal aid, 558
Agricultural Adjustment Act, 301
Airports, 168, 190, 375–376
Akron, Ohio, 378
Albright, Horace M., 271
Allegheny Conference on Community Development, 433, 489
Allen, Frederick H., 458
Ambler Realty Company, 238–240, 587
American Academy, Rome, 37
American Architect and Building News, 38
American Association of State Highway Officials, 539, 541
American City Bureau, 149
American City Planning Institute (ACPI). *See* American Institute of Planners (AIP)
American Civic Association: predecessor organizations, 66; sponsored model street, 71; secretary proposed federal department, 181; F. A. Delano president of, 189; aided development of city planning, 249; member of FSPP, 271; merger forming American Planning and Civic Association, 331; joint conference, 333; mentioned, 121, 175, 181, 302
American Community Builders, 457
American Construction Council, 284
American Council on Race Relations, 420
American Council to Improve Our Neighborhoods (ACTION), 503-504
American Federation of Labor, 328, 388
American Industrial Development Council, 484
American Institute of Architects (AIA): D. H. Burnham as president, 37; Cleveland chapter's proposal, 43; interest in plan of Washington, 49–50; *City Planning Progress,* 166–169; southern California chapter endorsed proposal for city planning commission, 204; nominated members of art jury, 233; mentioned, 211
American Institute of Park Executives, 271
American Institute of Planners (AIP): formation as ACPI, 163; charter members, 163–164; nominated members of art jury, 233; joint conference, 331, 333; member-

American Institute of Planners (AIP) (continued)
ship in late 1940s, 467; statement on urban development, 474–475; statement on research, 477–479; represented in National Industrial Zoning Committee, 484; represented at Sagamore Conference on federal highways, 539; newsletter report on Sagamore Conference, 539, 540–541; workshops for subprofessionals, 542; members in government agencies, 543; appraisals of Housing Act of 1959, 551; policy report on need for national development program, 552–553; unsuccessful in proposing federal scholarships, 568; reexamination of profession, 614–618; constitutional amendment broadening scope of profession, 616–618; fiftieth anniversary conference, 644; Task Force on New Communities, 648
American Legislators' Association, 325
American Municipal Association, 404, 539, 549
American Park Society, 271
American Planning and Civic Association. *See* American Civic Association
American Public Welfare Association, 325
American Railway Development Association, 484
American Society for Municipal Improvements, 252
American Society of Civil Engineers, 199, 298, 484
American Society of Landscape Architects, 298
American Society of Municipal Engineers, 325
American Society of Planning Officials (ASPO): formation of, 331; joint conferences, 333; distributed *Action for Cities,* 404; special institutes for public officials, 414; nationwide contest on organization of regional councils, 430–433; among organizations supervising Urban Redevelopment Study, 489; represented at Sagamore Conference on federal highways, 539; outlook for metropolitan planning, 558–559; comment on Housing Act of 1961, 569; report on scholarships, 636
Andrews, W. Earle, 403
Anthony, Susan B., 36
Armour, Philip D., 37
Army Corps of Engineers: prevented from constructing dams on Potomac, 304; attitude toward navigable waters, 309; opposed proposal for regional authorities, 357–359; unfriendly to NRPB, 408

Cleveland, Ohio (continued)
general plan of, 492
Coffin, George H., Jr., 242
Colby, Charles C., 468
Colean, Miles L.: attended Baltimore housing conference, 325; *Housing for Defense,* 394; *The Role of the Housebuilding Industry,* 399; *Renewing Our Cities,* 497; members of President's Advisory Committee on Government Housing, 498
Colmer, William F., 411
Columbia, Md., 644–645, 646
Comey, Arthur C.: paper in *City Planning,* 146; proposal for a state plan, 152; charter member of ACPI (AIP), 164; member of Urbanism Committee, 311; studies of planned towns, 345
Commerical Club of Chicago, 102, 105, 109
Commission form of municipal government, 67
Commission of Housing and Regional Planning, State of New York, 247
Commission on Building Districts and Restrictions, New York City, 154
Commission on Congestion of Population, New York City, 153
Commission on Distribution of Population, New York, 88
Committee for Economic Development, 407
Committee on City Plan, New York City, 153
Committee on Congestion of Population, New York City, 83, 84–86
Committee on Post-War Economic Policy and Planning, U.S. Senate, 410, 462
Committee on Recent Economic Change, 273–274
Committee on the Regional Plan of New York and Its Environs (CRPNY): steps toward formation of, 199–201; appointment of members, 202; initial studies, 203–204; progress of planning program, 223–225; comments of T. H. Reed on execution of plan, 225–226; presentation of *The Graphic Regional Plan,* 261–265; publication of *The Building of the City,* 289–290; criticisms of plan, 290, 292; T. Adams's defense of plan, 292–293; disbandment of Committee, 293
Commonwealth Club of San Francisco, 199
Community renewal program. *See* Urban renewal; Racial issues
Community Service Society of New York, 424
Conant, James Bryant, 614
Conference on Home Building and Home Ownership, 323

Conference on Metropolitan Area Problems, 557
Connor, Edward, 516, 517
Cooke, Morris L., 191
Cookingham, L. P., 401
Coolidge, Calvin, 189
Coolidge, J. Randolph, Jr., 114, 115, 116, 132, 175
Coolidge, T. Jefferson, 71
Copeland, Melvin T., 393
Copenhagen, Denmark, finger plan, 577
Copland, Aaron, 362
Corpus Christi, Tex., 388, 404, 405
Council of Economic Advisers, 602
Council of State Governments, 557
Councils of governments: Supervisors Inter-County Committee, Detroit area, 516–519; Metropolitan Regional Council, New York area, 519; Metropolitan Washington Council of Governments, 519–520, 580, 611; Association of Bay Area Governments, 520, 584–585, 611; Southern California Association of Governments, 520; Metropolitan Atlanta Council of Local Governments, 520; Mid-Willamette Valley Council of Governments, 520; Puget Sound Governmental Conference, 520; Regional Conference of Elected Officials, Philadelphia area, 520; interest in areawide planning, 559; role of Penjerdel in formation of Regional Conference of Elected Officials, 582–583; Metropolitan Council of the Twin Cities, 584; supporting grants authorized in Housing Act of 1965, 611; councils designated by Bureau of Budget to review applications for federally aided projects, 633–635; role in giving direction to areawide development, 651
County planning commissions: Los Angeles County Regional Planning Commission, 206; initial program in Los Angeles County, 206–209; Allegheny County [Pa.] Planning Commission, 213; Lucas County [Ohio] Planning Commission, 213; other commissions formed in 1920s, 214; planning studies of Los Angeles County Regional Planning Commission in 1930s, 281; land use plan of Marin County [Calif.] Planning Commission, 350; Louisville and Jefferson County [Kentucky] Planning and Zoning Commission, 400
Coyle, Grace L., 370
Crane, Jacob L., Jr.: planner for Illinois Chamber of Commerce, 294, 296; Iowa Conservation Plan, 296–297; believed

Open-space land (continued)
grants under Housing Act of 1965, 611; in Washington area, 577–580 *passim;* proposal of Second Regional Plan, New York, 648
Operations Research Society of America, 544
Orton, Lawrence M., 470
Osborn, F. J., 448
Our Cities To-day and To-morrow, by H. V. Hubbard and T. K. Hubbard, 266

Pacific Northwest Regional Planning Commission, 309
Palmer, Charles F., 369, 375
Paris, France, 45, 47, 96
Palos Verdes Estates, Calif., 242
Park, Robert E., 468
Park Forest, Ill., 456–457
Park systems: park movement, 11–12; Kansas City, Mo., 13–16; Boston area, 17–23; Dallas, Tex., 124; Cook County, Ill., Forest Preserve System, 210; expansion in Chicago area, 1925–1955, 212
Parkins, Maurice Frank, 527, 551
Patten, Simon, 84
Pearl, Raymond, 271
Peets, Elbert, 338, 340, 457
Pendergast, James, 16
Penjerdel (Pennsylvania–New Jersey–Delaware Metropolitan Project, Inc.), 582–583, 584
Perkins, Dwight H., 104, 211
Perkins, Frances, 328
Perkins, G. Holmes, 464, 522
Perloff, Harvey: ideas on education of planners, 545, 546, 547; urged political action, 580; lecture on links between physical and social planning, 606–607, 610, 620
Perry, Clarence Arthur: forerunner of his neighborhood concept in St. Louis, 72; residence in Forest Hills Gardens, 91; studies of residential areas, 188; member of RPAA, 223; neighborhood unit, 258; mentioned, 236, 335, 457, 644
Phelan, James Duval, 64
Philadelphia, Pa.: population increase in 1880s, 2; department of surveys, 5; park area in 1880, 11; Fairmount Parkway (now Benjamin Franklin Parkway), 58–60; diffusion of population, 169; Regional Planning Federation, 216–220; recommendation of charter commission, 354; population loss in 1930s, 378; employment increase in Second World War, 387; program of public works, 401; redevelopment

Philadelphia, Pa. (continued)
in, 489; Regional Conference of Elected Officials, 520; *CURA Report,* 522–524; comprehensive plan, 531–536; Better Philadelphia Exhibition, 532; financial effect of legislative malapportionment, 556; Penn-Jersey Transportation Study, 581–584 *passim;* Greater Philadelphia Movement, 583
Phillips, Walter M., 582
Pickwick Landing, Tenn., 314
Pico, Rafael, 480, 481
Pinchot, Gifford, 191, 297
Pinney, Harvey F., 432
Pittsburgh Plate Glass Company, 636
Pittsburgh, Pa.: Pittsburgh Survey, 93–95; influence of Survey on D. H. Burnham, 108; Olmsted report, 124–126; Regional Planning Association, 354–355, 433, 498; population loss in 1930s, 378; employment increase in Second World War, 387; redevelopment, 489
Planning Foundation of America, 267–268
Platt, Geoffrey, 305
Plumber and Sanitary Engineer, The, 6–7
Polk, Willis, 64
Pomeroy, Hugh R., 206–207, 319, 350, 416–417
Pope, Robert Anderson, 96–97, 98, 99
Populists, 36
Portland, Ore., 378, 390, 402–404
Portland Cement Association, 211
Post, Langdon W., 325
Postwar planning: creation of state development agencies, 411–412. *See also* National planning
Potter, Henry C., 90
Poverty in America: report of Council of Economic Advisers, 602; Economic Opportunity Act, 602; "war on poverty," 602; housing and urban development acts of 1966 and 1968, 624–634
Pratt, Edward E., 130
Pratt Institute, 542
Pray, James Sturgis, 101, 164
Preservation of historic sites and structures, 623
President's Research Committee on Social Trends, 300, 305
Prichard, Frank P., 41–42
Principles of Scientific Management, The, by F. W. Taylor, 122
Prospect Park, Brooklyn, 126
Public Administration Clearing House, 320, 325, 453, 458, 489, 504
Public Administration Service, 404